High
Performance
Cluster Computing:

Programming and Applications, Volume 2

ISBN 0-13-013785-5

9 780130 137852

90000

High Performance Cluster Computing:

Programming and Applications, Volume 2

Edited by
Rajkumar Buyya

(rajkumar@dgs.monash.edu.au)

School of Computer Science and Software Engineering
Monash University
Melbourne, Australia

Prentice Hall PTR
Upper Saddle River, New Jersey 07458
http://www.phptr.com

Library of Congress Cataloging-in-Publication Data

   High performance cluster computing / edited by Rajkumar Buyya.
       p.   cm.
   Includes bibliographical references and index.
   Contents: v. 2. Programming and applications.
   ISBN 0-13-013785-5 (v.2)
   1. High performance computing. I. Buyya, Rajkumar
QA76.88.H489   1999
004'.3--DC21   99-17906
                                    CIP

Editorial/Production Supervision: *Joan L. McNamara*
Acquisitions Editor: *Greg Doench*
Editorial Assistant: *Mary Treacy*
Marketing Manager: *Bryan Gambrel*
Cover Design Director: *Jerry Votta*
Cover Designer: *Anthony Gemmellaro*
Cover Illustration: *Rob Colvin (The Stock Illustration Source)*
Manufacturing Manager: *Alexis R. Heydt*

© 1999 Prentice Hall PTR
Prentice-Hall, Inc.
Upper Saddle River, New Jersey 07458

Prentice Hall books are widely used by corporations and government agencies for training, marketing, and resale. The publisher offers discounts on this book when ordered in bulk quantities.

For more information, contact: Corporate Sales Department, Phone: 800-382-3419;
FAX: 201-236-7141; email: corpsales@prenhall.com

Or write: Corp. Sales Dept., Prentice Hall PTR, 1 Lake Street, Upper Saddle River, NJ 07458

All product names mentioned herein are the trademarks of their respective owners.

Printed in the United States of America
10 9 8 7 6 5 4 3 2 1

ISBN 0-13-013785-5

Prentice-Hall International (UK) Limited, *London*
Prentice-Hall of Australia Pty. Limited, *Sydney*
Prentice-Hall Canada Inc., *Toronto*
Prentice-Hall Hispanoamericana, S.A., *Mexico*
Prentice-Hall of India Private Limited, *New Delhi*
Prentice-Hall of Japan, Inc., *Tokyo*
Prentice-Hall (Singapore) Pte. Ltd., *Singapore*
Editora Prentice-Hall do Brasil, Ltda., *Rio de Janeiro*

Contents at a Glance

Contents

Preface

The initial idea leading to cluster[1] computing was developed in the 1960s by IBM as a way of linking large mainframes to provide a cost-effective form of commercial parallelism. During those days, IBM's HASP (Houston Automatic Spooling Priority) system and its successor, JES (Job Entry System), provided a way of distributing work to a user-constructed mainframe cluster. IBM still supports clustering of mainframes through their Parallel Sysplex system, which allows the hardware, operating system, middleware, and system management software to provide dramatic performance and cost improvements while permitting large mainframe users to continue to run their existing applications.

However, cluster computing did not gain momentum until three trends converged in the 1980s: high performance microprocessors, high-speed networks, and standard tools for high performance distributed computing. A possible fourth trend is the increased need of computing power for computational science and commercial applications coupled with the high cost and low accessibility of traditional supercomputers. These building blocks are also known as killer-microprocessors, killer-networks, killer-tools, and killer-applications, respectively. The recent advances in these technologies and their availability as cheap and commodity components are making clusters or networks of computers (PCs, workstations, and SMPs) an appealing vehicle for cost-effective parallel computing. Clusters, built using commodity-off-the-shelf (COTS) hardware components as well as free, or commonly used, software, are playing a major role in redefining the concept of supercomputing.

The trend in parallel computing is to move away from specialized traditional supercomputing platforms, such as the Cray/SGI T3E, to cheaper and general purpose systems consisting of loosely coupled components built up from single or multiprocessor PCs or workstations. This approach has a number of advantages, including being able to build a platform for a given budget which is suitable for a large class of applications and workloads.

This book is motivated by the fact that parallel computing on a network of computers using commodity components has received increased attention recently, and noticeable progress towards usable systems has been made. A number of re-

---

[1]Cluster is a collection of interconnected computers working together as a single system.

searchers in academia and industry have been active in this field of research. Although research in this area is still in its early stage, promising results have been demonstrated by experimental systems built in academic and industrial laboratories. There is a need for better understanding of what cluster computing can offer, how cluster computers can be constructed, and what the impacts of clustering on high performance computing will be.

Though a significant number of research articles have been published in various conference proceedings and journals, the results are scattered in many places, are hard to obtain, and are difficult to understand, especially for beginners. This book, the first of its kind, gathers in one place the current and comprehensive technical coverage of the field and presents it in a tutorial form. The book's coverage reflects the state of the art in high-level architecture, design, and development, and points out possible directions for further research and development.

Organization

This book is a collection of chapters written by leading scientists active in the area of parallel computing using networked computers. The primary purpose of the book is to provide an authoritative overview of this field's state of the art. The emphasis is on the following aspects of cluster computing:

- Requirements, Issues, and Services

- System Area Networks, Communication Protocols, and High Performance I/O Techniques

- Resource Management, Scheduling, Load Balancing, and System Availability

- Possible Models for Cluster-Based Parallel Systems

- Programming Models and Environments

- Algorithms and Applications of Clusters

The work on High Performance Cluster Computing appears in two volumes:

- Volume 1: Systems and Architectures

- Volume 2: Programming and Applications

This book, Volume 2, consists of 29 chapters, which are grouped into the following three parts:

- Part I: Programming Environments and Development Tools

- Part II: Java for High Performance Computing

- Part III: Algorithms and Applications

Part I focuses on various programming paradigms, models, and environments, including MPI, PVM, tuple space programming, component based programming, debuggers, and OS services for wide area applications. Part II covers Java for high performance computing, focusing on Java variants supporting MPI, JVM, SPMD paradigm, and web-based computing. Part III discusses various parallel algorithms and applications designed for your cluster programming environments. The application areas discussed include the use of clusters in image processing, electromagnetics, ocean modeling, CFD simulation, and biological applications modeling.

Readership

The book is primarily written for graduate students and researchers interested in the area of parallel and distributed computing. However, it is also suitable for practitioners in industry and government laboratories.

The interdisciplinary nature of the book is likely to appeal to a wide audience. They will find this book to be a valuable source of information on recent advances and future directions of parallel computation using networked computers. This is the first book addressing various technological aspects of cluster computing in-depth, and we expect that the book will be an informative and useful reference in this new and fast growing research area.

The organization of this book makes it particularly useful for graduate courses. It can be used as a text for a research-oriented or seminar-based advanced graduate course. Graduate students will find the material covered by this book to be stimulating and inspiring. Using this book, they can identify interesting and important research topics for their Master's and Ph.D. work. It can also serve as a supplementary book for regular courses taught in Computer Science, Computer Engineering, Electrical Engineering, and Computational Science and Informatics Departments, including:

- Advanced Computer Architecture and Its Applications

- Parallel Programming

- Scalable Computing Environments

- Parallel Programming Environments

- Programming Network of Workstations

- Cluster Programming and Applications

- Applications Development on Clusters

- Distributed and Concurrent Systems and Programming

- Parallel Algorithms and Applications.

Cluster Computing Resources on the Web

The various software systems discussed in this book are freely available for download through the Internet. Please visit this book's website,

- http://www.phptr.com/ptrbooks/ptr_0130137855.html

for pointers/links to further information on downloading Educational Resources, Cluster Computing Environments, and Cluster Management Systems.

Acknowledgments

First and foremost, I am grateful to all the contributing authors for their time, effort, and understanding during the preparation of the book.

I thank Albert Zomaya (University of Western Australia) for his advice and encouragement while starting this book project.

I would like to thank Kennith Birman (Cornell University), Marcin Paprzycki (University of Southern Mississippi), and Hamid R. Arabnia (The University of Georgia) for their critical comments and suggestions on improving the book.

I thank Toni Cortes (Universitat Politecnica de Catalunya) for his consistent support and invaluable LaTeX expertise.

I thank Mark Baker (University of Portsmouth), Erich Schikuta (Universitaet Wien), Dror G. Feitelson (Hebrew University of Jerusalem), Daniel F. Savarese and Thomas Sterling (California Institute of Technology), Ira Pramanick (Silicon Graphics Inc), and Daniel S. Katz (Jet Propulsion Laboratory, California Institute of Technology) for writing overviews for various parts of the book.

I thank my wife, Smrithi, and my daughter, Soumya, for their love and under-standing (my long absences from home) during the preparation of the book.

I acknowledge the support of the Australian Government Overseas Postgradu-ate Research Scholarship, the Queensland University of Technology Postgraduate Research Award (Programming Languages and Systems Research Centre Scholar-ship), the Monash University Graduate Scholarship, and the Distributed Systems and Software Engineering Centre Scholarship.

I thank Clemens Szyperski (Queensland University of Technology) and David Abramson (Monash University) for advising my Ph.D research program.

Finally, I would like to thank the staff at Prentice Hall, particularly Greg Doench, Mary Treacy, Joan L. McNamara, Barbara Cotton, Mary Loudin, Lisa Iarkowski, Anne Trowbridge, and Bryan Gambrel. They were wonderful to work with!

Rajkumar Buyya
Monash University, Melbourne, Australia
(rajkumar@dgs.monash.edu.au / rajkumar@ieee.org)

March, 1999

Part I

Programming Environments and Development Tools

In order to effectively exploit the power of parallel computers in general, and a cluster of computers in particular, good programming environments and development tools are a must. This is particularly necessary for parallel processing and distributed computing to become the preferred programming model for a typical programmer, as opposed to being limited to an esoteric group of experts. The last two decades have seen a significant development of various kinds of programming environments, together with a plethora of associated programming aids including parallel debuggers and tracing/monitoring tools. Many of these environments have emerged as standards, which in turn are ushering in portable parallel programming models. This in turn is leading to an explosion in the popularity of parallel computing. This part of the book examines some of the main parallel environments that have emerged during the past twenty years, and some of the associated programming tools.

Chapter 1 introduces the common parallel programming models in use today for implementing parallel applications. It discusses the master/slave model, the single-program multiple-data model, data pipelining, the divide-and-conquer paradigm, speculative parallelism, and various hybrid methods. It ends with a section on templates for parallel programming.

Chapter 2 describes several popular parallel programming languages and environments. It begins with a discussion on parallel constructs used during the infancy of parallel programming, including primitives such as semaphores, monitors, sockets, and remote procedure calls. It then describes commonly used shared memory paradigms, including pure and virtual shared memory environments. The chapter then focuses on various distributed memory programming environments, and finally concludes with a section on parallel declarative languages.

A distributed memory model best fits cluster computing, although there have been some attempts to provide a shared memory interface for such systems, as discussed in the second chapter of this book. Chapter 3 describes the two most popular distributed memory message-passing environments that have become the standards of message-passing programming today, namely, MPI and PVM. The chapter illustrates programming in the two models through MPI and PVM implementations of two different parallel algorithms for the all-pairs shortest path problem. In addition to demonstrating the use of the basic functions in these two environments, it points out their differences where relevant. The chapter ends with porting hints from MPI to PVM and vice versa.

Chapter 4 examines the interoperability of different message passing environments for use in cluster computing. It describes three software packages available for linking MPI and PVM, namely, PACX-MPI, PLUS, and PVMPI. Next, it details the resource management support available in the PLUS-library. Adding new message environments to an existing environment is then illustrated together with performance results for experiments that were conducted toward this end.

Chapter 5 explores active objects for cluster computing. It presents the differences between active and passive objects, and then examines the atomicity requirement of objects. The chapter has a section on BaLinda K objects, and another one on speculative processing as it applies to active objects.

Chapter 6 describes the use of scoped behavior to optimize data sharing idioms using the example of the Aurora system. Aurora is a distributed shared data system. This chapter first gives an overview of the process models, shared-data objects, and scoped behavior in Aurora, illustrating these concepts via a matrix multiplication example. It then moves on to the implementation overview of Aurora. Experiences with three different applications, matrix multiplication, 2-D diffusion, and parallel sorting by regular sampling, are described.

Chapter 7 demonstrates a component-based approach for development of parallel applications on clusters. It first touches upon the main available approaches, and then moves on to the TRACS approach, focusing on its ability to reuse design components. It describes the TRACS approach through its API, the capability to reuse components, how to compile and run a distributed application within this model, and alternative design styles, among other things. It ends with an example of reusing sequential software in a distributed environment.

A fault tolerant tuple space system, LiPS (Library for Parallel Systems), is discussed in Chapter 8. It describes the cooperating run-time systems in LiPS, focusing on the fault tolerance, system runtime, and application run-time aspects. It then discusses the LiPS development system, with example applications such as distributed data structures, living data structures, message passing, and file use.

Tuple space programming in a cluster environment is the topic of discussion in Chapter 9. After an overview of tuple space programming, this chapter discusses the compilation environment for such systems with respect to basic translation and optimizing compilers. The run-time environment is next described with respect to both centralized and distributed data. Finally, extensions to the paradigms of multiple tuple spaces, persistent tuple spaces, fault-tolerant tuple spaces, and adaptive parallelism are detailed.

Chapter 10 discusses an important aspect of cluster computing, namely debugging parallelized codes. It focuses on the concept of debugging with code liberation, and discusses global renaming, name reclamation, and the debugging interface in that context. It also has a section on the additional benefits of code liberation in a cluster environment. It ends with some experimental results.

The last chapter in Part I, Chapter 11, focuses on WebOS, a framework for supporting geographically distributed, highly available, incrementally scalable, and dynamically reconfiguring applications. WebOS provides support for wide-area naming, persistent storage, security, and process execution. The chapter demonstrates how these primitives can be combined to develop Rent-A-Server, a Web server capable of dynamically replicating itself across a wide area in response to client access patterns. Performance measurements indicate that the system reduces latency and consumed wide-area bandwidth relative to existing static approaches to replication.

Chapter 1

Parallel Programming Models and Paradigms

Luís Moura e Silva[†] and Rajkumar Buyya[‡]

[†] Departamento de Engenharia Informática
Universidade de Coimbra, Polo II
3030 Coimbra - Portugal

[‡] School of Computer Science and Software Engineering
Monash University
Melbourne, Australia

Email: *luis@dei.uc.pt, rajkumar@ieee.org*

1.1   Introduction

In the 1980s it was believed computer performance was best improved by creating faster and more efficient processors. This idea was challenged by parallel processing, which in essence means linking together two or more computers to jointly solve a computational problem. Since the early 1990s there has been an increasing trend to move away from expensive and specialized proprietary parallel supercomputers (vector-supercomputers and massively parallel processors) towards networks of computers (PCs/Workstations/SMPs). Among the driving forces that have enabled this transition has been the rapid improvement in the availability of commodity high-performance components for PCs/workstations and networks. These technologies are making a network/cluster of computers an appealing vehicle for cost-effective parallel processing and this is consequently leading to low-cost commodity supercomputing.

Scalable computing clusters, ranging from a cluster of (homogeneous or heterogeneous) PCs or workstations, to SMPs, are rapidly becoming the standard platforms for high-performance and large-scale computing. The main attractiveness of such systems is that they are built using affordable, low-cost, commodity hardware (such as Pentium PCs), fast LAN such as Myrinet, and standard software components such as UNIX, MPI, and PVM parallel programming environments. These systems are scalable, i.e., they can be tuned to available budget and computational needs and allow efficient execution of both demanding sequential and parallel applications. Some examples of such systems are Berkeley NOW, HPVM, Beowulf, Solaris-MC, which have been discussed in Volume 1 of this book [8].

Clusters use intelligent mechanisms for dynamic and network-wide resource sharing, which respond to resource requirements and availability. These mechanisms support scalability of cluster performance and allow a flexible use of workstations, since the cluster or network-wide available resources are expected to be larger than the available resources at any one node/workstation of the cluster. These intelligent mechanisms also allow clusters to support multiuser, time-sharing parallel execution environments, where it is necessary to share resources and at the same time distribute the workload dynamically to utilize the global resources efficiently [4].

The idea of exploiting this significant computational capability available in networks of workstations (NOWs) has gained an enthusiastic acceptance within the high-performance computing community, and the current tendency favors this sort of commodity supercomputing. This is mainly motivated by the fact that most of the scientific community has the desire to minimize economic risk and rely on consumer based off-the-shelf technology. Cluster computing has been recognized as the wave of the future to solve large scientific and commercial problems.

We have presented some of the main motivations for the widespread use of clusters in high-performance parallel computing. In the next section, we discuss a generic architecture of a cluster computer and the rest of the chapter focuses on levels of parallelism, programming environments or models, possible strategies for writing parallel programs, and the two main approaches to parallelism (implicit and explicit). Within these two approaches, we briefly summarize the whole spectrum of choices to exploit parallel processing: through the use of parallelizing compilers, parallel languages, message-passing libraries, distributed shared memory, object-oriented programming, and programming skeletons. However, the main focus of the chapter is about the identification and description of the main parallel programming paradigms that are found in existing applications. At the end of the chapter, we present some examples of parallel libraries, tools, and environments that provide higher-level support for parallel programming through the use of skeletons or templates. This approach presents some interesting advantages, for example, the reuse of code, higher flexibility, and the increased productivity of the parallel program developer.

1.2   A Cluster Computer and its Architecture

A cluster is a type of parallel or distributed processing system, which consists of a collection of interconnected stand-alone computers working together as a single, integrated computing resource.

A computer node can be a single or multiprocessor system (PCs, workstations, or SMPs) with memory, I/O facilities, and an operating system. A cluster generally refers to two or more computers (nodes) connected together. The nodes can exist in a single cabinet or be physically separated and connected via a LAN. An inter-connected (LAN-based) cluster of computers can appear as a single system to users and applications. Such a system can provide a cost-effective way to gain features and benefits (fast and reliable services) that have historically been found only on more expensive proprietary shared memory systems. The typical architecture of a cluster is shown in Figure 1.1.

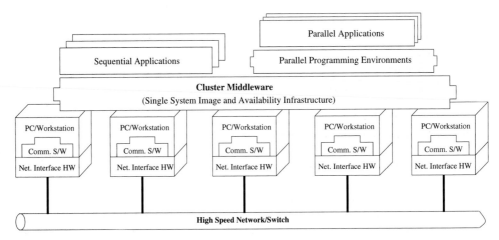

Figure 1.1 Cluster computer architecture.

The following are some prominent components of cluster computers:

- Multiple High Performance Computers (PCs, Workstations, or SMPs)

- State-of-the-art Operating Systems (Layered or Micro-kernel based)

- High Performance Networks/Switches (such as Gigabit Ethernet and Myrinet)

- Network Interface Cards (NICs)

- Fast Communication Protocols and Services (such as Active and Fast Messages)

- Cluster Middleware (Single System Image (SSI) and System Availability Infrastructure)

  - Hardware (such as Digital (DEC) Memory Channel, hardware DSM, and SMP techniques)

  - Operating System Kernel or Gluing Layer (such as Solaris MC and GLUnix)

- Applications and Subsystems
  * Applications (such as system management tools and electronic forms)
  * Run-time Systems (such as software DSM and parallel file-system)
  * Resource Management and Scheduling software (such as LSF (Load Sharing Facility) and CODINE (COmputing in DIstributed Networked Environments))

- Parallel Programming Environments and Tools (such as compilers, PVM (Parallel Virtual Machine), and MPI (Message Passing Interface))

- Applications

  - Sequential
  - Parallel or Distributed

The network interface hardware acts as a communication processor and is responsible for transmitting and receiving packets of data between cluster nodes via a network/switch.

Communication software offers a means of fast and reliable data communication among cluster nodes and to the outside world. Often, clusters with a special network/switch like Myrinet use communication protocols such as active messages for fast communication among its nodes. They potentially bypass the operating system and thus remove the critical communication overheads providing direct user-level access to the network interface.

The cluster nodes can work collectively as an integrated computing resource, or they can operate as individual computers. The cluster middleware is responsible for offering an illusion of a unified system image (single system image) and availability out of a collection on independent but interconnected computers.

Programming environments can offer portable, efficient, and easy-to-use tools for development of applications. They include message passing libraries, debuggers, and profilers. It should not be forgotten that clusters could be used for the execution of sequential or parallel applications.

1.3   Parallel Applications and Their Development

The class of applications that a cluster can typically cope with would be considered demanding sequential applications and grand challenge/supercomputing applications. Grand Challenge Applications (GCAs) are fundamental problems in science and engineering with broad economic and scientific impact [18]. They are generally considered intractable without the use of state-of-the-art parallel computers. The scale of their resource requirements, such as processing time, memory, and communication needs distinguishes GCAs.

A typical example of a grand challenge problem is the simulation of some phenomena that cannot be measured through experiments. GCAs include massive crystallographic and microtomographic structural problems, protein dynamics and biocatalysis, relativistic quantum chemistry of actinides, virtual materials design and processing, global climate modeling, and discrete event simulation.

Although the technology of clusters is currently being deployed, the development of parallel applications is really a complex task. First of all, it is largely dependent on the availability of adequate software tools and environments. Second, parallel software developers must contend with problems not encountered during sequential programming, namely: non-determinism, communication, synchronization, data partitioning and distribution, load-balancing, fault-tolerance, heterogeneity, shared or distributed memory, deadlocks, and race conditions. All these issues present some new important challenges.

Currently, only some specialized programmers have the knowledge to use parallel and distributed systems for executing production codes. This programming technology is still somehow distant from the average sequential programmer, who does not feel very enthusiastic about moving into a different programming style with increased difficulties, though they are aware of the potential performance gains. Parallel computing can only be widely successful if parallel software is able to accomplish some expectations of the users, such as:

- provide architecture/processor type transparency;
- provide network/communication transparency;
- be easy-to-use and reliable;
- provide support for fault-tolerance;
- accommodate heterogeneity;
- assure portability;
- provide support for traditional high-level languages;
- be capable of delivering increased performance;
- and finally, the *holy-grail* is to provide parallelism transparency.

This last expectation is still at least one decade away, but most of the others can be achieved today. The internal details of the underlying architecture should be hidden from the user and the programming environment should provide high-level support for parallelism. Otherwise, if the programming interface is difficult to use, it makes the writing of parallel applications highly unproductive and painful for most programmers. There are basically two main approaches for parallel programming:

1. the first one is based on *implicit parallelism*. This approach has been followed by parallel languages and parallelizing compilers. The user does not specify, and thus cannot control, the scheduling of calculations and/or the placement of data;

2. the second one relies on *explicit parallelism*. In this approach, the programmer is responsible for most of the parallelization effort such as task decomposition, mapping tasks to processors, and the communication structure. This

approach is based on the assumption that the user is often the best judge of how parallelism can be exploited for a particular application.

It is also observed that the use of explicit parallelism will obtain a better efficiency than parallel languages or compilers that use implicit parallelism.

1.3.1   Strategies for Developing Parallel Applications

Undoubtedly, the main software issue is to decide between either porting existing sequential applications or developing new parallel applications from scratch. There are three strategies for creating parallel applications, as shown in Figure 1.2.

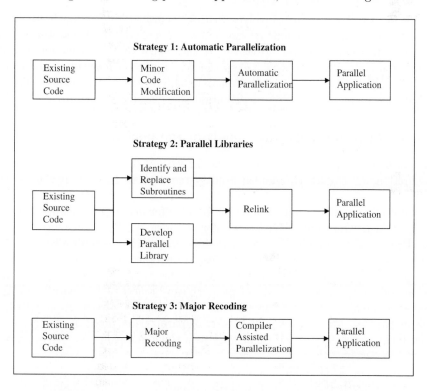

Figure 1.2 Porting strategies for parallel applications.

The first strategy is based on automatic parallelization, the second is based on the use of parallel libraries, while the third strategy—major recoding—resembles *from-scratch* application development.

The goal of automatic parallelization is to relieve the programmer from the parallelizing tasks. Such a compiler would accept *dusty-deck* codes and produce efficient parallel object code without any (or, at least, very little) additional work by the programmer. However, this is still very hard to achieve and is well beyond the reach of current compiler technology.

Another possible approach for porting parallel code is the use of parallel libraries. This approach has been more successful than the previous one. The basic idea is to encapsulate some of the parallel code that is common to several applications into a parallel library that can be implemented in a very efficient way. Such a library can then be reused by several codes. Parallel libraries can take two forms:

1. they encapsulate the control structure of a class of applications;

2. they provide a parallel implementation of some mathematical routines that are heavily used in the kernel of some production codes.

The third strategy, which involves writing a parallel application from the very beginning, gives more freedom to the programmer who can choose the language and the programming model. However, it may make the task very difficult since little of the code can be reused. Compiler assistance techniques can be of great help, although with a limited applicability. Usually the tasks that can be effectively provided by a compiler are data distribution and placement.

1.4   Code Granularity and Levels of Parallelism

In modern computers, parallelism appears at various levels both in hardware and software: signal, circuit, component, and system levels. That is, at the very lowest level, signals travel in parallel along parallel data paths. At a slightly higher level, multiple functional units operate in parallel for faster performance, popularly known as *instruction level parallelism*. For instance, a PC processor such as Pentium Pro has the capability to process three instructions simultaneously. Many computers overlap CPU and I/O activities; for instance, a disk access for one user while executing instruction of another user. Some computers use a memory interleaving technique – several banks of memory can be accessed in parallel for faster accesses to memory. At a still higher level, SMP systems have multiple CPUs that work in parallel. At an even higher level of parallelism, one can connect several computers together and make them work as a single machine, popularly known as cluster computing.

The first two levels (signal and circuit level) of parallelism is performed by a hardware implicitly technique called hardware parallelism. The remaining two levels (component and system) of parallelism is mostly expressed implicitly/explicitly by using various software techniques, popularly known as software parallelism.

Levels of parallelism can also be based on the lumps of code (grain size) that can be a potential candidate for parallelism. Table 1.1 lists categories of code granularity for parallelism. All approaches of creating parallelism based on code granularity have a common goal to boost processor efficiency by hiding latency of a lengthy operation such as a memory/disk access. To conceal latency, there must be another activity ready to run whenever a lengthy operation occurs. The idea is to execute concurrently two or more single-threaded applications, such as compiling, text formatting, database searching, and device simulation, or parallelized applications having multiple tasks simultaneously.

Table 1.1 Code Granularity and Parallelism

Grain Size	Code Item	Parallelised by
Very Fine	Instruction	Processor
Fine	Loop/Instruction block	Compiler
Medium	Standard One Page Function	Programmer
Large	Program-Separate heavyweight process	Programmer

Parallelism in an application can be detected at several levels. They are:

- very-fine grain (multiple instruction issue)
- fine-grain (data-level)
- medium-grain (or control-level)
- large-grain (or task-level)

The different levels of parallelism are depicted in Figure 1.3. Among the four levels of parallelism, the first two levels are supported transparently either by the hardware or parallelizing compilers. The programmer mostly handles the last two levels of parallelism. The three important models used in developing applications are shared-memory model, distributed memory model (message passing model), and distributed-shared memory model. These models are discussed in Chapter 2.

1.5   Parallel Programming Models and Tools

This section presents a brief overview on the area of parallel programming and describes the main approaches and models, including parallelizing compilers, parallel languages, message-passing, virtual shared memory, object-oriented programming, and programming skeletons.

1.5.1   Parallelizing Compilers

There has been some research in parallelizing compilers and parallel languages but their functionality is still very limited. Parallelizing compilers are still limited to applications that exhibit *regular* parallelism, such as computations in loops. Parallelizing/vectorizing compilers have proven to be relatively successful for some applications on shared-memory multiprocessors and vector processors with shared memory, but are largely unproven for distributed-memory machines. The difficulties are due to the non uniform access time of memory in the latter systems. The currently existing compiler technology for automatic parallelization is thus limited in scope and only rarely provides adequate speedup.

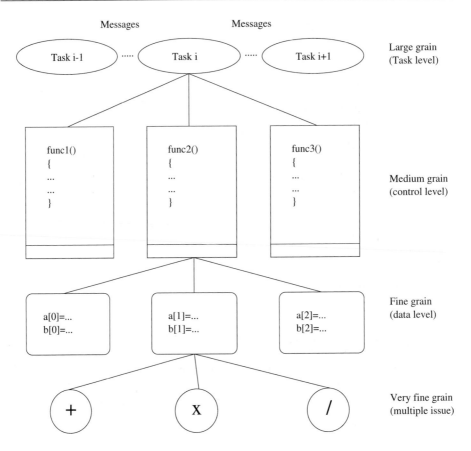

Figure 1.3 Detecting parallelism.

1.5.2 Parallel Languages

Some parallel languages, like SISAL [11] and PCN [13] have found little favor with application programmers. This is because users are not willing to learn a completely new language for parallel programming. They really would prefer to use their traditional high-level languages (like C and Fortran) and try to recycle their already available sequential software. For these programmers, the extensions to existing languages or run-time libraries are a viable alternative.

1.5.3 High Performance Fortran

The High Performance Fortran (HPF) initiative [20] seems to be a promising solution to solve the *dusty-deck* problem of Fortran codes. However, it only supports applications that follow the SPMD paradigm and have a very regular structure. Other applications that are missing these characteristics and present a more asynchronous structure are not as successful with the current versions of HPF. Current and future research will address these issues.

1.5.4   Message Passing

Message passing libraries allow efficient parallel programs to be written for distributed memory systems. These libraries provide routines to initiate and configure the messaging environment as well as sending and receiving packets of data. Currently, the two most popular high-level message-passing systems for scientific and engineering application are the PVM (Parallel Virtual Machine) from Oak Ridge National Laboratory and MPI (Message Passing Interface) defined by the MPI Forum.

Currently, there are several implementations of MPI, including versions for networks of workstations, clusters of personal computers, distributed-memory multiprocessors, and shared-memory machines. Almost every hardware vendor is supporting MPI. This gives the user a comfortable feeling since an MPI program can be executed on almost all of the existing computing platforms without the need to rewrite the program from scratch. The goal of portability, architecture, and network transparency has been achieved with these low-level communication libraries like MPI and PVM. Both communication libraries provide an interface for C and Fortran, and additional support of graphical tools.

However, these message-passing systems are still stigmatized as low-level because most tasks of the parallelization are still left to the application programmer. When writing parallel applications using message passing, the programmer still has to develop a significant amount of software to manage some of the tasks of the parallelization, such as: the communication and synchronization between processes, data partitioning and distribution, mapping of processes onto processors, and input/output of data structures. If the application programmer has no special support for these tasks, it then becomes difficult to widely exploit parallel computing. The easy-to-use goal is not accomplished with a bare message-passing system, and hence requires additional support.

Other ways to provide alternate-programming models are based on Virtual Shared Memory (VSM) and parallel object-oriented programming. Another way is to provide a set of programming skeletons in the form of run-time libraries that already support some of the tasks of parallelization and can be implemented on top of portable message-passing systems like PVM or MPI.

1.5.5   Virtual Shared Memory

VSM implements a shared-memory programming model in a distributed-memory environment. Linda is an example of this style of programming [1]. It is based on the notion of generative communication model and on a virtual shared associative memory, called tuple space, that is accessible to all the processes by using *in* and *out* operations.

Distributed Shared Memory (DSM) is the extension of the well-accepted shared-memory programming model on systems without physically shared memory [21]. The shared data space is flat and accessed through normal read and write operations. In contrast to message passing, in a DSM system a process that wants to fetch some data value does not need to know its location; the system will find and fetch it automatically. In most of the DSM systems, shared data may be replicated to enhance the parallelism and the efficiency of the applications.

While scalable parallel machines are mostly based on distributed memory, many users may find it easier to write parallel programs using a shared-memory programming model. This makes DSM a very promising model, provided it can be implemented efficiently.

1.5.6 Parallel Object-Oriented Programming

The idea behind parallel object-oriented programming is to provide suitable abstractions and software engineering methods for structured application design. As in the traditional object model, objects are defined as abstract data types, which encapsulate their internal state through well-defined interfaces and thus represent passive data containers. If we treat this model as a collection of shared objects, we can find an interesting resemblance with the shared data model.

The object-oriented programming model is by now well established as the state-of-the-art software engineering methodology for sequential programming, and recent developments are also emerging to establish object-orientation in the area of parallel programming. The current lack of acceptance of this model among the scientific community can be explained by the fact that computational scientists still prefer to write their programs using traditional languages like Fortran. This is the main difficulty that has been faced by the object-oriented environments, though it is considered as a promising technique for parallel programming. Some interesting object-oriented environments such as CC++ and Mentat have been presented in the literature [24].

1.5.7 Programming Skeletons

Another alternative to the use of message-passing is to provide a set of high-level abstractions which provides support for the mostly used parallel paradigms. A programming paradigm is a class of algorithms that solve different problems but have the same control structure [19]. Programming paradigms usually encapsulate information about useful data and communication patterns, and an interesting idea is to provide such abstractions in the form of programming templates or skeletons. A skeleton corresponds to the instantiation of a specific parallel programming paradigm, and it encapsulates the control and communication primitives of the application into a single abstraction.

After the recognition of parallelizable parts and an identification of the appropriate algorithm, a lot of developing time is wasted on programming routines closely related to the paradigm and not the application itself. With the aid of a good set of efficiently programmed interaction routines and skeletons, the development time can be reduced significantly.

The skeleton hides from the user the specific details of the implementation and allows the user to specify the computation in terms of an interface tailored to the paradigm. This leads to a style of skeleton oriented programming (SOP) which has been identified as a very promising solution for parallel computing [6].

Skeletons are more general programming methods since they can be implemented on top of message-passing, object-oriented, shared-memory or distributed memory systems, and provide increased support for parallel programming.

To summarize, there are basically two ways of looking at an explicit parallel programming system. In the first one, the system provides some primitives to be used by the programmer. The structuring and the implementation of most of the parallel control and communication is the responsibility of the programmer. The alternative is to provide some enhanced support for those control structures that are common to a parallel programming paradigm. The main task of the programmer would be to provide those few routines unique to the application, such as computation and data generation. Numerous parallel programming environments are available, and many of them do attempt to exploit the characteristics of parallel paradigms.

1.6   Methodical Design of Parallel Algorithms

There is no simple recipe for designing parallel algorithms. However, it can benefit from a methodological approach that maximizes the range of options, that provides mechanisms for evaluating alternatives, and that reduces the cost of backtracking from wrong choices. The design methodology allows the programmer to focus on machine-independent issues such as concurrency in the early stage of design process, and machine-specific aspects of design are delayed until late in the design process. As suggested by Ian Foster, this methodology organizes the design process into four distinct stages [12]:

- partitioning

- communication

- agglomeration

- mapping

The first two stages seek to develop concurrent and scalable algorithms, and the last two stages focus on locality and performance-related issues as summarized below:

1.6.1   Partitioning

It refers to decomposing of the computational activities and the data on which it operates into several small tasks. The decomposition of the data associated with a problem is known as *domain/data decomposition*, and the decomposition of computation into disjoint tasks is known as *functional decomposition*. Various paradigms underlying the partitioning process are discussed in the next section.

1.6.2   Communication

It focuses on the flow of information and coordination among the tasks that are created during the partitioning stage. The nature of the problem and the decomposition method determine the communication pattern among these cooperative tasks of a parallel program. The four popular communication patterns commonly used in parallel programs are: local/global, structured/unstructured, static/dynamic, and synchronous/asynchronous.

1.6.3   Agglomeration

In this stage, the tasks and communication structure defined in the first two stages are evaluated in terms of performance requirements and implementation costs. If required, tasks are grouped into larger tasks to improve performance or to reduce development costs. Also, individual communications may be bundled into a *super* communication. This will help in reducing communication costs by increasing computation and communication granularity, gaining flexibility in terms of scalability and mapping decisions, and reducing software-engineering costs.

1.6.4   Mapping

It is concerned with assigning each task to a processor such that it maximizes utilization of system resources (such as CPU) while minimizing the communication costs. Mapping decisions can be taken statically (at compile-time/before program execution) or dynamically at runtime by load-balancing methods as discussed in Volume 1 of this book [8] and Chapter 17.

Several grand challenging applications have been built using the above methodology (refer to Part III, Algorithms and Applications, for further details on the development of real-life applications using the above methodology).

1.7   Parallel Programming Paradigms

It has been widely recognized that parallel applications can be classified into some well defined programming paradigms. A few programming paradigms are used repeatedly to develop many parallel programs. Each paradigm is a class of algorithms that have the same control structure [19].

Experience to date suggests that there are a relatively small number of paradigms underlying most parallel programs [7]. The choice of paradigm is determined by the available parallel computing resources and by the type of parallelism inherent in the problem. The computing resources may define the level of granularity that can be efficiently supported on the system. The type of parallelism reflects the structure of either the application or the data and both types may exist in different parts of the same application. Parallelism arising from the structure of the application is named as functional parallelism. In this case, different parts of the program can perform different tasks in a concurrent and cooperative manner. But parallelism may also be found in the structure of the data. This type of parallelism allows the execution of parallel processes with identical operation but on different parts of the data.

1.7.1   Choice of Paradigms

Most of the typical distributed computing applications are based on the very popular client/server paradigm. In this paradigm, the processes usually communicate through Remote Procedure Calls (RPCs), but there is no inherent parallelism in this sort of applications. They are instead used to support distributed services, and thus we do not consider this paradigm in the parallel computing area.

In the world of parallel computing there are several authors which present a paradigm classification. Not all of them propose exactly the same one, but we can create a superset of the paradigms detected in parallel applications.

For instance, in [22], a theoretical classification of parallel programs is presented and broken into three classes of parallelism:

1. processor farms, which are based on replication of independent jobs;

2. geometric decomposition, based on the parallelisation of data structures; and

3. algorithmic parallelism, which results in the use of data flow.

Another classification was presented in [19]. The author studied several parallel applications and identified the following set of paradigms:

1. pipelining and ring-based applications;

2. divide and conquer;

3. master/slave; and

4. cellular automata applications, which are based on data parallelism.

The author of [23] also proposed a very appropriate classification. The problems were divided into a few decomposition techniques, namely:

1. Geometric decomposition: the problem domain is broken up into smaller domains and each process executes the algorithm on each part of it.

2. Iterative decomposition: some applications are based on loop execution where each iteration can be done in an independent way. This approach is implemented through a central queue of runnable tasks, and thus corresponds to the task-farming paradigm.

3. Recursive decomposition: this strategy starts by breaking the original problem into several subproblems and solving these in a parallel way. It clearly corresponds to a divide and conquer approach.

4. Speculative decomposition: some problems can use a speculative decomposition approach: N solution techniques are tried simultaneously, and (N-1) of them are thrown away as soon as the first one returns a plausible answer. In some cases this could result optimistically in a shorter overall execution time.

5. Functional decomposition: the application is broken down into many distinct phases, where each phase executes a different algorithm within the same problem. The most used topology is the process pipelining.

In [15], a somewhat different classification was presented based on the temporal structure of the problems. The applications were thus divided into:

1. synchronous problems, which correspond to regular computations on regular data domains;

2. loosely synchronous problems, that are typified by iterative calculations on geometrically irregular data domains;

3. asynchronous problems, which are characterized by functional parallelism that is irregular in space and time; and

4. embarrassingly parallel applications, which correspond to the independent execution of disconnected components of the same program.

Synchronous and loosely synchronous problems present a somehow different synchronization structure, but both rely on data decomposition techniques. According to an extensive analysis of 84 real applications presented in [14], it was estimated that these two classes of problems dominated scientific and engineering applications being used in 76 percent of the applications. Asynchronous problems, which are for instance represented by event-driven simulations, represented 10 percent of the studied problems. Finally, embarrassingly parallel applications that correspond to the master/slave model, accounted for 14 percent of the applications.

The most systematic definition of paradigms and application templates was presented in [6]. It describes a generic tuple of factors which fully characterizes a parallel algorithm including: process properties (structure, topology and execution), interaction properties, and data properties (partitioning and placement). That classification included most of the paradigms referred so far, albeit described in deeper detail.

To summarize, the following paradigms are popularly used in parallel programming:

- Task-Farming (or Master/Slave)

- Single Program Multiple Data (SPMD)

- Data Pipelining

- Divide and Conquer

- Speculative Parallelism

1.7.2   Task-Farming (or Master/Slave)

The task-farming paradigm consists of two entities: master and multiple slaves. The master is responsible for decomposing the problem into small tasks (and distributes these tasks among a farm of slave processes), as well as for gathering the partial results in order to produce the final result of the computation. The slave processes execute in a very simple cycle: get a message with the task, process the task, and send the result to the master. Usually, the communication takes place only between the master and the slaves.

Task-farming may either use static load-balancing or dynamic load-balancing. In the first case, the distribution of tasks is all performed at the beginning of the computation, which allows the master to participate in the computation after each slave has been allocated a fraction of the work. The allocation of tasks can be done once or in a cyclic way. Figure 1.4 presents a schematic representation of this first approach.

The other way is to use a dynamically load-balanced master/slave paradigm, which can be more suitable when the number of tasks exceeds the number of available processors, or when the number of tasks is unknown at the start of the application, or when the execution times are not predictable, or when we are dealing with unbalanced problems. An important feature of dynamic load-balancing is the ability of the application to adapt itself to changing conditions of the system, not just the load of the processors, but also a possible reconfiguration of the system resources. Due to this characteristic, this paradigm can respond quite well to the failure of some processors, which simplifies the creation of robust applications that are capable of surviving the loss of slaves or even the master.

At an extreme, this paradigm can also enclose some applications that are based on a trivial decomposition approach: the sequential algorithm is executed simultaneously on different processors but with different data inputs. In such applications there are no dependencies between different runs so there is no need for communication or coordination between the processes.

This paradigm can achieve high computational speedups and an interesting degree of scalability. However, for a large number of processors the centralized control of the master process can become a bottleneck to the applications. It is, however, possible to enhance the scalability of the paradigm by extending the single master to a set of masters, each of them controlling a different group of process slaves.

1.7.3   Single-Program Multiple-Data (SPMD)

The SPMD paradigm is the most commonly used paradigm. Each process executes basically the same piece of code but on a different part of the data. This involves

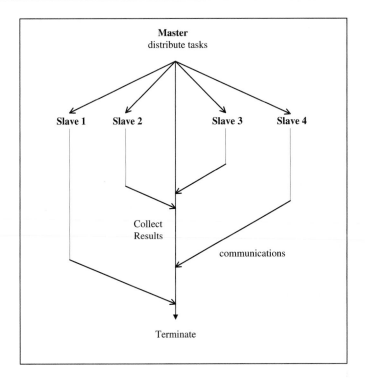

Figure 1.4 A static master/slave structure.

the splitting of application data among the available processors. This type of parallelism is also referred to as geometric parallelism, domain decomposition, or data parallelism. Figure 1.5 presents a schematic representation of this paradigm.

Many physical problems have an underlying regular geometric structure, with spatially limited interactions. This homogeneity allows the data to be distributed uniformly across the processors, where each one will be responsible for a defined spatial area. Processors communicate with neighbouring processors and the communication load will be proportional to the size of the boundary of the element, while the computation load will be proportional to the volume of the element. It may also be required to perform some global synchronization periodically among all the processes. The communication pattern is usually highly structured and extremely predictable. The data may initially be self-generated by each process or may be read from the disk during the initialization stage.

SPMD applications can be very efficient if the data is well distributed by the processes and the system is homogeneous. If the processes present different workloads or capabilities, then the paradigm requires the support of some load-balancing scheme able to adapt the data distribution layout during run-time execution.

This paradigm is highly sensitive to the loss of some process. Usually, the loss of a single process is enough to cause a deadlock in the calculation in which none of the processes can advance beyond a global synchronization point.

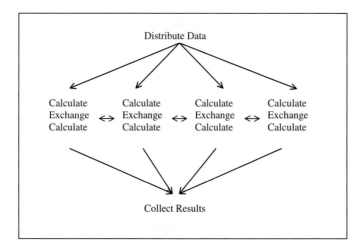

Figure 1.5 Basic structure of a SPMD program.

1.7.4   Data Pipelining

This is a more fine-grained parallelism, which is based on a functional decomposition approach: the tasks of the algorithm, which are capable of concurrent operation, are identified and each processor executes a small part of the total algorithm. The pipeline is one of the simplest and most popular functional decomposition paradigms. Figure 1.6 presents the structure of this model.

Processes are organized in a pipeline – each process corresponds to a stage of the pipeline and is responsible for a particular task. The communication pattern can be very simple since the data flows between the adjacent stages of the pipeline. For this reason, this type of parallelism is also sometimes referred to as data flow parallelism. The communication may be completely asynchronous. The efficiency of this paradigm is directly dependent on the ability to balance the load across the stages of the pipeline. The robustness of this paradigm against reconfigurations of the system can be achieved by providing multiple independent paths across the stages. This paradigm is often used in data reduction or image processing applications.

1.7.5   Divide and Conquer

The divide and conquer approach is well known in sequential algorithm development. A problem is divided up into two or more subproblems. Each of these subproblems is solved independently and their results are combined to give the final result. Often, the smaller problems are just smaller instances of the original

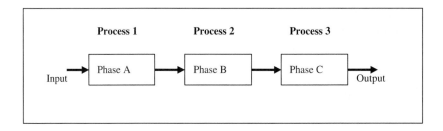

Figure 1.6 Data pipeline structure.

problem, giving rise to a recursive solution. Processing may be required to divide the original problem or to combine the results of the subproblems. In parallel divide and conquer, the subproblems can be solved at the same time, given sufficient parallelism. The splitting and recombining process also makes use of some parallelism, but these operations require some process communication. However, because the subproblems are independent, no communication is necessary between processes working on different subproblems.

We can identify three generic computational operations for divide and conquer: split, compute, and join. The application is organized in a sort of virtual tree: some of the processes create subtasks and have to combine the results of those to produce an aggregate result. The tasks are actually computed by the compute processes at the leaf nodes of the virtual tree. Figure 1.7 presents this execution.

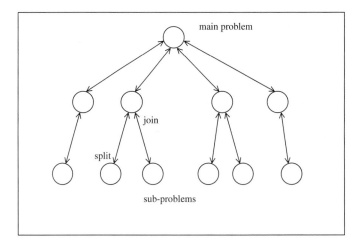

Figure 1.7 Divide and conquer as a virtual tree.

The task-farming paradigm can be seen as a slightly modified, degenerated form of divide and conquer; i.e., where problem decomposition is performed before tasks are submitted, the split and join operations is only done by the master process and all the other processes are only responsible for the computation.

In the divide and conquer model, tasks may be generated during runtime and may be added to a single job queue on the manager processor or distributed through several job queues across the system.

The programming paradigms can be mainly characterized by two factors: decomposition and distribution of the parallelism. For instance, in geometric parallelism both the decomposition and distribution are static. The same happens with the functional decomposition and distribution of data pipelining. In task farming, the work is statically decomposed but dynamically distributed. Finally, in the divide and conquer paradigm both decomposition and distribution are dynamic.

1.7.6   Speculative Parallelism

This paradigm is employed when it is quite difficult to obtain parallelism through any one of the previous paradigms. Some problems have complex data dependencies, which reduces the possibilities of exploiting the parallel execution. In these cases, an appropriate solution is to execute the problem in small parts but use some speculation or optimistic execution to facilitate the parallelism.

In some asynchronous problems, like discrete-event simulation [17], the system will attempt the *look-ahead execution* of related activities in an optimistic assumption that such concurrent executions do not violate the consistency of the problem execution. Sometimes they do, and in such cases it is necessary to rollback to some previous consistent state of the application.

Another use of this paradigm is to employ different algorithms for the same problem; the first one to give the final solution is the one that is chosen.

1.7.7   Hybrid Models

The boundaries between the paradigms can sometimes be fuzzy and, in some applications, there could be the need to mix elements of different paradigms. Hybrid methods that include more than one basic paradigm are usually observed in some large-scale parallel applications. These are situations where it makes sense to mix data and task parallelism simultaneously or in different parts of the same program.

1.8   Programming Skeletons and Templates

The term skeleton has been identified by two important characteristics [10]:

- it provides only an underlying structure that can be hidden from the user;

- it is incomplete and can be parameterized, not just by the number of processors, but also by other factors, such as granularity, topology and data distribution.

Hiding the underlying structure from the user by presenting a simple interface results in programs that are easier to understand and maintain, as well as less prone to error. In particular, the programmer can now focus on the computational task rather than the control and coordination of the parallelism.

Exploiting the observation that parallel applications follow some well-identified structures, much of the parallel software specific to the paradigm can be potentially reusable. Such software can be encapsulated in parallel libraries to promote the reuse of code, reduce the burden on the parallel programmer, and to facilitate the task of recycling existing sequential programs. This guideline was followed by the PUL project [9], the TINA system [7], and the ARNIA package [16].

A project developed at the Edinburgh Parallel Computing Centre [9] involved the writing of a package of parallel utilities (PUL) on top of MPI that gives programming support for the most common programming paradigms as well as parallel input/output. Apart from the libraries for global and parallel I/O, the collection of the PUL utilities includes a library for task-farming applications (PUL-TF), another that supports regular domain decomposition applications (PUL-RD), and another one that can be used to program irregular mesh-based problems (PUL-SM). This set of PUL utilities hides the hard details of the parallel implementation from the application programmer and provides a portable programming interface that can be used on several computing platforms. To ensure programming flexibility, the application can make simultaneous use of different PUL libraries and have direct access to the MPI communication routines.

The ARNIA package [16] includes a library for master/slave applications, another for the domain decomposition paradigm, a special library for distributed computing applications based on the client/server model, and a fourth library that supports a global shared memory emulation. ARNIA allows the combined use of its building libraries for those applications that present mixed paradigms or distinct computational phases.

In [7], a skeleton generator was presented, called TINA, that supports the reusability and portability of parallel program components and provides a complete programming environment.

Another graphical programming environment, named TRACS (see Chapter 7), provides a graphical toolkit to design distributed/parallel applications based on reusable components, such as farms, grids, and pipes.

Porting and rewriting application programs requires a support environment that encourages code reuse, portability among different platforms, and scalability across similar systems of different size. This approach, based on skeletal frameworks, is a viable solution for parallel programming. It can significantly increase programmer productivity because programmers will be able to develop parts of programs simply by filling in the templates. The development of software templates has been increasingly receiving the attention of academic research and is seen as one of the key directions for parallel software.

The most important advantages of this approach for parallel programming are summarized below.

1.8.1   Programmability

A set of ready-to-use solutions for parallelization will considerably increase the productivity of the programmers: the idea is to hide the lower level details of the system, to promote the reuse of code, and relieve the burden of the application programmer. This approach will increase the programmability of the parallel systems since the programmer will have more time to spend in optimizing the application itself, rather than on low-level details of the underlying programming system.

1.8.2   Reusability

Reusability is a hot-topic in software engineering. The provision of skeletons or templates to the application programmer increases the potential for reuse by allowing the same parallel structure to be used in different applications. This avoids the replication of efforts involved in developing and optimizing the code specific to the parallel template. In [3] it was reported that a percentage of code reuse rose from 30 percent up to 90 percent when using skeleton-oriented programming. In the Chameleon system [2], 60 percent of the code was reusable, while in [5] it was reported that an average fraction of 80 percent of the code was reused with the ROPE library.

1.8.3   Portability

Providing portability of the parallel applications is a problem of paramount importance. It allows applications developed on one platform to run on another platform without the need for redevelopment.

1.8.4   Efficiency

There could be some conflicting trade-off between optimal performance and portability/programmability. Both portability and efficiency of parallel programming systems play an important role in the success of parallel computing.

1.9   Conclusions

This chapter presented a brief overview about the motivations for using clusters in parallel computing, presented the main models of execution (parallelizing compilers, message-passing libraries, virtual shared-memory, object-oriented programming), and described the mostly used parallel programming paradigms that can be found in existing applications. At the end of the chapter we have underlined the most important advantages of using programming skeletons and environments for higher-level parallel programming.

In these past years there has been a considerable effort in developing software for exploiting the computational power of parallel, distributed, and cluster-based systems. Many advances have been achieved in parallel software but there is still considerable work to do in the next decade in order to effectively exploit the computational power of cluster for parallel high performance computing.

Acknowledgment

We thank Dan Hyde (Bucknell University, USA) for his comments and suggestions on this chapter.

1.10   Bibliography

[1] S. Ahuja, N. Carriero, and D. Gelernter. Linda and Friends. *IEEE Computer,* pages 26-34, August 1986.

[2] G.A. Alverson and D. Notkin. Program Structuring for Effective Parallel Portability. *IEEE Transactions on Parallel and Distributed Systems,* vol. 4 (9), pages 1041-1069, September 1993.

[3] B. Bacci, M. Danelutto, S. Orlando, S. Pelagatti and M. Vanneschi. Summarising an Experiment in Parallel Programming Language Design. *Lecture Notes in Computer Science,* 919, High-Performance Computing and Networking, HPCN'95, Milano, Italy, pages 7-13, 1995.

[4] A. Barak and O. La'adan. Performance of the MOSIX Parallel System for a Cluster of PC's. In *Proceedings of HPCN - Europe conference,* 1997.

[5] J.C. Browne, T. Lee, and J.Werth. Experimental Evaluation of a Reusability-Oriented Parallel Programming Environment. *IEEE Transactions on Software Engineering,* vol. 16 (2), pages 111-120, February 1990.

[6] H. Burkhart, C.F. Korn, S. Gutzwiller, P. Ohnacker, and S.Waser. em BACS: Basel Algorithm Classification Scheme. *Technical Report 93-03,* Univ. Basel, Switzerland, 1993.

[7] H. Burkhart and S. Gutzwiller. Steps Towards Reusability and Portability in Parallel Programming. In *Programming Environments for Massively Parallel Distributed Systems,* Monte Verita, Switzerland pages 147-157, April 1994.

[8] R. Buyya (editor). *High Performance Cluster Computing: Systems and Architectures.* Volume 1, Prentice Hall PTR, NJ, 1999.

[9] L. Clarke, R. Fletcher, S. Trewin, A. Bruce, G. Smith, and S. Chapple. Reuse, Portability and Parallel Libraries. In *Proceedings of IFIP WG10.3 Working Conference on Programming Environments for Massively Parallel and Distributed Systems,* Monte Verita, Switzerland, April 1994.

[10] M.Cole. *Algorithmic Skeletons: Structured Management of Parallel Computations.* MIT Press, Cambridge, MA, 1989.

[11] J. Feo, D. Cann, and R. Oldehoeft. A Report on the SISAL Language Project. *Journal of Parallel and Distributed Computing,* vol 10, pages 349-366, 1990.

[12] I. Foster. *Designing and Building Parallel Programs.* Addison Wesley, 1996, available at `http://www.mcs.anl.gov/dbpp`

[13] I. Foster and S. Tuecke. Parallel Programming with PCN. *Technical Report ANL-91/32,* Argonne National Laboratory, Argonne, December 1991.

[14] G. Fox. What Have We Learnt from Using Real Parallel Machines to Solve Real Problems. In *Proceedings 3rd Conf. Hypercube Concurrent Computers and Applications,* 1988.

[15] G. Fox. Parallel Computing Comes of Age: Supercomputer Level Parallel Computations at Caltech. *Concurrency: Practice and Experience,* vol. 1 (1), pages 63-103, September 1989.

[16] M. Fruscione, P. Flocchini, E. Giudici, S. Punzi, and P. Stofella. Parallel Computational Frames: An Approach to Parallel Application Development based on Message Passing Systems. In *Programming Environments for Massively Parallel Distributed Systems,* Monte Verita, Italy, pages 117-126, 1994.

[17] R. M. Fujimoto. Parallel Discrete Event Simulation. *Communications of the ACM,* vol.33 (10), pages 30-53, October 1990.

[18] *Grand Challenging Applications.* `http://www.mcs.anl.gov/Projects/grand-challenges/`

[19] P. B. Hansen. Model Programs for Computational Science: A Programming Methodology for Multicomputers. *Concurrency: Practice and Experience,* vol. 5 (5), pages 407-423, 1993.

[20] D. Loveman. High-Performance Fortran. *IEEE Parallel and Distributed Technology,* vol. 1 (1), February 1993.

[21] B. Nitzberg and V. Lo. Distributed Shared Memory: A Survey of Issues and Algorithms. *IEEE Computer,* vol. 24 (8), pages 52-60, 1991.

[22] D. Pritchard. Mathematical Models of Distributed Computation. In *Proceedings of OUG-7, Parallel Programming on Transputer Based Machines,* IOS Press, pages 25-36, 1988.

[23] G. Wilson. *Parallel Programming for Scientists and Engineers.* MIT Press, Cambridge, MA, 1995.

[24] G. Wilson and P. Lu. *Parallel Programming using C++.* MIT Press, Cambridge, MA, 1996.

Chapter 2

Parallel Programming Languages and Environments

IRA PRAMANICK

Silicon Graphics Inc.
Mountain View, California
USA

Email: *ira@sgi.com*

2.1 Introduction

Parallel computers or multiple CPU computers were born about two decades ago, and one of their main functions was to solve various types of problems faster by throwing the computational power of more than one CPU at a problem. To utilize the resources of a parallel computer, a problem had to be algorithmically expressed as comprising a set of concurrently executing subproblems or tasks. This was achieved via the use of parallel models, languages, and/or environments that encapsulate the way in which the various tasks cooperate to provide the solution to the original problem. Many ideas from a single CPU multiprogramming operating system environment were borrowed since these form the underlying principles for supporting more than one process on a computer.

Many of the early parallel computers supported very low level parallel primitives that typically rendered them difficult to use. This was not a problem initially since the use of such computers was limited to a small set of programmers, both because these computers presented a novel challenge for solving problems and because such computers were very expensive resources. However, the increasing popularity of such computers for solving large problems quickly, and their decreasing cost over the past two decades, led to demands for better programming environments. Also, as various new applications were considered as candidates for parallel processing, new models for effective cooperation among the tasks were proposed. The result has been the introduction of a multitude of parallel programming languages and environments over the years. These have different features and cover the entire spectrum of requirements, ranging from providing easy to use, high level primitives to very low level primitives that give the programmer a greater amount of flexibility in controlling the execution of the tasks in their parallel programs. Also, since the interaction between tasks of a program can be performed in many ways, each language focuses on a subset of these paradigms.

Orthogonal to these features are the types of hardware architectures for which such environments and languages are best suited. A parallel computer consists of a set of CPUs, memory modules, and an interconnection network (or switch or bus) that connects together the first two types of components. The interconnection of CPUs and memory modules of a parallel computer may be represented by two different kinds of models: the pure shared memory model, where the entire memory space is globally addressable from any of the CPUs in the computer; and the distributed memory model, where each memory module is only addressable from the CPU to which it is attached. These define the two ends of the memory-CPU spectrum with various hybrid models in between. A notable one is a distributed shared memory model or DSM where each memory module is physically attached to one or a subset of the CPUs, but the entire memory is globally addressable by an application. The underlying hardware together with the operating system running on top of it take care of translating the physically distributed memory space to a globally addressable one. Such systems are also referred to as virtual shared memory systems.

This chapter presents an overview of the more popular parallel programming languages and environments. As will be evident, many of these distinct parallel processing models are not necessarily distinct programming languages in the traditional sense of that term. For instance, parallel environments such as MPI and PVM, discussed in Section 2.4, are available in C, C++, and FORTRAN. Finally, this chapter will refer to the parallel components of a program as tasks for the sake of uniformity, be they processes or threads or some vendor-specific entities.

The various parallel environments discussed in this chapter have been classified into four different categories based on the paradigms that they support. Table 2.1 lists these four categories together with their representative examples discussed in this chapter. The first category, described in Section 2.2, consists of early parallel programming primitives that were used to coordinate tasks at a fairly low level. Many of these primitives, or their variants, are used in the implementation of the higher level parallel environments that fall in the other categories. The next section describes parallel languages used in the shared memory paradigm, and includes constructs for both pure shared memory, and those for virtual shared memory. Section 2.4 discusses the third category of parallel languages, namely the ones used for distributed memory machines. Note that parallel constructs for pure shared memory models can be used for virtual shared memory machines and vice versa, although each language is best suited for the particular model for which it was created. Similarly, parallel distributed memory languages can be used on shared memory machines, but their performance may not be as good as the corresponding shared

Table 2.1 Categories of Parallel Programming Environments

Early Mechanisms	Shared Memory		Distributed Memory	Parallel Declarative	
	Pure	Virtual		Logic	Functional
Semaphores	Pthreads	Linda	Ada	IC-Prolog	Multilisp
CCRs	Java Threads	SHMEM	MPI	PARLOG	Sisal
Monitors		OpenMP	PVM	GHCs	
Sockets		HPF	DCE		
RPCs		Rthreads	Dist. Java		
Rendezvous					

memory languages. The fourth category consists of parallel declarative languages, which includes parallel logic and functional languages, and these are discussed in Section 2.5. The chapter ends with a short summary in Section 2.6.

2.2   Early Mechanisms

During their infancy in the 1970s, parallel programs were expressed in terms of very basic parallel primitives that were mostly borrowed from concepts in operating system design. For tasks communicating via shared memory, the more popular techniques were semaphores, conditional critical regions, and monitors. These provide different mechanisms for mutual exclusion to any resource in the system, whereby a task A has access to a resource, and any other task B attempting to acquire access to that resource must block till task A relinquishes control of that resource. For tasks communicating via distributed memory using messages between them, the more popular methods were sockets, remote procedure calls or RPCs, and rendezvous.

2.2.1   Semaphores

A semaphore [1] is a synchronization primitive used to control access to shared resources by different tasks. A semaphore is a non-negative integer-valued variable that indicates the availability of a shared resource. To obtain access to a resource, a task needs to test or wait on the semaphore that controls the resource. If the value of the semaphore is greater than zero, then this value is decremented by one and access is granted. If the value is zero, then the task must wait until this value becomes greater than zero. To release a resource that a task has acquired access to, the task needs to signal the semaphore in question; this operation increments the value of the semaphore. If some other task has been waiting on this resource, this task can now be granted access to the resource.

If the semaphore only assumes the values 0 and 1, it is called a binary semaphore. A semaphore which can take arbitrary non-negative integer values is called a general semaphore.

While semaphores are powerful basic constructs for controlling access to a shared resource, they can result in potential deadlock situations if not used carefully. For instance, consider two resources A and B to be shared between two tasks $T1$ and $T2$. $T1$ would like to acquire both the resources, in the order A followed by B, and $T2$ would also like to acquire both the resources, but in the opposite order, namely B followed by A. Then, if both of the tasks start at the same time such that $T1$ has acquired A and is waiting to acquire B, and $T2$ has acquired B and is waiting to acquire A, neither task can make progress because each task is waiting for access to a resource held by the other. This results in deadlock.

2.2.2   Conditional Critical Regions

The preceding example illustrates a serious weakness of semaphores. There is no way to conditionally enter or leave a wait and there is no way to examine the value of the semaphore without executing a wait and becoming vulnerable to being blocked. Thus, there is no way to test multiple semaphores at the same time. Conditional critical regions [2] or CCRs avoid such problems by providing a structured synchronization mechanism.

A critical region is a primitive for mutual exclusion, and consists of a sequence of statements. If several tasks try to enter a critical region simultaneously, then only one successfully enters and the others must wait on a queue. When a task leaves a critical region, another task from the queue is allowed to enter. Finally, when a task attempts to enter a region while another task is within the region, the new task must join the queue of waiting tasks.

In a conditional critical region, competition for entry to the critical region is allowed only if an entry condition is satisfied. This entry condition is a Boolean expression and if it evaluates to true, then the task may enter the competition to enter the critical region; if the region is free, then the task succeeds in entering the region. If the entry condition evaluates to false, the task enters the queue of waiting tasks. Whenever a task leaves a critical region, all the queued tasks are released, and each of these tasks reevaluate their entry conditions.

Each task can evaluate its own condition, which can include expressions of arbitrary complexity, making conditional critical regions a very powerful and flexible synchronization primitive.

2.2.3   Monitors

Monitors [3] take structured synchronization a step further by defining a set of resources and operations that can manipulate these resources. The operations defined inside a monitor can only access local variables defined within the monitor and parameters passed to it; similarly, the local variables can only be accessed by these monitor operations. In other words, the scope of the monitor variables is the monitor itself. Communication between a monitor and the outside world (*viz.* tasks) is accomplished via the parameters to these operations. The monitor construct ensures that only one task can be active in the monitor at a time. Hence, the programmer does not have to explicitly take care of mutual exclusion to the resources that belong to the monitor.

2.2.4   Sockets

For tasks that reside on different address spaces in a system, as in different machines in a cluster connected by one or more networks, any form of intertask communication needs to be done by passing messages of some kind from one task to another. A socket [4] represents an endpoint of such a communication and typically has an address bound to it. To complete the communication, there must be a socket at the other endpoint of this communication channel, with a corresponding address. Sockets provide a general interface not only for communication over a network, but also for communication within a machine. There are several socket types that provide different classes of service ranging from reliable, duplex, sequenced data streams to unreliable, and unordered, packet oriented service. A pair of communicating tasks can choose a particular socket type, depending upon their needs. They can then use the communication channel between two sockets to send data to one another. In addition to different socket types, there are several socket options that can also be set to control the communication mode. That is, this intertask communication paradigm has a large degree of flexibility associated with it; however, it requires that the programmer handle the associated networking details.

2.2.5   Remote Procedure Calls

Remote procedure calls [5] or RPCs hide most of the networking details from the programmer by providing a higher level abstraction of communication between tasks than do sockets. RPCs provide the abstraction of a procedure call, but between tasks on different machines. In an RPC, a task referred to as the *client* on one machine invokes a procedure that is executed by a task referred to as the *server* on another machine. To the client, the procedure invocation and return appear as a normal (local) procedure call and return. The client calls a client stub, which is a local procedure. The stub marshals the arguments to the procedure and sends it off to the remote machine where a server stub procedure is waiting for the client's request. The server stub unmarshals the arguments and invokes the actual procedure on the server. The results of the procedure execution are handed back to the server stub, which marshals the results back to the client machine. The client stub on the client machine unmarshals the results and hands them back to the client. All the network details are thus encapsulated in the stub procedures of the RPC layer, facilitating the writing of distributed programs.

2.2.6   Rendezvous

The rendezvous mechanism [6] is another paradigm that can be used by tasks to exchange data in a distributed system. Two tasks communicate by synchronizing with each other as follows: one task calls an entry on the other one, and the latter responds with an accept for that entry. The crux of the rendezvous model is that a task which arrives earlier is required to wait for the task that it needs to communicate with.

With rendezvous, a server task A exports operations that can be called by others. Task A can now rendezvous with a caller of any of these operations by executing an *in* statement. A client task B invokes one of these operations by means of a call statement, which names task A and one of its exported operations. Just as with RPC, task B blocks at the call until the server task A executes the called operation. Similarly, the task A will also block if it reaches an *in* statement and there are no pending invocations. However, unlike RPC, with rendezvous server task A is an active task that executes both before and after servicing a remote invocation.

This paradigm is used as the basic intertask communication mechanism in Ada, which will be discussed in Section 2.4.1.

2.3   Shared Memory Environments

As parallel computers matured, demand for a higher abstraction for programming such machines grew. Most of the early parallel computers consisted of tens of CPUs connected together and to a globally addressable shared memory, via a bus. That is, a task running on any CPU could access any memory location in the computer with equal speed. Such systems are referred to as Uniform Memory Access or UMA architectures. For these machines, their respective vendors started providing shared memory languages. Such languages typically consist of a means for spawning multiple tasks for a problem, synchronization constructs for tasks to exchange data via shared memory, and mechanisms to allow synchronization with each other via barriers and related functions. Such environments are characterized in this chapter as pure shared memory environments.

As the number of CPUs started increasing on parallel computers, bus-based architectures exhibited limited performance improvements, since the bus bandwidth requirement reached its saturation point. Hence, larger parallel computers adopted switch interconnects for connecting CPUs to memory modules. For such systems, the distance of a memory module from a CPU is not constant, resulting in a non-uniform memory access speed by a task. Such systems are referred to as Non Uniform Memory Access or NUMA architectures.

Typically, on NUMA architectures, each CPU has local memory that is only addressable by tasks on that CPU, and the collection of all these local memory modules forms the entire memory of the system. Programming to this model involves explicitly passing information or messages from a task on one CPU to another, since no shared memory exists that can be utilized for this purpose. This message passing programming model is viewed by many as difficult, when compared to the shared memory model. To overcome this difficulty in using distributed memory machines, vendors of such systems started providing simulated globally addressable shared memory environments to the user, taking care of the translation to the physically distributed local memories in the operating system. Such systems are referred to as distributed shared memory or DSM. Since the memory is not really shared in hardware, but is available as such to the programmer, such a shared memory paradigm will be characterized as a virtual shared memory paradigm in this chapter.

2.3.1   Pure Shared Memory Environments

These languages are designed for systems where the entire memory in the system is uniformly globally addressable, and these environments do not make any provisions for, nor do they have any tuning hooks for, applications to take care of nonuniform memory accesses. While these languages will continue to work on virtual shared memory systems, they have no inherent features to support any NUMA characteristics that virtual shared memory machines exhibit. Most of the early parallel machines had their own shared memory parallel environments, and all these had a similar flavor. From these languages evolved the concept of threads. Threads are lightweight entities, which are similar to processes except that they require minimal resources to run. A process may consist of several threads, each of which represents a separate execution context; hence, a separate program counter, stack, and registers. All threads of a process share the remaining resources with the other threads in the process. Two types of thread environment are gaining widespread popularity across various platforms: Pthreads and java threads.

Pthreads

Pthreads [7] is an abbreviation for POSIX threads and refers to a standard specification for threads developed by the POSIX committee. The Pthreads environment provides two types of synchronization primitives: mutex and condition variable. Mutexes are simple lock primitives that can be used to control access to a shared resource, and the operations supported on a mutex to achieve this are lock and unlock primitives. Only one thread may own a mutex at a time and is thus guaranteed exclusive access to the associated resource.

Synchronization using mutexes may not be sufficient for many programs since they have limited functionality. Condition variables supplement the functionality of mutexes by allowing threads to block and wait for an event and be woken up when the event occurs.

Pthreads are limited to use within a single address space, and can not be spread across distinct address spaces.

Java Threads

The Java [8] language also provides a threads programming model, via its Thread and ThreadGroup classes. The Thread class implements a generic thread that, by default, does nothing. Users specify the body of the thread by providing a run method for their Thread objects. The ThreadGroup class provides a mechanism for manipulating a collection of threads at the same time, such as starting or stopping a set of threads via a single invocation of a method.

Synchronization between various threads in a program is provided via two constructs: synchronized blocks and wait-notify constructs. In the Java language, a block or a method of the program that is identified with the synchronized keyword represents a critical section in the program. The Java platform associates a lock with every object that has synchronized code. The wait construct allows a thread to relinquish its lock and wait for notification of a given event, and the notify construct allows a thread to signal the occurrence of an event to another thread that is waiting for this event.

2.3.2   Virtual Shared Memory Environments

The parallel environments that fall under this category provide a shared memory interface to the programmer. That is, to the programmer the entire memory in the system is globally addressable. The underlying hardware may consist of physically separate memory modules. In some cases, the operating system may take care of the distributed nature of the system memory, providing a shared memory view to these environments. In other cases, the memory is still presented to these environments as logically distinct modules, and these languages need to hide that detail from the programmer. These languages do this by providing a shared memory environment to the programmer and by performing the translation to the actual distributed memory at their layer. In either case, memory access becomes nonuniform, and virtual shared memory environments typically provide hooks to the programmer to manipulate the placement of data, placement of tasks on processors, movement of data relative to the tasks, and/or migration of tasks from one CPU to another. These hooks can be used by a parallel program in an attempt to maximize the performance of the system by controlling the placement of data, both statically and dynamically, so it is near the tasks that access that data. The biggest advantage of such an environment is that it still preserves a shared memory programming interface which is considered by many to be a simpler programming model than a message passing programming interface. Popular examples of such environments are described below.

Linda

Linda [9], [10] allows tasks to communicate with each other by inserting and retrieving data items, called tuples, into a distributed shared memory called tuple space. A tuple consists of a string which is the tuple's identifier, and zero or more data items. A tuple space is a segment of memory in one or more computers whose purpose is to serve as a temporary storage area for data being transferred between tasks. It is an associative memory abstraction where tasks communicate by inserting and removing tuples from this tuple space. When a task is ready to send information to another task, it places the corresponding tuple in the tuple space. When the receiver task is ready to receive this information, it retrieves this tuple from the tuple space. This decouples the send and receive parts of the communication so that the sender task does not have to block until the receiver is ready to receive the data being communicated.

Tuples can be active or passive. Active tuples contain at least one value that is not evaluated, as, for instance, when it is designated by a corresponding function name. The insertion of such a tuple in the tuple space results in the creation of another task to evaluate the function that will compute this value. When the value gets evaluated, it replaces the function call in the tuple. When all the values of a tuple are evaluated, it becomes a passive tuple.

Linda provides six functions to bring about this exchange of data between tasks. Passive tuples are inserted in the tuple space by the *out*() function, whereas active tuples are inserted by the *eval*() function. The functions *in*() and *rd*() retrieve a tuple from tuple space, with *in*() removing the matched tuple from the tuple space and *rd*() leaving it there. Both these functions block until a matching tuple is found. Their predicate counterparts, *inp*() and *rdp*(), return immediately with a 1 if the match was found and a 0 otherwise. These six functions can be added to any sequential programming language conforming to that language's function call syntax.

Linda works very well for smaller parallel programs with a few component tasks. However, as the number of tasks increases in a program, controlling access to a single tuple space and managing the tasks becomes difficult. This is mainly because there is no scoping in the tuple space, making the probability of access conflicts higher, which places an onus on programmers to be extra careful when the number of tasks becomes large.

SHMEM

The SHMEM [11] environment provides the view of a logically shared, distributed memory access to the programmer and is available on massively parallel distributed memory machines as well as on distributed shared memory machines. It enables tasks to communicate among themselves via low-latency, high-bandwidth primitives. In addition to being used on a shared memory architecture, SHMEM can be used by tasks in distinct address spaces to explicitly pass data among each other. It provides an efficient alternative to using message passing for intertask communication.

SHMEM supports remote data transfer through *put* operations, which can transfer data to another task, and through *get* operations, which can retrieve data from another task. This one-sided style of communication offered by SHMEM makes programming simpler since a matching receive request need not match every send request. SHMEM also supports broadcast and reduction operations, barrier synchronization, and atomic memory operations.

SHMEM is implemented on the Cray T3D, T3E, PVP, and Silicon Graphics' Origin systems.

OpenMP

OpenMP [12] is a new standard that has been defined by several vendors as the standard Application Programming Interface or API for the shared memory multiprocessing model. It attempts to standardize existing practices from several different vendor-specific shared memory environments. OpenMP provides a portable shared memory API across different platforms including Dec, HP, IBM, Intel, Silicon Graphics/Cray, and Sun. The languages supported by OpenMP are FORTRAN, C, and C++. Its main emphasis is on performance and scalability.

OpenMP consists of a collection of directives, library routines, and environment variables used to specify shared memory parallelism in a program's source code. It standardizes fine grained (loop level) parallelism and also supports coarse-grain parallelism.

Fine grain parallelism is achieved via the fork/join model. A typical OpenMP program starts executing as a single task, and on encountering a parallel construct, a group of tasks is spawned to execute the parallel region, each with its own data environment. The compiler is responsible for assigning the appropriate iterations to the tasks in the group. The parallel region ends with the end do construct, which represents an implied barrier. At this point, the results of the parallel region are used to update the data environment of the the the original task, which then resumes execution. This sequence of fork/join actions is repeated for every parallel construct in the program, enabling loop-level parallelism in a program.

For enabling coarse-grain parallelism effectively, OpenMP introduces the concept of orphan directives, which are directives encountered outside the lexical extent of the parallel region. This allows a parallel program to specify control from anywhere inside the parallel region, as opposed to only from the lexically contained portion, which is often necessary in coarse-grained parallel programs.

Advanced concepts such as data distribution control are absent from the OpenMP specification. Vendors may provide this added capability in their implementations, as does the OpenMP implementation for Silicon Graphics, Inc. Some vendor implementations of OpenMP provide interoperability with other parallel processing APIs. For instance, Silicon Graphics' OpenMP implementation is interoperable with the MPI and PVM, both of which are discussed in Section 2.4. Its interoperability with SHMEM and Pthreads is being evaluated.

High Performance Fortran

High Performance Fortran [13] or HPF is a standard defined for Fortran parallel programs with the goals of achieving program portability across a number of parallel machines, and achieving high performance on parallel computers with nonuniform memory access costs. HPF supports the data parallel programming model, where data are divided across machines, and the same program is executed on different machines on different subsets of the overall data. The HPF environment provides software tools such as HPF compilers that produce programs for parallel computers with nonuniform access cost.

There have been two versions of this standard to date. The first version, HPF-1, defined in 1993, was an extension to FORTRAN 90. The second version, HPF-2, defined in 1997, is an extension to the current FORTRAN standard (FORTRAN 95).

The HPF extensions to the FORTRAN standard can be classified into four categories. The first consists of compiler directives that give facts and/or hints to the compiler about a program. These directives generally indicate to the compiler which CPU gets what subset of the data. The second category consists of new language features, such as the *FORALL* construct in HPF-1. The FORALL statement represents a tightly-coupled parallel execution based on the structure of an index space, where indices may have associated masks to preclude the corresponding computation. The third category consists of new library routines, which are used to explicitly express parallelism in the program, such as array reduction and scatter functions. These functions are collected in the HPF library. Finally, HPF imposes some restrictions on the underlying FORTRAN language's definition of storage and sequence associations, since these are not compatible with the data distribution features of HPF.

An HPF programmer expresses parallelism explicitly in his program, and the data distribution is tuned to control the load balance and to minimize intertask communication. On the other hand, given a data distribution, an HPF compiler may be able to identify operations that can be executed concurrently, and thus generate even more efficient code.

HPF's constructs allow programmers to indicate potential parallelism at a relatively high level, without entering into the low-level details of message-passing and synchronization. When an HPF program is compiled, the compiler assumes responsibility for scheduling the parallel operations on the physical machines, thereby reducing the time and effort required for parallel program development.

Remote Threads

In Section 2.3.1, it was seen that Pthreads can not be extended across distinct address space boundaries such as a cluster of workstations. Remote threads [14] or Rthreads extend Pthreads-like constructs between address spaces. They provide a software distributed shared memory system that supports sharing of global variables on clusters of computers with physically distributed memory. Rthreads use explicit function calls to access distributed shared data. Its synchronization primitives are syntactically and semantically similar to those of Pthreads.

The Rthreads environment consists of a precompiler that automatically transforms Pthreads programs into Rthreads programs. The programmer can still change the Rthreads code for further optimization in the transformed program. Also, Pthreads and Rthreads can be mixed within a single program. Heterogeneous clusters are supported in Rthreads by implementing it on top of portable message passing environments such as PVM, MPI, and DCE, which are discussed in Section 2.4. The associated overhead seems to be minimal, as shown by performance evaluations reported in [14].

2.4   Distributed Memory Environments

As parallel computers started getting larger, scalability considerations resulted in a pure distributed memory model. In this model, each CPU has local memory associated with it, and there is no shared memory in the system. This architecture is scalable since, with every additional CPU in the system, there is additional memory local to that CPU, which in turn does not present a bandwidth bottleneck for communication between CPUs and memory. On such systems the only way for tasks running on distinct CPUs to communicate is for them to explicitly send and receive messages to and from other tasks. While many environments have attempted to provide a virtual shared memory paradigm on top of pure distributed systems, as discussed in Section 2.3, message passing languages grew in popularity very quickly and a few of them have emerged as standards in the recent years. This section discusses some of the more popular distributed memory environments.

2.4.1   Ada

Ada is a programming language originally designed to support the construction of long-lived, highly reliable software systems. It was developed for the U.S. Department of Defense for real-time embedded systems. Intertask communication in Ada is based on the rendezvous mechanism discussed in Section 2.2. The tasks can be created explicitly or declared statically. A task must have a specification part which declares the entries for the rendezvous mechanisms. It must also have a body part, defined separately, which contains the accept statements for the entries, data, and the code local to the task.

Ada uses the select statement for expressing nondeterminism. The select statement allows the selection of one among several alternatives, where the alternatives are prefixed by guards. Guards are boolean expressions that establish the conditions that must be true for the corresponding alternative to be a candidate for execution. Another distinguishing feature of Ada is its exception handling mechanism to deal with software errors. The disadvantages of Ada are that it does not provide a way to map tasks onto CPUs, and does not provide conditions to be associated with entry declarations.

2.4.2   Message Passing Interface

The Message Passing Interface [15], [16] or MPI is a standard for message passing that has been developed by a consortium consisting of representatives from research laboratories, universities, and industry. The first version MPI-1 [15] was standardized in 1994, and the second version MPI-2 [16] was developed in 1997. MPI is an explicit message passing paradigm where tasks communicate with each other by sending messages. The two main objectives of MPI are portability and high performance.

The MPI environment consists of an MPI library that provides a rich set of functions numbering in the hundreds. MPI defines the concept of communicators which combine message context and task group to provide message security. Intra-communicators allow safe message passing within a group of tasks, and inter-communicators allow safe message passing between two groups of tasks.

MPI provides many different flavors of both blocking and non-blocking point to point communication primitives, and has support for structured buffers and derived datatypes. It also provides many different types of collective communication routines for communication between tasks belonging to a group. Other functions include those for application-oriented task topologies, profiling, and environmental query and control functions. MPI-2 also adds dynamic spawning of MPI tasks to this impressive list of functions, although it is not clear when vendor implementations supporting this functionality will be released for public use.

The standard does not have a specification for allocating tasks to CPUs, this being left to individual vendor implementation. Also, the standard does not specify how different MPI implementations can talk to each other. This hinders the use of MPI in a network consisting of a wide variety of machines, each with its own MPI implementation.

MPI has been widely adopted as the message passing standard by many vendors including DEC, Hitachi, HP, IBM, 0 Graphics/Cray, and Sun Microsystems. Besides these vendor-specific implementations of MPI, there are a few public domain implementations also available.

2.4.3   Parallel Virtual Machine

Parallel Virtual Machine [17], or PVM, was the first widely accepted message passing environment that provided portability and interoperability across heterogeneous platforms. The first version was developed at Oak Ridge National Laboratory in the early 1990s, and there have been several versions since then. PVM allows a network of heterogeneous computers to be used as a single computational resource called the parallel virtual machine.

The PVM environment consists of three parts: a daemon that resides on all the computers in the parallel virtual machine, a library of PVM interface functions, and a PVM console to interactively start, query, and modify the virtual machine. Before running a PVM application, a user needs to start a PVM daemon on each machine, thus creating a parallel virtual machine. The PVM application needs to be linked with the PVM library, which contains functions for point to point communication, collective communication, dynamic task spawning, task coordination, and modification of the virtual machine, among others. This application can be started from any of the computers in the virtual machine at the shell prompt or from the PVM console.

The biggest advantages of PVM are its portability and interoperability, primary causes for its widespread use today. Not only can the same PVM program run on any platform on which it is supported, tasks from the same program can run on different platforms at the same time as part of the same program. Furthermore, different vendor's PVM implementations can also talk to each other, because of a well-defined inter-PVM daemon protocol. Thus, a PVM application can have tasks running on a cluster of machines, of different types, and running different PVM implementations.

Another notable point about PVM is that it provides the programmer with great flexibility for dynamically changing the virtual machine, spawning tasks, and forming groups. It also provides support for fault tolerance and load balancing.

The main disadvantage of PVM is that its performance is not as good as other message passing systems such as MPI. This is mainly because PVM sacrifices performance for flexibility.

PVM was quickly embraced by many programmers as their preferred parallel programming environment when it was released for public use, particularly by those who were interested in using a network of computers and those who programmed on many different platforms, since this paradigm helped them write one program that would run on almost any platform. The public domain implementation works for almost any Unix platform, and Windows/NT implementations have also been added. Additionally, almost all parallel computer vendors provide their proprietary implementations.

2.4.4   Distributed Computing Environment

Distributed Computing Environment [18], or DCE, is a suite of technologies available from The Open Group, a consortium of computer users and vendors interested in advancing open systems technology. DCE enables the development of distributed applications across heterogeneous systems.

The three areas of computing in which DCE is most useful are security, internet/intranet computing, and distributed objects. DCE provides six classes of service. It provides a threads service at the lowest level, to allow multiple threads of execution. Above this layer, it provides a remote procedure call (RPC) service which facilitates client-server communication across a network. Sitting on top of the RPC service are time and directory services that synchronize the system clocks and provide a single naming model throughout the network, respectively. The next service is a distributed file service, providing access to files across a network, including diskless support. Orthogonal to these services is DCE's security service, which authenticates the identities of users, authorizes access to resources in the network, and provides user and server account management.

DCE is available from several vendors including Digital, HP, IBM, Silicon Graphics, and Tandem Computers. It is being used extensively in a wide variety of industries including automotive, financial services, telecommunications, engineering, government, and academia. Some common tools built on top of DCE are transaction monitors and network management tools.

2.4.5   Distributed Java

The popularity of the Java language stems largely from its capability and suitability for writing programs that use and interact with resources on the Internet in particular, and clusters of heterogeneous computers in general. The basic Java package, the Java Development Kit or JDK, supports many varieties of distributed memory paradigms corresponding to various levels of abstraction [8]. Additionally, several accessory paradigms have been developed for different kinds of distributed computing using Java, although these do not belong to the JDK.

Sockets

At the lowest level of abstraction, Java provides socket APIs through its set of socket-related classes. The classes Socket and ServerSocket provide APIs for stream or TCP sockets, and the classes DatagramSocket, DatagramPacket and Multicast-Socket provide APIs for datagram or UDP sockets. Each of these classes has several methods that provide the corresponding APIs.

Remote Method Invocation

Just like RPCs provide a higher level of abstraction than sockets, as discussed earlier in this chapter, Remote Method Invocation or RMI, provides a paradigm for communication between program-level objects residing in different address spaces. RMI allows a Java program to invoke methods of remote Java objects in other Java virtual machines, which could be running on different hosts. A local stub object manages the invocation of remote object methods. RMI employs object serialization to marshal and unmarshal parameters of these calls. Object serialization is a specification by which objects can be encoded into a stream of bytes, and then reconstructed back from the stream. The stream includes sufficient information to restore the fields in the stream to compatible versions of the class.

To provide RMI support, Java employs a distributed object model which differs from the base object model in several ways, including: non-remote arguments to and results from an RMI are passed by copy rather than by reference; a remote object is passed by reference and not by copying the actual remote implementation; clients of remote objects interact with remote interfaces, and not with their implementation classes; the semantics of some methods defined by class Object, viz. *equals()*, *hashCode()*, *toString()*, *clone()*, and *finalize()* have specialized semantics for remote objects; and additional exceptions can occur during an RMI.

URLs

At a very high level of abstraction, the Java runtime provides classes via which a program can access resources on another machine in the network. Through the URL and URLConnection classes, a Java program can access a resource on the network by specifying its address in the form of a uniform resource locator. A program can also use the URLConnection class to connect to a resource on the network. Once the connection is established, actions such as reading from or writing to the connection can be performed.

JavaSpace

The JavaSpace paradigm is an extension of the Linda concept, discussed in Section 2.3. Analogous to Linda creating a shared memory space called a tuple space, which is used as a storage repository for data to and from distinct tasks, the JavaSpace model provides a medium for RMI-capable applications and hardware to share work and results over a distributed environment. A key attribute of a JavaSpace is that it can store not only data but serialized objects, which could be combinations of data and methods that can be invoked on any machine supporting the Java runtime. Hence, a JavaSpace entry can be transferred across machines while retaining its original behavior, achieving distributed object persistence. Analogous to the Linda model, the JavaSpace paradigm attempts to raise the level of abstraction for the programmer so they can create completely distributed applications without considering details such as hardware and location. JavaSpaces is still under development at Sun Microsystems and is not yet available to the public.

JMPI

The MPI-2 specification includes bindings for FORTRAN, C, and C++ languages. However, no binding for Java is planned by the MPI Forum. JMPI is an effort underway at MPI Software Technology Inc. to integrate MPI with Java. JMPI is different from other such efforts in that, where possible, the use of native methods has been avoided for the MPI implementation. Native methods are those that are written in a language other than Java, such as C, C++, or assembly. The use of native methods in Java programs may be necessitated in situations where some platform-dependent feature may be needed, or there may be a need to use existing programs written in another language from a Java application. Minimizing the use of native methods in a Java program makes the program more portable. JMPI also includes an optional communication layer that is tightly integrated with the Java Native Interface, which is the native programming interface for Java that is part of the Java Development Kit (JDK). This layer enables vendors to seamlessly implement their own native message passing schemes in a way that is compatible with the Java programming model. Another characteristic of JMPI is that it only implements MPI functionality deemed essential for commercial customers.

jPVM

jPVM is an API written using the Java native methods capability so that Java applications can use the PVM software described earlier in this section. jPVM extends the capabilities of PVM to the Java platform, allowing Java applications and existing C, C++, and FORTRAN applications to communicate with each other via the PVM API.

2.5   Parallel Declarative Environments

Parallel declarative languages encompass both parallel logic languages which express parallelism at the clause level, and parallel functional languages which express parallelism at the expression level. There are two main properties of declarative languages that make them amenable to parallel processing. First, their operational semantics have an inherent nondeterministic nature. Second, declarative languages have the property of single-assignment statements, which implies that only a single value can be assigned to each named variable in each scope. Both of these properties permit an arbitrary order of execution of different operations without affecting the results. In particular, such operations can be executed in parallel.

Some notable representatives from each category are discussed below.

2.5.1   Parallel Logic Languages

A popular model for sequential logic programming languages is based on the procedural interpretation of Horn clauses [19]. A Horn clause consists of a set of procedure calls or subgoals, and the proof procedure for such programs solves the subgoals in a sequential manner. Parallel logic languages aim to exploit parallelism in logic programs via parallel proof strategy. The parallelism can be either explicit, where the programmer explicitly specifies the parallelism in the program, or it can be implicit, where the parallelism is extracted by the language support during static analysis and at runtime. This chapter only considers explicit parallelism in logic programs since the implicit model depends only on the run-time support.

There are two main types of parallelism in logic programs: *AND* parallelism, which entails the parallel evaluation of each subgoal; and *OR* parallelism, which entails the parallel evaluation of only those subgoals that match the goal.

IC-PROLOG

IC-PROLOG [20] was one of the first parallel logic programming languages. It implements stream-*AND* parallelism, where subgoals communicate incrementally via values bound to their shared variables. This language incorporated concepts such as the pseudo-parallel evaluation of calls in a conjunction and a data-flow like execution mechanism. In the data-flow model, computations are represented as operations, and the execution of these operations is determined by their data only. Operations that do not depend on mutual data may execute concurrently.

PARLOG

PARLOG [21] stands for a Parallel Logic programming language and it uses mode declarations of predicate arguments to define access restrictions for variables. A logical variable shared between two subgoals provides a communication channel in PARLOG. This language has been used for applications in system programming, object-oriented programming, and discrete event simulation.

Guarded Horn Clauses

Guarded Horn Clauses [22] or GHC inherits the basic concepts of PARLOG, but is simpler and allows a more efficient implementation. The most characteristic feature of GHC is that the guard is the only syntactic construct added to Horn clauses because synchronization is realized by the semantic rules of the guards.

2.5.2   Parallel Functional Languages

In functional languages, parallelism is encoded at the expression level. Functional languages lend themselves very well to parallel implementation, since they express a problem in terms of their subproblems rather than a mechanism for solution. Furthermore, they are referentially transparent and have no state.

There are several important issues to note when dealing with parallel functional programs. First, the normal order evaluation of expressions in a functional setting does not yield much parallelism. Second, the order of functions that are allowed in the language also determines the ease of use of such languages for parallel implementation. Finally, there is the trade-off between explicit parallelism where programmers specify the parallelism via annotations, versus implicit parallelism where compilers discover parallelism.

There are three main ways in which parallelism can be exploited in such a paradigm: speculative computation, graph reduction, and dataflow languages. Two common parallel logic languages, employing some of these principles, are discussed below.

Multilisp

Multilisp [23] is an extension of the Lisp language, falling in the speculative computation category listed above. It tries to gain parallelism by performing computations in parallel before their results are known to be required. Multilisp uses futures to achieve this. A future is a promise to provide the value of a computation if needed. It is an object that can be passed around regardless of its internal status, and allows eager evaluation of an expression in a controlled way. The runtime decides when futures should create new tasks. Typically, a future applied to an expression creates a task to evaluate that expression which begins immediately, i.e., eagerly. A subsequent attempt to use the result of a future is suspended until the value has been computed.

Sisal

Sisal [24] began as an abstract dataflow language. Dataflow languages are single-assignment languages, the idea being to execute them in a data-driven manner on special-purpose hardware.

Sisal has syntactic structures looking like loops, which create a new context for each execution of the loop iteration. Structures for arrays, records, and streams exist, but their elements have the same semantics as ordinary variables. Most of the parallelism in Sisal programs is derived from parallel loops, whose bounds are defined by range operators. The generators impose an ordering on loop bodies.

2.6 Summary

This chapter presented an overview of various parallel programming environments that have been introduced in the last two to three decades since the advent of parallel computers. The parallel languages and environments have been classified into four categories: primitives provided by early parallel processing mechanism; shared memory environments, including both pure shared memory and virtual shared memory environments; pure distributed memory environments; and parallel declarative languages.

2.7 Bibliography

[1] E. W. Dijkstra. Cooperating Sequential Processes. In *New Programming Languages*, F. Genyus (editor), Academic Press, pages 43-112, 1968.

[2] P. Brinch Hansen. *Operating Systems Principles*. Prentice-Hall, Upper Saddle River, NJ, 1973.

[3] C. A. R. Hoare. Monitors: An Operating System Structuring Concept. In *Communications of the ACM*, vol. 17, pages 549-557, 1974.

[4] W. Richard Stevens. *Unix Network Programming*. Prentice Hall Software Series, Upper Saddle River, NJ, 1990.

[5] Sun Microsystems. RPC: Remote Procedure Call, Protocol Specification, Version 2. *RFC 1057*, June 1988.

[6] C. A. R. Hoare. Communication Sequential Processes. In *Communications of the ACM*, vol. 21, pages 666-677, 1978.

[7] B. Nichols, D. Buttlar, and J. P. Farrell. *Pthreads Programming*. O'Reilly, September 1996.

[8] M. Campionie and K. Walrath. *The Java Tutorial: Object-Oriented Programming for the Internet (Java Series)*. Addison Wesley, March 1998.

[9] S. Ahuja, N. Carriero, and D. Gelernter. Linda and Friends. In *IEEE Computer*, vol. 19(8), pages 26-34, August 1986.

[10] N. Carriero and D. Gelernter. Technical Correspondence on Linda in Context. In *Communications of the ACM*, vol. 32(10), pages 1255-1258, October 1989.

[11] K. Feind. Shared Memory Access (SHMEM) Routines. Presented at the *Cray Users' Group Meeting*, Cray Research, Denver, 1995.

[12] L. Dagum and R. Menon. OpenMP: An Industry-Standard API for Shared-Memory Programming. *IEEE Computational Science and Engineering*, vol. 5, pages 46-55, January-March, 1998.

[13] High Performance Fortran Forum. *High Performance Fortran Language Specification*, January 31, 1997, Version 2.0.

[14] B. Dreier, M. Zahn, and T. Ungerer. The Rthreads Distributed Shared Memory System. In the *Third International Conference on Massively Parallel Computing Systems*, Colorado Springs, CO, April 1998.

[15] Message Passing Interface Forum. *MPI: A Message-Passing Interface Standard*, May 5, 1994.

[16] Message Passing Interface Forum. *MPI-2: Extensions to the Message-Passing Interface*, July 1997.

[17] A. Geist et. al. *PVM3 User's Guide and Reference Manual*, September 1994.

[18] B. C. Johnson. A Distributed Computing Environment Framework: An OSF Perspective. *Open Group Research Institute White Paper.* DEV-DCE-TP6-1, presented at the *1991 EurOpen Conference*, Tromso, Norway.

[19] R. Kowalski. Algorithm = logic + control. *Communications of the ACM*, vol. 22, pages 424-431, 1979.

[20] K. L. Clark and F. G. McCabe. The Control Facilities of IC-PROLOG. In *Expert Systems in the Micro-Electronic Age.* Edinburgh University Press, pages 122-149, 1979.

[21] K. L. Clark and S. Gregory. PARLOG: Parallel Programming in Logic. *ACM Transactions on Programming Languages and Systems*, vol. 8(1), pages 1-49, January 1986.

[22] K. Ueda. Guarded Horn Clauses. *Technical Report*, ICOT, Tokyo, vol. TR-103, 1985.

[23] R. H. Halstead. MultiLisp: A Language for Concurrent Symbolic Computation. *ACM Transactions on Programming Languages and Systems*, vol. 7(4), pages 501-538, October 1985.

[24] J. T. Feo, D. C. Cann, and R. R. Oldehoeft. A Report on the Sisal Language Project. *Journal of Parallel and Distributed Computing*, vol. 10(4), pages 349-366, December 1990.

Chapter 3

MPI and PVM Programming

IRA PRAMANICK

Silicon Graphics Inc.
Mountain View, California
USA

Email: *ira@sgi.com*

3.1 Introduction

The needs of high performance computing are varied and many. While the goals of high speedup and efficiency are of chief importance when using parallel processing, other issues such as scalability, load balancing, utilization of idle resources, effective use of heterogeneous computing resources, and cost have become significant practical aspects in long term parallel processing perspective. As opposed to a couple of decades ago when parallel programming was synonymous with the use of (a few) supercomputers of that time, today the popularity of parallel programming has spread across the entire spectrum of computing, ranging from supercomputers to clusters of single CPU or symmetric multiprocessing (SMP) machines. In fact, a significant portion of parallel program development is now done on clusters of computers (personal computers, workstations or SMP machines). In the remainder of this chapter, unless otherwise specified, the discussion will implicitly focus on parallel processing on such clusters. Many of the issues discussed will also be directly relevant to noncluster parallel processing environments such as supercomputers and massively parallel processors (MPPs).

The increasing ease of parallel programming and the portability of such programs (and the time savings thereof in moving from one architecture to another) are becoming key factors for scientists and engineers as they are faced with a plethora of parallel programming and distributed computing alternatives. Among the multitude of parallel programming libraries, both public domain as well as vendor-specific, the clear winners are the Message Passing Interface (MPI) standard [1] and the Parallel Virtual Machine (PVM) [2] environment. PVM was developed at

Oak Ridge National Laboratories and the University of Tennessee starting in 1989, and MPI was a result of a consortium consisting of various universities and national laboratories with a goal of establishing a standard for a message passing library a few years later.

This chapter describes the use of MPI and PVM for cluster computing through the use of two different solutions to the all pairs shortest path problem [3]. The all pairs shortest path problem constitutes an important class of graph theoretic problems and finds extensive use in the study of transportation and communication networks. Section 3.2 gives a high level comparative overview of MPI and PVM. This is followed by a description of the all pairs shortest path problem, two sequential solutions attributable to Dijkstra and Floyd, and their parallel versions, in Section 3.3. Section 3.4 focuses on MPI and illustrates its salient features through the implementations of the two parallel algorithms mentioned above. Section 3.5 does the same for PVM. Both Sections 3.4 and 3.5 use code snippets to demonstrate the use of MPI and PVM library calls. These sections also discuss the basic intertask communication models supported by MPI and PVM, respectively. Finally, porting a PVM program to an MPI one and vice versa is the topic of discussion in Section 3.6, which gives several hints to achieve those goals. The chapter ends with a summary in Section 3.7.

3.2   Comparison of MPI and PVM

An introduction to MPI and PVM is given in the second chapter of this book, and the reader is referred to that chapter for a basic understanding of the two frameworks. This section briefly compares these two paradigms from several perspectives. As will be amply evident from the examples illustrating the use of MPI and PVM in the following sections, both these message passing libraries have their own strong points and, at the same time, have disadvantages in some other areas. Before focusing on their differences, it should be noted that due to the fact that it was the first popular, portable, message passing library of its kind, PVM has an enormous code base which is constantly growing. MPI is also growing in popularity and is the standard message passing library adopted by most vendors and research centers.

Although both MPI and PVM provide message passing libraries to their users, the basic framework under which they operate differs considerably. The PVM environment not only consists of a message passing library, but also a standard way to create the cluster on which to run one or more PVM programs. This cluster is called a parallel virtual machine. It also provides a mechanism for specifying the allocation of tasks to physical processors, both at the start of the parallel program as well as dynamically during runtime. On the other hand, MPI is a specification for a message passing standard, and consists of a rich set of library functions to do both point-to-point message passing communication and collective communication among parallel tasks. However, it does not specify any method to perform allocation of tasks to physical processors, leaving such details to vendor-specific implementations.

As far as library functions are concerned, both MPI and PVM have similar sets of functions, with one providing more in certain areas than the other. Both have routines to initialize the message passing environment in a task through the task registering with the environment. There are routines for the two main types of intertask communication: point-to-point communication between tasks where there is a sender and a receiver of a message; collective communication within a group of tasks where the communication is between the members of a group and not directly between two tasks. Finally, they have different sets of utility functions that have varied uses. Both MPI and PVM support the FORTRAN, C, and C++ programming languages, and support for Java is in the works.

The differences in the basic environment framework and the library functions supported result in different advantages and disadvantages among the two paradigms.

The biggest advantage of PVM is its flexibility – including portability, interoperability between heterogeneous platforms, and fault tolerance. Not only can the same PVM program be run on almost any platform (virtually all platforms are supported), but it can be run in a heterogeneous environment consisting of different platforms. This makes it very amenable to its use as a parallel programming tool in typical clusters which consist of heterogeneous platforms. Also, the public domain implementation of PVM can interface seamlessly with vendor-specific implementations, thus allowing a better use of resources in a heterogeneous environment. PVM provides various other runtime flexible features such as dynamic spawning of tasks, dynamic changes to the cluster on which a PVM program is being run, and dynamic process groups. These allow a PVM application to incorporate fault tolerance and load balancing by allowing it to detect changes in the cluster and to move tasks from one machine to another in that cluster in response to such cluster changes. The chief disadvantage of PVM is its performance – because of the flexibility that its framework supports, its performance suffers. Additionally, the set of library functions supporting point-to-point communication in PVM is not as rich as that of MPI. For example, PVM does not support the truly asynchronous receive of a message sent from one task to another, as MPI does.

Among the advantages of MPI are its higher performance in general, a richer set of point-to-point communication models, derived data types, and a larger set of collective communication calls. However, it is not as flexible as PVM in that it does not support dynamically changing the cluster or creating dynamic groups. Additionally, the first version of MPI, called MPI-1, which is what almost all vendors currently implement, does not support dynamically spawning tasks. The second version of the MPI specification, called MPI-2 [4], does have support for dynamically spawning tasks, but this standard has not been implemented by most vendors at this time. Towards this end, for the remainder of this chapter, our reference to MPI will typically be to MPI-1, with comments added for MPI-2 where appropriate. Finally, in general, MPI can not be run on a heterogeneous cluster consisting of machines of different types, since interoperability is not a requirement of the MPI standard. Related to this issue is the fact that the standard also does not define several details of a parallel programming environment, such as allocation of tasks to processors. These are left to individual implementations of the standard, and thus result in diverse ways to accomplish the same goal, leading to a further variation between the MPI environment across platforms.

Both the message passing environments have gone through several cycles of changes, and the difference in their feature lists is indeed decreasing as more functionality is added to each with every new version. This will make porting a program from one environment to the other easier, although each library will still remain different in its underlying philosophy and goals (flexibility versus performance for PVM versus MPI, respectively).

3.3   The All Pairs Shortest Path Problem

3.3.1   Description of the Problem

The all pairs shortest path problem can be stated as follows:

Given: A directed graph $G = (V, E)$ where V is the set of vertices of G and E is the set of edges of G, the number of vertices being n, and a weight matrix W representing the weights of edges between each pair of vertices.

Find: For every pair of vertices, determine the shortest path along the edges of G. Let this solution be represented by an $n \times n$ matrix A, where an element A_{ij} of this matrix represents the shortest path from vertex i to vertex j.

Figure 3.1 shows a graph with $n = 5$ vertices, and edges labeled with the corresponding weights as shown. Considering a single pair of vertices, a and b, the various paths between them are shown in **bold**, and are:

(i) (a, b) of path length 15,

(ii) (a, c, b) of path length 14, and

(iii) (a, d, c, b) of path length 11.

The shortest path among these is (a, d, c, b).

3.3.2   Dijkstra's Algorithm

Dijkstra's sequential algorithm [3] is a very popular algorithm for the single-source shortest path problem. An application of this algorithm for each vertex considered as a source in turn results in the solution to the all pairs shortest path problem. Dijkstra's algorithm is shown in Algorithm 3.1.

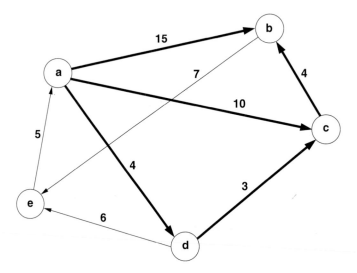

Figure 3.1 Illustrating shortest path computation.

1. $s =$ source vertex, $T = V$ (set of all vertices).

2. Perform steps 3 through 5 till T is empty (i.e. n times).

3. From T, find the vertex that is closest to s. Call it t.

4. For each vertex u in T, if the sum of the distances between s and t and between t and u is less than that between s and u, then update the distance between s and u to this sum.

5. Remove t from T.

Algorithm 3.1 Sequential Dijkstra's.

Hence, in terms of the result matrix A, as each source vertex is considered in turn, the corresponding row of the matrix is updated for each application of the basic algorithm at a time.

3.3.3   Floyd's Algorithm

Floyd's sequential algorithm [5] for the all pairs shortest path problem is considered the best sequential algorithm for this problem. As opposed to using Dijkstra's algorithm, where each vertex is considered in turn to be the source vertex and the entire algorithm repeated for the source vertex in question, Floyd's algorithm considers all the vertices as source vertices for its entire invocation. Floyd's algorithm is shown in Algorithm 3.2.

---

1. A = matrix representing the distances between pairs of vertices, initialized to the weight matrix W.

2. For $k = 0$ to $(n-1)$, perform steps 3 through 5.

3. For $i = 0$ to $(n-1)$, perform steps 4 through 5.

4. For $j = 0$ to $(n-1)$, perform step 5.

5. If $A_{ij} > (A_{ik} + A_{kj})$, then $A_{ij} = A_{ik} + A_{kj}$.

Algorithm 3.2 Sequential Floyd's.

Hence, in terms of the result matrix A, the entire matrix is updated throughout the algorithm application.

3.3.4   Parallel Algorithms

The parallel versions of the above two algorithms for the all pairs shortest path problem represent two distinct approaches to parallel processing, in terms of their communication and computation patterns. In this section, we will also see that their parallel implementations use two distinct parallel processing paradigms, the master-slave paradigm and the all-peers paradigm, for mapping the algorithm onto parallel tasks.

In the master-slave paradigm, one of the tasks is designated the master task; it controls the operations of the remaining tasks which are designated the slave tasks. In general, the master assigns each slave some work to do, and then collects the results from all the slaves and combines these into a solution. The slaves typically participate in the computation and the master oversees the entire procedure. Depending on the algorithm being implemented, the slaves may or may not communicate among themselves while they are computing their results. The slave tasks are also often referred to as worker tasks. This paradigm is illustrated in Figure 3.2.

In the all-peers paradigm, all tasks participate in the computation and are referred to as worker tasks in this scenario. Each of these tasks decides what portion of the problem it will solve, based on some common algorithm. In general, all tasks control the computation as a whole, communicating with each other as necessary both for computation and control purposes. Only one of the peer tasks may still read in the input data and distribute it to the rest of its peers, and then collect the results in the end. This paradigm is illustrated, in its most general form, in Figure 3.3, where it is assumed that a task communicates with all other tasks.

Since PVM has a dynamic task spawning capability, where a task spawns other tasks, most PVM implementations tend to fall naturally in the master-slave paradigm. Here, the first task that is started by hand takes the role of the master task, spawning several slave tasks according to the requirements of the application.

In the two versions of the all pairs shortest path problem solution that are discussed in this chapter, for the parallel Dijkstra's solution, the master-slave paradigm is employed for both the MPI and the PVM implementation. On the other hand,

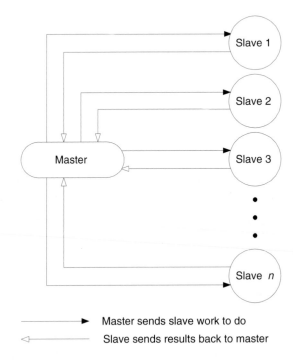

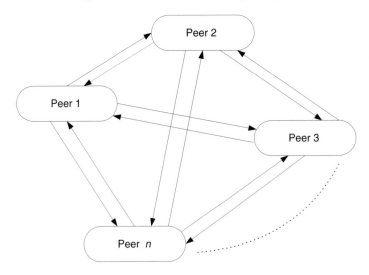

Figure 3.2 The master-slave paradigm.

Figure 3.3 The all-peers paradigm.

for the parallel Floyd's solution, the all-peers paradigm is used for the MPI implementation and the master-slave paradigm is used for the PVM implementation. The PVM parallel implementations have been reported in [7] and the corresponding MPI implementations have been coded thereafter.

Parallel Dijkstra's Algorithm

Parallel Dijkstra's solution uses concurrent applications of the sequential algorithm for distinct sets of vertices, with each set assigned to different processors in the cluster. The collection of results from these tasks constitutes the all pairs solution. Each task needs the entire weight matrix for its calculation. This solution fits naturally into a master-slave paradigm. The master task has the input graph W, and it broadcasts this graph to all the slave tasks and waits for results back from the slaves. A slave, upon receiving the input matrix W, computes the shortest paths for its subset of vertices and sends its partial result back to the master. The master collects all the partial results and forms the complete result. The slave or worker tasks each execute Algorithm 3.3.

---

1. Wait for matrix W from master.
2. $p =$ number of slaves.
3. $m =$ my instance id.
4. For $i = m$ to $(n-1)$, in increments of p, perform Dijkstra's algorithm with source i.
5. Send results to master.

Algorithm 3.3 Worker task for parallel Dijkstra's.

We will refer to the MPI implementation of the parallel Dijkstra's algorithm as PDIJK_MPI and to its PVM implementation as PDIJK_PVM.

Parallel Floyd's Algorithm

In the parallel Floyd's solution [6] used in this chapter, the matrix A is partitioned into distinct stripes assigned to distinct tasks. A stripe consists of a set of consecutive columns of the matrix. A task is responsible for updating its stripe according to Floyd's algorithm (discussed in Section 3.3.3). Each stripe consists of contiguous columns of A. This solution lends itself well to the master-slave paradigm for PVM, and to the all-peers paradigm for MPI. In the master-slave approach used for PVM, the master assigns an instance ID to each of the slaves, and sends each slave its stripe of W. In the all-peers approach used for MPI, each task is a worker, with the *task identifier* (*taskid*) assigned by MPI serving as its instance identifier. One of the tasks is designated as the one responsible for reading in the input matrix and distributing the relevant portions to its peers. This task is the one with the taskid of 0 in our implementation. At the end, it collects the results from its peers, which together yield the solution to the all pairs problem. The workers each execute Algorithm 3.4.

---

1. $p =$ number of slaves.

2. Determine my stripe by dividing n by p, the first instance taking any remainder columns.

3. For $k = 0$ to $(n - 1)$ do steps 4 and 5.

4. If column k belongs to my stripe, then broadcast that column to all other peers. Else, wait to receive the kth column from the owner peer of that column.

5. Update the elements of my stripe, according to Floyd's basic sequential algorithm.

Algorithm 3.4 Worker task for parallel Floyd's.

We will refer to the MPI implementation of the parallel Floyd's algorithm as PFLOYD_MPI and to its PVM implementation as PFLOYD_PVM.

3.4   The MPI Programming Environment

This section describes the MPI programming environment by first giving a brief overview, then discussing the most commonly used library functions in a typical program, and finally illustrating the above points via example programs that implement the two parallel algorithms described in the previous section. In the discussion that follows, the places where MPI calls are listed, only the C function from the MPI library is listed, for the sake of brevity. The corresponding FORTRAN call can be easily derived by converting all the letters in the C function to upper case. For example, the C call `MPI_Recv()` corresponds to the FORTRAN call `MPI_RECV()`. Additionally, the reader is referred to [1] for a complete listing of all library functions, both in C and FORTRAN, available in MPI-1. The example code excerpts given in this section have been stripped of variable declaration sections, error checking in most parts, and diagnostic information print statements, for the sake of brevity. Also, only those statements that pertain to MPI calls and associated comments are included in the excerpts as C program statements and comments; the other steps having been replaced with corresponding comments describing their general functionality.

As mentioned in Section 3.2, MPI consists of a specification of a set of library functions that tasks of a parallel program can use to communicate among themselves. By itself, the standard does not specify the exact method of program invocation and the run-time environment, although some of the conventions adopted by the public domain implementations of MPI have also been adopted by several vendor implementations. For example, there is a command called `mpirun`, which is almost the universal way to launch an MPI program. Additionally, each implementation of the MPI standard may come with different sets of environment variable that need to be set to achieve different options for the run-time environment. A simple example of this is MPI_DIR, which denotes the working directory for an MPI program on a remote host for some implementations.

An MPI parallel program consists of MPI tasks, all of which may be the same or different executables. Each MPI task needs to register with the MPI environment before it can start using the MPI library.

Once an MPI task has registered with the MPI environment, it can start communicating with other MPI tasks, either directly between itself and a destination task using point-to-point communication primitives from the MPI library, or between all members of a group to which it belongs using collective communication functions. The group can be the default group that it belongs to (corresponding to when it registers), or a new group to which it has explicitly become a member.

Once the MPI task has completed its job, which will typically consist of some computation interspersed with communication with other tasks, it can unregister from the MPI environment.

3.4.1   Communication Models in MPI

Intertask communication in MPI is based on the concept of communicators. A communicator is used to specify a communication context for a communication operation and the set or group of tasks that share this context. That is, communication within a communicator is limited to the group or groups of tasks that belong to that communicator. When a task registers/initializes itself with the MPI environment, the task is automatically placed in a base, predefined communicator called MPI_COMM_WORLD. An MPI program may define other communicators to which subsets of its component tasks may belong, depending on the communication requirements among them. There are two types of communicators in MPI: intra-communicators, which are used to provide safe communication, both point-to-point and collective, within a group of tasks; and inter-communicators, which are used to provide safe communication between groups of tasks.

The process group within an intra-communicator such as MPI_COMM_WORLD is ordered and processes are identified by their rank within this group. This rank lies in the range $(0 .. n-1)$ where n is the number of processes in the group. Considering the communicator MPI_COMM_WORLD, to which all MPI tasks belong, the rank of a task in the corresponding group is unique across all MPI tasks within an MPI program, and hence can be used as its task identifier, commonly referred to as its taskid. This is done in most MPI applications that need a task identifier. Similarly, the size of the group corresponding to MPI_COMM_WORLD denotes the number of parallel tasks in the program. In MPI-2, which will support dynamic spawning of tasks, this size may change depending on whether new tasks are being spawned or not.

Point-to-Point Communication

For direct communication between a source and a destination task, MPI provides various point-to-point send and receive functions. For each flavor, the sender task puts data in a send buffer and sends it off to a specific destination which receives this data from a corresponding receive buffer. The two main types of point-to-point communication functions are blocking and non-blocking communication, depending on whether the return from the send/receive function signals the availability of the send/receive buffers for reuse by the application. This is illustrated in Figure 3.4. Additionally, a blocking send can be matched with a non-blocking receive and vice versa. Within each of these categories, there are several flavors depending on when the send or receive of a message can start and/or complete. The reader is referred to [1] for a detailed explanation of each of these flavors.

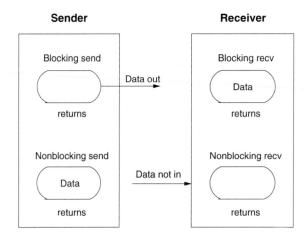

Figure 3.4 Point-to-point communication in MPI.

Collective Communication

For communication between a group of MPI tasks, where all tasks belonging to that group participate in the communication, MPI provides a rich set of collective communication primitives. Each such communication is characterized for a communicator, which defines the group of participating tasks. In collective communication, more than a single task may be the source of a message and more than a single task may be its destination. Each task participating in a collective communication operation calls the corresponding function with outgoing data in one or more send buffers and one or more receive buffers to receive incoming data. This is shown in Figure 3.5. For some types of such operations, there is a single sender or a single receiver in the group, and such a task is referred to as the root.

3.4.2   Creating an MPI Program

The MPI environment supports both the all-peers and the master-slave programming models very well. The only restriction as far as task control goes is that in

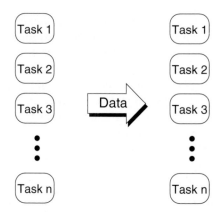

Figure 3.5 Collective communication in MPI.

MPI-1, the number of tasks in an MPI program has to be fixed prior to running the program, and no tasks can be spawned dynamically during runtime. MPI-2 will remove this restriction; however, implementations of MPI-2 will not become common in the immediate future. Although the MPI library is rich with several functions, all MPI programs will typically use the following minimum set of functions, arranged according to their type, and some additional functions depending on their requirements. The examples given in this section will illustrate the use of these and some additional MPI functions.

Environment Management

The first MPI function to be called in an MPI program must be MPI_Init(), and this must be called exactly once. As the name suggests, this function initializes the MPI environment for the program. The last MPI function to be called in an MPI program must be MPI_Finalize(). This function cleans up all MPI state in the program.

After MPI_Init() has been called in a program, the base communicator MPI_COMM_WORLD is established which includes all the tasks in the program and can be used to determine a task's rank and the number of tasks. To determine the number of tasks in the program, an MPI task needs to call the function MPI_Comm_size() with MPI_COMM_WORLD as the communicator. Similarly, the rank or taskid of an MPI task can be determined via the function MPI_Comm_rank().

Point-to-Point Communication

MPI provides various flavors of both blocking and non-blocking point-to-point communication for each, including standard, buffered, synchronous and ready modes. Each flavor differs from the others in the mode of buffering used for the message in question, and the dependence of a matching receive for the send call to complete or even start. The send call can be one of `MPI_Send()`, `MPI_Bsend()`, `MPI_Ssend()`, and `MPI_Rsend()` for blocking sends and similar ones for non-blocking sends. The corresponding receive functions are `MPI_Recv()` and `MPI_Irecv()`. For the asynchronous primitives, there are various flavors of wait and test functions to check whether the corresponding send/receive call has completed and whether the associated buffer can be reused by the application. Messages sent using blocking sends can be received using non-blocking receives and vice versa.

Collective Communication

As happens often in a parallel program, all MPI tasks within an MPI group want to exchange data among each other, and this can be done through one of the collective communication calls. A collective communication routine has to be called by all tasks in a group with matching arguments. A simple barrier synchronization is achieved via the `MPI_Barrier()` function. The remaining collective communication tasks take a root argument, which defines a single originator/receiver task. Then, depending on how the data is distributed from/to/among the root and the remaining tasks, there is `MPI_Bcast()` and various flavors of scatter/gather functions. Finally, there are `MPI_Reduce()` and `MPI_Allreduce()` which are used to perform reduction operations across the group.

3.4.3   Running an MPI Program

Once an MPI program is completely written and compiled using the platform and language specific compilers, it can be invoked by the environment-specific MPI program launcher. The most popular of these is `mpirun`, which typically takes, for each host in the cluster, at least the following arguments: number of tasks, arguments to each task, working directory. Depending on the platform in question and the MPI implementation being used, several environment variables need to be defined to be able to run the application, and some environment variables need to be defined to fully exploit the platform specific features of the underlying architecture. For example, on a Silicon Graphics DSM hardware, the environment variable `MPI_DSM_MUSTRUN` is used to pin MPI tasks to CPUs on the DSM, which can be useful for MPI jobs running on dedicated systems. An example of a typical command line using `mpirun` to start a program consisting of one instance of a master task, `master_mpi` and four instances of slave tasks, `slave_mpi`, with `master args` and `slave args` as their arguments, respectively, is:

```
mpirun -d <working directory> <hostname> \
    1 master_mpi <master args> : <hostname> 4 slave_mpi <slave args>
```

The `-d` option of `mpirun` is used to specify the location of the MPI task executables and other related files.

3.4.4   PDIJK_MPI

The parallel version of Dijkstra's algorithm, PDIJK_MPI, can be naturally implemented by a master-slave paradigm. The program consists of one master task
and several slave tasks. The master is called st_dijk_mpi, and the slave is called
pdijk_mpi. Relevant excerpts from these files are shown in listings 3.1 and 3.2.
Each task, on starting up, determines the number of tasks started, and its rank in
MPI_COMM_WORLD (which corresponds to its *taskid*). The number of slaves is one less
than the total number of tasks.

The master reads in the input data, distributes it to the slaves, and waits for
results from the slaves. It packs the input data, consisting of the number of vertices
and the input matrix, into a send buffer and then sends this message to each of
its slaves. It then waits for a message from each of its slaves, indicating this by
wildcarding the source field using MPI_ANY_SOURCE in the receive function. After
receiving a message, the master unpacks it into its receive buffer. Finally, it puts
the results sent to it by its slaves together and outputs the data.

The slaves, after registering with the MPI environment, wait for a message
from the master task. Since the master rank is only determined at runtime, it
can not be specified to the slaves a priori. This is not a problem since they can
use MPI_ANY_SOURCE in the receive function, and once they have received their
first message (from the master), they can determine the master's rank (taskid)
by examining the MPI_Source field of the MPI_Status variable returned by their
MPI_Recv() call, as shown in the code excerpt that follows. After unpacking their
input data, they perform their computation on it, pack the results into a send buffer,
and send that message to the master.

This program uses explicit packing and unpacking of data before and after the
corresponding send and receive functions to pack discontiguous data into the send
and receive buffers, respectively. Packing and unpacking primitives can be replaced
in MPI programs via the use of derived data types in general. Derived datatypes
provide a way for a program to send or receive discontiguous data by transferring
them directly from where they reside, without copying. In the case of this program,
however, packing and unpacking are needed since the master is sending two pieces of
information, and the slaves need the first piece of information to allocate sufficient
space before receiving the second piece of information.

Also, the tasks here use point-to-point communication primitives for exchanging
data between them, since the communication is always between a master and one
of its slaves.

Listings 3.1 and 3.2 are code excerpts for st_dijk_mpi and pdijk_mpi, respectively,
with the MPI calls being **highlighted**.

```
main(int argc, char *argv[])
{
    MPI_Init(&argc, &argv); /* Initialize MPI. */
    /* Get our task ID (our rank in the basic group). */
    MPI_Comm_rank(MPI_COMM_WORLD, &myTid);
```

```
        (void)printf(" Master tid = <%d>.\n", myTid);
        /* Get the number of tasks and slaves. */
        MPI_Comm_size(MPI_COMM_WORLD, &nTasks);
        nSlaves = nTasks - 1;

        /*
         * Read in the number of vertices, nVert, and the input matrix,
         * inMatrix, from the specified file.
         */
        .
        .
        /* Send work and receive answers from "pdijk_mpi" processes. */
        calcShort(nTasks, myTid, nVert, inMatrix, outMatrix);
        /* Write results in the specified output file. */
        .
        .
        /* Exit MPI. */
        MPI_Finalize();
        exit(0);
} /* end of "main" */

void calcShort(int nTasks, int myTid, int nVert,
               int *iMatrix, int **oMatrix)
{
        /* Send the input data to all the slaves. */
        sqNvert = nVert * nVert;
        bufPos = 0;
        MPI_Pack(&nVert, 1, MPI_INT, buf, BUFSIZE,
                 &bufPos, MPI_COMM_WORLD);
        MPI_Pack(inMatrix, sqNvert, MPI_INT, buf, BUFSIZE, &bufPos,
                 MPI_COMM_WORLD);
        for (i = 0; i < nTasks; i++) {
            if (i != myTid) {
                MPI_Send(buf, bufPos, MPI_PACKED, i,
                         WORK_MSG, MPI_COMM_WORLD);
            }
        }

        /* Collect results and put it together in the output matrix. */
        for (i = 0; i < nSlaves; i++) {
            MPI_Recv(buf, BUFSIZE, MPI_PACKED, MPI_ANY_SOURCE,
                     RESULT_MSG, MPI_COMM_WORLD, &status);
            bufPos = 0;
            slaveTid = status.MPI_SOURCE;
            if (slaveTid < myTid) j = slaveTid;
            else if (slaveTid > myTid) j = slaveTid - 1;
            /* Get size of result obtained, allocate space, and read in resMat[j]. */
            MPI_Unpack(buf, BUFSIZE, &bufPos, &sizeResMat, 1,
                       MPI_INT, MPI_COMM_WORLD);
            resMat[j] = (int *)malloc(sizeResMat * sizeof(int));
            MPI_Unpack(buf, BUFSIZE, &bufPos, &(resMat[j][0]), sizeResMat,
                       MPI_INT, MPI_COMM_WORLD);

            /* Put results in outMatrix. */
            .
            .
```

```
        }
} /* end of "calcShort" */
```

Listing 3.1 MPI steps for st_dijk_mpi.

```
main (int argc, char *argv[])
{
    /* Initialze MPI. */
    MPI_Init(&argc, &argv);
    /* Get our task id. */
    MPI_Comm_rank(MPI_COMM_WORLD, &myId);
    /* Get the number of tasks. */
    MPI_Comm_size(MPI_COMM_WORLD, &nTasks);
    nSlaves = nTasks - 1;
    /* Get data from master */
    MPI_Recv(buf, BUFSIZE, MPI_PACKED, MPI_ANY_SOURCE, WORK_MSG,
             MPI_COMM_WORLD, &status);
    masterTid = status.MPI_SOURCE;
    /* Unpack data. */
    bufPos = 0;
    MPI_Unpack(buf, BUFSIZE, &bufPos, &nVert, 1, MPI_INT,
               MPI_COMM_WORLD);
    sqNvert = nVert * nVert;
    inMatrix = (int *)malloc(sqNvert * sizeof (int));
    MPI_Unpack(buf, BUFSIZE, &bufPos, inMatrix, sqNvert,
               MPI_INT, MPI_COMM_WORLD);
    /*
     * Calculate the number of vertices I have to take care of, and allocate
     * space for output matrix, and other arrays needed for Dijkstra's algorithm.
     */
        .
        .
        .
    /* Calculte shortest paths for my set of vertices. */
    iterNo = 0;
    for (i = myTid; i < nVert; i += nSlaves) {
        /*
         * Calculate the shortest paths for source vertex i using Dijkstra's
         * single source shortest path algorithm, implemented in the
         * function dijkstra(). No MPI calls there.
         */
        dijkstra(i, ...);
        iterNo++;
    }

    /* Send the results back. */
    bufPos = 0;
    MPI_Pack(&totElem, 1, MPI_INT, buf, BUFSIZE, &bufPos,
             MPI_COMM_WORLD);
    MPI_Pack(outMatrix, totElem, MPI_INT, buf, BUFSIZE, &bufPos,
             MPI_COMM_WORLD);
    MPI_Send(buf, bufPos, MPI_PACKED, masterTid, RESULT_MSG,
             MPI_COMM_WORLD);
    /* Close MPI. */
    MPI_Finalize();
```

```
        exit(0);
    } /* end of "main" */
```

Listing 3.2 MPI steps for pdijk_mpi.

3.4.5 PFLOYD_MPI

The parallel Floyd solution described in Section 3.3.4 has been implemented in
MPI using the all-peers SPMD model. The peer tasks are called `pfloyd_mpi`.
excerpts from which are given in listing 3.3. Each peer task determines the number
of tasks in the program and its own taskid by querying the size and its rank in
`MPI_COMM_WORLD`. One of the tasks, the one with taskid of `MASTERTID`, acts as a
pseudo-master in that it reads in the input data from a file, distributes the data
to its peers, collects results from them, and then writes the output data back to
a file. It also participates in the computation of the output together with all its
peers. So, from the standpoint of receiving input data and sending results back,
the pseudo-master does not send itself a message, but just copies over the data and
results into appropriate data structures.

Each peer, after registering with MPI, waits for its input stripe matrix. After
receiving and unpacking the input data, each peer synchronizes with all its peers by
calling a barrier function. After this synchronization takes place, the main computation (interspersed with communication) phase starts. During this phase, the peers
work on their respective stripes of the input data matrix, and they need to communicate among themselves in every iteration of updates to the matrix to get the most
up-to-date value of the next column in question. In other words, there is a fairly
tight synchronization among them, and this is achieved here via the `MPI_Bcast()`
function. Hence, for each update communication, depending on which column needs
to be broadcast to all the peers, the corresponding task is the originator of data
(i.e., the root in the collective communication) for the `MPI_Bcast()` call.

At the end of this main phase of the algorithm, the peers send their results to the
pseudo-master. Since all the tasks are peers, and the pseudo-master is arbitrarily
chosen to be the task with rank `MASTERTID`, all the peers know a priori who to send
the results back to.

This example illustrates the use of both point-to-point and collective communication in MPI. As in the previous example of parallel Dijkstra's MPI solution,
packing and unpacking of data is needed here for the same reasons: the receiver of
a message needs the first piece of data before it can unpack the next piece.

Listing 3.3 is a code excerpt from the Parallel Floyd's MPI program, with the
MPI calls again being **highlighted**.

```
    main(int argc, char *argv[])
    {
        /* Initialize MPI. */
        MPI_Init(&argc, &argv);
```

```
      /* Get our task ID (our rank in the basic group). */
      MPI_Comm_rank(MPI_COMM_WORLD, &myTid);

      /* Get the number of tasks. */
      MPI_Comm_size(MPI_COMM_WORLD, &nTasks);

      /* The master reads the input, and distributes it to the workers. */
      if (myTid == MASTERTID) {
          /*
           * Read in the number of vertices and the input matrix itself from a
           * specified file.
           */
              .
              .
              .
          /* Assign stripes to everyone, including ourselves. */
          sendWork();
      }
      else {
          collectWork();
      }

      /* Calculate shortest paths for the stripe assigned to us. */
      calcShort();

      if (myTid == MASTERTID) {
          /* Receive results from others and consolidate with our own. */
          collectResults();

          /* Write results in the specified output file. */
              .
              .
              .
      }
      else {
          sendResults();
      }

      /* Say goodbye to MPI. */
      MPI_Finalize();
      exit(0);
} /* end of "main" */


void sendWork()
{
      for (i = 0; i < nTasks; i++) {
          if (i == MASTERTID) {
              /* Read in my stripeMatrix entries directly from inMatrix. */
                  .
                  .
                  .
          }
          else {
              /* Calculate the stripe for each peer task and send it to them. */
              bufPos = 0;
              MPI_Pack(&nVert, 1, MPI_INT, buf, BUFSIZE, &bufPos,
                      MPI_COMM_WORLD);
```

```
                for (j = 0; j < nVert; j++) {
                    MPI_Pack(&(inMatrix[j][begCol]), width, MPI_INT,
                              buf, BUFSIZE, &bufPos, MPI_COMM_WORLD);
                }
                MPI_Send(buf, bufPos, MPI_PACKED, i, WORK_MSG,
                          MPI_COMM_WORLD);
            }
        }
    } /* end of "sendWork" */


    void collectWork()
    {
        bufPos = 0;

        /* Get stripe matrix from master. */
        MPI_Recv(buf, BUFSIZE, MPI_PACKED, MPI_ANY_SOURCE, WORK_MSG,
                  MPI_COMM_WORLD, &status);

        /* Unpack data. */
        MPI_Unpack(buf, BUFSIZE, &bufPos, &nVert, 1, MPI_INT,
                    MPI_COMM_WORLD);

        /* Calculate my stripe width and allocate stripeMatrix. */
             ⋮

        for (j = 0; j < nVert; j++) {
            MPI_Unpack(buf, BUFSIZE, &bufPos, stripeMatrix[j],
                        stripeWidth, MPI_INT, MPI_COMM_WORLD);
        }
    } /* end of "collectWork" */


    void collectResults()
    {
        /*
         * Collect results and put it together in the output matrix.
         * First, myself directly.
         */
             ⋮

        /* Then, others. */
        for (i = 0; i < nTasks-1; i++) {
            MPI_Recv(buf, BUFSIZE, MPI_PACKED, MPI_ANY_SOURCE, RESULT_MSG,
                      MPI_COMM_WORLD, &status);
            peerTid = status.MPI_SOURCE;

            /* Calculate starting column and stripe width for the results sent. */
                 ⋮

            for (j = 0; j < nVert; j++) {
                MPI_Unpack(buf, BUFSIZE, &bufPos, &(outMatrix[j][begCol]),
                            width, MPI_INT, MPI_COMM_WORLD);
            }
        }
```

```
} /* end of "collectResults" */

void
sendResults()
{
    /* Send stripeMatrix results back. */
    bufPos = 0;
    for (j = 0; j < nVert; j++) {
        MPI_Pack(&(stripeMatrix[j][0]), stripeWidth, MPI_INT, buf, BUFSIZE,
                &bufPos, MPI_COMM_WORLD);
    }
    MPI_Send(buf, bufPos, MPI_PACKED, MASTERTID, RESULT_MSG,
            MPI_COMM_WORLD);
} /* end of "sendResults" */

void calcShort()
{
    /* All peers need to synchronize here. */
    MPI_Barrier(MPI_COMM_WORLD);

    /* Determine amount of data exchanged at each broadcast. */
    bcastSize = nVert * sizeof(int);

    /* Begin processing the kth (outermost) loop. */
    for (k = 0; k < nVert; k++) {
        /* Determine the broadcasting task. */
        rootTid = k/(nVert/nTasks);
        if (rootTid >= nTasks)
            rootTid = nTasks-1;

        if ((k >= begCol) && (k < begCol+stripeWidth)) {
            /* Broadcast column to all other "pfloyd_mpi" processes. */
            bufPos = 0;
            for (i = 0; i < nVert; i++) {
                MPI_Pack(&(stripeMatrix[i][k-begCol]), 1, MPI_INT, buf,
                        BUFSIZE, &bufPos, MPI_COMM_WORLD);
            }
            MPI_Bcast(buf, bcastSize, MPI_PACKED, rootTid,
                    MPI_COMM_WORLD);

            /* Update my stripe. */
                .
                .
                .
        }
        else {
            /* Wait for the kth column from another process */
            bufPos = 0;
            MPI_Bcast(buf, bcastSize, MPI_PACKED, rootTid,
                    MPI_COMM_WORLD);
            MPI_Unpack(buf, BUFSIZE, &bufPos, colRecd, nVert, MPI_INT,
                    MPI_COMM_WORLD);
            /* Update my stripe. */
                .
                .
                .
        }
```

```
    }
} /* end of "calcShort" */
```

Listing 3.3 MPI steps for pfloyd_mpi.

3.4.6   Tools for MPI Programs

The MPI standard includes support for tools for MPI programs by supporting communicators, contexts, and topologies, details of which can be found in [1]. Among visualization tools, XMPI [8], a public domain tool which has been also adopted by some vendors, is the most widely used. Among parallel debuggers, TOTALVIEW [9], and P2D2 [10] are the notable ones with support for MPI program debugging. In addition, there are several resource management tools available for clusters that have MPI support, including general purpose load balancers such as Platform Computing's LSF, vendors' proprietary load balancers for their parallel environment such as Silicon Graphics' NQE and IBM's LOADLEVELER, in addition to several public domain ones.

3.5   The PVM Programming Environment

This section describes the PVM programming environment by first giving a brief overview of this environment, followed by a discussion of the most commonly used library functions in a typical program. It illustrates the use of PVM via example programs that implement the two parallel algorithms described in Section 3.3. In the discussion that follows, at the places where PVM calls are listed, only the C functions from the PVM library are listed for the sake of brevity. The corresponding FORTRAN call is easy to extrapolate by replacing the "_" with the letter "f" in the pvm_ part of the C function name. For example, the FORTRAN counterpart for the C function pvm_recv() is pvmfrecv(). Also, the entire set of library routines (both C and FORTRAN) available in the latest PVM version, PVM 3.4, is listed in [2]. The example code excerpts given in this section have been stripped of variable declaration sections, error checking in most parts, and diagnostic print statements, for the sake of brevity. Also, only those statements that pertain to PVM calls and associated comments are included in the excerpts as C program statements and comments, the other steps having been replaced with corresponding comments describing their general functionality.

The PVM environment consists of a set of library routines to perform parallel/cluster communication between tasks, a defined start method for the parallel environment, and a console that allows a user to manipulate the parallel virtual machine by adding to and deleting hosts from it. The console also allows a user to start, monitor, and stop PVM programs. Finally, it has a set of other useful functions for debugging both the PVM environment and a PVM program. An alternative to setting up the parallel virtual machine via the console is to use a hostfile, and directly invoke the PVM daemon on the local host, which in turn invokes PVM daemons on remote hosts listed in the hostfile.

Once a parallel virtual machine or cluster of machines is set up, a PVM program can be run only on a subset of these hosts, including the entire set. One of the distinctive advantages of PVM is that the cluster can consist of heterogeneous hosts, as long as all of them have compatible versions of PVM installed on them.

A PVM program can either be started from within the PVM console or by hand. A PVM task can dynamically spawn other tasks. In fact, this is very commonly used in the master-slave approach where the master process spawns n copies of slave PVM tasks. A PVM task can also dynamically add or delete hosts to the parallel virtual machine during its execution. This feature can be used in load balancing or fault tolerant applications where a host can be dynamically added or deleted from the cluster and the application can spawn more tasks on the new machines, or, in the case of a machine getting deleted, restart the corresponding tasks on existing machines in the cluster.

A standard set of environment variables exist for the PVM environment and are specified in its public domain implementation. Vendors may add specific environment variables to achieve better performance or for added functionality, if any, on their platforms.

A PVM program consists of a set of PVM tasks, which may all be the same executable or different executables. A task first registers with the PVM environment, and once registered, can use any of the PVM library functions. As a result of registering, it is assigned a task identifier, referred to as the *tid* of the task. This *tid* is a number formed by combining a host number assigned globally (with respect to the cluster) to the host on which the task has been started and a task number assigned locally. Unlike in MPI, a task does not belong to any group by default. It can add or delete itself from any number of groups it desires if it needs to perform collective communication calls across a set of tasks. The number of tasks in the program can be determined via one of the utility functions available. A PVM task may also spawn another PVM task, and the spawned task can enquire about the *tid* of its parent via a library routine.

After a process is done with using the PVM environment, it can unregister from it and carry on its non-PVM related computations. A process can register and unregister as many times as it wishes from the PVM environment.

3.5.1   Communication Models in PVM

Once registered, a PVM task can send messages directly to another task via one of the point-to-point communication primitives, or communicate across a set of tasks by first joining the corresponding group and then using the appropriate collective communication primitive. PVM groups can be dynamically created.

Point-to-Point Communication

For direct communication between a sender and a receiver task, PVM provides a set of point-to-point PVM functions, although this set is not as rich as its MPI counterpart. In particular, the send functions in PVM are all blocking in nature, i.e., they block until the underlying PVM implementation has copied the contents of the send buffer into its own area and the buffer is available for reuse by the application. The receive functions are also not truly non-blocking – all but `pvm_nrecv()` are blocking in nature, and even with `pvm_nrecv()`, the call returns immediately if the matching message has not arrived, but the receive buffer is available for reuse by the application. That is, a receive operation can not be posted before the corresponding message has arrived at the destination. The point-to-point communication model of PVM is illustrated in Figure 3.6.

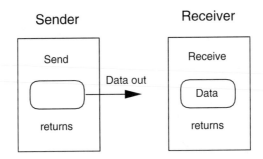

Figure 3.6 Point-to-point communication in PVM.

Collective Communication

PVM provides several functions for use by groups of processes to communicate among themselves. However, while some of these collective communication routines have to be executed by all the tasks in the group in question, some routines can be invoked by a task which is not even a member of the group. For example, a PVM task can broadcast a message to all members of a group, even though it may not belong to that group. Also, a message sent via a broadcast can be received through point-to-point calls. Finally, because PVM supports dynamically changing groups, some collective communication functions in PVM allow the non-participation of all group members in the call. For example, not all group members need participate in a `pvm_barrier()`, rather the number of tasks to be synchronized at a barrier is specified in the call itself. The scatter, gather and reduce functions, however, behave like their counterparts in MPI, where all tasks in the group have to participate in the collective communication operation. Figure 3.7 illustrates collective communication in PVM, where all participating tasks may not be part of the same group in general.

3.5.2   Creating a PVM Program

As we have seen, PVM is a very flexible parallel processing environment. It therefore supports almost all models of parallel programming, including the commonly used all-peers and master-slave paradigms and variations thereof. The chief reasons for the richness in the models it provides a framework for are its support for dynamic

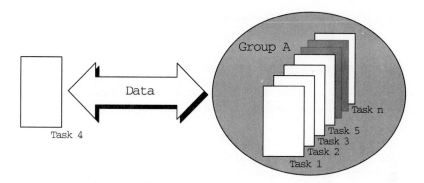

Figure 3.7 Collective communication in PVM.

cluster change and dynamic spawning of processes.

A PVM program will typically use the following minimum set of functions, arranged according to their type, and some additional functions depending on their requirements. The examples discussed in this section illustrate the use of these and some additional PVM functions.

Environment Management

The first PVM function a PVM program should call is `pvm_mytid()`. Some library implementations of PVM allow a PVM program to call any PVM function as its first PVM function, and the library calls `pvm_mytid()` for the program. The last PVM function in a program should be the `pvm_exit()` function, which denotes the unregistering of the program from the PVM environment, and the program may continue to do other non-PVM related tasks after this point. A program may register and unregister from PVM as many times as it desires. As noted earlier, a PVM program can manipulate the parallel virtual machine itself by adding or removing nodes from it, but this is not typically used in most PVM programs. Information about the tasks running in a PVM environment, such as the number of tasks in the virtual machine, can be determined via the `pvm_tasks()` function. Status of processes/tasks can be obtained through the `pvm_pstat()` call, and machine status of the members of the parallel virtual machine can be obtained from `pvm_mstat()`.

Dynamic Spawning of Tasks

If a PVM task needs to start other PVM tasks, it can accomplish this via the `pvm_spawn()` function. This function has several arguments, including the flexibility of starting an arbitrary (subject to system resource limitations) number of tasks of one or more kind (i.e. different executables), of starting these tasks on arbitrary or specified hosts in the parallel virtual machine, and of passing arbitrary argument strings to the new tasks. Any PVM task can find out its parent task via the call `pvm_parent()`. For a task started by hand directly on the shell, the parent is undefined; for a task started from the PVM console, the console is the parent, and for a task spawned by another PVM task, the parent is the latter.

Point-to-Point Communication

Although the set of functions to perform point-to-point communication in PVM programs supports various semantics of send and receive, it is not as rich as its MPI counterpart. In particular, asynchronous receive of a message is missing in PVM, in the true sense of the term. The send of a PVM message is asynchronous in the sense that the program hands off the send buffer contents to the daemon and returns as soon as the send buffer has been copied over to the daemon's area. That is, the program send buffer is ready for reuse. This is different from asynchronous sends where the send buffer may not be ready to be reused since the message to be sent may not have been copied out of it yet. The different types of sends supported by PVM are: pvm_send() and pvm_psend(), where the latter function obviates the need for packing of the message in to the active buffers before sending the message out. The different types of receives supported by PVM are pvm_recv(), pvm_precv(), pvm_trecv(), and pvm_nrecv(). The second receive function above does the unpacking and receiving of the message directly into the active message buffer. The third function performs a timed receive, and the last one performs a non-blocking receive, returning a message if one exists and matches the input parameters, or returning an error code otherwise. Thus, it is not a truly asynchronous receive as in MPI where the receive buffer is marked as such, and is filled in with a matching incoming message by the MPI environment asynchronously of what the program is doing at that point in time.

Before a message can be sent in PVM using pvm_send(), it must be packed into the send buffer using a variety of pvm_pk*() functions. Similarly, at the receiving end, the message needs to be unpacked using the corresponding flavor of the set of pvm_upk* functions, before being received via any of the above-mentioned receive calls (except for pvm_precv(), which does the unpacking as well).

Collective Communication

For several PVM tasks to communicate among themselves via collective communication calls, they all need to belong to the same group. There is no concept of a default group in PVM, and a PVM task must join a group if it needs to perform collective communication with other PVM tasks in the same group. A task can join a PVM group by calling pvm_joingroup(), and leave a PVM group that it is a member of by calling pvm_lvgroup(). A simple barrier synchronization can be implemented in a PVM program by using pvm_barrier(). Scatter and gather operations can be done via the pvm_scatter() and pvm_gather() calls. Different sorts of reduction operations across members of a group can be done by the pvm_reduce() function. A message can be broadcast to all members of a group via the pvm_bcast() function. Since groups can be dynamically changing in PVM, the members of a group for a collective communication call are those that belong to the group at the time of making the call.

3.5.3   Running a PVM Program

A PVM program can be compiled using the platform and language specific compilers. Certain environment variables need to be defined before the compilation to select the platform on which the program is to be run. These variables are PVM_ROOT, which indicates the root of the tree under which the PVM software resides, and PVM_ARCH, which indicates the architecture of the platform in question. Also, variables need to point to the path of the PVM daemon and console executable. The reader is referred to [2] for these details.

Once the program is compiled, the PVM console or a hostfile is needed to establish a parallel virtual machine. Then, the tasks of the PVM program can be started by hand or via the console, these tasks in turn spawning other tasks dynamically, if necessary, using the PVM functions mentioned in Section 3.5.2.

The PVM Console

This is a PVM program, pvm, that allows a user to start, modify, stop, and query the virtual machine. It may be started and stopped multiple times on any of the hosts in the cluster without affecting the PVM environment. Invoking the console starts PVM on the local machine if PVM is not already running on it; additional machines are included in the cluster by specifying these in a hostfile given as an argument to the console command, or by invoking the add command from inside the console prompt.

Once a virtual machine is established, a user can also start, stop, and monitor PVM programs from the console. The user can also send a signal to a given task through the console.

3.5.4   PDIJK_PVM

The parallel algorithm for Dijkstra's solution, described in Section 3.3.4, is implemented in PVM using the master-slave paradigm as in the case of MPI. The master task is called st_dijk_pvm, and the slave tasks are called pdijk_pvm.

The master reads in the input data, which includes the number of slaves to be spawned, $nTasks$. After registering with PVM and receiving a taskid or *tid*, it spawns $nTasks$ instances of the slave program pdijk_pvm and then distributes the input graph information to each of them. As a result of the spawn function, the master obtains the *tids* of each of the slaves. Since each slave needs to work on a distinct subset of the set of vertices, they need to be assigned instance IDs in the range $(0 .. nTasks - 1)$. Unlike in the case of MPI, the tids assigned to them by the PVM library do not lie in this range, so the master needs to assign the instance IDs to the slaves and send that information along with the input matrix. The slaves also need to know the total number of slaves in the program, and this information is passed on to them by the master process as an argument to the spawn function since, unlike the instance IDs, this number is the same for all *nTasks* slaves. To send the input graph and instance ID information, the master process packs these into the active send buffer, and then invokes the send function. It then waits to receive partial results from each of the slaves.

The slaves register with the PVM environment, and then wait for input data from the master, using a wildcard in the receive function to receive a message from any source. Once a message is received, each slave determines the master's *tid* from the received message buffer properties. Alternatively, the slaves could have determined the master's tid by calling the **pvm_parent()** function, which they could have used as the source in their receive function. On receiving the message from the master which contains the input matrix, a slave unpacks this data from the active receive buffer. Each slave then works on its input partition, and send its partial results to the master when it is done. The master collects these partial results into an output matrix and outputs the results.

Listings 3.4 and 3.5 are code excerpts from the Parallel Dijkstra's PVM program, with the PVM calls being **highlighted**.

```
main(int argc, char *argv[])
{
    /*
     * Read in the number of slaves, nSlaves, from the command line,
     * and the number of vertices, nVert, and the input matrix,
     * inMatrix, from a file specified on the command line.
     */
       .
       .
       .
    /* Allocate space for the output matrix. */
       .
       .
       .
    /* Enroll in pvm. */
    if ((myTid = pvm_mytid()) < 0) {
        pvm_perror("[Master] pvm_mytid");
        exit(1);
    }

    /* Create "nSlaves" instances of "pdijk_pvm". */
    taskIds = (int *)malloc(nSlaves * (sizeof(int)));
    /*
     * Form arguments list; we want to use pvm_spawn in one call, and hence are
     * not packing instnce ids via argList here. In argList, we supply a single
     * argument - the number of slaves, nSlaves - to be supplied as a command
     * line argument to each slave task.
     */
    (void)sprintf(work1S, "%d", nSlaves);
    argList[0] = work1S;
    argList[1] = NULL;
    numt = pvm_spawn("pdijk_pvm", argList, 0, (char *)0, nSlaves,
                     taskIds);
    if (numt < 0) {
        pvm_perror("[Master] pvm_spawn");
        (void)fprintf(stderr, "   Error rc from pvm_spawn = %d\n", numt);
```

```
            pvm_exit();            /* Un-enroll from pvm. */
            exit(1);
    }

    /* Send work and receive answers from "pdijk_pvm" slaves. */
    calcShort(nSlaves, nVert, taskIds, inMatrix, outMatrix);

    /* Write results in the outfile for comparison with serial output. */
        .
        .
        .
    /* Un-enroll from pvm. */
    pvm_exit();
    exit(0);
} /* end of "main" */


void calcShort(int nSlaves, int nVert, int *taskIds,
               int *inMatrix, int **outMatrix)
{
    /* Send the input data to all the processes */
    for (i = 0; i < nSlaves; i++) {
        pvm_initsend(PvmDataRaw);
        pvm_pkint(&i, 1, 1);                 /* Instance numbers. */
        pvm_pkint(&nVert, 1, 1);
        pvm_pkint(inMatrix, (nVert * nVert), 1);
        if (pvm_send(taskIds[i], WORK_MSG)) {
            pvm_perror("[Master] pvm_send");
            fprintf(stderr, " Error sending to task <%x>\n", taskIds[i]);
            pvm_exit();
            exit(1);
        }
    }
    /* Collect results and put it together in the output matrix. */
    for (i = 0; i < nTasks; i++) {
        if ((bufId = pvm_recv(-1, RESULT_MSG)) < 0) {
            pvm_perror("[Master] pvm_recv");
            fprintf(stderr, " Error %d receiving message type 2\n", bufId);
            pvm_exit();             /* Unenroll from pvm. */
            exit(1);
        }
        pvm_bufinfo(bufId, (int *)0, (int *)0, &slaveTid);
        /* Identify which slave is responding. */
            .
            .
            .
        /* Get size of result obtained, allocate space, and fill in resMat[j]. */
        pvm_upkint(&sizeResMat, 1, 1);
        resMat[j] = (int *)malloc(sizeResMat * sizeof(int));
        pvm_upkint(&(resMat[j][0]), sizeResMat, 1);
        /* Fill in the outMatrix entries. */
            .
            .
            .
    }
} /* end of "calcShort" */
```

Listing 3.4 PVM steps for st_dijk_pvm.

```
main(int argc, char *argv[])
{
    /* Enroll in pvm. */
    if ((myTid = pvm_mytid()) < 0) {
        pvm_perror("[Slave] pvm_mytid");
        (void)fprintf(stderr, "  Error rc from pvm_mytid = %d\n", myTid);
        exit(1);
    }
    /* Get number of tasks. */
    nSlaves = atoi(argv[1]);
    /* Get data from master. */
    if ((bufId = pvm_recv(-1, WORK_MSG)) < 0) {
        pvm_perror("[Slave] pvm_recv");
        (void)fprintf(stderr, "   Error rc from pvm_recv = %d.\n", bufId);
        pvm_exit();
        exit(1);
    }
    pvm_bufinfo(bufId, (int *)0, (int *)0, &masterTid);
    pvm_upkint(&myIdNum, 1, 1);
    pvm_upkint(&nVert, 1, 1);
    sqNvert = nVert * nVert;
    inMatrix = (int *)malloc(sqNvert * sizeof (int));
    pvm_upkint(inMatrix, sqNvert, 1);
    /* Calculate the number of vertices, numVert, that I have to take care of. */
        .
        .
        .
    totElem = numVert * nVert;
    /* Allocate space for o/p matrix and arrays needed for Dijkstra's algorithm. */
        .
        .
        .
    /* Calcuate shortest paths for my set of vertices. */
    iterNo = 0;
    for (i = myIdNum; i < nVert; i += nSlaves) {
        /* Calculate the shortest paths for source vertex i using Dijkstra's
         * single source shortest path algorithm, implemented in the
         * function dijkstra(). No PVM calls there. */
        dijkstra(i, ...);
        iterNo++;
    }
    pvm_initsend(PvmDataRaw);
    pvm_pkint(&totElem, 1, 1);
    pvm_pkint(outMatrix, totElem, 1);
    if ((rc = pvm_send(masterTid, RESULT_MSG)) < 0) {
        pvm_perror("[Slave] pvm_send");
        (void)fprintf(stderr, " Slave %d <%x>: ", myIdNum, myTid);
        (void)fprintf(stderr, "  Error rc from pvm_send = %d\n", rc);
        pvm_exit();
        exit(1);
    }
    pvm_exit();
    exit(0);
} /* end of "main" */
```

Listing 3.5 PVM steps for pdijk_pvm.

3.5.5   PFLOYD_PVM

Since the PVM framework supports the master-slave paradigm most naturally, the parallel implementation of Floyd's algorithm in PVM is also done using the master-slave paradigm. The master task is called `st_floyd_pvm`, and it dynamically spawns the slave tasks, which are called `pfloyd_pvm`.

The master reads in the input data, including the number of slaves, $nTasks$, and the input matrix. It registers with the PVM environment, as a result of which it is assigned a *tid*. It then spawns $nTasks$ instances of the slave program, passing $nTasks$ as an argument to the slave tasks. It then packs the input data for each slave into the active send buffer, where this input data consists of the instance ID it assigns to a slave, the number of vertices, and that slave's stripe of the matrix. After sending this input data message to its slaves, the master waits for results back from them.

The slaves first register with the PVM environment and are assigned *tids* as a result of that. They then call the receive function to obtain input data from the master. Since the parallel computation for this algorithm proceeds in a tight synchronization loop among the slaves, the slaves need to call collective communication primitives for which they need to be members of a group. For this purpose, each slave enrolls in a group. Before starting the main computation phase, the slaves synchronize at a barrier. Once they enter the computation phase, they need to synchronize with each of their peers in each iteration of the update of the matrix. The owner of the column of the matrix that corresponds to the iteration number needs to broadcast new information to all its peers, and it does that via the broadcast function available, `pvm_bcast()`. The other slaves do a corresponding receive to obtain this data and update their matrices. After computing their partial results, the slaves send their results to the master, who collects these and outputs the results.

Listings 3.6 and 3.7 are code excerpts from the parallel Floyd's PVM program, with the PVM calls being **highlighted**.

```
main(int argc, char *argv[])
{
    /*
     * Read in the number of slaves, nSlaves, from the command line,
     * and the number of vertices, nVert, and the input matrix,
     * inMatrix, from a file specified on the command line.
     */
      .
      .
      .
    /* Enroll in pvm. */
    if ((myTid = pvm_mytid()) < 0) {
        pvm_perror("[Master] pvm_mytid");
        (void)fprintf(stderr, "   Error rc from pvm_mytid = %d.\n", myTid);
        exit(1);
    }

    /*
```

```
 * Allocate space for PVM assigned taskids for nSlaves slaves; this will get
 * filled in as a result of a pvm_spawn() call.
 */
taskIds = (int *)malloc(nSlaves * (sizeof(int)));
/*
 * Form arguments list --- want to use pvm_spawn in one call,
 * hence not packing inst number via argList here
 */
(void)sprintf(work1S, "%d", nSlaves);
argList[0] = work1S;
argList[1] = NULL;

/* Create "nSlaves" instances of "pfloyd_pvm" */
numt = pvm_spawn("pfloyd_pvm", argList, 0, (char *)0, nSlaves,
                    taskIds);
if (numt < 0) {
    pvm_perror("[Master] pvm_spawn");
    (void)fprintf(stderr, "    Error rc from pvm_spawn = %d.\n", numt);
    pvm_exit();
    exit(1);
}

/* Procedure to send work and receive answers from processes. */
calcShort();

/* Write results in the specified output file. */
    :
/* Un-enroll from pvm. */
pvm_exit();
exit(0);
} /* end of "main" */


void calcShort(void)
{
    /* Calculate the segment of inMatrix for each slave. */
    :
    /* Send each slave its instance number and input data. */
    begCol = 0;
    for (i = 0; i < nSlaves; i++) {
        pvm_initsend(PvmDataRaw);
        pvm_pkint(&i, 1, 1);        /* This is their instance id. */
        pvm_pkint(&nVert, 1, 1);

        if (i == (nSlaves-1)) endCol = nVert;
        else endCol = begCol + stripeWidth;

        for (k = 0; k < nVert; k++) {
            pvm_pkint(&(inMatrix[k][begCol]), (endCol - begCol), 1);
        }
        begCol = endCol;

        if (pvm_send(taskIds[i], WORK_MSG)) {
```

```
                                pvm_perror("[Master] pvm_send");
                                (void)fprintf(stderr, "   Error sending to task <%x>\n",
                                         taskIds[i]);
                                pvm_exit();
                                exit(1);
                        }
                }


        /* Collect results and put it together in the output matrix. */
        for (i = 0; i < nSlaves; i++) {
                if ((bufId = pvm_recv(-1, RESULT_MSG)) < 0) {
                        pvm_perror("[Master] pvm_recv");
                        (void)fprintf(stderr, "   Error receiving message type 2\n");
                        pvm_exit();   /* Unenroll from pvm. */
                        exit(1);
                }

                pvm_bufinfo(bufId, (int *)0, (int *)0, &slaveTid);

                /* Identify which slave (index j) is responding. */
                    .
                    .
                    .
                /* Calculate size of, allocate and read in entries for result matrix. */
                    .
                    .
                    .
                pvm_upkint(resMat[j], sizeResMat, 1);

                /* Fill in the corresponding entries for the outMatrix. */
                    .
                    .
                    .
        }
} /* end of "calcShort" */
```

Listing 3.6 PVM steps for st_floyd_pvm.

```
main(int argc, char *argv[])
{
        /* Enroll in pvm. */
        if ((myTid = pvm_mytid()) < 0) {
                pvm_perror("[Slave] pvm_mytid");
                (void)fprintf(stderr, "   Error rc from pvm_mytid = %d.\n", myTid);
                exit(1);
        }

        /* Get number of tasks. */
        nTasks = atoi(argv[1]);

        /* Enroll in a group --- needed for broadcasting. */
        if ((myGid = pvm_joingroup(gName)) < 0) {
                pvm_perror("[Slave] pvm_joingroup");
                (void)fprintf(stderr, "   Error rc from pvm_joingroup = %d.\n",
                                myGid);
                pvm_exit();
                exit(1);
        }
```

```
/* Receive data from master. */
if ((bufId = pvm_recv(-1, WORK_MSG)) < 0) {
    pvm_perror("[Slave] pvm_recv");
    (void)fprintf(stderr, "   Error rc from pvm_recv = %d.\n", bufId);
    pvm_exit();
    exit(1);
}

pvm_bufinfo(bufId, (int *)0, (int *)0, &masterTid);
pvm_upkint(&myIdNum, 1, 1);
pvm_upkint(&nVert, 1, 1);

if (myIdNum == nSlaves-1) {
    width = (nVert/nSlaves) + (nVert%nSlaves);
    endCol = nVert;
    begCol = endCol - width;
}
else {
    width = nVert/nTasks;
    begCol = myIdNum * width;
    endCol = begCol + width;
}

/* Allocate inMatrix array. */
    .
    .
for (i = 0; i < nVert; i++) {
    pvm_upkint(&(inMatrix[i][0]), width, 1);
}

/* Synchronization point --- among all slaves. */
pvm_barrier(gName, nTasks);

/* Calculate shortest paths for its stripe */
calcShortestPaths(begCol, endCol, width);

/* Send final result back to master. */
pvm_initsend(PvmDataRaw);
for (i = 0; i < nVert; i++) {
    pvm_pkint(&(inMatrix[i][0]), width, 1);
}
if ((rc = pvm_send(masterTid, RESULT_MSG)) < 0) {
    pvm_perror("[Slave] pvm_send");
    pvm_exit();
    exit(1);
}

pvm_exit();
exit(0);
} /* end of "main" */
```

```
void calcShortestPaths(int begCol, int endCol, int width)
{
    /* Initialize local variables and arrays. */
    ⋮
    for (k = 0; k < nVert; k++) {
        if ((k >= begCol) && (k < endCol)) {
            /* Broadcast column to all other "pfloyd_pvm" processes. */
            pvm_initsend(PvmDataRaw);
            pvm_pkint(&k, 1, 1);
            for (i = 0; i < nVert; i++) {
                pvm_pkint(&(inMatrix[i][k-begCol]), 1, 1);
            }
            if ((rc = pvm_bcast(gName, INTER_MSG)) < 0) {
                pvm_perror("[Slave] pvm_bcast");
                (void)fprintf(stderr, " Error broadcasting\n");
                pvm_exit();
                exit(1);
            }

            /* Update my stripe. */
            ⋮

        } /* if k is in my stripe ... */
        else {
            if (kLeast != k) {
                success = FALSE;
                while (!success) {
                    /* Wait for the kth column from another process. */
                    if ((rc = pvm_recv(-1, INTER_MSG)) < 0) {
                        (void)fprintf(stderr,
                                        "error receiving msg. type 3\n");
                        pvm_exit();
                        exit(1);
                    }
                    pvm_upkint(&colNoRecd, 1, 1);
                    if (colNoRecd == k) {
                        success = TRUE;
                        pvm_upkint(colRecd, nVert, 1);

                        /* Update my stripe. */
                        ⋮

                    }
                    else { /* k not recd. */
                        if (colNoRecd > k) {
                            /*
                             * This column corresponds to a future k;
                             * Store it for later.
                             */
                            ⋮

                            pvm_upkint(tempc1->colMembers, nVert, 1);
                        }
                    }
                } /* while (!success) */
```

```
            } /* if kLeast != k */
            else { /* I have this column stored. */
                /* Update my stripe from the stored column directly. */
                    ⋮
            }
        } /* else */
    } /* for k */
    return;
} /* end of "calcShortestPaths" */
```

Listing 3.7 PVM steps for pfloyd_pvm.

3.5.6 Tools for PVM Programs

The PVM library has a rich set of functions to support and aid seamless integration of parallel processing tools into the PVM environment, and many PVM tools have been written both in research institutions and by vendors. Among visualization tools, the most notable one is the XPVM [11] visualization tool written by the PVM group at Oak Ridge National Laboratories, the authors of the public domain version of PVM. XPVM not only works with its counterpart PVM, but also with any vendor implementation of PVM that adheres to all PVM APIs. XPVM has support for both on-line monitoring of events in a virtual machine, as well as post mortem trace playback, and is a valuable tool for both performance and functional analysis of a PVM program. Among parallel debuggers, the notable ones supporting debugging of PVM programs are TOTALVIEW [9] and P2D2 [10]. Finally, many resource management tools support PVM programs, and the notable ones in this arena are Platform Computing's LSF, Silicon Graphics' NQE, IBM's LOADLEVELER, and University of Wisconsin's CONDOR [12] project.

3.6 Porting Hints

Having gone through the preceding sections in this chapter, it must be amply evident that for most programs, porting from one environment to another will not be unreasonably difficult. The exception to this will of course be PVM programs that use PVM functions not supported by the MPI standard, and vice versa. Most of even these programs may be ported from the source to the target environment, albeit with difficulty and entailing some minor modifications to the underlying algorithm. However, there will remain a subset of such programs that simply can not be ported since no equivalent functionality exists in the other library. An example would be a PVM program that has fault tolerance or load balancing built into it and thus needs the PVM functions that let it manipulate the cluster itself. This functionality is not available in MPI. Similarly, an MPI program that relies heavily on asynchronous receives may need a significant change to the underlying algorithm to fit in the PVM model.

In the following subsections, we examine a program in terms of each of the major phases in its life cycle. For each phase, the differences between the two environments are discussed and hints to port from one to the other and vice versa are suggested.

3.6.1   Initial Environment Setup

Before a parallel program can be run on a cluster, the cluster needs to be defined. As as has been mentioned in the preceding sections of this chapter, the MPI standard does not specify a fixed way to do this, and different implementations of MPI may use different means of determining the cluster and launching the MPI program on the cluster. Once the cluster is fixed, it can not be changed by adding or deleting hosts to the cluster dynamically during the execution of the MPI program. On the other hand, in PVM, the cluster or the parallel virtual machine is set up via the PVM standard ways, *viz.* either by specifying a hostfile to the local PVM daemon as its run-time argument, or via the PVM console. Once the cluster has been initialized, it can be changed dynamically either via the PVM console commands, or by the PVM program itself via PVM library routines. This is often used by PVM programs that have built-in support for load balancing and fault tolerance.

So this phase of a program is easy to set up when going from the MPI to the PVM domain, since the cluster initialization is simple to translate, and no further changes are necessary as the cluster definition is static. Similarly, if the PVM program in question does not dynamically change the cluster, then the translation to its MPI counterpart is straightforward. On the other hand, going from a PVM domain to an MPI one may prove difficult for those programs that employ dynamic cluster changes. Essentially, the underlying algorithm needs to be changed to fit the static cluster model, although this would in many cases detract from the usefulness of the program, at least in its load balancing and fault tolerant capabilities. Essentially, all the PVM calls that manipulate and monitor the cluster dynamically from within the program need to be removed and an assumption needs to be made in the program that the cluster is static. If the algorithm can not be changed to operate in a static cluster environment, then it can not be ported to the MPI domain.

3.6.2   Parallel Tasks Setup

Once a cluster is determined, MPI tasks can be started on this cluster through the vendor-specific launcher program with a static initial allocation of tasks to the hosts in the cluster. For MPI-2 programs, these tasks can be dynamically spawned too, although, as mentioned before, most MPI implementations will not provide this feature of MPI-2 in the immediate future. In the PVM environment, there is complete flexibility in the manner in which a PVM task can be started: manually inside the PVM console, manually at a shell prompt, or from within another PVM task dynamically.

Porting a statically allocated tasks-on-hosts MPI program to a PVM program is straightforward. If the program is a pure SPMD where n copies of the same program are started, this can be easily done in the PVM domain on the console, or by starting the n copies by hand on the hosts in the cluster. Going from PVM to MPI-1, all dynamic spawning of tasks needs to be removed from the PVM program, with the assumption that all the tasks need to be started by hand (via some MPI launcher command).

In the future, where MPI-2 support will exist, there will be a one-to-one correspondence between the dynamic spawning capabilities of the two environments. Nonetheless, the arguments and the options implied therein will be different in the two domains, and these need to be translated carefully.

3.6.3   Group Management

The chief difference between MPI and PVM groups is that MPI groups are static in nature, whereas PVM groups can be created on the fly. Additionally, arbitrary groups can be created in PVM, whereas all groups in MPI must be derived from existing groups. There are two predefined groups in MPI, `MPI_GROUP_EMPTY`, and the group associated with the initial communicator, `MPI_COMM_WORLD`, consisting of all processes. Again, porting this part of an MPI program to the PVM domain is straightforward since PVM allows for great flexibility in creating groups. However, to translate a PVM program using groups to a corresponding MPI program requires that the program be changed such that it only deals with static groups. Most applications do not use dynamic groups, so this translation will not be too difficult for typical PVM programs.

3.6.4   Intertask Communication

Point-to-Point Communication

For direct communication between MPI tasks, the MPI standard provides a rich set of communication primitives. On the other hand, the set of point-to-point communication primitives in PVM is limited. Hence, for this phase of the program, porting from MPI to PVM will probably be more difficult than vice versa. The semantics of what the communication primitives are aiming to achieve in the MPI program need to be understood before picking the corresponding PVM function. Also, the algorithm may need to be changed if the MPI program uses asynchronous receives since this functionality is not available in PVM. On the other hand, porting from PVM to MPI should be fairly straightforward for this case. The only PVM call here that does not have an MPI counterpart is the timed received, `pvm_trecv()`, but this functionality can be easily simulated at the application layer for the corresponding MPI program.

Collective Communication

Although the set of collective communication functions are about the same in MPI and PVM, the semantics of the calls is slightly different for some of the calls. Also, MPI has a few more functions for collective communication than PVM, such as `MPI_Allreduce()`. This is not a big problem when porting to PVM since these calls can be simulated at the application level in a straightforward manner by calling the corresponding single instance call (ex. `MPI_Reduce()`) multiple times. As far as semantics go, some of the calls in PVM are non-blocking in nature, such as `pvm_reduce()`, but none of these calls in the MPI standard are required to return as soon as their participation in the call is over. Furthermore, in MPI, these calls must be made by all the members of a communicator. In PVM, for some of the calls, all the members of a group need not call that function. Also, some of the collective communication calls such as `pvm_bcast()` do not need to have corresponding collective communication receives, but can have simple point-to-point receives instead. In general, the collective communication calls in MPI are based on a stricter set of rules than their corresponding PVM calls.

Hence, porting from an MPI program to a PVM program should be relatively straightforward as it involves replacing MPI calls with PVM calls, with additional looping in the case of some of the all-to-all calls with no counterparts in PVM. Going from PVM to MPI may entail more work, especially if the PVM program has mixed in the collective communication calls with point-to-point calls as in the use of `pvm_bcast()` and `pvm_recv()`. Here, the correct point-to-point calls will need to be identified and then replaced with the corresponding collective MPI call.

3.6.5   Utility Functions

By definition of being a flexible, parallel environment, PVM provides a much richer set of utility functions than does MPI, which is strictly a standard library specification and hence leaves some of the setup issues (and the resulting utility functions) to vendor implementations. Since these are utility functions, these do not affect the solution algorithmically; rather, these are convenient tools for programmers. As such, they can be easily done away with when one ports from the PVM to the MPI world. Porting from MPI to PVM is not a problem since MPI does not have any utility function which has no counterpart in the PVM world.

3.7   Summary

This chapter discussed parallel message passing programming using the two most popular message passing paradigms: MPI and PVM. The all pairs shortest path problem was used as the example problem to illustrate programming in these two paradigms. Two different algorithms, Dijkstra's and Floyd's, that solve this problem were parallelized algorithmically, and these parallel algorithms were in turn implemented using MPI and PVM. The four resulting programs, two for each paradigm, demonstrated the key issues in programming with these message passing systems. Lastly, porting hints from one paradigm to the other were given.

3.8   Bibliography

[1] Message Passing Interface Forum. *The Message-Passing Interface Standard,* May 5, 1994.

[2] A. Geist et al. *PVM 3 User's Guide and Reference Manual,* September 1994.

[3] E. Dijkstra. A Note on Two Problems in Connexion with Graphs. In *Numerische Mathematik,* vol. 1, pages 269–271, 1959.

[4] Message Passing Interface Forum. *MPI-2: Extensions to the Message-Passing Interface,* July 1997.

[5] R. W. Floyd. Algorithm 97: Shortest Path. In *Communications of the ACM,* vol. 5, page 345, 1962.

[6] J. Jenq and S. Sahni. All Pairs Shortest Paths on a Hypercube Multiprocessor. In *Proceedings of the International Conference on Parallel Processing,* pages 713–716, 1987.

[7] I. Pramanick. Distributed Computing Solutions to the All-Pairs Shortest Path Problem. In *Proceedings of the International Symposium on High Performance Distributed Computing,* pages 196–203, 1993.

[8] `http://www.mpi.nd.edu/lam/xmpi/xmpi21.html`, XMPI — A Run/Debug GUI for MPI.

[9] Dolphin Interconnect Solutions, Inc. *TotalView Multiprocess Debugger User's Guide,* 1997.

[10] Robert Hood. The P2D2 Project: Building a Portable Distributed Debugger. In *Proceedings of SPDT–96,* May 1996.

[11] J. Kohl and A. Geist. The PVM 3.4 Tracing Facility and XPVM 1.1. In *XPVM 1.1 Technical Report 33c.*

[12] D. H. J. Epema et al. A Worldwide Flock of Condors: Load Sharing Among Workstation Clusters. In *Journal on Future Generation of Computer Systems,* vol. 12, 1996.

Chapter 4

Linking Message-Passing Environments

MATTHIAS BRUNE[†], JÖRN GEHRING[‡], AND ALEXANDER REINEFELD[†]

[†]Konrad-Zuse-Zentrum für Informationstechnik
Takustrasse 7, D-14195 Berlin

[‡]Paderborn Center for Parallel Computing
University of Paderborn, Fürstenallee 11, D-33102 Paderborn

Email: *brune@zib.de, joern@uni-paderborn.de, ar@zib.de*

4.1 Interoperability Between Message-Passing Interfaces

In the last few years, clusters of LAN- or WAN-connected systems have become a reasonable and cost-effective alternative to the use of expensive, dedicated monolithic high performance systems. The notion of a metacomputer has been coined, denoting a "network of heterogeneous, computational resources linked by software in such a way that they can be used as easily as a personal computer" [15]. Clearly, building a metacomputer is an ambitious task, and several obstacles must be overcome before such a system may eventually become reality.

One such obstacle lies in the incompatibility of the vendor-specific message-passing libraries, e.g., MPL, NX, and PARIX. On the one hand, these message-passing libraries provide optimal communication on the corresponding hardware, but on the other hand, it is usually not possible with these communication libraries to exchange messages with other vendor's systems. Vendor-specific message-passing libraries support only 'closed world communication' within a single environment. Even with the two vendor-independent message-passing standards, PVM [7] and MPI[12], it is not possible for an application to communicate from one programming environment to another.

4.1.1   Message Passing Between Programming Environments

PLUS (Program Linkage by Universal Software interfaces) provides a fast communication interface between different message-passing methods, including both vendor-specific and standard models. PLUS can be used, for example, to send the output of a massively parallel application to a high resolution graphics system, operating under a different programming environment.

PLUS supports communication over LANs, MANs, and WANs. With only four new commands, `plus_init`, `plus_exit`, `plus_info`, `plus_system`, existing applications can be easily modified to communicate with other applications operating under other message-passing models. The original send and receive operations need not be modified in the application's source code: PLUS automatically distinguishes between 'internal' and 'external' communication partners.

The design of the PLUS software package is modular to allow for easy extension to other programming environments. Much emphasis has been put on the communication speed. The internal communication taking place within a single programming environment is not affected by PLUS.

4.1.2   Access to Resource Management Systems

When spawning a new process on another system – possibly running other programming models – PLUS calls the remote resource management system [2] to allow for an optimal process mapping on the target platform. In the case of space-sharing parallel systems, the native mapping strategies of the resource management system are used for determining an optimal mapping strategy with minimum partition waste and best job throughput. For time-sharing systems, the mapping scheme is usually based on processor availability, processor load, and the load of the interconnection network.

In the following section, we give an overview on the PLUS architecture and show some practical examples on how to use PLUS. We then illustrate the PLUS interface to resource management systems and present our declarative resource and service description RSD for specifying available hardware configuration and resource requests. Section 4.3 presents the PLUS system architecture (consisting of a library and daemons) modules in more detail. Section 4.4 describes a scheme on how to extend PLUS to new message-passing environments. In Section 4.5, we present some performance benchmarks measured in wide area networks.

4.2   An Overview of the PLUS Library

The design of PLUS was driven by the need for an efficient, portable interface between different communication models without using low-level socket routines. The rationale was to create a small interface that can be linked to existing applications to allow them to communicate to applications executing under other programming models.

PLUS consists of daemons and a modular library that is to be linked to the application code. Only four new commands make it easy to integrate PLUS into an existing code:

- `plus_init()`   for signing on at the nearest PLUS daemon

- `plus_exit()`   for logging off

- `plus_system()`   for spawning a task on another (remote) system

- `plus_info()`   for obtaining information on the accessible (remote) tasks

From an applications' view, the PLUS communication is completely hidden behind the native communication routines used in the application. By means of macro substitution, PLUS provides linkage to external systems without modifying the source code. Thereby, an MPL application, for example, makes implicit use of PLUS when using MPL communication routines. Data conversion between different data representations on the participating hardware platforms (e.g., little or big endian) is transparently handled by PLUS.

Moreover, PLUS is modular to allow for easy extension to other new communication methods. Only few communication routines in the translation library must be modified to include a new programming model to PLUS (see Section 4.4).

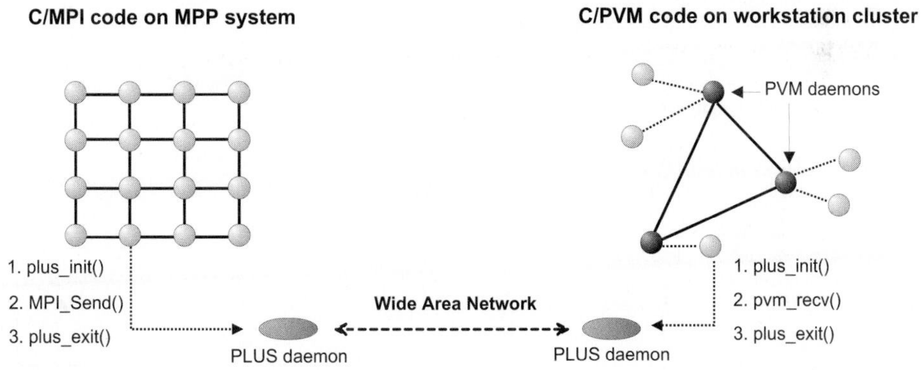

C/MPI code on MPP system   **C/PVM code on workstation cluster**

1. plus_init()
2. MPI_Send()   **Wide Area Network**
3. plus_exit()
        PLUS daemon   PLUS daemon

1. plus_init()
2. pvm_recv()
3. plus_exit()

Figure 4.1 Process communication via PLUS between different programming environments.

In the following, we describe an illustrating example (Fig. 4.1) on a process communication between C/MPI and C/PVM. The corresponding program code is shown in Fig. 4.2. Both applications have to 'sign on' at the PLUS master daemon using the `plus_init()` command with the daemon location and a logical name of the programming environment as parameters. As a result, the successful initialization of `plus_init()` is returned. The daemons will then autonomously exchange process tables and control information with each other.

After successful initialization, the remote processes are able to communicate with each other via PLUS. From the MPI application, the communication is done by

```
#include "mpi.h"
#include "plus_mpi.h"
#define MSG_TAG 1

void main( int argc, char* argv[ ] ) {
    int MPI_Size;
    MPI_Init ( &argc, &argv );
    MPI_Comm_Size ( MPI_COMM_WORLD, &MPI_Size );
    partner_ID = MPI_Size;

    /* Connect to the PLUS system */
    if( plus_init( argv[1], "MPI_sender" ) < 0 ) exit( -1 );

    /* Send a message to a non-MPI process */
    MPI_Send( "Hello world", 12, MPI_CHAR, partner_ID, MSG_TAG,
            MPI_COMM_WORLD );

    /* Disconnect from PLUS and MPI */
    plus_exit(); MPI_Finalize();
}
```

```
#include "pvm3.h"
#include "plus_pvm.h"
#define WORLD 0
#define MSG_TAG 1

void main(int argc,char* argv[]) {
  int ntask, partner_ID; char buffer[32];
  struct pvmtaskinfo *taskpt;

  pvm_initsend( PvmDataDefault );
  pvm_tasks( WORLD, &ntask, &taskpt );
  partner_ID = ntask;

  /* Connect to the PLUS system */
  if (plus_init( argv[1], "PVM_receiver" ) < 0 ) exit (-1);

  /* Recv a message from a non-PVM-process */
  pvm_recv( partner_ID, MSG_TAG );
  pvm_upkstr( buffer );
  plus_exit(); pvm_exit();
}
```

Figure 4.2 An MPI application (above) communicating with a PVM application (below) via PLUS.

calling MPI_Send() with a partner identifier that is greater than the last (maximum) process identifier managed by MPI in the communicator group MPI_COMM_WORLD.

In general, PLUS recognizes an external communication by a process identifier outside the ID range of the corresponding programming model. Within PLUS, all process identifiers are given relative to the number of active tasks. For situations involving more than two programming models, the plus_info() function can be used to identify remote communication partners. It returns a data structure identifying the accessible remote programming environments and corresponding processes in consecutive order.

Most of the PLUS system code is contained in the daemons. Thereby, it was possible to keep the PLUS library small. The daemons are used to hide the application processes from the slow internet communication. Whenever a message is to be transferred between different environments, it is first sent to the nearest PLUS daemon, which immediately acknowledges the message to allow for message latency hiding. The daemon then takes responsibility for delivering the message while the application process proceeds with its computation.

4.2.1   Process Creation and Management

Today's programming environments have succeeded in making the communication aspect easier, but powerful mechanisms for the dynamic creation of new processes are still missing. As an example, the current MPI-1 standard does not provide a dynamic process model at all. Moreover, MPI-2 and PVM cannot spawn dedicated processes that do not belong to the parallel program. Since message-passing environments are mainly used by communicating parallel programs, this situation is less than satisfying. We need a flexible and powerful interface between programming environments and resource management systems. Although both PVM and MPI-2 have interfaces to the resource management, this may only be used for creating independent subjobs. In Section 4.2.1 we describe how PLUS enables message-passing environments to efficiently spawn interdependent subtasks to message-passing environments. A core tool of this facility is the Resource and Service Description (RSD) described in Section 4.2.1.

Interface Between Multiple Resource Management Systems

For programming environments lacking a process model (such as MPI-1) PLUS provides `plus_system()` and `plus_info()` to spawn new processes and to obtain information on remote processes. Fig. 4.3 illustrates the spawning of new processes. Each daemon maintains a small database listing all available machines with the corresponding commands to be used for spawning processes. When an application calls `plus_system()`, the remote PLUS daemon invokes the corresponding command for allocating the requested number of computing nodes at the target machine. This is either done with the default parameters found in a local configuration database or with the user-supplied parameters in the `plus_system()` function. As a side effect, a new PLUS daemon may be brought up at the remote site to provide faster access.

If information about the resource requirements of the new process is available, this can be passed to the management system as an additional parameter. Thus, it is sometimes advisable to use this function explicitly, although it could be hidden behind a corresponding call of the programming environment. The function `plus_system()` accepts complex program descriptions written in RSD. For resource management systems that are not compatible with RSD, a filter translates the information into the required form. However, this may reduce the available data, if the target language is not as powerful as RSD.

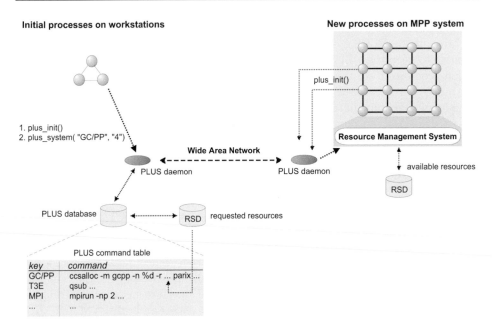

Initial processes on workstations

New processes on MPP system

1. plus_init()
2. plus_system("GC/PP", "4")

plus_init()

Wide Area Network

Resource Management System

PLUS daemon   PLUS daemon

available resources

RSD

PLUS database   RSD   requested resources

PLUS command table

key	command
GC/PP	ccsalloc -m gcpp -n %d -r ... parix...
T3E	qsub ...
MPI	mpirun -np 2 ...
...	...

Figure 4.3 Remote process creation with PLUS on a Parsytec operating under the
CCS resource management system.

Resource and Service Description (RSD)

In order to achieve an optimal mapping of communicating processes onto a set of
heterogeneous machines, a management system needs to know the communication
structure of the program as well as the properties of the available hardware. Most
common resource management systems describe resources and requirements by a
set of attribute/value pairs. While this may be sufficient for independent sequential
jobs, it does not allow to express the communication structure of a parallel program
or to specify the topology of networked computers. RSD [5] has been developed to
overcome this weakness.

In RSD every resource consists of nodes interconnected by an arbitrary topology. Active nodes are indicated by the keyword NODE. Depending on whether RSD is
used to describe hardware or software topologies, the keyword NODE is interpreted
as a "processor" or a "process." Communication interfaces are declared by the
keyword PORT. A PORT may be a socket, a passive hardware entity like a network
interface card, a crossbar, or a process that behaves passively within the parallel program. A NODE definition consists of three parts: In the optional DEFINITION section,
identifiers and attributes are introduced by $Identifier[=(value,...)]$. The
DECLARATION section declares all nodes with corresponding attributes. The notion
of a 'node' is recursive. They are described by NODE *NodeName* {PORT *PortName*;
attribute 1, ...}. The CONNECTION section is again optional. It is used to define

```
NODE Ring_Application {
 // DEFINITION: define attributes, values and ranges
    CONST N = 128; // number of processes
    VAR i;

 // DECLARATION:
    FOR i=0 TO N-1
       NODE i {
          PORT Comm; CPU=MPC601; OS=AIX; MEMORY=128; DISK=4; LOAD=2;}

 // CONNECTION:
 // build the bidirectional ring
    FOR i=0 TO N-1
       EDGE i {
          NODE i PORT Comm <=> NODE ((i+1)MOD N) PORT Comm;}
 // process 0 provides a TCP socket connection to the world
    ASSIGN TCP_SocketConnection {
       NODE 0 PORT Comm <=> PORT TCP_Socket;}
};
```

Figure 4.4 RSD specification of a parallel program.

attributed edges between the ports of the nodes declared above: EDGE *NameOfEdge*
{NODE *w* PORT *x* <=> NODE *y* PORT *z; attribute 1; ...*}. In addition, the notion of a 'virtual edge' is used to provide a link between different levels of the
hierarchy in the graph. This allows to establish a link from the described module to the 'outside world' by 'exporting' a physical port to the next higher level.
These edges are defined by: ASSIGN *NameOfVirtualEdge* { NODE *w* PORT *x* <=>
PORT *a*}. Note, that NODE *w* and PORT *a* are the only entities known to the
outside world.

Figure 4.4 shows a simple example where we have a program of N processes
communicating via a ring topology. In this example there are 128 processes, each
requiring an MPC601 CPU, AIX operating system, 128 MByte memory, 4 MByte
disk space and causing a load factor of two. Each process communicates with its
successor via link one and with its predecessor via link zero. Only one of them
makes additional I/O via link two.

Since real world systems are rather complex, we do not expect RSD specifications
to be created by hand. For this reason, we are currently developing a set of graphical
tools that help programmers and system administrators in generating the RSD
descriptions automatically [5].

4.3   System Architecture

4.3.1   Library

The PLUS library `libplus.a` contains a translation module and a communication
module. The translation module interfaces between the programming environment
and the PLUS system. By means of macro substitution in the application code,

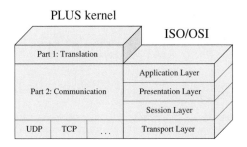

Figure 4.5 The PLUS system library `libplus.a` and the ISO/OSI model.

PLUS checks whether the communication is internal or external. In the first case, the native message-passing call is performed at runtime, whereas in the latter case, a PLUS routine takes care of the communication with the remote system.

The communication module in PLUS is responsible for all external communication. It supports various network protocols, e.g., TCP/IP, UDP/IP, thereby providing flexible communication between various programming models via the fastest available network protocol.

Initially, we used TCP/IP for the underlying communication layer. It provides a reliable, connection-oriented service. Later, we found TCP/IP to be inappropriate because of its high overhead, especially when opening several connections via the WAN. As TCP/IP keeps a file descriptor for each connection in main memory, the maximum number of descriptors might not be sufficient to allow for many concurrent external connections.

Therefore, this implementation uses the unreliable, connectionless UDP/IP protocol with a maximum packet length of 8 kBytes. With UDP/IP, it is possible to communicate with an unlimited number of processes over a single descriptor. For providing a reliable service, we implemented a segmentation and desegmentation algorithm and also a flow control with recovery. The segmentation/desegmentation algorithm splits the message into packets of 8 kBytes and reassembles the packets at the receiving node.

For error recovery, PLUS uses a sliding window mechanism with a variant of the selective reject, where only those packets that got lost (unacknowledged) are resent. The sender sends the packets from its window until either a timeout occurs or the window is empty. When a timeout for a sent packet occurs, the packet is resent and a new timeout is calculated. The receiver sorts the packets into its window and acknowledges receipt.

4.3.2 Daemons

Before running an application program, a PLUS master daemon must be brought up by the UNIX command `startplus <target_machine>`. Thereafter, the master daemon autonomously starts additional daemons that are (logically) interconnected

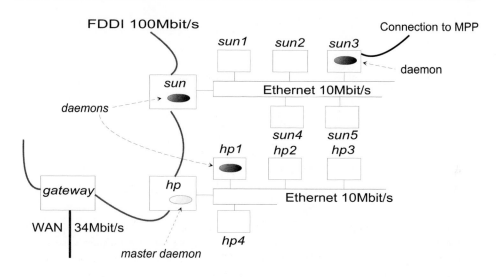

Figure 4.6 Network positions of PLUS daemons.

in a clique topology. Clearly, the daemons' location in the network are essential for the overall communication performance. As illustrated in Fig. 4.6, PLUS daemons should be run on network routers (e.g., machine 'sun'), or on powerful workstations (e.g., 'hp1'). Moreover, it is advisable to run a daemon on the frontends of a parallel systems (e.g., machine 'sun3' in Fig. 4.7).

Figure 4.7 shows a network configuration file used by the PLUS master daemon to identify suitable locations for the mapping of additional daemons. The configuration file consists of the following sections

- DEFS defines whether automatic mapping is enabled

- USERNAME provides network addresses and user IDs for remote domains

- NETWORK INFORMATION contains a list of hosts for each subnet where daemons may be started. The order of choice is top down.

- MPP FRONTENDS specifies frontends to MPP systems, where daemons are to be started.

In each subnetwork there exists at least one daemon. Depending on the actual communication load in the subnetwork, more daemons may be started by the master daemon on request of 'normal' daemons. Any daemon that has a workload (number of supported user tasks) larger than a certain threshold can ask the master to bring up further daemons.

```
SECTION DEFS
        MAPPING        1
        STARTUP        1

SECTION USERNAME
# external domains
        paragon.zam.kfa-juelich.de    zdv516
        parix1.mi.uni-koeln.de        pccs

SECTION NETWORK INFORMATION
# local domain uni.paderborn.de
        SUB:   sun                    # name of subnet
               sun1                   # hosts in descending order
               sun2
               sun3
        SUB:   hp                     # name of subnet
               hp1                    # hosts in descending order
               hp2
SECTION MPP-FRONTENDS
        sun3
```

Figure 4.7 Network configuration file of a PLUS master daemon.

4.4 Adding New Message-Passing Environments

PLUS has been kept rather small and modular to allow for future extension. At the time of writing, PLUS supports MPI, PVM, and PARIX. Other communication methods can be incorporated by extending the translation module of `libplus.a` (Figure 4.5). Assume we want to include a communication method to PLUS which provides two communication routines, `send` (`taskid, msgid, message`) and `recv` (`taskid, msgid, message`). We then have to:

- write an `include` file with two macros overlaying the original function calls in the application code by two new functions, `mysend(taskid,msgid,message)` and `myrecv(taskid, msgid, message)`.

- check in the `mysend(...)` and `myrecv(...)` functions whether the specified task-ID is internal or external. In the case of internal communication, we have to invoke the original send/receive function, otherwise we call `send_plus(...)` or `recv_plus(...)` provided by the PLUS communicator module of `libplus.a`.

- finally, `libplus.a` has to be recompiled.

Often, the parameters of the original communication functions and the corresponding PLUS calls are very similar, allowing to code the above `if`-statement directly into the macro definition.

4.5   Performance Results

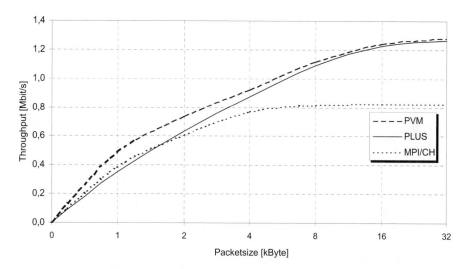

Figure 4.8 PLUS on a 34 Mbps ATM-WAN.

Figure 4.8 shows the communication throughput of PLUS in comparison to that of PVM and MPI via a 34 Mbps ATM network. In the runs, the same PVM (resp. MPI) code has been used: once communicating via PVM (resp. MPI) and the other time via PLUS. As can be seen, PVM and PLUS exhibit nearly the same performance. Both use the asynchronous UDP/IP network transport service between their daemons. The PLUS routing overhead does not influence the throughput too much, because on a WAN the bottleneck is not caused by software latencies at the daemons but rather by the message transfer time through the WAN. PLUS' asynchronous transport layer outperforms MPICH, which is based on the synchronous TCP/IP protocol. This is because the PLUS communication does not block while transmitting the messages to the receiver.

Note that PLUS was designed for message-passing in wide area networks. Its asynchronous communication layer utilizes the full bandwidth of wide area networks without wasting time to wait for acknowledgement packets.

4.6   Related Work

Much work has been done in the field of heterogeneous programming environments. However, most of the commonly used packages like PVM [7] or MPI [12] propose the use of a single homogeneous environment. This approach is not well suited, if existing code is to be ported to a heterogeneous environment. Furthermore, the high abstraction level of these tools make it difficult for the user to exploit the heterogeneity of the underlying infrastructure.

The MPICH [9] implementation of MPI, which has been developed at Argonne National Laboratory, offers support of heterogeneous networked environments at a lower layer. This MPI system has the ability to use multiple protocols and select the most appropriate for a specific situation. However, these facilities are not visible to the application developer.

Two other approaches similar to PLUS somewhat alleviate the problem by providing a linkage between standard programming models:

- *PACX* [4] is a similar approach, but it aims at linking two or more homogeneous systems. It was used in a transatlantical experiment to link two Cray T3Es for running a large simulation code under MPI.

- *PVMPI* [6] is an extension of MPI that provides a communication link to tasks running under MPI. However, PVMPI lacks openness towards other models.

Despite transparent support of different communications environments, the generic interface to HPC management systems like NQS [1], PBS [3], Codine [8], Condor [11], or CCS [10] is another important aspect of PLUS. A similar facility is provided by the Carmi package [13]. But since Carmi has been developed for the support of large workstation clusters, it is currently not suited for connecting supercomputers on which neither PVM nor MPI is used.

4.7   Summary

Efficient and portable communication interfaces become more important in the popular field of distributed computing. We have presented PLUS, a lightweight, extensible, and efficient communication interface. It provides interprocess communication between different message-passing models such as MPI, PVM, and PARIX, and dynamic process creation with access to resource management systems for determining optimal process mapping.

With only four new commands (`plus_init`,`plus_exit`,`plus_info`, `plus_system`), the PLUS communication library can easily be integrated into existing parallel codes, allowing tasks to communicate transparently between the message-passing standards and the vendor-supplied communication methods. Our current implementation supports interprocess communication between PVM, MPI, and the Parsytec PARIX. Other programming models can be added to PLUS with little effort, requiring only a few hours of implementing a small interface module.

Part of our PLUS implementation is the resource and service description RSD used for specifying both hardware requests and hardware components in a computing center. RSD is a versatile tool for describing any kind of resource used in networked computing and metacomputing environments.

With PLUS, we deliberately decided to design a small, self-standing software module with the only purpose being to provide a portable and extensible communication between programming models and resource management systems. This is in contrast to other approaches that try to integrate additional features to existing programming models, making them even larger.

4.8   Bibliography

[1] Carl Albing. Cray NQS: Production batch for a distributed computing world. In *Proceedings of the 11th Sun User Group Conference and Exhibition*, December 1993, USA, Brookline, pages 302–309.

[2] M. Baker, G. Fox, and H. Yua. Cluster Computing Review. Northeast Parallel Architecture Center, Syracuse University, November 1995, New York.

[3] A. Bayucan, R.L. Henderson, T. Proett, D. Tweten, and B. Kelly. *Portable Batch System: External Reference Specification*. Release 1.1.7, NASA Ames Research Center, June 1996.

[4] T. Beisel, E. Gabriel, and M. Resch. An Extension to MPI for Distributed Computing on MPPs. In M. Bubak, J. Dongarra, J. Wasniewski (Eds.), *Recent Advances in Parallel Virtual Machine and Message Passing Interface*, LNCS, Springer, 1997, pages 25–33.

[5] M. Brune, J. Gehring, A. Keller, and A. Reinefeld. RSD – Resource and Service Description. In *12th Intl. Symp. on High-Performance Computing Systems and Applications HPCS'98*, Edmonton, Canada, Kluwer Academic Press 1998, pages 193–206.

[6] G. E. Fagg and J. Dongarra. PVMPI: An Integration of the PVM and MPI Systems. *Calculateurs Paralleles*, vol. 8, 1996, pages 151–166.

[7] A. Geist, A. Beguelin, J. Dongarra, W. Liang, B. Manchek, and V. Sunderam. *PVM: Parallel Virtual Machine – A User's Guide and Tutorial for Network Parallel Computing*. MIT Press, Cambridge, MA, 1994.

[8] GENIAS Software GmbH. Codine: Computing in Distributed Networked Environments. *http://www.genias.de/genias/english/codine.html*.

[9] W. Gropp and E. Lusk. MPICH Working Note: Creating a New MPICH Device Using the Channel Interface. Technical Report, Mathematics and Computer Science Division, 1995, Argonne National Laboratory.

[10] A. Keller and A. Reinefeld. CCS Resource Management in Networked HPC Systems. In *7th Heterogeneous Computing Workshop HCW'98 at IPPS/SPDP'98*, Orlando, FL, IEEE Comp. Society Press 1998, pages 44–56.

[11] M.J. Litzkow and M. Livny. Condor–A Hunter of Idle Workstations. In *Procs. 8th IEEE Int. Conf. Distr. Computing Systems*, June 1988, pages 104–111.

[12] Message Passing Interface Forum. MPI: A Message-Passing Interface Standard. *International Journal of Supercomputer Applications*, vol. 8(3/4), 1994.

[13] J. Pruyne and M. Livny. Parallel Processing on Dynamic Resources with CARMI. *Springer Lecture Notes in Computer Science*, 1995.

[14] A. Reinefeld, J. Gehring, and M. Brune. Communicating Across Parallel Message-Passing Environments. *Journal of Systems Architecture*, vol. 44, Elsevier Science B.V., Amsterdam, 1998, pages 261–272.

[15] L. Smarr and C.E. Catlett. Metacomputing. *Communications of the ACM*, vol. 6, 1992, pages 45–52.

Chapter 5

Active Objects

CHUNG-KWONG YUEN

School of Computing,
National University of Singapore,
Kent Ridge, Singapore.

Email: *yuenck@comp.nus.edu.sg*

5.1 Objects in Cluster-Based Parallel Systems

Cluster-based systems aim to support scalable parallel computing, typically with a two level hardware structure of tightly coupled processing units making up a set of loosely coupled clusters, such as multiple processors on a single PC bus with LAN linking multiple PCs. Each cluster runs a set of tasks that have high communication requiremets with each other, such as threads sharing a single environment, but engages in only occasional communication with remote clusters, such as to spawn off functions that return results but otherwise do not access the main thread environment.

Objects provide an obvious software structure to match this hardware structure because they encapsulate highly self contained data and code. Methods spawned off for parallel execution in the same object share direct access to the object's encapsulated information, but are less likely to share information with methods spawned from other objects. As a general rule, methods of the same object should execute on the same cluster, and whole objects are dispatched to other clusters for execution. Objects change their state in the course of execution and receive occasional calls from other objects so that the computed results of the objects' methods may be retrieved. From time to time, object migration to another cluster may also be required, either to better balance the workload of the whole system, or to better meet intensive communication needs with objects that are already there. We expect close links between cluster based systems and concurrent object languages [1].

The intersection of parallel processing and object-oriented programming generates a number of language design problems that must be addressed. In the present chapter we discuss these and outline the positions taken for the BaLinda languages.

5.2   Active Versus Passive Objects

Objects are defined by first specifying the generic structure and content in a class definition, and then by making instances of the class occupying memory allocated from the heap. Execution activities in an object are triggered by calls on its methods. With multiple objects existing independently, parallel execution can be readily introduced. However, this does not occur by default but by design, and decisions need to be made on a specific parallelization mechanism.

Consider the following example involving pre-existing objects X, Y, and Z:

```
X calls Y
X waits for result      Y executes
X receives result       Y idle
further processing
X calls Z
X waits for result      Z executes
X receives result       Z idle
...
```

Despite the existence of three separate objects, no parallel execution takes place between them. In comparison, we can instead have:

```
X calls Y
X continues without Y result       Y executes
X calls Z to execute a method      Z executes
X continues without Z result       ...
X demands results of Y and Z       ...
X idles waiting for responses      Y and Z reply
X resumes with Y and Z results     Y and Z idle
...
```

In other words, whether multiple objects produce parallel execution would depend, among other things, on the active/passive status of each object and the communcation protocol used between them.

The requirement here is somewhat different from the spawning of parallel procedures, because a procedure can return results by assigning them to variables in the main thread. In contrast, the execution effects of an object method remain in the object, unless some explicit step to retrieve them, after verifying its availability, is carried out. Some relevant mechanisms must be provided in the parallel object language.

One simple mechanism is for a called method to return a result token or "future" to the caller immediately, so that the caller can continue with its own execution while holding this token for later use. The token is a promise to deliver a result at some later time, and before the result becomes available, any access on it would suspend the thread making this unsuccessful demand. When the result does become available, the thread is resumed. Copies of the token could be passed to other threads so that a number of tasks can synchronize by blocking on a common result. Sequences and nestings of futures, with access of results between different sequences and nestings, can produce versatile parallel program structures.

However, copying future tokens and passing them through complex program structures carries risks and could result in deadlock, such as two futures waiting for each other or a child future suspending on the parent. Because a future token can be either a pointer to a piece of unfinished computation in another object, or a data item returned to the caller's data space at the end of computation, it has an uncertain scoping status. A thread entitled to copy the result after X has received it from Y may not be entitled to point into Y during the computation. Further, future tokens are not atomic as they may be shared, and do not provide information exchange during task execution, since a result is returned only upon termination. They are not convenient ways to produce repeated exchanges of information between two executing threads.

A more versatile technique is to return a task ID which may be used to check the execution status of a method, to look into the task's data space, to retrieve the result if execution has completed, and to control its execution such as terminating it or assigning it different execution priorities. While this gives the programmer much freedom and power, some sophistication and knowledge are required to use it effectively. In our experience, most application programmers would not be able to handle such a tool well because it requires a background of system programming. There is again the risk of deadlock when task IDs are passed to other threads.

Our view is that a call on an object method should be treated just like a procedure call: normally, the caller's execution suspends during the procedure call and continues upon return, but the programmer can choose to spawn the call as a parallel thread, and can use its result after the thread has ended. If the method is a procedure, then the call changes the object state, but the caller has to retrieve the result by further (nonparallel) calls on the public portion of the the the object:

```
make object X
spawn X.method
other processing
wait for end of thread
use X.public
```

If the method is a function, the result is returned upon function exit and may be assigned to a variable in the caller's environment:

```
spawn Y = X.method
other processing
wait for end of thread
use Y
```

Concerning the right way to wait for the end of a parallel thread, our view is that it should not be necessary to know task IDs, and indeed the spawning function should not return any such information. The wait (or in the BaLinda languages, SYNCHRONIZE) should simply wait for the end of the most recently spawn thread. When multiple threads are spawned, one merely waits for them individually in a last in first out order, or as a group using SYNCHRONIZE (N) where N is the total number of threads most recently spawned from the current thread.

The question of whether SYNCHRONIZE should retrieve the execution result, in addition to confirming is availability, is an intriguing one. Consider the example of adding up a set of results returned from a list of objects, evaluating in parallel (EXEC is the BaLinda task spawning command):

```
X = ListHead;
Count = 0;
Sum = 0;
{ Loop: EXEC X.method;
     Count = Count+1;
     { IF NOT (NULL (X.next))
     => { X = X.next;
          Loop
}   }   }
{ FOR I = 1 TO COUNT
  Sum = Sum + SYNCHRONIZE
}
```

Each SYNCHRONIZE retrieves the result of one most recently spawned thread, until all the results have been included.

The alternative of storing the result of each X.method in an array requires us to know beforehand the maximum list length so that the array could be declared, or to have some way of acquiring additional storage if the array turns out to be too short. Alternatively, the X.method results have to be stored in a linked list. Acquiring the result with SYNCHRONIZE where it is needed is more flexible. In the example, tail recursive calls cause the deletion of the stack section of a recursion, even though a parallel thread may be open, but formally the parent recursion does not end until the child ends, when a leaf is reached, by which time all parallel threads spawned in all the recursions would be verified as having terminated.

Next, we consider the issue of the object "body" or initialization code. A class definition has the following typical structure:

```
{ CLASS A...;
  PUBLIC...;
  LOCAL...;
  body
}
```

When an instance of A is made, the variables declared in the PUBLIC and LOCAL statements are assigned storage, as are the methods defined there; if the body is present, then the code specified is executed to initialize the object, before a pointer to the object is returned to the caller permitting access to the new A object. Such an object is passive, since no execution will take place inside it unless calls on its method are received.

However, consider the follow scenario:

```
EXEC X = makeinstance (A)
other processing
SYNCHRONIZE
```

While "other processing" is occurring, X already points to the storage area allocated to the object, and the public information is already visible, even though the body may still be executing and changing the information. It is possible for calls to be made on X, so that there is parallel execution between the body of X and its called method. X is no longer a passive object; it contains execution of its own, which may interact with its own methods if they are called from the outside.

A pointer to an active object, like a future token, is a link to an unfinished piece of computation, but whereas accessing a future token would block a thread until computation completes, an object has no definitive final state and the public part of its content can be accessed even as the computation proceeds. Doing this safely would, however, require some atomic facility, and we discuss this in the next section. One could also wait for the object initialization code to end with a SYNCHRONIZE, after which the object is no longer active, and then call its methods like a normal passive object.

5.3   Objects and Atomicity

An object encapsulates a relatively self-contained set of data and code. In parallel processing problems, it is natural to see an object as a unit of atomicity, which arises from the imposition of sequential entry into the object, i.e., only one call on any method is executed at any moment. Some form of call queue management is required to produce this effect. While this is not difficult to implement in itself, it is contrary to the idea of treating a method call like a simple procedure call, and has several consequences that need to be dealt with.

First, even to obtain a simple result computed in an object we have to send a call to it and wait for the reply. In parallel processing an atomic object may not immediately respond to an incoming message because it could be engaged in some execution started by an earlier call, even though the result requested is a very simple one and is immediately available. The call and wait overheads, if incurred for a large number of simple processing steps, could make execution very inefficient.

Second, suppose an object receives a call that causes it to start some processing, e.g., pop stack, but it then discovers that the necessary information is not available, e.g., stack is empty, what does it do? Should it reply "unsuccessful" to the requester, who will have to try again, perhaps repeatedly before the request would succeed? Or, should it store away the request and wait for a new call in the hope that some other object would do something to rectify the situation, e.g., a push request, before returning to process the unsuccessful request? Or, perhaps methods are conditionally defined, such that a call on a method starts execution only if certain conditions are satisfied, e.g., calls on the stack pop function are queued to wait if the stack is empty. Such decisions materially influence the execution overheads as well as programming techniques. In particular, having guarded methods leads to the so-called inheritance anomaly problem discussed below.

Third, in recursive processing, an object may need to call itself. It is therefore necessary to stack the previous call in some way while the object takes the next call. This problem is unrelated to parallel execution, and the technique of causing an "unsuccessful" return for the earlier call upon a new call is not useful here.

Moreover, conditioned calls lead to the problem of inheritance anomaly, which has been extensively discussed in the context of parallel object-oriented languages. In [2] three cases of inheritance anomaly were posed.

(a) State Partitioning. Suppose we have a class Stack and a subclass DStack is defined with a new method PPoP that takes the top only if there are at least two elements in the stack. Previously, we need to distinguish between the Empty and NonEmpty states of stack, permitting Pop calls only if a stack object is in the NonEmpty state, but in a DStack object, the NonEmpty state is subdivided into two: the One state which permits a Pop but not a PPop, and the More state in which both are permitted. A Push now changes One state to More state and Empty state to One state, while Pop changes states in reverse; hence, the introduction of the subclass causes the redefinition of the methods of the parent class, instead of simply inheriting them; hence, an inheritance anomaly. This is because states controlling the behavior of the child class are partitions of the states of the parent class, whose methods must change to recognize these.

(b) History Sensitivity. In this, the child class EStack has a QPop method that cannot be executed after a Push from the same object. Again, parent class methods must be modified to change an object between the AfterPush and AfterPop states.

(c) State Modification. This concerns the introduction of orthogonal states with a subclass that may lock an object and, hence, affect the processing of parent class methods.

These difficulties do not arise if parallel entries into an object are possible, because in the subclass pre- and post-processing can be carried out with parent class methods to deal with the new situations, whereas with conditional entries, the condition and the parent method form an integrated unit.

If one permits multiple threads in an object, some atomic structure must then be available in objects to enforce sequentialization in shared access of wanted results or in suspending to await relevant conditions. In BaLinda languages, this is provided by tuples.

5.4 BaLinda K Objects

The BaLinda Lisp/K parallel languages provide classes and objects within a functional framework [3]–[5]. To identify independently executable parts of a program, BaLinda languages use the EXEC keyword. For intertask communication, we use Linda tuples. An efficient compiler for BaLinda Lisp, including good load balancing and tuple space distribution, is available for PC/Transputer, SUN workstation, IBM SP2, and Fujitsu AP3000 systems. It was subsequently given a new user interface, resulting in the K version of the language which superficially resembles C ("K" is "hard C") used for illustration here.

A class is called and executed like a function, except that instead of returning a result but disposing the execution environment, a class call returns a pointer to the execution environment, which may contain public functions or methods. Calling such a public function causes an object reentry, and its execution changes the object's state that persists even after the function returns. Objects in BaLinda K are not in themselves atomic, and multiple threads can be attached to methods (or even the same method) in a single object. However, each object can have a private tuple space, and atomic execution can be enforced within an object using tuples. In short, an object offers a framework for atomicity, but is itself not atomic.

To show an example, below is a stack object definition. A call on Stack creates an object with entry points for the public functions Push and Pop:

```
{ CLASS Stack;
LOCAL ...;
PUBLIC { PROCEDURE Push <- New;
       LOCAL Pointer;
       IN ('Stack, - ? Pointer);
       OUT ('Stack, T, CONS (New, Pointer))
       },
       { FUNCTION Pop;
       LOCAL Pointer;
       IN ('Stack, T ? Pointer);
       OUT ('Stack, NOT NULL (&(Pointer)), &(Pointer));
       $(Pointer)
       };
  OUT ('Stack, FALSE, NIL)
};
X = Stack;
...
X.Push (something);
...
Y = X.Pop;
...
```

By having the stack pointer in a tuple, parallel tasks are forced to access the stack one at a time. If a Pop call on an empty stack occurs, the call suspends on the IN, until another task makes a Push call. Note that $ is the Lisp CAR, taking the head of a list, while & takes the remainder, i.e., CDR. Each object has a private tuple space, so that its IN/OUT/RD operations only affect its own space. The tuple functions may be declared PUBLIC, so that another object may use X.IN, etc., to access the tuples of object X. The global tuple space is accessed from inside an object using .IN, .OUT, etc.

Because objects are created by a call/return on a class, there is no need for a make-instance function. Initial values are assigned by defining them in the LO-CAL/PUBLIC statements, or by passing over appropriate arguments at object creation. The creation of an object can be done together with the attachment of a parallel thread through a command like EXEC X = Stack (Y), which returns an object pointer to X as soon as the environment for the class execution is established. The main program and the object now execute in parallel, and X is an active object rather than a passive one. If the object body of X suspends on an IN, resumption of X occurs immediately after the wanted tuple is provided. Normally, such a tuple would originate from outside the object by a call on a method in the object. The body can repeatedly suspend to await tuples that trigger further processing. Thus, an active object may have its body's execution being observed or controlled from the outside through calls on its methods.

To take a simple example, we wish to compute the absolute values of a list of numbers and observe from time to time the percentage of negative values encountered. The list may be very long, or even unbound, e.g., the numbers are being produced and added at the end of the list while the computation is proceeding.

```
{ CLASS Absolute <- Alist;
  LOCAL { Total, Zeros, Negative } : INTEGER = 0,
      { PROCEDURE Loop <- Alist;
        IN (? Total, Zeros, Negative);
        { IF NULL (Alist)
            =>;
            $(Alist)<0
            => { Negative = Negative+1;
               SET$ (Alist, -$(Alist))
               }
            $(Alist)==0
            => Zeros = Zeros+1
        }
        Total = Total+1;
        OUT (Total, Zeros, Negative);
        Loop (&(Alist))
      };
  PUBLIC { FUNCTION Extract <- Which;
          LOCAL Total, Zeros, Negative;
          RD (? Total, Zeros, Negative)
          { CASE <- Which;
            '+ => (Total-Zeros-Negative)/Total;
            '0  => Zeros/Total;
            '-  => Negative/Total
          } };
  OUT (0,0,0);
  Loop (Alist)
}
```

After EXEC X = Absolute (Y), X.Extract would return one of three relevant percentages. The values are taken from a tuple in order to ensure consistency.

In BaLinda K, just as function definitions can be nested, so can class definitions, with inner classes inheriting the variables and functions of the outer definition. Further, inner definitions can be made publicly visible by placing them in the PUBLIC part:

```
{ CLASS X <- A;
  LOCAL ...;
  PUBLIC { CLASS Y <- B;
        ... }
  ... }
```

To call an inner class, the outer class must be entered first to establish the object attributes and methods. Hence, to create an object of class Y we could use

$$C = X.Y (A, B)$$

This provides first for entry into X with argument A and establishment of object content for inheritance by Y, then for entry into Y itself. Subsequently, we can call a public function Z defined in Y using the name C.Z, which is just the usual way. Note that an object of class X was established temporarily, but not retained: X was only used as the environment for establishing Y. It is also possible to have

$$C = X \ (A);$$
$$D = C.Y \ (B);$$

This produces two objects C and D of classes X and Y, respectively.

An object directory system has to be maintained to uniquely identify all objects, including objects of the same name and class spawned from different ancestors. Because objects encapsulate a package of self contained information, they can be moved from cluster to cluster to achieve better load balancing. However, objects without their own tuples can potentially migrate more easily, because for faster searching, tuples are stored in hash tables and usually there is just one table per cluster to contain tuples from all objects at the cluster, and all associated tuples must be retrieved when an object is moved. By not inheriting the tuple functions, an object indicates the absence of a private tuple space.

5.5   Speculative Processing

Speculative processing is a method to maximize the utilization of the processing capacity of a parallel system by initiating tasks before knowing whether they will be actually needed, provided there is idle capacity in the system. If, subsequently, the results are indeed required, they may be made available immediately, thus reducing waiting and overall elapsed time. A speculative task has to be purged if, during its execution, new information becomes available to indicate that its result will not be needed. There are also issues such as how to attach the appropriate execution priority to a speculative task based on the likelihood of its usefulness, and adjusting this with changing execution conditions. It is desirable to do this without requiring application programmers to manage task status and priority directly because the expected level of system expertise is usually lacking.

In an earlier paper [3] we studied parallelism within conditional statements as the route to speculative processing: the spawning of THEN and ELSE modules with their Boolean guards in parallel, assigned priorities that decrease with their depth of nesting in IF statements and adjusted as Boolean results become available, provides a simple way to introduce speculative processing into application programs, one which does not require the programmer to get involved in system programming and task control mechanisms.

To preserve the semantic integrity of the program, the side effects of a speculative module must be confined to its private data space until it is confirmed by the Boolean conditional returning a TRUE for a parallel THEN module or a FALSE for an ELSE module. Unfortunately, this makes it impossible to decide whether to confirm or purge a speculative task by observing its own execution, and severely limits the usefulness of the speculative mechanism. The Boolean can only use external information to decide whether to confirm or purge a speculative task, not information from within the task itself.

For example, if we need the product of a number of factors that are being evaluated in parallel, and one factor turns out to be 0, then the evaluation of all remaining factors could be immediately abandoned. This could only be coded in our scheme as a set of nested IF..THEN.. blocks each returning one factor. A 0 result in one block causes a Boolean FALSE to be returned, purging all computation in inner blocks, but the outer blocks continue to completion, even though the result is already determined. The overall wasted processing may be reduced by putting factors most likely to be 0 in the outmost nestings, but this is not always easy to achieve.

While in terms of implementation it is quite simple to provide a window through which the Boolean block can look into the THEN and ELSE modules, the problem is to do it in a semantically satisfactory way. Take the following example:

```
X = ...
Y = ...
IF {...}
THEN { X = ...;
          Z = ...
     }
ELSE { X = ...;
          Z = ...
     }
```

The THEN or ELSE block overwrites the old value X, and defines a new value Z, depending on whether the Boolean returns TRUE or FALSE, but while the Boolean block is still executing, it should see the old value X and undefined Z. If it is able to see the X and Z in the THEN and ELSE modules, then various questions arise that require the formulation of new scoping rules that allow the unique identification of the different items, e.g., (a) how to specify a particular X out of the three; (b) how to declare Z which is defined inside the speculative module, and when it becomes visible from the Boolean module; (c) whether a speculative module need to declare which variables it intends to change; (d) whether a speculative module can reuse a variable name (e.g., Y in the above program, which the speculative modules do not use) and then discard its value at completion even if the module is confirmed, without impacting the main thread at all.

Reluctance to introduce such new and potentially untidy language rules has led us to leave the problem unsolved up to now.

The situation changed with the introduction of the idea of active objects [4]. Consider the construct

$$X = \{ \text{ IF boolean} => \text{EXEC A ( ) } \}$$

The IF function is meant to return a pointer for an object of class A if the Boolean module returns TRUE, but since the object execution is proceeding in parallel, a pointer is immediately returned to the main thread as it executes the Boolean part. This pointer is not visible outside the IF function, because the

Boolean part has not returned TRUE/FALSE and the assignment to X is not yet confirmed, but it is visible within the IF function as a speculative object pointer. The Boolean module is therefore able to obtain the public content of the speculative object using the unconfirmed but internally visible pointer X.

The use of a speculative object instead of a function eliminates the various scoping problems mentioned earlier, because an object call returns just one pointer to the main thread, with no other impact. Any new variables defined by the speculative module are encapsulated inside the object, and only the public parts of the information are visible from the outside. No new scoping rules need to be introduced at all.

For an example of how to use the speculative capability, take the multiplication of two factors:

```
{ CLASS A;
PUBLIC IN..., OUT...;
EXEC OUT (Factor (1));
OUT (Factor (2));
SYNCHRONIZE
}
...
X = { IF { X.IN (? Product);
          { IF Product==0
               => NIL
             T => T
          } }
        => EXEC A
     };
{ IF NOT (NULL (X))
   T => { X.IN (? Y);
          Product = Product*Y
}      }
...
```

The class A allows public access to its tuple operations IN and OUT; thus the tuple space of object X may be accessed from the outside using X.IN and X.OUT. Its body computes two factors in parallel and puts the values into the object tuple space. After the Boolean module retrieves one value, it returns NIL (FALSE) if the value is 0, thus purging the evaluation of the other value and returning NIL to X. If the value is non-zero, it confirms the computation of the other value. The main program retrieves it from X later and multiplies it to the previous value.

Another example is killing "deadbeats": a task that executes for too long and refuses to stop on its own:

```
{ CLASS A;
PUBLIC Status = NIL;
...
Status = T
}
...
X = { IF { DELAY;
          { IF NULL (X.Status)
```

```
                => NIL;
           T => T
       } }
       => EXEC A
   };
   ...
```

Note this one does not use A's tuple space, because if A hangs, any thread waiting for its tuples would also hang so that it would not be able to return NIL to kill A. Also note that if a number of parallel tasks are to be monitored and possibly killed, then a separate, parallel Boolean guard is needed for each, because only then can each independently return a NIL to kill the attached speculative object. This can be improved by the use of multiple speculative objects within a single speculative environment, but we will not discuss the issue further here.

5.6   Summary

We have discussed a number of aspects of BaLinda objects that make them useful for cluster based systems. The dispatch of active objects to remote clusters and spawning of functions on the local cluster provide a two-level parallel execution structure for both loosely coupled and tightly coupled problems. Active objects communicate via method calls, including calls on tuple access methods in another object, while functions within the same object share the object tuple space using local access functions. The technique of speculative objects can further increase parallelism where idle capacity exists in a large network of clusters.

5.7   Bibliography

[1] G. V. Wilson and P. Lu. *Parallel Programming Using C++*. MIT Press, Boston, 1996.

[2] S. Matsuoka, K. Taura, and A. Yonezawa. Highly Efficient and Encapsulated Re-use of Synchronization Code in Concurrent Object-Oriented Languages. *ACM Sigplan Notices*, vol. 28(10), pages 109-126, 1993.

[3] M. D. Feng and C. K. Yuen. Iterative Computation and Speculative Processing. *Software - Concepts and Tools*, vol. 16, pages 41-48, 1995.

[4] C. K. Yuen and M. D. Feng. BaLinda Plus, Adding Objects to Parallel. Languages, *Software - Concepts and Tools*, vol. 16, pages 95-105, 1995.

[5] C. K. Yuen, and M. D. Feng. BaLinda - A Simple Parallel Programming Model with Active Objects. *IEEE ISPAN*, December 1997, Taipei, pages 23-29.

Chapter 6

Using Scoped Behavior to Optimize Data Sharing Idioms

PAUL LU

Dept. of Computer Science
University of Toronto
10 King's College Road
Toronto, Ontario, M5S 3G4
Canada

Email: *paullu@sys.utoronto.ca*

6.1 Introduction

In distributed systems and applications, there are often archetypical reader, writer, and producer-consumer data sharing patterns or idioms. Therefore, in addition to general-purpose data sharing, it is advantageous for distributed systems to flexibly and efficiently support common idioms. Flexibility includes the ability to implement different idioms with minimal and localized changes to the source code. Efficiency includes exploiting the semantics of the idiom to optimize performance.

For example, all message-passing systems provide general-purpose mechanisms to send and receive data across distributed nodes. However, some systems (e.g., Message Passing Interface) also support commonly occurring group operations, such as all-to-all communication. The higher-level functions are implemented using the lower-level mechanisms. By prepackaging a data sharing idiom into a single function, the system facilitates code reuse and it can also exploit the semantics of the idiom to optimize, say, the overlapped sending of different messages.

However, parallel programming systems based on shared memory and shared data models are becoming more popular and widespread. Accessing local and remote data using the same programming interface (i.e., reads and writes) is often more convenient than mixing local accesses with message passing. On distributed-memory platforms, the lack of hardware support to directly access remote memories has prompted a variety of software-based, logically-shared systems. Broadly speaking, there are distributed shared memory (DSM) [4], [2] and distributed shared data (DSD) [3], [12], [7] systems. Some hybrid systems combine properties of both DSM and DSD.

At one end of the spectrum, DSM systems typically emulate hardware-based shared memory so that a C-style pointer (e.g., `int *`) can transparently name either local or remote data. DSM systems are usually based on fixed-sized units of sharing, often a page, because they are implemented using the same mechanisms as for demand-paged virtual memory. A single data sharing policy is often used for all shared pages, although per-page policies are supported by some DSM systems.

At the other end of the spectrum, DSD systems treat shared data as an abstract data type. Shared data is named and accessed through a programmer's interface and DSD systems usually have a variable granularity of sharing. Consequently, the unit of sharing and the sharing policy can be selected to match the form and function of the particular data.

The Aurora DSD system provides a familiar shared data programming model on distributed memory hardware using standard C++ [9]. All shared data are encapsulated as objects and are accessed through overloaded operators and other interface methods. Using the shared-data objects is designed to be syntactically the same as with built-in data types. Since each shared object is an independent unit of sharing and management, the data access behavior can be optimized on a per-object basis.

Aurora is unique in its use of the scoped behavior approach for applying optimizations (discussed further in Section 6.3.3). With scoped behavior, a new language scope (e.g., nested braces in C++) around selected source code can be used to optimize the data sharing behavior of specific objects. Without any language extensions or special compiler support, the optimizations can be applied on a per-context (i.e., portion of source code) basis. Therefore, the per-object and per-context optimization flexibility allows different loops and computational phases to be optimized in different ways, according to the needs of the application. When used with data placement mechanisms, scoped behavior simplifies the implementation and optimization of a number of common data sharing idioms.

6.2 Motivation: Data Sharing Idioms

In designing computer systems, it is natural to identify and optimize for commonly occurring structures and idioms. Therefore, in addition to general-purpose mechanisms, it is important for the system to easily and seamlessly support higher-level abstractions. For example, in concurrency control, the monitor concept builds upon the underlying lock and semaphore mechanisms.

Analogously, researchers have identified a number of data sharing patterns that reappear in various distributed systems and applications. Data sharing patterns such as read-intensive, write-intensive, producer-consumer, migratory sharing, and others have been noted [4], [6]. Consequently, researchers have explored various compiler and run-time techniques to optimize performance for common data sharing idioms.

Ideally, the distributed system should allow the data sharing behavior of each object to be optimized independently of other objects. False sharing, when performance is degraded by the interference between logically independent data located in the same unit of data management, is a potential problem with DSM systems. As the number of data sharing optimizations increases, the negative impact of interference between sharing policies will likely also increase. In DSD systems, false sharing is avoided by managing independent data as separate objects.

Also, it should be possible to optimize each portion of the source code (i.e., context) independently of other contexts. Therefore, as the data access patterns change from computational phase to phase, it is possible to alter the data sharing policy. In DSD systems, since shared data is an abstract data type, it is natural to consider different programmer interfaces for different contexts.

6.3   Aurora: A Distributed Shared Data System

In this section, we provide a tutorial of the design and mechanisms of the Aurora system.

Aurora is a C++ class library and run-time system that provides a shared data programming model on distributed-memory architectures. Scalar and vector data can be distributed across, and accessed from, different address spaces. To overcome the latency and bandwidth performance problems of typical distributed-memory platforms, Aurora provides a set of data sharing optimizations.

6.3.1   Process Models

Aurora's mixed-parallelism process model includes both task parallelism and data parallelism. Currently, the task parallelism is provided by the underlying ABC++ library through active objects [11]. Active objects are normal C++ objects that contain their own thread of control. Data parallelism is provided by a simple for_all() construct that invokes a parallel method on all distributed data.

Aurora also provides a fairly standard single-program, multiple-data (SPMD) process model. The model includes teams of threads, sequential sections (i.e., code to be executed by only one thread, usually the team's "master"), and synchronization barriers.

The various process models can be mixed, in reasonable ways, within a single application.

6.3.2   Shared-Data Objects

The basic shared-data model is that of a distributed vector object or a distributed scalar object. Once created, a shared-data object is transparently accessed, regardless of the physical location of the data, using normal C++ syntax. By default, shared data is read from and written to immediately (i.e., synchronously), even if

(a) Original Source Code	(b) With Scoped Behavior
`GVector<int> vector1( 1024 );`	`GVector<int> vector1( 1024 );`
	`{ // Begin new language scope` `  NewBehavior( vector1, GVReleaseC, int );`

`for( int i = 0; i < 1024; i++ )`
`  vector1[ i ] = someFunc( i );`
	`  for( int i = 0; i < 1024; i++ )`
	`    vector1[ i ] = someFunc( i );`
	`} // End scope`

`vector1[ 0 ] = 1;`	`vector1[ 0 ] = 1; // Still immediate update`

Figure 6.1 Applying a data sharing optimization using scoped behavior.

the data is on a remote node, since that data access behavior has the least error-prone semantics.

Aurora's data model requires that shared scalar and vector objects be created using Aurora's templated C++ classes `GScalar` and `GVector`:

```
GScalar<int>     scalar1;
GScalar<VNode>   scalar2;              // User-defined type VNode

GVector<int>     vector1( 1024 );   // 1024 elements
GVector<float>   vector2( vsize );  // vsize elements
GVector<VNode>   vector3( vsize );  // User-defined type VNode
```

`scalar1` is a C++ integer that is shared across address spaces. By default, updates to `scalar1` are immediately visible to other processors, which may require a message send for each update. Any of the C++ built-in types or any user-defined concrete type [5], as with `scalar2`, can be an independent unit of sharing.

Shared vectors, such as `vector1`, are similar to shared scalars, except that the vector elements can be distributed across nodes and the subscript operator is over-loaded to support indexing. By default, the vector elements are block distributed across all the nodes involved in the computation. Parameters to the constructor specify the size of the vector and (optionally) data placement on the nodes.

Consider the following examples of explicit data placement:

```
// Block distributed across Node 0 and Node 1
GVector<float>  vector4( 1024, Nodes( 0, 1 ) );

// All elements on Node 0
GVector<int>    vector5( vsize, Nodes( 0 ) );
```

Table 6.1 Current Scoped Behaviors

Scoped Behavior	Comment
Owner-computes	Threads access only colocated data.
Caching for reads	Create local copy of data.
Release consistency	Buffer write accesses.
Special-purpose data movement	Used with owner-computes for *specific* applications.

In the example, `vector4` has 1,024 elements block distributed across nodes 0 and 1, with each block containing exactly 512 elements. `vector5` has `vsize` elements all placed on node 0 (i.e., single block). The class `Nodes` is provided by Aurora and is used during object construction to list the nodes for data placement.

6.3.3   Scoped Behavior

For the system implementor, scoped behavior is a structuring technique to change the implementation of selected methods for the lifetime of a language scope [10]. For the Aurora programmer, scoped behavior is how an optimization is applied to a shared-data object.

For example, if a shared vector is updated in a loop [Figure 6.1(a)] *and* if the updates do not need to be performed immediately, then the loop can use release consistency [1] and batch the writes until the scope is exited [Figure 6.1(b), shown side-by-side for easy comparison]. Without any changes to the loop code itself, the behavior of the updates to `vector1` is changed within the language scope. The `NewBehavior` macro specifies that the release consistency optimization should be *applied* to `vector1` within the loop. Since the statement `vector1[ 0 ] = 1` is outside of the scope, it forms a different context and is not affected by the new behavior.

Therefore, scoped behavior is the main interface between the programming model and the data sharing optimizations (Table 6.1), providing:

- *Per-object* flexibility: The ability to apply an optimization to a specific shared-data object without affecting the behavior of other objects. Within a context, different objects can be optimized in different ways (i.e., heterogeneous optimizations).

- *Per-context* flexibility: The ability to apply an optimization to a specific portion of the source code. Different portions of the source code (e.g., different loops and phases) can be optimized in different ways.

```
 1:extern int dotProd( int * a, int * b, int j, int n );
 2:
 3:void mmultiply(    // SPMD thread and shared data among parameters
 4:   ProcessTeam * myTeam,
 5:   GVector<int> mA, GVector<int> mB, GVector<int> mC,
 6:   const int m, const int n, const int p )
 7:{
 8:   int i, j;
 9:
10:  { // Begin scoped behavior
11:    NewBehavior( mA, GVOwnerComputes, int );
12:    NewBehavior( mB, GVReadCache, int );
13:    NewBehavior( mC, GVReleaseC, int );
14:
15:    while( mA.doParallel( myTeam ) )   // Owner-computes
16:    {
17:      for( i = mA.begin(); i < mA.end(); i += mA.step() )
18:        for( j = 0; j < p; j++ )
19:          mC[i][j] = dotProd( &mA[i][0], mB, j, n );
20:    } // while
21:  } // End scoped behavior
22:}
```

Figure 6.2 Matrix multiplication in Aurora, SPMD-style.

6.3.4   Illustrative Example: Matrix Multiplication

Consider the parallel dense matrix multiplication function in Figure 6.2. The Aurora implementation uses the SPMD process model, distributed matrices,[1] and three different data sharing optimizations applied using scoped behavior. At the heart of the function are the nested loops and a C-style dot product function.

Three elements of the SPMD process model are shown in this example. First, the myTeam (line 4) parameter points to the local thread executing the function. Each thread has a unique number and each thread is part of a larger team of threads that is executing the same function in the application.

Second, the NewBehavior with mA (line 11), which uses a macro provided by Aurora, is an example of scoped behavior and owner-computes. Note that this macro exists within a new language scope (i.e., the braces on lines 10 and 21). Outside of the scope, matrix mA continues to behave as a object of type GVector<int>. Inside the scope, the macro changes the type of matrix mA to GVOwnerComputes<int>. This changes matrix mA's behavior such that only local data (i.e., the portions of mA colocated with, and "owned" by, the thread) can be accessed and it can be ac-

---

[1] As in C/C++, multidimensional matrices in Aurora are implemented using one-dimensional vectors and a simple indexing function. For clarity, matrix indexing is shown using matrices of static size.

cessed using C-style indexing. Since the scoped behavior is known at compile-time, `NewBehavior` actually changes the code generated by the compiler to use a faster access technique. The user's source code for accessing the shared data is unchanged.

Third, the combination of `doParallel()`, `begin()`, `end()`, and `step()` method calls (lines 15 and 17) guarantees that the computation will span all of the local data. These methods are *not* defined for class `GVector` so they can only be used with the owner-computes scoped behavior. For the local thread in `myTeam`, the `doParallel()` method guarantees to return `true` until all of the local data for the object has been processed. For each call to `doParallel()`, methods `begin()`, `end()`, and `step()` will return the correct parameters to cover a portion of the local data. Using owner-computes for matrix `mA` improves performance by avoiding a large number of remote read accesses and it is a convenient way to partition the parallel work among the different SPMD threads.

However, even after optimizing the accesses to matrix `mA`, performance problems remain because matrices `mB` and `mC` are also distributed. Therefore, the behavior of `mB` within the scope is modified so that each thread makes a local copy of the entire matrix before entering the loops (line 12). Since `mB` is reused many times and since its values do not change, it is cached in local memory for read accesses. Again, since `mB` is of type `GVReadCache<int>` within the scope, the code generated by the compiler is different than without the scoped behavior.

The behavior of `mC` within the scope is modified (line 13) so that all updates to the matrix are not immediately sent, but are buffered until a full network message can be sent or the scope is exited (line 21). Consequently, the cost of sending a message is amortized over many updates to improve performance. This behavior is functionally equivalent to the release consistent memory model for writes. But, in contrast, the synchronization point for remote updates is at the end of the scope and only the updates to the specific data object need to be communicated.

Note that the scoped behaviors of the matrices are all different and are independent of each other (i.e., per-object). They only share the lifetime of the language scope.

6.3.5   Discussion: Programming in Aurora

The typical methodology for developing Aurora applications consists of three main steps. First, the code is ported to Aurora. Shared arrays and shared scalars are converted to `GVectors` and `GScalars`. Although the default immediate access policy can be slow, its performance can be optimized after the program has been fully debugged.

Second, the work is partitioned among the processors and threads. Owner-computes and SPMD-style parallelism are common and effective strategies for many applications. However, the application programmer may implement other work partitioning schemes.

Lastly, various data sharing optimizations can be tried on different bottlenecks in the program and on different shared-data objects. Often, the only required changes are a new language scope and a `NewBehavior` macro. Sometimes, straightforward changes to the looping parameters are needed, as for owners-computes. Consider an alternate way of optimizing the matrix multiplication function: owner-computes can be applied to vector `mC` instead, with read caches used for both vector `mA` and vector `mB`. The `dotProd()` function and the data access source code remain unchanged. Admittedly, more memory for read caches is required in the alternate strategy, but, since `mC` is being updated, it is perhaps a more conventional application of owner-computes. Reverting back to the original strategy is also relatively easy. For the application programmer, the ability to experiment with different optimizations, with limited error-prone code changes, can be valuable.

6.4   Implementation Overview

We provide a brief overview of how Aurora's shared-data objects and how scoped behavior are implemented. A more detailed discussion is available elsewhere [10].

6.4.1   Handle-Body Composite Objects

Both shared scalars and vectors in Aurora are implemented through the handle-body idiom for composite objects [5]. The handle class implements the appropriate overloaded operators and type constructors. The handle also provides the location and distribution transparency required to access remote data. In contrast, the body objects contain the actual data. However, to the application programmer, handle and body objects operate as a single object.

Consider a vector of nine elements, say `GVector<int> a( 9 )`, block distributed across three (of four) nodes, as illustrated in Figure 6.3. Assuming block distribution, the bodies of the vector are distributed across three local objects, each (potentially) located in a different address space and on a different physical processor. Handles can be replicated cheaply and passed as parameters, but the local objects are shared among the handles.

Currently, Aurora implements handles as passive objects, but the local objects are implemented as ABC++ active objects. Operations on the member data of an active object are handled by the member functions, as is the case with passive objects. However, unlike passive objects, the member functions of an active object can also be remotely invoked with a smart message. In ABC++, smart messages resemble normal method invocations and automate parameter marshaling and demarshaling. Distributed memory and shared memory ABC++ run-time systems are available to Aurora applications.

By default, a read or write to a shared object is translated into a smart message from the handle to a local body object. Thus, Aurora uses smart messages, in part, for `put()`s to and `get()`s from remote memory.

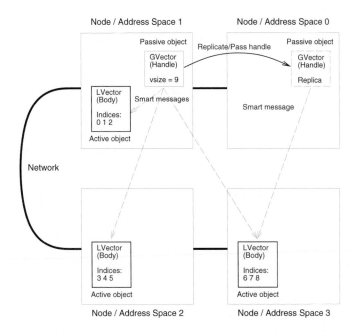

Figure 6.3 Basic handle-body architecture of Aurora.

6.4.2   Scoped Behavior Objects

The main motivation for using language scopes to define the context of scoped behavior is to exploit the property of name hiding. In block-structured languages, an identifier can be reused within a nested language scope, thus hiding the identifier outside of the scope.

Instantiations of a class that are designed to be used within a language scope, and which hide objects outside the scope, are called scoped behavior objects. Due to name hiding, the compiler will generate code according to the class of the scoped behavior object, instead of the original object's class. Aurora also uses the automatic construction and destruction of scoped objects in C++ to properly initiate the required coherence and data movement actions. Therefore, scoped behavior is a combination of compile-time and run-time techniques.

As previously shown in Figure 6.1, programming with scoped behavior under C++ requires a language scope and the `NewBehavior` macro. The macro merely hides the fact that a new handle of type `GVReleaseC<int>` is being created. The macro calls the constructor of class `GVReleaseC` with the old handle to `vector1` as a parameter. Without copying the bodies of `vector1`, the new handle now controls access to the shared vector elements within the scope. The behavior of the new handle is identical to the original handle except that updates are now batched. When the scope is exited, the scoped behavior object is destroyed and the batched updates are flushed by `GVReleaseC`'s destructor.

The new handle is also called `vector1`, thus it lexically hides the old handle, and all references to `vector1` within the new scope are compiled to use the new handle without changes to the user's source code. Consequently, it can be easy to add, change, and experiment with scoped behavior without requiring many error-prone lexical changes to the code.

There are three important aspects to Aurora's mechanisms and architecture:

1. Operator overloading supports location and distribution transparency across address spaces.

2. The handle-body architecture and scoped behavior substitutes handles for the lifetime of a language scope, thus altering the behavior of data accesses.

3. The lexical hiding semantics of nested scopes in C++ (and similar block-structured languages) causes the compiler to generate the appropriate scoped behavior code without changes to the programmer's code.

Although the current set of scoped behaviors is small, the behaviors can be combined on a per-context and per-object basis, and enhanced with explicit data placement, to support a variety of optimization strategies and idioms.

6.5   Experience with Parallel Programs

We discuss the use of scoped behavior in parallel programs and how the data sharing idioms found in these programs are optimized.

The hardware platform is a cluster of workstations assembled as part of the University of Toronto's Parallelism on Workstations (POW) project. Each workstation has a single 133 MHz PowerPC 604 processor and 96 MB of memory. The software includes IBM's AIX 4.1 operating system, POSIX threads (pthreads), the xlC C++ compiler, a prototype version of ABC++, and the MPICH (version 1.1.10) implementation of MPI for interworkstation communication. A single 100 Mbit/s Ethernet switch with half-duplex links is used for these experiments.

The speedups in Figure 6.4 and Table 6.2 are computed against C implementations of the same algorithm (or against quicksort in the case of parallel sorting). In particular, the sequential implementations do not suffer from the overheads of either operator overloading or scoped behavior. Overall, two trends can be noted in the performance results. First, for these three programs, additional processors improve speedup, albeit with diminishing returns. Second, as the size of the data set increases, the overall granularity of work and, thus, speedup also increases.

6.5.1   Matrix Multiplication

Figure 6.4 shows the speedups for a program that uses matrix multiplication. Speedups are given for data sets using 512×512 matrices and using 640×640

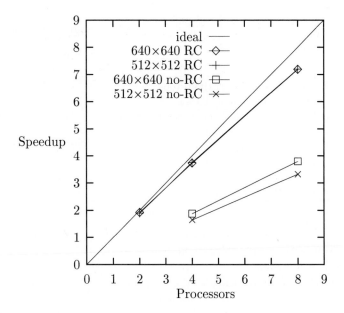

Figure 6.4 Matrix multiplication.

matrices. The real times for eight processors are about 18 seconds and 37 seconds, respectively. The data sets labelled "RC" are when all three scoped behaviors are used for each phase, as in Figure 6.2.

In Phase 1 of the program, mA is multiplied with mB and assigned to mC [i.e., mmultiply(..., mA, mB, mC, ...)]. In Phase 2, mA is multiplied with mC and assigned to mB [i.e., mmultiply(..., mA, mC, mB, ...)]. Of course, the same mmultiply() function is used for each phase, but it is called with different parameters. This is a form of per-context flexibility since, in Phase 1, a read cache is used for mB and release consistency is applied to mC, and vice versa for Phase 2.

Since matrix multiplication is known to be easy to parallelize, the speedups are very good and are virtually identical for the two data sets shown. In terms of data sharing idioms for Phase 1, matrix multiplication is characterized by the read-intensive matrices mA and mB, and the write-intensive matrix mC. In Phase 2, matrix mB is write-intensive. As we have seen, read-intensive shared data can be optimized using either owner-computes or a read cache. Write-intensive shared data can be optimized using release consistency. Aurora makes it easy to optimize the different access patterns of the different shared-data objects.

Another benefit of Aurora's scoped behavior approach is that one can easily experiment with and measure the performance impact of different optimization strategies. As a simple example, the program can be executed without the re-lease consistency optimization for matrix mC in Phase 1 (and matrix mB in Phase

Table 6.2 2-D Diffusion and Parallel Sorting by Regular Sampling

Program	Data Set	Speedup		
		2 PEs	**4 PEs**	**8 PEs**
2-D Diffusion	1536 × 1536, 32 time-steps (45.3 seconds on 1 PE)	1.9	3.2	6.6
	1024 × 1024, 32 time-steps (20.2 seconds on 1 PE)	1.9	2.8	5.9
PSRS	10 million keys (58.2 seconds on 1 PE)	n/a	2.5	4.4
	6 million keys (32.8 seconds on 1 PE)	1.3	2.3	4.0

2) by simply commenting out the relevant `NewBehavior` (Figure 6.2, line 13) and re-compiling. No other code changes are needed. Thus, by default, updates to `mC` are sent immediately and results in the performance labelled "no-RC" in Figure 6.4. Since many more update messages are generated, the performance decrease is substantial.

Finally, related to the owner-computes and read cache scoped behaviors, is the ability to bypass the overheads associated with operator overloading, under controlled circumstances. When debugging a program and for noncompute-intensive contexts, the overheads of operator overloading are tolerable. In compute-intensive loops and functions, it is desirable to access data using pointers. In this example, an important contributor to good performance is the use of C-style pointers in `dotProd()`. Note that `dotProd()` does not accept handles to shared-data object (Figure 6.2, line 1). Both the owner-computes and read cache scoped behaviors pass pointers as parameters in the function call to `dotProd()` (Figure 6.2, line 19). In effect, Aurora orchestrates any necessary data movement via scoped behavior and then provides a fast way to access the local data or local read cache through type constructors that return pointers. Not every shared data access needs to be optimized through the use of pointers, but scoped behavior allows the programmer to optimize the program when and where it matters most.

6.5.2   2-D Diffusion

Simulating the diffusion of matter involves data sharing idioms that are archetypical for a class of applications different from matrix multiplication. Therefore, it is important that scoped behavior be able to support idioms beyond the standard read-intensive and write-intensive patterns.

In our simplified simulation of 2-D diffusion, each floating point element of a matrix represents the density of matter at a given coordinate. Two matrices, `timeNow` and `timePrevious`, are used. For each time-step, the new density of matter at a coordinate in `timeNow` is computed by averaging the densities in `timePrevious`

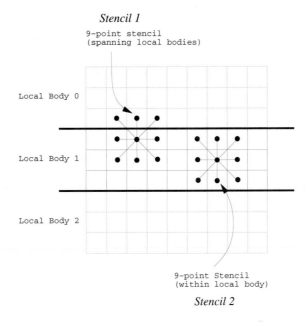

Figure 6.5 Stencils in 2-D diffusion simulation.

at the same coordinate and at its eight nearest neighbors. This computation is known as a 9-point stencil operation (Figure 6.5). For the next time-step, the two matrices are logically swapped.

Assuming a block-distributed matrix, the normal form of owner-computes is a problem because each thread needs to access some matrix elements from a different thread's local body. In particular, at the top and bottom borders of a local body, the nearest neighbors above or below the current coordinate can reside in a different local body. As an example, consider Stencil 1 in Figure 6.5.

Aurora addresses this form of data sharing by supporting block-distributed matrices with border padding and a modified form of owner-computes. These matrices are identical to normal block-distributed matrices except for the extra storage overhead required for the padding. Furthermore, the system automates the movement of the data at the borders into the appropriate border padding of the neighboring local bodies.

In essence, the new scoped behavior establishes a producer-consumer relationship between two neighboring local bodies. All local bodies are producers. The consumers are the neighboring local bodies. For example, Local Body 0 is a producer for Local Body 1, since the bottom row of Local Body 0 is used as part of computing Stencil 1 for Local Body 1. The data that is produced is moved into the border padding storage of the consumer. Once the automatic data movement is

Table 6.3 Per-context and Per-object Optimizations in PSRS

Phase	Algorithm	Main Optimizations
1	Sort local data and gather samples.	Sort local data using owner-computes. Samples are colocated with master and are gathered using release consistency.
2	Sort samples, select pivots, and partition local data.	Master sorts samples using owner-computes. Pivots are accessed from a read cache.
3	Gather partitions.	Partitions are gathered into a read cache using `distmemcpy()`.
4	Merge partitions and update local data.	Merge partitions from the read cache.

complete, the computationally-intensive 9-point stencil operation can be efficiently performed using a C-style pointers on the local body plus padding.

A total of 32 time-steps are simulated on a 1024 × 1024 grid and on a 1536 × 1536 grid, with the performance given in Table 6.2. Since a barrier synchronization is required after each time-step in the current implementation, the granularity of work is low. A larger data set and granularity of work would help improve the speedups for this parallel program.

Of course, the padding strategy used by Aurora is not new. However, Aurora abstracts the implementation details of the padding and automates the data movement using scoped behavior. Also, in keeping with the abstract data type approach, the new scoped behavior can be reused in similar applications.

6.5.3 Parallel Sorting by Regular Sampling

The Parallel Sorting by Regular Sampling (PSRS) application kernel [13], [8] has been implemented using Aurora. The performance of PSRS is given in Table 6.2. PSRS is a general-purpose, comparison-based sort with key exchange. It can be communication-intensive since the number of keys exchanged grows linearly with the problem size.

The basic PSRS algorithm consists of four distinct phases. Assume that there are p processors and the original vector is block distributed across the processors. Phase 1 does a local sort (usually via quicksort) of the local block of data. No interprocessor communication is required for the local sort. Then, a small sample (usually p) of the keys in each sorted local block is gathered by each processor. In Phase 2, the gathered samples are sorted by the master process and $p-1$ pivots are selected. These pivots are used to divide each of the local blocks into p partitions.

```
    GVector<int> Sample( vsize, Nodes( 0 ) );

    // Phase 1:  All nodes are producers
{
    NewBehavior( Sample, GVReleaseC, int );
    for( i = ... )
        Sample[ i ] = ...                    // Produce
}
```

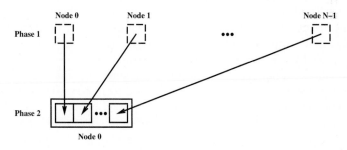

```
    // Phase 2:  Only Node 0 (i.e., master) is the consumer
MASTER
{
    NewBehavior( Sample, GVOwnerComputes, int );
    quicksort( Sample, 0, vsize - 1 );  // Consume
}
```

Figure 6.6 Producer-consumer idiom in PSRS.

In Phase 3, each processor i keeps the ith partition for itself and gathers the ith partition of every other processor. At this point, the keys owned by each processor fall between two pivots and are disjoint with the keys owned by the other processors. In Phase 4, each processor merges all of its partitions to form a sorted list. Finally, any keys that do not reside in the local data block are sent to their respective processors. The end result is a block-distributed vector of sorted keys.

A multiphase algorithm with several shared-data objects, like PSRS, is particularly suited for the per-context and per-object data sharing optimizations in Aurora. The optimizations required, and the objects that are optimized, differ from one phase to another phase. Table 6.3 summarizes the phases of PSRS and the main Aurora optimizations. Note that the data movement in Phase 3 is implemented with a memcpy()-like construct (called distmemcpy()) with full location and distribution transparency.

The programmer's knowledge of the application's data sharing idioms can also be exploited. For example, there is a multiple-producer and single-consumer sharing pattern during the gathering of sample keys in Phases 1 and 2 (Figure 6.6). Note that the vector `Sample` has been explicitly placed on Node 0. In Phase 1, the samples are gathered by all nodes and optimized using release consistency. Each node updates a disjoint portion of the vector. In Phase 2, the master node (i.e., Node 0) sorts all of the gathered samples. Since `Sample` is colocated with the master, we can use the owner-computes optimization and call `quicksort()` using a C-style pointer to the local data, for maximum performance.

Two other implicit optimizations are also present. First, `Sample` is updated in Phase 1 without unnecessary data movement and protocol overheads. With many page-based DSM systems, updating data requires the writer to first demand-in and gain exclusive ownership of the target page. However, with Aurora, the system does not need to demand-in the most current data values for `Sample` because it is only updated and not read in Phase 1. And, since the different nodes are updating disjoint portions of the vector, there is no need to arbitrate for ownership of the page to prevent race conditions. By design, the scoped behavior allows the programmer to optimize disjoint, update-only data sharing idioms involving multiple writers.

Second, since the local body for `Sample` is explicitly placed on Node 0, the updated values are sent eagerly and directly to the master node when the Phase 1 scope is exited. Therefore, there is no need to query for and demand-in the latest data during Phase 2, as would be the case for many DSM systems.

6.6   Discussion and Related Work

A large body of work has emerged in the area of DSM and DSD systems. These systems vary in their strategies to overcome false sharing, tolerance for high communication costs [4], [2], reliance on compiler support [3] and implementation techniques [12], [7], and their extensibility. Related work in High Performance Fortran (HPF) and parallel array classes have also addressed the basic problem of transparently sharing data.

One refinement in Aurora's implementation of release consistency is that only the affected data objects are made consistent at the end of a scope, instead of an entire page or all of memory. We refer to this as per-object release consistency. In this way, Aurora partitions the consistency namespace to avoid unnecessary updates of shared data.

The basic ideas behind scoped behavior are not new. The notion of nested scopes is fundamental to block-structured sequential languages. The association of actions with C++ constructors and destructors is also not new. For example, ABC++ also associates data movement actions with the scoped lock handles of its parametric shared regions [11]. Aurora's innovation is the application of scoped behavior, with the handle-body architecture, to the problem of per-context and per-object data sharing optimization.

In a largely C context, shared regions [12] and CRL [7], associate run-time coherence actions with programmer-inserted code annotations (i.e., function calls). One advantage of the automatic invocation of constructors and destructors in Aurora is that it is impossible to omit an annotation and miss a coherence action. Aurora is also able to exploit compile-time information to generate different code for different behavior.

More generally, scoped behavior, as an interface and mechanism, is similar to compiler directives and annotations. However, as an alternate implementation technique, scoped behavior does not require complex compiler support and its class library approach is easier to extend than modifications to a compiler [10].

6.7   Concluding Remarks

We have described and explored an all-software, standard C++-based DSD system called Aurora. The system is unique in its use of scoped behavior for data sharing optimizations. The advantages of Aurora's approach include its ability to support a variety of reader, writer, and producer-consumer data sharing idioms.

We have experimented with Aurora using three parallel programs and identified some of the data sharing idioms found in the applications. Matrix multiplication illustrates the effectiveness of Aurora at optimizing read-intensive and write-intensive access patterns. We also explored how a variety of optimization strategies can be tried with minimal error-prone source code changes. The 2-D diffusion program showed how special-purpose data movement idioms can be supported using scoped behavior. And the parallel sorting application demonstrates the value of per-context optimization for multiphase algorithms.

In distributed systems and applications, it is natural to identify and optimize for commonly occurring structures and idioms. Aurora's ability to combine scoped behaviors on a per-context and per-object basis, and to control data placement, allows important data sharing idioms to be optimized.

Acknowledgments

Thank you to Ben Gamsa, Kate Keahey, Bill O'Farrell, Eric Parsons, Karen Reid, John Reynders, Jonathan Schaeffer, Ken Sevcik, Michael Stumm, Roel van der Goot, Greg Wilson, and Songnian Zhou for their support during this work. Thank you to the Department of Computer Science and NSERC for financial support. Thank you to ITRC and IBM for their support of the POW Project.

6.8   Bibliography

[1] S.V. Adve and K. Gharachorloo. Shared Memory Consistency Models: A Tutorial. *IEEE Computer*, vol. 29(12), pages 66–76, December 1996.

[2] C. Amza, A.L. Cox, S. Dwarkadas, P. Keleher, H. Lu, R. Rajamony, W. Yu,

and W. Zwaenepoel. TreadMarks: Shared Memory Computing on Networks of Workstations. *IEEE Computer*, vol. 29(2), pages 18–28, February 1996.

[3] H.E. Bal, M.F. Kaashoek, and A.S. Tanenbaum. Orca: A Language for Parallel Programming of Distributed Systems. *IEEE Transactions on Software Engineering*, vol. 18(3), pages 190–205, March 1992.

[4] J.K. Bennett, J.B. Carter, and W. Zwaenepoel. Munin: Distributed Shared Memory Based on Type-Specific Memory Coherence. In *Proc. 1990 Conference on Principles and Practice of Parallel Programming*, Seattle, WA, pages 168–176, March 1990.

[5] J.O. Coplien. *Advanced C++: Programming Styles and Idioms*. Addison-Wesley, Reading, MA, 1992.

[6] B. Falsafi, A.R. Lebeck, S.K. Reinhardt, I. Schoinas, M.D. Hill, J.R. Larus, A. Rogers, and D.A. Wood. Application-Specific Protocols for User-Level Shared Memory. In *Proc. Supercomputing '94*, Washington, DC, pages 380–389, November 1994.

[7] K.L. Johnson, M.F. Kaashoek, and D.A. Wallach. CRL: High-Performance All-Software Distributed Shared Memory. In *Proc. 15th ACM Symposium on Operating Systems Principles*, Copper Mountain Resort, CO, pages 213–228, December 1995.

[8] X. Li, P. Lu, J. Schaeffer, J. Shillington, P.S. Wong, and H. Shi. On the Versatility of Parallel Sorting by Regular Sampling. *Parallel Computing*, vol. 19, pages 1079–1103, October 1993.

[9] P. Lu. Aurora: Scoped Behavior for Per-Context Optimized Distributed Data Sharing. In *Proc. 11th International Parallel Processing Symposium*, Geneva, Switzerland, pages 467–473, April 1997.

[10] P. Lu. Implementing Optimized Distributed Data Sharing Using Scoped Behavior and a Class Library. In *Proc. 3rd Conference on Object-Oriented Technologies and Systems*, Portland, OR, pages 145–158, June 1997.

[11] W.G. O'Farrell, F.Ch. Eigler, S.D. Pullara, and G.V. Wilson. ABC++. In Gregory V. Wilson and Paul Lu, editors. *Parallel Programming Using C++*. MIT Press, Cambridge, MA, 1996.

[12] H.S. Sandhu, B. Gamsa, and S. Zhou. The Shared Regions Approach to Software Cache Coherence. In *Proc. Symposium on Principles and Practices of Parallel Programming*, San Diego, CA, pages 229–238, May 1993.

[13] H. Shi and J. Schaeffer. Parallel Sorting by Regular Sampling. *Journal of Parallel and Distributed Computing*, vol. 14(4), pages 361–372, April 1992.

Chapter 7

Component-Based Development Approach

ALBERTO BARTOLI[†], GIANLUCA DINI[‡], AND COSIMO ANTONIO PRETE[‡]

[†]Dipartimento di Elettrotecnica, Elettronica, Informatica
University of Trieste
Via Valerio 10, I-34100 Trieste, Italy

[‡] Dipartimento di Ingegneria dell'Informazione
University of Pisa
Via Diotisalvi 2, 56126 Pisa, Italy

Email: *bartolia@univ.trieste.it, gianluca@iet.unipi.it, prete@iet.unipi.it*

7.1 Introduction

In this chapter we shall report on our experience regarding methods and techniques for simplifying the development of applications to be deployed on clusters by describing the design and implementation of a graphical programming environment, named Tracs, after the name of the project funded by the EECC Esprit III research program that supported its development.[1]

Tracs promotes a modular approach to the development of distributed applications for clusters of heterogeneous machines. Applications are constructed by assembling instances of a few types of design components. Low-level details such as communication of arbitrary data structures among heterogeneous machines, remote compilations, remote executions and the like are handled automatically. The existing prototype is based on OSF/Motif and runs on several flavors of Unix.

A distinguishing feature of Tracs is the novel way in which it provides several advanced facilities solely on the basis of a simple set of design components. The user does not need to define design components in their entirety. For certain components, the user can provide only part of the component and delegate its completion

---

[1]Tracs—Flexible real-time environment for traffic control systems—Project No. 6373, sector II.3.16.

to dedicated specialized tools that typically take care of low-level details and/or repetitive actions. For instance, such tools allow a programmer to define a task by supplying only part of the code, that is, the code devoted to processing. The code for communication and synchronization is generated automatically from a graphical description of the task communication pattern. Furthermore, the tools make it possible to build repetitive task graphs with a few mouse clicks and to automatically create tasks that are able to perform several kinds of message analysis and manipulation.

We shall present a real application of the above facilities to the reuse in a cluster of a large body of sequential software. This software is written in Fortran and is used daily at our department for simulating digital transmission systems. These simulations can be parallelized according to the process farm paradigm, and Tracs is able to complete the necessary design components out of programmer-provided sequential code. As a result, we were able to parallelize this software with very little engineering effort. Users can now transparently exploit the computational power of a cluster to speed up their simulations.

The core part of Tracs deals only with entire design components and it need not know who actually implemented which part of which component. It follows that new tools can be integrated easily, since they need not involve the core part of Tracs in any way. In fact, most of the tools that we have developed were not planned in the initial design of Tracs and have been implemented "on demand."

7.2   Component-Based Application Development

7.2.1   Overall Framework

Application design is subdivided in the definition phase and configuration phase. In the definition phase, the programmer builds the basic design components: message models, task models, and architecture models. In the configuration phase, the programmer constructs an application by assembling instances of the design components created in the definition phase. Both definition of design components and their assembling are performed through a specialized graphical interface. Design components can be made context-independent, thus promoting their reuse. A collection of components of the same kind can be saved as a separate library. As long as the existing components fulfill the need of a specific application, the definition phase may be skipped. The user does not need to define design components in their entirety. For certain components the user can provide only part of the component and delegate its completion to dedicated specialized tools that typically take care of low-level details and/or repetitive actions.

The programming model is a rather traditional one based on message passing. An application is composed of one or more tasks that can interact via services, a mechanism analogous to remote procedure call. A task that makes a service request is said to import that service. On the other hand, the task that implements the service is said to export the service. A service must be exported by exactly one task but can be imported by multiple tasks. Alternatively, tasks can interact through unidirectional typed channels. A task sees only one channel endpoint, which we call a port. The internal structure of each application is static, but applications can be dynamically created and destroyed. Interaction among tasks in different applications is allowed through services. Both ports and services are accessed through library functions. Tasks can be written in either the C language, the C++ language, or the Fortran language. Mixed-language programming is supported in the sense that communicating tasks may be written in different languages. The programming interface will be outlined in the next section.

Each port is associated with a message model, that is, a template for the structure of a message. Messages flowing through that port must observe the corresponding model. This constraint is automatically enforced in C++, while in C and in Fortran it is up to the programmer to use a port correctly. The run-time support takes care of performing the necessary marshaling and unmarshaling of messages transparently to the programmer-provided code. A service is associated with two message models, one describing the format of the request; the other describing the reply.

Names of ports and services are local to the task in which they are defined. Bindings among ports or services of different tasks are specified by the user during the configuration phase by drawing a line connecting the icons that represent the related ports or services. The binding information is used transparently during task start-up: when the programmer-provided code takes control, it can immediately start communicating through ports and services because all the necessary initialization has already been performed by the Tracs run-time support.

Tracs ensures that changing a binding does not involve recompiling the corresponding tasks. This feature makes it possible to write context-independent tasks (within the limits of use of the environment's communication primitives), that is, tasks whose code does not depend on which tasks they interact with or on which hosts they are placed in.

7.2.2   Programmer Interface

The programmer-provided code sees ports and services as variables created and initialized automatically during task start-up. These variables, called descriptors, are meant to be used only as parameters of the Tracs communication library. The names of these variables are identical to the names used in the graphical interface for the icons representing the corresponding ports and services. In the following we shall outline the programmer interface for tasks written in C.

Ports are variables of type `CHAN_DES`; imported services and exported services are variables of type `SRV_DES_C` and `SRV_DES`, respectively. The operations that can be done on descriptors are summarized in Figure 7.1. These operations are almost self-explanatory and we briefly discuss them in the following. All primitives return an integer describing the outcome of the invocation that we do not detail for brevity. The sending of a message through a port can be done either asynchronously (i.e., without waiting for an acknowledgment from the library at the remote destination) or synchronously. In the latter case, it is possible to specify a time-out after which the operation terminates even though the acknowledgment has not been received. The receiving of a message through a port can be done either by waiting until a message arrives or until a specified time-out expires. It is possible to wait for a message from any port in a set, by collecting pointers to these ports in a NULL-terminated array passed as parameters to either `PortSelect()` or `TimedPortSelect()`. Such operations wait until a message can be received from any port in the specified set or the optional timeout expires. In case multiple ports could be chosen, the `mode` parameter specifies whether the choice should be made at random or the elements with smallest indexes should be given priority. The use of primitives for using services is similar. Notice that no operations for initializing descriptors are available to programmers since this operation is performed by the Tracs runtime on the basis of the binding information collected during the configuration phase.

```
PortAsynchSend(CHAN_DES *port, void *msg)
PortSend(CHAN_DES *port, void *msg)
TimedPortSend(CHAN_DES *port, void *msg, unsigned timeout)
PortReceive(CHAN_DES *port, void *msg)
TimedPortReceive(CHAN_DES *port, void *msg, unsigned timeout)
PortSelect(CHAN_DES **plist, int mode)
TimedPortSelect(CHAN_DES **plist, int mode, unsigned timeout)
SrvCall(SRV_DES_C *srv, void *argin, *void argout)
TimedSrvCall(SRV_DES_C *srv,void *argin,*void argout,unsigned timeout)
SrvAccept(SRV_DES *srv, void *argin)
TimedSrvAccept(SRV_DES *srv, void *argin, unsigned timeout)
SrvReply(SRV_DES *srv, void *argin, void *argout)
SrvSelect(SRV_DES **slist, int mode)
TimedSrvSelect(SRV_DES **slist, int mode, unsigned timeout)
```

Figure 7.1 Interface of the communication library for the C language.

The interface for the C++ language can be found in [2]. In this case, the strong typing of the language allows Tracs to generate descriptors that cannot be misused by the programmer—e.g., it is not possible to send a message through an input port. The interface for the Fortran language is similar to that for the C language, except that messages must be placed in variables created automatically by the run-time support during start-up rather than in arbitrary memory buffers.

7.2.3 Building Reusable Design Components

To clarify our discussion, we shall consider the simple problem of implementing the multiscreen display of a moving "snake," whose body is made up of the string ">--0" [11]. Each screen supports a horizontal path where the snake can move.

The snake circulates through the screens. When it reaches the side of a screen, it moves to the beginning of the next and so on. Each screen also displays the number of times the snake has moved from one screen to another.

This problem may be solved by an application that consists of a set of identical tasks, each controlling a screen. Tasks are connected through ports to form a ring. Each task receives the snake from the previous task (character by character) displays the snake on the screen, and sends it to the next task.

Design components are constructed in the definition phase. Tracs supports three kinds of design components: message models, task models, and architecture models. For convenience, we shall not use architecture models in the example and we shall defer their discussion to a later section.

To define message models, the programmer has to identify the kinds of messages exchanged in the application. In our example, we need only one message model, which we call SNAKE. Messages following this model consist of: (i) the character of the SNAKE body that is moving from one task to the next, and (ii) an integer representing the number of screens that SNAKE has traversed so far. Figure 7.2 shows the window devoted to the definition of message models. It can be seen that the SNAKE model consists of two members: a character named body and an integer named jump. Tracs internally maps message models onto the XDR data definition language. All basic XDR types and constructors are available through dedicated buttons and windows. Once a message model has been defined graphically, the programmer can click on a button to see how that model interfaces with the programming language of interest. Figure 7.3 shows how the SNAKE message model is translated into C/C++. The p_hdl field, needed by the run-time support, is inserted automatically; its content is opaque to the programmer.

The second basic component is the task model. It is a complete description of a task that may be instantiated to one or more tasks. This description consists of the task interface—that is, ports and services together with their local names and message models—and the task code. In our example, all tasks are identical. Therefore, we need a single task model. A task model also includes such information as the programming language used and restrictions on the possible allocations of instances of that task model (if they cannot be executed on all the hosts).

Figure 7.4 shows a window supporting the definition of task models. The task model being defined is named path and has two ports, inp and outp, both associated with message model SNAKE. In particular, the figure shows the moment in which the message model SNAKE is going to be associated with the port outp. A new port is created by clicking on a button. The association between a port and a message model is established by clicking on the port and then choosing the message model from a pop-up menu. The code to be executed by the task model can be split into several files that are accessed through separate editing windows. The code of the task model is not shown for brevity. Essentially, each task executes a loop in which at each iteration it waits for a message from its input port, displays the relevant fields of the received message on the screen, constructs the message for the next task in the ring, and sends it.

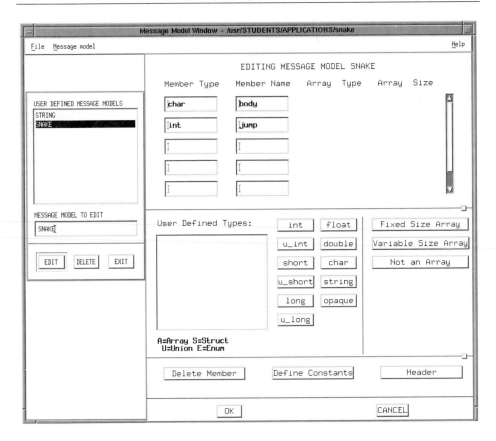

Figure 7.2 A window for defining message models.

7.2.4 Assembling Reusable Design Components

Design components are assembled to form a complete application in the configuration phase. Configuration consists of the following activities:

1. Definition of the logical structure of an application; that is, its constituent tasks, their interconnections, and the services exported to or imported from other applications; and

2. Definition of the placement of tasks on the available machines.

Figure 7.5 displays the logical structure of our example. There are four instances of the same task model named `path` connected to form a ring. These instances are named P1, P2, P3, and P4. The programmer can add a new task by clicking on a button and then associating it with a task model chosen from a pop-up menu. Connections between tasks—bindings between local names of ports—are established

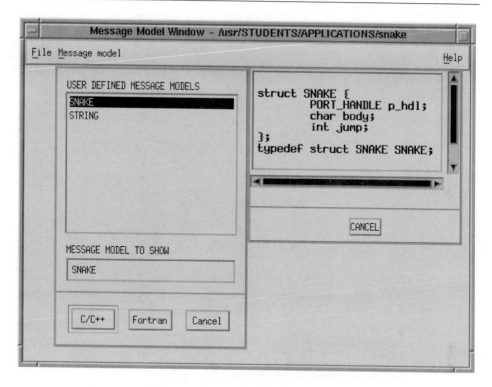

Figure 7.3 Translation of a message model into a programming language.

by drawing lines between the icons that represent the respective ports. Placement of tasks on machines is performed by clicking on the task and then selecting the host from a pop-up menu that will execute that task.

7.2.5   Compiling and Running a Distributed Application

When the configuration is complete, the programmer can ask Tracs to create the application. Tracs will generate automatically a Makefile containing all the rules for constructing the necessary executables. Because they embody knowledge of the architecture of the machines composing the system, the rules support remote compilations transparently and efficiently. If several instances of a given task model must run on machines that adopt the same executable format, only one compilation is made. Tracs makes remote copies of files only when there are accessing machines that do not share the filesystem with the programmer's machine.

Tracs also generates shell scripts for starting and killing the whole distributed application automatically. The default script associates each task with a separate window, but there are options for attaching the standard input, output, and error of each task to files (which are also transparently copied back and forth, if necessary).

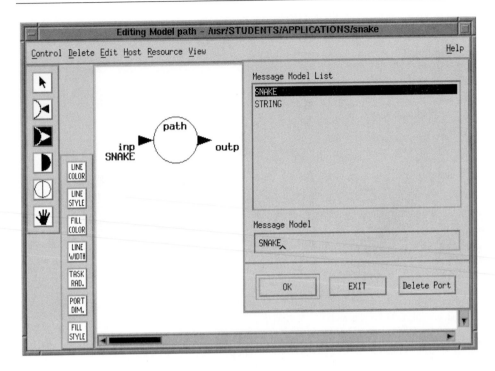

Figure 7.4 A window for defining task models.

7.2.6 Alternative Design Styles

Tracs supports more than the design style we have followed in this example. For instance, we could start by drawing in the configuration window a layout similar to that in Figure 7.5 by using only *empty* tasks and *untyped* connections. Then, we would refine the design by identifying tasks that perform similar actions and connections that carry structurally identical messages. Having thus decided on the necessary design components, we would switch to the definition phase to build them. Finally, we would use these components in the configuration phase to fill all the empty/untyped items. In particular, it would be necessary to click on each empty task and select from a pop-up menu the task model to associate with that task. Tracs would check that the association is consistent, thus rejecting, for instance, the association of a task having one input port and one output port with a task model having two input ports.

It is also possible to use components that have not yet been defined. For instance, when selecting the task model to associate with an empty task, the programmer could add a new item to the corresponding pop-up menu rather than selecting a pre-existing item. The newly-inserted task model will be defined later. This approach is also possible in the definition phase. For instance, when defining a task model, the

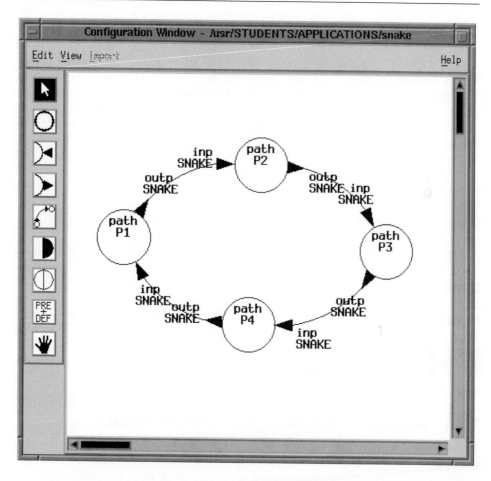

Figure 7.5 A window for configuring an application.

programmer could associate a port with a message model that does not yet exist, unlike what we did in the above example. In short, the programmer can freely switch back and forth between the configuration phase and the various definition sub-phases. In any case, Tracs does not allow the creation of an actual application until every component has been defined.

7.2.7   Consistency Checks

During the configuration phase, or upon its termination, Tracs automatically performs a number of consistency checks concerning the mixing of the design components. These checks include logical constraints and heterogeneity constraints. Logical constraints are violated, for instance, in the case of inconsistent intertask connections, such as connections between ports associated with different message models and connections between two input ports. On the other hand, checking heterogeneity constraints involves cross-checking host descriptions contained in a system-wide database against task model descriptions and placement information. So doing, it is possible to prevent, for instance, allocation of an instance of a task model written in Fortran to a machine that does not have a Fortran compiler.

Tracs performs every check as soon as possible so that, for instance, illogical connections are rejected immediately. Furthermore, the display uses colors to make the configuration more easily understandable. Each message model is associated with a programmer-defined color, which fills the icons of all the ports associated with that model. Each connection between tasks is drawn in the color of the message model associated with the corresponding endpoints. Each task model is also associated with a color, which fills all the tasks that instance that model. Tasks not yet instantiated to any task model are filled with a different default color.

This use of color makes a great deal of information immediately available to the programmer. For instance, in a set of tasks, colors show which connections between ports and services are allowed and which ones are not. For two or more tasks all with the same interface (that is, all associated with the same sets of ports and services), colors show which ones execute the same code and which ones do not. In an intricate graph of an application, colors show which connections carry which kind of messages.

7.3   Advanced Features

7.3.1   Architecture Models as Reusable Components

In addition to task models and message models, Tracs support architecture models as basic design component. An architecture model is a (possibly incomplete) description of a parallel program that is independent of what the single tasks actually do [8]. This description consists of a collection of tasks and connections. Instances of an architecture model can be used in the configuration phase, as part of a larger application, or as starting point for further design actions—removal of a connection, for instance. During the definition phase, Tracs provides some powerful graphic operations that greatly simplify the construction of architectures that include repetitive substructures, such as trees and arrays (Section 7.3.4).

In an architecture model, one or more ports or services can be left unbound. In addition, an architecture model is described in terms of formal message models and formal task models. A formal message model is a message model that has only a name, without any structure. A formal task model is a task model specified only in its interface (i.e., no code is associated with it) and such that message models associated with its ports and services may be formal ones. To use an architecture model in the configuration phase, the programmer must replace all its formal task models to actual task models, which specify both the code executed by the task and the structure of the corresponding message models. Tracs performs several checks to make sure that this operation is feasible—that is, that the interface of the formal and the actual task models are compatible.

For instance, if the programmer wants to define an architecture model describing a task farm, he has to define two formal task models, one for the master and the other for the workers. The former, m, exports a formal service s (a formal service is a pair of formal message models), whereas the latter, w, imports the same formal service s. Formal task models are defined through a window similar to the one for defining actual task models (Figure 7.4). The task farm architecture model consists of one instance of m, many instances of w and proper connections among them (Figure 7.6). The architecture model so defined may be saved for later use, as any other design component. Architecture models are defined through a window similar to the configuration window, since the actions are similar, such as creating tasks and defining interconnections. Connecting two tasks through a service is similar to connecting them through ports, i.e., by drawing a line between the icons representing the service at the importing and exporting task, respectively.

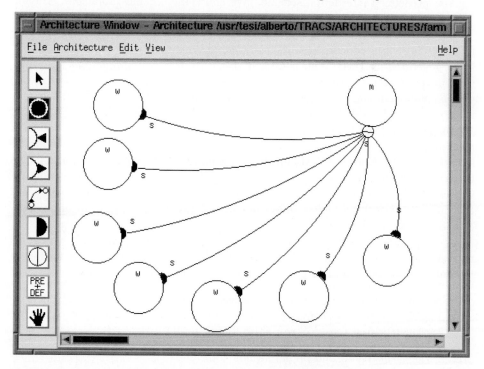

Figure 7.6 A window for designing architecture models. (Reprinted from [1], ©1995 IEEE.)

Similar to other design components, instances of architecture models can be added to the configuration window by clicking on a window and selecting a model from a pop-up menu (Figure 7.7). The instantiation of formal task models to actual task models that is necessary for specifying the code and actual message models of the corresponding tasks is performed through the usual mouse-driven actions. In this example, the actual task model for m should partition the problem to be solved into many independent jobs, whereas the actual task model for w should execute a loop in which it invokes a service s for returning the results of the previous job and getting a new one, and then carries out the new job. Of course, depending on the code executed by the actual task models, the task farm architecture model could be used for applications with a client-server structure.

7.3.2   Generation of Communication and Synchronization Code

The programming environment simplifies the creation of certain design components by automatically generating certain implementation details. In particular, the user may specify that a given task model must interact with the outside according to a given predefined interaction scheme. We call these schemes *behaviors*. Having associated a task model with a behavior, the programmer has to supply only the code that performs the "core" processing. The code necessary to complete the task model—that is, the code for communication and synchronization—will be automatically generated by Tracs. This code will deal with intertask interactions according to behavior-dependent rules. In other words, the programmer defines *part* of the design component and delegates its completion to an automatic tool. Each behavior is implemented by a dedicated tool.

Examples of behaviors include master and worker of a task farm. For instance, a master task model is composed of a part that depends on the specific problem to be solved—e.g., the code that splits up the problem into smaller jobs and that handles the corresponding results—and of another part that deals with intertask communication. While the former is problem-specific and is typically provided by the user, the latter is (largely) problem-independent and can be generated automatically. Master and worker behaviors are discussed in more detail in the following.

A task model with the master behavior exports a service through which the master dispatches jobs and collects results. The code executed by a master is basically composed of a main loop that carries out the following actions:

M1: Accept a service call issued by a worker requesting a new job. The service request message also conveys the results of the previous job dispatched to that worker (the first iteration recognize a null result).

M2: Process this result and prepare a new job.

M3: Reply to the service call to dispatch the newly prepared job to the worker.

The loop is exited and the master terminates when the last result has been received. The programmer must supply a subroutine that performs step M2. This subroutine has, essentially, one input parameter (a result) and one output parameter (a job). The remaining steps are performed by code generated automatically by the tool

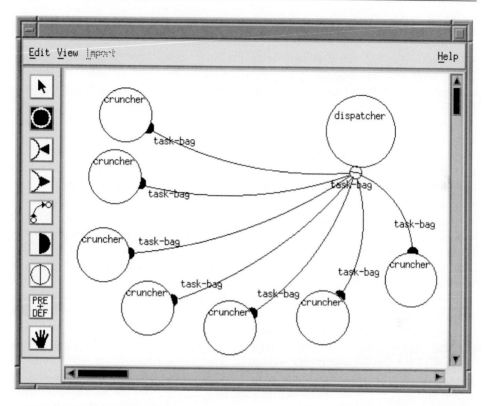

Figure 7.7 A configuration window that uses the farm architecture model. The formal task models w and m have been instantiated to the actual task models cruncher and dispatcher, respectively. (Reprinted from [1], ©1995 IEEE.)

supporting the master behavior. Of course, the programmer must also specify the structure of jobs and results, as this information is problem-specific. To this end, the programmer provides a pair of message models, one describing the input to the service exported by the master (results); one describing the output (jobs). The argument types of the subroutine performing M2 depend on these message models. More details can be found in [2].

A task model with the worker behavior imports the service exported by the master and executes the following loop:

W1: Call the service to send back the result of the previous job and get a new one (the first iteration automatically constructs a null result).

W2: Carry out the received job.

The loop is exited and the worker terminates when a null job is received. The programmer must provide only a subroutine that performs step W2, the remaining code being generated automatically. In short, the programmer supplies *part* of the code of the task models and delegates their completion to automatic tools. These tools will generate the necessary code for communication and management of distribution and combine it with the programmer-supplied code to build complete task models.

Other examples of behaviors include the server behavior, the grid-element behavior, and the filter behavior. To use any behavior, the programmer must know only a generic description of it. A server task model executes a loop in which, at each iteration, it waits for a service invocation, passes control to the user-provided code for carrying out the request, and then sends back the reply. The grid-element task model at each iteration sends part of its data to its neighbor tasks, applies a user-provided algorithm, and then gets some data from its neighbors. The filter task model at each iteration waits for a message from each input port, passes the messages to a user-provided function, and then sends the results along its output ports. The filter behavior is suitable for many interesting applications and is discussed in more detail in Section 7.3.3.

Behaviors have proven to be both a practical and powerful abstraction in the overall Tracs framework. The possibility of delegating to the environment the duty of managing intertask communication, in conjunction with the possibility of writing task codes in C, C++, and Fortran, is a powerful means of reusing existing sequential (i.e., non-concurrent) software. This feature speeds up and simplifies the development of distributed applications, since in many cases these tasks can be tested and debugged independently of other tasks. In Section 7.4, we shall illustrate a real experience of using of this technique to reuse existing simulation software in a distributed environment.

A task model associated with a certain behavior is a task model in which all source files are provided by the user except for one that is generated by the tool supporting that behavior. Since the core part of Tracs does not need to know which entity generated which parts of which components, it follows that it does not even know what behaviors actually are. No additional complexity is thus introduced into the core of the system. Furthermore, while developing the tool for a given behavior, all the basic features of Tracs are available from the very beginning: high-level interface for message-passing, transparent management of heterogeneity in data representation and in format of executables, transparent support for remote compilations and loading, and so on. This is an extremely useful feature because it substantially contributes to simplifying rapid prototyping of new ideas and facilities, allowing one to abstract from the corresponding low-level details and to focus only on the essential parts of the problems. Finally, the tool itself that implements a given behavior is often quite simple and, essentially, consists of a filter that specializes a template [2]. In short, adding new behaviors, as well as maintaining and enhancing those that already exist, is a smooth process.

7.3.3   Manipulating Messages

In this section we briefly present the filter behavior. The aim is to give some intuition on how the filter behavior can be used to perform several kinds of message analysis or manipulation that can be especially useful during application development.

A task model whose interface consists of one or more input ports and one or more output ports may be associated with the filter behavior. In this case, the task code will execute an endless loop that invokes a user-provided subroutine whenever there is a message on each input port. These messages are passed to the subroutine as input parameters. The subroutine returns a set of output parameters, one for each output port. These output parameters are sent asynchronously through the output ports. The programmer-provided code consists only of the subroutine. Tracs generates automatically the code that wraps around this subroutine to perform synchronization and intertask communication.

The filter behavior is useful to build applications structured according to the dataflow paradigm, for example. Furthermore, the filter behavior makes it possible to define components that are useful during the development of applications themselves. For instance, to manipulate and/or analyze messages traveling along a connection between tasks, it suffices to: define a task model T with one input port and one output port; define a manipulation and/or analysis subroutine; associate T with the filter behavior; and, finally, place an instance of the task model T "in the middle" of the connection to be monitored. Note that most of these operations can be performed by a few mouse clicks. Moreover, the last action does not require any recompilation of the other tasks, since tasks are context-independent.

The programmer can easily customize the predefined task model to perform several operations on messages, such as computing statistical properties (total number, total size, average size, and so on), saving and/or altering their content, altering their relative order, losing them according to a given probability, and simulating network partitions. Not only is this feature a simple yet powerful way to simplify many aspects of application development, it also supports the implementation of integrated testing and debugging tools. Moreover, altering the relative order of messages can be useful in many settings. For instance, the programmer might choose a random order to simulate different routings on wide-area networks, an order previously saved on a file to attempt to replay a specific execution, or an order that depends on the content of messages themselves to implement causal delivery protocols.

Notice that this technique is not intrusive on software. Message manipulation tasks can be freely inserted and removed without changing the code of the application, because the programming model uses local names for intertask communication. Such operations are performed quickly and with no possibility of errors due to a mismatch of versions of the various executables because programmer-written do not have to be compiled again.

7.3.4   Repetitive Substructures in Architecture Models

The definition of architecture models made up of repetitive substructures is greatly simplified thanks to powerful features of the graphical interface. By "repetitive substructures" we mean task graphs that consist of a number of identical "tiles" in which the connections between the borders of adjacent tiles are all the same. Such task graphs include most of the useful structures: farm, ring, array, grid, and so on.

    This facility is exploited as follows. While defining an architecture model, the programmer may select with the mouse the tile he wants to replicate and copy this tile into a dedicated replication window. A few mouse-driven actions, described below, allow replicating the tile quickly and easily and, when the replication window is closed, the architecture model window will automatically display the results of the replication process. The key features of the replication window are: (1) connections between tiles are defined automatically; and (2) the automatic replication can grow exponentially, depending on the tile structure.

    For instance, the definition of an architecture model describing an array of identical tasks can be based on the basic tile shown in the replication window of Figure 7.8 (left), where both ports are associated with the same formal message model. Then, the programmer should specify which border of a new tile must be connected to which border of an old tile. This information is necessary in order to define automatically the connections between the newly created tiles. In our example, these borders—that is, sets of ports—are, respectively, the input port and the output port of the only task in the tile. The three buttons on the lower part of the sidebar select the border of the old tile, the border of the new tile, and the part of the tile that does not belong to any border. Figure 7.8 (right) shows the resulting architecture model after three iterations—e.g., after three mouse clicks. Notice that Tracs defines the connections automatically. If the (formal) message models associated with the input ports had differed from those associated with the output ports, Tracs would have rejected the replication attempt.

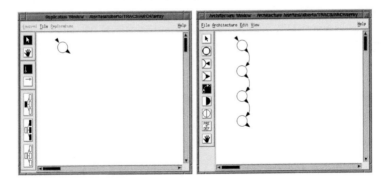

Figure 7.8 A replication window (left) and the architecture window resulting from three replications (right). (Reprinted from [1], ©1995 IEEE.)

In the more general case of tile borders that contain many ports or services, there may be a number of different ways to connect adjacent tiles. The number of possible combinations is reduced because, for instance, an input port can be connected only to an output port of the same message model. However, there may still be assignment conflicts, for example, when there are m input ports in the border of the old tile, n output ports in the border of the new tile $(m, n \geq 1)$, and all these ports are associated with the same message model.

Tracs handles all cases automatically thanks to a rule that, although not general, describes exactly what the programmer wants in most cases: (1) The set of ports and services composing a border is ordered according to the position of the corresponding icon on the display; (2) When there is an assignment conflict, Tracs resolves it by choosing the assignment satisfying this order, if such an assignment exists.

For instance, Figure 7.9 (left) shows a replication window containing a tile with four input ports and four output ports. For simplicity, all ports are associated with the same message model (whose name is not shown). The right picture shows the resulting architecture model after two replications. The old tile's border has been selected as the output port set left unbound; the new tile's border is the input port set left unbound. Notice that the output port of the task at the upper left corner of a tile might have been connected to any of the input ports of the newly created tile. However, Tracs defines connections automatically based only on the display position, so such an outcome is not possible.

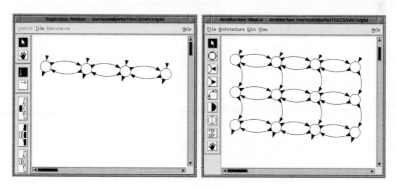

Figure 7.9 An example of architecture replication showing the rule for resolving assignment conflicts. A replication window (left) and the architecture window resulting from three replications (right). (Reprinted from [1], ©1995 IEEE.)

The exponential-growth feature of the replication window is described in more detail in [1]. Essentially, the idea is that with certain tiles the border constraints can be satisfied only by creating and attaching multiple tiles to each tile. For instance, if the tile has one input port and three output ports, Tracs figures out that it should generate three new tiles for each old one. Of course, if the replication does not proceed as expected, the programmer can undo it with a mouse click.

7.4   Reusing Simulation Software in a Distributed Setting

In this section, we outline a real application of behaviors as a tool for reusing
a large body of existing software in a cluster of heterogeneous workstations. This
software is written in Fortran and is used daily at our department to simulate digital
transmission systems [4]. The automatic parallelization performed with the Tracs
tools enables users to transparently distribute the processing load on the cluster,
thus speeding up their simulations.

The simulation software actually was not preexisting. It was generated automatically by a preexisting tool realized by the Telecommunication group in our
department. This graphical tool, called SPACE, makes it possible to graphically
specify a digital communication system in terms of block diagrams and automatically translates the graphical description into a Fortran program that simulates
that system. Some attributes of the configuration of the telecommunication system are specified as parameter values (filter bandwidth, signal-to-noise ratio, etc).
These may assume a finite set of values within user-defined ranges, and the system
is simulated for each combination of these values. Hence, a Fortran program generated by SPACE is basically structured as a collection of nested loops, one for each
parameter, where the innermost one carries out the simulation procedure. The key
point is that executions of the simulation procedure with different input data are
independent of each other. This kind of computation can thus be implemented in a
parallel fashion according to the task farm paradigm, which is one of the behaviors
supported in Tracs (Section 7.3.2).

Based on behaviors, automatic parallelization of SPACE-generated Fortran programs required only their restructuring to let them match the interface expected
by the Tracs task farm machinery. This restructuring is accomplished by a simple dedicated program that performs some filtering on the source file generated by
SPACE [3]. Essentially, this source file is split in two source files, one for the master
and one for the worker, that are structured in terms of the subroutines expected by
the master behavior and worker behavior, respectively.

The master and worker behavior exhibit some fault-tolerance properties. As
clarified below, they allow building farms that are resilient to host crashes and
to (temporary) network partitions. Such properties may be also useful in settings
where the hosts participating in the farm may be independently administered (e.g.,
workstations that lend CPU cycles at low priority, or that are part of clusters in
different organizations). In these cases, the application must be prepared to cope
with hosts that leave the farm without any prior negotiation (e.g., the host is shut
down or is withdrawn by his owner); otherwise such events could easily let the
application hang up or crash. These issues are particularly significant for long
simulations but, in practice, it is quite common to launch the application and hope
that it will complete without any failure occurring meanwhile.

The fault-tolerance properties of the master and worker behavior are obtained
by exploiting the semantics of process farms. Essentially, they consist in a proper
structuring of the template file that implement these behaviors (Section 7.3.2). The

fact that fault-tolerance is achieved in a way fully transparent to the programmer-provided code is especially important because proper handling of failures requires know-how that is typically orthogonal to the object of the application itself.

Failures in a cluster may affect a process farm in three ways. In the case of a worker crashing, the master would never receive the results for the job dispatched to that worker. In the case of the master crashing, it must be possible to restart the computation so that the jobs already carried out before crashing are not dispatched again, otherwise the computing resources would not be used efficiently. For the same efficiency reasons, it must be guaranteed that in the case of communication failures, for instance, transitory network partitions that isolate some workers from the rest of the system, results obtained by those workers are not lost.

Our solution assumes that worker execution is *idempotent*. This is a simplifying assumption but it is also a realistic one for the vast majority of applications of task farms. The Tracs-generated code for the master maintains internally these data structures: a completed list, containing all dispatched jobs whose results have already been received; and a pending list, containing all dispatched jobs whose results have not been received yet. When the master has no more jobs to dispatch, then it dispatches again those jobs that have been in the pending list for a "long" time. One might end up with more workers working on the same job because the master erroneously believes that a certain worker has crashed, while in fact it happens to be slow (or perhaps partitioned from the master). However, this is harmless both from the point of view of the correctness—jobs are idempotent—and of the efficiency—when the computation is about to finish, a worker would have nothing else to do.

Whereas jobs are idempotent, the processing of results could not be so. For instance, processing a result might involve writing on a file. To avoid this, the Tracs-generated code makes use of job identifiers, i.e., pieces of information that uniquely identify each job and are managed transparently with respect to the user-provided code: a job description sent by the master carries a job identifier that will be attached by the worker to the corresponding result; furthermore, job requests sent by a worker carry the identifier of the last job carried out by that worker. By making proper use of job identifiers and of completed and pending lists, the master is able to discard multiple results for the same job. The master could receive multiple results also because of retransmissions operated by workers that are necessary to cope with transitory network partitions and/or master unavailability. Retransmissions might also cause the delivery to a worker of multiple descriptions of the same job, which are discarded by means of mechanisms similar to those just outlined.

Finally, to cope with master crashes, the Tracs-generated code checkpoints on permanent storage the relevant master state every now and then, so that it may be restored when the master recovers. This strategy avoids restarting the farm from the very beginning, but it is possible that a job be scheduled multiple times or that a result be processed multiple times because the master state is volatile since the last checkpoint. However, as the master is usually idle for a large percentage of time, checkpointing the master very frequently is quite reasonable. However, the application may select the frequency that is most suitable to its own needs (e.g., the number of results that must be received between two consecutive checkpoints).

7.5   Comparison Between Approaches

The programming model supported by Tracs is purposefully a rather traditional one, based on unidirectional typed channels and remote procedure call-like communication. The resulting level of abstraction is higher than PVM or MPI (see Chapter 3, "MPI and PVM Programming"), but lower than that provided by LiPS (see Chapter 8, "Hypercomputing with LiPS") and Aurora (see Chapter 6, "Using Scoped Behavior to Optimize Data Sharing Idioms"). LiPS supports a communication paradigm based on the notion of tuple space, as introduced by the Linda system (see Chapter 2, "Parallel Programming Languages and Environments") and simplifies the development of fault-tolerant distributed programs by enabling the tuple space to survive (some forms of) failures. On the other hand, Aurora provides common data sharing idioms and allows programs to change data sharing policy as the access patterns to a given shared data item change from computational phase to phase.

Tracs is similar to Conic [11] in the emphasis placed on the context-independence of the design components, but is most similar to Parsec [8], which is based on a skeleton-template-module approach. Parsec lets the programmer select from a set of parameterized task graphs (farms, trees, and so on) and specify the required parameters. Whereas Parsec uses specialized windows for the various parallel-programming paradigms, the component-based approach of Tracs uses a special design component (the architecture model) to treat all the paradigms uniformly (see Chapter 1, "Parallel Programming Models and Paradigms"). Furthermore, Tracs provides powerful graphical procedures for building new architecture models quickly. Tracs exploits graphical interaction not only for choosing and connecting components, but also for the development of the components themselves. Moreover, the message type attains the status of a basic design component, greatly enhancing the system's modularity and making the interface between the other design components more explicit. A similar comparison can be made between Tracs and Code/ROPE [6], [7], another environment that emphasizes application structuring with basic design components and component reuse.

Enterprise [9] supports a fixed number of parallel-programming paradigms. The programmer specifies the required paradigm and provides part of its code, whereas the system generates the code needed for communication and synchronization. Tracs provides similar capabilities for certain frequently used process-interaction patterns, but allows dealing directly with tasks, channels, and messages. The HeNCE system [5] automatically generates message-passing primitives starting with a collection of subroutines combined in a graph built by the programmer. Tracs, instead, attempts to tackle the design process as a whole.

Tracs and P-RIO [10] display similarities concerning both the aims they pursue and the approach they take to achieve these aims. Like Tracs, P-RIO has great regard for properties of great concern in software engineering, such as reuse, modularity, and software maintenance. P-RIO addresses the above issues within an object-based framework. On the other hand, Tracs addresses them by the component-based methodology described in this chapter. Moreover, both programming environments exploit the notion of configuration paradigm that allows the assembly of a system or program by the external interconnection of modules, or components, from a library. Finally, Tracs and P-RIO give great importance to a graphical interface that provides immediate mapping of concepts associated with the software construction methodology to their graphical representations.

7.6   Concluding Remarks

Tracs exploits modularity in an original way. Support of message models, task models, and architecture models as basic design components provides programmers with a practical and easy to understand framework.

Not only does this framework simplify the development of distributed applications for clusters, it has also enabled us to enrich the environment by several advanced facilities with little implementation and integration effort. All facilities consist of specialized simple tools that may be used for automatically generating some implementation details of certain components. On the one hand, each tool inherits all the native facilities of Tracs—message-passing, data heterogeneity, mixed-language programming, remote compilations, and loading, etc.—from the very beginning of its development. On the other hand, the internals of the environment do not even need to know about which entity generated which parts of which components, therefore integrating new tools is fairly easy.

The kind of modular structuring proposed in Tracs has thus a great potential for simplifying application development as well as maintenance and enhancement of the overall programming environment. Furthermore, many of the ideas and techniques that characterize Tracs could be easily applied to other platforms based on message-passing. To sum up, we believe that the Tracs framework may constitute a sound basis for further engineering efforts in the area of message-based programming for clusters.

Acknowledgments

This work has been carried out in part under the financial support of the Commission of the European Community, Brussels (Esprit III, Tracs, project no. 6373), and in part under the financial support of the Italian Ministero dell'Università e della Ricerca Scientifica e Tecnologica (MURST) in the framework of the MOSAICO (Design Methodologies and Tools of High Performance Systems for Distributed Applications) Project.

7.7   Bibliography

[1] A. Bartoli, P. Corsini, G. Dini and C. Prete. Graphical Design of Distributed Applications through Reusable Components. *IEEE Parallel and Distributed Technology*, vol 3(1), pages 37–50, Spring 1995.

[2] A. Bartoli, and G. Dini. Automatic generation of distributed process farms. *Microprocessors and Microsystems*, vol 17(7), pages 413–422, September 1995.

[3] A. Bartoli, G. Dini, M. Luise, G. Pazzaglia, C.A. Prete and N. A. D'Andrea. Reusing sequential software in a distributed environment. *Distributed Systems Engineering*, vol 2(1), pages 2–13, March 1995.

[4] A. Bartoli, N. A. D'Andrea, G. Dini, V. Lottici, M. Luise and C.A. Prete. Parallelization of the Simulation Tool WING-SPACE for the Analysis and Design of Transmission Systems. *International Journal of Communication Systems*, vol 9, pages 213–222, September 1996.

[5] A. Beguelin, J. Dongarra, A. Geist, R. Manchek, and V. Sunderam. Graphical Development Tools for Network-Based Concurrent Supercomputing. In *Proc. of Supercomputing '91*, Albuquerque, NM, pages 435–444, 18–22 November 1991.

[6] J.C. Browne, M. Azam, and S. Sobek. Code: A Unified Approach to Parallel Programming. *IEEE Software*, vol 6(3), pages 10–18, July 1989.

[7] J.C. Browne, T. Lee, and J. Werth. Experimental Evaluation of a Reusability-Oriented Parallel Programming Environment. *IEEE Transactions on Software Engineering*, vol 16(2), pages 111-120, February 1990.

[8] D. Feldcamp, and A. Wagner. Parsec: A Software Development Environment for Performance-Oriented Parallel Programming. *Transputer Research and Applications: Proceedings of the Sixth North American Transputer Users Conference*, S. Atkins and A. Wagner, eds., IOS Press, Amsterdam, 1993.

[9] G. Lobe, P. Lu, S. Melax, I. Parsons, J. Schaeffer, C. Smith, D. Szafron. The Enterprise Model for Developing Distributed Applications. *Technical Report, TR 92-20*, Dept. of Computer Science, University of Alberta, 1992.

[10] O. Loques, J. Leite, and E. V. E. Carrera. P-RIO: A Modular Parallel-Programming Environment. *IEEE Concurrency*, pages 47–57, January-March 1998.

[11] J. Magee, J. Kramer, and M. Sloman. Constructing Distributed Systems in Conic. *IEEE Transactions on Software Engineering*, vol 15(6), pages 663–675, June 1989.

Chapter 8

Hypercomputing with LiPS

THOMAS SETZ

Technische Universität Darmstadt
Alexanderstr. 10
D-64283 Darmstadt
Germany

Email: *thsetz@acm.org*

The LiPS (Library for Parallel Systems) system enables users to implement distributed applications in heterogeneous networks of workstations connecting machines with different processor architectures and UNIX operating system flavors. The system ensures that only workstations which are considered idle by their users are used within the distributed computations. The system also guarantees successful completion of distributed computations in spite of failing machines or network links. LiPS supports a fault-tolerant communication paradigm based on the tuple space as introduced by the LINDA system. Furthermore, it provides its user with a development system to implement, document, and test his applications. The system itself is developed using the development system. Typical applications are in the area of computer algebra and cryptanalysis. This chapter gives an overview on the usage and implementation of the system.

The first section contains an introduction to tuple space based communication and gives example programs to work with this paradigm. The second section describes how the LiPS system and applications are started and controlled. The LiPS runtime systems are then explained in detail in section three. The last section highlights some parts of our development system which is used to implement, document and test the system and its applications.

8.1 Generative Communication

In order to implement distributed applications, a programmer must be supplied with primitives enabling him to create additional processes or tasks, and to exchange messages among them. A conventional programming language, when augmented by interprocess communication and process manipulation primitives, is sufficient for implementing distributed algorithms. Interprocess communication (IPC) may be established by accessing the network protocols, using systems like PVM, Express, or P4. Another approach is to use higher level paradigms such as the tuple space based generative communication [2] which is used throughout this work. These approaches differ with respect to usability, efficiency, and availability on different platforms. While IPC using direct access to network protocols permits highly efficient communication, applications implemented using this approach are rather cumbersome to maintain. The generative communication approach to IPC trades efficiency against ease of use, due to the overhead introduced by tuple space management. Although this overhead may be kept down to a reasonable amount by analyzing communication patterns at compile-time, it still is a main drawback in the usage of this paradigm.

This section first describes the shared memory tuple space and the possible operations on it. Following this, the benefits of tuple space based applications are stated. The section closes with some programming methods used to realize tuple space based distributed applications.

8.1.1 Tuple Space

The tuple space is an associative shared memory accessible to all application processes. It is called associative as it contains data tuples which may be retrieved addressable by their contents rather than by physical addresses, using a pattern-matching mechanism. The implementation of tuple space memory is hidden from the user and therefore may be realized on a shared-memory machine, a tightly-coupled parallel computer, or on a network of workstations. Data tuples consist of a list of simple data types. We distinguish active tuples generated with the `eval ()` operator from passive tuples generated with `out()`. Active tuples are used to create new threads of control within a distributed application, while passive tuples are merely used to store data items. A set of operations [`in()`, `rd()`, `inp()`, `rdp()`] is used to retrieve passive tuples. Both blocking and non-blocking versions of tuple retrieval operations are available. These operations thus may be used for synchronization *and* communication tasks. The tuple extracting operations `in()` and `inp()` read a data tuple and remove it from the tuple space. If no tuple is available, the non-blocking operation `inp()` immediately returns a boolean error code, as opposed to the blocking operation `in()` which suspends the calling thread until such a tuple is found. The tuple reading operations `rd()` and `rdp()` return a data tuple, again in a blocking and non-blocking manner, but do not extract the tuple from the tuple space.

The process of finding data tuples according to patterns passed to the tuple retrieval operations is called matching. Tuple matching is done by creating a template from the pattern passed as an argument to the retrieval operation. Tuples present in the tuple space are then matched against this template until a match is found.

Table 8.1 Matching

template	matches?	data tuple	rule
in("job", "ss", pc_a, pc_b)	no	("Name","ss","str1","str2")	1
in("Name", "s" , pc_a)	no	("Name","ss","string","f")	2
in("foo","Is", &i_j, "ab")	no	("foo","il", 5, 4.0)	3
in("bar", "i", &i_j)	no	("bar","i", 10)	4
in("karl", "s", pc_a)	yes	("karl","s","str1")	
in("sem")	yes	("sem")	
in("data", "i", &i_j)	yes	("data","i", 5)	
in("data", "I", &i_j)	yes	("data","i",5)	

Tuples and templates are split into three parts: their "logic name," their type list, and a variable-length list of data items, the so-called variable list.[1]

The "logic name" field is merely used to speed up tuple space operations at run-time as it is used to group data tuples into different hash chains, thereby restricting the search space for matching operations to a particular subset. The type list, also called "type descriptor," is used to indicate the data type for an individual tuple entry given in the variable list. Uppercase entries indicate formal variables; lowercase letters indicate actual variables. Formal variables are used in retrieval to indicate "any value" for tuple fields; actual variables define a value the matching tuple is assumed to have at the corresponding entry. Data type entries may be prefixed by modifiers, such as "array-of," or "unsigned." For example, a tuple containing three fields, an actual integer followed by an actual long integer and a formal character string, is defined with the type descriptor "ilS." In order to find a match, the template and the tuple must: (1) have equal logical names, (2) equal cardinality, (3) the same data types for corresponding elements, and (4) have the same values in corresponding actual parameter fields. The following examples assume the variables to be bound to: char *pc_a="str1"; char *pc_b="str2; int i_j=5;.

Table 8.1 illustrates the tuple matching rules. Successfully evaluated retrieval operations bind the values of the variables given in the retrieved tuple to the formal variables specified within the template.

Note the tuple space implements a true set of tuples, that is, it may contain several copies of identical data tuples. A given template may match several data tuples present in the tuple space; the matching algorithm is then allowed to return an arbitrary matching tuple.

8.1.2   Benefits of Generative Communication

As the tuple space is conceptually separated from an application process, its content is not lost across thread exits. Data tuples remain available until they are consumed by some other process, which may not necessarily be around at the time the tuple is created. As a result, interprocess communication is decoupled in time. As data

---

[1]Our Syntax differs from the C-Linda Syntax.

tuples are identified solely by their contents, and not by any other means such as
the senders or recipients process-ID, communication is made "anonymous" in that
communicating processes need no knowledge of their peers identity. IPC using the
tuple space thus decouples communicating processes logically and physically. This
eases application development when compared to using a message passing based
paradigm.

As processes in a distributed application have no notion of a peer locations,
migrating processes in the case that a machine becomes unavailable due to load
increase or crash is made easier. A process may still retrieve messages even when it
had to change to a different machine. This mechanism is transparent to the application programmer as no host addresses are involved. The tuple space communication
paradigm is not tied to a particular programming language, hardware or software
environment. It may thus be used for distributed applications running on a heterogeneous set of workstations. The paradigm also allows for adapting the number of
usable nodes at run-time, implementing what is called adaptive parallelism in [3].

Applications may use all available machines, shrink down to the usage of only
one, and switch between these bounds of possibility very easily. As shown in [4],
this is even true if machines participating in the distributed application crash.

Finally, integrating the tuple space based generative communication approach
into a conventional programming language requires only six additional operations.

Therefore, tuple space based applications turn out to be an adequate choice for
implementing distributed applications running on networks of workstations.

8.1.3   Example Applications

After having introduced the concept of tuple space in the previous section, we
now give some examples how the tuple space could be used to realize distributed
applications.

Gelernter [1] separates three general tuple space programming methods to work
with the tuple space: message passing, living data structures, and distributed data
structures. In this section we demonstrate each of the programming methods using
the LiPS syntax for tuple space operations. In the examples, we will compute the
prime numbers within an interval of 0 till 10000. The goal of the section is to
illustrate the usage of the different programming methods and not to write efficient
code for finding a prime number. We assume a function is_prime(int i) returning
1 if i is prime and 0 if i is not prime.

In the sequential case, the problem could be implemented in the following way:[2]

```
...

for(i = 1; i < 10000; i += 2)
   if(is_prime(i))
        printf("%d is prime\n", i);
```

---

[2]We use C Syntax, stick to the LiPS syntax for tuple space operations, and omit initializations
if not needed for the insight into the programming method.

To distribute the computation, we first start an initial process called master. The master then generates additional tasks with the `eval()`-operator.

The different programming methods describe the basic possibilities of how the master and the tasks reach consensus on the question: who tests which number whether it is prime or not.

The Message Passing Method

Now we will present how the prime numbers could be computed using the message passing method. We will first give a description of the master and then a description of the other tasks.

Assume the master process has a local variable `i_start`, initialized with 0 when the master is started. After having created additional tasks with `eval()`, the master removes job requests from tuple space. Each of the `Request_For_Job` tuples, created by the eval jobs, ships the task ID (TID) of the eval task asking for the new interval. The master now computes the new job description and adds the job description to tuple space. One variable of the `New_Interval` tuple is the task ID of the task asking for the new interval. As we are able to identify the requester for the job and as the master replies to the requester by means of the variable `i_his_tid`, we use a message passing style. After all jobs have been distributed, the master starts the distributed termination of the application, waits until all eval jobs are finished, and then prints out the results. The code for the master looks like:

```
main()
{
int i_start=0;
...

for(i = 0; i < i_num_worker; i++)           /* create additional tasks */
  eval worker(i);

while(i_start < 10000){                      /* distribute all intervalls */
   in("Request_For_Job", "I", &i_his_tid);   /* remove a jobrequest  */
   out("New_Interval", "iii", i_start,
       i_start + INTERVALL_SIZE, i_his_tid);   /* add the job description */
   i_start += INTERVALL_SIZE;
}
out("All_Done");                             /* start distr. termination */

for(i = 0; i < i_num_worker; i++)             /* wait for distr. termination */
   in("Terminated");

while(! inp("Prime", "I", &i))               /* print out results */
   printf("%d is prime", i);
}
```

Now we will present the code for the worker task. As already mentioned before, these tasks are created by the master. In the first step we send a message to the master requesting an interval to compute the prime number in. In the next step we wait for the reply of the master shipping the new interval. If no reply is available, we check if it is necessary to terminate. If neither the start of the distributed termination was detected nor a response from the master, we sleep a little bit and try again. The `sleep()` avoids saturation of the tuple space machine in case of a slow master process. The message passing style is based on the usage of the variable `i_my_tid_p` within the worker. This variable is used to distinguish the different requests submitted by the different eval tasks.

```
worker(int i_my_tid_p)
{
 ...

 while(TRUE){
    out("Request_For_Job", "i", i_my_tid_p);  /* send a message to the master */

    for(;;){
      if(inp("New_Interval", "IIi", &i_start, &i_end, i_my_tid_p)){
              /* No job description found */
          if(! rdp("All_Done")) {            /* check if we should terminate */
            out("Terminated");               /* indicate termination */
            return;                          /* terminate the task */
          }else{ sleep(1); }                 /* wait a little and try again */
      }else{
          break;                             /* We got the job description  */
      }
    }/* for */
    for(i = i_start; i<i_end; i+=2)          /* compute interval */
      if(is_prime(i))
          out("Prime","i",i);                /* put results into tuple space */
 }/* while */
}
```

Living Data Structures

If we use the programming method living data structures to solve the prime number application, the interval to be computed by the task is given as a parameter to the eval operator.

When a task completes, it leaves the result in the tuple space for later consumption. In our example, the tasks are generated in the master, but it is possible to generate additional tasks within the worker too.

After the master has created the different tasks (the task creation hands the interval to test as a parameter to the task), the master waits until all tasks have finished and then prints the prime numbers found.

In our prime number example the master code could look like the following:

```
main{}
{
 ...
 for(i=0; i<10000; i+=INTERVALL_SIZE, tasks++)
        eval worker(i, i+min(INTERVALL_SIZE, 10000-i)); /* create tasks */

 for(; tasks; tasks--)              /* wait till all tasks are */
    in("FINISHED");                 /* finished */

 while(! inp("IS_PRIME", "I", &i))  /* get all results */
     printf("%d is prime", i);
}
```

Each task computes their interval, writes all prime numbers found to the tuple space, and terminates. The interval a task should compute at is a parameter to the function. No additional communication is needed in order to get the interval.

```
worker(int i_start_p, int i_end_p)
{
  int i;
    for(i = i_start_p; i < i_end_p; i++)
      if(is_prime(i))
        out("IS_PRIME", "i", i);

  out ("FINISHED");
}
```

Distributed Data Structures

To use distributed data structures to solve the prime number problem, the master initializes a tuple SHARED_VARIABLE with the start and the end of the interval to search for prime numbers and puts this tuple out into tuple space. This tuple is shared among the eval tasks to agree on the number which will be tested next if it is prime or not. In the next step the master starts the tasks which will do the computation. These tasks will fill the distributed array being built out of tuples with the logic_name DISTRIBUTD_ARRAY. The master prints out all prime numbers found while traversing this array.

```
main()
{
int is_prime;
  ...

  for(i = 0; i < i_num_worker; i++)        /* generate the tasks */
      eval worker();

  out("SHARED_VARIABLE", "ii", 0, 10000);  /* initialize interval to compute */

  for(i = 0; i < 10000; i++){              /* walk through distributed array */
    in("DISTRIBUTED_ARRAY", "iI", i,&is_prime);
      if(is_prime)
        printf("%d is prime\n", i);        /* print out results  */
  }/* for */
}
```

The eval tasks remove (in()), the tuple SHARED_VARIABLE, from tuple space, get the size of the interval being in computation so far, add their own amount of numbers they are going to test to the interval, and put the tuple SHARED_VARIABLE back (out()) into tuple space again. In the next step, they check the numbers in their intervall if they are prime or not and create a tuple in the distributed array indicating this. (return).

```
worker()
{
  ...

  while(TRUE){
```

```
   in("SHARED_VARIABLE", "II", &i_start, &i_end);    /* get the interval to compute */
   out("SHARED_VARIABLE", "ii", min(i_start+INTERVALL_SIZE,i_end), i_end);

   if(i_start == i_end) return;

   for(i = i_start; i <= min(i_start+INTERVALL_SIZE,i_end) ; i++){
      if(is_prime(i))
         out("DISTRIBUTED_ARRAY", "ii", i,1);
      else
         out("DISTRIBUTED_ARRAY", "ii", i,0);
   }/* for */
 }/* while */
}
```

8.2   Using LiPS

LiPS provides its users with a development system to generate, document, and test executables. LiPS has different runtime systems to execute applications on a set of workstations. Several different UNIX flavors may participate in the execution of one application.

A LiPS application consists of two different executables: the master, being the initial process of the distributed application, and the eval-server (worker), executing tasks which were generated with `eval()`. Master and worker executables are generated from one source file and must be available for each architecture the application wants to work with. The first step in running a distributed application is the start of the LiPS runtime system. After the start of the LiPS runtime system a daemon process resides on each participating machine and checks the machines load restrictions. In the next step, the applications master process is started. After that, the LiPS runtime system will be asked to start eval-servers on idle machines. The eval-servers will execute the available eval-tasks. If a machine running a LiPS application becomes busy, this circumstance will be detected by the LiPS runtime system and the application process (eval-server or master process) will be killed. The application process will then be restarted on another machine immediately if an idle machine is available.

In this section we first show how an application code is generated from the users point of view. Then the different steps to start a distributed application are explained. The section closes with some hints on how to deal with nondeterministic behavior of fault-tolerant distributed applications.

8.2.1   Writing and Generating a LiPS Application

LiPS applications are written in CWEB, a language for literate programming. Literate programming enables the programmer to mix implementation and documentation within one file. The implementation part is in C Language, the documentation part uses LaTeX. CWEB files normally end in `.w`. The documentation part may additionally contain different test description parts. The minimal solution to make a CWEB file out of a C file is the addition of the characters "@@c" at the beginning

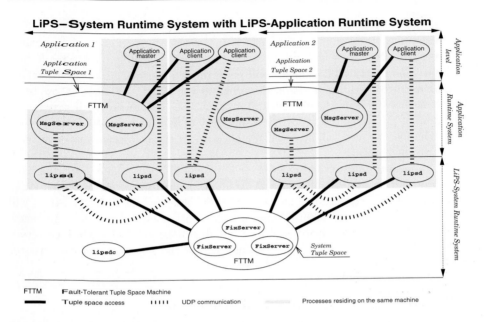

Figure 8.1 The different levels of the LiPS runtime systems. On each machine (gray-shaded) participating in the LiPS system, a server process called lipsd() provides access to the machine. lipsd() processes communicate through the System Tuple Space (solid line) or by exchanging UDP packets (dashed line). The Application Runtime System is based on the same communication mechanisms and uses services provided by the LiPS-System Runtime System.

to control the state of one or all machines and gives additional data about network bandwidth usage of the lipsd() processes. Now the LiPS-System Runtime System is up.

In order to start the application, the Applications tuple space server has to be started. Again, it could be defined in the WALKER file—how many tuple space servers should be up all the time. To distinguish the Applications tuple space servers from the System tuple space servers, the Application tuple space servers are called MsgServer. It now suffices to type make foo.run in the directory where the CWEB file lives and the distributed application will start.

8.2.3   Monitoring the System and its Applications

Currently there are two possibilities to get a glance about what is going on in the distributed application.

The first possibility is to trace the distributed application. You may use the same mechanism to trace the LiPS runtime systems behavior as well. The tracing mechanism is based on a printf-style syslog(3)-like macro in the code. This macro is

of the C file.[3]

If we assume a program foo living in a file `foo.w`, the documentation is generat
with `make foo.dvi`, `make foo.ps`, or `make foo.html` depending on which form
is wanted. The generated documents will be in the directories `.linkdvi`, `.linkp`
or `.linkhtml`. To perform[4] tests on the program you simply say, `make foo.tes`
The test results will be in the directory `.linktest`. The file `foo.log` will give you
description of the whole test, `foo.sum` a summary of which tests passed and whic
failed. The file `foo.cov` will give you the coverage of the performed tests as hint
to improve the coverage.

The application master and eval-server are generated with the command `mak
foo`. The results of the compilation will be found in the directory `.linkbinlink`
and will be named `foo-master` and `foo-client`. Each of these executables wil
end on the name for the architecture you have just compiled on (for instance
`sun4m_SunOS_5-5-1` for a sparc station 4 running Solaris 2.5.1). The director)
`.linkc` will hold intermediate C files needed within the generation of the mastei
and the eval-server.

8.2.2   Starting the System and its Application

The start of an application is divided into two main steps. In the first step the LiPS
-System Runtime System has to be started, and in the second step the Application
Runtime System is started along with the application. Figure 8.1 gives an overview
of a running LiPS application. In Section 8.3 the LiPS runtime systems will be
described.

Starting the LiPS-System Runtime System begins with the start of a tuple space
server called FixServer. A FixServer implements the functionality of the tuple space
and provides this functionality to its clients. It is possible to keep up several replicas
of a tuple space server. How many replicas there should be and on which machines
the replicas could reside is defined in a so-called WALKER file in the home directory
of the user. After the FixServer is started it tries to start as much replicas as there
are defined in the WALKER file. If, at run-time, a machine which a tuple space
server resides on crashes, another tuple space server will be started on another
machine if possible. The FixServer implements a tuple space called System Tuple
Space. This tuple space is used to store information about the Hypercomputers
state, e.g. machines load and kind of application processes on these machines.

In the next step the lips daemon controller `lipsdc()` is started with the name of
a so-called CLUSTER file as a parameter. The CLUSTER file holds a description
of machines participating in the Hypercomputer. This data is now inserted into the
System Tuple Space. In the next step the different `lipsd()` processes are started.
After a `lipsd()` process is started it will control the machine it resides on and
update the machines state in the System Tuple Space. The `lipsdc()` may be used

---

[3]In CWEB this simply means that there is only one code part having no documentation or test
cases specified.

[4]It is only possible to test sequential parts of the program, not the distributed program.

used in the entire system implementation and may be used on the application level as well. It distinguishes tracing output on different levels of priority within the code of a module. Within the configuration file, TRACEDEST/SYSTEM_TRACEDEST, the application/system-processes modules output can be configured to be talkative, e.g., all tracing information of the module having priority higher than 1 or silent— all tracing information of the module having priority higher than 9. At runtime, the output of these macros will be collected on a console process MsgCtl/SysCtl. The output behavior for each module can be configured independently at runtime. The implementation is based on the state of the tracing mechanism within a given process. The tracing mechanism is either in state enabled or in state off. On receipt of a SIGTRAP signal the current state will be changed. If the tracing mechanism is switched to state enabled, the configuration file is read again and the trace-level of the different modules are adapted to the values given in the file. If the tracing mechanism is switched to state off, the tracing mechanism stops sending messages to the console process.

Another possibility to analyze the application behavior is to generate a core dump of the application. The core dump's content is the tuple space and the tuple space access log of the different tasks working in the system. The core file implements a snapshot of the distributed application. It is generated by sending a SIGUSR1 to a tuple space server. On receipt of this signal the tuple space server will print a human readable output of its core into the `/tmp` directory. This core dump may be used to freeze the current state of an application. It is then possible to shut down the entire application and the runtime systems and restart the application from the core dump.

8.2.4   Some Remarks on Fault-Tolerant Applications

LiPS ensures that an application is able to finish successfully even if machines participating in the application crash (fail stop failures). The basic mechanisms used to ensure this are:

- tuple space replication, and

- recovery of crashed application processes.

Tuple space replication is scheduled with the help of a file in which the user specifies how many replicas should (normally 1-3) be maintained and on which machines these replicas could run. The replicas update themselves and start additional replicas if necessary.

The recovery of crashed application processes (eval-server or master) is based on a tuple space access log of the crashed task. If an application process (eval job) crashes, it is restarted, possibly on another machine. If a task is restarted, it is called recovering as long it is working on its tuple space access log. To be more precise, on the initial run of the crashed task, all tuple space accesses are logged and will be replayed in the same order and with the same data as in the first run while the task is recovering.

This circumstance assumes that eval jobs always have a deterministic behavior. In some cases nondeterministic application behavior could be simulated through the insertion of the random value into tuple space and thereby into the tasks tuple space access log.
Example:

```
int i=rand();          /* nondeterminism */
out("my_rand", "i", i);   /* add nondeterministic value to tuple space */
in("my_rand", "I", &i);   /* get the value again from tuple space */
```

In the first run the task chooses a random value `rand()`. This value will be used in case of a restart, too, as the variable will be set from the tuple space access log if available. This will overwrite the random value from the restarted run. Another possibility is to split the nondeterministic part into an additional eval task, as shown below.

```
int i=rand();            /* nondeterminism */
eval splitfunction(i);   /* add nondeterministic value to tuple space */
```

8.3   The LiPS Runtime Systems

In Section 8.2 we have seen how distributed applications are generated and started using the LiPS system. The following section describes how the LiPS runtime systems are realized using mechanisms that have been discussed in the previous section.

The main problem that arises in implementing and working with the system deals with the question of how to make a Tuple space resilient to faults like machine crashes. Obviously, the solution to this problem is a replication of the Tuple space among different machines. This approach is implemented in the so-called Fault-Tolerant Tuple Space Machine (FTTM) explained later in this section.

We distinguish two FTTMs in our runtime systems [5]. The FTTM of the LiPS-Runtime System implements the System Tuple Space maintaining data about the system state with processes called FixServers. The FTTM of the Application Runtime System maintains the Application tuple space and is implemented with processes called Message-Server. Several applications may exist concurrently,[5] each using a private FTTM. The System tuple space is shared by all applications. The relationship between the different runtime systems is depicted in Figure 8.1.

A designated server process called `lipsd()` resides on each machine participating in the LiPS system. The `lipsd()` processes update and retrieve information from the System tuple space. For example, node-state information, like load of a (the) machine, can be simply read (updated) through tuple space operations. The `lipsd()` processes update their own node-state information in the System tuple space in fixed intervals. A machine crash can be detected if this information is not received in time. In this case possible errors due to lost data are repaired, and

---

[5]This feature is not completely implemented so far.

watchdog mechanisms will reintegrate the crashed machine "automagically" after its recovery.

Fault-tolerance on application level is implemented with a Checkpointing and recovery mechanism integrated into the FTTM. A checkpoint is correlated to the evaluation of an `eval()` operation; recovery is based on the reexecution of a failed `eval()` together with the replay of the message logging of the first execution of `eval()`. Message logging is provided via the FTTM.

In this section we introduce the design of the FTTM being the basis for the LiPS-System Runtime System as well as for the Application Runtime System. In the following subsections we explain the `lipsd()` process in more detail and introduce a tool (`lipsdc()`, the `lipsd()` controller) to display the current state of the system configuration.

8.3.1   The Fault-Tolerant Tuple Space Machine

The Fault-Tolerant Tuple Space Machine (FTTM) [6] replicates the content of the tuple space among several machines. If a machine that a MessageServer (FixServer) resides on crashes, the data is still available on the replicas. Application processes being connected to a crashed server will switch to another server after they recognize the crash.[6] An additionally started server process joining the FTTM will be initialized with the data of an old replica. This feature makes the FTTM N-fault-tolerant.

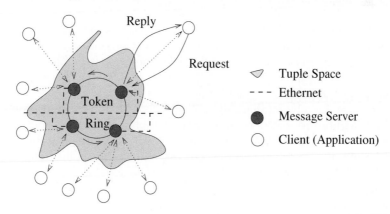

Figure 8.2 Processes of the tuple space machine.

In the FTTM, every tuple is tagged with a unique ID (sequence number) as a result of the protocol used to replicate data across the different machines. This unique ID is used to speed up replication of events, like reading or extracting tuple

---

[6]Recognition is based on timeout (machine-crash or network partition) and collapse of the communication link between application-process and server-process (server-crash).

space accesses among the different servers. The protocols used in the Fault-Tolerant Tuple Space Machine are based on those given in [7]. An in-depth description of the protocols used and their implementation are given in [9].

As depicted in Figure 8.2, the tuple space is managed by several Message-Server-processes residing on different machines. Message-Server must reside in the same broadcast domain i.e., broadcast packets must reach each machine hosting a Message-Server. The broadcast facility is utilized to replicate messages very efficiently among the different servers. A mutually exclusive token circulating among the servers schedules the permission to use the broadcast facility. This avoids Ethernet saturation due to collisions. The circulating token ships additional data enabling, among other things, flow control between the replicas. Additionally, each broadcast message (tuple) is tagged in sequence with a unique ID. This procedure establishes a linear order among the tuples of the FTTM and speeds up replication.[7]

As shown in Figure 8.2, an application process sends requests to the Message-Server which is assigned to it. A request can either contain a tuple or a template. In the following, we explain how a Message-Server processes a tuple, and then how templates are handled.

An application client doing an `out()` will send the tuple to its correlated Message-Server. As all Message-Server processes share the same broadcast domain, a Message-Server is able to broadcast the tuple and hence replicate it on multiple Message-Servers with only one physical operation. At any time only one Message-Server may broadcast a tuple, namely, the Message-Server holding the token message. After a Message-Server has finished broadcasting messages (tuples), it sends the token to the next Message-Server. With respect to this token transfer, the Message-Server processes form a logical token ring. Messages being broadcast are tagged with a unique sequence number. The sequence number of the last broadcast message of a Message-Server is sent within the token. The next Message-Server intending to broadcast knows the sequence number of the last broadcast message and continues the sequence, thereby establishing a total order on the messages (tuples) being broadcast. Within one token rotation several tuples may be broadcast by each Message-Server. The Message-Server will acknowledge the receipt of the tuple after successful replication to the application process, and on the application level `out()` will return.

If a Message-Server receives a template, it first tries a match on its local tuple space. If no tuple matching the template is found, the Message-Server notifies the requesting application process (NACK). Otherwise, if the Message-Server finds a match, it must first synchronize with the other Message Servers. In order to notify the other Message Servers of the tuple access, it is sufficient to send the sequence number (4 bytes), the ID of the application process accessing the tuple and the event number in the application processes message logging (4 bytes) as well as the type of access (1 byte) to identify the operation to the replicas. These items of

---

[7]If a broadcast message was not received on a replica, this circumstance is easily detected as there is a gap in the sequence of received messages. In this case, a retransmission could be requested immediately.

access information now are added to the circulating token. The size of the token then determines the number of reading and extracting tuple space operations which may be replicated within one token rotation.

The FTTM is based on different layers. The bottom layer of is the network layer where the socket mechanism is used in order to send and receive messages. Based on the network layer, the membership layer provides mechanisms to find out about the set of working processes in the FTTM and provides mechanisms to initialize new started processes with the needed data. The total order protocol layer, coming next, replicates tuples and locks among the processes of the FTTM and establishes a total order among the tuples. By means of the total order protocol every tuple is tagged with a unique ID. This ID is used on the event space layer to replicate reading accesses very efficiently, and to minimize memory requirements for the message log of the application processes. The event space layer additionally provides the FTTM with recovery and connection management. The upmost layer of the FTTM is the client/server layer, where the interactions with the master and eval-servers are handled. Depending on the amount of replication beeing done in the current version of the FTTM, the time to out() and then in() a tuple of 800 byte lies between 5.8 ms (one server, one client) and 80 ms (4 server, 40 clients).[8]

A detailed description of the implementation and additional performace data are given in [9], [6].

8.3.2   Performance

In this section, we present some run-time measurements for tuple space accesses using the Fault-Tolerant Tuple Space Machine. The machines used for the FTTM timings are Sun SPARCstation 20 with 128 MB main memory under the operating system Sun-OS 4.1.4. The replication of messages was done in a 10 Mb/s Ethernet. The machines hosting the different application processes were of different flavor connected through different medias providing enough bandwidth. The test measured the time needed for Tuple space operations with a number of application processes concurrently accessing the Tuple space. The test is based on the ping pong benchmark given in [8]. In this report, the tests were performed using PVM version 3.2.6, p4, TCGMSG, and SCA Linda on a network of IBM RS/6000 model 560 workstations under the operating system AIX 3.2. The test presented here was executed within another environment[9] and for this reason, the timings are not really comparable to the timings taken from [8]; however, they are in the same order of magnitude.

In the ping-pong test, the time needed by an application process to write a tuple into the Tuple space and read the same tuple afterwards is measured. The run-time for a different number of application processes and a different number of Message-Servers is given in Figure 8.3. The run-time for one application process

---

[8]These data have been accumulated on Sun Sparcstation 20 (server) and Sun SLC/ELC (clients) connected via 10 MBit/s Ethernet.

[9]Sparc station 20 running SunOS 4.1.4.

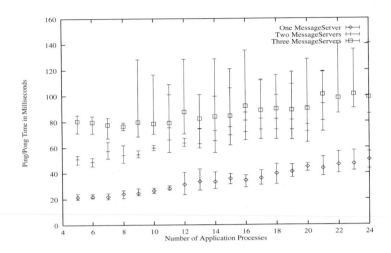

Figure 8.3 The ping/pong test.

and one Message-Server was 5.8 ms. ([8] TCGMSG 2.3 ms, P4 2.3 ms, PVM 2.8 ms, SCA Linda 3.4 ms)

8.3.3   The LiPS Daemon (`lipsd()`)

Besides the FTTM described in detail in the previous section, a major component of the LiPS runtime systems is the system server process called `lipsd()`. This process resides on each machine in a LiPS installation. It gives the LiPS system access to the machine and is responsible for obeying the idle-time restrictions for the machine this particular `lipsd()` is residing on. Furthermore, the `lipsd()` processes provide services such as starting and controlling application processes. Each `lipsd()` updates the node state information of its machine held in the System Tuple Space within a given time. If a `lipsd()` fails to update this information within the given period of time, the machine it resides on is assumed to have crashed. In this case, all other `lipsd()` processes are informed of the crash of the machine, and possible corrupted data in the System Tuple Space is repaired. Additionally, all application processes residing on that machine are scheduled to be restarted on another machine. Informing all `lipsd()` processes of this event is realized with a signal indicator shipped with every tuple space operation. As every `lipsd()` updates its node-state information periodically, it will receive the signal indicator soon after the crash of a machine. On receipt of the signal indicator, the `lipsd()` process triggers appropriate signal handler functions. The 'first' `lipsd()`, finding himself in the signal handler, will repair possibly corrupted data structures (lost tuple) and, if necessary, will schedule lost application processes to be restarted. All other `lipsd()` processes only update their locally cached data. The 'first' `lipsd()`

mentioned above is identified with the help of an automatically (FTTM) generated tuple which will be destructively read (`inp()`) by the 'first' `lipsd()` and is not available to the other `lipsd()` processes (`inp()` returns an error). Within the `lipsd()` process all destructive read operations (`in()`, `inp()`) are immediately followed by a tuple generating operation (`out()`). This eases the restoring of corrupted data after a crash as the FTTM simply reinjects the tuple into the System Tuple Space if the last tuple space operation of a crashed `lipsd()` has been a destructive read. These mechanisms enable us to handle recursive crashes of `lipsd()` processes e.g., if a `lipsd()` crashes while it was recovering the data for a formerly crashed `lipsd()`.

As already mentioned, each `lipsd()` process maintains a tuple for its machine in the System Tuple Space which contains the node state information. This information is based on the nodes status (running, idle etc.), number of users, load average, number of application processes, and the time of the last update of this tuple. This information is considered when starting new application processes to achieve a well-balanced process and load distribution. In order to detect failing application processes, the System Tuple Space holds a table for each running application process. When this information gets updated by a `lipsd()`, this old table is compared with the new information. The processes which are marked as running within the old table but, marked as non-running in the new one, need to be restarted. This data is periodically read by the applications' FTTM which in turn is able to request a restart of crashed application processes.

As the `lipsd()` processes are permanently running on all machines in a LiPS installation, in particular, even if a machine is unavailable to run a LiPS application process due to idle-time restrictions, they are implemented such that they cause minimal overhead for the machine. In the first place, the run-time and memory requirements are minimized, e.g., in the case that a machine is idle, the load is updated every 15 seconds, otherwise every 5 minutes. As the LiPS system was used in relatively fast networks so far, the network overhead was not yet optimized. When using LiPS in a huge installation or in wide-area networks, more attention must be paid to reducing the communication traffic.

8.3.4   The LiPS Daemon Controller (`lipsdc()`)

The `lipsdc()`tool can be used for two purposes: on one hand it is the means to initialize the global data structures of the LiPS System Runtime System in the System Tuple Space during the start-up of a LiPS configuration. On the other hand, it enables the administrator of a LiPS installation to interactively change the configuration during run-time and provides users with the information about their application processes in the LiPS system.

If used during the start-up of a LiPS configuration, a number of global tables are created in the form of tuples in the System Tuple Space. Moreover, a configuration file is read containing entries for each machine becoming a member of the LiPS installation such as the machine architecture, or a specification of what it means for that machine to be idle. Finally, several configuration files are created or updated which then have to be copied together with the architecture-dependent `lipsd()` binary to each machine taking part in the newly set-up LiPS installation. These files hold data about the FixServers' ports, the process IDs for the different `lipsd()` processes, and trace level data.

In the interactive mode, the `lipsdc()` allows displaying and changing the current LiPS configuration such as: request the load state of each machine, add or remove machines in the installation, change the idle-time specifications, or display all application processes, including information about the user to which each process belongs or which machine each process is distributed on within the network.

8.4   The LiPS Development System

The LiPS development system provides mechanisms to ease the job of documenting, porting, and testing the system and its applications.

The LiPS system and its applications are written in CWEB, a tool for literate programming with the C language. The benefit of this approach is the possibility to mix code and documentation in one file. The resulting documents may be translated automatically to the hypertext mark-up language (HTML) enabling us to view the whole project's documentation and implementation as a hypertext document. A test tool for executing tests being defined in a CWEB file is integrated into our development system and enables the user and the system developer to write and execute tests. Additional mechanisms (autoconf, imake ...) ease the job of configuring the system to a given machine or operating system, but will not be explained in detail here.

In this section we first give an example of writing and structuring a CWEB program. Then we show the different translation tools needed to generate program code as documentation from a CWEB file. The last section gives a short insight into the integrated test system.

8.4.1   Programming in CWEB

The CWEB package [11] is a front-end lead to the C programming language; it is not an entirely new system. So everyone familiar with programming in C will be able to write code in CWEB. Allthough we integrated better documentation features (using LaTeX instead of TeX, automatic translation to HTML format) and added a test-environment, we tried to stay compatible with the original tool. A CWEB program holds both documentation and C code in one file, so the system is helpful to improve structured documentation. The documentation is written in LaTeX-style, and therefore every CWEB file is a mixture of LaTeX and C code. First, we will give a very small example of the simplest way to write a CWEB program.

```
@
@c
#include <stdio.h>
int main()
```

```
{
        printf("Hello, world!\n");
        return 0;
}
```

The only difference between the CWEB file (typically ending with `.w`) and the well known Hello world example in C can be found in the first two lines. The first @ sign introduces the documentation part of the CWEB Hello world program and the @c starts the C part of the program. The minimal difference between a C file and a CWEB file is @ @c.

In the rest of this section we will first present a high level view on the structure of a CWEB file and explain some tools needed in the process of translating a CWEB file into different document and program representations. The section closes with the description of our integrated test environment.

A High Level View on a CWEB File

Each source file consists of multiple sections each of which is further divided into a documentation part and a code part. As shown in Figure 8.4, the translators

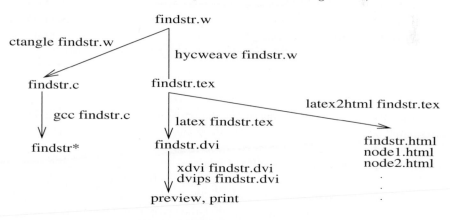

Figure 8.4 How to work with CWEB.

`ctangle` and `hycweave` are used to get the documentation or program code from the CWEB file. The `ctangle` command extracts the C code from the `.w`-file and throws away all comments. The resulting `.c`-file can be fed to a C compiler like cc or gcc. The documentation is prepared using the command `hycweave` which creates a `.tex`-file that can be fed to LaTeX to create DVI files or to LaTeX2Html in order to build an html document.

Together with LaTeX2Html and our CWEBTEX package we are able to generate an HTML presentation from the CWEB file. Within the HTML document we may jump back and forth between refinements (bubbles), specific locations of variables, the index or the glossary, and much more. The main benefit of this approach is that we are able to follow a thought maybe in a master thesis down to its implementation easy. Additionally, we now have a presentation ready for the Internet.

8.4.2   The LiPS Test Environment

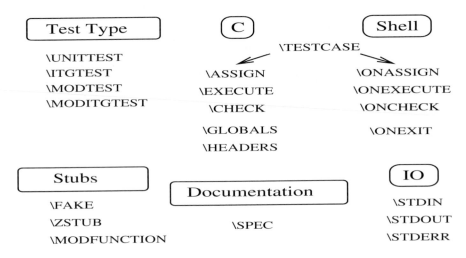

Figure 8.5 The test description language.

Implementing and documenting is not the only thing to be done while building a distributed system and applications. Code changes over time, bugs are fixed, and code is ported to other architectures. Needless to say that some code being originally implemented on one architecture will not work on another one, or even worse, may not behave as expected. The same condition holds for bug fixes, which will make the system work on one architecture but may introduce some more errors on another architecture. It is hard work to find out what the error is and why it appears. This is especially true for fault-tolerant distributed systems and applications. The field asked for more tools to be integrated into the development system.

In the first step we wrote a tool called spectest which is able to generate an executable test program from a C function and a test description. The test description is written in a test description language [10] defining the test case by its preconditions, the tests to be performed, and the expected results to be reached. Multiple tests can be performed with one test description. Each documentation part of a CWEB file may contain several different test descriptions. The LiPS development system will generate executable programs from the test descriptions and perform the tests. The possible test cases distinguish unit tests from integration tests. Within a unit test it is possible to define stubs for functions being called from the tested functions in order to investigate the tested function in isolation (unit test). It is also possible to call the "real" function, thereby making an integration test. The main advantage of our `spectest` tool, in comparison to other test tools in this area, e.g., dejagnu, is the possibility to perform the tests on the basis of a function instead of being able only to test a main program. In the next step we integrated gct [12] tool into our development system. The integration of gct enables us to find the coverage of the performed tests. The coverage measurements determine whether the set of tests applied to the module have test cases e.g., such that every branch of a function is walked through at least once while the tests are performed. The integration of our development system and Expect enable us to simply type `make findstr.test`, and all tests for this module are performed automatically. After the tests are finished, a file named `findstr.sum` gives a summary on the performed tests. A more detailed description, especially a description of what failed if the test failed, is given in the correlated file `findstr.log`. The coverage of the performed tests are given in the file `findstr.cov`.

```
-- Test Summary for /lippmann/test/findstr.w
------------------------------------------------
-- Working revision:      Repository revision:
-- RCS Id: findstr.w,v 1.1  11:28:19 lippmann Exp

UNITTESTfindstr.t: PASS
test1: PASS
test2: PASS

BINARY BRANCH INSTRUMENTATION (4 conditions total)
1 (25.00%) not satisfied.
3 (75.00%) fully satisfied.

LOOP INSTRUMENTATION (3 conditions total)
2 (66.67%) not satisfied.
1 (33.33%) fully satisfied.
```

The description of the tests to be performed is integrated into the documentation part of the CWEB file. Each test case distinguishes C commands to assign values to local and global variables: `ASSIGN`, `GLOBALS`, define stub functions (unit tests only): `FAKE`, `ZSTUB`, `MODFUNCTION` and check the values of variables after the test has been performed: `CHECK`. It is possible to write additional shell scripts to be called before the corresponding C action is performed: `ONASSIGN`, `ONEXECUTE`, `ONCHECK`, `ONEXIT`. Additionally, it is possible to control the input/output behavior of the tested unit (`STDIN`, `STDOUT`, `STDERR`).

8.5 Bibliography

[1] N. Carriero and D. Gelernter. How to Write Parallel Programs: A Guide for the Perplexed. *ACMCS*, vol. 21(3), September 1989.

[2] D. Gelernter. Generative Communication in Linda. *ACM Transactions on Programming Languages and Systems*, vol. 7(1), pages 80–112, January 1985.

[3] N. Carriero, E. Freeman, D. Gelernter, and D. Kaminsky. Adaptive Parallelism and Piranha. *Technical Report*, YALEU DCS Yale University, Department of Computer Science, February 1994.

[4] T. Setz. Dynamic Load Adaption in LiPS. In *7th Euromicro Workshop on Parallel and Distributed Processing*, February 3-5, 1999, Funchal, Portugal. IEEE Computer Society Press, 1999.

[5] T. Setz and T. Liefke. The LiPS Runtime Systems based on Fault-Tolerant Tuple Space Machines. In *Proceedings of the Workshop on Runtime Systems for Parallel Programming (RTSPP), 11th International Parallel Processing Symposium (IPPS'97)*, Geneva, Switzerland, April 1997.

[6] T. Setz. Design, Implementation and Performance of a Fault Tolerant Tuple Space Machine. In *Proceedings: ICPADS'97: 1997 International Conference on Parallel and Distributed Systems*, December 10–13, 1997, Seoul, Korea. IEEE, December 1997.

[7] Y. Amir, P. Dolev, P. Melliar-Smith, D. Agarwal, and P. Ciarfella. Fast Message Ordering and Membership using a Logical Token-Passing Ring. In *13th International Conference on Distributed Computing Systems (ICDCS)*, vol. 13 IEEE, pages 551–560, Pittsburgh, May 1993.

[8] T. G. Mattson. The Efficiency of Linda for General Purpose Scientific Programming. *Scientific Programming*, vol. 3(1), pages 61–71, 1994.

[9] T. Setz. Integration von Mechanismen zur Unterstützung der Fehlertoleranz in LiPS. *PhD Thesis*. Universität des Saarlandes, Germany, February 1996. Fachbereich Informatik.

[10] T. Setz and J. Lippmann. An Integrated Test-Environment for in Cweb Written C-Programs. In *9th International Symposium on Software Reliability Engineering*, Nov 4-7, 1998, Paderborn, Germany. IEEE Computer Society Press, 1998.

[11] D.E. Knuth and S. Levy. *The CWEB System of Structured Documentation* Addison Wesley, 1994.

[12] Brian Marick. *The Craft of Software Testing*. Prentice Hall, NJ 1995.

Chapter 9

An Efficient Tuple Space Programming Environment

JAMES B. FENWICK, JR.[†] AND LORI L. POLLOCK[‡]

[†]Department of Computer Science
Appalachian State University
Boone, North Carolina, USA

[‡]Department of Computer & Information Sciences
University of Delaware
Newark, Delaware, USA

Email: *jbf@cs.appstate.edu, pollock@cis.udel.edu*

9.1 Introduction

Writing efficient message passing programs can be difficult, error-prone, and tedious. An alternative paradigm of parallel programming in a cluster environment is distributed shared memory, in which a shared memory abstraction is presented to the programmer, despite the physically distributed memory. The shared memory abstraction provides an easier transition from a sequential to a correct parallel program. While a shared memory, parallelizing compiler provides an application programmer with an easy avenue to parallel computing, programming languages allowing the user to explicitly specify parallel constructs are prevalent. Sometimes it is difficult to express a parallel algorithm using a sequential language, even with annotations. Similarly, it may sometimes be easier to use parallel constructs and synchronization than to provide the compiler with sufficient annotations about data access patterns.

Tuple space is a structured distributed shared memory paradigm, as it offers programmers a shared space of structures as opposed to a linear array of bytes, and each structure is an individual shared unit. Explicitly created processes share a data space rather than sharing variables. Messages are not sent between processes,

175

but are instead placed in the shared data space for other processes to access. To reinforce this differentiation, messages in this paradigm are called tuples; hence, the shared data space holding these tuples is called tuple space[10].

The tuple space paradigm, or more succinctly just tuple space, provides parallel programmers with an abstraction that hides the specific underlying mechanisms implementing process creation, communication, and synchronization. The actual implementation of the parallel program on the target architecture is hidden from the programmer, and the architecture can be any number of platforms ranging from shared or distributed memory to a cluster of workstations. In short, tuple space offers the simplicity of shared memory programming and the benefits of distributed memory architectures without the false sharing and memory consistency concerns of unstructured distributed shared memory systems.

Unfortunately, any abstraction of this kind necessarily introduces a trade-off for the application programmer between ease of use and control over performance. Indeed, implementation of the tuple space paradigm on a distributed memory architecture has raised concerns regarding efficiency and performance. However, several researchers have demonstrated that distributed tuple space implementations can be efficient [14]. These experimental studies considered a wide variety of real applications that encompassed a large scope of parallel algorithm classifications.

This chapter presents an overview of tuple space programming, and techniques for effectively and efficiently compiling and executing tuple space parallel programs in a cluster environment. After describing the basics of translation necessary for correctness of tuple space programs in a distributed memory environment, techniques for optimizing compilation are described. Issues involved in implementing the shared data space abstraction of tuple space in a cluster environment are detailed, along with an overview of Deli, a UNIX-based distributed tuple space implementation.

9.2   Tuple Space Programming

Tuple space is central to the generative communication parallel programming model most notably embodied by Linda.[1] Linda is a coordination language consisting of a small number of primitive operations that are added to a base computation language. Example base languages include C, Fortran, and Lisp. The result is an explicitly parallel programming dialect of the base language (for example, C-Linda). The operations manipulate the fundamental objects of Linda, tuples and tuple space, to perform the communication and synchronization necessary for parallel programming.

---

[1]Linda is a registered trademark of Scientific Computing Associates, Inc., New Haven, Connecticut.

9.2.1 Fundamentals

Tuples and tuple space

A tuple is an ordered collection of typed fields, where the type of each field is dependent upon the underlying computation language and may be subject to restriction. Each field of a tuple is either an actual, which contains a data value, or a formal, which receives a data value. A field is distinguished as formal through the use of a syntactic element; for example, C-Linda uses the '?' character to indicate a formal field. Thus, $\langle$?i$\rangle$ is a single field tuple with the field being designated as a formal. The field variable i will receive a value from some tuple space process.

Tuple space is a shared memory because any process can reference any tuple regardless of where it is stored. Tuple space is a logically shared memory because it provides the appearance of a shared memory but does not require an underlying physical shared memory. Tuple space is also an associative memory, which means that tuples are accessed not by their address but rather by their content. The identification of tuples via an associative search is described in more detail in Section 9.2.3. The tuple space communication model is termed generative because a tuple generated by a process has an independent existence in tuple space. Any process may remove the tuple, and the tuple is bound to no process.

Gelernter noted two properties that distinguish tuple space from other parallel paradigms: space and time uncoupling [10]. Space uncoupling refers to the fact that tuple producers are unaware of where tuple consumers exist in the parallel machine. The reverse is also true; tuple consumers do not know from where tuples are generated. Time uncoupling means that tuple space processes do not have to co-exist in order to communicate. This is possible because tuple space has an existence outside of any individual process.

Operations

Linda defines six operations that manipulate tuples and tuple space. These operations divide naturally into three classes: operations that generate, extract, and examine tuples.

Generation operations (out() and eval())

The out() operation inserts a passive tuple into tuple space. Each field of the operation is evaluated by the process issuing the operation, and the resulting values are collected and deposited into tuple space.

Parallelism is explicitly specified by using the eval() operation to insert an active tuple into tuple space. New threads of control are created to evaluate each of the fields of an active tuple. However, in response to the high cost of process creation, most distributed tuple space implementations limit new threads of control to only the function-valued fields of an active tuple. For example, upon receiving the active tuple $\langle$5,x+y,foo(),x+foo()$\rangle$, a typical distributed tuple space creates only one new process to evaluate the third field. The fourth field contains a function

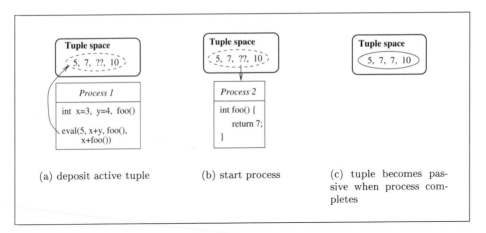

(a) deposit active tuple   (b) start process   (c) tuple becomes pas-
                                                             sive when process com-
                                                             pletes

Figure 9.1 Snapshots of `eval()` operation in action.

call, but the field is determined to not be function-valued since the call is a part of
an expression; therefore, a new process is not created to evaluate the fourth field.
An active tuple quiesces into a passive one upon completion of the evaluation of
each of its fields. Figure 9.1 diagrams a possible behavior of an `eval()` operation.
The active tuple, indicated by the dashed ellipse, is not available for matching via
an extraction or examination operation. The resultant passive tuple of Figure 9.1(c)
is available for matching.

Both the `out()` and `eval()` are non-blocking asynchronous operations, meaning
that these generation operations immediately return control back to their issuing
process. Specifically, a tuple generated by a process does not have to be consumed
before the process can continue.

Extraction operations (IN and `inp()`)

The IN operation extracts a tuple from tuple space and copies the values of the
tuple's actual fields into corresponding formal fields of the IN operation. Technically,
an extraction operation generates a description of the tuple it wants to extract. This
description of the desired tuple is called a template (or an anti-tuple). Data is sent
from one process to another by having the sender issue an `out()` operation while
the receiver issues an IN operation that has a formal field of the same type in the
same position. Figure 9.2 shows a possible behavior of two processes issuing IN and
`out()` operations.

The IN is a blocking, synchronous operation. Unlike the generation operations,
the process issuing an IN operation does not resume until it receives an extracted
tuple. The `inp()` operation behaves like an IN except rather than blocking when
no tuple is currently available, a boolean false value is returned, indicating that no
tuple was removed and no copying into formal fields was performed.

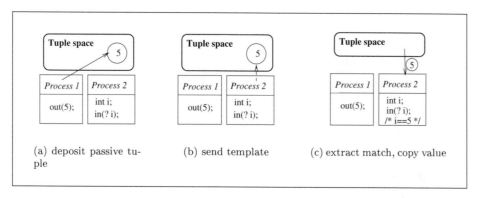

Figure 9.2 Snapshots of IN and out() operations in action.

Examination operations (rd() and rdp())

The rd() operation is also a blocking and synchronous operation like the IN. The only difference is that a tuple is not removed from tuple space in response to a rd() operation. However, data values are copied into formal fields of the rd(). The rdp() operation is a predicate form of the rd().

9.2.2   Example Linda Program

Figure 9.3 shows a Linda program to perform matrix multiplication. Each element of the result data structure is computed by a separate process. This example intends to demonstrate the tuple space operations on a well-known problem, but is not a particularly efficient solution, especially on a cluster. The emphmain() procedure creates N^2 active tuples. Each process executes the *worker()* function but with different input arguments, which tell the process the element of the result matrix to compute. The inner product computation requires a specific row and column from the input matrices. Thus, the *main()* procedure deposits each row of **A** as a tuple and each column of **B** as a tuple after a transposition of **B** to accommodate the row-major ordering. Since each row and column is used in many computations, the worker processes read their required data, then return the inner product. This return value is placed into the active tuple, making it passive. The *main()* process extracts the resultant passive tuples, which may come in any order, thus requiring the row and column identification in this tuple.

9.2.3   Associative Memory Analysis

An important characteristic of the Linda generative communication model is the associativity of tuple space, which necessitates the comparison of tuples and templates. Simplistic implementation approaches could, in the worst case, require a number of comparisons equal to the number of tuples generated at run-time. Carriero assuaged early Linda critics of this fear by developing compiler analysis to

```
main()  {
  int A[N][N], B[N][N], C[N][N];
  int r,c,e,i,worker(int,int);

  for (r=0; r < N; r++)
    for (c=0; c < N; c++)
      eval("C", r, c, worker(r,c));
                                        int worker(int myrow, int mycol)  {
  init(A, B);                             int i, value=0, row[N], col[N];
  transpose(B);
  for (i=0; i < N; i++) {                  rd("row of A", myrow, ?row);
    out("row of A", i, A[i]);             rd("col of B", mycol, ?col);
    out("col of B", i, B[i]); }           for (i=0; i < N; i++)
                                            value += row[i]*col[i];
  for (i=0; i < N*N; i++) {
    in("C", ?r, ?c, ?e);                   return value;
    C[r][c] = e; }                       }
}
```

Figure 9.3 Example Linda program performing matrix multiplication.

partition a program's tuple space operations into disjoint sets, thus limiting the associative search to a single partition rather than all of tuple space, and significantly decreasing the impact of the associative memory [5].

There are two cases in which tuple space must attempt to find a match between a tuple and a template. In the case where a tuple has been generated by an out() or eval() operation, the tuple space system must decide if this newly arriving tuple into tuple space has already been requested by a user process; that is, a process is blocked on an IN or rd() operation awaiting this tuple. If no request for this tuple has been made, the tuple is stored. In the case where a template has been generated by an IN or rd() or inp() or rdp() operation, the tuple space system must decide if a stored tuple matches this request. In both cases, the tuple space system must answer the question, *Does tuple X match the tuple description of template Y?*, for some tuple X and template Y. A tuple and a template are said to match if the tuple and template (1) agree on the number of fields, (2) agree on the types of corresponding fields, (3) agree on the value of corresponding actual fields, and (4) have no corresponding formal fields.

9.3   Compilation Environment

9.3.1   Basic Translation

Because Linda extends a base computation language, a Linda compiler is a source-to-source translator. A basic Linda compiler for C, for example, accepts a C-Linda program as input, performs tuple space partitioning to increase the efficiency of the

associative search, maps the tuple space operations to a Linda run-time library, and
outputs a C program. This C program is then compiled with a native C compiler
to generate an executable image, which is then executed in a distributed Linda
run-time environment.

9.3.2   Optimizing Compilers

Several methods for increasing the efficiency of distributed tuple space programs
have been developed. Some approaches involve the run-time system dynamically
managing its resources and gathering statistical information that triggers alternative
processing[13], [3]. Other approaches to increasing tuple space efficiency involve
collaboration between the compiler and run-time system [12], [3]; however, the
analyses and transformations are very localized. Carriero and Gelernter outline
several ideas for achieving increased performance through more global compiler
analysis [4]. They describe commonly used patterns of tuple space operations which
can be improved, and speculate about information that an optimizing compiler
would need to perform analysis.

Fenwick and Pollock [7], [9] have realized some of these visions by designing and
building the Deli optimizing C-Linda compiler. The optimizing compiler performs
global and interprocess data flow analyses and uses the results from these analyses
to identify the safety and profitability of several compile-time transformations for
improving run-time tuple space communication. This section describes the intermediate program representation, data flow analysis framework, and several of the
optimizing analyses and transformations in the Deli optimizing C-Linda compiler.

Program Representation

All of the information available in tuple space operations is needed in order to perform compile-time analysis to identify opportunities for tuple space communication
optimizations. Unfortunately, most tuple space programming systems lose this high
level information in much the same way as high level array access information is
lost in low level intermediate representations. This information is lost because tuple space operations are typically mapped to calls to a message passing library. To
retain the necessary high level information in the Deli optimizing C-Linda compiler,
compile-time analysis is performed on a high level intermediate program representation. Standard data flow analyses remain feasible, while tuple space communication
analysis is also effectively supported.

In particular, the high level representation developed for the Stanford University
Intermediate Format (SUIF) shared memory parallelizing compiler [17] has been
extended to support the additional tuple space operation syntax and to include
information about tuple space operations. Each tuple space operation outwardly
appears like a procedure call, but is further annotated with high level information,
including its tuple space partition, an indication of whether each field is formal
or actual, and other useful information. Processes are identified by examining the
EVAL tuple space operations, which contain the name of the procedure that will

be executed in parallel. The definitions of the named procedures are annotated to indicate that they are process entry points. Tuple space communications are modeled by constructing directed edges from tuple space generation operations to extraction/examination operations.

The entire program is a forest of process intermediate representations, where each process is a collection of procedures. The current version of the Deli optimizing C-Linda compiler builds an interprocedural flow graph similar to [6] for each process. Each procedure is represented in the form of the SUIF intermediate representation, and it is not necessary to have all procedure representations in memory at once. Interprocedural execution paths are not explicitly represented by edges in the intermediate representation, and similarly there are no edges from process invocation sites to process entry points. The communication edges connecting these process representations create the Linda intermediate representation.

Figure 9.4 depicts an example representation of a program with two processes

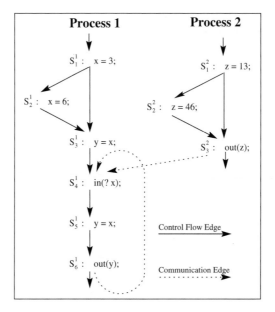

Figure 9.4 Example program representation.

that are connected by tuple space edges. In this example, there is only one tuple space partition, so each OUT is connected to every IN operation.

Data Flow Analysis

Data flow analysis plays a key role in ambitious optimizing compilers for sequential programming languages, but current compilers for parallel programs with user-specified parallelism restrict the scope of this analysis due to the complex issues involved in analyzing shared memory programs. In contrast, tuple space parallel programs are quite amenable to data flow analysis.

Intraprocess Data Flow Analysis

Tuple space processes share access to a logically global data space, but address spaces of the tuple space processes are distinct. Intuitively, a memory location in one process can not be accessed by another process. Therefore, only the actions of process i itself need to be examined in order to analyze how definitions and uses of variables accessible to process i flow within process i. While the concept of "last value written" is not well defined in other shared memory systems, it can be conservatively determined for the local variables of tuple space processes by analyzing only the process in which the variable is declared. As such, it is not difficult to understand that standard data flow analysis *within a process* remains feasible in the context of tuple space parallel programming, unlike other shared memory parallel programming systems [15].

The precision of the standard data flow analyses for tuple space programs can be improved by maintaining and using the high level information of tuple space operations. In particular, a straightforward modification of the computation of GEN and KILL examines the statement to determine whether it is a tuple space operation. If so, then formal fields become *un*ambiguous definitions of the associated variable, and actual fields are not considered to be definitions at all.

Interprocess Reaching Definitions

In a sequential program, a definition of a variable is said to reach a program point p if there is a definition-free path in the control flow graph from that definition to p. In addition to classic optimizations for individual processes, interprocess reaching definitions information is useful for improving the tuple space partitioning and tuple space communication operations[9].

The data flow system for computing reaching definitions across tuple space process boundaries extends the sequential reaching definitions data flow analysis. The GEN and KILL data flow sets are computed as described in the intraprocess data flow analysis. The IN set is unchanged and represents the definitions reaching a point p as the union of the definitions leaving all its control flow predecessors. The OUT data flow set is the most significantly changed. In addition to definitions generated and those coming in that are not killed, definitions coming in from tuple space communication edges are included. For example, in addition to the definition of y generated at S_3^1, the OUT set for statement S_4^1 of Figure 9.4 would also include the definitions at statements S_5^1, S_1^2, S_2^2 that are present due to the two communication edges. A slight technical consideration is necessary to accommodate mapping a definition of a variable in one process context to another process context. For example, the definition of z at S_1^2 becomes a definition of x at S_4^1. This accommodation is also required in interprocedural reaching definitions.

In [7], the interprocess reaching definitions problem is shown to be monotone.

To compute the reaching definitions using these equations, the standard $\mathcal{O}(N^2)$ algorithm is run to iterate over the program nodes, N, until a fixed point is reached.

Tuple Space Edge Elimination

More precise interprocess data flow information is possible if the number of tuple space edges connecting tuple space generation operations to extraction/examination operations can be reduced. This reduction can be achieved by propagating control flow information. In the example in Figure 9.4, the edge connecting the OUT operation in S_6^1 to the IN operation in S_4^1 can be eliminated because there is no control flow path from S_6^1 to S_4^1. That is, it is not possible for a tuple generated by the OUT in S_6^1 to be consumed by the IN in S_4^1.

In [9], Fenwick and Pollock present an algorithm for eliminating tuple space edges based on computing and using NREACH information, where NREACH(n) is the set of extraction/examination operations that node n cannot reach. A tuple space edge from x to y can be safely eliminated if $y \in$ NREACH(x).

Analysis and Transformation

Carriero and Gelernter [4] describe several classes of tuple usage that are commonly found in tuple space programs and can be transformed into more efficient communications. These tuple usage classes include: shared variable tuples, distributed queues, and message tuples. Being able to distinguish a tuple as belonging to one of these tuple usage classes enables detection of the safety and profitability of communication improving transformations. These tuple usage patterns, a method for automatic identification of the pattern, and transformation for increased performance are described in this section.

Shared Variable Tuples

Shared data is common in tuple space parallel programs. In a shared memory context, a shared location contains only a single value, and processes must synchronize among themselves to ensure exclusive access to the shared location. In a tuple space context, a partition that never contains more than a single tuple is said to contain a shared variable tuple. Removal of a shared variable tuple by a process implicitly synchronizes access to the tuple. Inserting the shared variable tuple into the empty partition makes the value available for other processes. Figure 9.5 depicts shared variable tuple space operations.

```
IN("shared variable", ?value);
newvalue = compute(value);
out()("shared variable", newvalue);
```

Figure 9.5 Shared variable tuple space operations.

Finding a tuple space partition that never contains more than one tuple requires determining the number of tuples, the tuple count, that may be present in the partition during program execution. In [7], Fenwick presents a data flow analysis framework that answers the question: For each tuple space partition, may there ever be more than one tuple in that partition? This data flow analysis is the crucial component in the analysis to automatically identify shared variable tuples.

The in/out collapse optimization [3] can be applied to many shared variable tuples. This transformation collapses an IN and a subsequent out() into a single operation. This reduces underlying communication and the time spent allocating storage for the tuple. In addition, the basic synchronization tuple is a specialization of the shared variable tuple, and can be optimized by identifying the synchronization and replacing it with a more efficient method native to the host architecture.

Distributed Queues in Tuple Space

In a comparative study of several parallel programming languages, Bal observed that the concept of distributed data structures is an important contribution of the tuple space communication model [2]. Distributing a queue essentially involves distributing the individual data elements across the memories of the cluster. A distributed queue used by a group of processes requires additional shared variable tuples to coordinate access to the front and rear of the queue. Thus, a distributed queue in tuple space is a multipartition data structure.

Figure 9.6 shows operations used to remove an item from a queue. The "front" shared variable tuple coordinates removing data from the distributed queue among multiple processes, but at the cost of efficiency. As Figure 9.6(a) shows, five network accesses may be necessary. Figure 9.6(b) illustrates an improvement to this default tuple space handling of distributed queues, which Wilson terms triangular messaging [18]. Triangular messaging does not eliminate any of the required messages, but rather changes when and who initiates messages. At best, the triangular messaging scheme results in the user process experiencing no delay at the second IN operation because the tuple space manager has already sent the tuple.

Wilson did not specify how or when the improvement can be applied safely. In [7], Fenwick presents a compiler analysis to detect and transform the set of tuple space operations acting on a distributed queue. The analysis links the value of the shared variable tuple to the IN operation that uses this value as a position in the queue. After detecting distributed queue operations, the compiler transforms the program so that triangular messaging is performed during program execution. This involves augmenting the shared variable tuple request with information so that the tuple space run-time system can send the template for the queue data item, and ensuring that the user process does not send this template. In addition, triangular messaging requires that the run-time system support the sending of a template on behalf of a user process.

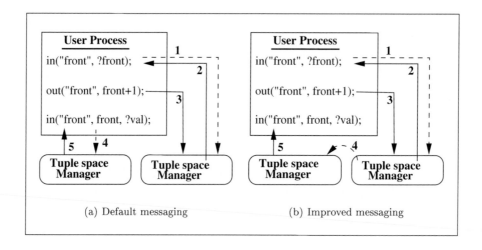

Figure 9.6 Messages required to access a distributed queue.

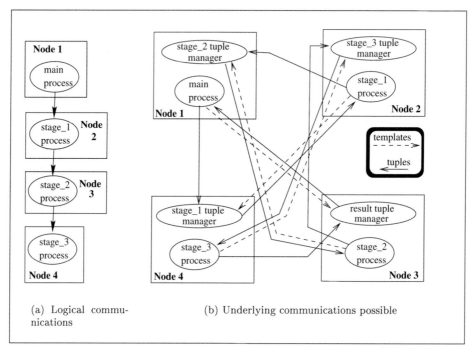

Figure 9.7 Communications of using a tuple space message tuple.

Tuples as Messages

A tuple space process needing to communicate data to a specific process may suffer an unwanted latency. Figure 9.7(a) shows a logical communication of a pipelined calculation that sends a message from *main* to *stage_1*, which then sends a message to *stage_2*, etc. However, the uncoupling property of tuple space described in Section 9.2 means that the messages will probably be stored at cluster nodes that are not executing the receiving process. This scenario is depicted in Figure 9.7(b), illustrating the source of the unwanted latency in sending a directed communication through tuple space.

In [7], Fenwick presents an analysis that is able to detect some tuples that are received by a single process invocation, and thus are messages. The identification of a message tuple requires the identification of a tuple that is intended to be received by a single, specific target process. In the intermediate representation of a tuple space program, this is characterized by a generation operation that has all of its communication successor nodes residing in the same process. Additionally, this process must be invoked only once.

The compiler transforms the program to invoke a dynamic transformation of the tuple space run-time system ensuring that the message tuple will be stored at the cluster node executing the process that receives the message tuple. The Deli tuple space implementation allows the process receiving the message tuple to run anywhere in the cluster. Once a node has been selected to execute this process, the run-time system reassigns the original node for the message tuple to this node, and lazily informs the other nodes of the reassignment.

Footprinting

In [12], Landry and Arthur describe the tuple space operations footprinting optimization that divides each IN and `rd()` operation into two suboperations that send the template and receive the tuple. Efficiency is improved by allowing the movement of noninterfering computation between the suboperations, thus, overlapping computation with communication.

9.4   Run-time Environment

The run-time environment of a tuple space system is composed of several subsystems. The cluster execution environment is the subsystem enabling the compiled tuple space application to execute in a cluster environment. This environment must unite distinct cluster nodes into a logically parallel machine. The tuple space data subsystem implements the storing, searching, and matching of run-time tuples and templates. This subsystem must determine which node of the cluster has the requested data and efficiently access this data on that node. The process execution subsystem is responsible for concurrently executing the user-specified processes. This subsystem must find a node in the cluster to execute a user process. The interface subsystem is a run-time library that connects the application to the other subsystems. To maximize the opportunities for compiler optimization, these subsystems are bundled together with the application program.

Figure 9.8 illustrates the relationships between these subsytems. The application interfaces to the data subsystem through its uses of the out(), IN, inp(), rd(), and rdp() operations. The eval() operation interfaces to the process execution and data subsystems. The application does not directly interface to the cluster execution environment; rather, the compiler imperceptibly inserts this code into the application. In Figure 9.8 the cluster execution environment is using cluster nodes 2–6 for the current execution of the application. Another run of the application may result in the cluster execution environment selecting a different subset of nodes. The major implementation issues for a distributed tuple space are described in this section.

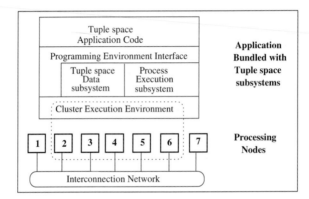

Figure 9.8 Overview of tuple space subsystem relationships.

9.4.1   Processor Location of Data

Supporting the sharing of data necessitates that processes be able to locate and retrieve the data they require. In a cluster environment, this means that processes must determine the node (processor) that is holding the data. In the tuple space programming paradigm, processes may need to determine the node that will hold the data in the event that the data has not yet been produced. There are two primary approaches to resolving this question: centralizing the data in the cluster, or distributing it in a controlled fashion.

Centralized Data

A logical choice for implementing tuple space is to use a client/server approach. Using this strategy, clients are the concurrent processes executing on nodes throughout the cluster, and the server manages all the tuples and templates. Several tuple space implementations follow this approach of centralizing all the tuple space data on a single server node. Consequently, a client process can easily locate the node holding the data it requires; it is the preselected server node. However, centralizing the data serializes data access and may become a communication bottleneck.

Distributed Data

Distributing the tasks of tuple storage and management over some subset, possibly all, of the nodes of the system increases parallelism as data requests can be concurrently handled by different nodes. However, locating a tuple becomes more difficult. There are two primary approaches to distributing tuples and templates throughout the nodes of the cluster: hash-based and operation-based tuple distribution.

A hash-based distribution method deterministically maps tuples and templates to a specific node using a hash function, which requires every tuple and template to contain an input to the hash function. Some tuple space implementations require a dedicated key field in all tuples and templates [5]. Others use a combination of the tuple space partition information and the values of actual fields [3]. A thorough investigation of the effectiveness of hash functions of this sort was performed by Bjornson [3]. Hashing is one of the best methods for efficient tuple distribution, and it does not assume any particular communication topology (i.e., broadcast/multicast).

An operation-based tuple distribution method uses the tuple space operation itself to determine the processor responsible for the tuple or template. One possibility is for tuples to be stored locally on the node executing the out() or eval() operation. [2] Then, templates, which are generated by the IN, RD, INP, and RDP operations, are sent to all nodes. Bjornson termed this scheme *negative broadcast*, and it is used in Leichter's implementation [13]. A second operation-based possibility, called *positive broadcast*, is the inverse of negative broadcast. In this case, it is the tuples that are broadcast to all nodes, and templates are sent locally [5]. A hybrid of these two methods multicasts tuples and templates to a subset of nodes. The intersection of these subsets must not be null; otherwise, templates can not find matching tuples. Restricting the intersection to a single node simplifies matching of tuples and templates. Methods using broadcast or multicast require a coherence protocol, which is discussed later.

Whichever tuple distribution method is selected, it should evenly distribute the load of managing the tuples since this requires CPU time and memory. The tuple distribution method should also strive to have tuples found locally, thus reducing network access and tuple space operation latency. Unfortunately, achieving one of these goals often conflicts with the achievement of the other goal.

It is uncertain which technique is superior, so attempts to safely hybrid these methods are justified. One such technique is sophisticated compiler analysis to estimate the tuple space access patterns of processes[7]; another has the tuple space implementation itself gather run-time statistics[3]. Both techniques attempt to circumvent the underlying distribution scheme when beneficial.

---

[2]Tuple in this context refers to the resultant passive tuple generated by an eval() and not any tuples created by the processes spawned by the eval().

9.4.2   Data Structures for Efficient Data Access

After the node managing a desired tuple is identified, the tuple must be retrieved from that processor's memory. There are several efficient data structure paradigms for tuple storage (hence, tuple access): trees, hash tables, queues, counters, and lists.

The tuple space implementor can use a single data structure for all of tuple space, or use different paradigms for different tuple space partitions. Both hash tables and trees require a key in each tuple (template) so that its location in the hash table (i.e., its location within the memory of this node) can be determined. The ordering properties of trees are an unnecessary overhead; hence, trees are not generally used. Recall the operations from Section 9.3.2 and Figure 9.6 that act on the data elements of the distributed queue. The second field in all those operations was always an actual; thus, this partition could use a hash table with this field serving as the key. If a hash table key consists of every actual field in the tuple, then access is $\mathcal{O}(1)$. However, most implementations use a subset of the tuple's actual fields for the key. In this case, different tuples may have the same hash value thus necessitating a search of the colliding tuples.

The worst case for representing tuple space is as a list. Every tuple in the list must be examined to determine that no match exists in the list. Partitioning tuple space is an improvement as it divides a single list into smaller sublists, only one of which needs to be searched, but the potential for expensive tuple access remains. Sophisticated compilers may perform analysis revealing that a tuple space partition never requires run-time matching; that is, any tuple may satisfy any template. For example, a partition containing the operations `out()("data",value)` and `IN("data",?item)` meets these restrictions regardless of when, where, or how often the operations occur in the application. In this case, the list can be viewed as a queue, and the access becomes constant. Compiler analysis can also determine that not only is no run-time matching required, but also there is no data copying necessary. In this situation, no data needs to be stored, and a simple counter provides efficiency. Example operations qualifying as a counter are `out()("lock")` and `IN("lock")`.

The Deli and Bjornson tuple space implementations represent tuple space as a table of partitions [7], [3]. Each partition can be any of the available data structures: a hash table, a queue, a counter, or a list. In the case of queues and lists, the partition data structure maintains two chains, one for unmatched tuples and another for unsatisfied templates. In the case of counters, the partition data structure maintains a single counter field for tuples and a chain for templates. If the partition data structure is a hash table, then each element of the hash table contains chains for tuples and templates.

Using appropriate data structures can allow a template to find a matching tuple efficiently, often in constant time. However, the converse may not be true. This is because an arriving template is satisfied by a single tuple, which can be found in constant time with efficient data structures. In contrast, an arriving tuple can satisfy multiple templates. Consider tuple space containing several RD and IN templates when a matching tuple arrives. The tuple can satisfy at most one of the IN templates and a subset, possibly empty, of the RD templates. This requires special attention by the tuple space implementor.

9.4.3   Data Transfer Protocol

There are a number of protocols that a tuple space implementor must support. In tuple space as a whole, a coherence protocol is necessary for any replicated tuples or templates. This is similar to the problem of keeping caches coherent in a multiprocessor, and the solutions are likewise similar. The physical transmission of tuples and templates requires a low level transport protocol providing reliability, retransmissions, reassembly, etc. In response to requests for tuples, a protocol is needed to ensure that multiple matching tuples are properly managed.

This tuple transfer protocol controls the movement of tuples and templates among nodes of the machine. A template travels between nodes to find a matching tuple. A tuple travels between nodes to find a matching template and then onward to the node issuing the tuple. The tuple transfer protocol must that ensure the atomicity of the tuple space operations while simultaneously attempting to minimize unnecessary movement. The tuple distribution method and the cluster's communication architecture have effects on appropriate tuple transfer protocols. In [8], Fenwick and Pollock explore the issues faced in selecting a tuple transfer protocol. The tuple space implementor must also realize that the protocol may work well for some tuple access patterns, and poorly (even terribly) for others. Again, sophisticated compiler analysis for estimating tuple space access patterns and/or run-time statistics gathering of actual access patterns may be able to allow the selection of alternative protocols. Because each application has its own tuple space access patterns, Shekhar and Srikant suggest that the tuple space implementation itself should be reconfigurable for each application so as to minimize inefficiencies [16].

9.4.4   Process Creation

The `eval()` operation is the tuple space programmer's vehicle for explicitly expressing parallelism through the creation of a new process. There are several issues requiring attention, including the semantic difficulties of the `eval()` operation, deciding upon a node to execute a new process, and establishing communication between the new process and other nodes.

Eval Semantics

Unfortunately, the semantics of the `eval()` operation are not well-specified. Specifically, the tuple space model does not define whether the new process shares global variables with its parent, or if a process can modify parameters passed by reference [16], [18]. In the absence of a clear semantic definition, implementations generally seem to let the machine's available process creation primitives dictate the definition of the eval() semantics. In a cluster environment, the most restrictive semantic interpretation is most feasible; that is, a new process only has access to the r-values of explicitly passed parameters.

Eval Implementation Alternatives

While several possibilities exist [8], a general machine-independent approach that is particularly well-suited for clusters is to use an *eval server* [3], [7]. An eval server runs on every node and monitors tuple space for active tuples created by an eval() operation. In the Deli tuple space implementation, a single active tuple is actually a set of passive tuples created by the compiler when translating an eval() operation. One of these tuples describes the overall eval() operation and holds the known values of all the fields of the resultant tuple. The other tuples describe the processes created. For example, eval()(matmul(),eigenvals()) is an eval() operation with an active tuple consisting of three compiler-created tuples; one for the eval() operation, one to describe the *matmul()* process, and another to describe the *eigenvals()* process. A unique tag associates these tuples as belonging to the same set. The eval server requests tuples describing an overall eval() operation. This gives it the tag for a specific eval() operation. Then this tag is used to request one of the associated tuples that describes a process. In turn, this tuple identifies a specific process which is then executed by the eval server. The result of the process execution is placed back into the overall eval() operation tuple, and the eval server begins anew.

9.4.5   Cluster Execution Environment

The execution environment is the tuple space subsystem that facilitates, transparently to the user, both the utilization of available cluster nodes and the preparation of these nodes for participation in the execution of the user's tuple space parallel program. The Deli tuple space implementation refers to these operations collectively as *bootstrapping* the execution environment [7]. When bootstrapping is complete, the execution environment is poised to commence execution of the user's tuple space parallel program. The bootstrapping process in Deli is described here as an example.

The user initiates the bootstrapping sequence by invoking Deli directly at one node, called the host node. The invocation of Deli specifies the tuple space executable program to run and the number of additional cluster nodes desired. A local interprocess communication channel is established for the data and process subsystems that will run on the host node. Next, an external communication port is obtained for communication with other cluster nodes. A communication subsequence then commences with other nodes in the cluster. This subsequence results in each node of the cluster that is participating in the execution obtaining a communication port that can be used by the other nodes. All participating nodes are informed of the communication ports of the other nodes. Determination of which other cluster nodes to include in the execution environment can vary. A list of available nodes can be maintained either statically within the tuple space implementation or read from an external file. The nodes in this list can be selected sequentially or randomly. A nice feature allows a selected node to refuse participation if it is already busy.

After the appropriate number of nodes are included, each node is responsible for instantiating its data and process subsystems. These subsystems have access to the communication ports of all the nodes participating in the application execution. The process subsystem on the original host node begins execution of the user's *main()* routine. The process subsystem on all the other nodes acts as an eval server ready to execute an application-specified process.

9.4.6 Run-time Optimizations

In [3], Bjornson describes several run-time optimizations incorporated into his hash-based tuple space implementation. Inspection of tuple space programs showed that some shared data is only read with the `rd()` operation; thus, these tuples can be safely replicated at each node. Bjornson's tuple space continually monitors itself at runtime, gathering statistics about application communications. If tuple space determines that the tuples of a partition are predominantly being sent to a particular node, then the task of managing these tuples will be dynamically reassigned to the node using the tuples. Lastly, in spite of distributing tuple space data throughout the cluster, it remains possible for a single node to be overwhelmed with data. In this case, Bjornson's tuple space further subdivides the data manager responsibilities at runtime. The application processes are informed lazily of the subdivision and may then direct data to an alternate node. Bjornson also describes the additional protocols necessary for this technique.

9.5 Extensions

The basic tuple space system described thus far can be extended in a number of interesting ways. Extensions accommodating heterogeneity, multiple tuple spaces, persistence, and fault tolerance are discussed here.

Clusters are increasingly being populated with nodes of different capabilities and architectures. Cluster-based systems such as tuple space should accommodate this heterogeneity. Allowing heterogeneous nodes to participate in the distributed, parallel execution of a single application presents several additional implementation issues including data formats (big/little endian, word size, etc.), and binary incompatibility of nodes (e.g., binary image for an Alpha will not execute on an Intel). A typical solution to the data format problem is the use of the XDR extended data representation. Binary incompatibility requires multiple versions of the application executable.

The model of tuple space described in this chapter uses a single tuple space equally accessible by any operation in any process of the application. Some researchers are exploring ways for an application to use multiple tuple spaces; thus, treating a tuple space as a fundamental *object* of the model. Multiple tuple spaces allow for several interesting possibilities: the coordination of distinct applications; levels of security, or access permissions, for an individual tuple space; and new distributed data abstractions.

Another extension has the tuple space memory persist beyond the lifetime of an application, thus decoupling invocations of an application over time. Some communication optimizations may not be possible in a persistent tuple space setting since the tuple space data manager cannot be bundled with the application. There are several open issues including how an application connects to a persistent tuple space and how the tuple space is initially created.

Fault tolerant tuple space systems prevent the loss of entire computations through transactions and checkpoints [1], [11]. Failures can occur for a variety of reasons, both hardware- and software-related. Fault tolerance is especially difficult in a cluster environment since defining a consistent global state across multiple, asynchronous nodes is problematic. Supporting fault tolerance for tuple space is facilitated by the characteristics of tuple space itself. Only a few operations require extension for transactions, and the uncoupled communication and synchronization of tuple space simplifies the recreation of processes during recovery.

9.6 Conclusions

The associative tuple space access and uncoupled communication of tuple space parallel programs are the key to the power and flexibility of this model, but also lie at the heart of the compiler and run-time system implementation challenges, especially in a cluster environment. Compile-time analysis can structure tuple space to significantly reduce the time to find data in tuple space. Run-time strategies counteract some communication inefficiencies. However, gains in performance in a cluster environment can also be made through sophisticated optimizing compiler techniques and corresponding run-time system modifications. The viability of classical intraprocess data flow analyses of tuple space parallel programs has been demonstrated, and a technique for interprocess data flow analysis via analysis of tuple space operations has been developed. Analyses for identifying common tuple usage patterns at compile time and code transformations for improving the underlying message communication in a distributed memory architecture have led to good performance gains at runtime[7]. The static analysis can be performed on a traditionally-based program representation, which also enables standard, sequential analysis of the parallel programs.

9.7 Bibliography

[1] David E. Bakken and Richard D. Schlichting. Supporting Fault-tolerant Parallel Programming in Linda. *IEEE Transactions on Parallel and Distributed Systems*, vol 6(3), pages 287–302, March 1995.

[2] Henri E. Bal. A Comparative Study of Five Parallel Programming Languages. *Distributed Open Systems*, F. Brazier and D. Johansen (Eds.), pages 134–151, IEEE Computer Society Press, 1994.

[3] Robert D. Bjornson. Linda on Distributed Memory Multiprocessors. *PhD Thesis*. Yale University, November 1992.

[4] Nicholas Carriero and David Gelernter. A Foundation for Advanced Compile-time Analysis of Linda Programs. *Languages and Compilers for Parallel Computing*, pages 389–404, Springer-Verlag, 1992.

[5] Nicholas John Carriero, Jr. Implementation of Tuple Space Machines. *PhD Thesis*. Yale University, December 1987.

[6] Evelyn Duesterwald, Rajiv Gupta, and Mary Lou Soffa. Demand-driven Computation of Interprocedural Data Flow. *22nd ACM SIGPLAN-SIGACT Symposium on Principles of Programming Languages (POPL '95)*, pages 37–48, January 1995.

[7] James B. Fenwick, Jr. Compiler Analysis and Optimization of Tuple Space Programs for Distributed-memory Systems. *PhD Thesis*. University of Delaware, August 1998.

[8] James B. Fenwick, Jr. and Lori L. Pollock. Issues and Experiences in Implementing a Distributed Tuple Space. *Software–Practice and Experience*, vol 27(10), pages 1199–1232, October 1997.

[9] James B. Fenwick, Jr. and Lori L. Pollock. Data Flow Analysis Across Tuple Space Process Boundaries. *Proceedings of the International Conference on Computer Languages*, pages 272–281, May 1998.

[10] David Gelernter. Generative Communication in Linda. *ACM Transactions on Programming Languages and Systems*, vol 7(1), pages 80–112, January 1985.

[11] Karpjoo Jeong and Dennis Shasha. PLinda 2.0: A Transaction/Checkpointing Approach to Fault-tolerant Linda. *Proceedings of the 13th IEEE Symposium on Reliable Distributed Systems*, pages 96–105, 1994.

[12] Kenneth Landry and James D. Arthur. Achieving Asynchronous Speedup While Preserving Synchronous Semantics: An Implementation of Instructional Footprinting in Linda. *The 1994 International Conference on Computer Languages*, pages 55–63, May 1994.

[13] Jerrold Sol Leichter. Shared Tuple Memories, Shared Memories, Buses and LAN's – Linda Implementations Across the Spectrum of Connectivity. *PhD Thesis*. Yale University, July 1989.

[14] Timothy G. Mattson. The Efficiency of Linda for General Purpose Scientific Programming. *Scientific Programming*, vol 3(1), pages 61–71, 1994.

[15] Samuel P. Midkiff and David A. Padua. Issues in the Optimization of Parallel Programs. *Proceedings of the International Conference on Parallel Programming*, vol II, pages 105–113, 1990.

[16] K.H. Shekhar and Y.N. Srikant. Linda Sub-system on Transputers. *Computer Languages*, vol 18(2), pages 125–136, 1993.

[17] Stanford SUIF Compiler Group. *The SUIF Parallelizing Compiler Guide Version 1.0*. Stanford University, 1994.

[18] Gregory V. Wilson. *Practical Parallel Programming*. The MIT Press, 1995.

Chapter 10

Debugging Parallelized Code

Patricia Prather Pineo

Department of Mathematics and Computer Science
Edinboro University of Pennsylvania
Edinboro, Pennsylvania, USA

Email: *ppineo@edinboro.edu*

10.1 Introduction

The increased availability of multiprocessor computing environments, including cluster computing environments, has posed a challenge to the traditional von Neumann computational model. In the von Neumann model, memory is tightly held by a processor and is assumed to be a scarce resource. As a result, traditional computing emphasizes memory reuse in order to preserve the resource, which has the unfortunate side effect of reinforcing centralized control.

However, in the emerging parallel and cluster computing environments it becomes evident that the opportunity for distributed control increases when the emphasis on *variable* use is replaced by the definition and availability of *values*. This concept has been explored in a theoretical way by earlier research on dataflow languages and paradigms, and research on functional languages.

It is also possible to achieve freedom from strict sequentiality in the variable space using a traditional declarative language. This chapter describes a two-part process termed Code Liberation. The name Code Liberation reflects the reality that the program is freed from debilitating and unnecessary data dependencies using this technique.

The Code Liberation technique employs both global renaming and name reclamation. Global renaming is the translation of the original program to an equivalent *single assignment* (SA) form. Single Assignment is an equivalent transformation of a program where each value computed is stored in a unique variable name and is never reassigned. It is distinguished from Static Single Assignment form (SSA) wherein variables are reassigned when they occur within repeated code (i.e., loops).

Single assignment removes the unnecessary dependencies between variable names and allows values to be stored and recovered in a unified way, without consideration of applied code transformations. Because each value is carried in a unique name, renamed code can be transformed by unrestricted parallelizing transformations and still be successfully debugged.

Global renaming of a program, however, creates an explosion of names and storage associated with single assignment programs. This problem is resolved in this work by the application of a second stage, Name Reclamation, that eliminates selected single assignments, thus reclaiming names not needed for either parallel execution or debugging before execution occurs. Therefore, additional storage is only needed during execution either to enhance the parallelizability of the program or to enable symbolic debugging of the program.

There are several advantages of using the Code Liberation approach for debugging transformed code. First, it supports high-level debugging in the face of both parallelizing and optimizing transformations. Second, it is transformation-independent, so that the introduction of new parallelizing transformations does not require changes to the method. Third, it is architecture-independent, and can thus be used with a wide variety of target machine specifications, including cluster environments. Fourth, the technique provides for the *recovery* of expected variable values, not just the *discovery* of noncurrency. Fifth, the renaming allows the exploitation of additional parallelism in program code by reducing data dependencies. The first three sections will describe the debugging problem and its solution.

Finally, an overview is given of a prototype system built to solve the debugging problem for FORTRAN 77 code. This section reports results of experiments showing modest storage expansion and superior parallelization using the technique. Overall, this chapter demonstrates that single assignment code, once dismissed as being an extravagant waste of storage space, can be used sparingly and creatively to produce significant economies with the Code Liberation technique.

10.2 Automatic Parallelization

The increasing availability of parallel architectures dictates that appropriate techniques be developed to enable the production of high quality code that effectively exploits the power of these architectures. For example, new parallel programming languages have been developed that enable the construction of explicitly parallel programs. An alternative approach has been to develop parallelizing transformations that convert sequential code into a parallel form targeted for a particular architecture.

The latter approach is attractive for three reasons. First, there are millions of lines of code already written and debugged that cannot feasibly be rewritten for the parallel architecture. Second, programmers find it less difficult to produce correct sequential code than to produce correct parallel code. Third, and most important, the lack of uniformity in parallel architectural styles discourages the development of portable parallel programs. The knowledge necessary to achieve reasonable speedup of a program is heavily dependent on a given parallel architecture.

In the last several years there has been a considerable research effort toward the development of automatic parallelization and partitioning tools. These tools seek to convert portable sequential code to a parallel version, exploiting only the parallelism appropriate to a given parallel processing or distributed architecture. To the extent that these efforts are successful, they take an important step toward moving the architecturally dependent portion of code analysis into the compiler, thus shielding the programmer from low level architectural details. They also allow the automatic parallelization (and improved performance) of preexistent code.

10.3   The Debugging Problem

While automatic parallelization yields many advantages to users who hope to exploit the power of their parallel or distributed computing environments, it complicates the problem of debugging such code. The code that is written may vary significantly from the code that is executed. Because of code modification, deletion, reorganization and parallelization, the *actual* values of variables seen at breakpoints during runtime will often differ from the values *expected* by the programmer viewing the sequential, untransformed code. Such variables are termed *noncurrent*. A variable is noncurrent at a program statement if, at a given program step during execution due to the program transformations that have been applied, the variable contains a value different from the expected value at that program step.

This debugging problem is similar to the problem of debugging optimized code, but more difficult. The extra difficulties arise from the more intrusive nature of the applied transformations and the additional complexities of parallel execution. While transformations typically reorder, delete, or copy code, parallelizing transformations may vectorize loops, unroll loops, segment code into parallel segments, rename variables, or completely reorganize a program. The requirements of execution on a distributed architecture may have introduced synchronization code, task initiation and termination code, or code that downloads variables from shared to private memory spaces. In addition, optimizations are typically applied as part of the parallelization process.

To illustrate this problem, suppose the original code shown in Figure 10.1(a) were to be run on a vector machine. The code cannot be directly vectorized due to the data dependencies that exist in the loop. However, after application of the transformations of scalar expansion, loop splitting, loop interchange and then vectorization, the code appears as shown in Figure 10.1(b). In the debugging of such code, the programmer may insert a breakpoint after statement 4 in the original code and ask for the value of T or I. How is the debugger to respond to such a request? Several distinct approaches to the debugging of transformed code have been used.

One approach is to debug the programs prior to the application of transformations. But there are several strong arguments against this practice. First, the behavior of the transformed program might be different in subtle ways than that of the untransformed code. This is true even though both the compiler and the trans-

1. T=0	1. T(0..M) = 0
2. do 100 I = 1,M	2. do 100 I = 1,M
3. T = T + sqrt(I)	3. T(I) = T(I-1) + sqrt(I)
	100 continue
4. do 100 J = 1, N	4. do 200 J = 1, N
5. A(I,J)=A(I,J-1)/T	5. A(I..M,J)=A(I..M,J-1)/T(I..M)
6. 100 continue	6. 200 continue
(a) original code	(b) vectorized code

Figure 10.1 Syntax changed by parallelizing transformations.

forming software are "correct." Second, the execution time and memory demands of the untransformed code may make it impractical or impossible to debug the original code. This is particularly true of programs that require a real time response. Third, the insertion of communication commands among the many processors may introduce nondeterminism that is absent in the sequential code. Finally, the practice of debugging untransformed code that is then parallelized prior to being put into production requires the simultaneous maintenance of multiple consistent compilers. This is an unnecessary expense incurred by the development environment. For all of these reasons it is preferable to execute and debug the program in its transformed state.

An alternative approach is to force the programmer to directly view and debug the transformed code. This approach requires the user to have familiarity with the parallel constructs available, the architecture, and the mapping from the source to transformed code. It may be very difficult to map certain transformations back to source code (e.g., renaming). Even when the user interacts with the transforming tool in order to direct transformations, it is desirable to shield the user from the complexities of the parallel code where possible, especially since the code was originally written as sequential code.

A preferable approach, and the one advocated here, is to allow the user to execute the transformed code on the parallel system but to debug the code from the viewpoint of the sequential code. This approach allows users to view the form of the program with which they are most familiar, while still debugging the program in its final parallelized form. This approach has been advocated by those studying the related problem of high-level debugging of optimized code[12], [27], [7], [21], [1], [6]. It requires the determination, upon reaching a breakpoint, of whether a requested variable is noncurrent, followed by the retrieval of the variable's expected value if possible. Each of these techniques that attempts to retrieve expected values employs some method for storing values for later retrieval.

10.4   Debugging with Code Liberation

10.4.1   Overview of the Technique

Practical high-level debugging with global renaming is accomplished in five stages. An overview of the technique is given in the algorithm below. Two stages (stages one and three) are introduced to bracket the application of parallelizing transformations (stage two). Their primary purpose is the renaming of the code and the production and maintenance of AVAIL sets (defined below).

Algorithm – Code Liberation Debugging

1. *Globally rename code (IN: original code, OUT: single assignment code; AVAIL sets)*

2. *Apply user chosen parallelization transformations(IN: SA code, OUT:parallelized SA code)*

3. *Reclaim unneeded names (IN:parallelized SA code, OUT: reduced name parallelized code, INOUT: AVAIL)*

4. *Compile (IN:reduced name parallelized code, OUT:executable code)*

5. *Execute code through debugger modified to access AVAIL sets when values are requested*

An AVAIL set is defined for each original source program statement. An AVAIL set contains one entry for each variable in the program, giving the current name (version) in use for that variable following the execution of the statement. Conceptually, AVAIL sets represent the values that should be reportable by the debugger following the execution of this program statement. In a single assignment program, this name will change each time the variable is reassigned and it might be thought of as a version number. For example, the following program segment would be associated with the AVAIL sets as shown. (Undefined variables carry the zero version number). These sets provide the value tracking capability used by the debugger at execution time. Data dependence refers to the implied ordering requirement be-

1. $A = B + C$	1. $A1 = B1 + C1$	$\{A1,B1,C1,D0\}$
2. $D = A - 3$	2. $D1 = A1 - 3$	$\{A1,B1,C1,D1\}$
3. $A = C / D$	3. $A2 = C1 / D1$	$\{A2,B1,C1,D1\}$
(a) original code	(b) renamed code	(c) AVAIL sets

Figure 10.2 Example program representation.

tween two program statements created by reuse of a variable. In Figure 10.2, we say statement 2 is flow dependent on statement 1 (S1 δ S2) because the value A is defined in statement 1 before being used in statement 2. Statement 3 is antidependent on statement 2 (S2 δ^{-1} S3) because variable A must be used in statement 2 before being defined in statement 3. Output dependence occurs when two statements both define a variable; statement 3 is output dependent on statement 1 (S1 δ^o S3).

In Figure 10.3, a simple program is shown passing through the stages of the system. Initially, the code is globally renamed. This first stage produces a semantically equivalent version of the program in single assignment form, which assigns each (potentially non-current) value a unique storage name. The current names at each statement are retained in the AVAIL sets. The reduction of undesirable data dependencies by the renaming can be observed in Figure 10.3. Antidependencies (e.g., S1 δ^{-1} S3) and output dependencies (S6 δ^o S7) are removed in the renamed code. The resulting code has been freed from about half of the original data dependencies and thus allows a more aggressive exploitation of parallelism.

The single assignment code can now be parallelized by software targeted for any desired architecture. The choice of transformations applied in this process is not important to the debugging system. Regardless of where variables are moved, their version names carry the tag required by the debugger for later inquiries. Once the parallelized code has been finalized, it may be that not all the names introduced through renaming are necessary. Some variables must be retained because they enable the reporting of a non-current value at debug time. In Figure 10.3, the programmer (debugging from the viewpoint of the sequential code) may insert a breakpoint after statement 5 and request the value of Z. This breakpoint maps to statement 5 of the parallelized code and the associated AVAIL set indicates that Z2 (see AVAIL set 5) is the proper version of Z to report from the transformed code. Since Z2 must be reported (and not Z1), it is necessary to distinguish between the Zs and therefore the Z2 name must be maintained.

The other reason for not reclaiming names is to allow multiple copies of a variable to be live on different concurrent tasks, thereby enabling the exploitation of parallelism. In this example, A3 cannot share storage with A1, because A1 is simultaneously live on a concurrent process. Similarly, A2 cannot share storage with A1 or A3.

The B2 variable is reclaimable because neither B1 nor B2 needs to be available for debugging purposes on a concurrent task, nor is B1 live on any concurrent task. The decision to reclaim B2 will result in a change in statement 7 of the parallelized code where B2 becomes B1, and an accompanying update to the database in the B entry AVAIL set associated with statement 7 (not shown).

This parallelized program with names reclaimed (which is no longer single-valued) can now be compiled and executed. The programmer, debugging from the viewpoint of the sequential code, places a breakpoint in the sequential code. This breakpoint maps through to the transformed code. When the breakpoint is encountered, a request for a value made by the programmer is trapped by the run-time interface. The interface in turn replaces the variable name requested with the version name associated with the breakpoint position which is stored in the AVAIL data set. The debugger then proceeds to fill the revised request in the ordinary way. In this example, if the programmer places a breakpoint after statement 3, a request for X, T, A or Z will be replaced with requests for X1, T1, A2, or Z1, respectively

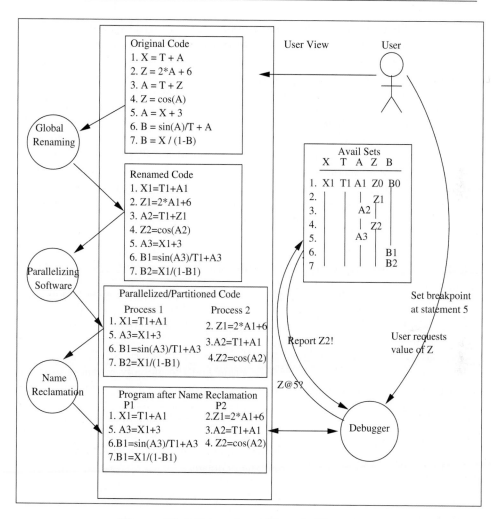

Figure 10.3 Debugging with code liberation.

and these modified requests filled by the debugger. The global renaming and name reclamation processes are presented in greater detail in the following sections.

10.4.2   The Single Assignment Form via Global Renaming

A basic requirement of Code Liberation is the conversion of the input program to single assignment form. This has necessitated development of renaming techniques capable of renaming all structures and data types supported by the source language.

The design decision was made to develop this technique for FORTRAN 77 code. FORTRAN was chosen to remain consistent with the research efforts in parallelization of FORTRAN code and has served as a context for prototyping the method. The technique can be extended to other languages as well.

Thus, the task of global renaming requires developing techniques to rename scalars and arrays found in the structures of FORTRAN, including straight line code, conditionals, counted (DO) loops, uncounted (WHILE) loops, and parameters to subprograms. The objective is to associate with each defined value a uniquely named variable. This requirement is relaxed for compiler-generated control variables, e.g., looping subscripts, but it is firmly upheld for all source program variables. The following sections define transformations for renaming these structures and types. We first consider structured programs with simple types. The following section develops methods for array types. Finally, a generalization of the renaming techniques to handle unstructured code is considered.

10.4.3   Renaming Simple Variables in Structured Code

In this section techniques are developed for scalar variables to ensure that each new value is assigned to a unique variable name, and that no variable name is ever reassigned. The techniques developed for scalars will also serve as models for array renaming techniques.

While the renaming progresses, AVAIL sets are also generated. These sets provide a mapping between the original program and the globally renamed program showing which version number is alive at each statement of the original program for each variable. The sets serve two purposes. During renaming they are used to track the current name space, which reflects the current name of each variable. The current name is used to replace variable uses and is also incremented when variable definitions are encountered. When global renaming is complete, the AVAIL sets are stored for later use by the system and the debugger.

Renaming Sequences and Conditionals

Scalars in straight line code require a new name whenever a variable definition occurs. When the definition of a scalar is encountered in a conditional statement, one new name is generated for each definition, plus one for each variable leaving the conditional as a way to establish a common exit name. It is also important in this transformation to provide for a set of variables entering the ELSE clause that is equivalent to that entering the THEN clause. These principles are illustrated in Figure 10.4. In the code of Figure 10.4(b) X5 and Y3 represent structure exit names and the use of Y1 in statement 6 shows the reinitialization of the name environment when entering the ELSE. This reinitialization of the name environment is also evident in the AVAIL sets shown in Figure 10.4(c). The AVAIL set associated with statement 5 shows Y1 as the reinitialized current name of Y, replacing the Y2 of statement 4.

1. if (P .gt. X) then	1. if (P1 .gt. X1) then	{P1, X1, C1, Y1, B0}
2. X = C + 1	2. X2 = C1 + 1	{P1, X2, C1, Y1, B0}
3. X = X / 2	3. X3 = X2/2	{P1, X3, C1, Y1, B0}
4. Y = C	4. Y2 = C1	{P1, X3, C1, Y2, B0}
	X5 = X3	
	Y3 = Y2	
5. else	5. else	{P1, X1, C1, Y1, B0}
6. X = Y	6. X4 = Y1	{P1, X4, C1, Y1, B0}
	X5 = X4	
	Y3 = Y1	
7. endif	7. endif	{P1, X5, C1, Y3, B0}
8. B = X	8. B1 = X5	{P1, X5, C1, Y3, B1}
(a) original code	(b) renamed code	(c) AVAIL sets

Figure 10.4 Renaming conditionals.

Renaming DO Loops

Scalars defined in loops are renamed by the explicit definition of an array subscripted by a compiler-generated loop iteration variable. Thus X defined in the first loop iteration might be stored in X3(1), X3(2) in the second iteration, and so on. This *expansion* of scalar variables in loops avoids the redefinition of renamed variables in repeated code, and is the distinction between SA code and SSA code. Scalar expansion is the source of much of the additional parallelism exposed by global renaming. The SSA form allows these values to be tracked during debugging.

Though this appears to increase the complexity of the code, it should be remembered that the user will not view the renamed code, but only the original code during debugging. The loop iteration variable is a compiler variable, and thus it is not required to be single-valued. The transformation requires normalization of the iteration variable and the allocation of space at runtime. The allocation is logically a dynamic memory allocation, but is implemented through a function call added to the FORTRAN code since FORTRAN does not directly support dynamic memory allocation. The loop normalization leads to a consistent naming approach in the transformed code and also anticipates work that is done later in loop vectorization and processor assignment phases. In those cases it is natural to assign code by iteration to processors, then to generate the loop variable from the iteration number. Scalars with values entering the loop then redefined within the loop are termed wraparound variables and require special handling. A wraparound variable is a variable that is first used in a loop and later defined. At each loop iteration the value exiting the loop must "wraparound" to the top of the loop. The scalar loop algorithm identifies these variables and generates code that uses the entry value on the first loop iteration, and the appropriate loop wrap value on each subsequent iteration.

```
                              alloc(10)
                              N2(0)=N1                        {entry name}
1. do I = 3, 7, 0.5           do LS = 1,9                     {normalization}
                        1.    I1(LS)=(LS-1)*0.5+3             {generate subscript}
2.  M=TEST * I          2.    M1(LS)=TEST1*I1(LS)
3.  N=cos(M/N)          3.    N3(LS)=cos(M1(LS)/N2(LS-1))
4.  N=TEST + N          4.    N2(LS)=TEST1+N3(LS))           {wrap value}
5.  end do              5.    end do
                              M2 = M1(9)                      {exit values}
                              N4 = N2(9)

(a) original code       (b) renamed code
```

Figure 10.5 Renaming DO loops.

In Figure 10.5 the loop generates nine iterations. The compiler generated Looping Subscript (LS) becomes the normalized iteration variable, allowing the user variables I, M, and N, to be single-valued. The function call *alloc(10)* allocates ten element arrays (0..9) for each of the variables altered in the loop: I1, M1, N3, and N2. Because of its use in statement 3, N2 is identified as a wraparound value and thus is given an entry value before entering the loop and a wrap value in statement 4. Uses of wrap values are designated by the "LS-1" subscript, for example, the use of N2(LS-1) in statement 3. This provides a clear indication that the value originated in the prior iteration. Variables that are computed before being used in the loop, such as M1 and N3, are simply expanded with the LS. Variables used without being defined in the loop, such as TEST1, are not expanded. At the loop termination the final value in each array representing an expanded scalar is renamed to a new scalar, allowing the loop vectors and bounds to die when execution leaves the loop. At the loop head, the AVAIL set entry for each variable modified in the loop is set to a name such as N2(LS-1) or M1(LS-1). This signifies that the value that reaches this program line originates from the prior loop iteration. When the statement of assignment is reached, the AVAIL entry is changed to the current iteration name, e.g., M1(LS).

The example of Figure 10.5 shows that some root names (e.g., N) are now associated with two distinct types; N1 and N4 are scalars while N2 and N3 are arrays. In general, the naming convention will allow creation of objects with the same root name to be of the same type as the root name or to be an array of any size with elements of the root type.

The transformation just described is similar to the parallelizing transformation scalar expansion, extended to expand wraparound variables as well as those defined before use, and to address and regulate the relationship between the expanded scalars' subscripts and the iteration variable. Cytron and Kuck[10] have identified scalar expansion as the single most important transformation to enhance vectorization over a wide variety of programs. This builds the expectation that global renaming may significantly enhance attempts to parallelize sequential programs. Experimental results of this work support this conjecture, showing that useful parallelism in single-valued code increases dramatically.

Renaming WHILE Loops

WHILE loops require incremental allocation of expanded scalar arrays in some cases. First there is an attempt to convert the WHILE loop to an equivalent DO loop. If a variable is discovered within the loop with the qualifications of a loop control variable (constant increment, initial value and termination condition), then conversion is made. Otherwise the loop is retained as a WHILE loop. Entry and exit values are handled in a way similar to DO loops.

1. X = 15	1. X1 = 15
	alloc(MAX)
	X2(0) = X1 {entry names}
	A2(0) = A1
	B2(0) = B1
	LS = 1
2. do while (f(X) .gt. 0)	2. do while (f(X2(LS-1)) .gt. 0)
3. A = X	3. A2(LS) = X2(LS-1)
4. X = f(X)	4. X3(LS) = f(X2(LS-1))
5. B = X	5. B2(LS) = X3(LS)
6. X = g(X)	6. X2(LS) = g(X3(LS)) {wrap value}
	LS = LS + 1
	if (LS mod MAX .eq. 0)
	alloc(MAX)
7. end do	7. end do
	A3 = A2(LS-1)
	Y2 = Y1(LS-1)
	X4 = X3(LS-1)
	B3 = B2(LS-1)
(a) original code	(b) renamed code

Figure 10.6 Renaming WHILE loops.

Since the virtual arrays of scalars being created in WHILE loops have unknown bounds it is necessary to allocate the arrays in chunks. This technique contrasts to an earlier method devised by Cytron and Ferrante[9] that dynamically allocates a scalar on each iteration, using a pointer. Although the objects are unique, the pointer variable itself is *not* single-valued, and the ambiguities arising from its use lead to code which is not parallelizable. The method presented here allows more flexible exploitation of parallelism in the WHILE loop code, especially where pipelining

approaches are relevant. Figure 10.6 shows the renaming of a WHILE loop. When
the attempt to find an iteration variable fails, making conversion to a DO loop impossible, the loop is renamed as a WHILE loop. A looping subscript is used in the
same way, but is explicitly incremented (after statement 6). Only X2 is identified
as a wrap value, but all three expanded names are given entry values, in case the
loop may be entirely skipped. This ensures that the exit values are correct in all
cases. Memory is allocated in chunks of size *MAX* as needed.

Renaming Parameters and Procedures

A method has also been developed for renaming scalar pass-by-reference parameters.
This method applies equally well to pass-by-value and copy-restore parameters. An
analysis of subprograms is first performed to determine which pass-by-reference (or
copy-restore) parameters are redefined in procedure bodies. The formal parameter
list is expanded with a new name for each of these redefined parameters, the second
name being used to return new values to the calling program. These are referred
to as IN and OUT parameters in the discussion below. The procedure calls are
similarly expanded for the actual parameters. In Figure 10.7, subroutines ASUB

```
{main program}              {main program}
    X = 3                        X1 = 3
    call ASUB(X)                 call ASUB(X1)
    call BSUB(X)                 call BSUB(X1,X2)
    print(X)                     print(X2)

subroutine ASUB(X)          subroutine ASUB(X1)
    Y = sqrt(X)                  Y1 = sqrt(X1)
    print(Y)                     print(Y1)
end ASUB                    end ASUB

subroutine BSUB(X)          subroutine BSUB(X1,X4)
    X = X + 1                    X2 = X1 + 1
    X = X / 2                    X3 = X2 / 2
    X = tan(X)                   X4 = tan(X3)
end BSUB                    end BSUB
(a) original code           (b) renamed code
```

Figure 10.7 Renaming parameters and call sites.

and BSUB are renamed first. In ASUB, since X1 is only used, the parameter is not
expanded to IN and OUT values. However, in BSUB, where X1 is modified, the
parameter is expanded to include an X-IN value, X1, and an X-OUT value, X4.
When the main program encounters calls to these subroutines, the revised subroutine definition signals which of the actual parameters will be modified and which

will not. The actual parameter list in the calling program is expanded accordingly. In the call to ASUB, X1 is used only and is not renamed; however, in the call to BSUB, X1 will be updated and is therefore renamed in the context of the calling environment.

This treatment allows additional instances of parallelism to be discovered at procedure call sites, since only expanded parameters will receive output values. For example, in Figure 10.7, both CALLs could be initiated in parallel. In addition, the code maintains strict single-valued properties across procedure calls, except in rare cases where aliases exist.

Since no storage location is ever reassigned, the only alias problem (in FOR-TRAN with COMMON excluded) that persists in this method occurs when the same input parameter is used twice in the actual parameter list. The following code illustrates this problem. Consider the following code:

$$\text{SUBROUTINE CSUB (x,y)}$$
$$x = x + 1$$
$$y = y + 1$$
$$\text{end CSUB}$$
$$\text{main}$$
$$M = 3$$
$$\text{Call CSUB (M, M)}$$

FORTRAN's execution of the above will compute $M = 5$. The renamed CSUB becomes

$$\text{SUBROUTINE CSUB (X1, X2, Y1, Y2)}$$
$$X2 = X1 + 1$$
$$Y2 = Y1 + 1$$
$$\text{end CSUB}$$

If the Main is renamed

$$M2 = 3$$
$$\text{call CSUB ((M2,M3,M2,M4)}$$

the incorrect result $M4 = 4$ will be achieved. The ambiguity arises when choosing the name for the second M in the call CSUB (M,M). If resolved in favor of

$$\text{call CSUB (M2,M3,M3,M4)}$$

then the correct result would be achieved. However, the correctness of this result is determined by the order of the operations in the subroutine and is arbitrary. Such ambiguities invariably result from use of the same variable for more than one of the actual parameters in the call. The ambiguities can only be resolved by costly procedure analysis or through programmer interaction. Since such cases are rare, in this work they are resolved by issuing a warning message to the programmer.

10.4.4   Array Renaming

Arrays can be redefined by partial redefinition, where one specific array element is changed, or by a total redefinition. Generally in renaming arrays, a change to any element will cause the entire array to be copied and a new array object created.

However, when an entire array is redefined, without intervening uses, this can be construed as a total array definition and done on a single array object.

A problem unique to arrays is the implied data dependence inherent in a partial array definition. Consider the assignment statement, $A(7) = X$, that might be found in original code. This assignment changes A and so should cause the creation of a new copy of A, which depends on X in element 7, *and* on the last instance of A to generate all other elements. This introduces an additional complexity into the dependence analysis. Assuming that array A has been renamed to A1, the dependence is expressed explicitly in this work as[1]

$$A2 \left[\Leftarrow A1\right] (7) = X$$

which can be read, "A2 is a copy of A1 except in element 7, which equals X." Figure 10.8 shows that renaming methods for arrays used in straight line and conditional code closely follow the methods developed for scalars.[2]

1. if $A(I) < 100$ then	1. if $A1(I1) < 100$ then
2. $A(I+1) = 0$	2. $A2[\Leftarrow A1](I1+1) = 0$
	$A4 = A2$
3. else	else
4. $A(1) = 3$	4. $A3[\Leftarrow A1](1) = 3$
	$A4 = A3$
5. end if	5. end if
6. $X = A(1)$	6. $X1 = A4(1)$
(a) original code	(b) renamed code

Figure 10.8 Renaming arrays in conditionals.

Renaming Arrays in Loops

Figure 10.9 shows the renaming of arrays in loops. Just as scalars renamed in loops become loop-bounded arrays, so arrays found in loops become arrays of arrays. A new array object is created for each assignment to an array in the loop, and the object number is assigned equal to the iteration variable driving the loop. This iteration id is shown as a superscript in Figure 10.9.[3]

Figure 10.10 illustrates the effect on statement dependencies when renaming arrays in loops. While anti and output dependencies are destroyed, additional flow dependencies are created. The original code contains dependencies

$$S_4 \ \delta^{-1} \ S_5$$
$$S_5 \ \delta \ S_7$$
$$S_7 \ \delta^{-1} \ S_4$$

which prohibits either vectorization or parallelization of the code. Application

---

[1] An equivalent FORTRAN-legal syntax, copy(A1,A2,7,X), is actually inserted into the code.

[2] Equivalent FORTRAN-legal syntax for A4 = A2 is copyall(A2,A4).

[3] Equivalent FORTRAN-legal syntax for $A2^{LS}(I)$ is A2(LS,I).

$$\text{alloc(N1+1)}$$
$$\text{A2}^0 = \text{A1}$$
$$\text{do LS} = 1,\text{N1}$$

1. do I = 1,N   1. I1(LS)=LS
2. A(I)=A(I)+B(2*I)   2. $\text{A2}^{LS}[\Leftarrow \text{A2}^{LS-1}](\text{I1(LS)})=\text{A2}^{LS-1}(\text{I1(LS)})$
                                        $+\text{B1}(2*\text{I1(LS)})$

3. enddo   3. enddo
                                   $\text{A3} = \text{A2}^{N1}$

(a) original code   (b) renamed code

Figure 10.9 Renaming arrays in loops.

of renaming strategies described thus far yields the renamed code shown in Figure 10.10(b).

This code retains only the flow dependence S5 δ S7, but adds the following implied flow dependencies arising from the creation of array copies.

$$S_4 \ \delta \ S_4 \quad S_4 \ \delta \ S_7$$
$$S_5 \ \delta \ S_5 \quad S_7 \ \delta \ S_7$$
$$S_5 \ \delta \ S_4$$

In addition, note that the determination of data dependence in the original code has required an analysis of subscripts, whereas in the renamed code only the named array object is required.

This feature can also be observed in the original code of Figure 10.8(a). Here S_6 is antidependent on both S_4 and S_2 (when I = 0) because the subscripts can be equal, whereas in the renamed code (Figure 10.8(b)) S_6 is flow dependent on S_5 (the creation of A4 is associated with the termination of the IF structure) and does not depend on the subscript choice.

DEF/USE Analysis of Array Names

A further analysis of array definitions (DEF) and references (USE) within the loop is done in an attempt to reduce these added flow dependencies. This analysis does evaluate subscripts in array references to determine whether the particular element used has been altered since loop entry. In Figure 10.10(b), for example, it can be seen that the use of $\text{C2}^{LS-1}(\text{I1(LS)})$ in S_4 refers to an element not yet changed by the loop. Therefore, the same element value could have been drawn from the loop entry version, or C1(I1(LS)). Changing the C array reference name in S_4 from C2 to C1 eliminates $S_5 \ \delta \ S_4$.

The DEF/USE analysis described here is similar to array reference disambiguation described by Wolfe, Nicolau, and others[26],[14], [5], in earlier work but simplified by the renaming that has occurred. First, after renaming, only flow dependencies persist, therefore pseudodependencies need not be considered. Second, the name of the object being used makes its unique birthpoint (definition) explicit.

(a) original code	(b) renamed code
1. X = X + 3	1. X2 = X1 + 3
2. Y = X / 5 - Y	2. Y2 = X2 / 5 - Y1
	alloc(N1+1)
	$A2^0$ = A1 {entry values}
	$C2^0$ = C1
	do LS = 1,N1
3. do I = 1, N	3. I1(LS)=LS {generate subscript}
4. A(I) = B(I) + C(I)	4. $A2^{LS}[\Leftarrow A2^{LS-1}]$(I1(LS))=B1(I1(LS)) + $C2^{LS-1}$(I1(LS))
5. C(I) = D(I) * X	5. $C2^{LS}[\Leftarrow C2^{LS-1}]$(I1(LS))=D1(I1(LS))*X2
6. if (I .lt. N) then	6. if (I1(LS) .lt. N1) then
7. E(I) = C(I)+A(I+1)	7. $E1^{LS}[\Leftarrow E1^{LS-1}]$(I1(LS))=$C2^{LS}$(I1(LS)) + $A2^{LS}$(I1(LS)+1)
8. endif	8. endif
9. enddo	9. enddo
	A3 = $A2^{N1}$
	C3 = $C2^{N1}$
	E2 = $E1^{N1}$
10. X = A(N) + C(N)	X3 = A3(N1)+C3(N1)

Figure 10.10 Renamed arrays in loops before DEF/USE analysis.

Only objects born within the loop are considered. The analysis identifies array objects defined and used within a loop structure and attempts to discard the use.

When it can be shown through analysis that the particular element accessed has not been changed between the loop entry and the access, it will replace the intermediate array name with the loop entry array name. In addition, if there is only a definition and no use of a given array name remaining in the loop, the definition can be handled as a complete object definition and done on a single object (thereby removing the superscript).

Each array use marked with an iteration ID is matched with its definition in the analysis. The analysis is done only if both the Subscript$_{USE}$ and the Subscript$_{DEF}$ have linear form. Suppose Subscript$_{DEF}$ = a*I + b and Subscript$_{USE}$ = c*I + d. In addition, from loop normalization we have I = incr * (LS-1) + init where incr is the loop increment and init is the initial value. In the bounds below, e is -incr if USE subscript is LS -1, 0 otherwise. From these facts, boundary conditions for the iteration variable, I, can be derived.

$$\text{Bound 1:} \quad I = (d - b - e*c)/(a-c)$$
$$\text{Bound 2:} \quad I = (d - b - e*a)/(a-c)$$

If neither boundary condition occurs within the range of I, the used array element has not been changed since the beginning of the loop. In this case it is safe to change the array name to the loop entry name.

When the divisor is zero, a second test is developed. If this inequality is false, it is safe to change the array name.

$$\text{Test 2:}\quad d - b \le e * a$$

Using the appropriate test gives a succinct determination of the dependence relationship between the given use and definition. If there are multiple subscripts in the expression, the DEF/USE analysis considers only the subscript associated with the iteration variable of the loop. Other subscripts are generally related to exterior looping subscripts and are nonvariant for the purposes of this analysis.

In the application of this method to the first DEF/USE pair above, where the components considered are

DEF   USE

(S5) C2LS(I(LS))   (S4) C2 LS-1(I(LS)),

the DEF subscript (I(LS)) yields a = 1, b = 0 (1 * I(LS) + 0), and the USE subscript (I(LS)) yields c = 1, d = 0. Since the USE superscript is LS-1, e = -incr. The increment is extracted from the multiplier in the loop normalization step, S_3: I1(LS) = 1 * LS + 0, giving e = -1. Since a = c, the second test is applied, giving the test

$$d - b \le e * a\ ?$$
$$0 \le -1\quad \text{(false)}$$

The empty solution leads to the change of the USE name to the loop entry name, C1(I(LS)).

Once it is determined which array uses can be safely renamed to the loop entry name, it may be the case that a particular array definition has no further uses within the loop. Recall that arrays that are completely defined without intervening uses are assigned only one array object for the complete definition. Having removed unnecessary array object uses, the loop is now scanned for objects defined but not used within the loop. E1 and A2 are both such objects in Figure 10.10. $E1^{LS}$ will be compressed to E1 and A2 will be similarly changed. The resultant code shown in Figure 10.11 can now be successfully parallelized or vectorized. Thus, the renaming of arrays in loops is accomplished in a two step process, first to rename the arrays, and then to resolve introduced dependencies where possible.

In debugging the code above, the AVAIL range of arrays A and C are marked with a condition, "if I1(LS) < I, report A1 (or C1) else report A2 (or C2)." So, if a breakpoint is set after statement 3, a request for C(3) in iteration 2 would report C1(3), whereas a request for A(6) in iteration 8 would report A2(6).

10.4.5   Renaming Unstructured Code

Techniques have also been developed to rename unstructured code, code modeled as a sequence of simple statements into which GOTO statements (and labels) have been arbitrarily inserted, such as intermediate code. As in structured global renaming, renaming of unstructured code creates single assignment (SA) code in which no variable, once assigned, will ever be altered. The techniques developed here work

1. X2 = X1 + 3
2. Y2 = X2 / 5 - Y
    alloc(N1+1)
    $C2^0$ = C1
    do LS = 1,N1
3. I1(LS)=LS
4. A2(I1(LS))=B1(I1(LS))+C1(I1(LS))

5. $C2^{LS}[\Leftarrow C2^{LS-1}]$(I1(LS))=D1(I1(LS))*X2
6. if (I1(LS) .lt. N1) then
7.   E1(I1(LS))=$C2^{LS}$(I1(LS))+ A1(I1(LS)+1)

8. endif
9. enddo
    C3 = $C2^{N1}$
10. X = A(N) + C(N)

(a) After DEF/USE Analysis

1. X2 = X1 + 3
2. Y2 = X2 / 5 - Y1
    alloc(N1+1)
    C2 = C1
    forall LS in 1..N1 do
3. I1(LS)=LS
4. A2(I1(LS))=B1(I1(LS))
    +C1(I1(LS))
5. C2(I1(LS))=D1(I1(LS))*X2
6. if (I1(LS) .lt. N1) then
7.   E1(I1(LS))=C2(I1(LS))+
    A1(I1(LS)+1)
8. endif
9. enddo

    X3 = A3(N1)+C3(N1)

(b) Parallelized

2. A2(1..N1)=B1(1..N1)+C1(1..N1)
3. C2(1..N1)=D1(1..N1)*X2
4. E1(1..N1-1)=C2(1..N1-1)+A1(2..N1)
(c) Vectorized

Figure 10.11 Array example after DEF/USE analysis is completed.

for any unstructured code, including irreducible code. This algorithm is able to assert join points without the production of a Control Flow Graph. So although it is very general, it still operates in linear time. Details of this approach can be found in[18].

10.4.6   Name Reclamation

After the globally renamed program has been partitioned, parallelized, or otherwise optimized, it is the task of name reclamation to eliminate the unnecessary names. This is accomplished in three steps. First, a maintenance range is computed for each renamed value. This is the set of program statements in the transformed program at which the value may be requested by either the executing program or the debugging programmer. Then using this information, names are reclaimed in the second step. Finally, the AVAIL sets are updated to reflect the name changes.

Maintenance Ranges

As seen previously, there are two reasons for maintaining a name at a program point: 1) it is still **live**, or 2) it still needs to be **available**, for debugging. This determination requires the computation of a maintenance range for each value that includes the entire Live Range of the value and also its Available Range.

The Maintenance Range of a value is a range of program statements in the parallelized (transformed) program over which the value must be retained because it is needed either for execution or may be requested by the debugger. Symbolically,

$$\text{MR}_v = \text{R}_{Av} \cup \text{R}_{Lv}$$

where R_{Av} is the range of original program statements in which the value should be available, now mapped into the transformed code, and R_{Lv} is the *live* range of the value in the transformed code.

It is straightforward to calculate R_{Av} by standard live range analysis with extensions to include statements up through the value redefinition. This is computed by the global renaming stage and stored in the AVAIL data set. However, it is then incumbent upon the name reclamation stage to map these availability ranges into the transformed code. In this stage it is necessary to view both the AVAIL sets and the transformed code to determine when specific variables must be available to serve debugging requests in the transformed program. Discrete locales of availability are combined into one contiguous availability range, since variables are assigned only once and can therefore become available only once.

In the computation of R_{Lv}, it is assumed that the transformed program may be modified for some form of parallel execution. A live range for a value may end on a certain processor, but if the value is also live in a parallel task, it cannot be considered dead until there is a synchronization point between the tasks. Therefore live range analysis in a parallel environment requires an inspection of all tasks that will be in concurrent execution. If a variable is live in only one task P1, then the variable dies when the last use is past. However, if the variable is also live on another task P2, then the variable is not dead on P1 until the P1-P2 synchronization following the last use in P1. Furthermore, the variable is not completely dead until dead on all tasks.

To illustrate these computations using the code of Figure 10.3, the A1 variable is available at statements S1-S2, and must be live at S1-S2. However, since S1 and S2 are on concurrent tasks, the live range is extended to the synchronization point. Therefore, MR_{A1}=S1-S7. Variable Z1 has an AVAIL range of S2-S3 and live range of S2-S3, giving MR_{Z1}=S2-S3. For variable Z2 the AVAIL range, S4-S7, and live range, S4, cross parallel tasks giving a maintenance range MR_{Z2}=S1-S7.

Two variables are said to have overlapping maintenance ranges if they must both be maintained at the same time, as in the case of Z1 and Z2 above. When the two variables have the same root name, e.g., B1 and B2, and nonoverlapping ranges, it is always safe to reuse the address(name). Symbolically, given values V1 and V2,

$$\text{if} \quad \text{MR}_{v1} \cap \text{MR}_{v2} = \emptyset$$
$$\text{and} \quad \text{Root}(V_1) = \text{Root}(V_2)$$

$$\text{then} \quad \mathrm{Addr}\,(V_2) = \mathrm{Addr}\,(V_1).$$

The availability of a value can be seen as a further use in generating maintenance ranges. If viewed in this way, the maintenance range within a basic block can be simply defined as beginning at the first position of use of the variable and extending to the last.

Computation of Maintenance Ranges

In name reclamation, maintenance ranges are computed for each variable in each basic block. These "per block" maintenance ranges are used to create summary maintenance information, such that at each statement it is known whether the maintenance of a particular variable is required at any time prior to this statement, or at any time beyond this statement. This information is derived from the Control Flow Graph (CFG) of the program. Backedges are removed from this graph since the reaching definitions of loop variables are handled by explicit mechanisms in renaming. In addition, irreducible flow graph constructs are resolved by removing edges representing backward branches in the written code. The resulting acyclic CFG is used to determine predecessor and successor blocks. Since there may also be concurrent blocks in the CFG, a block X that is concurrent to a block Y is considered both a predecessor and successor to Y.

This graph is then used to create three maintenance sets per block. A Maintenance Range$_i$ set is computed, which holds a minimum and maximum program location for each variable used or available in basic block$_i$ (BB_i). The computation of availability makes use of original statement line numbers that have been appended to the statement during renaming. These numbers indicate the original statement locations of lines of program code. After the application of program transformations, these numbers will normally be unordered and, in addition, may contain duplicated or missing numbers. However, these numbers provide crucial mapping information. Each time a statement line number is encountered, the associated AVAIL set is queried and any variable available at this line has its maintenance range updated with the present program location (in the transformed program).

After the MR_i sets are computed for the blocks, they are used to compute boolean sets, Pre_i and Post_i, for each block. Given a basic block, BB_i, Pre_i is a set of bits, one for each variable in the renamed program, in which a true value (one) indicates that the variable has a maintenance range in any predecessor of BB_i (including concurrent blocks). Pre_i is calculated from the immediate predecessors of BB_i by $\mathrm{Pre}_1 = \emptyset$ and $\mathrm{Pre}_i = \cup\,(\mathrm{Pre}_j \cup \mathrm{MR}_j)$ where a nonzero entry in $\mathrm{MR}_i.\min_k$ defines a true state and j is an immediate predecessor or concurrent block.

Post_i similarly indicates variables that have maintenance ranges in any successor to BB_i. Post_i is calculated in inverse program order from immediate successors and concurrent blocks by $\mathrm{Post}_{last} = \emptyset$ and $\mathrm{Post}_i = \bigcup\,(\mathrm{Post}_j \cup \mathrm{MR}_j)$, where j is an immediate successor of BB_i or concurrent block.

10.4.7   Reclaiming the Names

Modeled as a Graph Coloring Problem

After the maintenance sets have been computed, names can be reclaimed from the code. The injunction against values sharing a variable name when they have overlapping maintenance ranges allows name reclamation to be modeled as a graph coloring problem[11]. The graph consists of vertices v_i corresponding to each value generated. There is an edge from v_i to v_j whenever v_i and v_j may not share a variable name. Specifically, this results when any of the following is true:

> 1) the variables have different root names,
> 2) the variables have differing dimensionality, or
> 3) the variables have intersecting maintenance ranges.

At the beginning of the name reclamation process, this graph contains n vertices and is colored in n colors, where n is the number of variables in the globally renamed program. Name reclamation seeks to *recolor* this graph, using fewer colors. The reclaimed colors represent names that will not appear in the final executable program.

The graph is traversed starting from any arbitrary node. A color pool is maintained which represents the set of names that have been evaluated and will be retained. This set corresponds to the set of names finally held by the *visited* nodes. As the graph is traversed, an attempt is made to recolor each new node encountered with a color already in the color pool. Each candidate color is tried until one is found that has no conflict with the new node, or the list is exhausted. If the node cannot be recolored (the name cannot be reclaimed), then the node's original color is retained and added to the color pool. Figure 10.12 shows a globally renamed pro-

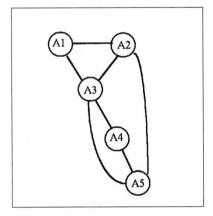

Figure 10.12 Name reclamation by coloring.

gram containing five names, with maintenance range intersections (conflicts) shown as edges. The recoloring starts with an empty color pool and immediately adds A1 to the color set. A2 and A3 are also added because conflicts in the graph do not allow any of these names to share storage. In processing node A4, all colors in the pool (in *last-added* order) will be tested until one is found that does not conflict with A4. If no such color were found, A4 would be retained. However, in this case, after A3 is rejected, A2 is selected to replace A4. In the processing of the A5 node, A3 and A2 are rejected but A1 is selected. The resultant graph contains three names.

An Efficient Implementation for Reclamation

A criticism of coloring algorithms may be that implementation becomes prohibitively expensive because the graphs involved get quite large. This is especially true for graphs created with single assignment programs. In practice, the reclamation algorithm may be implemented without building the graph, using the pre, post and MR sets described above. Collectively they allow the existence of a conflict edge to be easily computed.

At each statement the name of a defined variable, V2, may be reclaimed if there exists another active variable, V1, previously unreclaimed, such that V1 has the same root name and dimensionality as V2 and the two variables possess nonintersecting maintenance ranges. This last condition is computed by checking that $MR_{V1} \cap MR_{V2} = \emptyset$ within the block, that V2 has no maintenance range in a predecessor block, and that V1 has no maintenance range in a successor block. If the

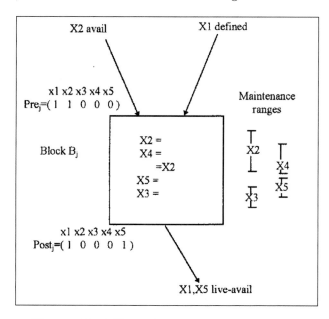

Figure 10.13 Example program representation.

maintenance ranges are disjoint, then the active name replaces the new name and the new name is reclaimed. This causes maintenance sets for the active variable to be updated. If no suitable active name can be found, the new name is retained and added to the active set.

Figure 10.13 illustrates the action of name reclamation. The example is simplified by showing only a single root name. The basic block shown is associated with a pre and post set. These indicate that X1 and X2 have maintenance ranges prior to B and that X1 and X5 have maintenance ranges after B. Beside the block, the (contiguous) maintenance ranges are displayed. Active names that reach the block are {X1}. During the processing of the block, X2 will not be reclaimed by X1 because X2 has a previous maintenance range, and also because X1 has a later maintenance range. X2 is then added to the active set. X4 is also retained because it has a nonempty intersection with X2, and X1 has a post maintenance range. X5 will be subsumed by X4 because pre (X5) is false, post (X4) is false, and X4 and X5 have an empty intersection. This reclamation causes updates to Pre(X4) and Post(X4) such that

$$\text{Pre(X4)} = \text{Pre(X4)} \mid \text{Pre(X5)}$$
$$\text{Post(X4)} = \text{Post(X4)} \mid \text{Post(X5)}.$$

The inblock maintenance ranges of X4 and X5 are also merged and information is retained that X5 is henceforth known as X4 in the *ref-pointer* set. Now X3 cannot be subsumed by X4 because X4 has inherited post(X5). However, X3 can be subsumed by X2, and similar set updates are initiated. The block will finally contain only X2 and X4.

Another form of name reclamation occurs within loops. The name reclamation algorithm will recover the expansion of objects when the loop in question was not chosen for parallelization. In the case of nested loops, each loop is associated with a unique looping subscript. Those associated with parallelized loops are retained while the others are reclaimed. The reconstruction of the looping subscript portion of each name is done whenever the name is added to the active set. At the end of a block's processing, the exiting active set is saved for use by successor blocks. After all blocks are processed, the AVAIL database is updated with the name changes and rewritten for later use by the debugger.

The name reclamation algorithm has three stages. First, the program dependence graph is computed along with the maintenance sets (MR_i, Pre_i, Post_i). Then the Basic Blocks are processed, reclaiming the names. Finally, the AVAIL data base is updated with named changed in the reclamation. The efficiency of this algorithm is bounded by O(plen x $|var|$), where plen is the length of the transformed program, and $|var|$ is the number of variables in the transformed program.

10.4.8   The Debugging Interface

The third piece of software necessary for a full implementation of Code Liberation is the debugging interface. This is a module designed to interface an existing debugger with the Avail database stored and updated by the first two stages of Code Liberation (see Figure 10.3). Its purpose is to enable the debugger to report the expected value when variables are requested by the user at runtime.

Operation of the Debugging Interface

It is assumed that a debugger implements a technique for reporting the present value of a variable when requested. The premise of debugging from the viewpoint of the original code implies that breakpoints will be placed in the original code (which maps through to related locations in the transformed code) and that requests will be made for variables using original names that no longer exist because of the renaming that has occurred. The runtime interface traps a request made for a variable at a breakpoint and replaces it with a request for the particular version of the same variable current at that breakpoint in the unparallelized code. The AVAIL database retains this information from the global renaming stage, with later updates by the name reclamation stage. The debugger can then proceed to fill the new request in the context of the transformed program.

For example, if a breakpoint is placed at statement 17 of some input code, this breakpoint may map to statement 12 of the transformed code. Upon encountering the breakpoint, the programmer may request variable X. This request traps into the debugging interface as a request for X at statement 17. Appealing to the AVAIL database, we may discover that $AVAIL_{17} = [A1, B2(LS), X5]$. The debugging interface will check to see whether X5 has yet been computed. If so, it replaces the request for X with a request for X5. The debugger can then fill the request for X with the value of X5. In the same example, if the value of B is requested, the runtime interface will respond by asking the user which loop iteration is desired. If the answer is "6," then the request for B will be filled with the value of B2(6).

Using this technique all noncurrent data variables can be tracked except for those whose computation has been moved forward past the inserted breakpoint, or entirely removed (as in dead code elimination). In these cases the value will not have been computed and is reported as unavailable due to the transformations performed. A significant advantage of this technique is that it is not dependent on the choice or order of transformations performed, and it is therefore able to provide debugging capabilities across a wide range of transformational environments. Minor modifications allow this technique to enable high-level debugging of optimized programs as well.

10.5   Experimental Results

Global renaming and name reclamation were implemented in about 3500 lines of C code in a system designed for structured FORTRAN 77. The experimental testbed consisted of a group of FORTRAN programs ranging in size from one to several pages, taken from the EISPACK and FFTPACK collections. Programs were renamed, parallelized, names were reclaimed, and programs were examined to determine the occurrence of noncurrent variables in the resulting code.

The issues experimentally investigated were:

1) What is the storage increase associated with Code Liberation?
2) Is parallelization more successful when applied to globally renamed code?
3) Are there significant numbers of noncurrent variables in parallelized code?
4) What is the cost of debugging associated with Code Liberation?

It was discovered that storage increases dramatically when renaming is applied to sequential code, but the increases mostly disappear when name reclamation is applied. The average program's storage increased 3900 times with the creation of Single Assignment code. However, after the application of name reclamation, the final storage requirements were only 2.5 times the original program's requirements.

The degree to which storage is reclaimed varies inversely with the amount of parallelism inherent in the program. Highly parallel programs reclaim fewer names, while programs that undergo no parallelizing transformations have virtually all their introduced names reclaimed. The increases in the test programs ranged from 1.1 to 7.3 times.

It was found that parallelization was dramatically more successful when applied to a globally renamed code. In original code only very small loops could be parallelized and code restructuring was inhibited by the data dependencies. After Code Liberation, many additional loops and larger loops were parallelizable. On the average, the number of lines of code in parallelized loops increased 6.4 times using the Code Liberation technique. In further experimentation [23], attempts were made to tie the increase in program parallelism (which might be viewed as "lexical speedup") with actual speedup measurement figures. A subgroup of programs was executed on the Cray C90 machine at the Pittsburgh Supercomputer Center. Programs were run unoptimized, compiler optimized (unrenamed), and compiler optimized applied after global renaming. Average speedups improved from 12.63 times to 25.39 times using single assignment input.

In an effort to determine the cost of debugging using Code Liberation, further analysis was made of unreclaimed names. Names that are retained because the multiple versions of a variable need to be simultaneously live (as in a parallel loop) were charged to the parallelism column. Conversely, names retained for the purpose of tracking noncurrent variables were charged to debugging. Where code is reordered aggressively, this number of variables charged to debugging can be high, but normally this number is eclipsed by the variables enabling additional parallelism. Over the group of test programs, about 82 percent of the introduced variables enabled parallelization. The remaining 18 percent were required for value tracking noncurrent variables.

Finally, measurements were made of the degree of noncurrentness that exists in the parallelized programs. The number of variable instances was computed as the number of program variables multiplied by the number of program lines. This corresponds to the places at which breakpoints could be set. After transformations were applied to unrenamed sequential programs, the number of noncurrent variable instances was computed by counting the number of lines at which each variable is noncurrent (unreportable at debug time) and summing them over the variable set. The percentage of noncurrent variable instances was unexpectedly high. Almost

10 percent of variables are unreportable at any given program checkpoint on the average.

The number of unreportable variable instances using the Code Liberation technique was then counted. These are places where, if a variable value were requested during debugging, the software would report that the value is unavailable due to transformations applied. This can occur when computations are moved forward or eliminated by the transformations applied. Using the Code Liberation technique only 0.01 percent of variables are noncurrent during debugging.

10.6   Conclusions

These results demonstrate the viability of the method. Not only do they show that the rather invasive nature of parallelizing transformations produces a large percentage of noncurrent variables, but they also seem to indicate that the cost of debugging such code is small. One could argue that only 18 percent of the 2.5x storage increase is due to debugging. Since 18 percent of 1.5x (new unreclaimed names) = .27 it can be concluded that the storage enlargement cost of debugging transformed code is about one quarter of the original storage.

As compilers become increasingly autonomous with respect to the restructuring of code, the problem of debugging such transformed code grows in importance. The approach presented in this chapter offers significant advantages to the user. It can be used with any transformational package without placing requirements or limitations on the transformations chosen. While the benefits of modular systems design are well-known, this characteristic is particularly useful with parallelizing packages, since the rapid evolution of defined transformations cripples a transformation-dependent approach.

The formation of single assignment code conveys advantages to later stages of code analysis as well. Parallelization is far more successful and all transformations requiring data dependence analysis are simplified. Code partitions are also computed easily. This work suggests that single assignment code captures properties of flow dependence that are so fundamental to the further manipulation of code, especially in a parallel environment, that it is a very appropriate first step to create this form from the input code via global renaming.

Name reclamation makes this a practical and workable approach by removing the unnecessary name allocations. Using this technique, parallelized programs are constructed in modestly expanded spaces, with far more parallelized code. And, most importantly, these programs can be successfully debugged.

10.7   Bibliography

[1] Ali-Reza Adl-Tabatabai and Thomas Gross. Source-Level Debugging of Scalar Optimized Code. In *ACM Programming Language Design and Implementation*, pages 33-43, June 1996.

[2] Randy Allen and Ken Kennedy. Automatic Translation of FORTRAN Programs to Vector Form. *ACM Transactions of Programming Languages and Systems*, vol. 9(4) pages 491–542, October 1987.

[3] Francis Allen. Compiling for Parallelism. In *Proceedings of the IBM Europe Institute Course on Parallel Processing*, North-Holland, 1986.

[4] L. Bic, M. Nagel, and J. Roy. Automatic Data/Program Partitioning Using the Single Assignment Principle. In *Supercomputing 89*, pages 551–556, August 1989.

[5] Michael Burke and Ron Cytron. Interprocedural Dependence Analysis and Parallelization. In *Proceedings of the SIGPLAN Symposium on Compiler Construction*, pages 162-175, July 1986.

[6] Max Copperman. Debugging Optimized Code Without Being Misled. In *ACM Transactions on Programming Languages and Systems*, pages 387-427, May 1994.

[7] D. Coutant, S. Meloy and M. Ruscetta. DOC: A Practical Approach to Source-Level Debugging of Globally Optimized Code. *SIGPLAN '88 Conference on Programming Language Design and Implementation*, pages 125-134, June 1988.

[8] Ron Cytron, Jeanne Ferrante, Barry Rosen, Mark Wegman, and Kenneth Zadeck. Efficiently Computing Static Single Assignment Form and the Control Dependence Graph. *ACM Transactions on Programming Languages and Systems*, vol. 13(4) pages 451–490, October 1991.

[9] R. Cytron and J. Ferrante. What's in a Name? -or- The Value of Renaming for Parallelism Detection and Storage Allocation. In *Proceedings of ACM Conference on Parallel Processing*, pages 19–27, 1987.

[10] R. Cytron, D. Kuck and A. Veidenbaum. The Effect of Restructuring Compilers on Program Performance for Highspeed Computers. In *Computer Physics Communications*, vol. 37, pages 39-48, 1985.

[11] G. J. Chaitin. Register Allocation and Spilling via Graph Coloring. In *SigPlan 82 Symposium on Compiler Construction*, pages 98–105, 1982.

[12] John Hennessy. Symbolic Debugging of Optimized Code. *ACM Transactions on Programming Languages and Systems*, vol. 4(3) pages 323–344, July 1982.

[13] Holzle, Chambers, and Ungar. Debugging Optimized Code with Dynamic De-optimization. *SigPlan 92 Conference on Programming Language Design and Implementation*, pages 32-43, June 1992.

[14] A.A. Nicolau Runtime Disambiguation: Coping with Statically Unpredictable Dependencies. *IEEE Transactions on Computers*, pages 663-678, May 1989.

[15] P. P. Pineo. The High-level Debugging of Parallelized Code using Code Liberation. Ph.D. Thesis Department of Computer Science, University of Pittsburgh, *Technical Report 93-07*, April 1993.

[16] P. P. Pineo. Code Liberation – A Tool for Refitting code to a Parallel Environment. PARLE '94 Conference, *Lecture Notes in CS #817*, Springer-Verlag, pages 167-179, July 1994.

[17] P. P. Pineo. An Efficient Algorithm for the Creation of Single Assignment Forms. In *Proceedings of Hawaii International Conference on System Sciences, HICSS-29*, vol. 1, pages 213–222, January 1996.

[18] P. P. Pineo. The Efficient Creation of Single Assignment Forms from Unstructured Code. In *Journal of Parallel Algorithms and Applications*, pages 1–22, Winter 1997.

[19] P. P. Pineo and M. L. Soffa. A Practical Approach to the Symbolic Debugging of Parallelized Code. In *Proceedings of the Intl Conference on Compiler Construction, Lecture Notes in CS #786*, Springer-Verlag, pages 339-356. April 1994.

[20] P. P. Pineo and M. L. Soffa. A Practical Approach to the Creation of Single Assignment Code. In *Proceedings of PACT '95*, pages 149–158, June, 1995.

[21] Lori Pollock and Mary Lou Soffa. High-Level Debugging with the Aid of an Incremental Optimizer. In *Proceedings of the 21st Hawaii Intl Conference on System Sciences*, January 1988.

[22] V. C. Sreedhar and G. R. Gao. A Linear Time Algorithm for Placing ϕ-nodes. In *Proceedings of POPL '95*, pages 62-73, January 1995.

[23] B. Walters and P. Pineo. Parallelizing Single Assignment Code for a Vector Supercomputer. *Technical Report 95-8*, Allegheny College Department of Computer Science, June 1995.

[24] Roland Wismuller. Debugging of Globally Optimized Programs using Dataflow Analysis. ACM SIGPLAN *Conference on Programming Language Design and Implementation*, pages 278–289, June 1994.

[25] Michael Wolfe. *Optimizing Supercompilers for Supercomputers.* MIT Press, Cambridge, MA, 1989.

[26] Michael Wolfe and Uptal Bannerjee. Data Dependence and its Application to Parallel Processing. In *Intl Journal of Parallel Programming*, vol. 16(2), pages 137-178, 1987.

[27] Polle Zellweger. An Interactive High-Level Debugger for Control-Flow Optimized Programs. In *Proceedings of the ACM Software Engineering Symposium on High-Level Debugging*, pages 159-171, March 1983.

Chapter 11

WebOS: Operating System Services for Wide-Area Applications

Amin Vahdat*, Thomas Anderson† and Michael Dahlin‡

*Department of Computer Science
Duke University
Durham, NC, USA
Email: *vahdat@cs.duke.edu*

†Department of Computer Science and Engineering
University of Texas
Austin, TX, USA
Email: *dahlin@cs.utexas.edu*

‡Department of Computer Science
University of Washington
Seattle, WA, USA
Email: *tom@cs.washington.edu*

11.1   Introduction

While the World Wide Web has made geographically distributed read-only data easy to use, geographically distributed computing resources remain difficult to access. As a result, wide-area applications that require access to remote CPU cycles, memory, or disk must be programmed in an ad-hoc and application-specific manner. For example, many popular services, such as Digital's Alta Vista or Netscape's download page, are geographically replicated to improve bandwidth, reduce latency, and improve availability because no single connection onto the Internet can support tens of millions of users. Today, such replication is manually managed on both the server and the client side—users are forced to poll several essentially equivalent services and system managers must manually distribute updates to replicas. This situation will only get worse as Internet usage continues to grow at exponential rates.

To address these problems, we have built WebOS, a framework for supporting geographically distributed, highly available, incrementally scalable, and dynamically reconfiguring applications. WebOS includes mechanisms for global naming, persistent storage, remote process execution, resource management, authentication, and security. We use WebOS to demonstrate the synergy of these services in simplifying the development of wide-area distributed applications and in providing more efficient global resource utilization. The WebOS framework enables a new paradigm for Internet services. Instead of being fixed to a single location, services can dynamically push parts of their functionality out onto Internet computing resources, and even all the way to the client.

Dynamically reconfiguring and geographically mobile services provide a number of advantages, including: (i) better end-to-end availability (service-specific extensions running in the client mask Internet or server failures), (ii) better cost-performance (by dynamically moving information closer to clients, network latency, congestion, and cost can all be reduced while maintaining server control), and (iii) better burst behavior (by dynamically recruiting resources to handle spikes in demand). For example, Internet news services experience an order of magnitude increase in traffic as a result of breaking news stories (e.g., a U.S. presidential election or the recent release of the Starr report). The WebOS framework enables services to handle such demand through dynamic replication. Recently, there has been a push toward the distribution of active components in the network through technologies such as Active Networks [15] and Java. One goal of WebOS is to provide a framework to enable application developers to utilize programmable and active network components.

This chapter presents an overview of the individual components that make up the WebOS design and prototype implementation. The end goal is to provide a platform for the development and deployment for wide-area applications. Toward this end, we demonstrate an extensible mechanism for running service-specific functionality on client machines and show that this allows for more flexible implementation of name resolution, load balancing, and fault tolerance. Second, we provide a file system abstraction that combines persistent storage with efficient wide-area communication; this combination simplifies the implementation of a number of wide-area applications, including Internet chat described below. Next, we describe a security infrastructure that facilitates the fine-grained transfer of rights between multiple wide-area administrative domains.

To demonstrate the utility of WebOS as a substrate for the development of wide-area applications, we motivate and describe our implementation of Rent-A-Server, an application that allows for transparent, automatic, and dynamic replication of HTTP service across the wide area in response to client access patterns. Rent-A-Server also demonstrates the power of exporting operating system abstractions

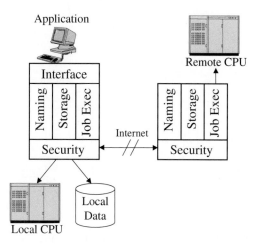

Figure 11.1 High-level system design.

to wide-area applications. Our experience with developing Rent-A-Server quantitatively demonstrates improved application behavior, as measured by client latency and consumed wide-area bandwidth. Further, our experience qualitatively demonstrates that WebOS services simplify both the design and implementation of Rent-A-Server.

The rest of this chapter is organized as follows. In Section 11.2 we present an overview of WebOS system components, before describing individual system components in more detail in Sections 11.3-11.6 which present: (i) programmable location and retrieval of wide-area resources through Active Names, (ii) WebFS, a global cache coherent filesystem, (iii) authentication for secure access to global Web resources, and (iv) a process control model supporting secure program execution and mechanisms for resource allocation. Section 11.7 describes in detail the design, implementation, and performance of one application built on WebOS, Rent-A-Server. Section 11.8 presents related work, leading to our conclusions in Section 11.9.

11.2   WebOS Overview

In this section, we provide a brief overview of the major WebOS components; together, they provide the wide-area analogue to local-area operating system services, simplifying the use of geographically remote resources. Figure 11.1 presents the design of the system at a high level. Applications are presented with a uniform interface to global computational resources. The three primary system interfaces include naming, persistent storage, and job execution. A security system cuts across all three interfaces, allowing, for example, authenticated access to global data or re-

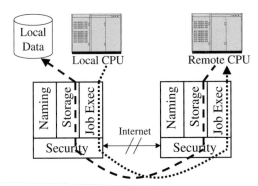

Figure 11.2 Transparent access to remote resources.

mote computational servers. Individual interfaces allow for existing applications to take advantage of new functionality (i.e., transparent access to network resources) without, in many cases, requiring redesign or even recompilation of the application.

The system interface attempts to make remote resources as easy to access as local ones. Thus, the job execution interface allows for the spawning of processes both locally and remotely. For remote execution, the job execution system on one machine contacts its counterpart on a remote machine to request remote execution, as illustrated in Figure 11.1. The security system mediates all cross-domain requests to ensure that the communication is secure (through encryption), that the identity of the requester is authenticated, and that access control lists are properly consulted for authorization on the remote site.

To illustrate the utility of the system design, consider the following example. A user wishes to spawn multiple simulations. To distribute load, some of the simulations will run on a local processor, while others will run on a remote processor. Job requests for both local and remote execution will utilize the same interface. For local execution, the request will flow from the application to the job execution system. In turn, the security system is used to authenticate the identity of the principal requesting execution and also to determine whether the principal is authorized to run jobs on the local processor. If so, the requested job is spawned in a virtual machine to ensure that a buggy or malicious program does not compromise local system integrity. The steps for remote execution are similar and summarized in Figure 11.2. The request for remote execution flows from the local processor through the job execution system and into the local security system. The local security system then establishes a secure channel to the security system on the target host. The job execution request is transmitted over this channel along with the identity of the requester. Once the request reaches the remote host, authentication, authorization, and execution in a virtual machine proceeds as in the local case.

Continuing with this example, simulations spawned on remote hosts will still require data files stored on the user's local host. To satisfy such data requests, the application utilizes the system interface to access the persistent storage system as described in Figure 11.2 (e.g., using a globally unique name provided by the naming system to uniquely identify the desired data file). Requests flow from the remote processor into the storage system and then to the security system. The security system establishes the identity of the process requesting the data file. As with job execution, the security systems on the remote and local nodes establish a secure channel to transmit the file request along with the identity of the process making the request. The local storage system, in cooperation with the local security system, determines if the requester possesses the proper set of privileges to obtain the identified data file. If so, the contents of the file are returned encrypted to the remote node for processing by the simulation. The remote storage system caches the contents of the file for optimal performance, avoiding the need for potentially slow wide-area access on subsequent file accesses. The local and remote storage systems cooperate to provide cache consistency in the case where the data file is updated to ensure proper behavior of the simulation program.

Given this description of the WebOS system architecture, the next four sections describe in more detail the design and implementation of the four primary WebOS components: naming, persistent storage, security, and remote execution.

11.3   Naming

In this section, we present the design of Active Names to address the problem of locating resources distributed and replicated across the wide area. Active Names support performance and flexibility in the deployment of network services. An Active Name extends the traditional name/binding translation by executing a program to directly retrieve a resource (not just its binding). Interposing a program on the naming interface provides a natural way to express semantics desired by wide-area network services. For example, code for an Active Name can: (i) manage server replicas, choosing the least loaded, closest server to a particular client, (ii) utilize application-specific coherence policies to locate caches with fresh entries, or (iii) store user preferences for page contents (e.g., specific headlines, stock quotes, weather reports). As an added advantage, the code for an Active Name is location independent, meaning that it can run at various points in the network to exploit, for example, locality, available computation, and/or available bandwidth.

The principal contribution of Active Naming is a unified framework for extensible and application-specific naming, location, and transformation of wide-area resources. Specifically, the goals of the system are to: (i) conveniently express in a unified framework a wide variety of existing approaches to replication, load balancing, customization, and caching, (ii) allow simple implementation and deployment of new naming extensions as they become necessary and available, (iii) compose any number of Active Name extensions into a single request (as opposed to the more ad-hoc, often mutually exclusive, nature of existing techniques), and (iv) minimize latency and consumed wide-area bandwidth in evaluating Active Names by integrating naming with higher level Web services.

Thus, Active Names provide a framework for binding names to programs and for chains of programs to cooperate in translating a name to the data that name represents. We chose Java as the implementation language for Active Name programs to leverage a number of system features, such as portability, object serialization, remote method invocation, and stack introspection. At a high level, Active Names are strings that take the following format:

```
namespace/name
```

The namespace field of an Active Name uniquely identifies a *Namespace Program* to be run to translate the name field of an Active Name into the resource it represents. A Namespace Program owns a portion of the global namespace (e.g., CNN) and has the freedom to bind subnames (e.g., CNN/frontpage) in a service-specific manner. Active Name evaluation requests are transmitted to *Active Name Resolvers*. These resolvers are arranged in a cooperating mesh distributed across the wide area, with a local resolver assumed to be available on client machines or on local proxies in the case of underpowered clients. Active Name Resolvers export a standard environment for the execution of Active Name code. The resolver allows, for example, access to a local cache and also enforces security and resource limitations. In designing the interface to system resources, we focus on the twin (and often contradictory) goals of simplifying the implementation of the code bound to an active name, and of allowing the maximum flexibility with respect to performance optimizations.

Namespace programs are location independent, meaning that they can be evaluated at the Active Name Resolver capable of most efficiently evaluating a particular Active Name. Responsibility for name resolution is often successively passed from resolver to resolver. Since name resolution can take place multiple hops away from the client, our name resolution model supports multiway RPCs. In this way, we reduce latency by avoiding multiple round-trip communications in returning the resource represented by an Active Name back to the client. With multiway RPCs, the resolver that successfully evaluates an Active Name transmits the resource directly back to the client. We support this model with *after-methods*, a list of additional Namespace Programs that run after evaluation of the initial Active Name completes. One instance of an after-method supports multiway RPC by encapsulating the state necessary to transmit results back to the client. After-methods also conveniently express client or service-specific filters on data once the raw resource is produced at an Active Name Resolver. For example, one application implemented using after-methods is distillation [7], transformation of Web content to better match client characteristics (e.g., before transmitting an image to a device with a small screen and a slow network, the image is first reduced in size and converted to black and white).

The process of evaluating Active Names is summarized in Figure 11.3. Clients transmit an Active Name to a nearby Active Name Resolver that is either colocated with the client or available on a local proxy. The resolver consults its local cache

Active Name Resolver

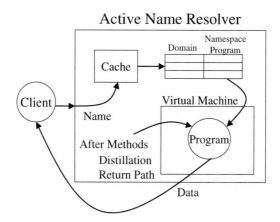

Figure 11.3 The Active Name evaluation process.

for the availability of the resource corresponding to the Active Name. Assuming a miss, the resolver consults a table mapping Active Name domains to the Namespace Program responsible for evaluating it. If the code is not available locally, the system falls back on HTTP and a well-known transformation on the namespace to retrieve the program remotely (the code is then cached to amortize this cost over multiple references to the same namespace). The resolver executes the Namespace Program in a virtual machine to enforce security and resource consumption limitations. The resolver also associates a list of per-client after-methods with the Namespace Program, e.g., a distillation program responsible for returning data back to the client once evaluation of the Active Name completes. Note that, if necessary, Active Name evaluation can be handed off to a remote resolver and that Namespace Programs can attach additional after-methods.

A number of services have been implemented in the Active Naming framework [18]. In this chapter, we will describe the application of Active Names to one such service, load balanced access to replicated Web services. Today, many service providers are replicating their services across both the local and wide area to achieve better performance, scalability, and availability. A principal problem with replication is determining which replica to access from the client's perspective. Current techniques range from placing the onus entirely on the end user to randomly directing requests to a set of replicas at the IP level to providing network support for sending requests to the nearest replica. Unfortunately, a large number of variables must be considered to optimally choose among replicas. Considerations include replica load/processing power, network connectivity, and incomplete replication (as is often the case with, for example, FTP mirror sites where only portions of a site are actually replicated). For example, even considering only variable CPU load and network connectivity (bandwidth, latency), one replica will often be optimal for one

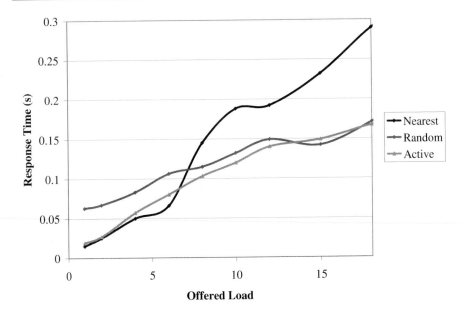

Figure 11.4 Performance of multiple wide-area load balancing algorithms.

client, whereas a different replica is optimal for a second client.

Active Naming allows service-specific programs to account for any number of variables in choosing a replica, including client, server, and network characteristics. Figure 11.4 summarizes the results of an experiment demonstrating the importance of introducing programmability into the decision-making process. For these measurements, between one and 18 clients located at U.C. Berkeley attempt to access a service made up of two replicated servers, one at U.C. Berkeley and the second at the University of Washington. The clients use one of the three following policies to choose among the replicas. *DNS Round Robin* (labeled "Random" in Figure 11.4) maps hostnames to multiple IP addresses. The binding returned to clients requesting hostname resolution is done in a round robin fashion, distributing requests evenly across available replicas. *Distributed Director* [3] (labeled "Nearest" in Figure 11.4) runs specialized code in routers to allow services to register their current replica membership. Requests (at the IP packet level) bound for a particular service are automatically routed to the closest replica (measured by hop count), achieving some level of geographic locality. *Active Names* (labeled "Active" in Figure 11.4) uses the number of hops (as reported by traceroute) from the client to the replicas to bias the server choice. Replicas farther away are less likely to be chosen than nearby replicas. However, this weighing is biased by a decaying histogram of previous performance. Thus, if a replica has demonstrated better performance in the recent past, it is more likely to be chosen.

Figure 11.4 shows the average latency perceived by clients continuously requesting the same small 1 KB file from the replicated service. The x-axis presents offered load, varying the number of clients simultaneously requesting the file (varying from 1 to 18). The y-axis shows the average latency in seconds perceived by the clients. The graph shows that at low load the proper replica selection policy is to choose the "nearest" replica in Berkeley because accessing the Seattle server would consistently incur higher latency as a number of wide-area links must be traversed. This is the policy implemented by Distributed Director and this policy shows the best performance at low load. However, as load increases, the Berkeley replica begins to become overloaded, and the proper policy is to send approximately half the requests to the Seattle replica. In this regime, the cost of going across the wide area is amortized by the high load at the Berkeley server. Such load balancing is implemented by DNS round robin, which achieves the best performance at high load.

The simple Active Naming policy is able to track the best performance of the two policies by accounting for not just distance, but also previous performance. At low levels of load, both distance and previous performance heavily bias Active Naming toward the Berkeley replica. However, as load increases and performance at the Berkeley replica degrades, an increasing number of the requests are routed to Seattle, achieving better overall performance.

11.4   Persistent Shared State

WebOS seeks to raise the level of abstraction for large-scale distributed programs that manipulate shared state. Today, many such applications share state and transfer control using a network communication abstraction that relegates caching, cache consistency, security, transactional updates, and location-independence to application programmers. Following the analogy that it is often simpler to program parallel applications using shared memory as opposed to message passing, we contend that a global cache coherent filesystem abstraction will simplify the implementation of many applications. For example, our experience with our prototype system, WebFS, demonstrates that the caching, consistency, and security provided by the system greatly simplifies the implementation of a number of wide-area applications, including Internet chat and Rent-A-Server, described below.

Providing these abstractions to diverse applications in a wide-area network is challenging. For example, some applications require strong cache consistency while other applications, such as an Internet news service, may prefer weaker consistency to reduce overhead or to ensure that network failures do not delay updates. Therefore, a focus of our design is to provide flexibility so that demanding applications can control details of how key abstractions are implemented. We believe this approach is crucial for an Internet filesystem both because different applications have different demands and because the Internet's scale, limited performance, and unreliability can make it expensive to provide stronger guarantees than applications strictly require. WebFS associates a list of user-extensible properties with each file to extend basic properties such as owner and permissions, cache consistency policy, prefetching and cache replacement policy, and encryption policy. These properties are set and accessed through the UNIX `ioctl` system call.

Currently, WebFS implements the last writer wins [10] cache consistency protocol to support traditional file access, an append-only coherence policy supporting applications such as Internet chat or whiteboard, and an IP multicast-based [5] update/invalidate protocol for widely-shared, frequently updated data files. We believe that providing IP multicast support at the filesystem interface will simplify the development of applications, such as news services, that disseminate nearly identical information to large user populations. To demonstrate this point, we have implemented a stock ticker application that regularly distributes (through multicast file writes) updated stock prices to interested clients performing blocking read operations.

WebFS is implemented as a dynamically loadable Solaris filesystem extension interfacing at the kernel's vnode layer. The vnode layer makes upcalls to a user level WebFS daemon for file accesses not cached in virtual memory. WebFS uses a URL-based namespace, and the WebFS daemon uses HTTP for access to standard Web sites. Thus, WebFS allows unmodified UNIX programs to take URLs (and URLs in a pathname syntax) in place of conventional file names (e.g., `ls /http/now.cs.berkeley.edu/WebOS/`). We chose to use URLs as the global namespace and HTTP for transport because of its wide deployment and our desire to provide backward compatibility with existing distributed applications. Since it is preferable to export a namespace with location independent names, we are currently investigating combining Active Names with WebFS to provide Uniform Resource Name (URN) support for WebFS file names. Additionally, if the server site is also running WebFS, then authenticated read/write access and cache consistency are enabled through our own custom extensions to HTTP.

To quantify the benefits available from the WebFS framework, we implemented two versions of an Internet chat application with identical semantics. One version of the application is message-based, with statements sent over sockets to all parties within a chat room. The second version utilizes a WebFS file to represent a "log" of the conversation within a given room. The filesystem interface is well-matched to chat semantics in a number of ways: (i) file appends and reads abstract the need to send and receive messages, (ii) the chat file provides a persistent log of chat activity, and (iii) access control lists allow for private and secure chat rooms (through the security mechanisms described in Section 11.5). The initial implementation consisted of 1200 lines of Java code in the client and 4200 lines of C++ code in the server. By using WebFS to handle message transmission, failure detection, and storage, the size of the chat client code was reduced to 850 lines, while the WebFS interface entirely replaced the 4200 lines of chat server code. The main reason for this savings in complexity was the replacement of separate code for managing communication and persistent storage of chat room contents with a single globally accessible and consistent file.

11.5   Security and Authentication

Applications operating across the wide area are susceptible to a variety of potential attacks by sophisticated adversaries. To motivate the need for a wide-area security system, consider the simple example of a user wishing to run a simulation. Typically, if the simulation were executed locally, the program would run with all the user's privileges. When running the same simulation remotely, however, it is necessary to assign to the program the least set of privileges necessary to complete its task (e.g., read access to an input file and write access to an output file). This confinement of privileges protects users if the remote machine is compromised; while the simulation data may be usurped, the user's identity and other private files will hopefully remain secure. To provide this level of protection, a wide-area security system must provide fine-grained transfer of rights between principals in different administrative domains. The goal of our security abstraction is to transparently enable such rights transfer.

11.5.1   Validating and Revoking Statements

A principal contribution of our security architecture, called CRISIS, is the introduction of *transfer certificates*, lightweight and revocable capabilities used to support the fine-grained transfer of rights. Transfer certificates are signed statements granting a subset of the signing principal's privileges to a target principal. Transfer certificates can be chained together for recursive transfer of privileges. The entire chain of transfers is presented to reference monitors for validation, allowing for confinement of rights (e.g., a reference monitor can reject access if any principal in a chain of transfers is not trusted). Transfer certificates form the basis of wide-area rights transfer in WebOS, supporting operations such as delegation, privilege confinement, and the creation of roles (as described below).

   All CRISIS certificates must be signed and counter-signed by authorities trusted by both endpoints of a communication channel. A Certification Authority (CA) generates *Identity Certificates*, mapping public keys to principals. In CRISIS, CAs sign all identity certificates with a long timeout (usually weeks) and identify a locally trusted on-line agent (OLA) that is responsible for counter-signing the identity certificate and all transfer certificates originating with that principal. The endorsement period of the counter-signature is application-specific, but typically on the order of hours. Redundancy employed in this fashion offers a number of advantages: (i) to successfully steal keys, either both the OLA and CA must be subverted or the CA must be subverted undetected, (ii) the CA is usually left off-line since certificates are signed with long timeouts, increasing system security since an off-line entity is more difficult to attack, (iii) a malicious CA is unable to revoke a user's key, issue a new identity certificate, and masquerade as the user without colluding with the OLA [4], and (iv) system performance is improved because certificates can be cached for the timeout of the counter-signature, removing the need for synchronous three-way communication in the common case.

Transfer certificates can be revoked modulo a timeout. Revocation is used not only for exceptional events such as stolen keys, but also applies to common operations such as revoking the rights of a remote job upon its completion or revoking the rights of a login session upon user logout. To revoke a particular privilege, the OLA that endorses the certificate must be informed that the certificate should no longer be endorsed. Once the timeout period for the endorsed certificate expires, the rights described by the certificate are effectively revoked because the OLA will refuse reendorsement for that certificate.

11.5.2 Processes and Roles

Given the ability to authenticate principals, CRISIS also requires a mechanism for associating privileges with running processes. Each CRISIS node runs a security manager responsible for mediating access to local resources and for mapping privileges to security domains. In CRISIS, all programs execute in the context of a security domain. For example, a login session creates a new security domain possessing the privileges of the principal who successfully requested login. A security domain, at minimum, is associated with a transfer certificate from a principal to the local node allowing the node to act on the principal's behalf for some subset of the principal's privileges. Restricting the rights available to a process is further detailed in Section 11.6.

In the wide area, it is vital for principals to restrict the rights they cede to their jobs. For example, when logging into a machine, a principal implicitly authorizes the machine and the local OS to speak for the principal for the duration of the login session. It is often convenient to associate names with a specific subset of a principal's privileges. This functionality is achieved in CRISIS through named roles. A principal (user) creates a new role by generating an identity certificate containing a new public/private key pair and a transfer certificate that describes a subset of the principal's rights that are transferred to that role; an OLA chosen by the principal is responsible for endorsing the certificates. Thus, in creating new roles, principals act as their own certification authority [14]. The principal stores the role identity certificate and role transfer certificate in a purse of certificates that contains all roles associated with the principal.

11.5.3 Authorization

Once a request has been securely transmitted across the wide area, and properly authenticated, the remaining task is authorization, determining whether the principal making the request should be granted access. CRISIS employs Access Control Lists (ACLs) to describe the principals and groups privileged to access particular resources. File ACLs contain lists of principals authorized for read, write, or execute access to a particular file. Process execution ACLs are a simple list describing all principals permitted to run jobs on a given node.

To determine whether a request for a particular operation should be authorized, a reference monitor first verifies that all certificates are unexpired and signed by a public key with a current endorsement from a trusted CA and OLA. In doing so, the reference monitor checks for a path of trust between its home domain and the domains of all signing principals. The reference monitor then reduces all certificates to the identity of single principals. For transfer certificates, this is accomplished by working back through a chain of transfers to the original granting principal. Finally, the reference monitor checks the reduced list of principals against the contents of the object's ACL, granting authorization if a match is found.

11.6   Process Control

To simplify development of wide-area applications, WebOS makes execution of processes on remote nodes as simple as forking a process on the local processor. As with the local case, the WebOS process control model addresses issues with safety and fairness. On local machines, safety is provided by execution in a separate address space, while fair allocation of resources is accomplished through local operating system scheduling mechanisms.

A resource manager on each WebOS machine is responsible for job requests from remote sites. Before executing any job, the resource manager authenticates the remote principal's identity and determines if the proper access rights are held. To maintain local system integrity and to ensure that running processes do not interfere with one another, the resource manager creates a virtual machine for process execution. These virtual machines interact with the CRISIS security system to enforce rights restriction associated with different security domains. Thus, processes will be granted variable access to local resources through the virtual machine depending on the privileges of the user originally responsible for creating the process.

We use Janus [8] to create such a virtual machine. Processes in the virtual machine execute with limited privileges, preventing them from interfering with the operation of processes in other virtual machines. Janus uses the Solaris /proc filesystem to intercept the subset of system calls that could potentially violate system integrity, forcing failure if a dangerous operation is attempted. A Janus configuration script determines access rights to the local filesystem, network, and devices. These configuration scripts are set by the local system administrator on a per-principal basis.

11.7   Rent-A-Server

This section describes the design, implementation, and performance of Rent-A-Server, a general model for graceful scaling across temporal and geographic spikes in client demand for a particular service. Our particular implementation focuses on Web service, and enables overloaded HTTP servers to shed load onto idle third-party servers called surrogates that use the WebOS framework to coherently cache data from the primary server. The surrogate is able to satisfy the same HTTP requests as the original server, including requests for both static and dynamically generated objects (e.g., data pages and CGI script results). The implementation and performance of Rent-A-Server illustrates the power of using a unified system interface to wide-area resources and of dynamically migrating services across the Internet.

11.7.1   Current Approaches

Current efforts to distribute HTTP server load focus on either distributing load across a fixed set of machines maintained by the owner of the data or distributing data across (proxy) caches under client (not server) control. Many HTTP server implementations achieve scalability by replicating their data across a fixed set of servers at a single site and then using the Domain Name Service (DNS) to randomly distribute requests across the servers. Unfortunately, this approach requires that each site purchase enough computing power and network bandwidth to satisfy peak demand.

Mirror sites are also used to improve locality and to distribute load, but this manual approach requires more effort to set up the mirrors and to maintain data consistency across the mirrors. Further, users must specify which mirror to use, which is both inconvenient and unlikely to yield a balanced load across sites. Finally, as with the approach of running multiple servers at one site, mirror sites are allocated statically. The system must always maintain enough mirrors to deal with its peak loads, and the location of mirrors cannot be shifted to address shifts in geographic hotspots.

Another approach to distributing load, caching proxies, is used to reduce server load and to improve network locality. To use a proxy, groups of clients send all of their requests to their proxy machine. The proxy machine attempts to satisfy the requests from its local cache, sending the requests to the remote server if the cache cannot supply the data. If proxies satisfy many requests to the server through their caches, both server load and network congestion are reduced.

However, proxies are conceptually agents of Web clients rather than of Web servers. Thus, in some instances they provide a poor match to the requirements of overloaded services. First, proxy servers cache only data pages. A proxy must send all requests for CGI scripts to the original server (a separate publication [17] describes an approach for relaxing this limitation). Second, because servers regard proxies as ordinary clients, the proxy can supply stale data to its clients because of the limitations of HTTP cache consistency protocols. As an example of the importance of having server-controlled rather than client-controlled load distribution, some sites have recently asserted that proxy caches violate copyright laws by storing site content. In effect, the proxies are reducing generated advertising revenues by hiding page access counts.

11.7.2   System Design

In this subsection we demonstrate how WebOS services simplify the implementation of this application. The architecture of the Rent-A-Server is described in Figure 11.5. Active Names are used for load balanced access to HTTP services.

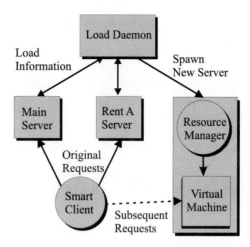

Figure 11.5 Rent-A-Server architecture. HTTP servers periodically send load information to a load daemon. In response to an update, the load daemon transmits the state of all servers. In turn, the HTTP servers transmit this state information as part of the HTTP header to Active Name programs. The clients use this information to determine which server to contact for their next request. When the load daemon notices that the service as a whole is becoming overloaded, it contacts the resource manager on an available surrogate to create another server replica. WebFS is used to securely transmit any executables or data files needed to start the server.

Periodically (currently every tenth response), servers piggyback service state information to clients in the HTTP reply header. This state information includes a list of all servers currently providing the service. The following information is included for each server: its geographic location, an estimate of its processing power, an estimate of current load, and a time period during which the server is guaranteed to be active.

Each Rent-A-Server maintains information about client geographic locations (location is sent by Active Name programs as part of the HTTP request) and its own load information in the form of requests per second and bytes transmitted per second. Each Rent-A-Server periodically transmits this state information to a centralized load daemon. The load daemon is currently a separate process; however, its functionality could be rolled into an elected member of the server group. The load daemon is responsible for determining the need to spawn or to tear down Rent-A-Servers based on current load information and client access patterns. It also transmits server group state (e.g., membership and load information) to each member of the server group, which is in turn piggybacked by the servers to clients as part of HTTP replies, as described above.

Once the load daemon determines the need to spawn an additional server, it first

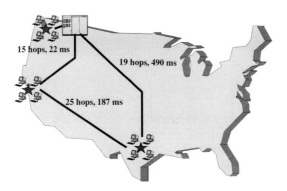

Figure 11.6 Rent-A-Server experimental setup. Clients at Seattle, Berkeley, and Austin act as clients of a service. For fixed server measurements, only a single server exists at the Seattle site. For Rent-A-Server measurements, the system begins with the single Seattle server, but additional servers are spawned at Berkeley and Austin in response to client load.

determines a location for the new Rent-A-Server. The new server should be located close to any hotspots in client access patterns to conserve bandwidth and minimize client latency (this policy has not yet been implemented). Once the target machine is selected, the load daemon establishes an SSL channel with the surrogate's resource manager. The load daemon then creates transfer certificates for the surrogate to access the WebFS files containing the executables (e.g., HTTP server) or internal service state (e.g., CGI scripts or internal database).

When setup negotiation is completed, the surrogate site builds a Janus virtual machine to execute the necessary programs (in our case an arbitrary HTTP server) to establish a service identity at the surrogate. The virtual machine ensures that the surrogate's system integrity is not violated by a buggy executable or a malicious server. Both the service executable and any necessary service state are securely accessed and cached on demand through WebFS. The load daemon propagates the identity of the new surrogate to other members of the server group, which in turn transmit the identity and location of the new server to Active Name programs. Tear down of a surrogate is accomplished when client demand subsides and the load daemon decides not to renew leases with a surrogate. The load daemon removes the surrogate from the appropriate ACLs.

11.7.3 Performance

To demonstrate the power of dynamic resource recruitment available from our approach, we measure the performance of Rent-A-Server when placed under a heavy synthetic load. While our measurements are preliminary and the system is not ready for production deployment, the measurements in this section suggest that further refinement of this model can potentially lead to improved wide-area Web service. Figure 11.6 depicts our wide-are experimental setup. Eight Sun Ultra workstations at each of Seattle, Berkeley, and Austin acting as clients of a Web service. Each client continuously requests the same 1 KB HTML file. Initially, there is a single HTTP server located in Seattle running Apache 1.2b6 on a Sun Ultra workstation. As described below, two surrogate Sun Ultra's are available at Berkeley and Austin to demonstrate the utility of Rent-A-Server. All the machines run Solaris 2.5.1.

Figure 11.6 also depicts the relative connectivity of the three sites, as measured by `traceroute` and `ping` on a weekend night. The reported numbers demonstrate best-case connectivity information. As shown in the figure, connectivity between Berkeley and Seattle is quite good, with only 22 ms round trip latencies reported by ping. Packets traveling from Berkeley to Austin have 187 ms latency, with approximately two percent of the packets dropped. Connectivity between Seattle and Austin is quite poor, with 490 ms latency and 20 percent of packets dropped.

During the experiment, each client machine starts eight client processes that continuously retrieve copies of the same 1 KB HTML file through an Active Name program. The results of our tests are summarized in Figure 11.7. The graphs plot average client-perceived latency in seconds as a function of elapsed time, also in seconds. Figure 11.7(a) shows performance for the case where only a single server is available in Seattle. The graph shows that performance for clients at Berkeley and Seattle is quite poor, averaging approximately 3 seconds to retrieve the 1 KB HTML file from the Seattle server. Clients at Austin suffer from even worse performance, widely varying in average latency between 4 and 10 seconds. The poor performance of the Berkeley and Seattle results from an overloading of the single HTTP server in Seattle. The performance for the Austin clients relative to the Berkeley and Seattle clients is explained by the poor network connectivity between Austin and the HTTP server located in Seattle.

Figure 11.7(b) shows the improved performance available from using Rent-A-Server. In this case, approximately 90 seconds into the experiment, Rent-A-Server's load daemon spawns off an additional server at Berkeley. At this point, latency for both the Berkeley and Seattle improves into the .75 second latency range. Latency for the Austin clients is still poor because of the poor network connectivity between Austin and both Seattle and Berkeley. Thus, 200 seconds into the experiment, a third server is spawned at Austin, with a corresponding improvement in latency for the Austin clients. What is not shown on this graph is the corresponding savings in wide-area bandwidth as clients at Berkeley and Seattle fall back to local servers as opposed to traversing wide-area links to reach the Seattle server.

The performance of Rent-A-Server demonstrates the power of dynamically recruiting resources for wide-area services. However, it is equally important to provide a convenient interface for application development. Our implementation of Rent-A-Server in WebOS consists solely of the load daemon and additions to the Apache HTTP server to transmit state information to the load daemon and to transmit aggregate service state (in HTTP headers) to the clients. The load daemon consists

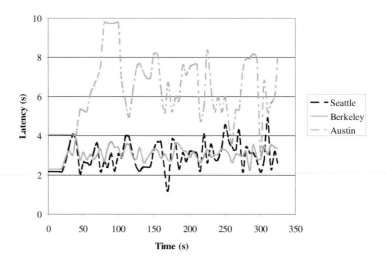

(a) Fixed Server

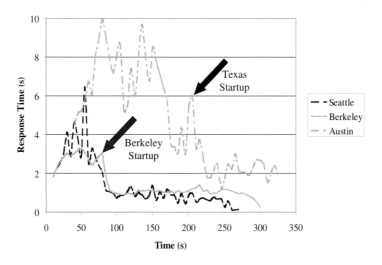

(b) Rent-A-Server

Figure 11.7 Rent-A-Server performance.

of 1000 lines of C++ code, and we added 150 lines of C code to Apache. Beginning with the WebOS framework, our prototype of Rent-A-Server was operational in less than one week.

11.8   Related Work

A number of recent efforts exploit computational resources available on the Internet for wide-area parallel programming, including Legion [9], Globus [6], and Globe [19]. WebOS shares a need for similar underlying technology with these systems (such as the need for a global namespace and filesystem). However, these systems focus on a programming model for computing across the wide area, while our work focuses on system level support for building and running wide-area applications.

Our work draws upon a large body of previous work in filesystems exporting a global namespace, including AFS [10], Alex [2], Coda [11], and Bayou [16]. The main differentiating point between WebFS and these earlier works is backward compatibility with the HTTP namespace and a security model appropriate for wide-area access. We plan to build on the work done in Coda and Bayou to address issues of replication and fault tolerance in the wide area.

The CRISIS security work is loosely based on the DEC SRC security model [12]. Relative to their work, one of our contributions is to simplify the model by using transfer certificates as the basis of fine-grained rights transfer across the wide area. Transfer certificates provide an intuitive model for both rights transfer and account-ability, as they allow a complete description of the chain of reasoning associated with a transfer of rights. Neuman [13] discusses distributed mechanisms for authorization and accounting. Neuman's work has much the same vision as our own, namely limited capabilities in addition to ACLs. His work proposes a more general capability model. However, the capabilities are not auditable because proxies do not carry a chain of transfers. Further, Neuman's work is secret key as opposed to public key, meaning that synchronous communication is required for each transfer of rights.

The Active Networks proposal is to modify Internet routers to be dynamically programmable, either at the connection or packet level [15]. The goal is to make it easier to extend network protocols to provide new services, such as minimizing network bandwidth consumed by multicast video streams. As in our work, a major motivation is to move computation into the Internet to minimize network latency and congestion. WebOS can be seen as a logical extension of Active Networks, where the active computing elements in the Internet can be servers in addition to the individual processors inside of routers operating on packet streams.

11.9   Conclusions

This chapter describes the design and implementation of WebOS, a system infra-structure supporting efficient development and deployment of wide-area applica-tions. Our experience with the system demonstrates the synergy available from exporting traditional operating system functionality to wide-area applications. In addition, we make the following specific contributions within the system framework. First, we show that extending server functionality onto client machines allows for more flexible implementation of name resolution, load balancing, and fault tolerance. Second, by providing a filesystem abstraction combining communication and persistence with flexible support for coherence protocols, we simplify the implementation of a number of wide-area applications. Next, we present a security system enabling the fine-grained transfer of rights between multiple wide-area protection domains. We also show how this combination of system abstractions supports the implementation of Rent-A-Server, an HTTP server capable of dynamically replicating itself across the Internet for both improved client latency and more efficient utilization of wide-area link bandwidth.

11.10   Bibliography

[1] Eshwar Belani, Amin Vahdat, Thomas Anderson, and Michael Dahlin. The CRISIS Wide Area Security Architecture. In *Proceedings of the USENIX Security Symposium*, San Antonio, TX, pages 12–26, January 1998.

[2] Vincent Cate. Alex – a Global Filesystem. In *Proceedings of the 1992 USENIX Filesystem Workshop*, pages 1–12, May 1992.

[3] Cisco Systems. Distributed Director. `http://www.cisco.com/warp/public/751/distdir/technical.shtml`, 1997.

[4] Bruno Crispo and Marc Lomas. A Certification Scheme for Electronic Commerce. In *Security Protocols International Workshop*, pages 19–32, Cambridge UK, April 1996. Springer-Verlag LNCS series vol. 1189.

[5] Stephen E. Deering. Multicast Routing in a Datagram Internetwork. *Ph.D. Dissertation*, Stanford University, December 1991.

[6] Ian Foster and Carl Kesselman. Globus: A Metacomputing Infrastructure Toolkit. *International Journal of Supercomputer Applications*, vol 11(2), pages 115–128, February 1997.

[7] Armando Fox, Steven Gribble, Eric Brewer, and Elan Amir. Adapting to Network and Client Variability via On-Demand Dynamic Distillation. In *Proceedings of the Seventh International Conference on Archictectural Support for Programming Languages and Operating Systems*, pages 160–170, October 1996.

[8] Ian Goldberg, David Wagner, Randy Thomas, and Eric Brewer. A Secure Environment for Untrusted Helper Applications. In *Proceedings of the Sixth USENIX Security Symposium*, July 1996.

[9] Andrew Grimshaw, A nhNguyen-Tuong, and William Wulf. Campus-Wide Computing: Results Using Legion at the University of Virginia. *Technical Report CS-95-19*, University of Virginia, March 1995.

[10] John Howard, Michael Kazar, Sherri Menees, David Nichols, M. Satyanarayanan, Robert Sidebotham, and Mike West. Scale and Performance in a Distributed Filesystem. *ACM Transactions on Computer Systems*, vol 6(1), pages 51–82, February 1988.

[11] James Kistler and M. Satyanarayanan. Disconnected Operation in the Coda Filesystem. *ACM Transactions on Computer Systems*, vol 10(1), pages 3–25, February 1992.

[12] Butler Lampson, Martín Abadi, Michael Burrows, and Edward Wobber. Authentication in Distributed Systems: Theory and Practice. In *The 13th ACM Symposium on Operating Systems Principles*, pages 165–182, October 1991.

[13] B. Clifford Neuman. Proxy-Based Authorization and Accounting for Distributed Systems. In *Proceedings of the 13th International Conference on Distributed Computing Systems*, May 1993.

[14] Ronald Rivest and Butler Lampson. SDSI–A Simple Distributed Security Infrastructure. `http://theory.lcs.mit.edu/~cis/sdsi.html`, 1996.

[15] David Tennenhouse and David Wetherall. Towards an Active Network Architecture. In *ACM SIGCOMM Computer Communication Review*, pages 5–18, April 1996.

[16] Douglas Terry, Marvin Theimer, Karin Petersen, Alan Demers, Mike Spreitzer, and Carl Hauser. Managing Update Conflicts in Bayou, a Weakly Connected Replicated Storage System. In *Proceedings of the Fifteenth ACM Symposium on Operating Systems Principles*, pages 172–183, December 1995.

[17] Amin Vahdat and Thomas Anderson. Transparent Result Caching. In *Proceedings of the 1998 USENIX Technical Conference*, pages 25–37, June 1998.

[18] Amin Vahdat, Michael Dahlin, Amit Aggarwal, and Thomas Anderson. Active Names: Flexible Location and Transport of Wide-Area Resources. *Technical Report*, Duke University, February 1999.

[19] Maarten van Steen, Philip Homburg, and Andrew Tanenbaum. The Architectural Design of Globe: A Wide-Area Distributed System. *Technical Report IR-422*, Vrije Universiteit, March 1997.

Part II

Java for High Performance Computing

Java inherently supports computing across a distributed network of computers where each computer may be a different platform. As the Java language and platform matures, vendor implementations of the Java Virtual Machine (JVM) and associated tools place a greater focus on better performance. This in turn makes high performance computing over a cluster of various computers using Java as the underlying platform a viable alternative. This part explores the various features of Java that make it a good candidate for high performance computing.

The basic object model in Java needs to be extended to correctly support distributed computation involving cooperating objects from distinct JVMs. Chapter 12 describes the distributed object model in general, and then focuses on the Java distributed object model that is the basis of Remote Method Invocation (RMI) in Java. It then discusses the CORBA model, which is now supported in Java. This is followed by a comparison of the RMI and CORBA models.

Orthogonal to the distributed object model is the parallel programming models that are supported on Java. Chapter 13 describes the various flavors of parallel programming models currently supported in Java. Some of these are included in the Java Development Kit (JDK), including the Java threads API. Others, such as jMPI and JPVM, are being developed outside Sun Microsystems and are Java implementations of popular message passing libraries for high performance computing. Finally, others such as JavaSpaces is under development at Sun Microsystems and is not yet released as part of the JDK.

A Java language binding for structured SPMD programming is the topic of discussion in Chapter 14. It starts with a description of process groups, subgroups, and subranges, following that with issues that arise in a language binding for global variables, program execution control, and operators. It ends with two programming examples, namely, Cholesky decomposition and Fox's algorithm for matrix multiplication.

The last chapter of this part, Chapter 15, focuses on web-based parallel computing with Java, differentiating it from cluster-based parallel computing. It discusses the various issues that arise when considering Java as a viable platform for web-based parallel computing. The chapter ends with a case study for the JET platform, giving some performance results.

Chapter 12

Distributed-Object Computing

Rajeev R. Raje, Zhiqing Liu, Sivakumar Chinnasamy, Joseph Williams,
Wilfred Mascarenhas, Ming Zhong

Department of Computer and Information Science
Indiana University Purdue University Indianapolis
Indianapolis, Indiana 46202-5132, USA

Email: {*rraje, zliu, schinnas, jwilliam, wmascare, mzhong*}*@cs.iupui.edu*

12.1 Introduction

The enormous growth and the popularity of the Internet and the World-Wide Web
have emphasized the power of distributed (or clustered) computing. As we approach
the next millennium it is safe to predict that the next generation of computing systems will be based upon the distributed paradigm. The technological advances in
the processor and the networking architectures are providing us with the appropriate facilities to migrate towards this new paradigm. Distributed systems exhibit
the following characteristics: a) a presence of interconnected machines, b) open
(heterogeneous) hardware and software systems, c) complete autonomy (local or
decentralized control) over the hardware and software resources, d) dynamic system configuration and integration, and e) (in some cases) time-sensitivity of the
expected solution.

These inherent characteristics require a different software-development approach
for distributed systems from the one practiced for centralized systems. Due to its
properties of encapsulation and inheritance, the Object-Oriented (OO) approach
has been accepted as an effective solution to manage the complexity of developing
any industrial strength software system [1]. Encapsulation provides a clean separation between the interface and the implementation, thereby avoiding the ripple-
carry effect of changes in implementations. Inheritance provides an evolutionary
approach to the development of complex software systems than a revolutionary one,
thus making them more resilient to changes. The advantages of the OO approach
for centralized systems have been extensively studied and well understood. We

249

believe that the OO approach can provide similar benefits to distributed systems. The concept of a large number of autonomous objects ("a sea of objects"), each with a specific functionality, residing in different address spaces, dynamically discovering each other and communicating/collaborating/integrating with each other by message passing, meshes well with the distributed computing model, thus giving rise to the distributed-object model. Hence, it is hardly a surprise that distributed systems can be effectively and efficiently programmed using the principles of the distributed-object model.

Related Work

As appealing as it may be, the application of OO principles to distributed systems is far from simple due to the presence of heterogeneity and the lack of centralized control. Also, distributed systems are more prone to failures as compared to centralized systems. Many models and environments [3]–[7] have been suggested by academia and industry for distributed-object computing.

Among the above mentioned alternatives for distributed-object computing, the prominent ones are CORBA [4], [5], Java-RMI [3], [5], DCOM [6], [8], and Voyager [7]. We briefly explore these four alternatives in this chapter. We describe their characteristics, programming details, and performance via a simple matrix multiplication example. Due to the space constraints, we are not able to provide the entire code-listings for this example. However, we are providing code-templates to the sufficient level of detail to enable the reader to write applications using these alternatives.

For the purpose of brevity, this chapter is not intended to present the most comprehensive details of each of these approaches. It will, however, provide a general overview to allow the readers to understand the principles and to write applications programs using these paradigms.

12.2 CORBA

Object Management Group (OMG)[1] was formed by eight companies in 1989 as a non-profit organization to hasten the introduction of standardized object software and reduce the cost and complexity of software applications. OMG's mission is to promote the theory and practice of object technology for the development of distributed computing systems. Now a consortium of over 800 vendors, OMG is the driving force behind Common Object Request Broker Architecture (CORBA). It should be noted that all the information about OMG, including its objectives and background, is obtained from OMG's website, http://www.omg.org.

---

[1]OMG, CORBA, ORB, IIOP, CORBAservices, OMG Interface Definition Language (IDL) are registered trademarks of the Object Management Group.

12.2.1   Basic Model – CORBA 2.0 Architecture

Object Management Architecture (OMA) forms the basis for all OMG specifications, including the Reference Model and the Object Model. The OMA provides the conceptual infrastructure on which all OMG specifications are based. The Object Model defines the way an object and its visible characteristics are described in a heterogeneous environment and the Reference Model defines object-interactions. The CORBA specification [9], [10] is the widely referenced specification adopted by OMG. Many commercial implementations of CORBA, such as VisiBroker and Orbix, are available.

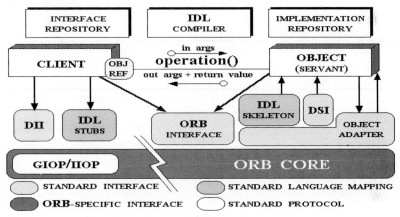

Figure 12.1 CORBA 2.0 architecture.

Figure 12.1 [11] shows the CORBA 2.0 architecture. The central theme of the architecture is the presence of the ORB (Object Request Broker). A Client is an object requesting a service. Clients invoke the services of Object implementations (servers) only through the ORB and there is no direct object to object connectivity. The Object Implementation contains the data and realization of methods for objects.

The ORB Core delivers requests to servers and returns the responses to corresponding client(s). The ORB is a set of programs that implement the interfaces and provide for IIOP (Internet Inter Object Protocol). The ORB Core hides the location, implementation, and execution state of the server objects. It also provides an easy way for clients to create a new object and to get a reference to it. The ORB provides object references for uniquely identifying CORBA objects.

ORB Interfaces are basic interfaces that are common to everyone using the ORB. They provide functionalities for *stringification* (conversion of the object references to strings for storage purposes), *destringification*, and the creation of argument lists for DII (Dynamic Invocation Interface).

Interoperability between different ORBs is made possible through GIOP (Global Inter ORB Protocol), IIOP, and ESIOP (Environment Specific Inter ORB Protocol). The GIOP specifies the standard transfer syntax and a set of message formats for communication between ORBs over any connection-oriented network architecture. It uses CDR (Common Data Representation) for underlying data representation. The IIOP provides a common framework for mediated Inter ORB bridging. CORBA 2.0 specifies a common format for object references that are exchangeable over IIOP, referred to as Interoperable Object Reference (IOR). ESIOPs are out-of-the-box interoperation mechanisms for networks using distributed computing framework(s) other than CORBA. While ESIOPs are optional, GIOP and IIOP (or a half-bridge connecting to an IIOP transport) are mandatory.

IDL (Interface Definition Language) stubs and skeletons provide an illusion of a remote method call to appear like a local call.They are described in subsection 12.2.2.

Interface Repository (IR) is a CORBA object that allows applications to get on-the-fly knowledge of other IDL interfaces. It makes CORBA a self-describing system by providing the information of all the registered IDL interfaces.

Implementation Repository is a run-time repository containing relevant information, such as the classes and their IDs, about object implementations. It is used by the ORB to locate and activate an object.

Dynamic Invocation Interface (DII): All the IDL interfaces have been derived from CORBA::Object. Hence, all objects support an operation *create_request*, which, by invoking, a client can create a dynamic request for the server object. Dynamic invocation can be either synchronous or asynchronous.

Dynamic Skeleton Interface (DSI) is the server side counterpart of DII. Using DSI, servers can be implemented without having the static precompiled IDL skeletons. DSI can service both static and dynamic invocations.

Object Adapter (OA) acts as the intermediary between the Object implementations and the ORB core. Although CORBA 2.0 provides only the Basic Object Adapter(BOA), object implementations can support multiple OAs. An OA performs functions such as activation/deactivation of objects, generation and interpretation of object references, and registration of object implementations.

12.2.2   OMG IDL(Interface Definition Language) and its Mapping

The CORBA model allows interoperability between heterogeneous objects (i.e., objects implemented in different languages). This is achieved by using OMG's Interface Definition Language (OMG IDL). It is used to describe object interfaces in a standard manner. IDL is a declarative language and its interfaces are similar to the interfaces in Java and abstract classes in C++. The grammar of IDL is an extension of a subset of the ANSI C++ standard. The IDL compiler generates the client-side stub and the server-side skeleton. These stub and skeleton act as a connection between the client and the server. The stub is a proxy of the remote methods of the server. The client can invoke operations on the stublike local methods. The skeleton is the counterpart of the stub on the server side. OMG provides mappings from IDL to different implementation languages (such as C and C++).

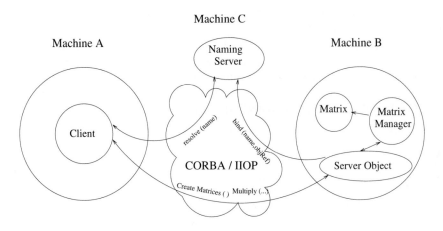

Figure 12.2 A Matrix Multiplication Example.

12.2.3   CORBA Object Services

CORBA Object Services are nothing but a set of interfaces and objects used for the handling of objects (invoking and implementing). Currently, CORBA provides about 15 object services. The prominent ones are: a) Naming Service, which helps the clients in finding the object implementations based on their name, b) Trading Service, which is similar to 'Yellow Pages,' allows objects to advertise their services and to bid for contracts, and c) Event Service, which provides for an event-channel interface that distributes events among components. Other services are Persistent Object Service, Life Cycle Service, Transaction Service, Concurrency Control Service, Relationship Service, Externalization Service, Query Service, Licensing Service, Property Service, Time Service, Security Service, and Collection Service.

12.2.4   A Matrix Multiplication Example

We now describe, as an example, the development of a CORBA-based matrix multiplication using the naming service. Figure 12.2 shows the classes and the objects involved in this example. The entire setup can be configured in a single workstation or distributed across a network. The `Matrix` class contains the necessary attributes and methods used to describe the concept of a matrix. The `MatrixManager` class exports the matrix creation and manipulations operations, such as multiplication and addition. The `MatrixServer` contains the server program, which initializes the ORB and registers the object with CORBA naming service. The `MatrixClient` implements the client code. The overall development process is: a) create a IDL file containing the interfaces to be supported and the user defined exceptions; b) use the code generated by the *idl2java* (supplied with the *VisiBroker*) compiler as a template and write the object implementations; c) implement the server program; and d) implement the client code.

We have implemented this example using JDK1.1, VisiBroker 3.1 and WinNT 4.0. This example does not use any VisiBroker-specific utilities and, hence, it should be easily portable to other CORBA 2.0 compliant ORBs.

Step 1: Create the .idl file–MatrixCalculator.idl

```
MatrixCalculator{
    // Specify the declarations of datatypes and methods to be used.
    typedef sequence<float> oneDArray;
    typedef sequence<oneDArray> twoDArray;
      // Specify the interfaces for Matrix class.
      interface Matrix {
         attribute unsigned short Row;
         attribute unsigned short Col;
         attribute twoDArray myMatrix;
         void Initialize (in float val);
         void Randomize ();
         float getElement (in unsigned short row, in unsigned short col);
         void setElement(in unsigned short row,in unsigned short col,in float val);
         void Display();
    };
      //Specify the Exception.
      exception IncompatibleSizeException {string explanation;};
      // Specify the interface for Matrix Manager class.
      interface MatrixManager {
        Matrix newMatrix();
        Matrix newFixedMatrix(in unsigned short row, in unsigned short col);
        Matrix Multiply (in Matrix A, in Matrix B) raises(IncompatibleSizeException);
      };
};
```

Step 2: Generate stubs, skeletons and implement the interfaces

Compile the .idl file using the command: `idl2java MatrixCalculator.idl -no_comments -no_tie`. The `-no_comments` option suppresses the comments and `-no_tie` option declares that we are not using 'ties' (which are meant for delegation based implementations for non-OO languages) [5]. The idl2java compiler creates a separate directory, `MatrixCalculator`, and puts all the files generated in this directory. The idl2java compiler also provides the template for the object implementation.

Step 3: Implement the Matrix class–Matrix.java

Use `_example_Matrix.java`, generated by the idl2java compiler, as the template for implementing the Matrix class.

```
import java.util.*;
import java.io.*;
public class Matrix extends MatrixCalculator._MatrixImplBase {
      private short Row; private short Col;
      private float[][] myMatrix; private short MAX_SIZE = 100;
```

```
        //Constructors
            .....
        // Functions for accessing the values of matrix elements
            .....
        // Functions to initialize and display the matrix
            .....
    }
```

Step 4: Implement the MatrixManager class–MatrixManagerImpl.java
Use _example_MatrixManager.java, generated by the idl2java compiler, as the template for implementing the MatrixManager class.

```
import java.io.*;
public class MatrixManagerImpl extends
    MatrixCalculator._MatrixManagerImplBase {
        private MatrixCalculator.Matrix resultMatrix;
        private short MAX_SIZE = 100;

        //constructor
            .....

        public synchronized MatrixCalculator.Matrix
          newFixedMatrix (short row, short col) {
            MatrixCalculator.Matrix temp = new Matrix(row,col);
            // Make the matrix available to ORB.
            _boa().obj_is_ready (temp);
            return (temp);}

        public synchronized MatrixCalculator.Matrix Multiply
          (MatrixCalculator.Matrix A, MatrixCalculator.Matrix B)
             throws MatrixCalculator.IncompatibleSize{
          //Code to perform matrix multiplication and generate resultMatrix
              .....

          _boa().obj_is_ready (resultMatrix);
          return (resultMatrix);
        }
    }
```

Step 5: Implement the Server program–MatrixServer.java

```
import java.io.*;
import org.omg.CosNaming.*;
public class MatrixServer {
    public static void main(String[] args){
      try {
        // Initialize the ORB.
        org.omg.CORBA.ORB orb = org.omg.CORBA.ORB.init(args,null);
        // Create the Matrix Calculator object.
        MatrixManagerImpl matManager = new MatrixManagerImpl();
        // Export the newly create object.
        orb.connect(matManager);
        // Get a naming service reference
        org.omg.CORBA.Object nameServiceObject =
          orb.resolve_initial_references ("NameService");
        org.omg.CosNaming.NamingContext namingService =
          org.omg.Cosnaming.NamingContextHelper.narrow (nameServiceObject);
        // Bind the matManager object in the naming service.
        NameComponent[ ] MatCal = {new NameComponent ("MatCal","")};
```

```
        namingService.rebind (MatCal, matManager);
        System.out.println( matManager + " is ready.");
        // As it is the ORB's responsibility to create threads
        // to receive requests, there is no need to enter an event
        // loop, so just wait forever (till the current thread dies)
        Thread.currentThread().join();
      } catch(Exception e){System.err.println("Exception:   " + e);}
    }
  }
```

As seen from the code, the object implementation (server) binds a name to one of
its objects within a *namespace* [12]. The client application will use that namespace
to resolve a name and obtain an object reference. As the namespace is implemented using *Namingcontext* objects, we are dealing with `NamingContext` objects.
We first obtain an 'initial naming context' using the `resolve_initial_references`,
method, then narrow it down to the *Naming context type*. The `org.omg.CosNaming`
package contains Helpers and Holders for the Naming Service classes. The *Naming-
ContextHelper* is one of the Helper objects automatically generated by the CORBA
compiler. We then create a naming context for the MatrixCalculator by creating
a naming component and assigning it to an array of naming components. We use
`rebind` utility to bind our object with the Naming service.

Step 6: Implement the client–MatrixClient.java

```
import java.io.*;
import org.omg.CosNaming.*;
import MatrixCalculator.*;
  public class MatrixClient {
   public static void main(String[] args) {
     try {
       short mat_size=100;
       // Initialize the ORB.
       org.omg.CORBA.ORB orb = org.omg.CORBA.ORB.init(args, null);
       // Get a naming service object reference.
       org.omg.CORBA.Object nameObject =
            orb.resolve_initial_references ("NameService");
       // Narrow the Object
       org.omg.CosNaming.NamingContext nameService =
            org.omg.CosNaming.NamingContextHelper.narrow (nameObject);
       // Locate the object - MatCal
       NameComponent[] MatCal = {new NameComponent("MatCal","")};
       MatrixCalculator.MatrixManager MatManager =
            MatrixManagerHelper.narrow (nameService.resolve (MatCal));
       //Create two 100 * 100 float matrices
       MatrixCalculator.Matrix MatA = new
Matrix(mat_size,mat_size);
       MatA.Randomize ();
       MatrixCalculator.Matrix MatB = new Matrix
(mat_size,mat_size);
       MatB.Randomize ();
       MatrixCalculator.Matrix result = MatManager.newMatrix ();
       // Multiply 2 100 * 100 float matrices
       for (int count = 0; count < 5; count ++)
          result = MatManager.Multiply (MatA , MatB);
```

```
        }
      catch (Exception e) {System.err.println ("Exception"+e);}
    }
  }
```

After initializing the ORB, the client obtains the naming service object reference, narrows it down to naming context type, locates the matrix manager object, and invokes the multiplication function on it by passing two 100X100 matrices as arguments.

Step 7: Create the `makefile` and launch the application

The makefile, with appropriate comments, for this application is shown below:

```
@echo off
rem MakeFile
if "%1" == "" goto all
if "%1" == "server" goto server
if "%1" == "client" goto client
:all
echo Building the MatrixCalculator...
call idl2java MatrixCalculator.idl -no_comments -no_tie
vbjc Matrix.java
vbjc MatrixManagerImpl.java
vbjc MatrixClient.java
vbjc MatrixServer.java
echo starting the OSAgent (Broker)...
start osagent -c
echo starting the Naming service...
vbj -DORBservices=CosNaming -DSVCnameroot=MatManager -DJDKrenameBug

com.visigenic.vbroker.services.CosNaming.ExtFactory MatManager namingLog
goto end
:server
start vbj -DORBservices=CosNaming -DSVCnameroot=MatManager MatrixServer
goto end
:client
vbj -DORBservices=CosNaming -DSVCnameroot=MatManager MatrixClient "%2"
:end
```

Launch this example, by the following commands:

```
prompt> make
prompt> make server
prompt> make client
```

12.3   Java RMI

When Sun released the Java[2] language, the only mechanism provided to allow objects, residing in different address spaces, to communicate was the low-level socket-based networking paradigm. Soon the need for a communication mechanism at a higher level of abstraction was felt, which resulted in Sun extending the basic Java object model to incorporate distributed objects. This extended model, called Java

---

[2]Java and RMI are registered trademarks of Sun Microsystems Incorporated.

RMI (Remote Method Invocation), allows the objects to communicate at their natural level of abstraction, the method-invocation. There are many research efforts that aim at creating high performance implementations of RMI. One notable example is the Albatross project. A part of it involves the design of Manta [2]. Manta is an alternative implementation of RMI designed for use in high-performance clusters.

12.3.1 Basic Model

The basic idea behind RMI is the concept of a remote-enabled object. When an object is remote-enabled, other objects, regardless of their virtual machines, can interact with it.

When an object A (client) is communicating with a remote-enabled object B (server), which resides in a separate Virtual Machine (VM), it must interact with the remote interface of B. The remote interface defines the methods on B that are visible to nonlocal objects. One implication of this is that A never directly interacts with an object of type B, it only interacts with interfaces of B. A receives a reference to B through a naming service, called *Registry*.

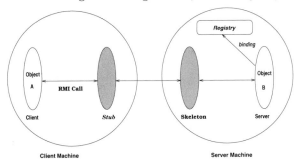

Figure 12.3 Basic model of RMI.

When A invokes a method on a remote interface a proxy object, called the *stub*, receives the method invocation. The stub then forwards the call across the network, where a *skeleton* receives it. The skeleton will then invoke the method on the object B. When the invocation is done, any return arguments are forwarded back across the network to object A through the same mechanism. Figure 12.3 depicts a remote method invocation scenario.

In RMI, remote objects may be passed as arguments or returned as results from any method invocation, whether local or remote. A remote object, as an argument, is passed-by-reference. A remote object may be typecast into any of the remote interface that it supports. Local objects are passed by value.

12.3.2 RMI Features

Java RMI provides many useful features to a programmer for constructing distributed applications. Many of the RMI features stem from the fact that RMI is a

Java-specific distributed-object model. For instance, an interface definition is written by using the standard notion of the Java interface and does not need any special interface definition language. The special interfaces and classes required by RMI for developing a distributed application are shown in Figure 12.4.

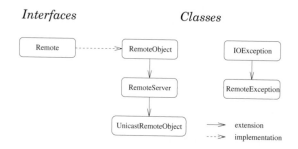

Figure 12.4 Class framework for RMI.

Interfaces and Server Setup

In RMI, the programmer defines an *interface* to express the remote methods to be exported to the clients. Once this interface is created, the programmer of the server class must specify an implementation of these methods. All interfaces for remote objects must extend the `Remote` interface defined within the `java.rmi` package and declare that remote methods throw a `RemoteException`. The `RemoteException` is necessary due to the lack of stability of remote calls (i.e., network errors, a server may be down, etc.) in contrast with local calls. The server class must then implement this interface to export these methods to clients. The server class must explicitly extend the `UnicastRemoteObject` class, supplied by RMI. The server registers itself with the registry service. Then, prior to a remote method invocation, the client asks the registry service for a stub to the server. The `Naming` object (standard in RMI) is responsible for the actual registration of objects and retrieval of stubs. Once the stub is available, the client can invoke remote methods on it.

The detailed steps will become clear as we discuss the matrix multiplication example below.

12.3.3   Matrix Multiplication

Now, we rewrite the matrix multiplication example (discussed earlier in the CORBA section) in Java RMI. The necessary classes and their deployments on the client and server machines are similar to the ones used in the CORBA example, shown in Figure 12.2.

Step 1: Define the Remote Interface for Matrix–MatrixInterface.java

```
import java.rmi.*;
interface MatrixInterface extends Remote {
    public short Row() throws RemoteException;
```

```
public short Col() throws RemoteException;
public void Initialize(float val) throws RemoteException;
public void Randomize() throws RemoteException;
public float Element(short Row, short Col)   throws RemoteException;
public void setElement(short Row, short col, float val)
   throws RemoteException;
public void Display() throws RemoteException;
}
```

This interface defines all the functions which are to be exported to the remote client. As stated earlier, it extends the standard interface `Remote` and all its methods explicitly throw the `RemoteException`.

Step 2: Define the Remote Interface for MatrixManager – MatrixManagerInterface.java

```
import java.rmi.*;
interface MatrixManagerInterface extends Remote
{
    public MatrixInterface newMatrix() throws RemoteException;
    public MatrixInterface newFixedMatrix(short row, short col)
      throws RemoteException;
    public MatrixInterface Add(MatrixInterface A, MatrixInterface B)
      throws RemoteException;
    public MatrixInterface Multiply(MatrixInterface A, MatrixInterface B)
      throws RemoteException;
}
```

Step 3: Define the Matrix class–Matrix.java

```
import java.util.*;
import java.io.*;
import java.rmi.server.UnicastRemoteObject;
import java.rmi.*;
public class Matrix extends UnicastRemoteObject implements MatrixInterface{
        private short Row;
        private short Col;
        private float[][] myMatrix;
        private short MAX_SIZE = 100;

        //Constructors
          .....

        // Functions for accessing the value of private members.
          .....
}
```

As stated earlier, this class extends `UnicastRemoteObject` and implements the `MatrixInterface`, i.e., provides the implementations to all the remote methods of `MatrixInterface`.

Step 4: Define the MatrixManager class–MatrixManager.java

```
import java.rmi.*;
import java.rmi.server.UnicastRemoteObject;
import MatrixManagerInterface;
class MatrixManager extends UnicastRemoteObject implements MatrixManagerInterface{
    private MatrixInterface resultMatrix;
    private short MAX_SIZE = 100;
```

```
        public MatrixManager() throws RemoteException { ..... }
        public synchronized MatrixInterface newMatrix() throws RemoteException
            { ..... }
        public synchronized MatrixInterface newFixedMatrix(short row, short col)
            throws RemoteException  { ..... }
        public synchronized MatrixInterface Add(MatrixInterface A,
            MatrixInterface B) throws RemoteException { ..... }
        public synchronized MatrixInterface Multiply(MatrixInterface A,
            MatrixInterface B) throws RemoteException { ..... }
    }
```

The `MatrixManager` class extends the `UnicastRemoteObject` class (similar to the `Matrix` class) and provides concrete implementations of the functions declared in the `MatrixManagerInterface`.

Step 5: Define the Server class–Server.java

```
    import java.rmi.*;
    class Server {
        public static void main(String args[]) {
          System.setSecurityManager(new RMISecurityManager());

          try {
            System.out.println("Server: Creating a Server");
            String name = "Matrix Manager";
            MatrixManager matManager = new MatrixManager();
            System.out.println("Server: Binding it to "+ name);
            Naming.rebind(name, matManager);
            System.out.println("Server ready");
          } catch (Exception e) { System.out.println("ServerImpl:an
                exception occurred: " + e.getMessage());
            e.printStackTrace();
          }
        }
    }
```

The `Server` class instantiates the `RMISecurityManager` (available with RMI to handle the security-related issues), creates an instance of the `MatrixManager` class, binds with the registry, and prints out the appropriate messages indicating its readiness.

Step 6: Define the Client class–Client.java

```
    import java.io.*;
    import java.rmi.*;
    public class Client {
        public static void main(String[] args) {
          try {
    // Get a naming service object reference.
        String name = "//"+args[0]+"/Matrix Manager";

        System.out.println ("Locating the object Matrix Manager");
        MatrixManagerInterface MatManager =
          (MatrixManagerInterface) Naming.lookup(name);

        //Create two 100 * 100 matrices and multiply them
        short mat_size = 100;
        MatrixInterface MatA = MatManager.newFixedMatrix (mat_size, mat_size);
        MatA.Randomize ();
```

```
MatrixInterface MatB = MatManager.newFixedMatrix (mat_size, mat_size);
MatB.Randomize ();
MatrixInterface result = MatManager.newMatrix ();
result = MatManager.Multiply(MatA, MatB);
} catch (Exception e) { System.err.println ("Exception");
System.err.println (e);
}
  }
}
```

The `Client` obtains the reference to the `MatrixManager` object by looking at the Registry (by using the `lookup` method). It creates two $100 X 100$ floating point matrices and sends them as arguments to the `Multiply` function of the `MatrixManager`. The resultant matrix is returned back to the client.

Step 7: Compilation
Compile all the Java source programs by using the appropriate Java compiler. After the successful compilation, create the `stub` and `skeleton` for the remote objects (`Matrix` and `MatrixManager`) by the `rmic` compiler provide with RMI. This is achieved by the commands: `prompt> rmic MatrixManager.class` and `prompt> rmic Matrix.class`

Step 8: Starting the Registry
Before starting the execution of relevant objects, start the Registry on the machine which will house the server-side objects. This is achieved by:
`prompt> rmiregistry` command.

Step 9: Starting all the Objects
Start `Server`, `MatrixManager`, and `Matrix` on one machine and the `Client` on the another. These, being Java class files, are invoked by the Java interpreter in the usual fashion, e.g., `java Matrix` command.

12.4 DCOM

Distributed Component Object Model (DCOM)[3] is Microsoft's answer to the distributed world [8], [6]. It is a binary standard that allows components (objects) to communicate with each other regardless of their platform and implementational languages. DCOM was first released in 1996, and is now available on all modern Windows operating systems. DCOM is COM (Component Object Model) in a distributed environment. Hence, understanding COM is essential to understanding DCOM. Currently, COM is available on Windows NT, Windows 98, MacOS, Linux, Sun-Solaris, DEC-Unix, and IBM-MVS, among others.

12.4.1 Basic Model

Each DCOM component can be thought of as an encapsulated object. The internal object implementation and data structures are completely hidden from the outside. A DCOM object offers its services to clients through interfaces. An interface is a

---
[3]DCOM and COM are registered trademarks of Microsoft Corporation.

contract of the object with the outside world. As long as the contract is honored, a client can communicate and use the services offered by that component. An interface may support multiple functions. For example, the following `IMatrix` interface (represented in Java) defines two methods, `getElement` and `putElement`:

```
public interface IMatrix {
    public float getElement (int row, int col);
    public putElement (int row, int col, float val);};
```

As long as the contract is honored, an implementation can be revised without affecting clients. If the new implementation requires a revision to the contract, such as adding new functions or changing the number of parameters of a method, then a new contract has to be written. The methods supported by the old interface are honored in the revised interface using inheritance.

Each interface has a corresponding component class (coclass) that defines the implementation of the interface functions. By convention, class names begin with an uppercase `C` while interface names begin with an uppercase `I`. For example, following is the definition of a class implementing the methods of interface `Imatrix`:

```
public class CMatrix implements IMatrix {
    public float getElement (int row, int col) { return myMatrix[row][col];}
    public putElement (int row, int col, float val) {myMatrix[row][col]=val;} };
```

12.4.2   Identification of DCOM Interfaces and Classes

In DCOM, each interface and coclass is identified by a globally unique identifier (GUID). The interface identifier is called IID (interface identifier) while the coclass identifier is referred to as CLSID (class identifier). Each identifier is a 128-bit structure formed by using the machine's network card ID, the current time, and other alpha-numeric data. These identifiers are globally unique and are automatically created by a utility called `GUIDGEN.EXE` supplied by Microsoft. The use of GUIDs ensures all interfaces and classes can be uniquely identified without any naming conflicts or ambiguities.

12.4.3   IDL and its Mapping

A DCOM object is language-independent and is defined in Microsoft's Interface Definition Language (MIDL). MIDL is similar to the C++ declarative statements, with support for attributes such as [in], [out], interface, etc. For example, the `IMatrix` interface and `Cmatrix` coclass definitions in MIDL would be:

```
[uuid (D3A74E81-6B7B-11d2-A1CB-00C04F734AA8)]
interface IMatrix : IUnknown{
    HRESULT getElement([in] int row, [in] int col, [out] float val);
    HRESULT putElement([in] int row, [in] int col, [in] float val);}
[uuid (D3A74E82-6B7B-11d2-A1CB-00C04F734AA8)]
coclass CMatrix{
    [default] interface Imatrix;};
```

The UUIDs (Universally Unique Identifiers) define the interface and class IDs. The attributes [in] and [out] specify whether the parameters are inputs (passed in) or outputs (passed out) to the function. Almost all DCOM interfaces should return HRESULT (although this is not a requirement). HRESULT is used to communicate to the client if the function call was successful or not. HRESULT provides a standard way for error checking in DCOM. The IDL file is compiled by the MIDL compiler to generate the client-side stub and the server-side skeleton. A stub resides in the client address space and is responsible for marshaling parameters via RPC (Remote Procedure Call) to the corresponding skeleton. The skeleton residing on the server machine receives the parameters, unmarshals them, and makes the necessary calls to the server function. Upon completing execution, the skeleton passes the result back to the stub, which in turn passes it to the client.

12.4.4   Creation of Objects

All DCOM applications begin with a call to the `CoInitialize` function to initialize the DCOM library, and end with a call to `CoUnInitialize` to close the DCOM library, free any resources held by the component, and close all RPC connections. After initializing the library, a client would need an instance of the DCOM object. This is achieved by the function `CoCreateInstanceEx`. This function uses the class ID, server context (inprocess, local, or remote) and server location information to return a pointer to the desired interfaces of the DCOM object.

The client would use `CoCreateInstanceEx` as follows:

```
HRESULT hr = CoCreateInstance(CLSID_Matrix, NULL,
                CLSCTX_REMOTE_SERVER, &ServerInfo, n, qi);
```

where n is the number of interface pointers desired. The interface pointers are returned in the array qi, which is of type `MULTIQI` defined below:

```
typedef struct MULTIQI {
    const IID* pIID; // Interface ID (input to function)
    Iunknown* pItf; // Pointer to the interface (return value)
    HRESULT hr; // Error code
} MULTI_QI;
```

12.4.5   Using COM Interfaces and Object Lifetime

All DCOM objects must support the `IUnknown` interface with the following functions:

```
HRESULT QueryInterface(REFIID iid, void** pObj);
ULONG AddRef(void);
ULONG Release(void);
```

The `QueryInterface` method is used to obtain references to other interfaces on an object once the object's interface pointer is known (using `CoCreateInstance`). Thus, if pMatrix is the interface pointer obtained by calling `CoCreateInstance`, a reference to another interface supported by the same Matrix component is obtained as follows:

```
IAnotherInterface *pNext = NULL;
hr = pMatrix->QueryInterface(IID_IAnotherInterface, (void**)pNext);
```

```
if (SUCCEEDED(hr))
    pNext->MultiplyMatrix(. . .);
else { // handle error}
```

The `AddRef` and `Release` methods are used to control the object lifetime of a DCOM object by reference counting. `AddRef` increments the count whenever a client requests a reference to the interface whereas `Release` decrements the count when a release operation is called upon the interface. `AddRef` is automatically called before `CoCreateInstanceEx` returns. `Release` has to be explicitly called by the client. An interface is unloaded only when its reference count reaches zero. The object is eventually unloaded when the reference counts for all interfaces supported by an object reach zero.

12.4.6   DCOM Programming in Java

Java simplifies DCOM programming by relieving the programmer from knowing the intricacies of DCOM. Microsoft's VJ++ provides an Integrated Development Environment (IDE) for Java development and Java-DCOM integration tools. The integration of Java-DCOM has been achieved through Microsoft's Java Virtual Machine (msjava.dll) which translates Java byte code into the native code. VJ++ also provides tools such as ActiveX Wizard for Java/COM and Java Type Library Wizard to help generate the IDL file from Java source code and to register type libraries. Java provides automatic garbage collection and, hence, calls to `Addref` and `Release` are not required. Also, the object instantiation is automatic via the Java Virtual Machine and is transparent to the user. In the next section, we present the same matrix multiplication example implemented in Java-DCOM.

12.4.7   Matrix Multiplication Example

In this example, we create a single component, `MatrixCalculator`, having two interfaces, `IMatrix` and `IMatrixManager`. The DCOM component offers matrix creation and manipulation services such as adding two matrices, multiplying two matrices, etc. We now describe the steps involved in creating the server and then accessing the services offered by it through a client running on a remote machine.

Create the Server - Server Machine

Step 1: Construct the IDL file : MatrixCalculator.idl

```
[uuid(D3A74E80-6B7B-11d2-A1CB-00C04F734AA8),
    helpstring("MatrixCalculator Type Library"), version(1.0)]
library MatrixCalculator{
    importlib("stdole32.tlb");
        [object, uuid(D3A74E81-6B7B-11d2-A1CB-00C04F734AA8), dual,
        oleautomation, pointer_default(unique), helpstring("IMatrix Interface")]
    interface IMatrix : IDispatch {
        [id(1), helpstring("fixedMatrix Method")]
```

```
HRESULT fixedMatrix([in] long p1, [in] long p2);
[(id(2),helpstring("Randomize Method")] HRESULT Randomize();
[(id(3),helpstring("Row Method")] HRESULT Row([out, retval] long * rtn);
[(id(4),helpstring("Col Method")] HRESULT Col([out, retval] long * rtn);
[(id(5),helpstring("getElement Method")]
HRESULT getElement([in] long p1, [in] long p2, [out, retval] float * rtn);
[(id(6),helpstring("setElement Method")]
HRESULT setElement([in] long p1, [in] long p2, [in] float p3);
[helpstring("Multiply Method")]
HRESULT Multiply([in] IMatrix A, [in] IMatrix B, [out,retval] IMatrix *C);
};
[uuid(D3A74E82-6B7B-11d2-A1CB-00C04F734AA8),
 helpstring("Matrix Object")]
coclass Matrix{
    [default] interface IMatrix;};
};
```

Step 2: Compile the IDL file

The IDL file of the MatrixCalculator is compiled by using the MIDL compiler: `midl matrixcalculator.idl`. This creates a Type Library file `MatrixCalculator.tlb`, which is the binary version of the IDL file and contains the description of the component.

Step 3. Register the type library file

The command `javatlb /U:T matrixcalculator.tlb` results in two files being created in the `<windows>Java\TrustLib` directory, where `<windows>` indicates the windows directory on the machine. These files are `Imatrix.class` and `Matrix.class`. In addition, the interface and the type library are registered in the `HKCR\Interface` and `HKCR\TypeLib` entries in the registry. These entries can be verified by the `regedit` utility.

Step 4: Define the implementation of the Matrix interface

The implementation of the interface is given below.

```java
import java.util.*;
import java.io.*;
import com.ms.com.*;
import matrixcalculator.*;
public class Matrix implements IMatrix{
    private int Row;
    private int Col;
    private float[][] myMatrix;
    private int MAX_SIZE=100;

    // Member functions - Implementations of all functions
    // are NOT provided here. Any appropriate implementation
    // should be provided where-ever required.
    public int Row() throws ComException { return Row;}
    public int Col() throws ComException { return Col;}
    public void fixedMatrix(int row, int col) throws ComException
    { //Create a matrix of size row x col }
    public void Randomize() throws ComException
        { //Initialize matrix with random values }
    public float getElement(int row, int col) throws ComException
    { return myMatrix[row][col];}
```

```
public void setElement(int row, int col, float val) throws ComException
{ myMatrix[row][col]=val;}
public IMatrix Multiply (IMatrix A, IMatrix B) throws ComException
{//Multiply matrix A and B and return the resultant matrix}
}
```

Step 5. Compile the Matrix.java file

The Java file is compiled by using the `jvc` compiler. The resulting `Matrix` class file is moved to the `<windows>\Java\Lib` directory.

Step 6. Register the class file with the Windows Registry

The registration process is achieved by the command:

```
javareg /register /class:Matrix.class
    /clsid:{D3A74E82-6B7B-11d2-A1CB-00C04F734AA8} /surrogate
```

Step 7. Run the DCOM server locally

Follow the steps for Creating the Client (Steps 5, 6, and 7 in the next section) and run the MatrixClient.class locally (command: jview MatrixClient). The client should run locally before attempting to make the application work remotely.

Step 8. Make the server remotely accessible

Run DCOMCNFG and select the Default Security tab. In the Default Access Permissions, select Edit Default and add the SYSTEM account and the user who will access the DCOM server from the client machine. In the Default Launch Permissions select *Edit Default* and add the SYSTEM and INTERACTIVE accounts, and the user who will access the DCOM server.

Client Machine

Step 1. Register the interfaces

Copy the `matrixcalculator.tlb` file to the client machine and register the tlb file (command: javatlb /U:T matrixcalculator.tlb)

Step 2. Register the remote object classes

```
javareg /register /class:Matrix.class
    /clsid:{D3A74E82-6B7B-11d2-A1CB-00C04F734AA8}
```

Step 3. Specify the location of the server

Run DCOMCNFG. Select the JavaClass:Matrix entry and hit the Properties button. Select the Location tab and choose the Run application on the following *computer* option. Enter the name of the server machine. Ensure the other two checkboxes are clear. Select OK.

Step 4. Check settings in the windows registry

Run REGEDIT and search for Matrix. In the HKCR\AppID entry, the Remote-Server name should be set to the name entered in Step 3. Continue searching (Hit F3). In the HKCR\CLSID delete the InProcSever32 and LocalServer32 entries (if they exist). Further searching should find the IID for IMatrix registered in the HKCR\Interfaces location.

Step 5. Create the client code

Type the client java source code MatrixClient.java.

```
import java.io.*;
import matrixcalculator.*;
public class MatrixClient {
   public static void main(String args[]) {
   try {
   int mat_size = 100;
      // Bind to Matrix Object
   System.out.println("Creating Matrix Objects");
   IMatrix matA = (IMatrix)new Matrix();
   IMatrix matB = (IMatrix)new Matrix();
   IMatrix matC = (IMatrix)new Matrix();
      // Create matA and matB matrices of size 100 X 100
            .....
   // Invoke multiply function on matC and get the result
   matC = matC.Multiply(matA, matB);
   } catch(Exception e) {
   System.err.println("System Exception");
   System.err.println(e);
   }}
   }
```

Step 6. Compile the client code

Compile the client code to create the class file MatrixClient.class using the command: `jvc MatrixClient.java`.

Step 7. Run the client program

Run the client program using the command: `jview MatrixClient`.

12.5 Voyager

Due to space limitations, we now present a less comprehensive treatment of Voyager 1.0.1, without a step-by-step approach for the matrix multiplication example. However, we will compare its performance with other three approaches in the next section. It is largely based on the on-line documentation of Voyager [13], [7].

12.5.1 Basic Model

Voyager is a full-featured, intuitive Java ORB that combines the power of mobile agents and remote method invocation with complete CORBA support. Remote objects are constructed via regular Java syntax. Voyager objects communicate with each other by passing synchronous, one-way, future, or one-way multicast messages via the ORB. Voyager provides many services including database-independent persistence service, scalable group communication service, and federated directory service. We summarize fundamental features of Voyager 1.0.1 below.

12.5.2 Voyager Features

Remote construction and messaging

Voyager 1.0.1 provides a utility called vcc to generate a remote-enabled class from a regular Java class. Once a remote-enabled class is created, its instance can be created outside the local address space. The remote object can be accessed through a virtual reference (a special object). When a message is sent to a virtual reference, it forwards that message to the remote object. If the message requires a return value, the return value is passed back to the sender through the same virtual reference. When a remote exception occurs, it is caught and thrown to the sender in a similar way.

Each Voyager program has a network address consisting of its host name and a communication port number. By default, a Voyager-enabled program starts at a random port number. A Voyager server is a Voyager program that holds objects and agents created by other Voyager programs. Each remote instance has a random, 16-byte globally unique ID (GUID) and the object's address. Voyager does not require separate steps for name-binding; the user creates a remote object and assigns it an alias. To connect to an existing remote object, the user creates a new virtual reference and associates it with that remote object through its alias and GUID-based address.

Message Types

Voyager supports four message types: a) Synchronous Messages: Voyager messages are synchronous by default, b) One-way Messages: the sender discards the result, c) Future Messages: when a client sends a future message, it receives a placeholder from which results will be retrieved at a later time. If the client attempts to read the return value, it is blocked until the return value is received or the timeout period is exceeded, and d) One-Way Multicast Messages: this is used to send one-way messages to all objects in a *space*, a concept to be discussed later. Voyager also supports dynamic invocation.

Life Span

By default, a simple object has a reference-based life span. A simple object is garbage collected when all its local and virtual references are destroyed. The default life span for an agent, which is a special object, is one day. The user can control the life span of an object by explicitly sending to it different messages such as, dieNow() and liveForever().

Mobility and Agents

A serializable object can be moved even when it is receiving a remote message. This usually reduces the network traffic and increases the throughput. To move an object, the user invokes the moveTo function with the destination (Program or Object Destination) as the parameter. The object waits until all remote messages in progress are complete and then moves to the specific destination. If the move is successful, the original object leaves behind a forwarder to forward messages and future connection requests. If a callback function is specified, the object can continue to execute after the move.

An agent is a special object that has autonomy. An agent can independently move to a remote object or program or even a moving object. When an agent arrives at a remote object, it executes a callback with a native Java reference to the remote object. By default, the remote object is prevented from moving until the callback is completed. The classes, whose instances want to autonomously travel over the network, must extend the standard `Agent` class.

Space

To communicate with groups of objects, distributed systems need features like distributed messaging and distributed publish/subscribe. Unlike traditional systems, that use a single repeater object to replicate the message or an event, Voyager uses a *Space architecture*. Clusters of objects in the target group are stored in local groups called *subspaces*. These are linked together to form a space. A message sent to a subspace is cloned to each of the neighboring subspaces before being delivered to each object in the local space. Each subspace has a mechanism to guarantee that a message or an event is only processed once. One-way messages can be sent to all objects in a space by using one-way multicast. A multicast message can also be delivered selectively to objects by using subscription-based, one-way multicasts.

Applets

Voyager includes a lightweight software router to support applet-to-applet and applet-to-program connectivity. A Voyager-enabled applet needs to be associated with a Voyager program that acts as its server for network class loading and a software router. Multiple applets can share the same server. An object can communicate with objects in another applet even if the applet is on a different server.

Database Independent Persistence

Voyager supports database-independent, distributed-object persistence. The databases can be relational or object-oriented. Voyager also provides an object storage system, called *VoyagerDb*, that implements a database to persist any serializable object without modification. A Voyager program can be assigned to an optional database so that it supports persistence. Two different Voyager programs should not share the same database. If a persistent object moves, its persistent copy is automatically removed from the source database and saved in a destination database.

Security

Voyager includes a security manager, called `VoyagerSecurityManager`, which can be installed at the start of a program to restrict its operations. After it is installed, instances of a class loaded via the programs `CLASSPATH` are considered as native, and instances of a class loaded across the network are considered as foreign.

Federated Directory Service

Voyager provides a built-in lookup mechanism, called *Federated Directory Service*, to retrieve virtual references of remote and mobile objects. In order to use this service, users need to have an up-to-date knowledge of the current and past locations of the object. Users can register the objects in a distributed hierarchical directory structure and associate objects with path names consisting of simple strings separated by slashes.

Future Extensions

Voyage 2.0 has full native support for IDL, IIOP, and bidirectional Java/IDL mappings. The new Voyager naming service provides unified access to a variety of commercial naming services including Voyager federated directory service, CORBA naming service, JNDI, Microsoft Active Directory, and RMI registry. Voyager 2.0 also supports Dynamic Aggregation, which allows users to add secondary objects (facets) to a primary object at run time.

12.6   A Simple Performance Measurement

12.6.1   Matrix Multiplication

In order to compare the performance, we executed a floating-point matrix multiplication example using these four paradigms. Table 12.1 shows the result (time, in seconds, required to complete the execution) of multiplying two 100 * 100 floating-point matrix objects. The matrices were created by the client object and passed as parameters to the multiplying function of the server object. The client object ran on a DELL DIMENSION XPS Pro 180n (Pentium Pro 180 MHz processor) withe 32 MB DRAM, while the server object ran on a DELL Optiplex G1 3331 (Pentium II 333 MHz Processor) with 64 MB DRAM. Both these machines had Windows NT 4.0 operating system and were connected by a 10MB Ethernet. Also, these experiments were conducted when no other programs were running on these machines. The software environments used in the experiments were: JDK 1.1.5, Voyager 1.1 and 2.0, VisiBroker for Java 3.1, and Java Naming Service 3.1. We used `System.currentTimeMillis()` to obtain the timing values for these experiments.

Table 12.1 Time (in sec.) for a $100X100$ Floating-point Matrix Multiplication

Parameter Passing	CORBA	RMI	DCOM	Voyager 1.1	Voyager 2.0
By-reference	6355.637	5973.93	0.34	8500	5590
By value	2.864	4.736		4.7464	4.847

The following points should be noted while interpreting the results from Table 12.1:

- The time required by DCOM (pass-by-reference) is the least. However, it is the effect of two factors (a) For DCOM we used a JIT compiler (Microsoft VJ++), while other measurements were implemented using slower JDK1.1.5, and (b) The structure of the matrix multiplication, used in DCOM, was different from other implementations. This was necessary due to an internal error in Microsoft's JView.exe. It did not allow the passing of an interface pointer as an argument to a method of a different type. Our attempts to pass such a pointer always resulted in "access violation error." A similar error prohibited us from testing pass-by value with DCOM.

- Although CORBA 2.0 does not support pass-by-value, many Java ORB vendors (including VisiBroker) support that feature. OMG, in its CORBA 3.0 specification, has incorporated the pass-by-value feature.

12.6.2   Which Paradigm is Superior?

Each of these four paradigms have advantages and drawbacks. Here, we evaluate these four paradigms from the perspective of a developer.

- *Ease of Use:* RMI is the easiest, as it is integrated into the Java environment and does not require special interface language. Voyager comes a close second, as it is also a pure Java-based paradigm. CORBA, although very comprehensive, is next, as it needs the use of IDL and the broker. DCOM stands at the bottom, because in Windows environments it is tightly coupled with Windows registry and requires administrator privileges. However, the procedure for registering objects in DCOM might vary depending upon the platform.

- *Language Support (Implementational Independence):* CORBA and DCOM both fare well while JRMI and Voyager are, by definition, specific to Java. However, OMG's IDL is a bit simpler than MIDL. On the other hand, as RMI and Voyager use Java's inherent features, they are easier to learn and do not put an additional burden (of learning a new interface language) on the developers.

- *Platform Independence:* RMI and Voyager can be supported on all platforms that incorporate a Java environment. CORBA is virtually supported on all major operating systems including 16 bit windows. DCOM is also ported over most of the leading operating systems, but is not as time tested as CORBA.

- *Open Standard:* In this category, CORBA scores over its competitors. As it is just a specification, the implementation is up to the vendors. This makes it possible to create CORBA-compliant ORBs for specific domains such as high performance and real-time computing.

Irrespective of merits and drawbacks of these paradigms, one important fact is that the future generation of software systems will be interconnected and the distributed-object paradigm will be the vehicle to perform the migration into the net-centric world.

12.7 Bibliography

[1] G. Booch. *Object Oriented Design with Applications.* Benjamin-Cummings Publishing Company, Redwood City, 1991.

[2] R. Veldema, R. Nieuwpoort, J. Maassen, H. Bal, and A. Plaat. Efficient Remote Method Invocation. *Technical Report IR-450.* Vrije Universiteit, Amsterdam, 1998.

[3] *Java^{TM} Remote Method Invocation Specification.* Sun Microsystems, 1996.

[4] J. Siegel. *CORBA Fundamentals and Programming.* John Wiley & Sons, Inc., New York, 1996.

[5] R. Orfali and D. Harkey. *Client/Server Programming with JAVA and CORBA.* John Wiley & Sons, Inc., New York, 1998.

[6] R. Grimes. *DCOM Programming.* WROX Press Ltd., Birmingham, AL, 1997.

[7] G. Glass. Voyager: The New Face of Distributed Computing. *Object Magazine,* June 1997. http://www.sigs.com/publications/docs/objm/9706/9706.glass.html.

[8] *DCOM Specifications.* http://www.microsoft.com/oledev/olecom, Microsoft Corporation, 1998.

[9] *CORBA 2.2 Specification.* http://www.omg.org/Library/c2indx.html, Object Management Group, 1998.

[10] S. Vinoski. CORBA: Integrating Diverse Applications within Distributed Heterogeneous Environments. *IEEE Communications,* vol. 14(2), February 1997.

[11] Douglas C. Schmidt, David L. Levine, and Sumedh Mungee. The Design and Performance of Real-Time Object Request Brokers. *Computer Communications.* Elsevier, vol. 21(4), pages: 294–324, April 1998.

[12] VisiBroker Naming and Event Services 3.3, *Programmers Guide.* http://www.inprise.com/techpubs/book/visibroker/vbnes33, INPRISE Corporation, Inc., 1998.

[13] ObjectSpace, Inc. *ObjectSpace Voyager, Version 1.0.0 User Guide.* http://www.objectspace.com/voyager/documentation.html, 1997.

Chapter 13

Java and Different Flavors of Parallel Programming Models

DANIEL C. HYDE

Department of Computer Science
Bucknell University
Lewisburg, PA 17837 USA

Email: *hyde@bucknell.edu*

13.1 Introduction

Interest in the Java language continues unabated. It is clearly the most talked about language of the last few years. However, we ask, "Is Java useful for parallel computation?" At first glance you might say "No!" since most people are interested in parallel computation to achieve high performance, and Java is infamous for lack of high performance. But with new technologies, such as Just-In-Time (JIT) compilers and Sun Microsystem's effort to improve performance, that is changing.

Also, there are other reasons why many researchers are interested in Java as a language for parallel computation. First, Java promises platform independence, which is important for developing parallel computation programs in heterogeneous environments. Second, producing bug-free software is easier in Java than in C or C++. Third, Java has built-in primitives for writing multithreaded programs—though many question whether they are the "correct" primitives for the task. (More later.) Fourth, the Java Application Programming Interface (API) includes multi-level support for network communication. This includes the establishment of low-level sockets between hosts as well as higher-level support for distributed object schemes, i.e., Remote Method Invocation (RMI). These facilitate the development of software for clusters of machines that execute parallel programs. Perhaps the most important reason for the popularity of Java is the belief that Java is destined to become ubiquitous and, therefore, many parallel computing researchers have jumped on the Java bandwagon.

For the above and other reasons, many researchers are developing software tools and methodologies to combine Java and their "favorite" parallel programming models. This flurry of activity includes using Java to develop data parallel models similar to High Performance Fortran (HPF), CSP-based models similar to Occam, message passing models based on PVM and MPI, bulletin board models similar to Linda, and shared memory models. This chapter describes these activities in the context of levels of abstraction, portability, programmability, and performance.

13.2   Java Threads—Built-in Support for Parallelism and Concurrency

Java allows programs to do more than one thing at a time (*concurrency*) with a technique called *multithreading*, i.e., more than one thread of control through a program executing at the same time. For example, a web-based application could be loading a large file in one thread and waiting for user input in another. Unlike the programming languages C and C++, Java contains multithreading primitives as part of the language itself. This encourages programmers to use the multithreading features and ensures a level of portability that can't be achieved by the various C and C++ libraries.

Threads are central to the use of Java. For example, if an application programmer uses the Abstract Windowing Toolkit (AWT) package in the Java API, he or she is programming with multithreads. Also, Java's garbage collector runs as a separate thread to automatically reclaim dynamically allocated memory.

Java threads are a simple model. The following Java program demonstrates the ease of creating and running threads. We write a class `PrintThread` which extends the `Thread` class in the Java API package `java.lang.Thread`. The constructor for the `PrintThread` class sets the name of the thread and the instance variable `sleepTime` to how long the thread will sleep. The user provides the code for the thread by overriding the `run` method. In this program, a thread only sleeps for `sleepTime` milliseconds, then prints that it is finished. In the `main` method, we create the four threads and start them by invocation of the `start` method.

```
// Example 1 - demo of four non-interacting threads
// By Dan Hyde, Oct 22, 1998
public class Ex1{
    public static void main(String args[]){
        PrintThread th1, th2, th3, th4;
        th1 = new PrintThread("th1");
        th2 = new PrintThread("th2");
        th3 = new PrintThread("th3");
        th4 = new PrintThread("th4");
        th1.start();
        th2.start();
        th3.start();
        th4.start();
```

```
        }
}
class PrintThread extends Thread {
    public int sleepTime;                // instance variable
    public PrintThread(String name){  // constructor
        setName(name);
            // sleep between 0 and 5 seconds
        sleepTime = (int) (Math.random() * 5000);
        System.out.println("Thread " + getName() +
         " will sleep: " + sleepTime + " milliseconds.");
    }
    public void run(){
        try{
            Thread.sleep(sleepTime);
        }
        catch (InterruptedException e){
            System.err.println(e.toString());
        }
        System.out.println(getName() + " finished!");
    }
}
```

Here is a run of the above program.

```
% java Ex1
Thread th1 will sleep: 4026 milliseconds.
Thread th2 will sleep: 1481 milliseconds.
Thread th3 will sleep: 1492 milliseconds.
Thread th4 will sleep: 1537 milliseconds.
th2 finished!
th3 finished!
th4 finished!
th1 finished!
%
```

A thread is the independent execution of a sequence of instructions. If threads never interacted as in the above example, their design would be easy. However, threads must interact and such interaction raises many issues. For example, how do they communicate? How to coordinate shared data items?

In Java, this coordination or synchronization is based on C. A. R. Hoare's *monitor*[7]. A monitor is a body of code guarded by a mutual-exclusion semaphore, called a *mutex*. The mutex or lock allows only one thread to enter the body of code and, therefore, the thread has exclusive use of any shared date items. An analogy might be the bathroom on a plane where the narrow door only allows one person to enter. Once inside, the occupant automatically locks the door when he or she turns on the light. No one else may use the bathroom until the occupant leaves and releases the lock.

In Java, every object has the potential of having a monitor associated with it. A monitor is associated with any object whenever one of its class methods (or block of code) has the keyword `synchronized` attached. Before a thread may enter the code of a monitor, it must acquire the mutex or lock; otherwise, it must wait. After a thread acquires the mutex, it may proceed to execute statements in the protected code. After it exits the code, the mutex is released and another thread that was waiting may acquire the mutex and proceed.

To allow the user to coordinate a program's threads, Java provides a rich selection of methods. However, a programmer must carefully learn the semantics of each. For example, in the above, the method invocation `Thread.sleep (sleepTime)` suspends the thread for `sleepTime` milliseconds. Note, `sleep` does *not* release any mutex for use by another thread. This is consistent with our plane bathroom analogy, i.e., if anyone falls asleep inside, all others must wait. The method `suspend` suspends the thread indefinitely until a `resume` method is called. Like `sleep`, `suspend` does not release the mutex. Therefore, a missing `resume` will lock up a monitor, forcing other threads to wait forever (a type of *deadlock*). Similarly, a `stop` method does not release the mutex. Therefore, a `stop` is like entering our plane bathroom and killing oneself. No one can enter the locked door. For these problems, `suspend` and `stop` have been deprecated in JDK 1.2.

The method `wait` suspends a thread until a `notify` or `notifyAll` method is called. Unlike `suspend`, the `wait` method releases the mutex to allow other threads to execute. The methods `wait`, `notify`, and `notifyAll` are found in the Class `java.lang.Object`. The `yield` method causes the currently executing thread to temporarily pause, release the mutex, and allow other threads to execute.

Shown below is a simple and admittedly contrived example to demonstrate the interaction between two threads that share a counter object.

```
// Example 2 - incrementing and decrementing a shared counter
// Synchronized methods in Counter class
// By Dan Hyde, Oct 22, 1998
public class Ex2{
    public static void main(String args[]){
        DecThread dec;
        IncThread inc;
        Counter c;
        c = new Counter();
        // create one Counter object ''c''
        // which is passed to both threads
        dec = new DecThread("dec", c);
        inc = new IncThread("inc", c);
        dec.start();
        inc.start();
    }
}
class DecThread extends Thread{
    private Counter myCounter;
```

```java
    public DecThread(String name, Counter c){
        setName(name);
        myCounter = c;
    }
    public void run(){
        int i;

        for(i = 0; i < 10; i++){
            myCounter.decCounter();
            System.out.println("Thread " + getName() + " "
                                + myCounter.getCounter());
            try{
                Thread.sleep(100);
            }
            catch (InterruptedException e){
                System.err.println(e.toString());
            }
        }
    }
}
class IncThread extends Thread{
    private Counter myCounter;
    public IncThread(String name, Counter c){
        setName(name);
        myCounter = c;
    }
    public void run(){
        int i;
        for(i = 0; i < 10; i++){
            myCounter.incCounter();
            System.out.println("Thread " + getName() + " "
                                + myCounter.getCounter());
            try{
                Thread.sleep(100);
            }
            catch (InterruptedException e){
                System.err.println(e.toString());
            }
        }
    }
}
class Counter{
    public int count;
    public Counter(){
        count = 0;
    }
    public synchronized void incCounter(){
        int temp;
```

```
        temp = getCounter();
        temp++;
        setCounter(temp);
    }
    public synchronized void decCounter(){
        int temp;
        temp = getCounter();
        temp--;
        setCounter(temp);
    }
    public synchronized int getCounter(){
        return count;
    }
    public synchronized void setCounter(int value){
        count = value;
    }
}
```

Since the `dec` thread decrements the counter ten times, and the `inc` thread increments the counter ten times, the result should be zero. Without the `synchronized` keywords on the `Counter` methods, the value may be corrupted. Since some Java systems use preemptive scheduling, e.g., Windows NT, the code for `decCounter` and `incCounter` methods might be interleaved in such a way as to produce the wrong result. For example, one thread might call `setCounter` between another thread's calls to `getCounter` and `setCounter`. Adding the `synchronized` keywords guarantees that only one thread is allowed to be executing any one of the four `Counter`'s methods. However, adding `synchronized` keywords when they may not be needed will hurt a program's performance.

In Java, the monitor is associated with the "whole" object and not just the synchronized method or code. In this way, the monitor protects all the data elements or the state of the object. Remember that threads execute code and monitors protect objects.

In Java, an object has the monitor associated with it and not a class. That is, each instance of a class, i.e., an object, has a monitor. Therefore, two `Counter` objects in the above program would not share the same monitor. Forgetting this is a source of frustration for programmers.

Programmers with experience in multithreading in other languages may be tempted to use `int` variables as mutex variables. This does not work in Java! A monitor will not be associated with an `int` variable because primitive data types are not objects in Java. However, a one element `int` array may have a monitor since arrays are objects.

For more details on writing Java programs using threads, see the appropriate Java API and one of the many books on Java such as Deitel and Deitel[2]. For more advanced material on Java threads, see the books *Java Threads* by Scott Oaks and Henry Wong[12], *Concurrent Programming in Java: Design Principles and Patterns* by Doug Lea[11] and *Java: Distributed Computing* by Jim Farley[3]. Also, Allen

Holub has written several excellent articles on programming Java Threads for the on-line magazine *JavaWorld* (http://www.javaworld.com).

13.2.1   Are Java Threads the Correct Model?

Java threads are a simple model but they are not so easy to use correctly! Java threads are a common source of problems and thread-related problems can be difficult to diagnose. Here is one view on this matter from Prashant Jain and Douglas C. Schmidt:[1]

> While Java's simplicity is often beneficial, we encountered subtle traps and pitfalls with its concurrency model. In particular, Java's Monitor-based concurrency model can be nonintuitive and error-prone for programmers accustomed to developing applications using threading models (such as POSIX Pthreads, Solaris threads, or Win32 threads) supported by modern operating systems.

First, programmers have problems identifying and protecting shared objects, and if not done properly, a *data race* may occur where the value depends on the order of the execution of the threads. Second, with the possibility of threads waiting, the program may arrive at a state where a group of threads are all waiting for an event in which only one of the waiting threads can cause, therefore creating *deadlock*. The Java Virtual Machine specification has no guarantee of fairness in scheduling threads and this can lead to thread *starvation*. All three of these problems are timing-dependent and, therefore, very hard to detect and fix.

As to why Java threads have such problems, Peter Welch has said it best:[2]

> The problem with Java threads is that the language designers used the wrong Tony Hoare paper and based them on the concept of *monitors* (an idea from the late 60s and early 70s) rather than his later algebraic theory of *Communicating Sequential Processes* (CSP). A crucial benefit of CSP is that thread semantics are compositional (i.e., WYSIWYG), whereas monitor thread semantics are context-sensitive (i.e., non-WYSIWYG and that's why they hurt!).
>
> For example, to write and understand *one* synchronized method in a (Java) class, we need to write and understand *all* the synchronized methods in that class *at the same time*—we can't knock them off one by one! This does not scale—we get a combinational explosion of complexity!! As advertised, avoiding race hazards (etc.) becomes very hard.

---

[1] Prashant Jain and Douglas C. Schmidt, "Experiences Converting a C++ Communication Software Framework to Java," *C++ Report*, January, 1997.

[2] Peter Welch, "Teaching How to Use Java for Parallel and Multi-Threaded Computing," Uppsala97 Conference, Panel on Using Java in Computer Science Education, 1997.

The developers of Java threads lacked a sense of history. Operating systems researchers have known about these problems of data races, deadlock, and starvation and pondered their solutions for decades. In the 1960s, with the increasing complexity of time sharing systems, Dijkstra proposed his synchronization mechanism, the *semaphore*. Though Dijkstra's semaphore was an elegant solution at the time, experience proved it to be at too low a level of abstraction. Therefore, in 1974, C. A. R. (Tony) Hoare proposed his concept of monitors[7]. This 25-year-old concept is the basis of Java's synchronization mechanism. Much has happened in operating system research in the last two decades. Notable was the development of process algebras such as Hoare's CSP introduced in 1978[8]. An important facet of Hoare's CSP was the abandonment of shared variables. Since shared variables caused so many problems, Hoare proposed eliminating them and all their associated baggage, such as mutexes and conditional variables. In their place, CSP-based systems restrict interactions between processes to sending and receiving messages on point-to-point channels. (More on CSP and its relation to Java in a later section.) The point here is the thread problems that Java programmers are struggling with have been known and studied for decades.

Much of the research effort combining Java and parallel computing is investigating ways to overcome these problems with Java threads. Some are proposing changes to the Java language; most researchers are building on top of it.

13.2.2   Java Support for Parallelism

Parallelism is subtly different from concurrency. *Parallelism* is the performing of actions at the same time, e.g., a program running on multiple CPUs. For some researchers, concurrency is the illusion of a program running in parallel. For example, several Java threads may appear to run at the same time, but in reality the threads are interleaved in time on one CPU. The JVM performs instructions for one thread, then switches to perform instructions for another thread. I call this *virtual parallelism*. I reserve the word *concurrency* to mean capable of being performed in parallel in the abstract. An underlying implementation for this abstraction may be either *physical parallelism*, e.g., running on multiple CPUs, or *virtual parallelism*, e.g., timeslicing on one CPU.

Until Java Development Kit (JDK) 1.2, Java threads supported only virtual parallelism and not parallelism. With JDK 1.2, users of multiprocessor Solaris boxes will be able to take advantage of the multiprocessors within a single Java program. Sun Microsystems has added native-thread support, which the programmer may choose instead of the original (and still default) "green threads." However, if developers desire platform independence, they will avoid use of these new threads. Therefore, a platform-independent Java program may only use virtual parallelism, i.e., interleaving threads on one CPU.

The field of parallel computation's primary focus is on the use of parallelism to achieve higher performance, i.e., a program that runs faster or a program that handles a larger problem in the same amount of time. A secondary but still important focus is *availability*. (See Pfister's book for a discussion on availability within clusters of computers[14].)

To achieve platform-independent parallelism in Java, the programmer must write several Java programs that communicate between each other. The Java API includes multilevel support for network communication which includes the establishment of low-level sockets between hosts as well as higher-level support for distributed object schemes, i.e., Remote Method Invocation (RMI). These facilitate the development of software for clusters of machines that execute parallel programs.

However, splitting a Java program that uses Java threads into two or more Java programs that communicate by way of Java API sockets or RMI is not easy. The necessary primitives are available, but the rewrite requires a lot of effort and significantly increases the complexity of the programs. Due to these difficulties, parallel computation researchers are investigating ways to lessen the burden on the programmer.

13.3   Parallel Programming Models

A parallel programming model is the language abstractions presented to the programmer. Since these abstractions are the programmer's view of parallel computation, the model strongly influences how a programmer thinks about the problems he or she is solving. If the model is to be implemented on a real machine, the model must also interface with current or new machine architectures by way of a language processor such as a compiler.

Surprisingly, researchers have investigated dozens if not hundreds of parallel programming models with widely varying abstractions. A sample list includes data flow languages, functional languages, communicating sequential processes, message passing systems such as MPI[13], coordination languages such as Linda[1], and shared memory approaches like Pthreads[10]. The landscape is a jungle with no clear preferred choice. (For an excellent survey on the matter, see "Models and Languages for Parallel Computation" by David B. Skillicorn and Domenico Talia[18]. Skillicorn and Talia have also edited a book containing reprints of 23 key papers[17].)

There are several reasons why there exists such a proliferation of parallel programming models. First, the models have different purposes, e.g., the PRAM model's purpose is theoretical analysis of parallel programming behavior; MPI's purpose is to provide primitives for collective communication; and the LogP model's purpose is for cost estimation of performance.

Second, models focus on different problem domains, e. g., logic programming, functional programming, database, and digital systems (Verilog and VHDL).

Third, the models have different underlying assumptions. This third reason is the root cause of many "religious debates" we hear at conferences. For example, many researchers implicitly assume their parallel computational model is for transformational programs. A *transformational program* is one where the input is transformed into the output, i.e., a function in the mathematical sense. Dataflow and functional models usually assume this. A programmer wants and expects his large numerical simulation to reproduce the same answers given the same input. On the other hand, some researchers implicitly assume their model is for reactive programs. A *reactive program* is one that reacts to its environment, such as an operating system or a Graphical Users Interface (GUI). As an example, Hoare's CSP assumes reactive programs. Whereas researchers in dataflow and functional models work hard to eliminate any source of nondeterminism in order to preserve transformational semantics, researchers of reactive program models desire a way to intelligently model nondeterminism, an important aspect of reactive programs. Discovering and making explicit these underlying assumptions is difficult at times.

The fourth reason for many parallel programming models is the possibility of many different levels of abstraction. At a high level of abstraction, even the presence of parallelism may be abstracted away from the programmer, as in some functional languages. At a low-level of abstraction, the programmer must deal with all the messy details of parallel programming explicitly, e.g., determine the threads, how to allocate them to processors, how to express communication between them and how to schedule threads, and communication as required in Java. Mid levels of abstraction are possible as evidenced by JavaParty and CSP, which we discuss later. Determining the proper level of abstraction is a tension between many issues including expressibility, portability across machines, ability to perform cost estimates, efficiency, and ease of programming.

Many researchers agree that Java's built-in features are too low level for parallel computing. Higher levels of abstraction must be used for effective parallel programming such as on a cluster of workstations.

The following sections present a candy dish of different flavors of parallel programming models using Java. We discuss the ways researchers incorporate their favorite model into creating a higher-level abstraction for the purpose of improving the lives of Java programmers.

13.3.1   Functional Models

Functional languages are usually elegant and push the edge of parallel language technology. One interesting example is Pizza (http://www.cis.unisa.edu.au/~pizza/). Pizza is a super set of Java that compiles to ordinary Java Byte Code and interfaces with existing Java code. The first important new feature in Pizza is *parametric polymorphism*, which provides to the programmer the ability to write classes that operate on data without specifying the data's type (similar to C++ templates but with type checking). Many C++ programmers, especially ones programming scientific numerical codes, have lamented the lack of templates in Java. Pizza provides an elegant solution. Second, Pizza has *first class functions* which allow the programmer to use functions (in Java, they are called methods) as special kinds of data types. Pizza allows a programmer to store a function in a variable and access it without knowledge about the class it's defined in. In C++, a programmer would use function pointers. Pizza allows a function to be a parameter to a function.

13.3.2 Object-Oriented Models

Even though Java is already a well engineered object-oriented language, researchers are extending it to better suit parallel computation. One approach is to distribute objects.

One of the most promising projects on distributed objects is JavaParty by Michael Philippsen at the University of Karlsruhe, Germany[15] (http://www.icsi. berkeley.edu/~phlipp/JavaParty/). Think of JavaParty as a party of Java Virtual Machines cooperating on a common task. JavaParty transparently adds *remote* objects to Java. Starting with a working Java program using threads, the application programmer adds only the keyword `remote` to the thread objects she wants to execute remotely on another host. Through a preprocessor, the program is transformed to standard Java with RMI method invocations. The application programmer is spared the grief of splitting the program manually and dealing with the ugly details of explicit socket communication and RMI. While other research projects require extensions to the Java language and a customized JVM, JavaParty accomplishes its results with the standard Java compilers and JVMs.

JavaParty is purposely optimized for parallel computing on clusters of workstations. For example, if several remote threads are allocated by JavaParty on the same host, the system automatically uses pointer redirection and not RMI invocations with their severe time penalties. Since JavaParty can migrate objects, locality can be exploited and thus performance can be improved.

JavaParty provides a shared address space, i. e., although objects of remote classes may reside on different machines, their methods and variables (both non-static and static) can be accessed in the same way as in pure Java.

Other worthy projects with similar goals as JavaParty are the Proactive PDC Java library (formerly Java//, *Java Parallel*) (http://www.inria.fr/sloop/javall/), Parallel Java (http://charm.cs.uiuc.edu/papers/ParJavaPDPTA97.html) and Do! (http://www.irisa.fr/caps /PROJECTS/Do/Do.html).

Though JavaParty is an elegant way to program clusters of workstations with Java, the application programmer must still program with Java threads. Many researchers consider Java threads lacking in expressive power as well as being error prone.

13.3.3 Data Parallel Models

In a data parallel model, the same operator operates in parallel on separate but similar data objects. For example, consider the natural parallelism that exists in the many particles in a molecular dynamics computation. The same computation could be performed in parallel on the data object associated with each particle.

Data parallel provides to the programmer an abstraction of a single thread of control. The underlying implementation spreads the work across processors transparently to the programmer. Many programmers are comfortable with this single thread approach. Skillicorn and Talia claim the reason is that "Conscious human thinking appears to be sequential"[18]. This comfort may be only the result of over 50 years of our sequential programming tradition. When we think of a home heating system, we don't think sequential but hierarchically, i.e., as a collection of subsystems (objects) interacting for a common purpose.

A more important but often overlooked strength of the data parallel model is that the application programmer is presented an abstraction where he or she is free of worry from data races, starvation, and deadlock. Assuming the underlying implementation is carefully crafted, these hard to diagnose and fix troublemakers can't happen in the data parallel's single thread model.

HPF Flavors

Data parallel approaches to Java are intimately intertwined with efforts for a "High Performance" Java (http://www.npac.syr.edu/projects/pcrc/HPJava/), related to its namesake: High Performance Fortran (HPF). This multi-university effort is spearheaded by Geoffrey Fox[5] at the Northeast Parallel Architectures Center (NPAC) of Syracuse University. The HPJava Project proposes parallel extensions to Java including a HPF-like distributed array model as well as new distributed control concepts for data parallel. The plan is to construct a special HPJava compiler which generates Java Byte Code for standard JVMs.

13.3.4   Message Passing Models

As both clusters of workstations networked together and distributed memory parallel machines became popular, researchers investigated ways to effectively and efficiently pass messages between machines. Over the last decade, many communication packages have been developed to ease the burden for the application programmer. Some of the more popular approaches are incorporating Java.

PVM Flavors

The PVM (Parallel Virtual Machine) developed at Oak Ridge National Laboratory is a software package that permits a heterogeneous-interconnected collection of Unix-based computers to be used as a single large machine. PVM supports programs written in C, C++, and Fortran. PVM is popular, portable, and supported by most of the high performance computer vendors.

The jPVM project (formerly JavaPVM) (http://www.isye.gatech.edu/chmsr/jPVM/) at Georgia Tech is a native methods interface to PVM for the Java platform. This interface allows Java applications to interact with applications written in C, C++, and Fortran that adhere to the PVM protocols. However, jPVM is *not* an implementation of PVM written in Java, but the next project JPVM is!

The JPVM (with a capital J) project (http://www.cs.virginia.edu/~ajf2j/jpvm.html) at the University of Virginia is a PVM-like library of object classes implemented in and for use with Java. JPVM is a combination of the ease of programming in Java and the high performance parallel virtual machine concept borrowed from PVM. JPVM is *not* interoperable with standard PVM. It is designed to build

PVM-like systems across many computers written totally in Java.

MPI Flavors

The Message Passing Interface (MPI)[13] is an industry standard programming interface for transferring messages between processors on a parallel machine or a cluster of workstations. In contrast to PVM, MPI is typically faster but does not support the virtual parallel machine concept of PVM, e. g., no remote process creation.

The MPIJ project (http://notch.cs.byu.edu/DOGMA/online_docs/docs/mpij/ MPIJ.html) at Brigham Young University is a completely Java-based implementation of MPI. This enables MPIJ to run on multiple platforms (including web browsers) without the need for a native MPI implementation. MPIJ is part of the DOGMA project.

The mpiJava project (http://www.npac.syr.edu/projects/pcrc/mpiJava/ mpi-Java.html) at Syracuse University is part of the HPJava project mentioned earlier. mpiJava is an object-oriented Java interface to the standard MPI. mpiJava provides the full functionality of MPI 1.1 but requires a native MPI implementation.

CSP/Occam Flavors

A process is different from a thread. A *thread* is an independent execution of a sequence of instructions. A *process* is similar but the instructions execute inside an operating-system protected region of memory. Since threads share their memory region, there is much less context to save when a context switch occurs. Therefore, switching between threads is faster than between processes. However, threads require careful coordination because of the shared data areas.

The concept of process is a general abstraction of concurrent entities across machines as well as on the same machine. The process concept is central to Communicating Sequential Processes (CSP). Processes do not share data areas and communicate only by sending messages on point-to-point channels.

It is easy to fall into a tar pit with either naive use of threads or naive use of message passing. The timing-dependent beasts of data races, deadlock, improper synchronization, and starvation will rear their ugly heads. C. A. R. Hoare developed his CSP model[8], [9], [6] (CSP archive http://www.comlab.ox.ac.uk/archive/csp.html) to keep these beasts in check. He developed CSP as a process algebra to reason about concurrent programs. With CSP, the programmer can prove practical theorems such as his or her program can never deadlock. However, since CSP is a mathematical theory, it can be overwhelming to the typical programmer.

To hide the mathematics behind the elegant and secure abstractions of CSP, researches have developed CSP-based programming languages, the most notable being Occam. Unfortunately, Occam is a static language like Fortran and does not allow dynamic data allocation, recursive functions, or dynamic process creation. Fortunately, there is a way to build the CSP model on top of Java monitors. This approach is called JavaPP (Java Plug-and-Play) (http://www.cs.bris.ac.uk/~alan/

javapp.html). Research teams at University of Kent, UK[19]; University of Twente, the Netherlands (http://www.rt.el.utwente.nl/javapp/information/CTJ/CTJ-Tutorial-LT-3.pdf); and Oxford, UK have created JavaPP, a Java class library to support CSP-style concurrent programming.

From the formal work at Oxford, the company Formal Systems markets a product called FDR (Failures-Divergence Refinement) which allows the checking of many properties of finite-state systems and the investigation of systems which fail these checks. It is based on CSP theory and has been applied successfully in a number of industrial applications.

Dyke Stiles of Utah State University taught a graduate level course (http://www.engineering.usu.edu/classes/ece/6750/) where the students read Bill Roscoe's textbook on CSP[16], used the FDR tools, and programmed in JavaPP. Students very quickly learned how to specify concurrent systems using CSP, and could then use the CSP CASE tools from FDR to verify correctness with specifications and freedom from deadlock and divergence (livelock). The students' proven systems could then be implemented in Java using the CSP class libraries of JavaPP.

Fortran-M Flavors

Fortran M is a small set of extensions to Fortran where programs are constructed by declaring communication channels to plug together program modules (processes). See Ian Foster's book[4] for details. Similar to CSP, Foster's processes do not share data, and all interaction between processes is through message passing on the channels. With careful use of these communication channels, critical problems that plague message passing systems can be avoided. For example, operations on channels are restricted so as to guarantee deterministic execution, even in dynamic computations that create and delete processes and channels. Channels are typed, so a compiler can check for correct usage.

One project that is incorporating Fortran M-like channel communication in Java is at the Northeast Parallel Architectures Center (NPAC) of Syracuse University (http://www.npac.syr.edu/projects/pcrc/HPJava/beginnings.html).

13.3.5   Shared Memory Models

The shared memory models provide the programmer the abstraction that all the data objects are in the same data address space. Some models achieve the abstraction by relying on physically shared memory and special features in the operating systems. Others provide the abstraction by hiding the network communication between computers.

Thread Flavors

The Shared Memory Processor (SMP) architecture consists of several processors sharing a common main memory. The SMP architecture is popular today in the high-end server and workstation markets. Computer vendors sell models with up to 64 processors, and have developed features in their operating systems to allow a single program to utilize the multiple CPUs. This is typically done by providing a threads package[10]. Some Java implementations allow the programmer to use these "native threads," e.g., Sun Microsystems' recent JDK 1.2 under Solaris. In the near future, we can expect rapid advancement in this area of Java parallel computing.

The JavaParty project[15], which we discussed previously, is a threads-based approach to parallelism. Though one expects Michael Philippsen and his team to incorporate SMP features into JavaParty, JavaParty's strength is in providing the programmer the abstractions of remote objects, remote threads, and a shared address space across a network of computers. The details of the network communication is hidden from the programmer.

Linda Flavors

Developed by Gelernter and Carriero at Yale, Linda[1] is a coordination language which is easily added to existing sequential languages like C and Fortran. The Linda extensions support process creation on other networked machines and coordinate communication between them. Linda uses a bulletin board model of communication where processes can post a message (`out` operator), read a message (`rd` operator) and consume a message (`in` operator). The message posted is in the form of an n-tuple, a vector with n fields. Selection of a message in the universally visible tuple space (the bulletin board) is first by the signature, i.e., the types and number of fields, then by associative pattern matching of fields in the tuple. Consider the following two operations on two different parallel machines:

```
out(''T1'', 2 , 3)          in(''T1'', ?x, 3)
```

The `out` operation places the tuple ("T1", 2, 3) in tuple space and continues. The `in` operation will block until it finds a matching tuple. The fields of the `in` operation will match the tuple and thus remove it and assign the value of 2 to the variable x. This simple and elegant scheme is easy to understand and program.

The key contribution of the Yale research team is the development of compile-time optimizations that allows this simple model to be efficient on both distributed memory parallel machines and clusters of workstations. Linda versions in Fortran and C are commercial products marketed by Scientific Computing Associates. The Yale team is currently developing a Java-Linda (http://www.cs.yale.edu/users/asmith/cs690/cs690.html).

The database research group at IBM has developed a Linda-like product written in Java called T Spaces (http://www.almaden.ibm.com/cs/TSpaces/html/TSRole.html) that is a software package offering database services as well as group communication services. The ideas of Linda's tuple space were borrowed to create T Spaces as a persistent data repository as well as allow global communication across a network of computers.

Not in competition with T Spaces but sharing a similar name, Sun Microsystems has announced JavaSpaces (http://java.javasoft.com/products/javaspaces/ whitepapers/index.html). JavaSpaces uses Linda-like primitives to create a simple, fast, and unified mechanism for sharing, coordination, and communication of distributed resources, services, and objects in a network. JavaSpaces provides many of the same services we associate with a traditional operating system. JavaSpaces is still in development but worth watching.

13.4   Summary

Two years ago high performance Java was an oxymoron. Today, it is clear; the research community is very active in uniting Java and parallel computing. Production-level parallel computing in Java is being performed in the scientific and financial fields. Global computing resources through Java-based web browsers are working on significant problems like breaking RSA codes and the Search for Extraterrestrial Intelligence (SETI).

Researchers around the world are investigating and experimenting with Java as a platform to perform parallel computations. Some are extending the Java language in innovative ways. Others are building abstractions on top of Java.

Deadlock, the need for synchronization, starvation, and data races are major issues. Efficiency is very important, but a fast incorrect program is not acceptable. The search for the proper Java parallel abstractions continues.

13.5   Bibliography

[1] N. Carriero and D. Gelernter. How to Write Parallel Programs: A Guide to the Perplexed. *ACM Computing Surveys*, vol 21(3), September 1989.

[2] H. M. Deitel and P. J. Deitel. *Java: How to Program*. Prentice Hall, 1998.

[3] Jim Farley. *Java: Distributed Computing*. O'Reilly and Associates, 1998.

[4] Ian Foster. *Designing and Building Parallel Programs: Concepts and Tools for Parallel Software Engineering*. Addison Wesley, 1995.

[5] Geoffrey Fox and Wojtek Furmanski. Java for Parallel Computing and as a General Language for Scientific and Engineering Simulation and Modeling. *Concurrency, Practice and Experience*, vol 9(6) pages 415–425, 1997. URL: http://www.npac.syr.edu/pub/by_index/sccs/papers/html/ 0750/abs-0793.html.

[6] M.G. Hinchey and S.A. Jarvis. *Concurrent Systems: Formal Development in CSP*. International Series in Software Engineering. McGraw-Hill, 1995.

[7] C. A. R. Hoare. Monitors: An Operating System Structuring Concept. *CACM*, vol 17(10) pages 549–557, 1974.

[8] C. A. R. Hoare. Communicating Sequential Processes. *CACM*, vol 21(8) pages 666–677, 1978.

[9] C. A. R. Hoare. *Communicating Sequential Processes.* International Series in Computer Science. Prentice Hall, 1985.

[10] Steve Kleiman, Devang Shah, and Bart Smaalders. *Programming with Threads.* Prentice Hall, 1996.

[11] Doug Lea. *Concurrent Programming in Java: Design Principles and Patterns.* Addison-Wesley, 1997.

[12] Scott Oaks and Henry Wong. *Java Threads.* O'Reilly and Associates, 1997.

[13] Peter S. Pacheco. *Parallel Programming with MPI.* Morgan Kaufmann, 1997.

[14] Gregory F. Pfister. *In Search of Clusters: The Ongoing Battle in Lowly Parallel Computing.* Prentice Hall, 1998.

[15] Michael Philippsen and Matthias Zenger. JavaParty – Transparent Remote Objects in Java. *Concurrency: Practice and Experience,* vol 9(11) pages 1225-1242, November 1997.

[16] A. W. Roscoe. *The Theory and Practice of Concurrency.* Prentice Hall, 1997.

[17] David B. Skillicorn and Domenico Takia. *Programming Languages for Parallel Processing.* IEEE Computer Society Press, 1995.

[18] David B. Skillicorn and Domenico Takia. Models and Languages for Parallel Computation. *ACM Computing Surveys,* vol 30(2) pages 123–169, June 1998.

[19] Peter Welch et al. Response to Ted Lewis's article "If Java is the answer, what was the question?" *IEEE Computer,* July 1997. http://www.cs.bris.ac.uk/~alan/Java/ieeelet.html.

Chapter 14

The *HPspmd* Model and its Java Binding

Guansong Zhang, Bryan Carpenter, Geoffrey Fox,
Xinying Li, and Yuhong Wen

NPAC at Syracuse University
Syracuse, NY, 13244, USA

Email: {*zgs,dbc,gcf,xli,wen*}*@npac.syr.edu*

14.1 Introduction

In this chapter we introduce the *HPJava* language, a programming language that extends Java for parallel programming on message passing systems—from multiprocessor systems to workstation clusters.

HPJava owes much to High Performance Fortran (HPF) [4]. Its model of data distribution is adapted directly from the HPF model. The heritage of HPF can be traced back to Fortran dialects that were implemented most successfully on SIMD and other tightly-coupled MPP architectures. While it was always a goal of the HPF designers that the language should be efficiently implementable on the more loosely coupled MIMD clusters that dominate today, the complexity of the language—and notably the design goal of emulating exactly the semantics of a sequential Fortran program—have made efficient implementation on today's architectures quite hard.

HPJava, in contrast, starts from the assumption that the target hardware is a set of interacting MIMD processors, and exposes that assumption explicitly in its programming model. This greatly simplifies the task of the compiler, and increases the chance of obtaining efficient implementations on architectures including PC and workstation clusters. Instead of the HPF programming model, the language introduces a high-level structured SPMD programming style—the HPspmd model. A program written in this class of language explicitly coordinates well-defined process groups. These cooperate in a loosely synchronous manner, sharing logical threads of control. As in a conventional distributed-memory SPMD program, only a process owning a data item such as an array element is allowed to access the item directly. The language provides special constructs that allow programmers to meet this constraint conveniently.

Besides the normal variables of the sequential base language, the language model introduces classes of global variables that are stored collectively across process groups. Primarily, these are distributed arrays. They provide a global name space in the form of globally subscripted arrays, with assorted distribution patterns. This helps to relieve programmers of error-prone activities such as the local-to-global, global-to-local subscript translations which occur in data parallel applications.

In addition to special data types, the language provides special constructs to facilitate both data parallel and task parallel programming. Through these constructs different processors can work either simultaneously on globally addressed data, or independently to execute complex procedures on locally held data. The conversion between these phases is seamless.

In the traditional SPMD mold, the language itself does not provide implicit data movement semantics. This greatly simplifies the task of the compiler, and should encourage programmers to use algorithms that exploit locality. Data on remote processors is accessed exclusively through explicit library calls. In particular, the initial HPJava implementation relies on a library of collective communication routines originally developed as part of an HPF run-time library. Other distributed-array-oriented communication libraries may be bound to the language later. Due to the explicit SPMD programming model, low level MPI communication is always available as a fallback. The language itself only provides basic concepts to organize data arrays and process groups. Different communication patterns are implemented as library functions. This allows the possibility that if a new communication pattern is needed, it is relatively easily integrated through new libraries.

In our earlier work on HPF compilation [10] the role of run-time support was emphasized. Difficulties in compiling HPF efficiently suggested to make the run-time communication library directly visible in the programming model. Since Java is a simple, elegant language, we are implementing our prototype based upon this language.

Section 14.2 reviews the HPspmd model in the context of the HPJava language. Section 14.3 describes the class library packages used in code generated by the HPJava translator, and thus exposes many of the implementation issues. Some examples of simple algorithms expressed in HPJava are given in Section 14.4. Then Section 14.5 discusses the rationale of various design decisions in the language. The status of the project and future goals are summarized in Sections 14.6 and 14.7.

14.2 Java Language Binding

This section introduces the HPJava language. HPJava contains the whole of standard Java as a subset. It adds various built-in classes for describing process groups and index ranges, new global data types, and some syntax for accessing distributed data and specifying which processes execute particular statements.

14.2.1   Basic Concepts

Key concepts in the programming model are built around the process groups used to describe program execution control in a parallel program. Group is a class representing a process group, typically with a grid structure and an associated set of process dimensions. It has its subclasses that represent different grid dimensionalities, such as Procs1, Procs2, etc. For example,

```
Procs2 p = new Procs2(2,4);
```

p is a 2-dimensional, 2 x 4 grid of processes.

The second category of concepts is associated with distributed ranges. The elements of an ordinary array can be represented by an array name and an integer sequence. There are two parameters associated with this sequence: an index to access each array element, and the extent of the range this index can be chosen from. In describing a distributed array, HPJava introduces two new kinds of entity to represent the analogous concepts. A *range* maps an integer interval into a process dimension according to certain distribution format. Ranges describe the extent and the mapping of array dimensions. A *location*, or slot, is an abstract element of a range. For example,

```
Range x = new BlockRange(100, p.dim(0)) ;
Range y = new CyclicRange(200, p.dim(1)) ;
```

creates two ranges distributed over the two process dimensions of the group p. One is block distributed, the other is cyclic distributed. There are 100 different locations in the range x. The first one, for example, is

```
x [0]
```

Additional related concepts are subgroups and subranges. A subgroup is some slice of a process array, formed by restricting the process coordinates in one or more dimensions to single values. Suppose i is a location in a range distributed over a dimension of group p. The expression

```
p / i
```

represents a smaller group—the slice of p to which location i is mapped. Similarly, a subrange is a section of a range, parameterized by a global index triplet. Logically, it represents a subset of the locations of the original range. The syntax for a subrange expression is

```
x [1 : 49]
```

The symbol ":" is a special separator. It is used to construct a Fortran-90 style triplet, with lower- and upper-bound expressions defining an integer subset. The optional third member of a triplet is a stride.

When a process grid is defined, certain ranges and locations are also implicitly defined. As shown in Figure 14.1, two primitive ranges are associated with dimensions of the group p:

```
Range u = p.dim(0);
Range v = p.dim(1);
```

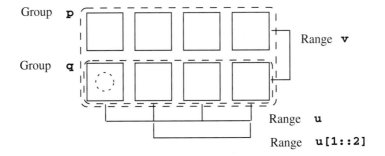

Figure 14.1 Structured process group.

`dim()` is a member function that returns a range reference, directly representing a processor dimension. We can obtain a location in range v, and use it to create a new group,

```
Group q = p / v [1] ;
```

In a traditional SPMD program, execution control is based on *if* statements and process ID or rank numbers. In the new programming language, switching execution control is based on the structured process group. For example, it is not difficult to guess that the following code:

```
on(p) {
   ...
}
```

will restrict the execution control inside the bracket to processes in group p. The language also provided well-defined constructs to split execution control across processes according to data items we want to access. This will be discussed later.

14.2.2   Global Variables

When an SPMD program starts on a group of n processes, there will be n control threads mapped to n physical processors. In each control thread, the program can define variables in the same way as in a sequential program. The variables created in this way are local variables. Their names may be common to all processes, but they will be accessed individually (their scope is local to a process).

Besides local variables, HPJava allows a program to define global variables, explicitly mapped to a process group. A global variable will be treated by the process group that created it as a single entity. The language has special syntax for the definition of global data. Global variables are all defined by using the **new** operator from free storage. When a global variable is created, a data descriptor is also allocated to describe where the data are held. On a single processor, an array variable might be parametrized by a simple record containing a memory address

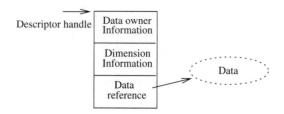

Figure 14.2 Descriptor.

and an `int` value for its length. On a multiprocessor, a more complicated structure is needed to describe a distributed array. The data descriptor specifies where the data is created, and how they are distributed. The logical structure of a descriptor is shown in Figure 14.2.

HPJava has special syntax to define global data. The statement

```
int # s = new int # on p ;
```

creates a global scalar replicated over process group `p`. In the statement, `s` is a data descriptor handle—a global scalar reference. The scalar contains an integer value. Global scalar references can be defined for any primitive type (or, in principle, class type) of Java. The symbol `#` in the type signature distinguishes a global scalar from a primitive integer. For a global scalar, a field `value` is used to access the value:

```
on(p) {
  int # s = new int # ;
  s.value = 100 ;
}
```

Note how the `on` clause can be omitted from the constructor: the whole of the active process group is the default distribution group. Figure 14.3 shows a possible memory mapping for this scalar on different processes. Note, the value field of `s` is

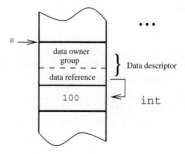

Figure 14.3 Memory mapping.

identical in each process in the distribution group. Replicated value variables are different from local variables with identical names. The associated descriptors can be used to ensure the value is maintained identically in each process, throughout program execution.

When defining a global array, it is not necessary to allocate a data descriptor for each array element—one descriptor suffices for the whole array. An array can defined with various kinds of range, introduced earlier. Suppose we have, as before,

```
Range x = new BlockRange(100, p.dim(0)) ;
```

and the process group defined in Figure 14.1, then

```
float [[]] a = new float [[x]] on q ;
```

will create a global array with range x on group q. Here a is a descriptor handle describing a one-dimensional array of float. It is block distributed on group q.[1] In HPJava a is called a global or distributed array reference.

A distributed array range can also be collapsed (or sequential). An integer range is specified, eg

```
float [[*]] b = new float [[100]] ;
```

When defining an array with collapsed dimensions an asterisk is normally added in the type signatures to mark the collapsed dimensions.

The typical method of accessing global array elements is not exactly the same as for local array elements, or for global scalar references. In distributed dimensions of arrays we must use named locations as subscripts, for example

```
at(i = x [3])
  a [i] = 3 ;
```

We will leave discussion of the *at* construct to Section 14.2.3, and give a simpler example here: if a global array is defined with a collapsed dimension, accessing its elements is modelled on local arrays. For example:

```
for(int i = 0 ; i < 100 ; i++)
  b [i] = i ;
```

assigns the loop index to each corresponding element in the array.

When defining a multidimensional global array, a single descriptor parametrizes a rectangular array of any dimension:

```
Range x = new BlockRange(100, p.dim(0)) ;
Range y = new CyclicRange(100, p.dim(1)) ;
float [[,]] c = new float [[x, y]];
```

---

[1]The on clause restricts the data owner group of the array to q. If group p is used instead, the one-dimenstional array will be replicated in the first dimenstion of the group, and block distributed over the second dimension.

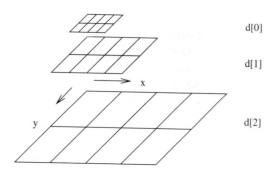

Figure 14.4 Array of distributed arrays.

This creates a two-dimension global array with the first dimension block distributed and the second cyclic distributed. Now c is a global array reference. Its elements can be accessed using single brackets with two suitable locations inside.

The global array introduced here is a true multidimensional array, not a Java-like array-of-arrays. Java-style arrays-of-arrays are still useful. For example, one can define a local array of distributed arrays:

```
int[] size = {100, 200, 400};
float [[,]] d[] = new float [size.length][[,]] ;
Range x[], y[];
for (int l = 0; l < size.length; l++) {
  const int n = size [l] ;
  x[l] = new BlockRange(n, p.dim(0)) ;
  y[l] = new BlockRange(n, p.dim(1)) ;
  d[l] = new float [[x[l], y[l]]];
}
```

This creates the stack of distributed arrays shown in Figure 14.4.

Like Fortran 90, HPJava allows construction of sections of global arrays. The syntax of section subscripting uses double brackets. The subscripts can be scalar (integers or locations) or triplets.

Suppose we have array a and c defined as above. Then a[[i]], c, c[[i, 1::2]], and c[[i, :]] are all array sections. Here, i is an integer in the appropriate interval (it could also be a location in the first range of a and c). Both the expressions c[[i, 1::2]] and c[[i, :]] represent one-dimensional distributed arrays, providing aliases for subsets of the elements in c. The expression a[[i]] contains a single element of a, but the result is a global scalar reference (unlike the expression a[i] which is a simple variable).

Array section expressions are often used as arguments in function calls.[2] Table

---

[2]When used in method calls, the collapsed dimension array is a *subtype* of the ordinary one, i.e., an argument of float[[*,*]], float[[*,]] and float[[,*]] type can all be passed to a dummy of type float[[,]]. The converse is not true.

Table 14.1 Section Expression and Type Signature

global var	array section	type
2-dimension	c	float [[,]]
	c[[:,:]]	float [[,]]
1-dimension	c[[i,:]]	float [[]]
	c[[i,1::2]]	float [[]]
scalar(0-dim)	c[[i,j]]	float #

14.1 shows the type signatures of global data with different dimensions.

The size of an array in Java can be had from its `length` field. In HPJava, information like the distributed group and distributed dimensions can be accessed from the following inquiries, available on all global array types:

```
Group grp()      // distribution group

Range rng(int d) // d'th range
```

Further inquiry functions on `Range` yield values such as extents and distribution formats.

14.2.3   Program Execution Control

HPJava has all the conventional Java statements for execution control within a single process. It introduces three new control constructs: *on*, *at*, and *overall* for execution control across processes. A new concept, the active process group, is introduced. It is the set of processes sharing the current thread of control.

In a traditional SPMD program, switching the active process group is effectively implemented by *if* statements such as:

```
if(myid >= 0 && myid < 4) {
  ...
}
```

Inside the braces, only processes numbered 0 to 3 share the control thread. In HPJava, this effect is expressed using a `Group`. When a HPJava program starts, the active process group has a system-defined value. During the execution, the active process group can be changed explicitly through an *on* construct in the program.

In a shared memory program, accessing the value of a variable is straightforward. In a message passing system, only the process which holds data can read and write the data. We sometimes call this SPMD constraint. A traditional SPMD program respects this constraint by using an idiom like

```
if(myid == 1)
  my_data = 3 ;
```

The *if* statement makes sure that only `my_data` on process 1 is assigned as 3.

In the language we present here, similar constraints must be respected. Besides *on* construct introduced earlier, there is a convenient way to change the active process group to access a required array element, namely, the *at* construct. Suppose array a is defined as in the previous section, then:

```
on(q) {
  a [1] = 3 ;     // error

  at(j = x [1])
    a [j] = 3 ;  // correct
}
```

The assignment statement guarded by an *at* construct is correct; the one without is likely to imply access to an element not held locally. Formally it is illegal because, in a simple subscripting operation, an integer expression cannot be used to subscript a distributed dimension. The *at* construct introduces a new variable j, a *named location*, with scope only inside the block controlled by the *at*. Named locations are the only legal element subscripts in distributed dimensions.

A more powerful construct called *overall* combines restriction of the active process group with a loop:

```
on(q)
  overall(i = x | 0 : 3)
    a [i] = 3 ;
```

is essentially equivalent to[3]

```
on(q)
  for(int n = 0 ; n < 4 ; n++)
    at(i = x [n])
      a [i] = 3;
```

In each iteration, the active process group is changed to q / i. In Section 14.4, we will illustrate with further programs how *at* and *overall* constructs conveniently allow one to keep the active process group equal to the data owner group for the assigned data.

14.2.4   Communication Library Functions

When accessing data on another process, HPJava needs explicit communication, as in a normal SPMD program. Communication libraries are provided as packages in HPJava. Detailed function specifications are given elsewhere. The next section will introduce a small number of top level collective communication functions.

---

[3]A compiler can implement overall construct in a more efficient way, using linearized address calculation. For detailed translation schemes for the overall construct, please refer to [2].

14.3   Java Packages for HPspmd Programming

The implementation of the HPJava compiler is based on a run-time system. It is actually a source-to-source translator converting an HPJava program to a Java node program, with function calls to the run-time library, called *adJava*.

The run-time interface consists of several Java packages. The most important one is the HPspmd runtime proper. It includes the classes needed to translate language constructs. Other packages provide communication and some simple I/O functions. Important classes in the first package include distributed array "container classes" and related classes describing process groups and index ranges. These classes correspond directly to HPJava built-in classes.

The first hierarchy is based on `Group`. A group, or process group, defines some subset of the processes executing the SPMD program. They can be used to describe how program variables, such as arrays, are distributed or replicated across the process pool, or to specify which subset of processes executes a particular code fragment. Important members of adJava `Group` class include the pair `on()`, `no()` used to translate the *on* construct.

The most common way to create a group object is through the constructor for one of the subclasses representing a process grid. The subclass `Procs` represents a grid of processes and carries information on process dimensions: in particular an inquiry function `dim(r)` returns a range object describing the *r*-th process dimension. `Procs` is further subclassed by `Procs0`, `Procs1`, `Procs2`, ... which provide simpler constructors for fixed dimensionality process grids.

The second hierarchy in the package is based on `Range`. A range is a map from the integer interval $0, \ldots, n-1$ into some process dimension (i.e., some dimension of a process grid). Ranges are used to parametrize distributed arrays and the *overall* distributed loop.

The most common way to create a range object is to use the constructor for one of the subclasses representing ranges with specific distribution formats. Simple block distribution format is implemented by `BlockRange`, while `CyclicRange` and `BlockCyclicRange` represent other standard distribution formats of HPF. The subclass `CollapsedRange` represents a sequential (undistributed range). Finally, a `DimRange` is associated with each process dimension and represents the range of coordinates for the process dimension itself—just one element is mapped to each process.

The related adJava class `Location` represents an individual location in a particular distributed range. Important members of the adJava `Range` class include the function `location(i)`, which returns the *i*th location in a range, and its inverse, `idx(l)`, which returns the global subscript associated with a given location. Important members of the `Location` class include `at()` and `ta()`, used in the implementation of the HPJava that *at* construct.

Finally, we have the rather complex hierarchy of classes representing distributed arrays. HPJava global arrays declared using `[[]]` are represented by Java objects belonging to classes such as:

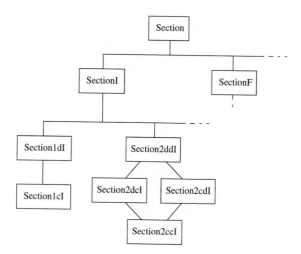

Figure 14.5 The adJava `Section` hierarchy

```
Array1dI, Array1cI,
Array2ddI, Array2dcI, Array2cdI, Array2ccI,
...
Array1dF, Array1cF,
Array2ddF, Array2dcF, Array2cdF, Array2ccF,
...
```

Generally speaking, the class "`Array`$nc|d\ldots T$" represents n-dimensional distributed arrays with elements of type T—currently one of I, F, ..., meaning `int`, `float`, ... [4] The penultimate part of the class name is a string of n "c"s and "d"s specifying whether each dimension is collapsed or normally distributed. These correlate with presence or absence of an asterisk in slots of the HPJava type signature. The concrete `Array...` classes implement a series of abstract interfaces. These follow a similar naming convention, but the root of their names is `Section` rather than `Array` (so `Array2dcI`, for example, implements `Section2dcI`). The hierarchy of `Section` interfaces is illustrated in Figure 14.5. The need to introduce the `Section` interfaces should be evident from the hierarchy diagram. The type hierarchy of HPJava involves a kind of multiple inheritance. The array type `int [[*, *]]`, for example, is a specialization of both the types `int [[*, ]]` and `int [[, *]]`. Java allows "multiple inheritance" only from interfaces, not classes.

Important members of the `Section` interfaces include inquiry functions `dat()`, which returns an ordinary one dimensional Java array used to store the locally held elements of the distributed array, and the member `pos(i, ...)`, which takes n subscript arguments and returns the local offset of the element implied by those

---

[4]In the inital implementation, the element type is restricted to the Java primitive types.

subscripts. Each argument of `pos` is a location or an integer (only allowed if the corresponding dimension is collapsed). These functions are used to implement elemental subscripting. The inquiry `grp()` returns the group over which elements of the array are distributed. The inquiry `rng(d)` returns the *d*th range of the array.

Another package in adJava is the communication library. The adJava communication package includes classes corresponding to the various collective communication schedules provided in the NPAC PCRC kernel. Most of them provide a constructor to establish a schedule, and an `execute` method, which carries out the data movement specified by the schedule. Different communication models may eventually be added through further packages.

The collective communication schedules can be used directly by the programmer or invoked through certain wrapper functions. A class named `Adlib` is defined with static members that create and execute communication schedules and perform simple I/O functions. This class includes, for example, the following methods, each implemented by constructing the appropriate schedule and then executing it:

```
static void remap(Section dst, Section src)
static void shift(Section dst, Section src, int shift, int dim, int mode)
static void copy(Section dst, Section src)
static void writeHalo(Section src, int [] wlo, int [] whi, int [] mode)
```

`Adlib.remap` will copy the corresponding elements from one array to another, regardless of their respective distribution format. `Adlib.shift` will shift data by a certain amount in a specific dimension of the array, in either cyclic or edge-off mode. `Adlib.writeHalo` is used to update ghost regions.

Given the classes described above, one can program in the HPspmd style in pure Java program. Then the idea of the HPJava compiler is just to translate the HPJava program onto this interface, in the meanwhile, to use optimized address calculation instead of function calls to access elements of arrays. (For a detailed translation scheme, please refer to [11].)

14.4 Programming Examples

In this section we give two example programs to show the new language features. The first example is the Choleski decomposition, seen in Figure 14.6. Here, `remap` is used to broadcast one updated column to each process. The function `idx` gets the global index of location `m` relative to the parent range `x`. The second example is the Jacobi iteration, seen in Figure 14.7. In the displayed code there is only one iteration, but it demonstrates how to define range references with ghost areas, how to use the `writeHalo` function, and how to use shifted locations as subscripts.

14.5 Issues in the Language Design

With some of the implementation mechanisms exposed, we can better discuss the language design itself.

```
Procs1 p = new Procs1(4);
on(p) {
  Range x = new CyclicRange(n, p.dim(0));
  float a[[*,]] = new float [[n, x]];
  ... some code to initialise 'a' ...
  float b[[*]] = new float [[n]]; // buffer

  for(int k = 0 ; k < N - 1 ; k++) {
    at(l = x[k]) {
      float d =  Math.sqrt(a[k,l]) ;
      a[k,l] = d ;
      for(int s = k + 1 ; s < N ; s++)
        a[s,l] /= d ;
    }
    Adlib.remap(b[[k+1:]], a[[k+1:,  k]]);

    overall(m = x | k + 1 : )
      for(int i = x.idx(m) ; i < N ; i++)
        a[i,m] -= b[i] * b[x.idx(m)] ;
  }
  at(l = x [N - 1])
    a[N - 1,l] = Math.sqrt(a[N-1,l]) ;
}
```

Figure 14.6 Choleski decomposition.


```
Procs2 p = new Procs2(2, 4);
Range x = new BlockRange(100, p.dim(0), 1),
      y = new BlockRange(200, p.dim(1), 1);
on(p) {
  float [[,]] a = new float [[x,y]], b = new float [[x,y]];
  ... some code to initialize 'a'

  Adlib.writeHalo(a);

  overall(i = x | : )
    overall(j = y | : )
      b[i,j] = 0.25 * (a[i-1,j] + a[i+1,j] + a[i,j-1] + a[i,j+1]);
  overall(i = x | : )
    overall(j = y | : )
      a[i,j] = b[i,j];
}
```

Figure 14.7 Jacobi relaxation.

14.5.1   Extending the Java Language

The first question to answer is why use Java as a base language? Actually, the programming model embodied in HPJava is largely language-independent. It can be bound to other languages like C, C++, and Fortran. But Java is a convenient base language, especially for initial experiments, because it provides full object-orientation—convenient for describing complex distributed data—implemented in a relatively simple setting, conducive to development of source-to-source translators. It has been noted elsewhere that Java has various features suggesting it could be an attractive language for science and engineering [6].

With Java as a base language, an obvious question is whether we can extend the language by simply adding packages, instead of changing the syntax. There are two problems with doing this for data-parallel programming.

Our baseline is HPF, and any package supporting parallel arrays as general as HPF is likely to be cumbersome to code with. Our run-time system needs an (in principle) infinite series of class names

```
Array1dI, Array1cI, Array2ddI, Array2dcI, ...
```

to express the HPJava types

```
int [[]], int [[*]], int [[,]], int [[,*]] ...
```

as well as the corresponding series for char, float, and so on. To access an element of a distributed array in HPJava, one writes

```
a[i] = 3 ;
```

In the adJava interface, it must be written as

```
a.dat()[a.pos(i)] = 3 ;
```

This is only for simple subscripting. Constructing array sections will be even more complex using the raw class library interface.

The second problem is that a Java program using a package like adJava in a direct, naive way will have very poor performance, because all the local address of the global array are expressed by functions such as pos. An optimization pass is needed to transform offset computation to a more intelligent style. So if a preprocessor must do these optimizations anyway, it makes sense to design a syntax to express the concepts of the programming model more naturally.

14.5.2   Why not HPF?

The design of the HPJava language is strongly influenced by HPF. The language emerged partly out of practices adopted in our efforts to implement an HPF compilation system [10]. For example:

```
!HPF$ POCESSOR     P(4)
!HPF$ TEMPLET      T(100)
!HPF$ DISTRIBUTE   T(BLOCK) ONTO P
```

```
        REAL        A(100,100), B(100)
!HPF$ ALIGN        A(:,*) WITH T(:)
!HPF$ ALIGN        B WITH T
```

have their conterparts in HPJava:

```
Procs1 p = new Procs1(4);
Range x = new BlockRange (100, p.dim(0));
float [[,*]] a = new float [[x,100]] on p;
float [[ ]] b = new float [[x]] on p;
```

Both languages provide a globally addressed name space for data parallel applications. Both of them can specify how data are mapped on to a processor grid. The difference between the two lies in their communication aspects. In HPF, a simple assignment statement may cause data movement. For example, given the above distribution, the assignment

```
A(10,10) = B(30)
```

will cause communication between processor 1 and 2. In HPJava, similar communication must be done through explicit function calls:[5]

```
Adlib.remap(a[[9,9]], b[[29]]);
```

Experience from compiling the HPF language suggests that, while there are various kinds of algorithms to detect communication automatically, it is often difficult to give the generated node program acceptable performance. In HPF, the need to decide on which processor the computation should be executed further complicates the situation. One may apply "owner computes" or "majority computes" rules to partition computation, but these heuristics are difficult to apply in many situations.

In HPJava, the SPMD programming model is emphasized. The distributed arrays just help the programmer organize data, and simplify global-to-local address translation. The tasks of computation partition and communication are still under control of the programmer. This is certainly an extra onus, and the language may be more difficult to program than HPF;[6] but it helps programmers to understand the performance of the program much better than in HPF, so algorithms exploiting locality and parallelism are encouraged. It also dramatically simplifies the work of the compiler.

Because the communication sector is considered an "add-on" to the basic language, HPJava should interoperate more smoothly than HPF with other successful SPMD libraries, including MPI [5], Global Arrays [7], CHAOS [3], and so on.

14.5.3   Datatypes in HPJava

In a parallel language, it is desirable to have both local variables (like the ones in MPI programming) and global variables (like the ones in HPF programming). The

---

[5]By default Fortran array subscripts starts from 1, while HPJava global subscripts always start from 0.

[6]The program must meet SPMD constraints, e.g., only the owner of an element can access that data. Run-time checking can be added automatically to ensure such conditions are met.

former provide flexibility and are ideal for task parallel programming; the latter are convenient especially for data parallel programming.

In HPJava, variable names are divided into two sets. In general those declared using ordinary Java syntax represent local variables and those declared with # or [[]] represent global variables. The two sectors are independent. In the implementation of HPJava the global variables have special data descriptors associated with them, defining how their components are divided or replicated across processes. The significance of the data descriptor is most obvious when dealing with procedure calls. Passing array sections to procedure calls is an important component in the array processing facilities of Fortran90 [1]. The data descriptor of Fortran90 will include stride information for each array dimension. One can assume that HPF needs a much more complex kind of data descriptor to allow passing distributed arrays across procedure boundaries. In either case the descriptor is not visible to the programmer. Java has a more explicit data descriptor concept; its arrays are considered as objects, with, for example, a publicly accessible length field. In HPJava, the data descriptors for global data are similar to those used in HPF, but more explicitly exposed to programmers. Inquiry functions such as grp and rng have a similar role in global data as the field length in an ordinary Java array.

Keeping two data sectors seems to complicate the language and its syntax. But it provides convenience for both task and data parallel processing. There is no need for things like the LOCAL mechanism in HPF to call a local procedure on the node processor. The descriptors for ordinary Java variables are unchanged in HPJava. On each node processor ordinary Java data will be used as local varables, as in an MPI program.

14.6   Projects in Progress

Projects related to this work include development of MPI, HPF, and other parallel languages such as ZPL[8] and Spar[9]. Here, we explain the background and future developments of our own project.

The work originated in our compilation practices for HPF. As described in [10], our compiler emphasizes run-time support. Adlib[2], a PCRC run-time library, provides a rich set of collective communication functions. It was realized that by raising the run-time interface to the user level, a rather straightforward (compared to HPF) compiler could be developed to translate the high level language code to a node program calling the run-time functions.

Currently, a Java interface has been implemented on top of the Adlib library. With classes such as Group, Range, and Location in the Java interface, one can write Java programs quite similar to HPJava proposed here. But a program executed in this way will have large overhead due to function calls (such as address translation) when accessing data inside loop constructs. Given the knowledge of data distribution plus inquiry functions inside the run-time library, one can substitute address translation calls with linear operations on the loop variable, and keep inquiry function calls "outside the loop."

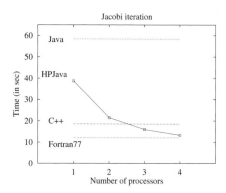

Figure 14.8 Preliminary performance.

At the present time, we are implementing the translator. Further research work will include optimization and safety-checking techniques in the compiler for HPspmd programming.

Figure 14.8 shows a preliminary benchmark for a hand-translated versions of our examples. The parallel programs are executed on 4 sparc-sun-solaris 2.5.1 with MPICH and the Java JIT compiler in JDK 1.2Beta2. For Jacobi iteration, the timing is for about 90 iterations; the array size is 1024X1024.

We also compared the sequential Java, C++, and Fortran version of the code, all with -O flag when compiling. The dotted lines shown in the figure only represent times for the one processor case. We can see that on a single processor, the Java program uses a language-supported mechanism for calculating an array element address, which is slower than HPJava mechanism (as HPJava uses an optimized address calculation scheme). We emphasize again that in the picture we are comparing *sequential* Fortran, etc., with *parallel* HPJava. This is not supposed to be an comparative evaluation of the various languages. It is just supposed to give an impression of the performance ballpark Java is currently operating in.

14.7   Summary

Through the simple examples in this chapter we have tried to illustrate that the programming language presented here provides the flexibility of SPMD programming, and much of the convenience of HPF. The language helps programmers to express parallel algorithms in a more explicit way. We suggest it will help programmers to solve real application problems more easily, compared with using communication packages such as MPI directly, and allow the compiler writer to implement the language compiler without the difficulties met in the HPF compilation.

The overall structure of the system is shown in Figure 14.9. The central DAD stands for the Distributed Array Descriptor. Around it, we have different run-

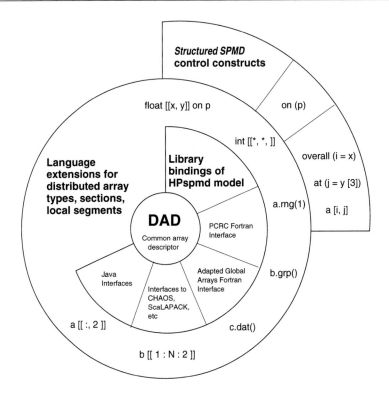

Figure 14.9 Layers of the HPspmd model.

time libraries. The Java interface is most relevant here. But the Java binding is only an introduction of the programming style. (A Fortran binding is being developed.) Initially, the Java version can be used as a software tool for teaching parallel programming. As Java for scientific computation becomes more mature, it will be a practical programming language to solve real application problems in parallel and distributed environments.

14.8 Bibliography

[1] Jeanne C. Adams, Walter S. Brainerd, Jeanne T. Martin, Brian T. Smith, and Jerrold L. Wagener. *Fortran 90 Handbook*. McGraw-Hill, 1992.

[2] Bryan Carpenter, Guansong Zhang, and Yuhong Wen. NPAC PCRC Runtime Kernel Definition. Technical Report CRPC-TR97726. Center for Research on Parallel Computation, 1997. Up-to-date version maintained at http://www.npac.syr.edu/projects/pcrc.

[3] R. Das, M. Uysal, J.H. Salz, and Y.-S. Hwang. Communication Optimizations for Irregular Scientific Computations on Distributed Aemory Architectures. *Journal of Parallel and Distributed Computing*, vol. 22(3), pages 462–479, September 1994.

[4] High Performance Fortran Forum. High Performance Fortran Language Specification. *Scientific Programming*, special issue, February 1993.

[5] Message Passing Interface Forum. *MPI: A Message-Passing Interface Standard*. University of Tenessee, Knoxville, TN, June 1995. `http://www.mcs.anl.gov/mpi`.

[6] Geoffrey C. Fox, editor. *ACM 1998 Workshop on Java for High-Performance Network Computing*. February 1998.

[7] J. Nieplocha, R.J. Harrison, and R.J. Littlefield. The Global Array: Non-Uniform-Memory-Access Programming Model for High-Performance Computers. *The Journal of Supercomputing*, vol. 10, pages 197–220, 1996.

[8] Lawrence Snyder. A ZPL Programming Guide. Technical Report, University of Washington, May 1997. `http://www.cs.washington.edu/research/projects/zpl/`.

[9] Kees van Reeuwijk, Arjan J. C. van Gemund, and Henk J. Sips. Spar: A Programming Language for Semi-Automatic Compilation of Parallel Programs. *Concurrency: Practice and Experience*, vol. 9(11), pages 1193–1205, 1997.

[10] Guansong Zhang, Bryan Carpenter, Geoffrey Fox, Xiaoming Li, Xinying Li, and Yuhong Wen. PCRC-Based HPF Compilation. In *10th International Workshop on Languages and Compilers for Parallel Computing*, August 1997. To appear in Lecture Notes in Computer Science.

[11] Guansong Zhang, Bryan Carpenter, Geoffrey Fox, Xinying Li, and Yuhong Wen. Considerations in HPJava Language Design and Implementation. In *11th International Workshop on Languages and Compilers for Parallel Computing*, August 1998. To appear in Lecture Notes in Computer Science.

Chapter 15

Web-Based Parallel Computing with Java

Luís Moura e Silva

Departamento de Engenharia Informática
Universidade de Coimbra, Polo II
3030 Coimbra - Portugal

Email: *luis@dei.uc.pt*

15.1 Introduction

The concept of Web-based metacomputing is becoming popular. The idea is to use geographically distributed computers through the Internet to solve large parallel problems. In practice, the idea behind Web-based parallel computing is just a new variation over NOW-based computing – the recycling of idle CPU cycles in the huge amount of machines connected to the Internet.

Both approaches have their domain of application: cluster-based computing is used to execute a parallel problem that is of interest to some institution or company. The parallel problem is typically of medium-scale and the network of computers usually belongs to the same administrative domain. Cluster-based computing is now well established, and libraries like PVM and MPI have been widely used by the HPC community.

On the other hand, Web-based computing is more suited for the execution of long-running applications that have a global interest, like solving some problems of cryptography, mathematics, and computational science. It uses computing resources that belong to several administrative domains. Web-based computing is not so widely used as cluster computing, though there are already some successful implementations of this concept.

This chapter discusses the main issues involved with the execution of number-crunching applications over the Web using Java. We describe the idea of Web-based parallel computing and we compare this approach with the traditional use of cluster-based computing. Then, we present some examples of applications that have been executed over the Internet and we discuss the possible use of Java in these environments. After that, we discuss a list of problems that have to be solved in Web-based computing and we briefly describe a case study for this model of parallel computing: the JET Platform. This system allows the execution of parallel applications over the Web by using Java applets and a set of servers. It solves some of the issues that will be presented and allows the integration of Web-based with cluster-based computing. The chapter ends up with some performance figures that were taken with some complex applications written in Java and using the JET platform.

15.2   Web-Based Parallel Computing

The popularity of the World Wide Web has lead to an impressive increase in the number of Internet hosts. According to the statistics presented in [10], in January of 1998 there were about 29.6 million computers connected to the Internet. This mass of processors connected together represents a very powerful parallel supercomputer with an incredible computational power. Most of these machines are only used for small interactive tasks, like the reading of electronic mail, the editing of files, or just the browsing of Web pages; most of them remain idle in a significant part of the time. Thus, it seems insightful to apply this vast computing resource for solving some problems of cryptography, mathematics, and computational science.

There are some quite interesting projects that use the computational power of machines that are connected to the Internet. Examples include the Bovine project for cracking RC5 and DES encryption keys [4], the GIMPS project to find Mersenne Primes [8], the RSA Factoring-By-Web effort that tries to crack RSA codes [17], the experimental study of cryptography presented in [19], the example described in [20] to solve a problem of molecular sequence analysis, and the announced project -SETI@home- that will try to use the spare power of Internet-connected computers in the Search for Extra-Terrestrial Intelligence (SETI) [3].

These examples demonstrate that thousands of computers can be harnessed as an Internet-based supercomputer to solve long-running problems using nothing but spare CPU time. None of those projects use Java: client programs are written in traditional languages like C and assembly. The download of code is done manually by the user that is also responsible by its installation and configuration. In most of the cases, the communication over the Internet is simply based on electronic mail.

In the past two years there has been impressive hype among the use of Java for distributed and Internet-computing [11]. In our opinion, it can bring some important advantages for this kind of Internet-based metacomputing: it solves the architectural heterogeneity of Internet hosts ensuring the portability of code; it is easy to install in Internet nodes by using downloaded Java applets; and it has built-in security mechanisms. Besides, Java applications are easier to develop and maintain than other languages.

We have developed a Java-based infrastructure to support the execution of parallel applications over the Internet called JET [18], but there are other ongoing projects that pursue the same goal. Examples include the Legion project [9], Globus [7], Charlotte [2], ParaWeb [5], and Albatross [1] among others. The vision of all these projects is to provide a unified high-performance virtual machine that may span across several worldwide institutions and may consist of several workstations and personal computers that are connected to the Internet. Some of these systems are also implemented in Java.

15.3   Comparing Cluster with Web-Based Parallel Computing

The use of PVM and MPI requires the installation of a daemon in all the machines that will be used by the computation. The applications should be compiled for the specific architecture of each machine and the binaries should be explicitly copied to the machines. Alternatively, there should be the existence of a shared filesystem. The user should have a login account and *rexec* permissions in all the machines that are used in a computation.

In Java-based Internet parallel computing there is no need to install any software in the client machines. The user is not required to have login accounts on participating machines: the worker processes can be downloaded as Java Applets and run inside a Web browser. There is no need to have a shared filesystem or to explicitly copy the binaries of the application. If the applications are written in Java, they are likely to be portable across different architectures and there is only one bytecode that can be used by any machine with JVM support.

In PVM and MPI the user must compile, debug, and install the different binaries of the application on each platform on which it runs. As a result, utilizing heterogeneous computing resources is rarely done in practice. The architecture-independence of Java bytecode will encourage and facilitate the use of heterogeneous platforms.

Basically, the use of clusters is usually done inside a single administrative domain and the applications are of interest to a particular group inside a company or a research institute. In Internet-based computing, the use of anonymous machines comprises several administrative domains and the applications should be of "public interest" to seize volunteer machines for the computation.

The communication latency in clusters of workstations is in the order of 10 to 100 microseconds. In wide-area systems the latency is in the order of milliseconds, and in the Internet is even higher. The typical bandwidth in clusters is between 10 and 100 Mbits/sec; the bandwidth in the Internet varies greatly. Due to these architectural differences, clusters can be used to execute loosely synchronous applications that may require intensive communication and tight synchronization between the processes. On the other side, the applications that execute in the Internet must be very coarse-grain and have limited communication. The applications should be really CPU-intensive, have a very high ratio of computation over communication, and should be able to tolerate the high latency of the communication. The best candidate applications should run for days or months and should not have strict deadlines for the execution.

The usefulness of Internet-based parallel computing depends on the number of applications that can be successfully executed. There are some studies in the literature [19], [20] which confirm that massive parallelism over the Internet or wide-area networks can be successfully applied for solving some complex computational problems. These problems should definitely have low requirements on communication bandwidth. Due to its coarse granularity they are mostly targeted at job-level parallelism. The number of appropriate applications for Web-based computing is relatively scarce, but it was already shown that, in some cases, it is possible to optimize medium-grain applications, taking into account the communication latency, in order to obtain high-performance in wide-area networks. With those optimizations, the range of applications suited for Web-based parallel computing can therefore be larger than previously thought.

15.4   Examples of Internet-Based Parallel Computing

On October 20th of 1997 one of the largest distributed-computing efforts ever seen, involving tens of thousands of computers connected to the Internet, happened: the Bovine cooperative effort [4] decrypted a message encoded with RSA Labs' 56-bit RC5 encryption algorithm. The search took 250 days of massive Internet computing. The medium computational power was equivalent to 14,685 Intel Pentium Pro 200 processors or to 58,163 Intel Pentium 133 processors. The lucky man that found the right key was Peter Stuer from Belgium.

There are some other good examples of number crunching over the Internet. In [19] another example of massively parallel computing is reported. The experiment used about 400 machines, located in three different continents, to factorize a 100-bits integer used by the RSA cryptographic algorithm. Each site received a set of polynomials to independently work with by electronic mail. The results computed by each task were also sent back by E-mail to some specific server that automates and coordinates the flow of tasks and relations. In April 1994 the famous 129-digit RSA code was cracked in the same project by using a quadratic sieve algorithm [17]. According to the inventors of RSA (Ron Rivest, Adi Shamir, and Len Adleman), this code would take 40 quadrillion years to factorize, but eight months of Internet number sieving was just enough to crack the code. In April 1996 a 130-bits number was successfully factorized. This time they used a number field sieve factoring method. The project is moving forward RSA-155.

Another interesting example was presented in [20]. That study describes the use of 800 workstations to solve a problem of molecular sequence analysis. The machines were dispersed over 31 different local area networks and five continents.

On January 28th of 1997 (9 am PST) the RSA Laboratories announced a set of 13 cryptographic contests — one using the DES government approved algorithm and the remaining 12 using the block cypher RC5 with a variable keysize.

The RC5 code with 40 bits was promptly cracked by a graduate student – Ian Goldberg — from the University of California at Berkeley in just 3.5 hours

(12:30pm PST of the same say). He used a network of 250 workstations to crack the code [12]. A very important achievement was then made: if someone with that computing power can break a random 40-bit key in three-plus hours it means Internet commerce based on 40-bit keys is unacceptable. Longer keys increase the cracking time exponentially. For instance, under those same circumstances, a 56-bit code would take 22 years to crack.

On February 10th of 1997 a team of researchers using 3500 computers spread across Europe were able to crack a RSA RC5 code of 48 bits in just 13 days [13]. The idea was to prove the weakness of a 48-bit encryption code and to show that current U.S. government regulations restrict the users to levels of encryption that are fairly unsecure: under the U.S. laws companies are only allowed to export software containing 56-bit or weaker encryption keys.

On June 17th of 1997, the only contest that used the Data Encryption Standard (DES) algorithm was also finished. Thousands of computers linked over the Internet managed to crack a message coded through 56-bit DES encryption. This time Michael Sanders of Salt Lake City went to the hall of fame earning $10,000 for cracking the code using a computer with a modest 90-MHz Pentium processor. This machine was just one of the thousand machines that contributed some CPU cycles to the computation.

Later on, in October of 1997, the RC5 56-bit was cracked by the Bovine cooperative effort [4]. The ongoing challenge is to crack a RC5 64-bit code. Just for curiosity, in this infrastructure the communication between clients and the server is done by E-mail (SMTP).

In August of 1997, Gordon Spence from Germany found the 36th Mersenne Prime on behalf of the GIMPS project (Great Internet Mersenne Prime Search) [8]. The computation comprised about 2000 users who volunteered their machines to that computation. Spence offered 15 days of calculation with his modest Pentium-based desktop computer.

Finally, it has been announced that a very appealing project called SETI@home will try to use the spare power of Internet-connected PCs in the Search for Extra-Terrestrial Intelligence (SETI) [3]. The program will execute as a special kind of screen saver: after some idleness period of time it will start computing in the client PCs and will analyze some data that was captured by the world's largest radio telescope. This project has not yet started but in September of 1997 there were more than 35,000 people that joined the SETI@home mailing list.

To summarize, there are some good examples of number-crunching applications that have been executing over the Internet. These examples demonstrate that thousands of computers can be harnessed as an Internet-based supercomputer to solve long-running problems using nothing but spare CPU time. What do these applications have in common?

First, all of them try to solve some problem that is of public interest. The Bovine cooperative effort is a good example where tens of thousands of users felt motivated to participate in a worldwide computation. It is foreseeable that the SETI@home project will motivate even more volunteers to donate their CPU cycles.

All these applications have some specific characteristics. They divide the problem into small tasks to be executed by different computers distributed over the Internet. The applications should be coarse-grained with a very high ratio of computation over communication, take a long time to execute (in the order of several hours, days or months), do not have real-time requirements, and should tolerate, to some extent, the low latency of the network.

15.5   Can Java be Used for Web-Based Parallel Computing?

None of those applications were written in Java. Although Java is still a very young language, it is claimed to be a language for the Internet [11]. But can Java be used for number-crunching computing?

In our opinion, yes. Java is intended to be used in distributed environments: it solves the architectural heterogeneity of Internet hosts; it is platform-independent, which ensures the portability that is required for Internet computing; it is easy to install in Internet nodes; and it has built-in protection mechanisms. Besides, Java applications are easier to develop and maintain than other languages.

Performance can be the only handicap of Java: interpreted Java executes very slowly and this can be a limiting factor. The use of Just-In-Time (JIT) compilers would speed up the execution of Java programs by a factor of 5 up to 30. Nevertheless, they still run slower than their C and C++ counterparts. Further performance improvements can be achieved with the use of native classes or advanced compiler techniques [6]. Even so, there is currently a common belief that Java is too slow to be used in scientific computing. This means that some more work is required in this issue to show that Java can execute with similar levels of performance of C and C++. Nevertheless, it is foreseeable that with the evolution of JIT compilers and the introduction of new technologies, like the new HotSpot JVM of Sun, the performance gap of Java will be reduced.

Despite the performance handicap there is a great potential for using Java in parallel computing. A "Java Grande" Forum was created to discuss the use of Java in parallel and scientific computing, and there are some efforts to develop consensus in the high-performance community about the potentialities of Java.

15.6   Problems to be Solved in Web-Based Parallel Computing

There are several problems to be solved in Web-based parallel computing. Issues like security and robustness are of paramount importance, the role of failures in the Internet environment is a great point of concern, and other factors, such as scalability, performance, and latency of communication should be studied in detail. The list can be stated as follows:

Security

A Web-based parallel virtual machine relies on the machines of several different people; therefore, it is extremely important that anonymous users should rely on the applications that are downloaded and executed in their machines. Java is supposed to be used in distributed environments in a safe way, and includes built-in protection against viruses and tampering. Although not perfect, Java provides more security than traditional languages like C and C++. Nevertheless, this issue of security requires some important support from the underlying environment.

Failures

Wide-area distributed systems represent a cost-effective solution for running scientific computations, but at the same time they are more vulnerable to the occurrence of failures. In [14] a more extensive study was presented concerning the reliability of heterogeneous workstation machines connected to the Internet. At the time of that study there were around 3 million hosts in the Internet. The results have shown that the measured aggregate time-to-failure of each machine was in the order of 311.8 hours (i.e., 12.99 days). This value reflects the time between interruptions of the machine's service. This is not the MTBF of permanent hardware failures: system crashes, reboots, and shutdowns for software maintenance were also considered in their definition. Thus, if we consider a typical distributed system composed by 100 workstations, where each machine exhibits a MTBF of 13 days, we can expect a failure every 3.1 hours. This is interesting: every application that takes more than three hours to execute will hardly terminate in such an unstable system.

The execution of parallel applications should be quite dynamic and quite unpredictable, taking into account that the MTBF of the overall application should be very low. The underlying system must provide some support for fault-tolerance in order to tolerate the failures of machines and network communication.

The latency of the communication   Current wide-area networks present a very low network bandwidth (tens of KB/s) and a huge latency (hundreds of milliseconds). In spite of the communication limitations of WAN computing there are some classes of applications that can take advantage of the potentially enormous computational power of multiple workstations and supercomputers. For instance, there are some applications that can asynchronously prefetch data while the computation is taken place. This approach, however, is only applicable to some algorithms. Some Master/Worker programs are potential candidates, provided they observe two important characteristics: they must be latency tolerant and present large-grain task parallelism.

Portability

The applications should be completely portable across multiple computing platforms. The platform-independent nature of Java bytecodes already provides most of the portability that is required. The parallel applications will run in a completely heterogeneous environment.

Scalability

The number of machines that can join a Web-based computation is surely unpredictable and the system must be able to manage hundreds or thousands of processors. It is absolutely necessary to avoid the bottleneck of a central point of control and provide some scalable solution; for instance, use several servers in separate machines and some software mechanism to distribute the load evenly among the machines.

Data-Integrity

Before running the applications over the Web we certainly need to protect the integrity of the application results. There is always the danger that a malicious Internet user could easily jeopardize a Web-based computation by sending dummy results to a server of the platform. It is absolutely necessary to prevent this situation and provide some integrity mechanisms to protect the data of application.

Java Support for Mathematical Libraries

Apart from performance, another issue to be solved is the lack of support for mathematical libraries, including the fundamental numerical algorithms. Fortunately, there is some ongoing work in this direction.

15.7   A Case Study: The JET Platform

JET is a software infrastructure that supports parallel processing of CPU-intensive problems that can programmed in the Master/Worker paradigm (more details about this platform can be found in [18]). Basically, there is a Master process that is responsible for the decomposition of the problem into small and independent tasks. The tasks are distributed among the Worker processes that execute a quite simple cycle: receive a task, compute it, and send the result back to the master. The Master is responsible for gathering the partial results and for merging them into the problem solution. Since every task is independent from each other, there is no need for communication between worker processes.

The Worker processes execute as Java applets inside a Web browser. The user that wants to volunteer his spare CPU cycles to a JET computation just needs to access a Web page by using a Java-enabled browser. Then the user just has to click somewhere inside the page and one Worker Applet is downloaded to the client machine. This Applet will communicate with a JET Master that executes on the same remote machine where the Web page came from.

The communication between the worker applets and the JET Master is done through UDP sockets. This class of sockets provides a higher scalability and consumes less resources than TCP sockets. The UDP protocol does not guarantee the delivery of messages, but the communication layer of JET implements a reliable service that insures sequenced and error-free message delivery. The library keeps a time-out mechanism for every socket connection in order to detect the failure or a shutdown of some worker applet.

The JET platform is easy-to-use and program. Participation in a Web-based parallel computation should be based mainly on volunteers, so the interface of the platform was made quite user-friendly. The application developers who are interested in using the potential computational power of JET will find an easy-to-use API. The complexity of the communication, the synchronization, the management of the parallel virtual machine, and the occurrence of failures are automatically supported by the library.

Only those users who are willing to borrow some CPU time from their machines will participate in the JET computations. There is no "hidden" applet that consumes the processor without the explicit authorization of the owner of the machine. Furthermore, the execution of the JET applets should have a minimal impact on the remote machine: if the user is running some interactive jobs and the load is high, then the JET applets should withdraw. The goal is to use the CPU cycles of the machines only during the non prime-time hours, but without disturbing the interactive tasks of the client user.

The volunteer machines may join and leave the computation at any moment in time. Thereby, the execution environment is completely dynamic. The JET system provides some mechanisms to tolerate the frequent changes on the parallel virtual machine and include support for dynamic task distribution.

The JET system provides some internal mechanisms to tolerate the high latency of the communication over the Internet. Those techniques are based on the prefetching of tasks by the remote machines and the asynchronous flush of output results back to the JET Master. There are some internal threads that perform the communication in a concurrent way with the normal execution of the application processes.

The number of machines that can join a JET computation is surely unpredictable, but the system should be able to manage hundreds or thousands of clients. To assure a scalable execution, we depart from the single-server approach and the second version of JET relies in a hierarchical structure of servers, as represented in Figure 15.1.

This scalable structure relies on multiple JET Masters: every Master will be responsible for a subset of worker machines dividing the load more evenly and increasing the reliability of the system. Every JET Master communicates with a centralized JET Server that maintains the global status of the application and a database with all the interesting statistics.

The JET system includes some fault-tolerance mechanisms based on task reconfiguration, checkpointing, and logging. It is able to tolerate any failure of a worker applet and a JET server. A mechanism of server checkpointing is used to assure the continuity of the application when there is a failure or a preventive shutdown of a JET Master or the main Server. The critical state of the application is saved

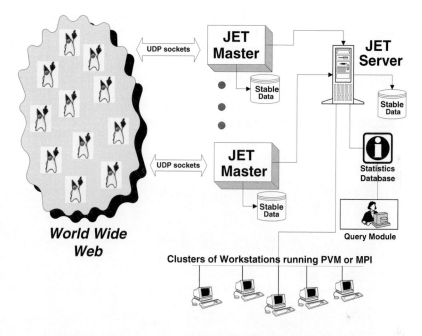

Figure 15.1 The structure of the JET virtual machine.

periodically in stable storage in some portable format that allows its resumption later on in the same or in a different machine.

The JET library maintains a task-reconfiguration scheme to tolerate the loss of stateless worker applets. The JET library keeps the jobs that have been sent to each worker applet. If one applet fails or withdraws from the virtual machine, the only part of the computation that is affected is the task that was being executed. Reallocating that task to another worker would reproduce the lost work without changing the ultimate outcome of the computation. This works for stateless processes. However, for those applications with very long-running tasks, it is important to save intermediate states of the task execution in the worker applets. Implementing client checkpointing is not trivial in a Java applet since it cannot write to the local disk. Thereby, the only way to implement the client checkpointing was to send the state over a socket stream to the associated JET Master.

The JET machine must keep the volunteers interested to participate in a worldwide computation. The best way to motivate people and increase their enthusiasm is to maintain statistics about their participation. The current status of the JET parallel virtual machine may be accessed through a Web page that contains the module of statistics. Information such as the list of volunteer machines, their contribution time, and performance will be automatically published in a public-domain Web page. The position in the JET rankings promotes a healthy competition between individual users and organized teams. In some sense, the information about the contribution of users to a particular JET computation is a way of paying back the CPU cycles that have been contributed. With all this information, there could be the idea to develop a CPU market where every contributed MIP/MFLOP would correspond to some electronic cash. Figure 15.2 presents a snapshot of the Web page with the JET statistics.

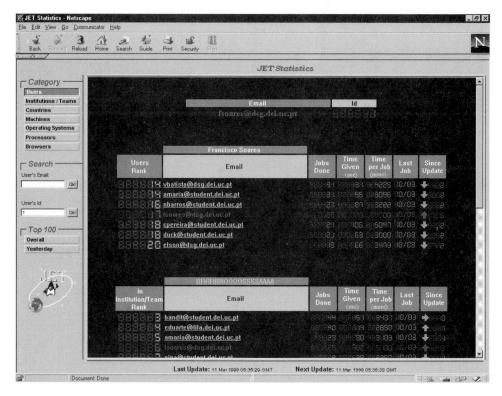

Figure 15.2 Global view of the JET statistical visual module.

JET computations will not be restricted to the Web. It is possible to use some other existing high-performance computing resources – clusters of workstations or parallel machines. The basic idea is to allow existing clusters of machines running PVM or MPI to interoperate with a JET computation. To achieve this interoperability, we have implemented a Java interface to the Windows version of MPI. The Java binding is described in [15]. We have also ported a Java interface to our implementation of PVM, called WPVM. Together, we have developed a module of software, called JET-Bridge, that merges the use of Web-based computing with cluster-based computing, therefore allowing the integration of JET with PVM/MPI applications.

The JET-Bridge was also implemented in Java and is represented in Figure 15.3.

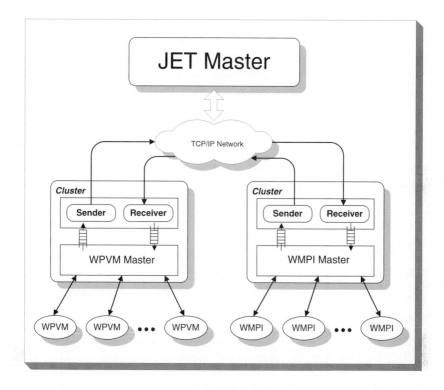

Figure 15.3 Interoperability of JET with PVM/MPI clusters.

The use of the JET-Bridge assumes that the cluster-based applications will have the Master as one of the processes of the cluster. Usually this is the process with rank 0 in a MPI program. The Master process is the only one that interacts with the JET-Bridge. Inside the cluster the application may follow any programming paradigm (SPMD, Task-Farming, or Pipelining).

The WPVM or WMPI Master is the only process of the cluster that connects directly with the JET machine and is also the only one that must to be written in Java. The Worker processes can be implemented in any of the languages supported by MPI/PVM libraries (i.e., C, Fortran, C++, Java) and all the heterogeneity is solved by using the Java bindings [15].

15.8 Some Performance Results

This section presents some performance measurements taken with JET. We have implemented three number-crunching applications: a program to find Mersenne primes; another one to crack the Secure Socket Layer (SSL); and a third application to crack the RC5 (64-bit key).

The study was conducted in a cluster of homogeneous machines, composed of six

PentiumPro-based machines, all of them running at 200 MHz with the Windows NT operating system. Two of the machines are dual-Pentiums so, overall, we have taken results in eight processors. The machines are connected through a nondedicated 10 Mbit/sec Ethernet. The worker applets execute on Netscape 4.01, while the Master process executes with JDK on a Sun Ultra-Sparc machine running Solaris V 4.0.

Figure 15.4 shows the speedup of the RC5 64-bits cracking algorithm. In this experiment the application was searching the key in a segment of 20,000,000 keys. The values obtained are quite good; with eight processors the speedup was 7.832. Although the application characteristics are good for parallel execution, it shows that the JET Library does not degrade the performance of the programs when the number of processors increases.

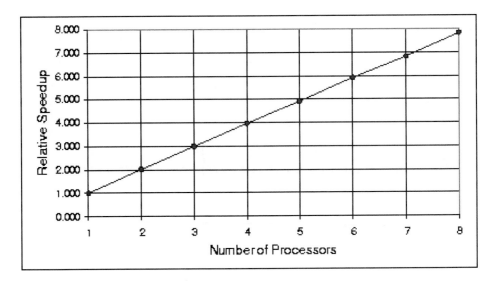

Figure 15.4 Relative speedup of the RC5 64-bits cracking algorithm.

Table 15.1 shows the key rate of the RC5 64-bits application. The performance penalty of Java is undoubtedly obvious. The Java version is four times slower than the C+assembly version used by the Bovine project. Thereby, more than four machines connected to JET are necessary to reach the performance of one machine contributing to the Bovine Project.

Table 15.1 Key Rate of the RC5 64-bits Cracking Application (Kkeys/sec)

	Bovine Version	Java Version	JET		
			1 Machine	4 Machines	8 Machines
Rate (Kkey/sec)	488,563	121,167	120,827	480,842	948,927

Figure 15.5 shows the speedup results of the Mersenne Primes application. The measurements were taken with the application seeking for all the Mersenne Primes less than 3000. Since the computational demands differ from task to task, we have conducted two different experiments. In the first one the scheduling of tasks was done from the beginning to the end of the searching space. This means that the first tasks take a small time to execute while the last tasks to be distributed are coarser-grain. This case may result in some load unbalanced situations at the end of the computation, where there are some workers that have long-running jobs to process while there are others that remain idle. In the second experiment we have gone the other way: first, we distributed the tasks from the end that take more time to execute, and we finished at the beginning of the search space.

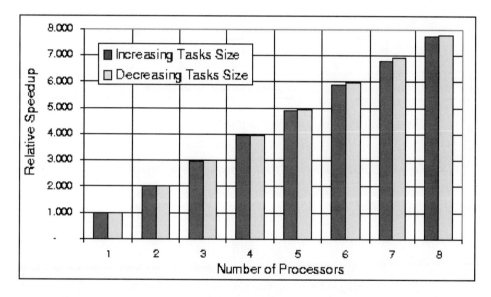

Figure 15.5 Relative speedup of the Mersenne Primes application.

Although in both cases the speedup was almost linear, there are some differences between the two task distribution policies. Figure 15.6 shows the average percentage of time that was actually spent by the processors in computing. It shows that when the longer tasks are the last ones to be computed, there is more idle time than in the other case.

The last results were taken with the Brute-SSL cracking application and are shown in Figure 15.7. The JET parallel machine had to search for the correct key in eight consecutive segments, which represents 134,217,728 ($8*2^{24}$) keys. Due to the even number of tasks we only took results with 1, 2, 4 and 8 processors. With eight processors we have obtained a speedup of 7.1 with the JET parallel version.

All the results that were taken with these applications were very encouraging. At this point, we can conclude that JET can be very efficient to execute number-

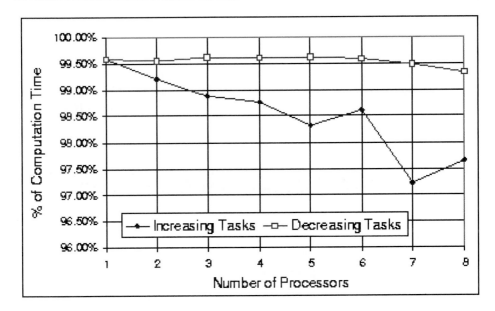

Figure 15.6 Percentage of computation time in both distributions.

crunching applications that have a coarse-grain task distribution.

15.9 Conclusions

The main goal of a tool like the JET project is to prove that massively parallel computing in the Internet can be feasible for some applications that take quite a long time to execute and have low communication requirements. Volunteer Web-based parallel computing is based on the idea of "scavenging" the idle CPU cycles of machines that are connected to the Internet. We have discussed some of the issues required by parallel computing software for the Internet and we presented some of the lessons we have learned with the implementation of some number-crunching applications in the JET parallel machine.

Hopefully we will soon see some of these or other similar Java based applications running over the Web and also using cluster computing. This is an important step to prove that Java can be used for scientific computing. Although there is no evidence about this goal, we can maintain the hope that someday some Java applet will be in the Hall of Fame for cracking the RC5 64-bits in the RSA cryptographic contest.

Acknowledgments

I would like to thank Hernâni Pedroso, Paulo Martins, Vitor Batista, Guilherme Soares, and Telmo Menezes for contributing to the JET project.

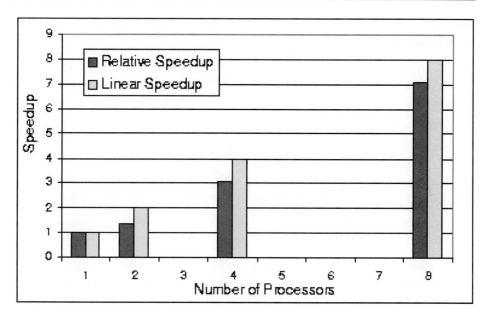

Figure 15.7 The relative speedup of the Brute-SSL application.

15.10   Bibliography

[1] H. Bal. Albatross—Wide Area Cluster Computing. `http://www.cs.vu.nl/albatross`

[2] A. Baratloo, M. Karaul, Z. Kedem, and P. Wyckoff. Charlotte: Metacomputing on the Web. *In Proceedings of ISCA Int. Conf. on Parallel and Distributed Computing,* PDCS'96, Dijon, France, pages 181-188, September 1996.

[3] `http://www.bigscience.com/`

[4] `http://www.distributed.net/`

[5] T. Brecht, H. Sandhu, M. Shan, and J. Talbot. ParaWeb: Towards World-Wide Supercomputing. *In Proceedings 7th SIGOPS European Workshop on System Support for Worldwide Applications,* 1996.

[6] Z. Budimlic and K. Kennedy. Optimizing Java: Theory and Practice. *1997 ACM Workshop on Java for Science and Engineering Computation,* Las Vegas, Nevada, June 1997.

[7] I. Foster and S. Tuecke. Enabling Technologies for Web-Based Ubiquitous Supercomputing. *In Proceedings 5th IEEE Int. Symposium on High-Performance Distributed Computing.* Syracuse, USA, pages 112-119, August 1996.

[8] The Great Internet Mersenne Prime Search. `http://www.mersenne.org/prime.html`

[9] A. Grimshaw and W. Wulf. Legion - A view from 50,000 Feet. *In Proceedings 5th IEEE Int. Symposium on High-Performance Distributed Computing*, HPDC-5, Syracuse, NY, pages 89-99, August 1996.

[10] Internet Domain Survey. `http://www.nw.com/zone/WWW/report.html`

[11] JavaSoft Homepage. `http://www.javasoft.com/`

[12] A. Lash. 40-bit Crypto Proves No Problem. *CNET: The Computer Network*, January 31, 1997. `http://www.news.com/News/Item/0,4,7483,00.html`

[13] A. Lash. 48-bit Crypto Latest To Crack. *CNET: The Computer Network*, February 11, 1997. `http://www.news.com/News/Item/0,4,7849,4000.html`

[14] D. Long, A. Muir, and R. Golding. A Longitudinal Survey of Internet Host Reliability. *In Proceedings 14th Symposium on Reliable Distributed Systems*, pages 2-9, Germany, September 1995.

[15] P. Martins, L. M. Silva, and J. G. Silva. A Java Interface for WMPI. *In Proceedings of EuroPVM/MPI*, Liverpool, UK, Springer-Verlag, September 1998. `http://dsg.dei.uc.pt/wmpi/`

[16] S. Mintchev and V. Getov, Automatic Binding of Native Scientific Libraries to Java. *In Proceedings of ISCOPE'97*, Springer LNCS, September 1997.

[17] RSA Factoring-By-Web. `http://www.npac.syr.edu/factoring.html`

[18] L. M. Silva, H. Pedroso, and J. G. Silva. The Design of JET: A Java Library for Embarrassingly Parallel Applications. *WOTUG'20 - Parallel Programming and Java Conference*, Twente, Netherlands, 1997. `http://serendip.dei.uc.pt/~jet`

[19] R. D. Silverman. Massively Distributed Computing and Factoring Large Integers. *Communications of the ACM*, vol. 34 (11), pages 95-103, November 1991.

[20] V. Strumpen. Parallel Molecular Sequence Analysis on Workstations in the Internet. *Technical Report 93-28*. Department of Computer Science, University of Zurich, 1993.

Part III

Algorithms and Applications

As large-scale parallel computing has developed and expanded over the past 10 to 20 years, a large amount of work has gone into the invention and evolution of algorithms and applications to efficiently use these resources. The development of cluster computing has brought in a new, larger set of users and developers, and thus has increased the need for good parallel methods for problem solving. Part III examines a number of newly-developed and newly-applied algorithms and applications.

The first chapter, Chapter 16, discusses parallel genetic algorithms. It first provides an overview, and then goes into more detail about its object-oriented implementation. This implementation includes a consideration of load balancing and I/O. Finally, the chapter builds an application framework, and examines a sample problem.

Chapter 17 focuses on load balancing on heterogeneous systems for a specific application; the solution of a Finite-Difference Time-Domain (FDTD) equation using the classical Yee scheme. The load balancing is done through a scheme called Application Data Movement (ADM), and the chapter discusses this scheme in general terms, provides examples of its use while solving the FDTD equation, then analyzes and generalizes the results.

Chapter 18 presents various issues involved in simulation of systems such as semiconductor manufacturing lines and military applications. It focuses primarily on ways of accelerating discrete event simulation and synchronization protocols through use of clustering.

Chapter 19 discusses using a number of systems connected by a local area network to simulate parallel computers using a fairly coarse grain simulation. This simulation uses User Datagram Protocol (UDP) for communications, and includes an implementation of checkpointing and rollbacks for fault tolerance. The basic simulator is the subject of a number of tests, then some extensions are added, followed by additional simulations. There is also a discussion of migration and load balancing for the simulator.

Chapter 20 discusses innovative Quality of Service management technology. This employs the "dynamic path" paradigm. An example of a shipboard system is used to describe three dynamic paths. The chapter then introduces an adaptive resource management middleware that provides integrated services for fault tolerance, distributed computing, and real-time computing. The chapter also describes how the presented approach differs from other models of real-time systems.

One of the many areas where cluster computers are being increasingly used is in database systems. Chapter 21 discusses how to allocate data to individual processing elements and disks in such systems. It introduces the basic concept of data placement, and then moves on to detail the three phases of a data placement strategy: declustering, placement, and redistribution. The chapter also considers dynamic reorganization, where data can be moved among processors to optimize performance for the type of query or queries being performed.

As the understanding of human cognition, including the constraints or real-time response and reaction times, has grown, the need for massive parallelism in the design of scalable intelligent systems has become more clear. Chapter 22 focuses on the Artificial Intelligence (AI) field of developing very large knowledge bases, and performing rapid reasoning with respect to such knowledge. This chapter uses a structured connectionist reasoning system called SHRUTI, which is mapped onto parallel machines. Then, this parallel application is analyzed, and some experiments are performed to check the analysis.

The next chapter, Chapter 23, deals with ray-tracing and its use in image synthesis. It introduces two potential methods for parallelization of ray tracing, employing and analyzing the two approaches to determine inherent tradeoffs in efficiency. The chapter then discusses sequential and parallel implementations of MaRT, a lazy ray-tracer. It uses the parallel version to create some test pictures, and analyzes the memory and timing results to discuss computational efficiency.

Chapter 24 shifts focus to image retrieval, specifically determining a method to query and retrieve an image by its content for a large image database. This involves extracting features from the images by using a wavelet transform. The chapter discusses how to index a large number of images, how to measure image similarity, and how to search a range of images. The proposed method is parallelized, and then used in some experiments which are then analyzed.

The next chapter, Chapter 25, discusses a science application—climate ocean modeling. Here, the large memory of parallel computers allows a dramatic increase in resolution of these models, and the performance of large numbers of processors makes possible long-running and large-scale simulations. This chapter discusses both a simple and a more efficient partitioning scheme, and then describes performance results on four different parallel computer systems, comparing the machines in terms of runtimes for various problems, and in terms of the scientific calculations that each machine will allow.

The final four chapters of this part focus on engineering problems. First, Chapter 26 discusses three electromagnetic algorithms, physical optics, finite-difference time-domain (also discussed in Chapter 17), and coupled finite-element integral-equation. Each algorithm is introduced with examples of its use, described in both sequential and parallel implementations, and run and analyzed on Beowulf-class computers. These runtimes are also compared with commercial parallel computers to show the outstanding price-performance for the Beowulf systems on these applications.

Chapter 27, examines a computational fluid dynamics code named TfC. This program is used as a case study in software engineering. The chapter first discusses the TfC program, which uses a finite volume discretization and an algebraic multi-grid solver, then describes the requirements that were considered when the code was parallelized. Next, a software engineering process is defined, and the use of this process in the parallelization of the code is explained. Then, the parallel code is evaluated, and the lessons learned are presented. The chapter also provides an example of object-oriented design for an element of the code. Finally, a discussion of actual use of the parallel code in a production environment is given, including pre- and post-processing, and collaborative design environments.

Next, Chapter 28 uses the modeling of complex gas phase systems to introduce quantum chemistry, specifically quantum reactive scattering calculations. It illustrates how the problem of calculating quantum reaction probabilities has been decomposed and how related algorithms are organized. It then analyzes parallel models that can be used to implement these algorithms on massively parallel architectures. Finally, it analyzes the performance measurements on two parallel computers.

The final chapter in this part of the book, Chapter 29, discusses two biomedical applications, chromosome reconstruction via ordering of clones for a genomic library, and analysis of heart rate variability from an electrocardiograph signal. The first application is implemented using both simulated annealing and microcanonical annealing, and these algorithms are discussed. Both applications are implemented on a cluster of UNIX workstations under PVM. The convergence, speedup, and scalability characteristics of the algorithms are analyzed and discussed.

Chapter 16

Object-Oriented Implementation of Parallel Genetic Algorithms

MARIAN BUBAK[†] AND KRZYSZTOF SOWA[‡]

[†]Institute of Computer Science, AGH, al. Mickiewicza 30, 30-059 Cracow, Poland
Academic Computer Centre CYFRONET, ul. Nawojki 11, 30-950 Cracow, Poland

[‡]Institute for Software Technology and Parallel Systems, University of Vienna,
Liechtensteinstr. 22, A-1090 Vienna, Austria

Email: *bubak@uci.agh.edu.pl, sowa@par.univie.ac.at*

16.1 Introduction

Genetic algorithms (GA), now becoming more and more popular, are universal methods of optimization as they are easy applicable to many practical problems. GA approach was introduced by John Holland [10] in 1975. It is based on the evolutionary process of Darwinian natural selection and on population genetics. In this technique, a solution to a problem is a set of parameters, usually in the form of string of values, which is called a *chromosome*, while each chromosome represents an *individual* [1], [8], [11].

GAs manipulate a population of individuals to find an optimal solution of a problem. The search with GAs is directed by the fitness function which is related to the function to be optimized. Fitness function is a measure of the quality of the evolution. A new population of individuals is generated from the previous one, typically with the following genetic operations: reproduction, crossover, and mutation. Reproduction copies individuals unchanged into new population, crossover chooses randomly two parents and combines them into two offsprings, and mutation changes each gene with a small probability. Crossover is responsible for rapidly exploring a search space whereas mutation introduces a small amount of random search. Selection of individuals for genetic operations is done according to their fitness factors. Worse fitted individuals are eliminated from the population because they do not survive the selection process, while best fitted individuals are recombinated to produce a generation of better offspring. In this way, individuals which are the best at solving the problem are most likely to be chosen in genetic operations.

There is no guarantee that solutions found with GAs are optimal ones; GAs may mostly find an acceptably good solution in relatively short time. GAs are particularly useful when methods based on domain specific knowledge are not yet developed or are not available because of the nature of a problem. GAs have proven to be suitable for hard optimization problems, classification, control of very large scale and varied data, financial and economic modeling and decision making, as well as in so-called bioinformatics (e.g., predicting protein structures) [13]. GAs are applied in engineering and industry to solve such problems as optimization in computational fluid dynamics, shape optimization and identification, load balancing of industry processes, and electromagnetic systems design [16].

GAs usually deal with extremely large search spaces that result in a need for their efficient implementation, and parallel approach seems to be the best way out. Most GAs systems are programmed in imperative languages, whereas it is known that an object-oriented approach may provide significant improvements in terms of the quality of the implementation.

In this chapter we present an approach to the object-oriented implementation of parallel genetic algorithms. Parallel GA library POOGAL is based on TOLKIEN – C++ [14] sequential GAs, and on Para++ [6] – C++ library for stream-based message passing. SPMD paradigm was applied as a base of the library architecture. Two models of GA parallelism have been chosen for implementation: island and global population [5], [15]. POOGAL is a C++ library of parallel genetic algorithms that enables easy development of parallel programs exploiting a genetic algorithm approach [4]. The library is portable; it was implemented on clusters of workstations as well as on parallel computer HP Exemplar SPP1x00/XA. The results of the investigation of the efficiency for the traveling salesman problem and for the maximization of the De Jong function have demonstrated the usefulness of the library.

16.2 Short Overview of GA Systems

GAs systems may be divided (according to their specific objectives) into three classes [9], [13]:

- *application-oriented*—designed for developing applications for specific domains (e.g., PC/BEAGLE for scheduling or telecommunication, OMEGA for finance modeling)

- *algorithm-oriented* implements specific genetic algorithms and may be incorporated into new specific applications after some adaptation of a source code.

In this class there are two systems:

- *algorithm-specific* consists of a single GA (e.g., ASPARAGOS, DGEN-ESIS, GALOPPS, GAMAS, HSDGA, PARAGENESIS) to be used to solve a specific problem

- *algorithm libraries* provide a set of genetic algorithms in a library format (e.g., PGAPack, OOGA, EM 2.1) to support a wide range of applications

- *toolkits* for programming various GAs. These are parameterized and equipped with a graphical user interface so a user can easily modify GAs and adapt them to specific needs. Toolkits may be used for introducing GA concepts to a novice (e.g., GA Workbench) or for modifying and developing a range of GA operators, algorithms, and applications (e.g., EnGENEer, GAME, PeGAsuS, RPL2, SPLICER, TOLKIEN).

As parallelism is an intrinsic feature of GAs, many implementation of parallel genetic algorithms are reported [2], [5]. The first approach to parallelization of GAs uses a single population, while evaluation of the individuals and application of genetic operators are done in parallel. This is the *global population model*. In the global population model, a temporary global population is created once for every several generations by gathering all individuals in one process and redistributing them randomly. A master performs the selection operations while the associated slaves perform the recombination, mutation, and evaluation of the fitness factors. Therefore, if there is a good load balance between individuals assigned to processor, a linear speedup can be expected. The following GA systems belong to this class: EnGENEer, PGAPack, and GENITOR.

The second class of parallel GA is called an *island model* or a *multiple-population coarse-grained GA*. In the island model, individuals are divided into several subpopulations assigned to concurrent processes which perform local genetic operations, and solutions are exchanged by migration. Each of these relatively large subpopulations evolves separately on different processors and periodically exchange individuals with other subpopulations. On each *island* the subpopulation undergoes exactly the same genetic operations on the same kind of genotype and the result is the best individual found in the overall population. The following GA systems belong to this class: CoPDEB, DGENESIS 1.0, GALOPS 3.1, GAMAS, PGA 2.5, RPL2, GDGA, PeGAsuS, and SGA-Cube.

Another approach to the development of parallel genetic algorithms is *cellular GAs* or *fine grained GAs*. In this model the population is partitioned into a large number of very small subpopulations assigned to individual processors. Logically, the population is mapped onto a connected processor graph. Less communication costs between neighboring processors imply that selection and recombination operations are done only between neighboring individuals, i.e., individuals stored on neighboring processors. The following GA systems belong to this class: ASPARA-GOS, and ECO-GA.

16.3   Object-Oriented Approach to PGAs

Most implementations of GAs are based on imperative languages like C or PAS-CAL. These languages enable the user to gain a relatively high computational speed; however, an object-oriented approach may provide significant improvements in the quality of the implementation. Very often existing software tools are too specific and cannot be used for solving other problems, or they are too general and thus ineffi-cient. Object-oriented implementation significantly reduces the time needed for the adaptation or incorporation of the software to the user needs, and helps in providing safety for this software. From the design point of view, the object-oriented approach provides a common architecture of classes for a genetic system that could be created and extended by different people. This enables the development of very flexible and sophisticated systems that allow for experimenting and combining different models, topologies, genetic operators, and even for hybridization or cooperation with other techniques to possibly gain some improvements.

After having analyzed publicly available libraries and systems of GAs [7], [9], we have decided to develop a parallel genetic algorithms library (POOGAL) which should enable easy creation of parallel programs exploiting the GA approach. The library should be flexible, easy maintainable, able to support maximal attainable performance of its routines, and portable to wide range parallel computing envi-ronments, including clusters of workstations and massively parallel machines. We have decided to reuse the existing code which implements sequential GAs and to apply the SPMD paradigm as a basis of the library architecture to ensure ease of programming. The library is based on:

- TOLKIEN – C++ sequential GAs library with clear and flexible architecture and extensive documentation [14],

- Para++ – C++ library, which is a very convenient layer of abstraction be-tween parallel GA code and underlying lower-level environments based on message passing—PVM and MPI [6].

Two models of GA parallelism have been chosen for implementation: the island model and the global population model [5], [15]. In order to reduce the execution time of parallel GA programs on clusters of workstations, the library is equipped with a load balancing facility.

Relations between components of the POOGAL library are shown in Figure 16.1. Local genetic operations are performed with the TOLKIEN's classes. Creation of processes and exchange of individuals is realized using Para++. New classes have been developed in order to run parallel genetic algorithms. These classes are com-bined with TOLKIEN's and Para++'s classes by inheritance. The abstract base class SPMD_PGA is the root of inheritance hierarchy of all models of PGA imple-mented in the library. The most important member function of SPMD_PGA is void generation(), which executes a single complete step of an genetic algorithm. This step includes local genetic operations and exchange of individuals between sub-

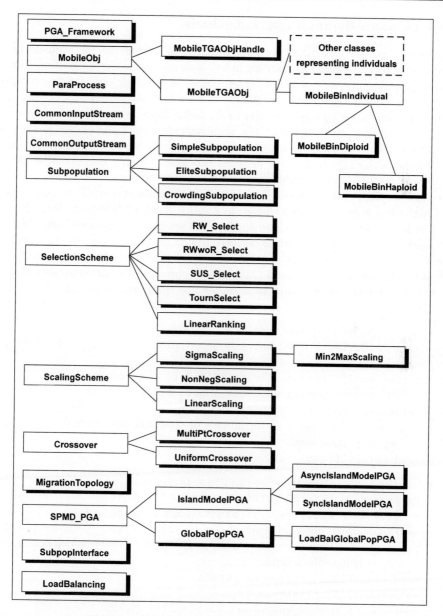

Figure 16.1 Components of POOGAL library.

populations. Local operations are organized in the same way for all subclasses of SPMD_PGA. Components of POOGAL are described in the subsequent sections.

16.4   Classes Representing Individuals

A part of a genetic algorithm program which is the closest to the problem being solved includes the way of representing individuals specific to the application domain and appropriate genetic operators. C++ classes responsible only for this range of functionality are derived from the `TGAObj` class of the TOLKIEN library [14]. The best example of such a class is `BinHaploid`, which implements the most frequently used binary string representation. The requirements concerning classes in the case of parallel genetic algorithms must be significantly extended. In particular, such classes should be able to be sent between processes running concurrently. As an additional feature, they should offer the possibility to save and to restore their complete internal state on files. To fulfill these requirements while retaining clear and uniform design, an abstract base class called `MobileTGAObj` has been derived from `TGAObj` (Figure 16.1). Such an approach, when there is one class from which all the individual classes used must be derived, has an advantage to make it possible to apply compile-time static type checking to ensure that the initial population state is valid. Thus, every new created class which represents the program should have defined two fundamental groups of member functions (which are pure virtual in `MobileTGAObj` class):

- genetic algorithm specific functions:
  `void randomize();` used for random initialization of individual representation,
  `TGAObj *oddPtCrossover(const TGAObj &, int) const;`
  `TGAObj *evenPtCrossover(const TGAObj &, int) const;`
  `TGAObj *uniformCrossover(const TGAObj &, float) const;`
  which implement the basic techniques of crossover operators appropriate to the representation used,
  `void mutate(float)` – mutation operator,

- functions supporting the space and time persistence:
  `ParaStreamOut &sendCopy(ParaStreamOut &) const;`
  `ParaStreamIn &receiveCopy(ParaStreamIn &) const;`
  used to send the internal state of objects using member functions of `ParaStreamOut` and `ParaStreamIn` classes from Para++ library, which enable only to send primitive data types,
  `void printAllOn(ostream &) const;`
  `void readAllFrom(istream &);`
  used to write/read internal object state to/from streams.

Two basic classes, `MobileBinHaploid` and `MobileBinDiploid`, which represent binary individuals and follow the rules described above, are included into the library and may be used in typical GA applications. All classes derived from `MobileTGAObj` should also support run-time type information mechanisms which are used mainly by the class `MobileTGAObjHandle`. This solution enables us to use a heterogeneous population of individuals, which, in turn, implies that objects of different types may co-evolve within the same run of program provided that crossover operators between them are implemented. To make this possible, the objects of class `MobileTGAObjHandle` act as wrappers to objects of arbitrary subclass of `MobileTGAObj`, which send their internal state through a network or write it to files together with unique type identifiers. When the reverse operations are executed (i.e., receiving from the network and reading from the file), default objects of the appropriate class are created by the `MobileTGAObjHandle` member functions using the identifier value received, and then their internal state is initialized according to flowing in data.

16.5   Local Genetic Operations

In any model of a parallel genetic algorithm, evolving individuals are distributed among available processors. As a result, in any run of a parallel GA there are two parts which are realized alternatively:

- local operations performed independently in every parallel process; they include evaluation of values of objective function for elements of subpopulation, transformation of these values into fitness factors, selection of individuals, and crossover, mutation and replacement of old population elements with new-created individuals

- exchange of individuals between processes, which requires communication and synchronization between them.

The user who will develop PGA programs should implement the evaluation of objective functions for each type of individual included into the population. A routine should have the form of C++ function with a prototype like

`double ObjectiveFunction(const TGAObj &individual)`.

This routine is used to evaluate the initial population and to compute the objective function for newly created individuals or for the entire population, e.g., when function characteristics change with time or with a generation number.

At the next step of local operations during one generation, the values of objective function are transformed into fitness factors. This is done to ensure that fitness factors used in the next phases are positive and to modify them slightly in order to achieve a better optimization efficiency. This operation and those following are implemented in TOLKIEN in several variants which are also reused in the PGA library. A natural way of expressing such a relationship in object-oriented languages is inheritance. Abstract base class `ScalingScheme` was created with several derived classes: `NonNegScaling`, `LinearScaling`, and `SigmaScaling`; their names are self-explanatory [8].

When fitness factors are calculated, one may choose a pool of individuals that will undergo further operations [8], [15]. This may be done with several new classes which have been derived from the common abstract base called `SelectionScheme`:

- RW_Select (roulette wheel selection with replacement),

- RWwoR_Select (roulette wheel selection without replacement),

- SUS_Select (stochastic universal sampling),

- TournSelect,

- LinearRanking.

All variants of crossover and mutation operations are implemented as member functions of classes which describe individuals because they must match the specific representation used. The Crossover class is therefore created only to choose the appropriate operation during runtime and execute it with given parameters (crossover probability). It has two subclasses: MultiPtCrossover and UniformCrossover.

As a result of genetic operations, a temporary pool of new individuals is created which must replace a part of the old population. In the TOLKIEN library, subclasses of Population hold the collection of individuals of types derived from TGAObj together with the objective function, and they implement several strategies of replacing old elements. In the PGA program, every individual may be sent to a subpopulation residing in other process; therefore, elements in a local population must be restricted to some subclasses of MobileTGAObj. That is why an abstract base class Subpopulation was introduced with the following subclasses:

- SimpleSubpopulation – replaced individuals are chosen randomly,

- EliteSubpopulation – elements with the worst fitness are deleted first,

- CrowdingSubpopulation – De Jong's crowding model.

16.6   Island Model

In the island model the data which represent individuals are sent according to a predefined migration topology represented by the MigrationTopology class. Subpopulations are treated as nodes of a graph with two defined parameters for each edge: migration interval and fraction of subpopulation (subpopFrac) sent.

The MigrationTopology object describes only the edges adjacent with local subpopulation and their parameters are set with functions:
void setDestination(int destNum, int interval, float subpopFrac);
void setSource(int destNum, int interval, float subpopFrac);
The MigrationTopology object defines connections between subpopulations; therefore, it can access all processes by a pointer to ParaProcess object from Para++ library which handles identifiers of all processes. The island PGA algorithm uses a SelectionScheme object to select individuals for migration. The flow of individuals and genetic operations in the island model consists of the following steps (see Figure 16.2):

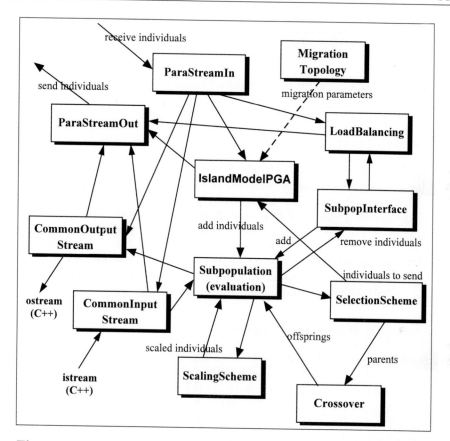

Figure 16.2 Flow of individuals and evolution steps in the island model.

1. Select individuals for crossover operations (class `SelectionScheme`),

2. Create offsprings by crossing over the parents (class `Crossover`),

3. Perform mutation on the offsprings,

4. Add the offsprings to a local population (class `Subpopulation`),

5. Evaluate new offsprings,

6. Perform fitness scaling if necessary (class `ScalingScheme`),

7. Select individuals for migration operations (class `SelectionScheme`),

8. Send copies of selected individuals (class `ParaStreamOut`),

9. Receive individuals (class `ParaStreamIn`),

10. Add received individuals to the local population,

11. Perform fitness scaling (class `ScalingScheme`),

12. Load balancing operations if necessary (class `LoadBalancing`),

13. I/O operations - write results (class `CommonOutputStream`).

Two island models are implemented:

- *synchronous*—represented by the `SyncIslandModelPGA` class; a local process has access to the numbers of individuals that are sent from other processes. In this algorithm, processes are partially synchronized during migration; therefore, there is a guarantee that every individual enters the destination subpopulation in the same generation in which it has left its origin

- *asynchronous*—represented by the `AsyncIslandModelPGA` class; individuals are received in a non-blocking manner so a local process does not wait and inserts all the arrived individuals into the subpopulation.

16.7   Global Population Model

The interchange of individuals keeps a variety of local population. In the global population model interchange is achieved by the creation of a temporary global population by sending individuals from all subpopulations to one process. It is then randomly permuted and next individuals are redistributed and sent back to processes. The frequency of the creation of a global population is controlled by a parameter defined in the constructor of the `GlobalPopPGA` class. Additionally, an object which implements this model needs a pointer to the `ParaProcces` object which describes the identifiers of processes taking part in the PGA run. This model is very convenient to apply a load balancing mechanism during the creation of a global population and redistribution phase. Therefore, there is the `LoadBalGlobalPopPGA` class, which should be used instead of the `GlobalPopPGA` class with load balancing switched on. In the global population model, the flow of individuals and genetic operations consists of the following steps (see Figure 16.3):

1. Select individuals for crossover operations (class `SelectionScheme`),

2. Create offsprings by crossing over the parents (class `Crossover`),

3. Perform mutation on the offsprings,

4. Add the offsprings to a local population (class `Subpopulation`),

5. Evaluate new offsprings,

6. Perform fitness scaling if necessary (class `ScalingScheme`),

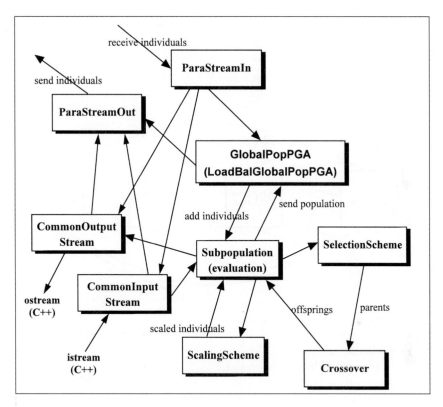

Figure 16.3 Flow of individuals and evolution steps in the global population model.

7. Send all individuals to a master process and create a global population (class `ParaStreamOut`),

8. Receive a new pool of individuals (class `ParaStreamIn`),

9. Add redistributed individuals to the local population,

10. Perform fitness scaling of the local population (class `ScalingScheme`),

11. I/O operations - write results (class `CommonOutputStream`).

16.8   Load Balancing

The functionality of the library described so far enables us to assign to processes a given number of individuals that remain unchanged during the whole run of a PGA program. This is a serious drawback when a GA program is running on the most frequently accessible computational systems, e.g., clusters of workstations and parallel machines which are shared by other users. The load is nonuniform and varying with time across available processors, so processes which are temporarily faster have to wait for their slower partners. This problem may be solved by adding load balancing facilities to the library. Figure 16.4 presents a scheme of the load balancing facility implemented within the library [3].

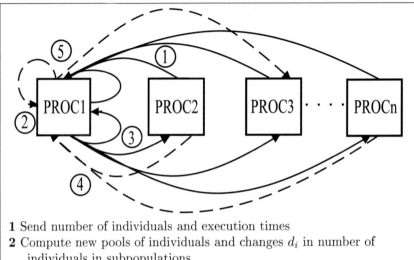

1 Send number of individuals and execution times
2 Compute new pools of individuals and changes d_i in number of
   individuals in subpopulations
3 Send changes d_i to subpopulations
4 If changes $d_i < 0$ send individuals to main process (PROC1)
5 If changes $d_i > 0$ receive individuals from main process
   (PROC1)

Figure 16.4 Load balancing scheme.

A new number of individuals n_k^{s+1} assigned to process k accordingly to relative temporary speeds of processors equals

$$n_k^{s+1} = n_k^s + \lambda \cdot \left(\frac{\frac{n_k^s}{t_k^s}}{\sum_{i=1}^{N} \frac{n_i^s}{t_i^s}} \cdot \sum_{i=1}^{N} n_i^s - n_k^s \right)$$

where:
n_i^s denotes the distribution of individuals in the previous stage of PGA program,
t_i^s are the recent computation times of processes,
$\lambda \in [0,1]$ is a parameter (*transfer*) which allows to reduce too rapid changes in number of individuals on processors.

   The implementation is contained in the class `LoadBalancing` with its member function `balance()`, which calculates new distribution of individuals and sends only the required part of individuals to processors. Elements of subpopulation are accessed with methods of the `SubpopInterface` class which provide the operations of addition and removal of individuals. This mechanism is universal and flexible, so it may be applied with each model implemented in the library. However, for the global population model, instead of the base class `GlobalPopPGA`, one should use the class `LoadBalGlobalPopPGA` which applies load balancing during the gathering of individuals and their redistribution.

16.9   File and I/O Operations

A large part of the PGA program consists of saving and restoring population state, reading in parameters, and storing the results obtained. These operations are especially hard to program because processes are executed on different machines. Therefore, some facilities have been developed to arrange access to a common file and input/output streams through a single process. They include two classes: `CommonOutputStream` and `CommonInputStream`, which provide overloaded `write()` and `read()` member functions for several data types, e.g., `double`, `MobileTGAObj`, `MobileTGAObjHandle`, and `Subpopulation`. These operations are realized with star topology communication.

16.10   PGA Application Framework

The `PGA_Framework` class constitutes the framework of typical PGA applications. An object of this class chooses appropriate components from the library according to the values of parameters specified by the user in the input configuration file.

```
#include "Poogal.hh"
double objFun(const TGAObj &)
{ ... }                 // Objective function definition.
void main(int argc, char **argv)
{
    ParaProcess p("pga", argc, argv);
    PGA_Init();        // Start processes
    PGA_Framework frw(MobileBinHaploid(30, RANDOMIZE),
                objFun, argv, argc, p);
                       // Create the framework of PGA application.
    frw.PGA_Run();     // Create all PGA objects and perform
                       // evolution steps.
    return;
}
```

Figure 16.5 Sample PGA program built with the PGA_Framework object.

The user is only responsible for defining the problem, i.e.:

- selection of classes which represent individuals. The constructor of `PGA_Fra-mework` class obtains an object representing an individual which is replicated inside the framework to the population size specified by the user. The purpose of this implementation is to allow the user to define a problem-specific representation of individuals, which is not currently implemented in the library

- evaluation of objective function.

Figure 16.5 presents the source code of evolution program that uses the `PGA_Framework` class and PGA components defined in the library. The goal of the program is defined by the objective function `objFun`, and the type of individual is specified by the first parameter of the `frw` object declaration. The values of various parameters used by the parallel genetic algorithms (population type, number of individuals in each subpopulation, number of generations, model of PGA and relevant intervals, and fractions of migration, probabilities of applying genetic operators, load balancing parameters, etc.) are specified by the user in the input configuration file. This allows users to ease the creation of programs which test efficiency of searching the solution for different values of PGA parameters.

16.11   Sample Results

This section presents the results of solving the traveling salesman problem for 105 points (*lin105* from TSPLIB [12]) with POOGAL. The values of the most important parameters are given in Table 16.1. The evaluation of obtained results is done with

Table 16.1 Values of Parameters for a TSP Test Problem

Parameter	Value
number of subpopulations	4
subpopulation class	elite
size of population	5000 per processor
number of generations	1000
scaling scheme	non-negative values
generation gap	0.7
selection scheme	roulette-wheel
crossover scheme	PMX
crossover rate	0.5
mutation rate	0.03
selection for migration	roulette-wheel
migration topology	undirectional ring
migration interval	30
migration fraction	0.2
global population interval	30

search quality which shows how the best value of an objective function obtained by PGA changes with the generation number, and with *search efficiency* being the most important criterion because it expresses the dependence of the best solution found on the computation time.

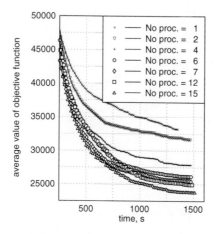
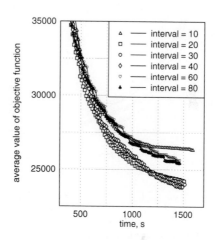

Figure 16.6 Average search efficiency of island model algorithm for TSP 105-point on Exemplar SPP1600 for different number of processors.

Figure 16.7 Average search efficiency of island model algorithm for TSP 105-point on Exemplar SPP1600 for different migration intervals.

Calculations on the cluster of workstations were done with g++ v2.7.2 compiler, PVM v3.3.8, and Para++ v1.03. On HP/Convex Exemplar SPP1600 Para++, TOLKIEN and PGA library as well as the test program were compiled with C++ v3.75.05 compiler, linked with PVM v3.3.10.1 and executed on a dedicated subcomplex with 16 processors in it, four processors on each hypernode.

The results obtained show that a larger population size enables us to achieve a lower value of the objective function. Additionally, for large computation intensive problems, communication time takes a smaller part of the total execution time and does not increase radically with the number of processors. In practical applications which run on the large-scale machines, this allows users to achieve a high search efficiency. Choice of parameters steering the intensity of individuals exchange influences significantly the efficiency and quality of the solution. Results presented in Figures 16.6, 16.7, and 16.8 for the island model, and in Figure 16.9 for the global population model show that there is a range of values which are the best for a given optimization problem. Too strong-separation of subpopulations leads to a worse search quality because of the fast local degeneration of individuals in each subpopulation. On the other hand, greater rates of individual exchange in the island model decreases diversity due to tighter coupling between subpopulations. Only for the

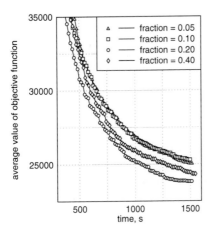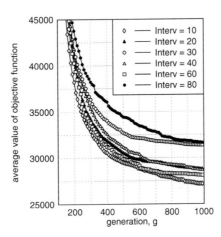

Figure 16.8 Average search efficiency of island model algorithm for TSP 105-point on Exemplar SPP1600 for different migration fractions.

Figure 16.9 Average search quality of global population model algorithm for TSP 105-point on a heterogeneous cluster.

global population model, a high frequency of creating global population increases diversity which is profitable for the evolution of individuals. However, it results in a greater communication overhead.

Figure 16.10 presents the search efficiency of the island model on a heterogeneous cluster (HP D-370/2, HP 712/60, IBM RS6000/520, IBM RS6000/320) for different intervals of load balancing, and Figure 16.11 shows the distribution of individuals onto processors for load balancing interval = 10. The user must be aware that load balancing can significantly influence the evolution of population. The frequent use of load balancing reduces the total computation time, but leads to a worse quality of solutions because the strongest machine may obtain most of the individuals; hence, the local diversity in each subpopulation radically decreases.

16.12   Concluding Remarks

C++ is usually used as a tradeoff between improvement of programming offered by OO techniques and the computation efficiency requirements. However, the adoption of the object-oriented design together with the definition of a GA-oriented application programming interface provide vast flexibility to application developers. The C++ implementation of TOLKIEN and Para++ libraries enabled an easy development of POOGAL and provided the user with a collection of reusable objects that

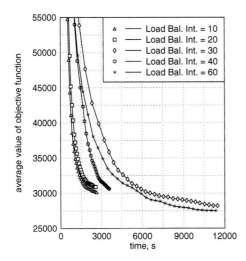

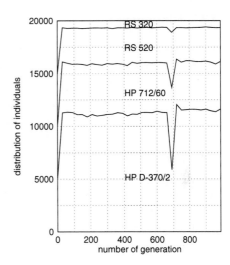

Figure 16.10 Average search efficiency of island model algorithm with load balancing for TSP 105-point on a heterogeneous cluster.

Figure 16.11 Redistribution of individuals due to load balancing in TSP 105-point problem, island model, on a heterogeneous cluster.

reduce the effort in developing genetic-based applications. Moreover, the library is easy extendable to new individual representations, genetic operators, migration topologies, and PGAs models. The C++ language also guarantees maximum portability for POOGAL.

The parallel GA library is a very useful and flexible tool which allows for quick implementation of parallel genetic algorithm programs on different parallel computer architectures. The user may easily start experimentation with a genetic program without going into details of communication, synchronization, debugging, and testing of parallel programs.

Acknowledgments

We are very grateful to Waldemar Cieśla for his contribution and to Jacek Mościński and Włodzimierz Funika for their helpful comments and discussion. We are indebted to Rajkumar Buyya for inspiring us to write this chapter and for his suggestions. The computations were carried out at ACC CYFRONET-KRAKÓW. This research was partly supported by the AGH grant.

16.13   Bibliography

[1] D. Beasley, R. D. Bull, and R. R. Martin. An Overview of Genetic Algorithms. *University Computing*, vol 15, pages 58-69 (Part 1), and pages 170-181 (Part 2), 1993.

[2] R. Bianchini, and C. M. Brown. Parallel Genetic Algorithms on Distributed Memory Architectures. Technical Report 436, University of Rochester, Computer Science Department, 1993. ftp://ftp.cs.rochester.edu/pub/papers/systems.

[3] M. Bubak, J. Mościński, M. Pogoda, and R. Słota. Load Balancing for Lattice Gas and Molecular Dynamics Simulations on Networked Workstations. In *Proceedings of the High Performance Computing and Networking – HPCN'95*, B. Hertzberger, and G. Serazzi (eds.), Milan, Italy, May 1995, *Lecture Notes in Computer Science*, vol 796, pages 329-334, Springer-Verlag, Berlin, 1995.

[4] M. Bubak, W. Cieśla, and K. Sowa. Object-Oriented Library of Parallel Genetic Algorithms and its Implementation on Workstations and HP/Convex Exemplar. In *Proceedings of the High Performance Computing and Networking – HPCN'97*, B. Hertzberger, and P. Sloot (eds.), Vienna, Austria, April 1997, *Lecture Notes in Computer Science*, vol 1225, pages 514-523, Springer-Verlag, Berlin, 1997.

[5] E. Cantú-Paz. A Summary of Research on Parallel Genetic Algorithms. *Technical Report No. 95007*, Illinois Genetic Algorithms Laboratory, 1995. ftp://gal4.ge.uiuc.edu/pub/papers/IlliGALs.

[6] O. Coulaud, and E. Dillon. Para++: C++ Bindings for Message Passing Libraries. *Technical Report*, Institute National de Recherche en Informatique et en Automatique, 1995. ftp://ftp.loria.fr/pub/loria/numath.

[7] J. R. Filho, C. Alippi, and P. Treleaven. Genetic Algorithm Programming Environments. *Technical Report*, Department of Computer Science, University College, London, 1994. ENCORE: ftp://ftp.egr.msu.edu/pub/EC/GA/.

[8] D. E. Goldberg. *Genetic Algorithms in Search, Optimization and Machine Learning.* Addison-Wesley, New York, 1989.

[9] J. Heitkoetter, and D. Beasley (eds.). The Hitch-Hiker's Guide to Evolutionary Computation: *A List of Frequently Asked Questions (FAQ) Issue 6.3.* http://www.etsimo.uniovi.es/pub/EC/FAQ/www.

[10] J. H. Holland. *Adaptation in Natural and Artificial Systems.* The University of Michigan Press, Ann Arbor, 1975.

[11] Z. Michalewicz. *Genetic Algorithms + Data Structures = Evolution Programs.* Springer-Verlag, Berlin, 1992.

[12] G. Reinelt. TSPLIB95. http://www.iwr.uni-heidelberg.de/iwr/comopt/soft.

[13] J. Stender, E. Hillebrand, and J. Kingdom (eds.). *Genetic Algorithms in Optimisation, Simulation and Modeling*. IOS Press, Amsterdam, 1994.

[14] A. Yiu-Cheung Tang. TOLKIEN: Toolkit for Genetics-Based Applications. Department of Computer Science, The Chinese University of Hong Kong, 1993-94. ENCORE: ftp://ftp.egr.msu.edu/pub/EC/GA/.

[15] D. Whitley. A Genetic Algorithm Tutorial. *Technical Report CS-93-103*. Colorado State University. Department of Computer Science, 1993. ENCORE: ftp://ftp.egr.msu.edu/pub/EC/GA/.

[16] G. Winter, J. Périaux, M. Galan, and P. Cuesta (eds.). *Genetic Algorithms in Engineering and Computer Science*. Wiley Computer Publishing, New York, 1995.

Chapter 17

Application-Specific Load Balancing on Heterogeneous Systems

KA-YEUNG KWOK, FU-MAN LAM, MOUNIR HAMDI, YI PAN[†],
AND CHI-CHUNG HUI

Department of Computer Science
The Hong Kong University of Science and Technology
Clear Water Bay, Hong Kong

[†]Department of Computer Science
University of Dayton
Dayton, OH, USA

Email: *hamdi@cs.ust.hk, pan@udcps.cps.udayton.edu*

17.1 Introduction

Heterogeneous workstations connected by local area networks have proven to be an attractive solution in academic and industrial research computing environments. The computational power of workstations, and the bandwidth of networks are increasing rapidly. As a result, the potential technological enhancement of network-based computing environments is boundless.

Researchers are increasingly interested in using networked workstations to perform large scale scientific computations. For example, the PVM system is a software package that allows a heterogeneous network of parallel and serial computers to operate as a single concurrent computational resource. PVM supplies the functions which automatically start up tasks on the virtual parallel machine and allows the tasks to communicate and synchronize with each other. Applications can be parallelized by using message-passing constructs provided by PVM. By sending and receiving messages, multiple tasks of an application can cooperate to solve a problem in parallel.

Recently, an application-driven parallel platform which provides a general and efficient parallel solution for time-dependent partial differential equations (PDEs) using the finite difference method has been designed and implemented [3]. Parallelism is extracted by partitioning the data and distributing each portion to a separate workstation. Each process then only performs the computation on its portion of the data. The results from the workstations are continually combined so that the overall solution evolves from the separate pieces. However, the load on individual workstations and the network varies dynamically. This unpredictable variation can degrade the performance of our PDE solver drastically. The entire platform can be slowed down by only one of its workstations which is having a heavy load. In addition to the CPU performance, other system resources such as virtual memory, physical memory, and network bandwidth fluctuate and strongly affect the execution of jobs on the system.

In this chapter, we present a performance analysis of a FDTD equation which is based on our developed PDEs solver. In particular, an adaptive load balancing scheme for the PDEs solver is proposed, implemented, and analyzed. We have to mention here that only a few attempts have been made towards providing parallel solutions for solving PDEs [9]. In particular, these solutions have been targeted towards specific problems and are not general enough [7], [8], [11].

This chapter is organized as follows. Section17.2 introduces a previously developed parallel solver of PDEs equations and details its implementation. Section 17.3 analyzes the performance of this parallel platform with a time-dependent complex differential equation. Section 17.4 introduces the load balancing scheme we used to solve the load variation of the workstations. Section 17.5 performs a performance analysis on the effectiveness of our load balancing scheme. Finally, Section 17.6 provides some concluding remarks.

17.2   System Overview

The parallel platform we are investigating uses the finite difference method [4] which provides approximate solutions to PDEs such that the derivatives at a point are approximated by difference quotients over a small interval. In solving the initial-boundary value problems, this method determines approximations using a finite number of points (grid points) in the domain. Therefore, continuous dependent variables are represented by their values at discrete time intervals at the set of grid points. The accuracy of the approximation of the exact solution depends on the number of grid points across the domain and how fine the time steps are. Each data point in the grid is given an initial value at the beginning of the execution. As time goes by, the value of each grid point is updated according to the PDEs provided. Based on the time step used in time differentiation and the order used in spatial differentiation, different dependencies among the grid points are resulted. Typically, the data at each grid point is updated at each time step by the surrounding points in the previous time steps, as depicted in Figure 17.1. The regular relationship among the data points is where the parallelization can be captured using a data parallelism paradigm.

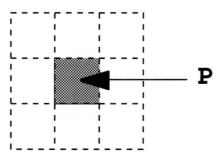

Figure 17.1 The nine surrounding points (including the central point) needed by P in the previous time steps. The central shaded point is the location of the point P that needs to be calculated.

The parallel processing environment we used consists of SUN IPX workstations. The workstations are connected by an Ethernet network, forming a common bus architecture. A single filesystem is being shared by all the workstations in the network. The PVM system has been used in the implementation of the platform. The actual number of workstations used can be easily configured in the PVM. Our platform views PVM as a parallel computing resource, in which individual machines communicate via message passing. The parallel programming model used is SPMD (Simple Program Multiple Data). As mentioned above, the platform developed is general in the sense that it can solve PDEs involving applications for numerous physical world problems. This requires the user to describe the details of the applications to the platform. The specifications of the PDEs for modeling a physical problem are given through the user interface which is then fed into a parser. The parser parses the specification and builds the corresponding executable programs. The user specifications are divided into three categories, which are the parameter section, the definition section, and the auxiliary section. The interface is flexible enough to allow the user to define C-style parameters, variables, and functions inside the appropriate sections. The parameter section allows the user to define all global data structures and constant parameters needed by the platform. These include the structure of the data point, initial values, dimension of the grid, data dependency, checkpointing options, computational mode (regular or irregular), and boundary conditions. In the definition section, the user needs to define the function which is used by the platform to perform iterative updates of the grid points. The auxiliary section contains any user-supplied subprograms that are needed by the three functions defined in the definition section. Moreover, for an efficient parallel implementation, the platform carries out a number of tasks including processor allocation, data partitioning, load balancing, computation, communication, and disk

I/O. It distributes blocks of grid points among the processors and monitors the flow of data across the processors' boundaries.

In this platform, parallelization is achieved by distributing the computation and data into different workstations. However, the number of workstations used, as well as the processors allocation scheme and the load balancing along the dimensions of the problem, are critical to the performance of the platform [2]. Thus, it should be very carefully taken care of to assure high performance of the platform. Unfortunately, there is a trade-off: The greater the number of workstations used, the higher the overall computing power will be, but also the higher the communication cost among the workstations will be. Hence, one must set up some means to determine a suitable number and allocation of processors with respect to the particular problem to be solved.

After determining the processor allocation scheme, the region of the grid that each processor should hold is determined. This job is done by the host process, and each node process is notified the region to get for computation. Note that the allocation obtained may not be optimal, and other factors (such as the processor speed, loading of the processors) may be added in computing the communication cost. However, the cost function is employed because it is rather simple and can be a guideline to the allocation procedure. Moreover, the data partitioning thus resulted is only initial and may be changed in future load balancing. The load balancing scheme will be discussed in Section 17.4 in detail.

17.3   Implementation of a Complex FDTD Equation

A complex FDTD equation was implemented in order to evaluate the performance of the platform in real cases [5], [6], [4]. The FDTD equations that we used in this example are the Maxwell's Curl Equations given below:

$$\frac{\partial \overline{H}}{\partial t} = -\frac{1}{\mu} \nabla \times \overline{E} - \frac{\rho}{\mu}\overline{H}$$

and

$$\frac{\partial \overline{E}}{\partial t} = \frac{1}{\varepsilon} \nabla \times \overline{H} - \frac{\sigma}{\epsilon}\overline{E}$$

where $\overline{E}$ is the electric field (V/m); $\overline{H}$ is the magnetic field (A/m); ρ is the magnetic resistivity(W/m); ϵ is the electric permittivity(F/m); σ is the electrical conductivity(W/m); and μ is the magnetic permeability(H/m).

Assuming that ϵ, σ, μ, and ρ are isotropic, the Maxwell's Curl equations can be transformed to the following system in terms of the rectangular coordinate system (x, y, z):

$$\frac{\partial H_x}{\partial t} = \frac{1}{\mu}\left(\frac{\partial E_y}{\partial z} - \frac{\partial E_z}{\partial y} - \rho H_x\right)$$

$$\frac{\partial H_y}{\partial t} = \frac{1}{\mu}\left(\frac{\partial E_z}{\partial x} - \frac{\partial E_x}{\partial z} - \rho H_y\right)$$

$$\frac{\partial H_z}{\partial t} = \frac{1}{\mu}\left(\frac{\partial E_x}{\partial y} - \frac{\partial E_y}{\partial x} - \rho H_z\right)$$

$$\frac{\partial E_x}{\partial t} = \frac{1}{\epsilon}\left(\frac{\partial H_z}{\partial y} - \frac{\partial H_y}{\partial z} - \sigma E_x\right)$$

$$\frac{\partial E_y}{\partial t} = \frac{1}{\epsilon}\left(\frac{\partial H_x}{\partial z} - \frac{\partial H_z}{\partial x} - \sigma E_y\right)$$

$$\frac{\partial E_z}{\partial t} = \frac{1}{\epsilon}\left(\frac{\partial H_y}{\partial x} - \frac{\partial H_x}{\partial y} - \sigma E_z\right)$$

The six partial differential equations given above form the basis of the FDTD algorithm for electromagnetic wave interactions with general three-dimensional objects [6]. In order to simplify the full three-dimensional case, it is assumed that neither the incident plane wave excitation nor the modeled geometry has any variation in the z-direction. As a result, the Maxwell's Curl equations are reduced to two decoupled sets of scalar equations. These two sets are named the transverse magnetic (TM) mode and the transverse electric (TE) mode which describe the two-dimensional wave interactions with objects.

The corresponding equations for the TM case are:

$$\frac{\partial H_x}{\partial t} = -\frac{1}{\mu}\left(\frac{\partial E_z}{\partial y} + \rho H_x\right)$$

$$\frac{\partial H_y}{\partial t} = \frac{1}{\mu}\left(\frac{\partial E_z}{\partial x} - \rho H_y\right)$$

$$\frac{\partial E_z}{\partial t} = \frac{1}{\epsilon}\left(\frac{\partial H_y}{\partial x} - \frac{\partial H_x}{\partial y} - \sigma E_z\right)$$

The corresponding equations for the TE case are:

$$\frac{\partial E_x}{\partial t} = \frac{1}{\epsilon}\left(\frac{\partial H_z}{\partial y} - \sigma E_x\right)$$

$$\frac{\partial E_y}{\partial t} = -\frac{1}{\epsilon}\left(\frac{\partial H_z}{\partial x} + \sigma E_y\right)$$

$$\frac{\partial H_z}{\partial t} = \frac{1}{\mu}\left(\frac{\partial E_x}{\partial y} - \frac{\partial E_y}{\partial x} - \sigma H_z\right)$$

The Maxwell's Curl equations can be represented by the finite-difference expressions using the Yee algorithm [6]. The finite-difference expressions that represent the space and time derivatives are:

$$\frac{\partial F^n(i,j,k)}{\partial x} = \frac{F^n(i+\frac{1}{2},j,k) - F^n(i-\frac{1}{2},j,k)}{\Delta x} + O(\Delta x^2)$$

$$\frac{\partial F^n(i,j,k)}{\partial t} = \frac{F^{n+\frac{1}{2}}(i,j,k) - F^{n-\frac{1}{2}}(i,j,k)}{\Delta t} + O(\Delta t^2)$$

To achieve good accuracy, $\overline{E}$ and $\overline{H}$ are evaluated at alternate half time steps. The resulting finite-difference time-stepping expressions for a magnetic and an electric field component are:

$$H_x^{n+\frac{1}{2}}(i, j+\tfrac{1}{2}, k+\tfrac{1}{2}) = \frac{1 - \frac{\rho(i,j+1/2,k+1/2)\Delta t}{2\mu(i,j+1/2,k+1/2)}}{1 + \frac{\rho(i,j+1/2,k+1/2)\Delta t}{2\mu(i,j+1/2,k+1/2)}} \cdot H_x^{n-\frac{1}{2}}(i, j+\tfrac{1}{2}, k+\tfrac{1}{2}) +$$

$$\frac{\frac{\Delta t}{\mu(i,j+1/2,k+1/2)}}{1 + \frac{\rho(i,j+1/2,k+1/2)\Delta t}{2\mu(i,j+1/2,k+1/2)}} \cdot$$

$$\{[E_y^n(i, j+1/2, k+1) - E_y^n(i, j+1/2, k)]/\Delta z +$$

$$[E_z^n(i, j, k+1/2) - E_z^n(i, j+1, k+1/2)]/\Delta y\}$$

$$E_z^{n+1}(i, k, k+\tfrac{1}{2}) = \frac{1 - \frac{\sigma(i,j,k+1/2)\Delta t}{2\epsilon(i,j,k+1/2)}}{1 + \frac{\sigma(i,j,k+1/2)\Delta t}{2\epsilon(i,j,k+1/2)}} \cdot E_z^n(i, j, k+\tfrac{1}{2}) +$$

$$\frac{\frac{\Delta t}{\epsilon(i,j,k+\frac{1}{2})}}{1 + \frac{\sigma(i,j,k+1/2)\Delta t}{2\epsilon(i,j,k+1/2)}} \cdot$$

$$\{[H_y^{n+1/2}(i+\tfrac{1}{2}, j, k+\tfrac{1}{2}) - H_y^{n+1/2}(i-\tfrac{1}{2}, j, k+\tfrac{1}{2})]/\Delta x +$$

$$[H_x^{n+1/2}(i, j-\tfrac{1}{2}, k+\tfrac{1}{2}) - H_x^{n+1/2}(i, j+\tfrac{1}{2}, k+\tfrac{1}{2})]/\Delta y\}$$

Similarly, the new value of the magnetic and electric field in other directions can be obtained. By the above finite-difference equations, the new values of the magnetic and electrical fields only depend on their previous values. Thus, the data space can be easily separated into various regions for several workstations to evaluate. The equations above were implemented by the parallel platform.

17.3.1   Implementation Details

In order to simplify the complexity of the equations, several assumptions are made. First, the electrical conductivity(σ), the electrical permittivity(ϵ), the magnetic resistivity(ρ), and the magnetic permeability(μ) are assumed to be constants within the efficient region. These parameters are also kept constant when time passes. The assumption greatly reduces the memory space that must be used in order to store all the parameters' values at each point of the region. Second, all points which are not located in the efficient region have a zero electric and magnetic field.

Since the computation requires alternative calculation of the electric and magnetic fields, and each calculation of electric or magnetic field is proceeded using a half logical time step, the platform uses two basic time steps to represent one logical time step. One time step is used for the calculation of the electric field in half logical time step, and the other time step is used for the calculation of the magnetic field in another half logical time step. In the implementation of the Maxwell's Curl equations, 1000 basic time steps are used in order to simulate 500 logical time steps.

17.3.2   Experimental Result

In this section, the experimental results for the Maxwell's Curl equations are presented. We measured all the factors that contribute to the total elapsed time for both parallel methods used in the platform; that is, the two-phase method and the precomputation method [3]. Tables 17.1 and 17.2 show the timing results in seconds of the experiments for the Maxwell's Curl equations using the two-phase method and the precomputation method, respectively. The grid size is 1000 x 20 x 20 with 500 logical time steps; that is, 1000 basic steps. Various SUN IPX workstations connected through an Ethernet network are used. The I/O time is the time that the node program spends in reading the initial data and writing the final results. The time decreases as the number of nodes increases due to the decrease of size of data that a processor stores which reduces the time for writing and reading from the disk.

Table 17.1 Timing Results in Seconds for the 3-D Maxwell's Curl Equations Using the Two-Phase Method

No. of Nodes	I/O Time	Computation Time	Communication Time	Elapsed Time	Speedup
1	65.34	11788.7	0.48	11897.80	1
5	84.77	2380.58	17.678	2662.62	4.46846
10	60.987	1185.2	20.165	1386.03	8.58409
15	57.8993	798.342	20.9413	1029.30	11.5591
20	47.7985	597.678	21.3	922.61	12.8958

Table 17.2 Timing Results in Seconds for the 3-D Maxwell's Curl Equations Using the Precomputation Method

No. of Nodes	I/O Time	Computation Time	Communication Time	Elapsed Time	Speedup
1	62.39	11568.9	0.66	11662.59	1
5	50.274	2593.57	19.1	2699.45	4.32036
10	42.772	1335.74	21.577	1442.88	8.08286
15	44.0567	906.949	21.882	1018.21	11.454
20	45.3745	705.912	22.3625	828.53	14.0762

As shown in the tables, the computation time used in the precomputation method is greater than those using the two-phase method. When the two-phase method is used, all the points are calculated in the same iteration. However, in the precomputation method, all interior points are calculated first. After receiving the boundary points, the new values of the boundary are calculated. If three dimensional space is used, it needs six extra six iterations in order to calculate all the boundary points on each surface. The extra iterations are attributed to the

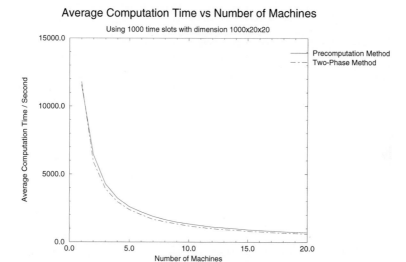

Figure 17.2 Average computation time as a function of the number of workstations.

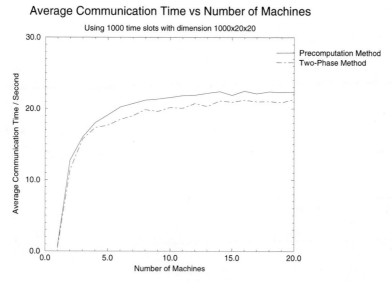

Figure 17.3 Average communication time as a function of the number of workstations.

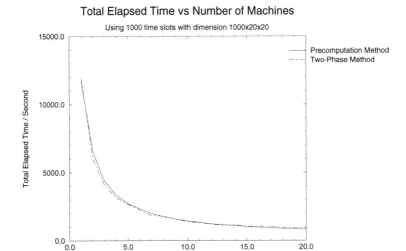

Figure 17.4 Elapsed time as a function of the number of workstations.

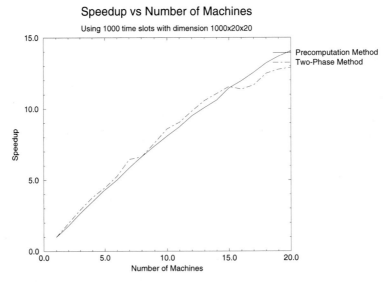

Figure 17.5 Speedup as a function of the number of workstations.

overhead of the platform. Thus, the computation time of the platform using the precomputation method is higher than using the two-phase method. Figure 17.2 illustrates the computation time of the precomputation method and the two-phase method as a function of the number of workstations. The communication time is the time that a node spends processing and waiting for the messages. The communication time using precomputation method is greater than that using two-phase method. Figure 17.3 illustrates the communication time of the precomputation method and the two phase method as a function of the number of nodes. The speedup of the precomputation method is better than that using two-phase method when smaller number of nodes are used. However, when more number of nodes are used (as seen in Figure 17.5), the speedup of the precomputation method is better. When the two-phase method is used, the overhead of iteration is smaller than that using the precomputation method. On the other hand, precomputation method allows overlapping of the computation time and the communication time. When small number of nodes are used, the overhead for iterations overcomes the overlap of the precomputation time and communication time. Thus, the speedup of the two-phase method is greater than that using the precomputation method. However, when large number of processors are used, the overlap of the precomputation time and communication time dominates and the speedup of precomputation method is higher than that using the two-phase method.

17.4   Load Balancing

17.4.1   Methodology

In this research, a load balancing scheme which can be used to perform even or uneven distribution is successfully implemented. We employ an application level approach, called Application Data Movement (ADM), to perform adaptive load distribution through data movement [1]. When the workloads on workstations are different, load balancing is performed to migrate some of the workload from heavily loaded workstations to lightly loaded ones. The load balancing scheme is designed in such a manner that it can also be used in a heterogeneous environment where the speeds of processors differ. Since the distribution of data can have a great impact on interprocessor communication, the message passing scheme needs to be designed carefully to achieve an acceptable performance. In order to minimize the complexity of the buffer management scheme and interprocessor communications scheme, the local regions kept by the nodes are always rectangular in shape. This way, our load balancing scheme considers a grid to be a collection of planes and columns in a three-dimensional Cartesian space. Partitioning along the x-axis partitions the grid into planes. Partitioning along the y-axis further partitions these planes into blocks. Figure 17.6 illustrates one simple example where the grid consists of two planes and each plane is divided among two processors. With load balancing, the division of data can be unequal. If the grid is very large and there are large number of processors available, load balancing allows further partitioning of data along the z-axis. This is shown in Figure 17.7, where the grid is divided along all three dimensions. Here the planes can be viewed as collections of columns.

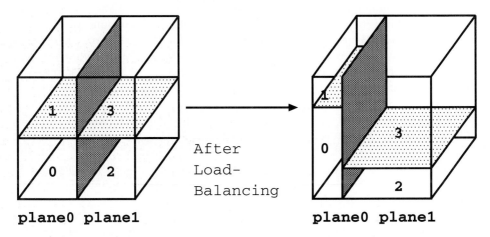

Figure 17.6 The load balancing scheme partitions the data across two dimensions.

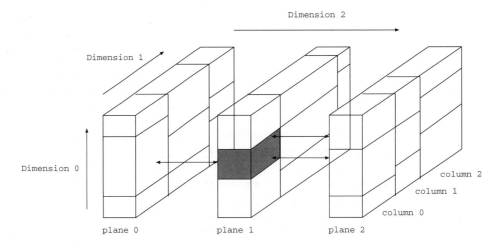

Figure 17.7 The load balancing scheme partitions the data across three dimensions.

17.4.2   Processor Weights

In this platform, for load balancing purposes, the speed of a process is defined by the amount of computational work which can be done in a logical time-step of computation. As each node station shares a portion of the data points, the workload depends on the elapsed time that a station needs to complete a computation work in a logical time-step. This elapsed time will be sent form node to host station in each user-defined constant interval. The host will then calculate the new region of each processor according to its individual processor's elapsed time information, and this load information is normalized with respect to the lightest weight processor to ease the comparison. The detail of the load equations are shown below. It should be noted that due to the limitation of the interprocessor communication, there should be a least one data point remaining in each dimension for each processor.

$$NewLoad(i) = \frac{e_i}{\min(e_j)}$$

where $NewLoad(i)$ is the new generalized load for workstation i, e_i is the elapsed time of workstation i in a logical time-step, and $\min(e_j)$ is the minimum of all e_i.

In the initialization step, a user-defined weight constant is defined to give some heuristic information about the old load information and new load information. It may help to avoid the sudden fluctuation of the unstable workload.

$$Load(i) = OLDWEIGHT \times OldLoad(i) + NEWWEIGHT \times NewLoad(i)$$

where $Load(i)$ is the resulting load for a load balancing decision for workstation i, $OldLoad(i)$ is the load for workstation i in pervious logical time-step, and $NewLoad(i)$ is the new generalized load for workstation i.

17.4.3   Application Data Movement (ADM)

ADM is a load balancing scheme that performs adaptive load distribution through data movement. The ADM model described in this research involves three steps: detecting when the data needs to be repartitioned, defining the points during computation when the data can be reshuffled, and defining the mechanism to perform the repartitioning. The first is done by the host check function, which can be written once and reused. The function is able to determine if the local processor is idle or busy, and return a signal indicating whether a load balancing event has occurred or not. It also determines what level of variation in processor activity is tolerated before a state change, and thus a migration event is declared. During the computation, all node processors will send the elapsed time of its previous time step spent in computation to host processor in a constant interval. With this information, the host check function can perform analysis and make a decision to perform load balancing or not. Since the computation on the analysis is independent of the computation of the node processes, there is an overlapping of time on performing load balancing analysis and the original computation of node processes. This overlapping can greatly reduce the overhead of performing the load balancing scheme. The host check function is in effect the key procedure to make a policy decision about when the program will adapt, and thus needs to be reasonably intelligent. For example, it would be detrimental for the host check function to be too eager to indicate a change in the host machine's state, because responding to every small change in machine activity might cause the program to spend all its time adapting and little time computing. The overhead in doing the load balancing is an important factor in a load balancing decision. A simple host-node relationship is shown in Figure 17.8. In the figure, there are three main steps: (1) During a predefined interval, all nodes send their load information to the host processor; (2) From the load information, the host makes a decision to perform load balancing or not; (3) If load balancing is required, the repartition time and new data regions are sent to all nodes. The load balancing algorithms for the host processor and node processors are given below.

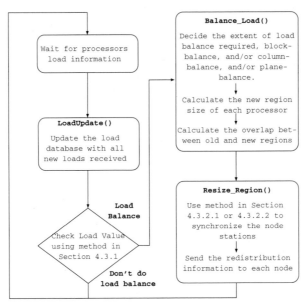

Heuristic for Repartition

The crucial part of implementing the load balancing scheme is how to decide when to perform load balancing on the data space. Bad criteria will not balance the time for computation and will increase the overhead on load balancing. The elapsed time will be even worse than the case without load balancing. In particular, a good heuristic function for deciding on load balancing should always gain savings on the total elapsed time and balance the computation time.

A efficient heuristic function is presented with the assumption that the computation time for each iteration is linearly related to the size of the data space. Under this assumption, if the data space is reduced by half, the computation time for each iteration will also be reduced by half. The assumption is valid when the computation of each iteration uses a certain portion of the CPU resource.

The basic idea is to compare the difference between the gain in saving when performing load balancing to the overhead on repartitioning. For each node in the N/multiple workstations' parallel platform, the computation times for the current

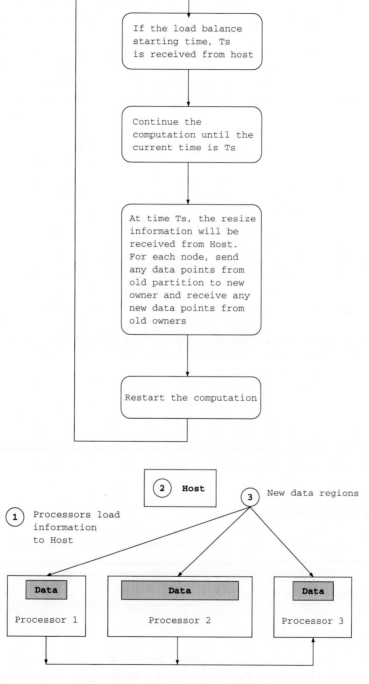

Figure 17.8 To simplify the Host-node relationship in load balancing, each node processor owns a portion of the data region.

iteration will be sent to the host in a constant interval. After receiving all data from the nodes, the host will calculate the average computation time for all the node processors, C_{aver}. The resulting computation time is the computation time of each iteration for all machines after load balancing is performed. The calculation is based on the linearity assumption stated above. The maximum computation time among the node processors, C_{Max}, approximates the computation time for all the node processors without using a load balancing scheme. This is because when one machine is highly loaded and the computation time is long, the other processors must wait for the data of that machine in order to continue the computation. Thus, the time used for each iteration is compared to the computation time of the highly loaded one. After calculating the average computation time, the difference between the average time and the maximum computation time, $C_{Max} - C_{aver}$, will be calculated. The difference is the time gained for each iteration after performing the load balancing. Multiplied with the remaining time steps for the process, the result is the total gain when performing load balancing. For each node, the time for the repartition procedure will be taken and sent to the host. After receiving the data, the host will select the maximum time which is the correct time for performing the repartitioning of data space, P_i. The times for the previous repartitioning will be summed up. The time of the previous repartition will be used to estimate the repartition time for the coming repartition time. The total time, $\sum P_i$, will be the total overhead on performing load balancing. The total gain on performing load balancing will be compared with the total overhead when performing load balancing. If the gain overcomes the overhead, that is, $[(C_{Max} - C_{aver}) \cdot T_{remain}] > \sum P_i$, load balancing will be performed. Otherwise, load balancing will not be performed.

The advantage of this heuristic function is that the savings in time between the current time and the time after the previous load balancing will be preserved. Since only the time saving after the current point and the overhead of performing load balancing are compared, the time saving from the previous load balancing before the current time will not be reduced. It guarantees that there is at least some savings in time for each load balancing process. Besides, it is very easy to implement. The heuristic function is also biased towards the small time steps. It is more likely to perform load balancing as early as possible in order to get higher savings in time in the following time steps.

The load balancing will start at the heaviest loaded machine which is selected by finding the maximum of $Load(i)$ information mentioned earlier. If $Max(Load(i)) > THRESHOLD$, where $Max(Load(i))$ is the normalized load of the heaviest loaded machine and the $THRESHOLD$ is a user defined constant, load balancing will be performed based on the method mentioned above.

Data Repartition Method

After the heaviest loaded machine is selected, the extent of the load balancing should be determined. The overhead of all the balance methods are compared. With this information, we can determine whether we should perform block-balance, block-balance and column balance, or column-balance and plane balance. The overhead of the latter case is the greatest, as it involves load balancing in all dimensions. As we know that transferring time in Ethernet depends on the amount of data transferred, the overhead can easily be calculated.

In order to repartition the data space at the same time, a synchronization scheme must be introduced in order to preserve the program correctness. The aim of the synchronization scheme is to: 1) make sure all machines can receive the time step for repartition in advance; and 2) make sure all data are updated at the same logical time for repartition. However, we need two synchronizations which are extremely expensive, since synchronizations only stand and wait without doing anything. In order to minimize the overhead, it is preferred to eliminate one of the synchronizations. Two implementation methods are used for data repartition. The first one is the synchronization method. The second one is the predefined method. The synchronization method uses two synchronizations as stated above. It is quite expensive but the program correctness can be guaranteed. The predefined method eliminates the second synchronization. That is, all machines receive the time step for repartition in advance. However, it cannot guarantee the correctness of the program, which means the machine may receive the time step for repartition that the machine has already computed.

Synchronization Method

In order to ensure that the repartition can be achieved correctly, the host machine must keep track of the logical time steps of each machine process at the time of repartition. In the synchronization method, when the host decides to repartition the data space, the host will send a STOP_NODE flag to all the node machines to inform them that repartition will proceed. Once the node receives the STOP_NODE flag, the node will send the time step which the node processed to the host and wait. The above procedure is necessary because all nodes can receive the repartition time which the nodes still do not process. Thus, the first goal stated above is achieved. After collecting all time steps form all the node processes, the host will find the highest time step that the machines process and send this time step to the node processes to inform them that repartition will take place at that time step. When the node processes receive the proposed time step for repartition, they will check whether they have finished the computation of the proposed time step. If the time step is reached, the node process will send the host a READY_PART flag to acknowledge the host to be ready for partition. If the time step is not reached, the node processes will continue computation until the time step is reached. After the host receives all READY_PART flags, it will send all nodes an acknowledgment to start the repartition. The READY_PART flag here is used to synchronize the start of the repartition. It is necessary, since synchronization can prevent nodes from receiving boundary data from those time steps before the repartition time. The synchronization method is shown in Figure 17.9.

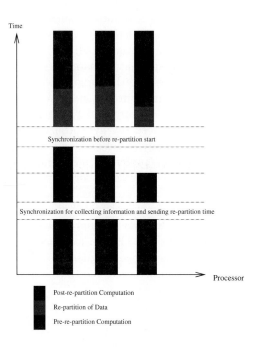

Time

Synchronization before re-partition start

Synchronization for collecting information and sending re-partition time

Processor

■ Post-re-partition Computation
■ Re-partition of Data
■ Pre-re-partition Computation

Figure 17.9 Synchronization method.

The Predefined Method

The weakness of the synchronization method is the big overhead for synchronization. It is necessary to reduce this idle time in order to decrease the overhead. Recall that each node cannot process and calculate data of time $t + 1$ if the boundary data of time step t - LEVEL has not been received. Thus, if there are N node processes, the maximum difference in the time steps between processors is N × LEVEL. When the host receives load balancing information every T time steps and the minimum logical time step that processors undergoing is t, time step $t + T + (N × LEVEL)$ is the minimum "safe" time step for repartition to occur. Using this "safe" time, the time for synchronization to receive repartition time steps can be eliminated. There are two important problems that need to be considered. First, the time that processors send load balancing information to the host is ignored. Second, the time that the host sends the repartition time step to the nodes cannot be determined. Since these two times are network dependent, they cannot be upper-bounded. Thus, the node processors may receive repartition time that they have already processed. However, as the host machine is a node processor, the time spent sending data to the host is very small and can be ignored. Thus, the host can at least receive one node's real time information. Although the time step that the host receives may not be minimum, it only enlarges the "safe" time region. The first problem can be solved. Besides, by the same assumption that the host processor is also the node processor, the time when the host sends the repartition time to the nodes should be the same as the time that the node process of the same machine sends the boundary data to other nodes. This time contributes one logical time step in advance. Therefore, the new minimum "safe" time step should be set to t + T + (N × LEVEL) + 1.

Although the minimum "safe" time step can be calculated, it cannot guarantee the correctness since two times cannot be guaranteed to be bounded. However, encouraging results are achieved. In the experiment, the platform is run using the predefined method for 200 times using different parameters (i.e., different time steps, different sizes of data region in different dimensions) and each time the executions are completed correctly.

Having determined and sent the repartition time step to the nodes, the nodes will continue until the repartition time is reached. If all boundary data is sent and received, the nodes will send the READY_PART flag to the host. The host will then send to the nodes an acknowledgment flag and start the repartition. The predefined method is shown in Figure 17.10.

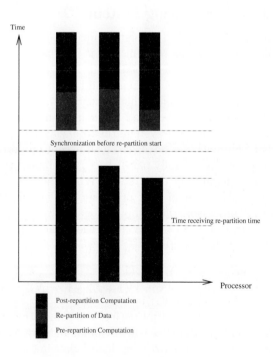

Figure 17.10 Predefined method.

The advantage of the predefined method is the reduction of synchronization time used. As the nodes need not stop and wait for the repartition time step, it sharply reduces the repartition time used. However, the predefined method cannot capture the real time situation of the network loading. As the predefined method only calculates the minimum time steps for repartition in the future, the repartition cannot reflect the real time network loading. There is a gap between the time of the decision and the time of implementation. For a network with fluctuating work load, the predefined method may not perform very well since the platform cannot catch the updated information of the network loading. We will see that the time gap between the time of the decision and the time of implementation has negative effects on the time performance of the platform. If the network loading is relatively stable, that is, the loading will not change very much in the time gap, the predefined method will be very efficient.

17.5   Analysis

In this section, the performance of the load balancing algorithm is examined and a detailed analysis is presented. We analyze the efficiency of the platform by checking the speedup of the platform in the loaded environment.

17.5.1   Perfect Load Balancing System

In order to compare the efficiency of the load balancing methods, a perfect (but not practical) load balancing is used as reference. It is used as an upper bound of our load balancing algorithm. This perfect load balancing case assumes that the load balancing and repartition involve no overhead and the load balancing is performed immediately after the load in the system has changed.

The total elapsed time for a perfect load balancing can be calculated as follows: Suppose there are N processors in the system; the total elapsed time for one machine without any load is E; all machines have zero load except one processor which has load L. Assume the system can be fully parallelized, the elapsed time for the system is E/N when there is no loading in the system. When there is one processor with load L, the computational power of that processor will become 1/L. Thus, if the platform is run in that processor, the computational power of that processor used by the parallel platform is 1/(1+L). Therefore, the total elapsed time, C for the platform in an unbalanced load system is

$$C = \frac{E}{(N-1) + \frac{1}{1+L}} = \frac{E(1+L)}{(N-1)(1+L)+1} = \frac{E(1+L)}{NL+N-L}$$

However, C cannot represent the actual perfect case since there was time that is used by the load balancing procedures which cannot be parallelized. Thus, $\delta(N)$, the total time difference between performing load balancing and without load balancing, is taken. Since the time that is used in the load balancing procedure which cannot be parallelized was dependent on the number of processors used, $\delta(N)$ was dependent on the number of processors, N. Besides, the equation stated above does not include the communication time for transmitting data between nodes. The total communication time, $T_{comm}(N)$, can be obtained experimentally. Similar to $\delta(N)$, $T_{comm}(N)$ is dependent on the number of processors used in the system. Thus, the new time $C' = C + \delta(N) + T_{comm}(N)$ can approximate the ideal total elapsed time for perfect load balancing.

17.5.2   Experimental Results

In this section, the experimental results for solving three-dimensional PDEs on the platform using the Maxwell's Curl equations are presented. The total elapsed times for using the two different repartitioning methods are also presented. The total elapsed times are taken using the two-phase method. In the experiments, a grid with a size of 500 x 20 x 20 points with 300 time steps is used with different numbers of SUN IPX workstations connected through an Ethernet network. The experiments are conducted in two different load environments. The first one is a complete idle environment. In this environment, no additional jobs are added in the system. The second is a loaded environment. In the loaded environment, one processor suffers a heavy load and the rest of the processors are idle. If there are N machines, one of the N machines is set to a certain load level. In the experiment, the load level is set to three. The remaining processors are completely free of load, that is, zero load level. The complete idle environment is used to give the original speedup and elapsed time for comparison. In the loaded environment, three sets of data are taken. The platform is run without the load balancing algorithm and the performance of the original platform is recorded. The platform is then run with the load balancing algorithm. The two repartition methods are also examined. Table 17.3 shows the elapsed time in seconds for the experiments for the three-dimensional Maxwell's Curl equations.

Table 17.3 Elapsed Time in Seconds for the 3-D Maxwell's Curl Equations

Number of Machine	Without Load Balancing	Perfect Load Balancing	Load Balancing (Synchronization)	Load Balancing (Predefine)
1	7201.02	7477.95	7224.06	7231.77
2	3656.54	1550.57	2240.14	1989.76
3	2484.73	876.54	1401.03	1505.66
4	1861.87	605.87	1056.96	1181.93
5	1517.80	461.19	934.29	915.36
6	1312.32	377.29	764.53	758.46
7	1178.60	318.00	638.17	538.25
8	1024.96	275.78	553.54	511.77

We present four values for comparison: the elapsed without using load balancing;

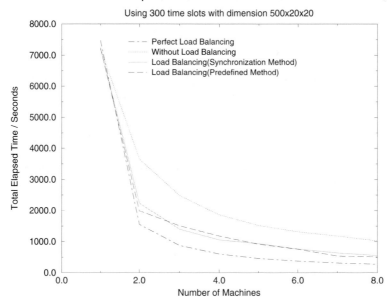

Figure 17.11 Total elapsed time as a function of the number of workstations.

the perfect elapsed time calculated by the procedure above; the elapsed time with load balancing using the synchronization repartition method; and the elapsed time with load balancing using the predefined repartition method. Figure 17.11 present the results graphically. As seen from the graphs, the total elapsed time is greatly improved by using the load balancing method. Nearly 40 percent of time is reduced by using the two load balancing methods. However, when compared with the perfect load balancing cases, overheads still exist. These overheads are mainly the time for performing repartition of data space and the time to perform calculations to determine the portion of data each processor needs to send and receive in the load balancing procedure. Moreover, it is shown that the performances of the two repartition methods, and the synchronization and predefined methods were very close to each other.

Table 17.4 shows the average time for each repartition procedure with a different number of machines using the synchronization and predefined methods. Figure 17.12 presents the results graphically.

As seen from the above graphs, the time for each repartition using the predefined method is less than the time using the synchronization method. As described above, the predefined method can save one synchronization procedure which was very time consuming. The difference between different numbers of machines in the above graphs is the time savings for the extra synchronization process. However, as we have seen from the previous table, the total elapsed time for the two methods is very

Table 17.4 Average Time for Each Repartition Procedure With Different Numbers of Machines

Number of Machines	Aver. Repartition Time (Synchronization Method)	Aver. Repartition Time (Predefined Method)
2	32.02	28.85
3	11.65	10.41
4	10.11	7.39
5	7.35	6.79
6	7.99	5.40
7	6.70	6.60
8	7.03	5.52

close. It is attributed to the late repartition when the predefined method is used. Since the predefined method uses the closest "safe" time step for repartition, there is a time gap between the time of decision and the time of processing the repartition. When the synchronization method is used, which performs repartitioning at the time of decision, this time gap is benefited by the load balancing. Nevertheless, load balancing is not processed in this time gap when the predefined method is used. Thus, inefficiency results and the time that is lost by the predefined method is nearly the same as the time gained by not performing the extra synchronization. Therefore, the overall performance of the two methods is very close, as illustrated by the speedup curves in Figure 17.13. In the speedup curves, we can see that both methods gain a significant speedup by using our load balancing algorithm. Compared with the speedup curves without load balancing procedures, the load balancing procedure can gain an improvement of about 80 percent.

Compared with the perfect load balancing case, however, there is a gap between our experimental results and the perfect load balancing case. Two factors are attributed to this overhead. First, there is an overhead of the load balancing algorithm which performs the computation in the load balancing algorithm and the time for repartitioning and synchronizing the data. Second, there is an inefficiency of the heuristic function and the region rearrangement. As described in the previous section, the computation of the load balancing algorithm is highly overlapped with the computation of the node processes. Thus, this computation time is relatively small. However, the overhead due to the repartitioning processes and synchronization processes which contribute to the major part of the overhead cannot be avoided. Besides, the heuristic function may not give the optimal decision on whether repartition of data should start. Thus, there are several time savings which should be saved in the perfect load balancing case but are lost. Moreover, since each region must restore at least one point in the previous region after repartitioning, several repartitions may be needed in order to rearrange the regions which perfectly correspond to the load of the processors. Thus, extra overhead results.

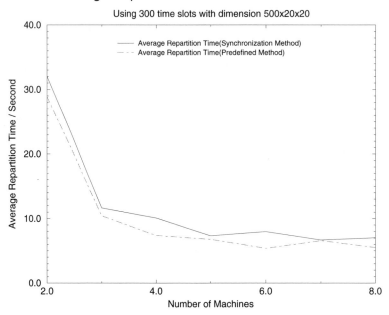

Average Repartition Time vs Number of Machines

Using 300 time slots with dimension 500x20x20

Figure 17.12 Average repartition time as a function of the number of workstations.

17.5.3 Future Improvements

The major overhead of the load balancing algorithm are the time to repartition the data and the time for synchronization. As for each time the data needs to be rearranged, time must be wasted in order to send and receive the data. This overhead can hardly be avoided. The synchronization in the partitioning procedure is also unavoidable. However, the time for synchronization can overlap with the computation of the node processes. The predefined repartition method is one kind of overlapping of synchronization with the computation of the node processes. Defining and improving the heuristic function used to decide when the repartition must start could improve the performance of the algorithm. Besides, the repartition algorithm can be modified so that the data space after repartitioning perfectly corresponds to the load of the processors.

17.6 Conclusions

The use of networks of heterogeneous workstations as parallel computers is a very attractive proposition for high performance computing. An efficient parallel platform was built on this computing environment to solve partial differential equa-

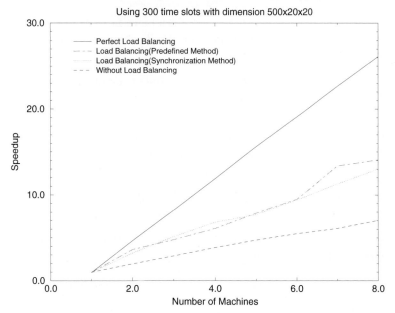

Figure 17.13 Speedup as a function of the number of workstations.

tions (PDEs). Maxwell's Curl equations, complex time-dependent partial differential equations, are implemented using the parallel platform in order to analyze the practicality and efficiency of the parallel PDEs solver. Significant speedups are indicated and it has been shown that the solver is practical enough to solve a wide range of PDEs.

However, the load on individual processors and the network varies dynamically. This unpredictable variation can degrade the performance of our PDE solver drastically. An efficient load balancing facility is important for the parallel platform to deal with practical applications. An effective load balancing scheme using Adaptive Data Movement is implemented on top of this parallel platform with two different repartition methods (synchronization method and predefined method). Experimental results proved that significant speedups are achieved using the load balancing schemes in heavily loaded environments. Although the two repartition methods have their own advantages and shortages, it is shown that the two methods perform equally well on the parallel platform. Finally, some guidelines concerning the improvement of the parallel platform are presented.

17.7   Bibliography

[1] J. Casas, R. Konuru, S.W. Otto, et al. "Adaptive Load Migration Systems for PVM," In *Proceedings Supercomputing '94*, Washington D.C., pages 390-399, 1994.

[2] M. Hamdi and C.K. Lee, "Dynamic Load-Balancing of Image Processing Applications on Clusters of Workstations," *Parallel Computing*, Vol. 22, no. 11, pages, 1477-1492, 1997.

[3] C.C. Hui, M. Hamdi and I. Ahmad, "SPEED: A Parallel Platform for Solving and Predicting Performance of PDEs on Distributed Systems," *Concurrency: Practice and Experience*, Vol. 8. no. 7 pages 537-568, 1996.

[4] G. D. Smith. *Numerical Solution of Partial Differential Equations: Finite Difference method.* Oxford University Press, New York, 1985.

[5] A. Kunz and S. Kari. *The Finite Difference Time Domain Method for Electromagnetics.* CRC Press, 1993.

[6] M. N. O. Mattew. *Numerical Techniques in Electromagnetics.* CRC Press, Boca Raton, Fla., 1992.

[7] S. McFaddin and J. R. Rice, "RELAX: A Software Platform for Partial Differential Equation Interface Relaxation Methods," In *Proc. of the 2nd IMACS Int. Conf. on Expert Systems for Numerical Computing*, Pages 175-194, 1992.

[8] N. H. Naik, J. K. Naik and M. Nicoules, "Parallelization of a Class of Implicit Finite Difference Schemes in Computational Fluid Dynamics," In *Int. J. High Speed Computing*, Vol. 5, no. 1, pages 1-50, 1993.

[9] M. A. Pinsky. *Introduction to Partial Differential Equations with Applications.* McGraw-Hill Publishing Co., New York, 1984.

[10] T. Schnekenburger and M. Huber, "Heterogeneous Partitioning in a Workstation Network," In *Proc. Heterogeneous Comput. Workshop*, Santa Barbara, pages 72-77, 1994.

[11] E. Verhulst, "A Prototype of a User Friendly Partial Differential Equation Solver on a Transputer Network," In *Proceedings of the User 1 Working Conference*, Belgium, Pages 232-239, 1998.

Chapter 18

Time Management in Parallel Simulation

AZZEDINE BOUKERCHE

Department of Computer Sciences
University of North Texas
Denton, TX 76203, USA

Email: *boukerch@cs.unt.edu*

18.1   Introduction

Simulations are widely used in analyzing systems such as large communication networks, computer-aided design (CAD) circuits, semiconductor manufacturing line, and many aerospace and military applications. The computational expense and/or the real time required to run significant simulation may inhibit the use of simulation in these areas. Parallel simulation offers a promising solution to this problem, but not without creating a new set of issues and trade-offs.

In this chapter, we shall describe ways of accelerating discrete event simulation using multiprocessor systems; in particular, we focus upon synchronization protocols with clustered processes.

18.1.1   Different Types of Simulations

We must draw distinctions between different types of simulations: *continuous, discrete, and hybrid. Continuous* simulation models the situation in which changes in state occur smoothly and continuously in time, e.g., the flow of liquid through a pipeline, weather modeling, and circuit level simulation of electronic components. Continuous simulation models often involve difference or differential equations that represent certain aspects of the system. *Discrete* simulation refers to the modeling technique in which changes to the state of the model can occur only at countable points in time. For example, in logic simulation, the circuit is simulated by assuming that node voltages take on values only from a finite set (say, 0 and 1) and that transitions between values are instantaneous; in switch-level simulation, transistors are simulated as switches that can be either opened or closed. Digital computing systems, computer and communication systems, and queueing systems (such as bank teller and job shops) are other examples of discrete event systems. Many systems are hybrid, that is, combinations of discrete and continuous characteristics. An example of a hybrid system is an unloading dock where tankers queue up to unload their oil through a pipeline. The decision of whether to use a discrete or continuous model for a particular system depends on the specific objectives of the study. For example, a model of traffic flow on a freeway would be discrete if the characteristics and movement of individual cars were important. Alternatively, if the cars can be treated in the "aggregate," the flow of traffic can be described by differential equations in a continuous model.

Discrete systems can be simulated by discrete-event simulations. Many methods have been proposed in the literature for implementing discrete systems. They can be broadly classified into two groups: the synchronous and the asynchronous methods. In synchronous discrete event simulation, all objects in the simulation progress forward in simulation time together, in synchrony, with no object ahead in time of any other. The usual queue implementations for sequential simulation are all synchronous methods. In contrast, an asynchronous method permits some objects to simulate ahead in time while others lag behind. Of course, an asynchronous method must include some mechanism for ensuring that when an object that is "behind" schedules an event for execution by an object that is "ahead," it does not cause any events to be executed in the wrong order.

Sowizral and Jefferson [17] showed that synchronous parallel discrete event methods are fundamentally unable to provide any speedup at all for many simulations, in particular the very common kind of simulation with low virtual concurrency. In synchronous parallel discrete event simulations, all events are synchronized by a global clock shared by all processors and each process can process events with the same timestamps that are equal to the global clock time. However, this type of simulation limits the degree of parallelism during the simulation, and the synchronization barrier becomes a bottleneck. We conclude that asynchronous methods are essential, and therefore we consider only asynchronous discrete event simulation[1] here.

18.2   Major Issues of Parallel Simulation

A central issue in any simulation carried out in parallel is the mechanism by which simulation time is advanced. In traditional discrete simulation, time is commonly advanced from event to event (*discrete*) or in fixed increments (*time-stepped*). The conventional uniprocessor algorithm for discrete event simulation relies upon a single event list from which events are removed and simulated in their correct time order. This is not readily executed in parallel because of the bottleneck inherent in access

---

[1] In the sequel, discrete event simulation refers to the asynchronous discrete systems.

to the event list. Consequently, a radically new approach must be adopted. Chandy and Misra [6] showed that parallelism can be achieved only by changing the structure of the event list from its traditional form; this is the goal of *parallel simulation*.

Indeed, parallel simulation shows the greatest potential in terms of exploiting the inherent parallelism of a system. However, many problems remain to be solved before parallel simulation can become commonplace. The problem of parallel simulation is a complex one, demanding the resolution of a number of issues. It contains classical parallel processing problems, such as distributed detection and resolution of deadlocks, distributed termination, synchronization, partitioning and mapping processes to processors, flow control, and memory management.

Before we proceed further, let us introduce the basic terminology and the major issues pertaining to parallel simulation.

18.3   Principles of Parallel Simulation

A parallel simulation should provide the same solution to a problem as a sequential simulation. Thus, in specifying and developing a parallel simulator, it is first important to understand the sequential nature of the simulation.

18.3.1   Distributed Programming: A Simulation Example

Simulation provides an interesting problem for the creation of distributed algorithms. Parallel discrete event simulation is a special case of parallel programs. It has relationships with parallel computation and also with simulation. Many scientists in the parallel computation community consider discrete event simulation as a challenge because of the inherently sequential nature of the simulation algorithms used. Indeed, the sequencing constraints that dictate the order in which computations must be executed relative to each other are, in general, quite complex and highly data-dependent, as we shall see in Figure 18.1. Indeed, let us consider two events E_1 at logical process LP_1 with timestamp 20 and E_2 at LP_2 with timestamp 30. Assume that processing E_1 causes the creation of event E_3 for LP_2 with a timestamp less than 30. E_3 might affect E_2; for instance, E_3 could modify a state variable used by E_2, necessitating sequential execution of all three events.

Discrete event simulation is a challenging algorithm to parallelize and presents a good test case to explore the limits of the parallelism [6], [9]. As a consequence, researchers in the parallel programming community are interested in this important problem.

18.3.2   The Apparently Sequential Nature of Simulation

The inherently sequential nature of event list manipulation limits the potential parallelism of standard simulation models. The head of the event list must be removed, the simulation clock advanced, and the event simulated. Several data structures have been proposed or adapted to solve the event set representation problem for discrete event simulation. All such data structures share a common

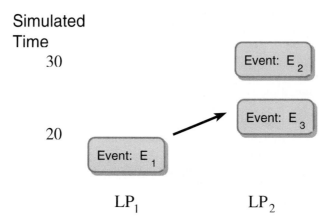

Figure 18.1 Sequencing constraints.

attribute: All future events are maintained in a single set and ordered by event time to permit the extraction of the event with minimum time. The events must proceed in a strict chronological order in order to mimic the real system. However, the execution of one event may possibly cause new events to be added to the event list. Thus, to ensure strict chronological order, events must be processed one at a time, resulting in an (apparently) sequential program. Only by eliminating the event list in its traditional form so as to capture the interdependence of the processes being simulated can additional parallelism be obtained [6]. This is the objective of parallel simulation.

The goal of parallel simulation [6] is (a) to partition the system being simulated into relatively independent subsystems which communicate with each other in a simple manner (such as passing customers or jobs from one subsystem to another), and (b) to simulate each subsystem on a different processor. In the next section, we shall discuss the natural correspondence between the physical system and the logical system (simulator).

18.3.3   A Natural Correspondence Between Problem and Solution

In order to guarantee the correctness of the simulation, the following property [6] must hold: The event message (e, t) is generated, received, processed, consumed (i.e., has reached its final destination) or transmitted, respectively, by LP_i in the simulation system if and only if the event e was generated, received, processed, consumed or transmitted, respectively, by PP_i (physical process) in the physical system at time t. We will not prove this statement. The interested reader may wish to consult [6] for more details.

A parallel simulation can be constructed in which every physical process (PP) is modeled by a corresponding logical process (LP) [6]. The logic of a process depends only upon the physical process that it is simulating; it is independent of the rest of the physical system. There is no restriction on the logic of any process, provided it can be simulated. For example, a multicomputer system might be divided into a collection of microcomputers and interconnection switches, e.g., a global bus. One could create one instance of the switch LP to model the bus and a processor LP to model each microcomputer. Any communication between physical processes is modeled by communication[2] of logical processes within the simulation. There is no central process which controls the synchronization among various processes. This implies there is no variable, such as simulated time, shared by all processes.

In a simulation, events must always be executed in increasing time order. Anomalous behavior might then result if an event is incorrectly simulated earlier in real time and affects state variables used by subsequent events. In the physical world this would represent a situation in which future events could influence the present. This is referred to as a *causality error*.

The lack of an overall global time in the simulation has profound consequences for the preservation of causality. A partial solution [6] is to use *timestamps* and to model the interactions between physical processes by exchanging timestamped event messages between the corresponding logical processes. They also represent sending times of events and the service time added to the received time (when the event is in an output queue). They ensure that events are simulated in the proper order.

Second, each LP must maintain its own clock representing the *local simulation time* (LST). This time is equal to the time when the last event (e) was processed, i.e., the time in the simulated system which indicates the end of an event that occurred at the corresponding PP; thus if the LST was the old local simulation time at LP, the new LST, after processing the event e, is computed as follows: LST = Max(LST, $e.time$), where $e.time$ is the time of the last event.

For instance, as shown in Figure 18.2, LP_i first determines which message bears the smallest timestamp in its input buffer that is to avoid the causality errors (the timestamp of each event appears between parentheses). Then LP_i processes event e_1, advances its LST to ($Max(LST_i, e_1.time) + Service_{time}$), where $Service_{time}$ represents the time that the physical process PP_i would have spent to process the event e_1 ($e_1.time = 5$), and generates the new event e_4. If we assume that $Service_{time} = 1$, then $e_4.time = 6$, and the local simulation at LP_i will be set to 6 ($LST_i = 6$).

Associated with each predecessor (LP_i), LP_j maintains a time value TNE_{ij}, which denotes the Time-of-Next-Event, for all predecessor empty links. Finally, an LP is allowed to execute an event e with timestamp $e.time$ if it can be sure that it will not receive any future events with timestamp less than $e.time$, i.e., if for all j, where link $l_{i,j}$ is empty, $TNE_{ij} \geq e.time$.

Consequently, events are always executed in chronological order and the time-

---

[2]Some authors use the concept of a directed link or channel between communicating logical processes. In this chapter, we also use the concept of directed link.

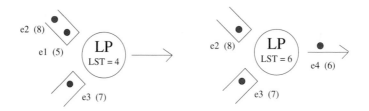

Figure 18.2 Schematics of events flow.

stamps of event messages sent by each LP are ordered in a non-decreasing order. An input buffer is assigned to each input link l_{ij}.

A system is simulated for some time period $[0,T]$, where T is referred to as termination or end-time of simulation. During this time, any LP sends a finite number of messages (or more accurately, initiates a finite number of message sends). A basic blocking algorithm run by each LP in a distributed (parallel) simulation is presented in Figure 18.3. LP blocking greatly influences the performance of a parallel simulation. If many of the LPs are blocked, a parallel simulation can degenerate into a sequential one with an even poorer performance than the corresponding sequential simulation run on a single machine.

The performance of parallel simulation executed on multiprocessors is determined by many other factors. Among these factors is the partitioning and mapping of processes to processors. It can affect the efficiency of a parallel simulation a great deal [3]. Indeed, as it is often the case, the number of logical processes (LPs), n, is much larger than the number of processors, k. These results indicate the need for clusters of processes to be selected and assigned to different processors. Selection from the set of processes may also be considered as partitioning of the problem into k components [3].

18.3.4   Logical Process Simulation

Before we present the parallel simulation algorithm at an LP, we must define what we mean by an unblocked LP. We begin with a discussion of what it means for an LP to be (un)blocked.

Definition 18.3.1: An *LP* is *unblocked* if:

1. Each of its input buffers contains at least one event message or

2. There exists an input event message with a timestamp smaller than or equal to the timestamp of messages expected on all empty input links or

3. It has an output event message to send.

Conversely, an LP is *blocked* if all of these three statements are not true.

Begin
   LST := 0 ;
   While Not Finished **Do**
     receive input *event messages* ;
     m:= earliest available message ;
     If *LP* is unblocked **Then**
       If no output *event messages* **Then**
         consume (m) ;
         LST := Max (LST,*m. time*);   /* *m.time* is the timestamp */
                                            /* assigned to *m*/
       simulate (m);
       $LST := LST + Service_{time}(m.\ event)$;
       EndIf
       await(a message arrival);
     EndIf;
   End;
 End.

Figure 18.3 Basic parallel simulation algorithm for LP_i.

During the course of the simulation, each logical process executes the basic blocking algorithm described in Figure 18.3. Notice that we have not included the deadlock detection and resolution algorithms. Unfortunately, blocking behavior may lead to deadlock, as depicted below in Figure 18.4. Each of the four LPs has an empty input queue, expecting messages from another LP. At the same time, each of the LPs has event messages in other input queues. LP_1 has a message bearing timestamp 11, LP_2 has a message with timestamp 7, LP_3 has one message bearing timestamp 13, and LP_4 has one message bearing timestamp 10.

In accordance with (our) protocols, LP_1 expects a message from LP_4, LP_4 expects a message from LP_3, LP_3 expects a message from LP_2, and LP_2 completes the circle. None of the LPs can respond because they cannot be certain that they will not receive a message from a neighbor which could change its response. Our deadlock cycle can be generalized to a knot of blocked LPs [4].

Two approaches to deadlocks in the conservative methodology are (1) to avoid them or (2) to allow the simulation to deadlock, detect deadlock, and then break it by providing additional information to LPs.

18.3.5   Conservative Vs. Optimistic Simulation

Several methods for parallel simulation have been proposed. Good surveys of the literature may be found in [9]. These techniques for parallel simulation can be classified into two groups: *conservative* algorithms and *optimistic* algorithms. While conservative synchronization techniques rely on *blocking* to avoid violation of dependence constraints, *optimistic* methods rely on detecting synchronization errors at

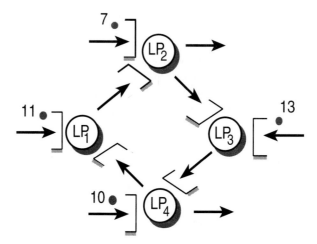

Figure 18.4 Empty cycle.

runtime and on recovery using a *rollback* mechanism. In both approaches, the simulated system is modeled as a network of logical processes (LP) which communicate only via *message passing*.

In the *conservative* approach [6], each process is allowed to proceed if and only if it is certain that it will not receive any earlier event. Consequently, events are always executed in chronological order at any LP. In the case where one or more queues are empty, the LP is blocked because an event with a smaller timestamp than the timestamp of the waiting events might yet arrive at an empty queue. This mechanism implies that only unblocked LPs can execute in parallel. If all the LPs were blocked, the simulation would be deadlocked. Ensuring synchronization and avoiding deadlocks are the central problems in the conservative approach.

In the *optimistic* approach [11], each process continues to receive and process the event messages out of its input queue until no messages remain or until a message arrives "in the past" (a *straggler*). Upon receiving a *straggler*, the process execution is interrupted and a *rollback* action takes place. Rollback consists of restoring the process to the appropriate state and sending cancellation notices for messages produced by the rollback portion of the computation using *antimessages*. There are two major versions of Time Warp: the original version that is intended for distributed memory architecture and that performs *cancellation by antimessage* [11], and a version that is intended for a shared memory architecture that uses *direct cancellation* without antimessages [9].

A Time Warp mechanism is itself deadlock free (if there is enough memory), but time is spent while rolling back and repeatedly simulating the same events. This mechanism requires a lot of memory to store the history at each LP as well as efficient garbage collection algorithms in order to remove old states. Most studies of Time Warp have been experimental [9], [16]. Despite these studies, the rollback mechanism is not well understood. A number of memory management schemes have been proposed to reduce the space usage of Time Warp. Some of these schemes reduce the average space utilization, but cannot be invoked to recover storage when simulation actually runs out of memory. Others are more adaptive and can run the simulation within the available memory (as long as there is some minimal amount of memory available, i.e., that which is required to execute the corresponding sequential simulation) and are able to recover memory "on demand." Lin, in [13], made a comprehensive study on space usage of different memory management schemes. However, there has been little work on the performance issues of theses schemes in terms of execution time.

This chapter focuses upon the algorithms of the conservative methodology. We believe that the implementation of the conservative method is simpler than the implementation of the optimistic method. However, ensuring synchronization and avoiding deadlocks are one of the central problems in the conservative paradigm. Several solutions to these problems exist, each requiring a certain amount of overhead. A substantial amount of work has been done to evaluate the performance of these strategies [19]. Some of these studies assumed that a single process was mapped into a single processor while other studies did not take advantage of the knowledge that several processes were assigned to a single processor. In our opinion, the mapping of one process to a single processor is, in most cases, not particularly efficient. Indeed, the parallelism between individual processes can easily be too low and the communication cost too high.

Intuitively, a way to exploit the inherent parallelism of distributed (parallel) simulation is to assign several processes to a single processor. This is true for several reasons. First, there is no communication overhead within the cluster. Second, efficient distributed algorithms [10] that exploit the parallelism can be employed in each processor, and deadlock detection [4] and resolution are easier [10]. Finally, clustering also enables the efficient control of event scheduling. This approach also fits a fundamental problem of parallel simulation, that of simulating a large number of objects with low computational granularity. These simulation models include queueing network models of computer and communication systems, finite state machines and VLSI systems.

18.4   Conservative Synchronization Protocols

18.4.1   Variants of the Chandy-Misra Null Message Protocol

Chandy and Misra [6] employ *null messages* to avoid deadlock and exploit the parallelism of distributed simulation. When an event message (e,t) is sent on an output link, a null message bearing the same timestamp t as the event message is sent on all other links. This enables the recipient to simulate all events bearing a timestamp *less than or equal to* the minimum timestamp of all of the null messages. However, the arrival of a null message at an LP can cause the recipient to generate yet another null message, resulting in the potential generation of an overwhelming number of null messages. As a result, a number of attempts to optimize this basic scheme have appeared in the literature. For example, in [18] the authors refrain from sending null messages until such time as the LP becomes blocked. They refer to this approach as eager events, lazy null messages. They reported some success in using variations of Chandy-Misra approaches to speed up *logic simulation.*

De Vries [8] has suggested considering the overall network of processes as composed of sub-networks. By using detailed knowledge of the local network of which it forms a part, an LP can improve lookahead and diminish the number of null messages required. Cai and Turner [5] attempt to diminish null message transmission by knowledge of the simulation network. They suggest that such information can be obtained dynamically with the use of an additional type of null message. This *carrier null message* is propagated through the system and carries additional information (Inf) on lookahead and the route taken. Once a logical process LP_{join} had received a carrier null message with its ID as source and sink in Inf, it can be sure not to receive an event message via that path, unless LP_{join} itself had sent an event message along that path. So it can— without further waiting— after having received the first carrier null message, process the event message from LP_{source}, and thus increment the local simulation times of all successors on the route in Inf considerably. Even with the carrier null messages, the Chandy-Misra (CM) algorithms still generate many null messages. Wood and Turner [20] have shown that the Cai-Turner scheme can fail to reduce null message traffic in simulations with certain communication graphs (in particular, those with nested cycles), and have modified the carrier null scheme approach in order to extend its applicability to arbitrary graphs. Their results seem to indicate, however, that the benefits which can be derived from the scheme are very sensitive to the simulation parameters, and therefore they feel the need for further experimental and analytic work to estimate the impact of specific parameters.

In order to increase the efficiency of the Chandy-Misra basic scheme, Boukerche and Tropper [2] employed the following approach: In the event that a null message is queued at an LP and a subsequent message (either null or event) arrives on the same channel, we overwrite the (old) null message with the new message. A single buffer is associated with each input channel at an LP to store null messages, thereby saving space as well as the time required to perform the queueing and de-queueing operations associated with null messages.

The use of demand-driven null messages is described in [6]. In this algorithm, an LP can query a predecessor *(via request message)* in an attempt to obtain a new lower bound on the timestamps of messages which it can consume. One possible choice for when to make these queries is the time at which the LP becomes blocked. Another possibility is to wait until the processor becomes idle. However, no analysis of the performance of their algorithm is given. In the event that the predecessor cannot increase this lower bound, then it can query its own predecessors via a request message. This, however, can lead to deadlock [9]. Consequently, a deadlock detection and breaking algorithm must also be employed [4].

18.4.2   Deadlock Detection and Recovery

In order to avoid the overhead of null messages, Chandy and Misra [7] have proposed a protocol that allows the simulation to deadlock, and have provided a mechanism to detect it and recover from it. A necessary and sufficient condition for a deadlock is given in the following theorem:

Theorem 18.4.1: *A deadlock exists if and only if there is a cycle of empty links all of which have the same time of next events, and (logical) processes which all are blocked because of these links and only these links, i.e., there exists a knot.*

Chandy and Misra's algorithm operates in two phases: (*i*) *parallel* phase in which the simulation continues to run until it deadlocks; (*ii*) *interface* phase, which initiates a computation allowing some LPs to advance their local simulation time. Chandy and Misra [7] have proven that in every parallel phase at least one event will be processed, generating at least one event message, which will be propagated before the next deadlock. A central controller is assumed in their algorithm. Distributed detection algorithms could be used instead, see [4], [9], [15].

To break the deadlock, it is easy to prove that unblocking the LP with the smallest timestamp will break the deadlock. Interested readers may wish to consult [7] for further details.

18.4.3   Global Vs. Local Lookahead

Groselj and Tropper [10] pointed out that the inherent parallelism of a distributed simulation must be exploited to the maximum possible extent. They cluster several processes into the same processor in order to achieve better efficiency, and propose a scheme referred to as the Time of Next Event algorithm (TNE). Their algorithm computes the greatest lower bound on all input links for processes assigned to the same processor. The algorithm is based on a *shortest path algorithm* [12]. It helps to unblock blocked processes within a processor, thus increasing the parallelism. However, it does not prevent global deadlock. TNE does not have global information, unfortunately making *inter-processor deadlocks* possible. In [10], the authors proposed a distributed deadlock breaking algorithm (DLTNE) to deal with inter-processor deadlock. Experimental results [2] showed that if the the DLTNE algorithm was invoked without a preliminary check to see if the initiator process of DLTNE is in a knot, DLTNE would be invoked too often in vain. Boukerche and Tropper [4] proposed an efficient distributed algorithm to deal with the detection of local cycles and knots, since deadlock takes the form of a cycle or knot.

Overview of Time of Next Event (TNE) Algorithm

In this section, we describe the intuition behind the TNE algorithm and present pseudo code for TNE. We employ the example presented in Figure 18.5 to informally describe TNE. The readers should consult [10] fo a detailed description.

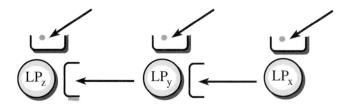

Figure 18.5 LPs connected by empty links.

Figure 18.5 shows three logical processes, LP_x, LP_y and LP_z, connected by directed empty links. Let LST_x, LST_y and LST_z be the local simulation times, and T_{min_x}, T_{min_y} and T_{min_z} be the smallest timestamp at LP_x, LP_y and LP_z respectively. $T_{smin_{i,j}}$ denotes the smallest time-stamp increment an event sent from LP_i to its neighbor LP_j. We define T_i to be the smallest timestamp which can be sent by LP_i and $T_{i,j}$ the TNE of the link (i,j).

Consider the empty link from LP_x to LP_y. LP_x cannot send an event message with a smaller timestamp than T_x, where $T_x = Max(LST_x, T_{min_x})$. On its way the message has to pass through LP_y as well.[3] A service time has to be added to each output sent by LP_x. Therefore LP_y cannot expect a message with a smaller timestamp than $T_{x,y}$, where $T_{x,y} = T_x + T_{smin_{x,y}}$. Thus, a new T_y is computed as: $T_y = Min(T_y, T_{x,y})$. LP_z cannot expect a message with a smaller timestamp than $T_{y,z}$ from LP_y for the same reason.

Based on these observations, a shortest path algorithm may be employed to compute the TNE. The TNE algorithm explores the directed graph of LPs connected by empty links. It finds estimates for the next timestamps on all empty links that belong to the same processor. If the estimate(s) of the future timestamps at all of an LP's empty links is higher than the LP's smallest timestamps, then the event with the smallest timestamp can be processed, i.e., the LP is unblocked. Provided that this algorithm will be executed independently and frequently enough in all of the processors, estimates on future timestamps can unblock several LPs.

We could improve the lower bound produced by the TNE by precomputing a portion of the computation for future events. The priority queue (PQ) might be implemented as a heap or even as a splay tree. The TNE algorithm is not computationally very expensive. It is easy to prove that TNE can be mapped to the shortest path problem [10], and therefore has the same complexity, i.e., $O(n \log (n))$, where n is the number of nodes in the graph. The TNE algorithm helps to unblock LPs and breaks all local deadlocks.

As a benchmark, the authors [2] used a FCFS (NxN) toroid queuing network model. It was chosen because of the large number of cycles which it has, making it a good stress test for the algorithms. They reported that TNE was 3-5 times faster when fewer than 10 processors were used. When more than 10 processors were used

---

[3]We assume that it is safe for LP_x to process the event with the smallest timestamp T_x.

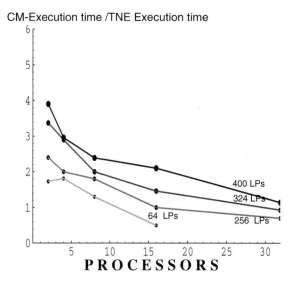

CM-Execution time /TNE Execution time

Figure 18.6 Runtime vs. number of processors.

for the same population of LPs, it was 2-3 times as fast (see Figure 18.6). Nevertheless, during the course of the experiments, the authors believed that improved performance was possible if the shortest path algorithm at the core of TNE could be executed over a cluster of *processors* instead of over only those LPs contained within a processor. It was felt that the algorithm would be able to produce better lookahead as a consequence of obtaining input from LP's resident on neighboring processors. Another motive was to inhibit the formation of inter-processor deadlocks, as these deadlocks do occur and the deadlock detection/breaking algorithms are expensive. These speculations led to the development of the Semi-Global TNE algorithm, or SGTNE [3].

SGTNE: Semi Global of the Time of the Next Event Algorithm

The Semi-Global TNE (SGTNE) algorithm is similar to the original TNE. While the original TNE is executed over a cluster of processes in each processor, Semi-Global TNE algorithm is executed over a cluster of processors. TNE algorithm helps to unblock local deadlocks, while SGTNE can break inter-processor deadlocks by accessing to data pertaining to processes assigned to different processors. Boukerche and Tropper [3] believed that this will help to reduce the number of inter-processor deadlocks and increase the parallelism by increasing the number of unblocked LPs in a single invocation of the algorithm, because information needed to unblock an LP could come from processors which are neighbors of the processor to which the LP belongs, to minimize the number of times the distributed knot detection is invoked.

SGTNE algorithm can be executed by a single processor (the *manager*) while the other processors are still running. Hence, a simulation can progress while SGTNE is running. SGTNE can unblock more processes within a single invocation of the algorithm.

Pseudo code of the SGTNE is contained in Figure 18.7 below.

Input : Graph G(V,E) and its subgraph $G_{cluster}(V_{cluster_p}, E_{cluster_p})$ where V are LPs
E are empty links, $V_{cluster_p}$ is the set of LPs assigned to all processors $\in Cluster_p$, and $E_{cluster_p}$ is the set of empty links belonging to each processor $q \in Cluster_p$; $cluster_p$ is the set of neighbor-processors to p,
$LST_u, T_{min_u}, T_{smin_{u,v}}, T_{w,u}$ such that $u \in V_{cluster_p}$, $v \in V$
and $w \in E(V - V_{cluster_p})$.
Output : time-of-next-event $T_{u,v}$ for all empty links (u,v), such that
$u \in V_{cluster_p}$ and $u \in V$.
Temporary data structure : priority queue PQ.

> **begin**
>> $PQ = $ empty ;
>> **for** all (u,v) s.t. $u \in V_{cluster_p}$ and $v \in (V - V_{cluster_p})$ **do** $T_v = 0$;
>>> **for** all $v \in V_{cluster_p}$ **do**
>>>> $Temp = Min_{w \in V - V_{cluster_p}}(T_{min_v}, T_{w,u})$; /* T_{min_v} is the smallest
>>>>   timestamp at LP_v*/
>>>> $T_v = Max(Temp, LST_v)$;
>>>> insert(v,PQ);
>>> **endfor**;
>>> **while** not empty (PQ) **do**
>>>> select $u \in$ PQ s.t. $T_u = Min_{v \in PQ}(T_v)$;
>>>> delete(u, PQ);
>>>> **for** all (u,v) s.t. $v \in V$ **do**
>>>>> $T_{u,v} = T_u + T_{smin_{u,v}}$;
>>>>> **if** $(T_v > Max(T_{u,v}, LST_v))$ **then** $T_v = Max(T_{u,v}, LST_v)$);
>>>> **endfor**;
>>> **endwhile**;
> **end.**

Figure 18.7 SGTNE algorithm over a cluster of processors $(Cluster_p)$.

Making use of SGTNE algorithm presented in this section (see Figure 18.7), we find estimates for the next timestamps on all empty links belonging to the same cluster of processors. If the estimates of the future timestamps at all of an LP's empty input links are higher than the LP's smallest timestamp, then the event with the smallest timestamp can be processed (i.e., the LP is unblocked). Provided that the SGTNE algorithm is executed frequently enough, estimates on future time-stamps can unblock several LPs and several processors, therefore speeding up the simulation.

Unlike TNE, SGTNE has more information pertaining to processes assigned to different processors. Consequently, SGTNE will help to unblock more LPs than TNE would, and although, SGTNE algorithm doesn't have complete information about the whole graph, it is easy to see that SGTNE alone can break inter-processor deadlocks. Indeed, a good choice of the neighbors of each processor and the execution of the SGTNE over several clusters of processors will soon or later break the inter-processor deadlocks, as we shall see later.

SGTNE, like the TNE, is basically a variation of the shortest path algorithm. The algorithm computes the greatest lower bound for the timestamp of each next event to arrive at each input link within a given cluster of processors. SGTNE has the same complexity as the original TNE—$O((N_{cluster_p} + E_{cluster_p})\ log(N_{cluster_p}))$, where $N_{cluster_p}$ is the number of processes and $E_{cluster_p}$ is the number of links within the cluster of processors ($cluster_p$).

Despite the fact that TNE and SGTNE are not computationally expensive, simulation efficiency must still be considered. Two basic questions must be addressed; *how and when do we schedule SGTNE/TNE suite of algorithms?*

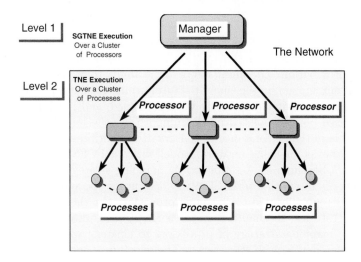

Figure 18.8 The two-level hierarchical scheduling scheme.

In an attempt to answer these questions, the two-level hierarchical strategy was investigated [2]. The basic motivation in using this scheme is to more aggressively exploit the inherent parallelism of the parallel simulation and to prevent the formation of deadlocks. In order to do this, at level 1, TNE is called locally when a processor becomes idle. In the event that it does not unblock the processor, SGTNE is called. Executing TNE will help to break local deadlocks while SGTNE algorithm will help to break more global deadlocks over a cluster of processors. This approach should speed up the simulation and increase the efficiency of the parallel simulation. Figure 18.8 illustrates a conceptual model for this two-level scheduling.

Once the *manager* receives a *request* message from processor p, it executes SGTNE algorithm. SGTNE is executed over a cluster of processors, i.e., neighbor-processors to p ($cluster_p$). If SGTNE algorithm helps to unblock some LPs, then the manager informs the processors p and q, where $q \in Cluster_p$, to resume the processing of their events. Pseudo-code of the two-level TNE scheduling is shown in Figure 18.9 below.

While (*Not Finished*) **Do**
    If (*Blocked*(Pr_i))   /* Processor Pr_i is blocked if all processes */
                                /* assigned to Pr_i are blocked */
        Execute TNE algorithm
        If (*Blocked*(Pr_i))   /* TNE did not help to unblock any process in Pr_i */
            Send a *request* message to the manager to execute SGTNE
        Else Select an LP to process its event
        EndIf
    Else Select an LP to process its event
    EndIf
EndWhile

Figure 18.9 Two-level TNE scheduling.

The efficiency of parallel simulation depends a great deal upon its ability to predict the next service time. This notion is captured in the idea of the lookahead of a service distribution. *Lookahead* refers to the ability to predict what will happen, or what will not happen, in the simulated future time based on the knowledge of the application, events that have already been processed, and pending events waiting to be processed [9]. As pointed in by Fujimoto [9], the lookahead ratio plays an important role in the performance of conservative algorithms.

An *N*x*N* torus queueing network model with an FCFS service discipline was employed as a benchmark. A simple static mapping strategy of LPs to processors was used [9], [2], in which a torus is subdivided into grids, and in which the LPs in the same grids are allocated to the same processor. For the proposed hierarchical scheduling strategies, the multicomputer is partitioned into clusters (spheres). A simple static mapping strategy of processors to clusters was used, in which each sphere is centered at a given processor p. The selection of each sphere is determined by the graphical covering radius r. Hence, a sphere centered by a given p is defined as:

$$Sphere_p = \{q, |Dist(p,q) = r\} \ and \ Cluster_p = Sphere_p \cup \{p\};$$

where $Dist(p,q) = min_{ij}(\delta_{ij})$, such that $LP_i \in p$ and $LP_j \in q$), δ_{ij} is the (shortest) number of hops between LP_i and LP_j.

It is easy to see that with this scheme of partitioning/mapping, the SGTNE can unblock all inter-processor deadlocks within a finite time, (see [4]).

The speedup curves of the parallel simulation algorithms using TNE and SGTNE are shown in Figure 18.10. The results obtained clearly show the superiority of the SGTNE algorithm for both population levels. We observe that the factor of improvement in speedup increases as the number of processors increases. We observe that the number of processes assigned to a single processor and the lookahead plays an important role in determining parallel simulation performance. The performance of the parallel simulation is very good. An intuitive explanation for this is that we don't need to access data pertaining to processors assigned to different processors to break local deadlock. Indeed, in a one-level scheduling strategy, SGTNE will unblock some LPs that TNE would unblock, in any case, if the (local) TNE would have been executed within the confine processor. One should also not forget that SGTNE is more expensive than TNE. Recall that TNE is executed over a cluster of processes while SGTNE is executed over a cluster of processors.

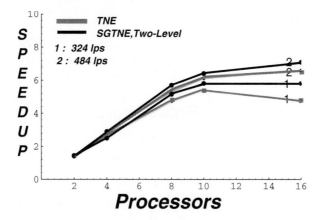

Figure 18.10 Speedup vs. number of processors.

Figure 18.11 show the success ratio (SR) of the SGTNE algorithm relative to the TNE algorithm. SGTNE success ratio is defined as the average of the number of times SGTNE is called successfully (SR_i) divided by the number of times SGTNE is called on each cluster of processors. The SGTNE is called successfully if it helps to unblock at least one LP within the cluster.

We see in Figure 18.11 that the success ratio decreases with an increase in the number of processors for both population levels and for all distributions. The figure indicates very clearly that the Semi-Global TNE algorithm has a higher success ratio than TNE. Indeed, by increasing the number of processors, we decrease the number of LPs in each processor, thereby decreasing the information available to the TNE algorithm. In addition to this, increasing the number of processors increases the number of executions of the deadlock detection and breaking algorithms [2] under TNE. SGTNE, on the other hand, has the advantage of access to data resident on other processors. Recall that in a two-level scheduling, a TNE is executed within each processor to break all local deadlocks, while SGTNE is executed to break the inter-processor deadlocks, and it helps TNE to break more LPs. As TNE makes use of information located only within the confines of one processor, making use of the SGTNE increases the ability of TNE to unblock an LP, as the information required to unblock the LP might be located in another processor.

18.4.4   Conservative Time Windows

All of the algorithms which we have described provide information about the future arrival of messages to an LP by making use of information obtained from neighboring

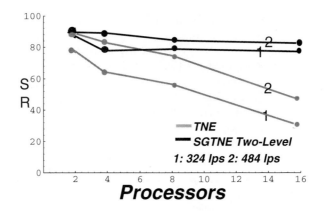

Figure 18.11 Success ratio vs. number of processors.

LPs. They rely either on the propagation of successive lower bounds between actual LPs, or make use of the information obtained from a snapshot of the state of all LPs within a processor. These techniques are very well suited for LPs that operate in an asynchronous way.

Another approach to conservative parallel simulation has been introduced by Ayani et. al. [1] using Conservative Time Windows (CTW). In this approach, a time window (W_i) is assigned to each LP. Events within the time windows are independents. Hence they are safe and can be processed concurrently. A conservative time window LP synchronously operates in two phases:

1. *Window Identification*: For every LP_i, a chronological set of events W_i is identified such that for every event $e \in W_i$, e is causally independent of any $e' \in W_j, j \neq i$.

2. *Event Processing*: Every LP_i processes events $e \in W_i$ sequentially in chronological order.

Both phases are accomplished by a barrier synchronization. The width of the windows is calculated in each iteration of the CTW-algorithm and may be different for different LPs. In contrast to other window-based schemes reported in the literature [14], the CTW-algorithm produces local bounds for the time windows. Their experiments indicate that this feature improves the performance of the CTW-algorithm. On the other hand, they revealed several limitations of the CTW-algorithm. First, it requires that the size of the application be very large, and not too complex for the hardware to process efficiently. Second, the CTW-algorithm performs poorly for heterogeneous applications [1].

18.5   Conclusion

The advent of massively parallel computers and multi-computer networks over the past few years has had a major impact in the simulation arena. Networks of workstations are becoming a commodity, and networking performance price and availability are improving dramatically, making all kinds of new applications of parallel simulations a possibility.

In this chapter, we are interested in parallel simulation algorithms for event-driven simulations and in mapping them onto multi-computer network. These algorithms help to maintain the correct order of (simulation) events through the execution of the model by means of constraints on simulation time advance. Several variants of Chandy-Misra algorithms were described, as well as a new class of conservative algorithms known as SGTNE/TNE. TNE is executed independently in each processor and helps to unblock all local deadlocks, while the SGTNE algorithm is executed over a cluster of processors, and helps to prevent the deadlock across processors. As shown in this chapter, SGTNE with a two-level scheduling provides a better performance compared to both approaches of the TNE algorithm and the Chandy & Misra algorithm. We have described a new emerging type of protocol that constrains all concurrent simulation activity to be within some window of global synchronization time, i.e, conservative time window protocols.

Another area for future research is to investigate the modification of parallel simulation protocols and to formalize a generic simulation model for which different specific simulators could easily be derived. Examples are verification of safety properties in a concurrent model of time, and verification of real-time software programs where it is convenient to utilize state variables that can be accessed by distinct logical processes. Last but not least, it is our belief that synchronization will always be a challenging and an interesting area of study.

18.6   Bibliography

[1] R. Ayani. Parallel Simulation Using Conservative Time Windows. *Proc. of the 1992 Winter Simulation Conference*, pages 709–717, 1992.

[2] A. Boukerche and C. Tropper. Parallel Simulation on the Hypercube Multi-processor. *Distributed Computing*, Springer Verglag, 1995.

[3] A. Boukerche and C. Tropper. SGTNE: Semi-Global Time of Next Event Algorithm. *Parallel Distributed Simulation (PADS'95)*, pages 68–77, 1995.

[4] A. Boukerche and C. Tropper. A Distributed Graph Algorithm for the Detection of Local Cycles and Knots. *IEEE Trans. on Parallel and Distributed Systems*, Vol. 9, pages 748–757, 1998.

[5] W. Cai and S. J. Turner. An Algorithm for Distributed Discrete Event Simulation- The *Carrier Null Message* Approach. *Proc. of the SCS Multiconf. on Distributed Simulation*, Vol. 22, January 1990.

[6] K. M. Chandy and J. Misra. Distributed Simulation: A Case Study in Design and Verification of Distributed Programs. *IEEE Trans. on Software Engineering*, SE-5, pages 440–452, 1979.

[7] K. M. Chandy and J. Misra. Asynchronous Distributed Simulation via Sequence of Parallel Computations. *CACM*, Vol. 24(3), pages 198–206, 1981.

[8] R. C. De Vries. Reducing Null Messages in Misra's Distributed Discrete Event Simulation Method. *IEEE Trans. on Soft. Eng.*, Vol 16, January 1990.

[9] R. M. Fujimoto. Parallel Discrete Event Simulation. *Communications of the ACM*, Vol 33, pages 30–53, October 1990.

[10] B. Groselj and C. Tropper. The Distributed Simulation of Clustered Processes. *Distributed Computing*, Vol. 4, pages 111–121, 1991.

[11] D. Jefferson. Virtual Time. *ACM Trans. Prog. Lang. Syst.* vol. 77(3), July 1985.

[12] D. B. Johnson. Efficient Algorithms for Shortest Paths in Sparse Networks. *Journal of the ACM*, Vol. 24(1), pages 1–13, January 1977.

[13] Y. B. Lin. Memory Management Algorithms for Optimistic Parallel Simulation. In *Proceedings of the 1992 SCS Western Simulation Multiconf. in Parallel and Distributed Simulation*, SCS Simulation Series, Vol. 24(3), pages 43–52, 1992.

[14] B. D. Lubachevsky. Efficient Distributed Event-Driven Simulations of Multiple Loop Networks. *CACM*, Vol. 32, pages 111–123, January 1989.

[15] J. Misra. Distributed Discrete-Event Simulation. *ACM Computing Surveys*, Vol. 18(1) pages 39–65, 1986.

[16] P. Reiher, R. Fujimoto, S. Bellenot, and D. J. Jefferson. Cancellation Strategies in Optimistic Execution Systems. *Proc. of the 1990 SCS Multiconference on Distributed Simulation*, 1990.

[17] H. A. Sowizral and D. Jefferson. *Synchrony Versus Asynchrony for Concurrent Simulation*. Rand Corporation, 1982.

[18] W. K. Su and Seitz, C. L. Variants of the Chandy-Misra-Bryant Distributed Discrete Event Simulation Algorithm. *Proc. of the SCS Multiconference on Distributed Simulation*, Vol. 21(2), March 1989.

[19] D. B. Wagner, E. D. Lazowska, and B. Bershad. Techniques for Efficient Shared Memory Parallel Simulation. *Proc. of the 1989 SCS Multiconf. on Distributed Simulation*, pages 29–37, 1989.

[20] K. Wood and S. J. Turner, A Generalized Simulation- The Carrier Null Message Approach, *Proc. of the SCS Multiconf. on Distributed Simulation*, Vol. 22(1), January 1994.

Chapter 19

Hardware System Simulation

D. K. Sharman[†] and D. M. W. Powers[‡]

[†]Motorola Australian Software Centre
Adelaide, South Australia

[‡]Department of Computer Science,
Flinders University of South Australia
Adelaide, South Australia

Email: *dsharman@asc.corp.mot.com, powers@ist.flinders.edu.au*

19.1   Introduction

Electronic devices are becoming increasingly larger, more integrated, powerful and difficult to design, so that simulation must play an ever-increasing and important role. With these increasingly large systems, simulation times are actually getting relatively longer with regard to the target systems being simulated [3]. The aim of this project was to ascertain the benefits of using a local area network as host for a parallelized simulator of coarser grain than has been implemented previously. The artifacts simulated in this project are parallel machines themselves. The choice of simulating parallel hardware comes from three factors, with the first two being able to effect the simulator's load. These factors are:

1. Each Processing Element (PE) can be varied in size/complexity,

2. The total number of PEs can be manipulated,

3. This is a real-world problem faced by engineers designing parallel hardware.

The design was primarily dictated by efficiency considerations. There are several ways in which network traffic can be minimized. The first is to use broadcast rather than point-to-point communication as much as possible, and we saved further on overheads by designing our protocol using the User Datagram Protocol (UDP) directly.

19.2   NEPSi

The Network Enabled Parallel Simulator (NEPSi) is the test bed for this project. It consists of a VHDL (Very High Speed Hardware Integrated Circuits Hardware Description Language) simulator augmented with communication primitives so that it can be distributed across a network of workstations.

19.2.1   ASIMUT

NEPSi is based on ASIMUT, a VHDL simulator which is part of the ALLIANCE CAD package[2]. The alliance CAD package is primarily intended as a teaching tool and as such supports only a subset of VHDL. However, it has been used in serious applications by the team at MASI and several large projects have been reported using the package. Most industry standard packages are priced in the tens of thousands of dollars plus annual licenses and high end workstations are required to do anything of a serious nature on them. ASIMUT, on the other hand, is happy to work with virtual memory, will run on a low end SPARC (an ELC at that) and comes in at a cost we can afford: nothing.

Concurrent Distributed Processing

NEPSi is a concurrent distributed simulator. By this we mean that the processes that comprise the simulator are not only spread across distributed machines, but that multiple copies of the simulator may also be run on each machine. Thus we not only have concurrency provided by the distribution process, but we also have concurrency provided through time sharing on each machine. This allows for flexibility in matching computation time and communication latency.

19.2.2   NEPSi as a Client Server Architecture

Data Distribution

UDP provides for broadcast transmission of a packet onto a subnet. Two network configurations were examined. The first setup is where packets would be broadcast

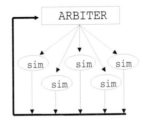

Figure 19.1 Communication flow in NEPSi.

from the arbiter and all return packets would be sent back to the arbiter for re-assembly and broadcast as shown in Figure 19.1. The alternative setup was for each simulator to broadcast its results and reassemble the resultant global broadcasts once all simulators had transmitted their data.

Early experimental results showed that the first setup was more appropriate. It reduced the cost of, or facilitated, a number of operations better than the alternative. Specifically, the arbiter needs to be the hub for the following reasons:

1. The arbiter needs to synchronize the start up of the client simulators. For process migration to be implemented, a centralized register of processes/machines is required.

2. The arbiter needs to compile the separate signals into one message to be broadcast. If all clients assemble their own packets, then network traffic will increase dramatically. If a central arbiter with 5 sub-nets is used then it needs to send only 5 broadcast messages (one to each sub-net); if a more distributed system is used, then each node will have to transmit 5 packets (one to each sub-net). Thus if we have 10 nodes in the network, we would have the following number of packets:

   - central arbiter 5 broadcast messages + 1 from each node =15
   - distributed control 5 messages from each node = 50

   Of course, if a single sub-net is used, then costs are about equal (10 pkts without arbiter, 11 pkts with an arbiter). Note, too, that a single UDP packet is of limited size, so multiple packets will be required once a large number of signals need to be transmitted over the network. Since the number of machines on each subnet is limited and it is necessary to use more than one subnet, we have adopted the centralized arbiter model.

3. Once large simulations are run, we need to detect bus conflicts. There are two ways in which this can be achieved. The arbiter can do the signal detection or every node can do its own conflict detection through merging of bussed signals from other nodes. The second method generates more redundant computation, which can be done in parallel with other computation in the central arbiter method.

For these reasons, the arbiter is the central point for all communication. This allows for broadcast messages to be used rather than point to point as is used in other message-passing schemes such as Parallel Virtual machine(PVM)[5], [6]. This increases parallelism dramatically, which is of utmost importance, although it is predicated on the total number of signals (G) being of the same order as the number of signals per node (L), the network overheads(H) & the number of sub-nets(S). The costs are:

central arbiter: $S*(H+G)+N*(H+L)$

distributed control: S*N*(H+L)

19.2.3   Overview of the NEPSi Network

NEPSi is comprised of many parts, each one relying on the others, and in total all working together to perform the simulation. The next sections deal with the implementation of each part of the network. We begin by looking at the simulation engine, NEPSi ASIMUT, then we look at the arbiter, the daemons, and finally the VHDL parser used to split the description into leaf cells.

NEPSi Client - ASIMUT

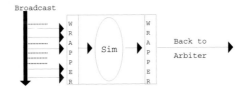

Figure 19.2 NEPSi client is an augmented ASIMUT simulator.

As can be seen in Figure 19.2 a simple function logically wraps around the ASIMUT simulator. This wrapper functionally is actually inside ASIMUT, as the simulator, as it stood, had no interactive input or Programming Language Interface(PLI). The wrapper function grabs its assigned signals from the broadcast packet and sends its resultant signals back to the controller.

The Arbiter

The arbiter is the heart of the NEPSi infrastructure; it is responsible for arbitrating all communication between the simulators and daemons. Figure 19.3 displays all the communication paths within the NEPSi network. As can be seen, outbound communication from the arbiter takes two forms: arbiter to daemon and arbiter to simulator. The arbiter is responsible for initiating the communications network. This is accomplished by issuing a ping to the daemons, arc one. On receiving the ping command the daemons simply respond with their daemon ID-number, arc two. The arbiter uses this information to establish which daemons are available and uses the response times as a rough indicator of the load on the replying machines. Given that we have n modules to be simulated, the arbiter will select the top n machines (in response time) as the hosts for the simulators. If there are more modules to be simulated than there are available machines, the arbiter will increase the number of simulators per machine to accommodate the required amount. The required number of simulators is then sent to the daemon in arc three. Arcs three and four represent the daemon interacting with the OS to invoke the first simulator. The

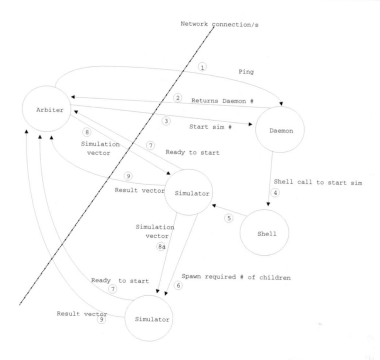

Figure 19.3 Communication flow diagram for NEPSi network.

first simulator started on each machine is then responsible for forking the desired number of children, shown here as arc six. The reasons for starting additional simulators on each machine using the simulator itself are twofold:

- We get a performance gain by the simulator cloning itself instead of the children having to parse and set up all the data structures: We get a bonus from the memory manager.

- All the communication is sent to one port on all the machines, and only one process can be bound to a port, so the parent has to open pipes to its children before it forks.

The fork is represented by arc 6 in Figure 19.3. Once all the internal data structures are set up and any required children have been created, each simulation process then informs the arbiter that it is ready to begin simulation, arc 7. The arbiter then transmits the simulation vector to the parent simulators on each machine, arc 8, and the parent gives this to the child, arc 8a. All simulators then send their result back to the arbiter, arc 9. The arbiter then assembles the signals for retransmission and sends them out again on arc 8. This process continues until the last test vector has been simulated. Then the arbiter sends a special test vector that informs all

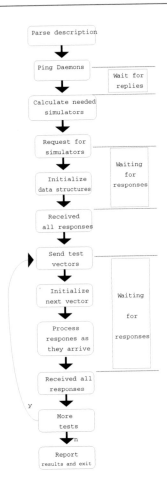

Figure 19.4 Operations performed in a typical simulation.

the simulators that they should exit. Daemons remain alive, sleeping, waiting to start up the simulators again.

These test vectors are represented compactly so that each byte reflects 4 signals. This allows us to have a total of approximately 4500 signals in a packet, depending upon the number of PEs in the design and the number of inter-PE signals. The simulation cycle has been designed in such a way that communication and calculation could be interleaved as much as possible. As can be seen in Figure 19.4, there is a delay slot after each message is passed to the simulators where the arbiter is waiting for a response. As much of the calculations needed to be performed has been rolled into these slots. Figure 19.4 illustrates the operations carried out during

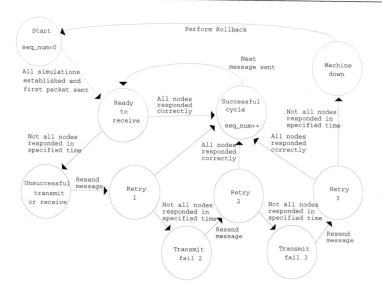

Figure 19.5 State transition diagram for arbiter communication model.

the execution of a simulation session. A lot of the initialization of the data has been folded into the slots where the arbiter is idle waiting for the responses from the simulators. Most of the test vector is constructed while waiting for the results of the present cycle. This reduces the amount of processing time the arbiter needs while the simulators are idle and minimizes the sequential bottleneck of the simulation algorithm.

NEPSi Daemons

The NEPSi daemon is simply a small program that acts as a remote shell. It has a specific port to which it listens and to which requests are made.

19.2.4   Communication Model

Communication in NEPSi is based directly on UDP, an unreliable communication medium in which packets are not guaranteed to arrive and if they do, they may arrive out of order. This sounds worse than it actually is. Packet loss is not as bad as one might expect, and this is a strength as much as a weakness of UDP. We have defined a communications model for NEPSi which exploits this.

Answers as Acknowledgment

As UDP is an unacknowledged protocol, the sender receives no notification of whether the packet arrived at its destination or not. This increases the speed obtainable from UDP as packets can be sent without having to wait for acknowledgment packets that would double the network overheads. So to make sure that our packets have arrived, we use the result as an acknowledgment. To facilitate this, it is necessary to number all packets with a sequence number. We send only one packet to each subnet in the system. Therefore there will be varying number of replys to each packet, as different subnets have different numbers of computers, and each computer can have more than one simulation process on it. Figure 19.5 shows the state transition diagram for the arbiter's communication scheme. As can be seen, the arbiter simply transmits its data and waits for a reply. If all the nodes reply correctly with the same sequence number, then it proceeds to simulate another vector. All packets received with the wrong sequence number are ignored. If the time limit is reached and not all simulators have replied correctly, then we enter the missed transmission state. A packet could have been lost on the simulator side, or we may have lost a packet on the arbiter side. When this occurs, we simply resend the last message. If the simulator receives this second transmission, it has either seen it before and simulated it, or it didn't receive it in the first place. If it has seen it before, it simply retransmits its last result with the previous sequence number. If it hasn't seen it before, then it simulates it and sends the response. This is why the arbiter can receive packets with the wrong sequence number. The reason why we have so many retries is that we need to know if a machine has gone down (or is very busy). If we retransmit four times unsuccessfully, then we assume that a machine has gone down. We then enter damage control mode where we kill all the simulators and do a rollback start. For brevity and clarity, Figure 19.5 has a large number of states involved in the rollback process represented as one transition; similarly, the startup process has been omitted for clarity. The state transitions for the simulators side of the communications scheme is very simple. It waits forever until it gets a message and replies to all given messages, with the last result it generated.

Checkpointing & Rollbacks

To make the system more secure with regard to long execution times, it has been necessary to implement a means by which checkpointing can be implemented. At a predetermined time interval, measured in simulation cycles simulated, the arbiter transmits a special packet that instructs the simulators to save their internal states to a file. Each simulator then saves its state to a file with a unique name based on its node number. These files are stored in a centralized account which relies upon the network file system (NFS) to save the files on the one machine. If a rollback is deemed necessary, the arbiter then performs the following tasks:

1. instructs all simulators to terminate;

2. ensures that all simulators have terminated;

3. pings the daemons;

4. recalculates what simulators are required on which machines;

5. asks the daemons to do a roll_start;

6. begins processing again from rollback point.

The rollback point is the simulation test vector immediately following the vector which preceded the checkpoint. The simulators are not guaranteed to be simulating the same node number after a restart, but this has no effect on simulators as all the checkpoint files are stored in a central point from which they all have NFS access. This scheme works well with two notable exceptions:

- If the machine with the host account in which the checkpoints are stored goes down, then the simulation cannot continue.

- All machines in the NEPSi network must reside within a single NFS domain.

19.2.5   VHDL Models Used

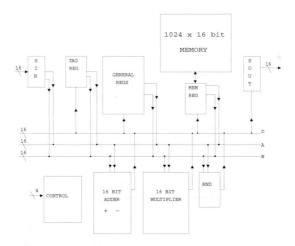

Figure 19.6 TNP processor.

The hardware we chose to simulate was the Toroidal Neural Processor(TNP) [4] which was designed to be used in neural network experiments, and it is theoretically infinitely scaleable. Large extensive test files were available for the TNP and experienced users (e.g., the author) of the TNP were available.

TNP Processor

Each of the modules in Figure 19.6 is written as a behavioural description. Interconnections between these modules is described in the top level structural description. The modules range in size from a single register to a 1024 sixteen bit memory array.

The varying size of these modules allows us to examine at what point the communication versus computation tradeoff favors switching to a parallel implementation.

19.2.6   Tests for TNP

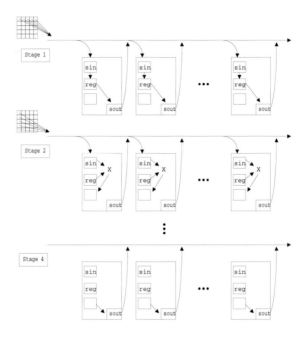

Figure 19.7 Stages of matrics multiplication.

As a small example of the kind of task the TNP was designed for, a vector dot product was calculated for the majority of our tests. Figure 19.7 outlines some of the stages involved in the multiplication. A row of the first matrix is first loaded into the array (stage 1 of diagram), then a column of the second matrix is passed through the array with a partial sum building up in each element as the column is passed through (stage 2). Once this is completed, all the products are passed out with the last element summing the products as they pass and then this is passed out (stage 4). This process is then be repeated for all the remaining rows and columns, but to aid test turn around times we do only the first row and column.

TNP Assembly Tests

Test programs were written for TNP arrays varying from 1 to 64 nodes. These programs were then used as the simulation vectors while the experimental variables were manipulated, which are as follows

- Number of machines used

- Number of processes on each machine

- Number of PEs per simulator

- Distance between simulators (all simulations on campus, or some at a remote campus)

These four variables and the combinations thereof provided for a large array of experiments.

19.2.7   Initial Tests

The following results were obtained from running a simple test program/pattern file through a simulated TNP array. The array consisted of 10 PEs in a linear array. The output from each PE is fed into the input of the next. Input to the array is from within the pattern file and the output is obtained from the 10th PE. The NEPSi network consisted of 10 machines on 4 subnets. Each machine was minimally loaded (0.0-0.05) with nova and baldrick being the exception. These had a load of 1 to 1.1. The graph in Figure 19.8 details the simulation times for a sequential (standard ASIMUT) simulation of the PE array and the time taken for NEPSi to do the same simulation as averaged over 10 runs. As can be seen, simulation times varied extensively with boomer being the fastest and karl being the slowest. NEPSi averaged at least half the execution times of most machines, and was up to 5 times faster than the slowest machine. To compensate for load

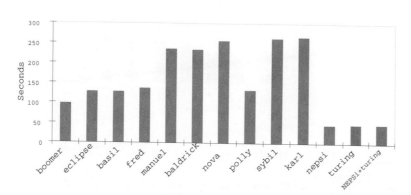

Figure 19.8 All machines compared to NEPSi.

differences, a further 10 iterations were run on each machine with NEPSi running concurrently. This increased the load on each machine, but it was intended to be a crude way of maintaining some load consistency between the test runs performed on NEPSi and the sequential version. As can be seen in Figure 19.9, the concurrent runs were slowed down with a consistent amount. From this we can assume that the sequential times vary directly with the load on each machine and the amount of physical resources available to them.

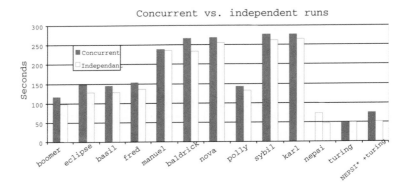

Figure 19.9 Concurrent runs compared to independent runs.

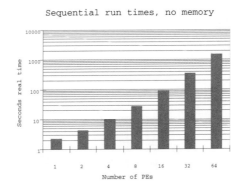

Figure 19.10 Average cycle times on Turing.

Since the NEPSi version is done in lock step, its simulation time will directly depend on the speed of the slowest machine in the network. In both Figures 19.8 and 19.9 we see that the best machine (NEPSi) is around 5 times faster than the slowest machine. The machines are all either Sparcs or SuperSparcs, but already the factor of two difference in power has meant that the faster machines are underutilized. The asterisked machines are presented for comparison and were not part of the original experiment. Karl was then supplanted by turing, an UltraSparc, after the initial experiments.

19.2.8   Varying Numbers of PEs and Simulators

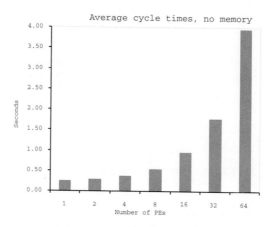

Figure 19.11 Average simulation times on Turing.

Once the initial tests had been conducted and had proved the applicability of our concept, we then moved on to slightly more complex testing. The following figures show the results for sequential runs on Turing using the simulation vector for a ring adder test as we varied the number of PEs simulated on the machine. Figure 19.10 shows the average simulation times for turing and Figure 19.11 shows its average cycle time. It should be noted that the simulation times are given on a

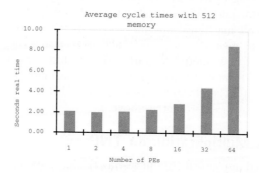

Figure 19.12 Cycle times on Turing with 512 byte memory.

logarithmic scale. The simulations were conducted using a reduced version of the TNP PE, which had only one memory location instead of 512 or 1024. Using the trivial memory aided in implementation and development as simulator start times

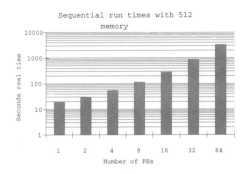

Figure 19.13 Run times on Turing with 512 byte memory.

were significantly reduced, as can be seen in Figure 19.14. The following Figures 19.12 and 19.13 display the simulation and cycle times for a TNP array that uses 512 bytes of memory in each PE. At first one would assume that simulating memory would be rather fast, as we recall the simulation is an event based simulator and as such must recalculate the internal state of all Binary Decision Diagrams (BDD) that have an input change state. But as all the memory is clocked, every memory location must be recomputed. Bryant [1] points out that simulating memories with BDDs is not efficient due to the high fanout that occurs as the BDD tree grows. Furthermore, we could see from the memory usage of the simulator itself that the BDD representation of the memory is inefficient. The memory usage of the simulator became extreme when simulating 64 PEs with a 1024 byte memory, with the executable growing to over 218 meg at runtime, with the result that at some point the process started to thrash and entered into a continuous I/O wait state. This happened on all machines, but just when they started thrashing depended on how much actual memory and how much swap space they had. Given that these processes also fork numerous children, the machines are liable to crash under these conditions and running tests of this size was considered antisocial in a shared resource environment. Therefore, the experiments with half the specified memory were undertaken instead, as presented above.

19.2.9   Matrix Multiplication on TNP

Once we had finished implementing and testing the basic simulator, we proceeded to extend it. The rollback/checkpoint system was implemented, packet compression, auto-daemon selection and top level preparsing/decomposition were added and the test file parser was developed. All these things either helped make the simulator easier to use or made it more stable. These additions added only a small amount to the startup times for the ring adder; it added around 4 seconds, which was largely due to the waits for the daemon startup/selection. With all these facilities in place we could then perform the tertiary tests. The results for these tests are

Runtimes, memories & number of PEs

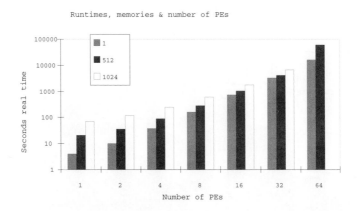

Figure 19.14 Comparison of memory sizes and number of PEs.

presented in Figures 19.15 and 19.16. Again we are using a logarithmic scale and the machines displayed are meant to represent the spectrum of the machines used in the NEPSi network. It should be noted that we used only 16 machines at a maximum, therefore the 32 and 64 PE simulations required that each PE simulate 2 and 4 PEs, respectively.

As can be seen, NEPSi is actually slower than turing for the simulations where there are less than 8 PEs being simulated. The slowest machines like manuel are only half the speed of NEPSi for a single PE simulation. This is due to the start-up time for NEPSi, which is comparatively larger for smaller simulations. As can be seen in Figure 19.15, this deficit is quickly made up in the larger simulations. Figure 19.16 details the cycle times for the Matrix multiplication as given in Figure 19.15. This is a very interesting graph and shows distinctly where the break-even points are for NEPSi. As can be seen, the cycle time for NEPSi is higher than for turing when the TNP arrays consist of less than 7 PEs. Comparing NEPSi directly to turing is not a good metric. NEPSi is constrained by the slowest machine in the network. In the case above, it is an ELC. What should become apparent from the graph is that we can obtain the performance of nearly twice that of an ULTRA Sparc from servers that are now very well dated. After we have an array larger than 7 Pes, NEPSi becomes viable. What is also of interest is the slopes of the lines. The turing line is nearly completely straight; this proves simulation speed is directly related to the simulation size. However, if we observe the line for boomer, we can see that the line increases in slope as we increase the number of PEs from 16 to 32. This shows the point where we also start to run out of compute resources (physical memory). Therefore, the time a simulation will take is directly related to the number of PEs being simulated and the amount of free resources available for this computation. Interestingly, the line for NEPSi is relatively flat until we reach the 8 PE mark. This may be due to three factors: Firstly, the arbiter selects the

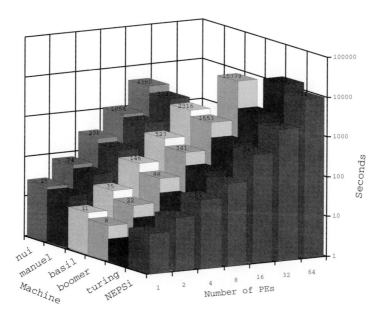

Simulation times while varying PE numbers

Figure 19.15 NEPSi and sequential version performing TNP matrix multiplication.

fastest machines first (network response plus some parsing in the daemon); as we go past eight machines, we start to use the slower machines and thus we increase the time required to simulate some of the PEs. Examining Figure 19.9 reveals that there are basically two levels of machine performance available in the Flinders computer science network. There are eight machines of relatively fast performance (this includes turing and boomer, which are faster again), then there is the second tier to which a lot of the student servers belong and some ELCs. These machine are nearly half the speed of the first tier machines. Once we go over the 8 machine mark we start using the slower machines. This is clearly visible in Figure 19.16; it is the first kink in the graph on the NEPSi line. Secondly, as we progress beyond 16 PEs we need to start doubling the number of PEs being simulated on a machine. Again we are doubling the simulation load on the machines so that the graph continues on the same slope as it did from the 8 PE mark. This increase in slope is not due to network overheads but is due to a resource shortage. If more machines were available then the graph may flatten out again. Thirdly, there is an effect upon the machine called manuel, which is the NFS server for the directory in which the executables and the test files are kept. This is the directory to which all the checkpoint files are written. Therefore, when we are simulating large numbers of PEs we get some NFS errors as the 64 simulators try to read and write to the same directory/file.

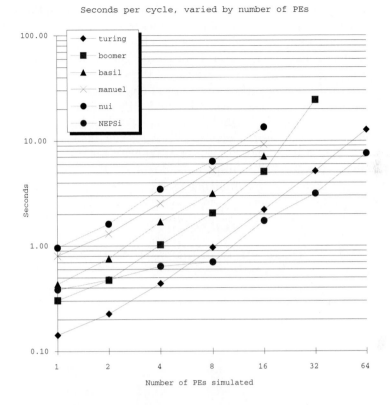

Figure 19.16 Machine comparrison with varying number of PEs.

Furthermore, as the arbiter is on a fairly crowded subnet, when all the responses start coming back from the simulators we may be flooding the network, although there appears not to be any significant increase in network collisions. This can be observed with the number of retries that are needed for a simulation; these increase with the number of PEs being simulated. However, many factors come into play here, including network load, the load on the arbiter, the machine it is running on and NFS server contention, etc. It is very hard to determine the exact cause of network behaviour as the experiments are conducted on a working academic network which is subject to all the trials and tribulations that students can put it through.

19.2.10 Variable Machines, Processes and PEs

To ascertain what effect simulation load has on throughput, a further test was carried out: We varied the number of PEs in a simulator over a specified range of array lengths. Then we conducted the same set of tests, but we varied the number of simulators on each machine rather than the number of PEs. Figure 19.17 shows the effect of having more than one simulator on a machine (the array numbers were kept small so as to allow homogeneous servers to be used). The single PE single simulator had the best average cycle time. As can be seen, the single process usually returns the fastest average cycle times. However, you will notice that the average for the 2 simulators per machine is actually faster for the 8 PE simulation than for the one simulator version. This may be caused by a quicker start time or just variation in the network traffic. As can be seen, 4 simulators per machine reduce the performance by about half. This directly shows the effect of the increase in average cycle times for four simulators per machine, as displayed in Figure 19.16. This does not support the increase in average cycle time from one to two processes that is also evident in the same figure. Most likely, network variation is the cause; this point is taken up in Section 19.2.14. To find the relationship between communication and computation,

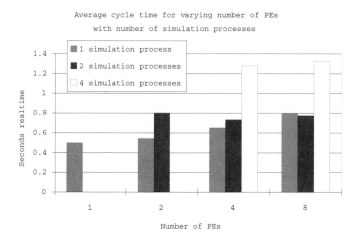

Figure 19.17 Varying number of PEs and processes.

a further experiment was undertaken where we measured the CPU time taken for a simulator to perform a simulation, and we compared this with the amount of CPU time used by the concurrent version. We used the machines that were as evenly matched as possible; thus, we had only eight machines available. As can be seen in Figure 19.18, we have been fairly successful in limiting the communication time compared to calculation. The distance between the NEPSi line and the bar is the communication time and system overhead for NEPSi, and the distance between the other line and the bar is the system overhead for the sequential version. A speedup factor of about 6 is evident again, and furthermore, we can see that the communications overhead is about a third of the time. The average node CPU usage is also given, and this indicates how much processing has been interleaved by the distribution process.

19.2.11   Rollback

The rollback mechanism was implemented through each simulator producing a save file at a given point in the simulation. The saving of a checkpoint takes approximately half a second, apparently independent of the number of processes involved (the actual time is most likely hidden in NFS delays and disk buffers). The rollback mechanism can take anywhere between 6 and 15 seconds. The arbiter must make

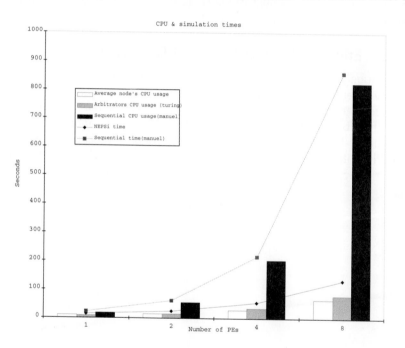

Figure 19.18 CPU usage and simulation time versus number of PEs.

sure that all the simulators are dead before it can ask the daemon to invoke a new set of simulations. When this occurs, primitive process migration takes place and the arbiter will select the best machines that it requires for the simulation. As can be imagined, the rollback process is quite costly and thus we need to make sure that if we are going to do one, we lose the least amount of time.

19.2.12   Multi Campus Simulation

The use of servers at Adelaide University served an interesting purpose. Adelaide University is connected to Flinders University via a 31 megabit link. The Flinders computer science network is connected to this backbone via 2 other network hops. Using the network utility ping reveals that we typically have a 5-8 millisecond round trip. The network here at Flinders is an unruly beast and it does get choked (especially when the AI class is running a robot soccer simulation); on average, the network delay is anywhere between 1 and 4 ms. The experiments run using the Adelaide machine showed no statistically significant slowdown in the performance of NEPSi. Some large delays occurred, but these usually originate here at Flinders so the simulation would have been effected whether the simulation was run here or not. One disadvantage of using machines at Adelaide is that if we are to implement checkpoints and thus migration, we need to keep a consistent copy of all the checkpoints at both locations without NFS.

19.2.13   Effect of Migration / Load Balancing

The migration code was added to NEPSi in an attempt to counteract the effects of increased network traffic that is sustained for medium lengths of time (such as student machines being used for a class). When a machine reaches a certain level of activity, the arbiter may decide to migrate the simulation to another machine which is not as busy. This is implemented through the rollback-checkpointing mechanism. The arbiter will ask a parent process on a machine to fork another child. This is an extremely quick process. The simulation node to be migrated performs its

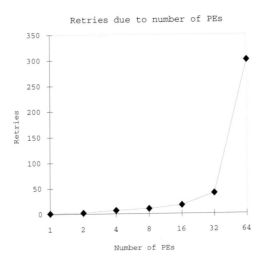

Figure 19.19 Retries versus number of PEs.

checkpoint at the normal designated point. Then on the next cycle the arbiter issues a special packet that informs the appropriate parent to spawn a new child using the checkpoint data from the to-be-spawned process. Then on the next cycle everything continues as normal. Preliminary tests show that this process works but has not been tested to its fullest. A checkpoint takes approximately half a second to perform, and a fork migration takes roughly half to one second as well. As was seen in Section 19.2.10, the rollback mechanism when activated can take anywhere from 6 to 15 seconds to do. Therefore, the fork method is far superior in time.

19.2.14   Network Traffic Effects

Network traffic plays a very large role in this project. So, too, do machine loads. If a machine is highly loaded, then it cannot adequately serve the incoming packets or respond in the allocated time specified by the arbiter. This can then cause a retry, which may not actually be needed yet, but the arbiter assumes that it is. This timeout variable is thus crucial to NEPSi's performance. If set too low, the arbiter will send a retry too early; if set too high, then a missed packet will not be sent for an extended period, which wastes time for all processors. Various methods were employed to try to automatically determine a heuristic for the optimal timeout. None proved to be any more successful than others. The methods tried were an increasing timeout period, setting the timeout from the first packet received and an average. The network fluctuations in a teaching environment based on X-terminals are dramatic. A network that consists of homogeneous dedicated workstations should prove to far be less troublesome. Figure 19.19 shows the average number of retries that are encountered during a simulation with a varying number of PEs.

19.3   Discussion

This project has achieved its major goals of exploring the utility of network enabled parallel simulation in a very dynamic and unruly network environment. The NEPSi simulator was developed with the accompanying testing resources. We have observed in most cases a general simulation speed increase by a factor of 5. Larger simulations produce larger amounts of speed, up to a point. This point is governed not necessarily by communications contentions but by resource contentions. Invariably we ran out of processors or increased the number of simulations per machine, which had a much more significant effect on the speedup factor than network overheads.

There are some possible measures which should improve the results. The network here is relatively lopsided and quite a number of the machines used in the project are located on the same subnet. The relatively fast machine used as the arbiter was on this overused subnet and should ideally have been located on a less populated network node, so that packets get through with fewer collisions. Also, the simulator relies on the NFS file system so that all machines have a consistent view of a central data repository. This means, however, that the machine on which the repository exists must service all the demands from the simulators as well as do any simulation that may have been assigned to it. This became a problem when we were conducting the 64 PE tests. Several NFS errors would occur during the simulation and on a couple of occasions this would cause the simulator to go into damage control mode and initiate a rollback; of course, this only made things worse and the whole simulation had to be aborted. This is a problem out of our control and the NFS errors experienced cannot be attributed to the simulator itself; it is at the mercy of the network environment. To counteract this problem, the simulator could be run so that when starting a simulation session all the relevant files are copied to the local temp directory on each host. This way the files would be local and would stop any problems with NFS. However, this then presents a problem for the checkpoint files in the event that a machine went down, but mirroring could be handled within a subnet if losing an entire subnet was deemed unlikely.

We also note that more useful speedup figures could be obtained with a homogeneous network. Also, while NEPSi has proven to be a highly effective implementation technique for hardware, the task allocation has been done in a very rudimentary manner. It would also be possible to have different functional entities on one processor and remove the present restriction that only one type of module can be simulated on each machine, allowing more freedom in the placement of modules.

Further reduction of the amount of network traffic on a single subnet should also be achievable by the following means:

1. Incorporate an arbiter into the daemon and have it transmit the message back to a central arbiter. This is what PVM does in some circumstances, but as explained earlier, this increases the number of packets required. As we saw, when a large simulation is being executed, the number of packets returned to the arbiter increases greatly and the subnet on which it resides can get flooded.

2. Equip the server on which the arbiter resides with multiple network adapters so that it becomes a hub for the simulation network. This will spread the traffic presently on the arbiter's subnet across several subnets. This becomes particularly attractive when one considers that one can equip a PC with several Ethernet cards for a very small outlay, and this would reduce the network contentions considerably.

Using the communications functions developed in this project, extending a commercial simulator should be the next logical step. Combining this with the above proposed extensions would produce a cheap extensible simulator than can make use of resources that are usually thought to be too slow to be of any practicable use. All this and more can be accomplished through employing networked enabled parallel simulation.

19.4   Bibliography

[1] R. E. Bryant. Bit-Level Analysis of an SRT Divider Circuit. *Technical report, CMU-CS-95-140*, Carnegie Mellon University, April 1995.

[2] CAO_VLSI team, ALLIANCE, ftp://ftp.ibp.fr/ibp/softs/masi/alliance/

[3] S. Gupta, and K. Pingali. Fast Compiled Logic Simulation Using Linear Bdds. *(TR95-1522)*, Cornell University, June 1995.

[4] S. R. Jones and K. Sammut. Learning in Linear Systolic Neural Network Engines: Analysis and implementation. *IEEE Transactions on Neural Networks*, vol. 5(4), pages 584-593, July 1994.

[5] A. Geist, A. Beguelin, J. Dongarra, W. Jiang, R. Manchek, and V. Sunderam. PVM: Parallel Virtual Machine, A User's Guide and Tutorial for Networked Parallel Computing, Web version.
http://www.netlib.org/pvm3/book/pvm-book.html, MIT Press Scientific and Engineering Computation, (ed.) Janusz Kowalik. Massachusetts Institute of Technology 1994.

[6] R. Rabenseifner and A. Schuch. Comparison of DCE RPC, DFN RPC, ONC and PVM. In Alexander Schill (ed.), DCE - The OSF Distributed Computing Environment, *International DCE Workshop, Proceedings*, pages 39-46, Karlsruhe, Germany, October 1993.

Chapter 20

Real-Time Resource Management Middleware: Open Systems and Applications

Lonnie R. Welch, Behrooz A.Shirazi, Carl Bruggeman†, Binoy Ravindran‡, Paul Werme, Michael W. Masters∗, Steve Sharp⋆

†Computer Science and Engineering Dept.
University of Texas at Arlington
Arlington, Texas USA 76019-0015
Email: *welch@cse.uta.edu*

‡The Bradley Dept. of Electrical and Computer Engineering
Virginia Polytechnic Institute and State University
Blacksburg, VA USA 24061

∗Naval Surface Warfare Center
Dahlgren, VA USA 22448

⋆Computer Sciences Corporation
Dahlgren, VA USA 22448

20.1 Introduction

Many real-time systems have rigorous, multi-dimensional Quality-of-Service (QoS) objectives. They must behave in a dependable manner, respond to threats in a timely fashion and provide continuous availability within hostile environments. Furthermore, resources should be utilized in an efficient manner, and scalability must be provided to address the ever-increasing complexity of scenarios that confront such systems, even though the worst-case scenarios of the environment may be unknown [1]. This chapter describes innovative QoS management technology for such systems, as well as experiences in applying the technology within the distributed shipboard computing systems domain.

418

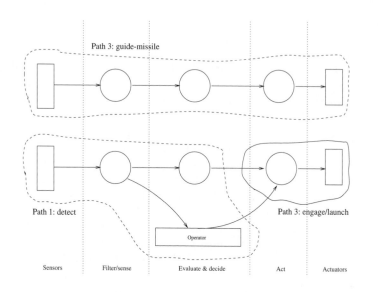

Figure 20.1 Paths from an AAW System.

The QoS management technology employs the "dynamic path" paradigm, which has proven useful for QoS assessment and for resource allocation during the engineering of the Navy's distributed anti-air warfare (AAW) prototype within the HiPer-D Testbed [11]. Figure 20.1 shows three dynamic paths from an AAW system. The detect path (path 1) performs the role of examining radar sensor data (radar tracks) and detecting potential threats to a ship or to a fleet. The sensor data are filtered by software and are passed to two evaluation components, one of which is software and the other is a human operator. When a threat is detected and confirmed, the engage path (path 2) is activated, resulting in the firing of a weapon to engage the threat. A typical engagement is the launching of a missile. After a missile is in flight, the guide missile path (path 3) tracks the threat and issues guidance commands to the missile. The guide missile path involves sensor hardware, software for filtering/sensing, software for evaluating and deciding, software for acting, and actuator hardware.

The real-time characteristics of the three paths are as follows. The detect path is a data-driven path (in contrast to a clock- driven periodic task as described in the real-time computing literature; see [8]) with desired end-to-end latencies for

evaluating radar track data and detecting potential threats. The path is not hard
real-time [8]. If it fails to meet the desired timeliness QoS, the path must continue
to process track data, even though desired end-to-end latencies cannot be achieved.
The sensor data is provided to the path periodically, but the periodicity changes
dynamically. If a potential threat is detected, the frequency of sensing increases.
Following the classification of a potential threat as a non-threat or a real threat,
the frequency of sensing decreases. Peak loads cannot be known in advance for
the detect path, since the maximum number of radar tracks can never be known.
Furthermore, average loading of the detect path is a meaningless notion, since the
variability in loading for the detect path is very large—it may be processing zero
tracks or it may be processing thousands of tracks.

The engage path is a sporadic, high-priority, "one-time" path. It is activated
by an event from the detect path. There is an end-to-end QoS timeliness objective
on the engage path, which has a higher priority than the timeliness QoS of the
detect path or the guide missile path. Each time the engage path is activated, it
executes only once. The guide missile path is a sporadically activated, periodic,
transient path. It is activated by the missile launch event. Once activated, the path
periodically issues guidance commands to the missile until it detonates. The period
is dynamically determined, based on characteristics of the threat. For example, a
fast-moving threat in close proximity to a ship will require issuing more frequent
guidance commands than a slower-moving threat that is farther away. Since it is
not possible to know all possible threats that will be engaged, it is impossible to
statically define a set of periodicities that the guide missile path will have. If multiple threat engagements are active simultaneously, the threat engagement path is
responsible for issuing guidance commands to all missiles that have been launched.
As the maximum number of engagements cannot be known in advance, the peak
load of the guide missile path is impossible to predict. Similarly, each engagement
scenario can vary significantly from other engagement scenarios, so the average loading of this path is not a highly useful metric for QoS management. Most previous
work in distributed real-time systems has focused on a lower level of abstraction
than the path and has assumed that all system behavior follows a statically known
pattern [8], [9], [2], [3], [10], [4]. When applying the previous work to some applications (such as shipboard AAW systems [11]), problems arise with respect to
scalability of the analysis and modeling techniques; furthermore, it is sometimes
impossible to obtain some of the parameters required by the models. The work described in this chapter addresses these problems. Also, [6] present dynamic models
and algorithms are based on static system profiles and dynamic measurements. A
resource management model for systems with multiple applications, each of which
have several Quality-of-Service (QoS) requirements, is described in [5]. The model
presented by the authors is intended for use with static allocation schemes, dynamic
allocation with admission control schemes, and allocation approaches where each
allocation has a duration of validity associated with it. The authors present necessary conditions for the optimality of allocations, and algorithms to achieve optimal
allocations.

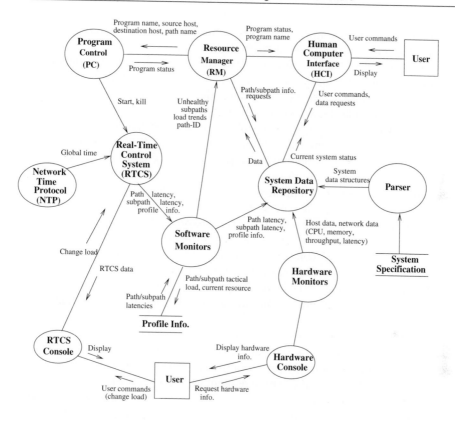

Figure 20.2 The architecture of the middleware.

The rest of the chapter is organized as follows. Section 2 provides an overview of a middleware architecture for dynamic QoS management of path-based systems. Section 3 describes the adaptive resource allocation approach employed by the middleware. In Section 4 we present our experiences with the QoS management middleware services. This includes a description of a distributed shipboard AAW system for which the techniques were employed, and experimental results showing the response times (end-to-end and component-wise), intrusiveness on CPU and network resources, bottlenecks, and boundedness.

20.2   Architecture of Dynamic QoS Management Middleware

The primary components of our dynamic resource management middleware include a resource manager, program control (PC), system data repository, software monitors, hardware monitors, and a human computer interface. The architecture of the middleware is shown in Figure 20.2. The components of the architecture are explained in the remainder of this section.

The core component of the middleware is the resource manager. It is activated when programs die, and when paths are missing their deadlines. In response to these events, it takes appropriate measures to maximize the quality of service delivered to the applications. Typical actions taken by the resource manager include restarting a program that "died," restarting the collection of programs that were running on a host that failed, and replicating the bottleneck program of an "overloaded" path. The reallocations made by the resource manager make use of information provided by the hardware and software monitors.

The system data repository component is responsible for collecting and maintaining all system information. A parser that is front-end to the repository reads a description of the system and its requirements, expressed using a specification language, and builds the data structures that model the system. Dynamically measured software QoS metrics are collected and maintained by the software monitors. The data repository obtains measurements of the dynamic attributes of the software from the software monitors. Hardware resource profiles are collected and maintained by the hardware monitors, and are fed to the repository on demand as well as periodically.

The hardware monitors consist of a host broker program and a set of host monitor daemons. The daemon programs act as "bidders" for both host and network resources. Host monitor daemons collect various host-level metrics such as CPU idle time, CPU ready queue length, and host free memory for each host in the system. The host-level metrics of individual hosts is send to the host broker by the daemons in a periodic manner. The host broker thus becomes a single repository of host information, and provides the data to the resource manager on demand.

The software monitors consist of a set of path manager programs. The objective of the path managers is to monitor path- level QoS metrics and to alert the resource manager of QoS violations. There is one path manager per dynamic path. Each path manager receives time-stamped event tags from the real-time applications, transforms them into path-level QoS metrics, and evaluates the metrics for QoS violations. When a QoS violation is detected by the path manager, it performs local diagnosis to determine subpaths of the path that are causing a poor QoS to the path. As an example, subpath programs that are exhibiting an increased execution latency may contribute to a poor real-time QoS of the path. In such a scenario, the path manager determines the set of subpath programs with an increased latency as the result of the diagnosis. The resource manager is notified of the result of the diagnosis by the path manager(s).

The program control (PC) component consists of a central control program and a set of startup daemons. When the resource manager needs to start a program on a particular host, it informs the control program, which notifies the startup daemon on that host. Each host contains a startup daemon, which starts and kills programs at the control program's request. Each startup daemon is also responsible for notifying the control program if a process that it started has died. In the event

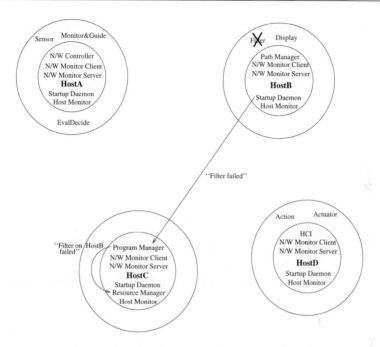

Figure 20.3 Detection of a failed program.

of a process death, the program control informs the resource manager, which in turn decides where (and if) to restart the process.

The human-computer interface (HCI) serves two main functions. It provides information to the user regarding the system configuration (the network topology, the hosts and the mapping of programs to hosts), the status of the applications (programs and paths), and information pertaining to reallocation decisions. It also allows the operator to dynamically modify the behavioral characteristics of the resource discovery and the resource manager components. The frequency of resource monitoring and the types of metrics collected by the resource discovery components can be dynamically changed through the HCI. Also, the automatic scalability and automatic survivability services of the resource manager can be toggled on and off.

20.3   Adaptive Resource Allocation

This section explains the techniques used to provide adaptive resource allocation. Sections 20.3.1 and 20.3.2 describe the automatic survivability and automatic scalability services, respectively. Section 20.3.3 describes assessment of real-time QoS and Section 20.3.4 presents the resource allocation and management strategy.

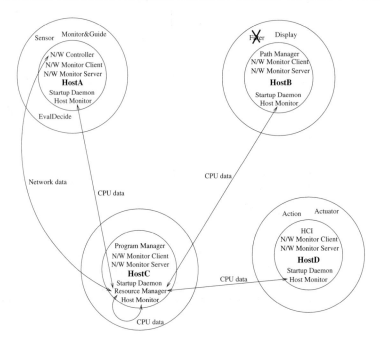

Figure 20.4 Discovery of resources.

20.3.1 Automatic Survivability

Survivability is provided to dynamic paths by the resource manager's ability to detect, reallocate, and restart dead programs. The survivability service is performed as follows:

1. Detection of a failed program: The startup daemon on the failed program's host informs the program manager. The program manager, in turn, informs the resource manager and the HCI (Figure 20.3).

2. Host and network resource discovery: The resource manager obtains host and network-level information from the system data repository (Figure 20.4).

3. Computing an allocation: The resource manager determines a candidate host for re-starting the failed program using a "best host" algorithm (Figure 20.10).

4. Enactment of allocation: The resource manager informs the program manager to re-start the program on the "best" host. The program manager notifies the startup daemon on the "best" host, which then starts a new process on the host (Figure 20.5).

5. Re-start notification: The startup daemon notifies the program manager of a successful program re-start. The program manager, in turn, notifies the resource manager and the HCI (Figure 20.6).

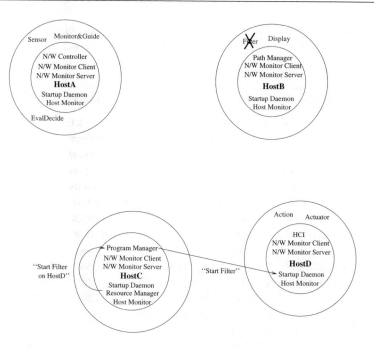

Figure 20.5 Re-start of failed program.

20.3.2   Automatic Scalability

The adaptive resource management middleware provides the ability to detect dynamic paths that are receiving poor QoS, and to "scale up" such paths via replication of the "bottleneck" of the path. This is illustrated in Figure 20.7. In part (a) of the figure, an overloaded path is depicted. For this path, its average latency exceeds the required latency. The bottleneck is the assessment application. In part (b), a scaled path is shown, wherein the bottleneck has been replicated. The steps involved in providing automatic scalability to the paths by the resource manager include (1) overload detection/QoS assessment, (2) resource discovery, (3) reallocation and (4) starting a program copy. Steps 2-4 are explained in Section 3.1. Step 1, QoS assessment, is explained in Section 20.3.3.

20.3.3   Assessment of Real-Time QoS

To assess the real-time QoS of dynamic paths, a moving window of path latency samples is collected for each path. The moving window consists of the set of the last ω path latency samples. A threshold value for the path latency is also defined for each of the paths. A path is said to be overloaded when any υ number of path latency samples among the ω samples of the window, exceeds the threshold value defined for the path. More formally, let $p_1, p_2, \cdots, p_\mu$ be the dynamic paths in

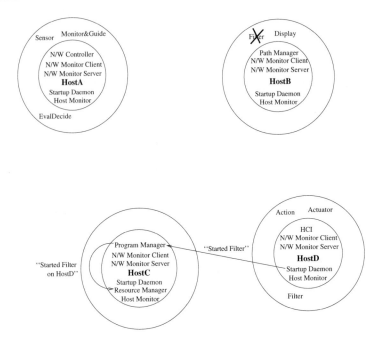

Figure 20.6 Notification of successful program re-start.

the system, and $\tau_1, \tau_2, \cdots, \tau_\mu$ be their path latencies. Let $THRESH_i$ be the path latency threshold for path p_i, and $\tau_i^1, \tau_i^2, \cdots, \tau_i^\omega$ be its last ω path latency samples, where ω is the size of the moving window. A path p_i is said to be *overloaded*, if there exists any v number of latencies $\tau_i^1, \tau_i^2, \cdots, \tau_i^v$ in the last ω path latency samples, such that $\tau_i^j > THRESH_i, \forall j : 1 \leq j \leq v$.

Figure 20.8 illustrates an example scenario where the path manager monitors the latency of a path. Time stamps from the beginning (t_1) and end (t_2) of the path are sent to the path manager by the respective programs in the path. The path manager computes the path latency $(t_1 - t_2)$, and updates the table of path latency samples (the moving window), on receiving the latest sample. The number of samples maintained in the table is determined by the size of moving window $(\omega = 6)$. When any v number of samples $(v = 3)$ exceeds the threshold value $(THRESH_i = 1.2$ seconds), the path manager notifies the resource manager.

20.3.4   Resource Allocation and Management

Path-level QoS requirements are used by the adaptive resource allocator to determine if the current configuration is achieving the desired QoS and to assist in selecting new configurations to improve QoS. This section describes the adaptive resource allocator, the core algorithm of the resource manager, and also presents the objective function employed for making resource allocation decisions.

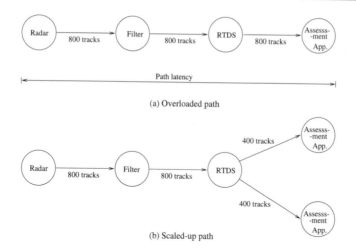

(a) Overloaded path

(b) Scaled-up path

Figure 20.7 An overloaded path and a path that has been "scaled up."

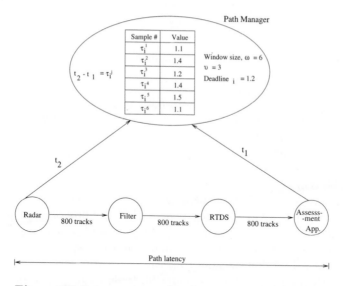

Figure 20.8 Assessment of real-time quality-of-service.

When a notification for performing resource allocation is received, the resource manager requests resource information from the system data repository, and determines a "best host" where a program may be (re)started. The best host is determined using an algorithm—the Best-Host algorithm (Figure 20.10)—that considers trend values from a moving window of hardware utilization levels. The algorithm determines the best candidate host using a *fitness* function that simultaneously considers both host-level metrics and network-level metrics.

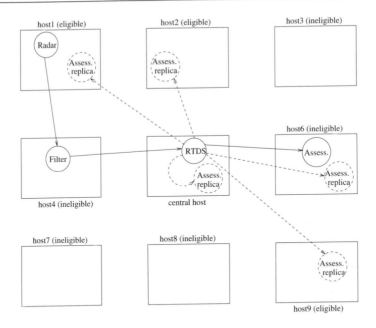

Figure 20.9 Program-to-host re-allocation scenario for scalability.

Figure 20.9 illustrates the program-to-host re-allocation scenario for achieving path scalability. Table 20.1 shows the host and network-level metrics for a set of eligible hosts. An eligible host is a host where a program is prepared for execution. The set of eligible hosts for each program in the application is user-defined . For each eligible host, the host-level metrics considered include CPU utilization (HOSTi values in Table 20.1) and utilization trends ($HOSTTREND_i$ values in Table 20.1). The network-level metrics (for each eligible host) are considered for every (*central host, eligible host*) pair. A central host is defined as any host where a program that was communicating heavily with the candidate program[1] is running. For each pair of programs in the application that communicate, the degree of communication is characterized based on domain knowledge. The network-level metrics considered include network throughput (NET_i values in Table 20.1) and throughput trends ($NETTREND_i$ values in Table 20.1). Network throughput is the number of unit size data packets transported between host pairs in unit time. Based on these resource discovery metrics, the $FITNESS_i$ (line 5.3 in Figure 20.10) for each host is evaluated. Host2 is judged as the *BestHost* by the algorithm, after evaluating the $FITNESS_i$ values for all eligible hosts, namely host1, host2, host5 and host9.

The computational complexity for the Best-Host Algorithm is $\mathcal{O}(mn^3)$ due to the complexity encountered during line 3 [7]. The complexity of the line 1 is $\mathcal{O}(kmn)$, where k is the number of programs, m is the number of host monitors and n the

---

[1]i.e., the program that has to be replicated or re-started.

Table 20.1 Computation of Host "Fitness"

Elgbl. Host	(Cntrl.-host, Elgbl.-host)	$NET_i \times 10^{-7}$ (bits/sec) weight = 0.2	$NET-$ $TREND_i$	$HOST_i$ (utlzn.%) weight = 0.8	$HOST-$ $TREND_i$	$FIT-$ $-NESS_i$ $(w = 0.25)$
host1	(host5,host1)	9	+1	0.98	0	3.7992
host2	(host5,host2)	8	0	0.80	+1	9.8982
host5	(host5,host5)	8.5	+1	0.70	-1	-4.5339
host9	(host5,host9)	7	-1	0.99	-1	-12.4569

number of hosts. Obtaining the resource discovery information, i.e., host-level (line 2.1) and network-level metrics (line 2.2), has a complexity of $\mathcal{O}(pm)$ where p is the number of eligible hosts. Extracting appropriate (central-host, eligible-host) pair network-metrics (line 3) has a complexity of $\mathcal{O}(nk + mn^3)$ for k programs, m host monitors and n hosts. Determining the maximum CPU and network utilization (line 4) has a complexity of $\mathcal{O}(m)$ for m eligible hosts. Finally, for lines 5 and 6 a combined complexity of $\mathcal{O}(m)$ is incurred. Since the complexity of line 3 ($\mathcal{O}(mn^3)$) overrides all other complexities, $\mathcal{O}(nk), \mathcal{O}(kmn), \mathcal{O}(pm)$ and $\mathcal{O}(m)$, the complexity of the algorithm is $\mathcal{O}(mn^3)$.

20.4   Experiences with the Adaptive Resource Management Services

This section describes our experiences with the QoS management middleware services. This includes a description of a distributed shipboard AAW system for which the techniques were employed, and experimental results showing the response times (end-to-end and component-wise), intrusiveness on CPU and network resources, bottlenecks, and stability/boundedness.

20.4.1   The Navy Testbed

The technology described in this chapter was evaluated within the Naval Surface Warfare Center High Performance Computing (NSWC HiPer-D) Testbed, which contains a distributed implementation of an AAW system. The software and hardware features of the Testbed are described in this section.

Figure 20.11 depicts the major software components of the AAW system, and categorizes them as sensors, filter and sense software elements, evaluate and decide software elements, act software elements, and actuators. The implementation includes the following capabilities:

- a simulated track source,

- track correlation and filtering algorithms,

- track data distribution services,

1. Identify the set of eligible hosts for the candidate program.
2. For each eligible host H_i do
    2.1 Request and collect host utilization $HOST_i$, and host trend $HOSTTREND_i$ from host monitor component running on host H_i.
    2.2 Request and collect network utilization NET_{ij} and $NETTREND_{ij}$ between host H_i and any host H_j from the host broker component.
    /* $HOSTTREND_i$ and $NETTREND_{ij}$ are real values that indicate an increasing or decreasing host and network utilization trends, respectively.*/
3. For each eligible host H_i do
    3.1 Set $NET_i = \infty$;
    3.2 For each *central* host H_j do
        3.2.1 if $NET_{ij} < NET_i$ then
                $NET_i = NET_{ij}$;
                $NETTREND_i = NETTREND_{ij}$;
4. Determine maximum host utilization $HOST_{max}$ from all $HOST_i$, and maximum network utilization NET_{max} from all NET_i, for all eligible hosts H_i.
5. For each eligible host H_i do
    5.1 $HOST_i^{weight} = 1.0 + \mathtt{atan}(HOSTTREND_i \times w)$;
        where w is a real constant.
    5.2 $NET_i^{weight} = 1.0 + \mathtt{atan}(NETTREND_i \times (1 - w))$;
        /* The *arctangent* function normalizes the $HOSTTREND$ and $NETTREND$ values to a value in the interval [0,1.57]. */
    5.3 $FITNESS_i = \left(\left[\frac{HOST_i}{HOST_{max}} \right] \times HOST_i^{weight} \right) \times HOST_{weight}$
        $+ \left(\left[\frac{NET_i}{NET_{max}} \right] \times NET_i^{weight} \right) \times NET_{weight}$;
        where $HOST_{weight}$ = weight allocated to host-level metrics, and NET_{weight} = weight allocated to network-level metrics.
6. Set *BestHost* as the host H_i that has the maximum value for $FITNESS_i$.

Figure 20.10 The Best-Host algorithm.

- a doctrine server and three types of doctrine processing ($semi-auto$, $auto-sm$, and $auto-special$), and

- an engagement server.

Further, the AAW system also has a display subsystem including X-windows based tactical displays, submode mediation, and alert routing surface operations (reengineered from CMS-2 to Ada) simulated weapons control system, and identification upgrade capabilities.

The HiPer-D Testbed is a distributed system providing functionality to support a standard missile path through the combat system. It consists of more than 50 processes (not including COTS components). It has both fault-tolerant and scalable components. The Testbed runs over a heterogeneous network configuration that includes Myrinet, ATM, FDDI, and Ethernet, on multiple heterogeneous platforms, including Dec Alpha's with OSF-1, Dec Sable with OSF-1, TAC-4's with HP-UX, Sun Sparc 10's with Solaris, and Pentiums with OSF-1RT (real-time).

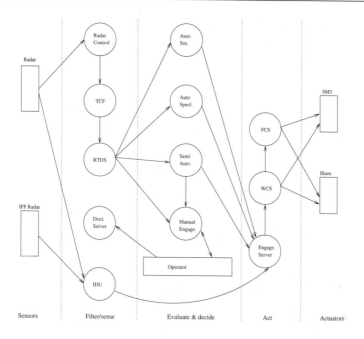

Figure 20.11 Elements of a shipboard AAW system.

Table 20.2 The HiPer-D Hardware Platform.

Processor (Quantity)	Operating System	Networks
Sun UltraServer 4000, 6 processor SMP (1)	Solaris 2.5.1	Ether/FDDI/Myrinet
Sun Server 1000, 8 processor SMP (1)	Solaris 2.5.1	Ether/FDDI/ATM
Sun Ultra 1 (2)	Solaris 2.5.1	Ether/FDDI/Myrinet
Sun Ultra 2, 2 processor SMP (1)	Solaris 2.5.1	Ether/FDDI/Myrinet/ATM
Pentium 90Mhz (6)	OSF RT	Ether/FDDI/Myrinet
HP TAC-4 J210 (7)	OSF PA RT or HPUX 10.10	Ether/FDDI/Myrinet or Ether/FDDI/ATM
Alpha Server 2100 4 processor SMP (1)	DEC Unix 3.2	Ether/FDDI
Alpha 3000 (4)	DEC Unix 3.2	Ether/FDDI/ATM
Alpha 200 (5)	DEC Unix 3.2	Ether/FDDI

Specifically, the tactical programs are distributed over the architecture summarized in Table 20.2.

20.4.2   A Real-Time Control System Benchmark

In addition to employing the middleware components within the NSWC HiPer-D Testbed, extensive experimentation was done using a real-time control system

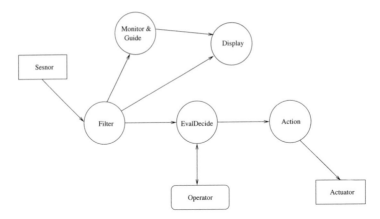

Figure 20.12 A real-time control system benchmark.

benchmark depicted in Figure 20.12. The benchmark contains three paths. They include a *continuous* path (consisting of components Sensor,Filter & EvalDecide), a *transient* path (consisting of components Action and Actuator), and a *quasi-continuous* path (consisting of components Sensor, Filter, Monitor & Guide). The three paths correspond to the detect, engage and guide paths, respectively, of the AAW system (Section 20.1). The continuous path is representative of a data acquisition/situation assessment path of a generic *real-time control system*, in which a sensor cyclically receives data from the external environment. The transient path is analogous to the path traversed during an action initiated by the control system. Finally, the quasi-continuous path simulates a path that provides continuous guidance to the result of the action, until the action accomplishes its objective. For each class of path, its timeliness is monitored using the respective path latencies which are determined as follows:

- Continuous path latency (Lat_C) is the time required for the data stream generated by the Sensor to travel from the Sensor to the Evaluate&Decide component during a single cycle and is given by $(Evaluate\&Decide_{End-Time}$ - $Sensor_{Start-Time})$.

- Transient path latency (Lat_T) is the time required for the event generated by the Evaluate&Decide component to travel from the Action component to the Actuator component, and is given by $(Actuator_{End-Time}$ - $Action_{Start-Time})$.

- Quasi-continuous path latency (Lat_Q) is the time required for the data stream generated by the Sensor to travel from the Sensor to the Monitor&Guide component during a single cycle, and is given by $(Monitor\&Guide_{End-Time}$ - $Sensor_{Start-Time})$.

The benchmark programs were distributed over a network of two sun SPARC-station5 and two sun SPARC-ultra1 machines. The communication link between

Table 20.3 Scalability Operation - Phases and Delays.

Event ID	Phase	Delay (seconds)
5	Path overload detection	0.002170
10	Pre-processing	1.006571
15	Network resource discovery	0.000447
20	Host resource discovery	0.190824
25	Allocation decision	0.069200
30	Post-processing	0.042757
35	RM-to-PM message transfer	0.074609
40	PM-to-SD message transfer	0.000648
45	SD-to-PM acknowledgment	3.129638
	Total response time	4.516864

Table 20.4 Survivability Operation - Phases and Delays.

Event ID	Phase	Delay (seconds)
5	Program failure detection	0.023941
10	RM notification	0.000456
15	Pre-processing	1.006571
20	Network resource discovery	0.000500
25	Host resource discovery	0.199455
30	Allocation decision	0.071756
35	Post-processing	0.045471
40	RM-to-PM message transfer	0.000410
45	PM-to-SD message transfer	2.109669
50	Program restart detection	0.000738
	Total response time	3.458967

the hosts is a 100 BaseT Ethernet LAN twisted pair connection.

20.4.3   Experiments

This section provides an experimental characterization of the survivability and the scalability services of the adaptive resource management middleware. Response time characterizations of these services include: (1) average end-to-end response time of each service, (2) standard deviation of service response times to characterize the boundedness of the services, and (3) step-by-step response times to identify the bottleneck step of each service. In addition to response time characterizations of services, we also measured the intrusiveness of the services to determine the host and network loads imposed by the middleware components, and to quantify the decrease in performance of the benchmark. The final experimental results characterize the scalability of the middleware service that provides survivability; this was accomplished by measuring the response times for handling increasing numbers of faulted programs.

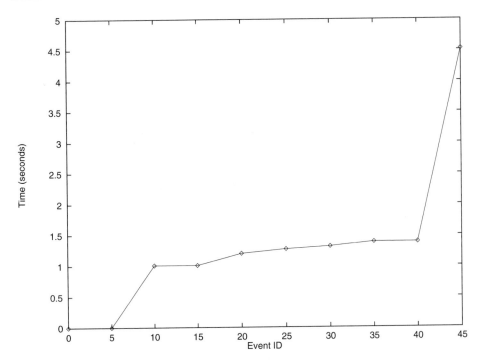

Figure 20.13 Scalability service—events vs. time.

Scalability and Survivability Experiments

As shown in Figure 20.13, the total response time of the resource manager for providing scalability service consists of the following phases:

- Path overload data transfer time (*Event 5*) is the time taken for the overloaded path information to reach the resource manager.

- Pre-processing time (*Event 10*) is the time interval after the receipt of a dead program message from the program manager and before network discovery begins. This time interval is internal to the resource manager.

- Network resource discovery (*Event 15*) is the time interval required to obtain network-level metrics from the network controller.

- Host resource discovery (*Event 20*) is the time interval required to obtain host-level metrics from all eligible host monitors.

- Allocation decision time (*Event 25*) is the time required by the best-host algorithm in determining the candidate host.

- Post-processing time (*Event 30*) is the time interval after finding the best

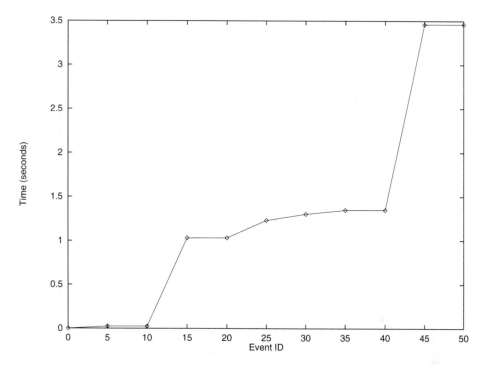

Figure 20.14 Survivability service—events vs. time.

host and before sending a program-start notification message to the program manager. This interval is internal to the resource manager.

- Program re-start notification time (*Event 35*) is the time required to inform the Program Manager to re-start a particular program on a particular host.

- Program Manager (PM) to Startup Daemon (SD) data transfer time (*Event 40*) is the time required to transfer the restart data to the appropriate startup daemon from the program manager.

- Program re-start detection time (*Event 45*) is the time required by the startup daemon to detect the re-start of the program.

The experimental results for scalability is summarized as follows. We obtained a total response time of 4.516864 seconds (Table 20.3) with a standard deviation of 0.005845. On comparison with the average path cycle latency of 2 seconds, the scalability service response time indicates that, on the average, we are able to recover from the timing failure of a path within, at most, *3 cycles* (of the path) since the occurrence of the failure.

Response time measurements for survivability service were also performed (Figure 20.14). The different phases of the survivability operation are almost similar to

Table 20.5 Intrusiveness Measurements.

Stg	Middleware Assignment	Expt. # 1 Avg. Path Lat. (Cycle Interval)	Expt. # 2 Avg. Path Lat. (Cycle Interval)	Expt. # 3 Avg. Path Lat. (Cycle Interval)	Avg. Path Lat. (Avg. Cycle #)	Std. Dev. of Path Lat.
1	Texas : BM0	10.088 (0 - 186)	10.24 (0 - 139)	9.66 (0 - 125)	10 (150)	0.3010
2	Texas: BM0, HM, HB	9.47 (187 - 310)	10.38 (140 - 218)	10.23 (126 - 208)	10.03 (245)	0.4879
3	Texas: BM0, HM HB, RM, PC HA, SD, PM Nujersy: BM1, HM, SD	10.42 (311 - 474)	10.18 (219 - 304)	10.05 (209 - 297)	10.22 (358)	0.1877
4	Texas: BM0, HM HB, RM, PC HA, SD, PM Nujersy: BM1, HM, SD	10.47 (475 - 589)	10.33 (305 - 393)	10.29 (298 - 393)	10.36 (458)	0.0945

that of the scalability service. It consists of:

- Program failure detection time (*Event 5*) is the time taken by the startup daemon to inform the program manager of a failed program.

- Resource manager notification time (*Event 10*) is the time taken by the program manager to inform the resource manager of the failed program.

- Resource manager processing time (*Events 15 - 35*) is the total time taken by the resource manager to determine a "good" host and notify the program manager.

- Re-start time (*Events 45,50*) is the time taken by the program manager and startup daemons to actually restart the program.

The summation of these response times will provide us with the total response time for the complete survivability operation. The resource manager processing time consists of five phases similar to that of the scalability operation. As seen in Table 20.4, we obtained a total response time of 3.458967 seconds with a standard deviation of 0.022354. On comparison with the average path cycle latency of 2 seconds, the survivability service response time indicates that, on the average, we are able to recover from the program failure of a path within at most *2 cycles* (of the path), since the occurrence of the failure.

Intrusion Experiments

To measure the intrusiveness of the middleware, we performed a series of experiments in which the real-time QoS of paths was measured in isolated and non-isolated conditions. First, all programs of the benchmark were assigned to a single host machine, and the path latency was measured without any middleware components running on the host. This constituted stage 1 of the experiment. We will refer to this copy of benchmark as *BM0*. Components of the middleware were then started on the host in an incremental manner. A host monitor daemon and a program startup daemon were first started on the host, and the path latency was measured

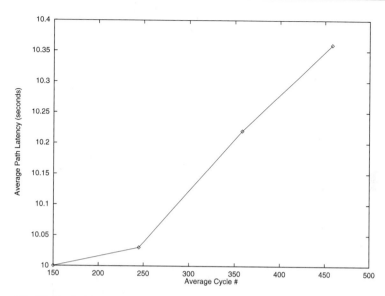

Figure 20.15 Path latency vs. "increased presence" of middleware components.

(stage 2). Stage 3 of the experiment was comprised of starting the rest of the middleware on the same host. This included the resource manager, program control, host broker, system data repository, and the software monitors. Host monitors and startup daemons were also started on another set of hosts. A second copy of the benchmark–$BM1$–was started on a different host for QoS monitoring, detection, and resource allocation. $BM0$ was not allowed to interface with the middleware throughout the experiment. The path latency of $BM0$ was again measured during this stage (stage 3). During stage 3 of the experiment, the track size of $BM1$ was substantially increased to force a real-time QoS violation and to "activate" the resource manager. Upon notification of a QoS violation by the software monitors, the resource manager performed a diagnosis of $BM1$ and a re-allocation of resources. The path latency of $BM0$ was measured during this stage when the resource manager was thus computationally active. This stage is referred to as stage 4 of the experiment. The entire experiment was repeated three times, and the results are summarized in Table 20.5. The graph in Figure 20.15 illustrates the average path latency of $BM0$ during each of the progressive stages. The x-axis of the graph in Figure 20.15 indicates the average of cycle numbers at which the path latency measurement was made, for different runs of the experiment. Since middleware components were completely absent during stage 1, and were completely present during stage 4 with the resource manager being computationally active as well, stages 1 and 4 may be referred to as minimal and maximal intrusive stages, respectively. The maximum (minimum) intrusiveness of the middleware may be computed as the percentage of maximal (minimal) increase in path latency due to

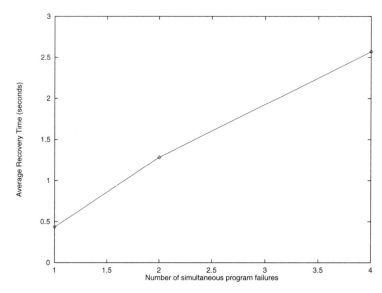

Figure 20.16 Response times for recovery from simultaneous program failures.

the maximal (minimal) presence of the middleware. The maximum and minimum intrusiveness have been thus determined to be 3.47% and 0.3%, respectively.

Middleware Scalability Experiments

The scalability of the resource management middleware for providing survivability service was also determined experimentally. The scalability of the middleware for survivability service is defined as its ability to recover from n simultaneous program failures of the benchmark, in n times the amount of time required to recover from a single program failure. In order to quantify this experimentally, different number of benchmark programs were faulted simultaneously, and the total amount of time that was taken by the middleware in completely recovering from each of the simultaneous failures was measured. Figure 20.16 illustrates recovery time measurements that were made for 1, 2, and 4 simultaneous program failures. We repeated the experiment five times and measured the total recovery time. The average recovery time for each case was found to be 0.436830, 1.283890, and 2.568578 seconds, respectively.

20.5   Conclusions

This chapter describes adaptive resource management middleware that provides integrated services for fault tolerance, distributed computing, and real-time computing. The system model on which the systems engineering toolset is based differs significantly from that used in related work; it is at a higher granularity, and it accommodates properties pertinent to dynamic real-time systems. Furthermore, the services have been applied to a shipboard AAW system and they have been experimentally characterized. The experiments show that the services provide bounded response times, scalable services, and low intrusiveness on host and network resources.

20.6   Bibliography

[1] G. Koob. Quorum. In *Proceedings of The Darpa ITO General PI Meeting*, pages A–59–A–87, October 1996.

[2] C. L. Liu and J. W. Layland. Scheduling Algorithms for Multiprogramming in a Hard Real-Time Environment. *Journal of the ACM*, vol. 20(1), pages 46–61, 1973.

[3] C. D. Locke. Software Architecture for Hard Real-Time Applications: Cyclic Executives Vs. Fixed Priority Executives. *Real-Time Systems*, vol. 4(1), pages 37–53, March 1992.

[4] A. K. Mok. *Fundamental Design Problems of Distributed Systems for the Hard-Real-Time Environment*. Ph.D. thesis, M.I.T, Cambridge, Massachusetts, 1983.

[5] R. Rajkumar, C. Lee, J. Lehoczky, and D. Siewiorek. A Resource Allocation Model for QOS Management. In *Proceedings of The 18th IEEE Real-Time Systems Symposium*, pages 298–307, 1997.

[6] D. Rosu, K. Schwan, S. Yalamanchili, and R. Jha. On Adaptive Resource Allocation for Complex Real-Time Applications. In *Proceedings of The 18th IEEE Real-Time Systems Symposium*, pages 320–329, December 1997.

[7] P. A. Shirolkar. Multi-Objective Dynamic Resource Allocation and Management. Master's thesis, University of Texas at Arlington, December 1997.

[8] S. H. Son, editor. *Advances in Real-Time Systems*. Prentice Hall, 1995.

[9] J. A. Stankovic and K. Ramamritham, editors. *Advances in Real-Time Systems*. IEEE Computer Society Press, 1993.

[10] J. P. C. Verhoosel. *Pre-Run-Time Scheduling of Distributed Real-Time Systems: Models and Algorithms*. Ph.D. thesis, Eindhoven University of Technology, The Netherlands, January 1995.

[11] L. R. Welch et al. Challenges in Engineering Distributed Shipboard Control Systems. In *Proceedings of The Work-In-Progress Session of The 17th IEEE Real-Time Systems Symposium*, pages 19–22, December 1996.

Chapter 21

Data Placement in Shared-Nothing Database Systems

SHAOYU ZHOU[†], M. HOWARD WILLIAMS[‡], AND KAM-FAI WONG[§]

[†]Microsoft Corp., One Microsoft Way, Redmond,
Seattle, Washington, USA.
Email: *shaozhou@microsoft.com*

[‡]Department of Computing and Electrical Engineering,
Heriot-Watt University, Riccarton, Edinburgh, Scotland.
Email: *howard@cee.hw.ac.uk*

[§]Department of Systems Engineering and Engineering Management,
The Chinese University of Hong Kong, Shatin, N.T., Hong Kong.
Email: *kfwong@se.cuhk.edu.hk*

21.1 Introduction

As databases become larger and hardware becomes less expensive, interest in parallel database systems [1] has greatly increased, with major database vendors such as Oracle and Informix producing parallel versions of their products to run on different hardware platforms.

Since for large databases, a shared-nothing architecture is believed to be more scalable than other architectures, much research has focused on this type of architecture for parallel database systems. A shared-nothing machine consists of a number of relatively autonomous nodes which communicate through messages sent via some interconnection device. The only shared hardware resource is the system interconnect. The same approach applies to cluster computing.

The way in which data is distributed about such a system can have a significant impact on the overall system performance. However, deciding how to distribute

440

the data is a non-trivial task. A given data distribution may be ideal for one type of query but may produce a load imbalance with consequential reduction in performance for another.

The process of deciding how to distribute data among the different nodes in the system is known as data placement. This involves breaking up each relation into a number of fragments and allocating each fragment to a node of the system (or to a particular disk of the node). Various strategies for data placement have been developed which attempt to achieve improved performance in different ways. Some focus on the complexity of operations such as joins, others are based on the accesses made to each fragment of a relation. However, there is no obvious choice among the different approaches which would provide the best results in all cases. The purpose of this chapter is to provide an understanding of different data placement strategies and their relative merits.

The rest of the chapter is organized as follows: In Section 21.2, the basic concept of data placement is introduced. A data placement strategy is divided into three phases: *Declustering, Placement* and *Re-Distribution*. Section 21.3 discusses the declustering phase in which a relation is partitioned into fragments. Section 21.4 describes placement strategies which allocate fragments of relations to processors. Section 21.5 concentrates on re-distribution of fragments in parallel database systems. In Section 21.6, consideration is given to dynamic re-organization of relations when performing some operations. Finally, Section 21.7 summarizes this chapter.

21.2   Data Placement

Data placement is a very important issue in shared-nothing parallel database systems. It is a key factor to be taken into account when trying to increase the overall system performance. In [2], Sacca and Wiederhold define the data placement problem as follows:

"Let **F** be a set of fragments of a given set of relations **R**. Let **T** be a set of transactions, **P** be a set of p processors, and Cef be a cost evaluation function, vi_i be the load in terms of the number of block accesses required in P_i, vc_i be the load in terms of the number of processor cycles consumed by P_i, vm_{ij} be the load due to the message traffic between P_i and P_j, CI_i be the input-output capacity of P_i, CC_i be the maximum number of cycles of P_i and CM_{ij} be the maximum volume of messages between P_i and P_j. Find an allocation **L(O,P)**, where $O = T \bigcup F$, such that

$$\sum_{i=1}^{p} (vi_i + vc_i) + \sum_{i=2}^{p} \sum_{j=1}^{i-1} vm_{ij}$$

is minimum, subject to

1. $vi_i \leq CI_i$ for all P_i in $\mathbf{P}$

2. $vc_i \leq CC_i$ for all P_i in $\mathbf{P}$

3. $vm_{ij} \leq CM_{ij}$ for all P_i, P_j in $\mathbf{P}$

where $< vi, vc, vm > = Cef(\ \mathbf{L(O,P)}\ )$. "

In summary, this defines the data placement problem as that of finding a placement of both data and transactions within the system capacity constraints so that the combined cost of I/O, processing and net communication is minimized. However, while this definition considers the overall load reduction, it does not take into account load balancing. Moreover, it does not give a time scale for completing the set of transactions. This will lead to the allocation of fragments to as few nodes as possible, since using fewer nodes reduces communication cost and therefore reduces the overall load of the system. Obviously, this kind of allocation does not balance the load among processors. For a system utilizing only inter-transaction or inter-query parallelism (i.e., a transaction/query is processed by only one processor) [1, Chapter 1], the average waiting time in the queue for a transaction will be significantly increased and therefore the average response time for a transaction will become longer. For a system utilizing intra-transaction or intra-query parallelism (i.e., a transaction can be processed by multiple processors), the response time for those transactions involving the heavily loaded processor will be increased. By not giving a time scale for completing transactions, this definition does not consider system throughput (in terms of transactions per second) since it could be a very long time to complete the set of transactions with the minimum cost.

Boral [3] associates data placement with load balancing. He has defined the problem as that of mapping several collections of data to several storage devices so that access is more or less uniformly distributed across the storage devices. This definition emphasizes load balancing, particularly I/O load balancing, but fails to take into account response time and load reduction. It also does not consider placement of transactions.

Copeland et al. [4] aimed at maximizing the overall throughput of the system by using some data placement heuristics, while trying to reach a compromise between load balancing and overall load reduction. Transaction response time was not taken into account.

To interpret the above definitions and aims of data placement in the context of shared-nothing parallel database systems, the objective of data placement should be defined as follows: A data placement strategy is that of finding an optimal placement scheme in order to obtain the minimum response time and/or maximum throughput. This is achieved by reaching the best compromise between load balancing and the overall load reduction. Load here refers to I/O, processing and communication costs. For a system utilizing only inter-transaction parallelism, the determining factor is the I/O load balance among processors and network traffic reduction, since the data operation cost (i.e., processing cost) in a transaction is the same regardless of the data placement. For a system utilizing intra-query parallelism, one needs to balance the CPU load of the processors which a transaction involves. Among examples of this type of system, the ones which exploit intra-operator parallelism (e.g., a **Sort** or **Join** operation can be distributed across a number of processors) place even more emphasis on processing cost balance. Data placement for these systems must take account of both I/O cost and processing cost for a parallel **Select** or **Join** operation. It also needs to consider relation co-location for **Join** operations to reduce network traffic. Moreover, the compromise between load balancing and the overall load reduction should be achieved in the presence of *data locality* (i.e., non-uniformity of access frequency).

Since data placement is one of those problems whose complexity is NP complete, one cannot guarantee finding an optimal solution in a reasonable amount of time. For this reason various heuristic methods have been developed to assist in finding good solutions. Some of these methods are based on reducing net traffic in order to minimize the response time for queries. Most of these methods were originally developed for distributed database systems, where net communication cost is a dominant one. Some methods are based on operation complexity, especially for **Join** operations. They are particularly useful for systems utilizing intra-operator parallelism. Since the main factor considered by them is processor load balance, these methods are particularly suitable for main memory parallel database systems. Most of these methods adopt data size as the indicator for operation complexity and will therefore be referred to as *size-based* approaches. Some other methods focus on the balance of I/O load among processors. The indicator that they use is the access frequency of data fragments. They try to achieve even I/O load distribution by having an even distribution of access frequency across processors. These methods will be referred to as *access-frequency-based*. There are also some methods which consider both operation complexity and access frequency distribution. These will be referred to as *size-and-access-frequency-based*.

In practice, a data placement strategy is divided into three phases: *Declustering*, *Placement* and *Re-Distribution*. A brief outline of each of these areas is given in the following sections.

21.3   Declustering

In the *Declustering* phase of a data placement strategy, relations are partitioned into a number of fragments which are subsequently allocated to the processors of a parallel machine. The number of fragments is not necessarily equal to the number of processors. Since it is relatively easy to obtain robust access statistics at the relation level (a program either accesses a relation or it doesn't) and since these access patterns remain static over long periods of time [3], only relation-level granularity is considered. The two fundamental types of partitioning of a relation are *horizontal* and *vertical*. In horizontal partitioning a fragment contains a subset of tuples from a relation, while in vertical partitioning it contains a projection of the relation over a set of attributes. It is possible to combine the two, which results in a *mixed* partitioning. A fragment of this latter kind can be thought of as being derived from a relation in two steps. First, a set of tuples is selected from a relation according to a given predicate; then the resulting relation is projected onto a set of attributes. Since most parallel database systems developed or under development adopt horizontal partitioning, this type of partitioning will be assumed throughout the remainder of this section.

Most of the declustering methods developed are for systems utilizing intra-operator parallelism, in which an operation can be distributed across a number of processors and proceeds in parallel. Hence, the discussions in this section are based on this type of system. Basically, there are two criteria used in partitioning a relation into fragments for data placement. First, the declustering scheme should be advantageous to evaluation time reduction for **Select** and **Project** operations; second, it should take into account relation co-location for **Join** operations.

21.3.1   Evaluation Time Reduction for Select and Project

In shared-nothing database systems, the use of parallelism for all types of queries is not necessarily a good idea [4]. In particular, it becomes questionable when the overhead associated with using parallelism to execute a particular query begins to constitute a significant fraction of the execution time of the query. On the other hand, for those queries consuming significant processor and I/O resources, the overhead associated with using parallelism may not be significant. In this case, additional processors can be used to improve the response time without adversely affecting the throughput of the system.

Ghandeharizadeh and DeWitt [5] proposed a new declustering strategy termed the *hybrid-range partitioning* strategy (HRPS) which utilizes the characteristics of the queries that access a relation to obtain the appropriate degree of intra-query parallelism. With this strategy, a relation is declustered into many small logical fragments so that each fragment contains a distinct range of the partitioning attribute value (the number of fragments is independent of the number of processors in the configuration). A response time function is given to calculate the optimal number M of processors that should participate in the execution of the query, based on the query information. This number is then used to obtain the optimal number of tuples in each fragment by dividing the expected number of retrieved tuples by M.

Two other declustering strategies which are common are *range* and *hash*. The range partitioning strategy does not perform as well as the hash partitioning strategy for queries with high resource requirements and, conversely, the hash partitioning strategy does not perform as well as the range partitioning strategy for queries with minimal resource requirements. The performance figures of the HRPS approach, presented in [5], indicate that by declustering a relation using HRPS, the number of processors that participate in the execution of the queries in the workload is optimized, resulting in a lower average response time and a higher average throughput when compared with the range and hash declustering strategies.

21.3.2   Relation Co-Location for Join

The Join operator is critical to the operation of any relational database management system (DBMS). Following the trend of applying parallelism to database processing, a number of researchers have addressed parallel implementations of the join operation. This section will focus on hash-based join methods because their performance has been demonstrated to be superior in systems with large memories. Hash-based algorithms partition a relation into a number of clusters called *buckets*, based on the hash value of the join attribute. Because a join operation is divided into small joins of buckets which can be carried out in parallel, hash-based algorithms perform much better than other algorithms such as nested-loop or sort-merge.

However, to conform to the basic principle of "to execute where the data lives" (i.e., exploit data placement as much as possible by sending operations to their data) in a system which utilizes intra-operator parallelism, the hash-based join algorithms require each operand relation to be declustered in the same way. The corresponding buckets of the two relations, which have the same hash value on the join attribute, are required to be co-located (i.e., placed onto the same processor). Usually these two buckets are grouped into one fragment called a *unit*. A *unit* is a logical grouping of tuples which should be placed together onto the same processor, and if necessary, moved together to other processors (i.e., it is a unit of data movement). For instance, if **R** and **S** are both declustered into n buckets using the same hash function on the join attribute, the operation Join(R, S) is equivalent to the union of n parallel operations Join(R_i, S_i), with $i = 1, ..., n$. Data placement strategies attempt to make such conditions available by grouping R_i and S_i $(i = 1, ..., n)$ into one unit.

From the above, it can be seen that when a hash-based join algorithm is applied statically (the dynamic re-organization for hash-based join algorithms will be discussed in Section 21.6), it requires hash-based declustering on the two operand relations. An access method based multi-attribute declustering method is also presented by Cheiney et al. [6].

The access frequency for each attribute of each relation can be a very useful source of information in determining declustering strategies for queries containing a set of join operations. If a set of join operations on different join attributes is executed on the same database using the same data placement scheme, only a compromise data declustering scheme is possible. In this situation access frequency is the major factor.

Hash-based declustering methods suffer from a major drawback, referred to as the *data skew* problem, due to non-uniform distribution of tuples and key values [7]. Data skew effects can be classified into *attribute value skew* and *partition skew*. Attribute value skew occurs when attribute values are not distributed uniformly, while partition skew occurs on parallel implementations when the work load is not balanced between nodes. In hash-based join algorithms, attribute value skew causes the time consumed by a particular sub-join to be much longer than other sub-joins and hence greatly increases the overall evaluation. Attribute value skew may also cause bucket overflow, i.e., the size of a unit exceeds the memory capacity of a processor.

A number of hash-based join algorithms have been proposed to solve the data skew problem. Most of them make use of dynamic re-organization, which will be discussed in Section 21.6.

21.4　Placement

In the *Placement* phase of a data placement strategy, the *units* (or *fragments*) obtained from the declustering phase are distributed across the processors of a parallel machine. This is a critical stage to achieve load balancing, maximum throughput and to reduce response time.

There are various placement strategies developed for parallel database systems. As previously stated, some of them are net-traffic-based [8], some are size-based [10], [9], some are access-frequency-based, and some are combined strategies [4]. For systems utilizing intra-operator parallelism, a number of placement strategies have been proposed following their declustering strategies. Some of them favor **Select** and **Project** operations [5], while others favor **Join** operations [11]. Since the declustering methods are built around the ideas of hashing and sorting of relations, relation operations applied to the partitioning attribute can be performed very efficiently. However, it is difficult for the placement strategies to support effectively queries that involve non-partitioning attributes.

Apers [8] presented an algorithm for placement in a distributed database environment where the processors are remote from each other and, presumably, close to their users. The strategy is based on a heuristic approach coupled with a greedy algorithm. It is a net traffic-based approach. A network is constructed in which each node represents a fragment of a relation and each edge, the cost of data transmission between two nodes. The transmission cost between each pair of nodes is then computed and the pair of nodes with the highest utilization is selected and united. This process is repeated until the network is unified with the actual network of machines.

Sacca and Wiederhold [2] extended the algorithm by using Apers' method to select the candidate fragments and then allocating these selected fragments with first-fit bin-packing. The allocation process considers load constraints which Apers did not take into account. However, like Apers' method, this approach failed to consider load balancing.

Probably the most thorough discussion of placement strategies is given in [4], which describes data placement in Bubba, a system utilizing intra-operator parallelism. Associated with each relation is its *heat* (frequency of access) and its *temperature* (heat/size). Heat is used in determining how many nodes to spread, and temperature determines whether a relation should be RAM resident. Fragments of relations are assigned to nodes in such a way that each node's temperature and heat are roughly equivalent to the others. While this study attempted to strike a compromise between load balancing and the overall load reduction in the presence of data locality, it did not consider the impact of alternative declustering strategies on the throughput of the system. In addition, the algorithms do not attempt to minimize the response time of a transaction. They consider only the overall access frequency of each relation, rather than the access frequency for each fragment of a relation which could be more useful in fragment placement.

Hua et al. [10] presented a size-based data placement scheme which balances loads of the nodes during query processing. The entire scheme is built on the well-known grid file concept. Relations are partitioned into large numbers of cells using a grid file structure, which are then assigned to the processors using a greedy algorithm so as to balance the data load for each processor. This algorithm is executed by first sorting, in descending order, the cell sizes in a list. The cells are then assigned to the processors in the sorted order. The assignment is done by allocating the currently largest cell in the sorted list to the currently smallest (in size) processor. The cell is then removed from the list. This process is repeated until the sorted list becomes empty. The adaptiveness of this scheme lies in the data rebalancing algorithm which will be discussed in the next section.

This initial placement scheme is also used in [9], where the concept of a cell is generalized to any logical unit of data partitioning and movement, i.e., all records belonging to the same cell are stored on the same processor.

In Hua et al.'s data placement scheme, the criterion for load balancing is to make sure that each of the processors assigned to store a given relation has about the same number of tuples from the given relation. It did not take account of the *heat* of each relation obtained from query frequencies. Moreover, in order to overcome the data skew effect, the cell sizes need to be quite uniform. For cells obtained from a range declustering method, it is easy to adjust the size of each cell by shifting the boundaries of the ranges. However, in the case of a hash declustering method, data skew cannot be easily balanced since the paper suggested that a cell be equal to a bucket. One proposed solution is to split a large cell into several which have the balanced sizes. But the placement strategy cannot guarantee relation co-location of these divided cells when a hash-based join is encountered, and therefore dynamic re-organization of the data is required.

To illustrate the difference in performance obtained when different data placement strategies are used to distribute data, consider some results obtained from a comparative study conducted using two standard benchmarks, TPC-B and TPC-C. The study was conducted using an analytical performance prediction tool developed for the ICL GoldRush parallel platform. Figure 21.1 shows how the throughput of the system varies for the TPC-B benchmark as the number of nodes increases, using several different data placement strategies. Figure 21.2 shows a similar set of results for a particular configuration of the TPC-C benchmark. Further details and an explanation of the different behavior patterns is given in [12]. What is important to note is the significant differences in throughput which can be obtained even for very simple benchmarks such as TPC-B.

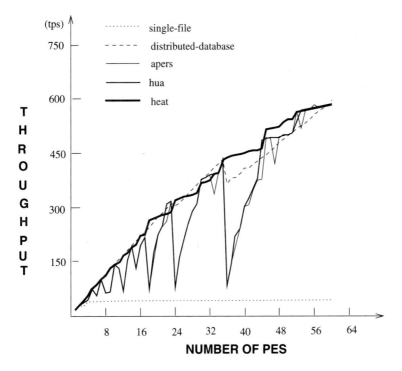

Figure 21.1 Performance of strategies of different types for TPC-B.

21.5   Re-Distribution

As insertions and deletions occur to the local data in each processor, the size and/or access frequency of the local partition of data may change so that gradually a non-uniform distribution of data will appear. This causes an unbalanced load of processors (i.e., data skew) which in turn increases the response time and degrades overall system performance. In this situation, a re-distribution of data is necessary to resume good system performance. This kind of re-distribution will be referred to as *update re-distribution.*

Sometimes, in systems which utilize intra-operator parallelism, an initial data placement scheme may be developed on the basis of optimizing performance for several queries. In the case that two of the queries contain hash-based join operations on different join attributes of a set of relations, the data placement scheme may favor one of the queries by declustering on its join attribute. The criterion for choosing this favored query may be based on its frequency. Under this data placement scheme, the favored query can be executed very efficiently because of relation co-location for join. However, the other query cannot be executed as efficiently as the favored one, since the join attribute is different. This means that for the second query a dynamic re-organization is required. This is reasonable since the frequency

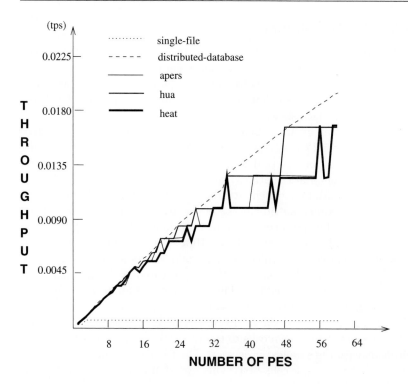

Figure 21.2 Performance of strategies of different types for TPC-C.

of the favored query is higher than that of the other query. However, after a period of time, the query frequency may change, with the result that the frequency of the second query may become greater than that of the favored one. In this case, the data may need to be re-clustered on the join attribute of the second query and then re-distributed in order to favor the second query. This is a more complicated re-distribution. This will be referred to as *query frequency change re-distribution*.

The cost of re-distribution may be even higher than the cost of processing data under the skewed circumstances, requiring the movement of large amounts of data. While this data movement could be done in the background, throughput would be severely degraded in a heavily-loaded system. This high cost dictates that re-distribution should be infrequent and should involve as little data as possible. In Bubba's data placement strategy, if the system estimates that the re-distribution cost is higher than the cost of processing data under the skewed situation, the re-distribution will not be performed. In other words, the system will tolerate a possibly high cost on processing skewed data simply because re-distribution of the entire relations would cost even more. In several other systems, re-distribution is performed manually in off-peak hours.

21.5.1   Update Re-Distribution

This kind of re-distribution does not involve deriving a new declustering of relations. It is concerned only with determining a revised placement of all the units previously placed on the processors. The key objective of a re-distribution algorithm is to minimize the re-distribution cost so that the system can rebalance its data load more easily to avoid serious data skew.

The data placement strategy in Bubba [4] uses a simple re-distribution algorithm. If the estimated cost of re-distribution is higher than the cost of processing data under the skewed situation, the re-distribution will not be performed. During the re-distribution, a few candidate relations are chosen, which are then distributed onto processors using the initial placement strategy. In this approach, however, the re-distribution process does not take advantage of the already balanced part of the data assigned to processors but performs a complete reshuffle of all data fragments.

In the previous section, it was mentioned that Hua et al. [10], [9] have proposed an adaptive data placement scheme which takes account of update re-distribution. In their first paper [10], a re-distribution algorithm is presented, which first sorts the cell sizes in each processor into a sorted list. The second step is an iterative process. In each iteration, the largest processor (i.e., has the most data) is determined, and its size (i.e., the count of retained data records) is used as the basis for other processors to offload some of their own cells to the respective retaining lists in order to balance their loads with the smallest processor. The priority for adding cells to a retaining list is to select the larger cells first. This iteration process continues until some processors run out of cells. The remaining cells are then merged into a single sorted list and they are allocated to the processors using the placement method mentioned in Section 21.2. This algorithm tries to leave as many larger cells at their current host processors as possible and this provides us a low re-distribution cost.

In Hua et al.'s second paper [9], a different re-distribution algorithm is proposed. This algorithm first sorts cell sizes in each processor into sorted lists. Thereafter the average number of tuples a processor should retain after the re-distribution is computed. Every processor retains its local cells up to the average number of tuples. The remaining cells are then merged into a single sorted list and allocated to the processors using the initial placement method. Except during the final data movement period, this algorithm is executed at a chosen coordinator that manipulates only the directory information. This algorithm is much simpler than the first one and achieves the same effect.

21.5.2   Query Frequency Change Re-Distribution

This kind of re-distribution has not been addressed in the literature. It is concerned with both determining a new clustering and a new placement. The re-distribution algorithm should first decluster the local data on each processor into sub-units, using a hash function on the new join attribute. The main task for the algorithm is to find a balanced distribution of new units obtained from the corresponding sub-units across the processors, with minimum data movement. Since the size of each unit in the new declustering is probably unknown, the problem becomes even more complicated.

Although there is currently no paper tackling this kind of re-distribution, some methods of dynamic re-organization for hash-based join operations, especially the *Bucket Spreading Parallel Hash* method and its extensions, provide good references. They will be discussed in the next section.

21.6 Dynamic Re-Organization

The previous sections discuss the three phases of *static* data placement. For systems utilizing intra-operator parallelism, the basic principle is "to execute where the data lives." In this case, it is sometimes better to dynamically re-organize the relations in order to increase the degree of parallelism, reduce response time and improve throughput.

For example, suppose there are two hash-based join operations in a query or set of queries which use different join attributes of the same relation. The data placement strategy can favor only one of the two joins by declustering on the join attribute of that join operation. Suppose that the declustering strategy is hash-based. This enables the favored join operation to be executed very efficiently, since it can be divided into a number of sub-joins which are executed in parallel. However, for the second join operation, the data has to be re-organized in order to perform sub-joins on a number of buckets to improve efficiency. The conditions for hash-based join can be achieved only by re-declustering the two operand relations on the second join attribute and dynamically placing the resulting units onto processors using some placement strategy.

It should be noted here that the dynamic loading takes the form of generating temporary (i.e., intermediate) relations. The placement of base relations resulting from the initial data placement scheme is not changed.

Various parallel join algorithms have been proposed in recent years. Most of them can be used for dynamic re-organization. The join algorithm selected usually determines the declustering strategy adopted for dynamic loading. Since hash-based join algorithms have proved to be superior to other join algorithms, they form the focus of this section. A study of the factors that can limit parallel join performance is given in [13].

Kitsuregawa and Ogawa proposed a dynamic hash join method, *Bucket Spreading Parallel Hash*, which is robust for data skew. During the re-declustering of relations, local data is again divided into sub-buckets of the same size and the sub-buckets are temporarily placed on processors one by one. This algorithm defers the allocation to sub-buckets until the data declustering process is completed. Since the distribution of the data among the sub-buckets then becomes known, the buckets can be assigned to the processors dynamically based on the bucket sizes to ensure a balanced data load at each processor. A scheduling strategy is proposed for collecting sub-buckets. To avoid a bottleneck during the collection phase, a special

Omega network is used to ensure that the sub-buckets are evenly spread across all processors. However, the network suffers from three major drawbacks. First, it does not scale well with the rest of the system. Second, unless other operations can be designed to take advantage of the data spreading feature of the Omega network, the complexity in the network design may affect its communication performance, and consequently the overall performance. Finally, the complexity explodes when one considers a multiuser environment.

Hua and Lee [14] improved the *Bucket Spreading Parallel Hash* method and proposed three parallel join algorithms with dynamic load balancing capability using the partition tuning concept introduced in [10].

The first of the three algorithms is the *Tuple Interleaving Parallel Hash* join method, which is quite similar to the *Bucket Spreading Parallel Hash* method. Instead of relying on a specially designed Omega network to maintain uniform spreading of sub-buckets across processors, it uses software control to interleave the tuples among processors as they are being distributed to their destinations.

The second algorithm is the *Adaptive Load Balancing Parallel Hash* join method. It introduces an additional step to the conventional parallel hash join algorithms, which relocates the excess sub-buckets from the larger processors to the smaller processors attempting to balance the data load prior to the join operations. The whole idea is quite similar to the re-distribution algorithm proposed in [9].

The other algorithm is the *Extended Adaptive Load Balancing Parallel Hash* join method. In this algorithm, each processor hashes its local portion of the relations into local sub-buckets. These local sub-buckets are stored in the local memory. After this partitioning process is completed, the distribution of the data in each bucket can be computed. The matching local sub-buckets are then distributed to their final destinations to form the corresponding buckets. The gathering of the sub-buckets is based on the bucket sizes to ensure a balanced work load for each of the processors during the join process.

21.7 Summary

In this chapter, two aspects of data placement strategies have been described, namely, *static* and *dynamic* data placement. Static data placement is divided into three phases, namely, *declustering, placement* and *re-distribution*. These three phases are not independent. The strategy adopted in one phase can have a considerable influence on the strategies used in the other two phases. In the description of each phase, a review of the current research in related fields is given. Furthermore, the notion of dynamic re-organization of data is discussed, and an introduction to some dynamic hash-based join algorithms is also given.

The data placement overview outlined in the chapter provides a background for the implementation of parallel database applications on cluster computers.

21.8   Bibliography

[1] M. Abdelguerfi and K.F. Wong. *Parallel Database Techniques*. IEEE-CS Press, June 1998. (ISBN 0-8186-8398-8)

[2] D. Sacca and G. Wiederhold. Database Partitioning in a Cluster of Processors. In *Proceedings of the 9th VLDB Conference*, pages 242–247, Florence, Italy, October 31-November 2, 1983.

[3] H. Boral. Parallelism and Data Management. In *Proceedings of the 3rd International Conference on Data and Knowledge Bases*, pages 362–373, Jerusalem, June 28-30, 1988.

[4] G. Copeland, W. Alexander, E. Boughter, and T. Keller. Data Placement in Bubba. In *Proceedings of ACM SIGMOD Conference*, 1988.

[5] S. Ghandeharizadeh and D. DeWitt. Hybrid-Range Partitioning Strategy: A New Declustering Strategy for Multiprocessor Database Machines. In *Proceedings of the 16th VLDB Conference*, pages 481–492, Brisbane, Australia, 1990.

[6] J. Cheiney, P. Faudemay, R. Michel, and J. Thevenin. A Reliable Parallel Backend Using Multiattribute Clustering and Select-Join Operator. In *Proceedings of the 12th VLDB Conference*, pages 220–227, Kyoto, Japan, January 1986.

[7] C. Walton, A. Dale, and R. Jenevein. A Taxonomy and Performance Model of Data Skew Effects in Parallel Joins. In *Proceedings of the 17th VLDB Conference*, pages 537–548, Barcelona, Spain, 1991.

[8] P. Apers. Data Allocation in Distributed Database Systems. *ACM Transactions on Database Systems*, Vol. 13(3), pages 263–304, September 1988.

[9] K. Hua, C. Lee, and H. Young. An Efficient Load Balancing Strategy for Shared-Nothing Database Systems. In *Proceedings of DEXA'92 Conference*, pages 469–474, Valencia, Spain, September 1992.

[10] K. Hua and C. Lee. An Adaptive Data Placement Scheme for Parallel Database Computer Systems. In *Proceedings of the 16th VLDB Conference*, pages 493–506, Brisbane, Australia, 1990.

[11] M. B. Ibiza-Espiga and M. H. Williams. Data Placement Strategy for a Parallel Database System. In *Proceedings of DEXA'92 Conference*, pages 48–54, Valencia, Spain, September 1992.

[12] M.H. Williams and S. Zhou. Data Placement in Parallel Database Systems. In *Parallel Database Techniques*, M. Abdelguerfi and K. Wong (eds), IEEE Computer Society Press, California, pages 203–219, 1998.

[13] M. Lakshmi and P. Yu. Limiting Factors of Join Performance on Parallel Processors. In *Proceedings of the 5th International Conference on Data Engineering*, pages 488–496, Los Angeles, California, February 1989.

[14] K. Hua and C. Lee. Handling Data Skew in Multiprocessor Database Computers. In *Proceedings of the 17th VLDB Conference*, pages 525–535, Barcelona, Spain, 1991.

Chapter 22

Parallel Inference with Very Large Knowledge Bases: A Connectionist Approach to Real-Time Reasoning

D. R. Mani[†] and Lokendra Shastri[‡]

[†]GTE Laboratories Incorporated
40 Sylvan Road
Waltham, MA 02154 USA

[‡]International Computer Science Institute
1947 Center Street, Suite 600
Berkeley, CA 94707 USA

Email: *mani@gte.com, shastri@icsi.berkeley.edu*

22.1   Introduction

Over the past decade, there has been growing consensus in the Artificial Intelligence (AI) community that massive parallelism must play an essential role in the design of scalable intelligent systems [2]. The need for massive parallelism is all the more evident when modeling human cognition, with its concomitant constraints of real-time response and reaction times [8]. The introduction and widespread availability of a variety of parallel machines, including cluster computers with fast networks, has made it feasible for researchers to experiment with parallel approaches to AI.

A core problem in AI is that of knowledge representation and reasoning. Research has shown that reasoning underlies even the most commonplace intelligent behavior. Furthermore, such common-sense reasoning occurs with respect to a very large knowledge base. Guha and Lenat have estimated that the size of such a knowledge base may easily run into several million items [3]. In view of this, it is crucial

455

that we develop effective knowledge representation and reasoning systems capable of encoding large bodies of knowledge and performing rapid reasoning with respect to such knowledge.

22.1.1   Parallel Reflexive Reasoning on Cluster Computers

We explore the design, analysis and implementation of a massively parallel knowledge representation and reasoning system that can encode very large knowledge bases and respond to a class of queries in real-time. *Real-time reasoning* is defined as reasoning that is fast enough to support real-time cognitive activity such as language understanding, where reasoning episodes span a fraction of a second.[1]

We use SHRUTI, a structured connectionist knowledge representation and reasoning system which attempts to model reflexive—i.e., effortless and spontaneous— reasoning [10], [6] as our knowledge representation formalism.[2] Our choice of SHRUTI is motivated by several factors: SHRUTI is an efficient, limited inference system which imposes psychologically and biologically motivated constraints in order to make reasoning tractable. SHRUTI is a structured connectionist system; it is therefore both inherently parallel and capable of representing structured knowledge. Finally, SHRUTI attempts to model common-sense reflexive reasoning and provides an opportunity to explore its cognitive aspects.

We map SHRUTI onto MIMD (Multiple Instruction Multiple Data) parallel machines—be they *cluster computers* built with commodity, off-the-shelf components, or proprietary *massively parallel processors* (MPPs)—to develop systems that can encode very large knowledge bases and perform a class of reasoning in real-time. Such systems, which we term *parallel reflexive reasoning systems*, exploit both the parallelism of the underlying hardware, and the biologically and psychologically motivated constraints imposed by SHRUTI, to achieve real-time performance.

The work presented in this chapter is valid irrespective of whether the target machine is a cluster computer or an MPP. Our parallel reflexive reasoning system implementation has been developed on the Connection Machine CM-5 (an MPP machine). This choice has been dictated more by availability and access than by any bias between cluster computers and MPP machines. Furthermore, the experimental results for the CM-5 may be extended to cluster computers by recalibrating the computation and communication costs (see Sections 22.5 and 22.7).

A Note on Terminology

In this chapter, we use the terms *cluster computer, massively parallel processor* (MPP) and *massively parallel machine* interchangeably, to describe supercomputers constituted by a significant number of processing elements which are relatively

---

[1]For example, we can understand written language at the rate of about 150–400 words per minute—i.e., we can understand a typical sentence in a second or two [1].

[2]The details of the SHRUTI system described here are current as of early 1995. For an up-to-date description of SHRUTI, see [9] and `http://www.icsi.berkeley.edu/~shastri/shruti`. Though SHRUTI has evolved, the basic premises on which this work is based continue to be valid.

tightly integrated through a high performance network. We also use *massive parallelism* to describe the parallel program execution effected by such machines.

22.1.2   Contributions

In designing real-time reasoning systems by mapping structured connectionist networks—SHRUTI in particular—onto parallel machines, we develop parallel reflexive reasoning systems on the Connection Machine CM-5. SHRUTI-CM5, the SPMD (Single Program Multiple Data) asynchronous message passing CM-5 implementation, achieves very good performance by using active messages for efficient, low-latency interprocessor communication. SHRUTI-CM5 encodes large artificial knowledge bases with over half a million (randomly generated) rules and facts, and responds to a range of queries requiring derivation depths of up to eight in well under a second. SHRUTI-CM5 running WordNet, a real-world lexical database, responds to queries in times ranging from a few to a few hundred milliseconds. We therefore develop viable technology for supporting large-scale knowledge base systems.

We also analyze issues involved in the design and implementation of parallel reflexive reasoning systems—both from machine dependent and machine independent points of view. In addition to optimizing system performance, the analysis provides some new insights into mapping structured connectionist networks onto distributed memory massively parallel machines, and results in interesting predictions about query response time and its relation to computation and communication costs. One such prediction, confirmed by experimental data, indicates that average response time is close to optimal when knowledge base elements are mapped to random processors—i.e., load balancing is more critical than locality—when communication cost is either small, or comparable to the computational cost of processing a knowledge base element. Such results help engineer performance improvements and steer the course of future research.

22.2   SHRUTI: **A Structured Connectionist Reasoning System**

SHRUTI, is a connectionist reasoning system proposed by Shastri and Ajjanagadde that can represent systematic knowledge involving *n*-ary predicates and variables [10]. SHRUTI can perform a broad class of reasoning with extreme efficiency. In principle, the time taken by the reasoning system to draw an inference is only proportional to the *length* of the chain of inference and is otherwise independent of the number of rules and facts encoded by the system. The reasoning system maintains and propagates variable bindings using temporally synchronous—i.e., in-phase—firing of appropriate nodes. This allows the system to maintain and propagate a large number of variable bindings simultaneously as long as the number of *distinct* entities participating in the bindings during any given episode of reasoning remains bounded. Reasoning in the system is the transient but systematic flow of rhythmic patterns of activation, where each phase in the rhythmic pattern corresponds to a distinct entity involved in the reasoning process and where variable bindings are represented as the synchronous firing of appropriate role and filler nodes. A fact behaves as a temporal pattern matcher that becomes "active" when it detects that the bindings corresponding to the fact are present in the system's pattern of activity. Rules are interconnection patterns that propagate and transform rhythmic patterns of activity.

SHRUTI attempts to model *reflexive reasoning*—efficient, effortless and spontaneous "common-sense" reasoning which does not require conscious thought—over a large body of knowledge. SHRUTI has been extended in several ways [9] to effectively reason with a more flexible set of rules and facts, thereby enhancing the system's ability to model common-sense reflexive reasoning. In this chapter, we confine ourselves to backward reasoning.

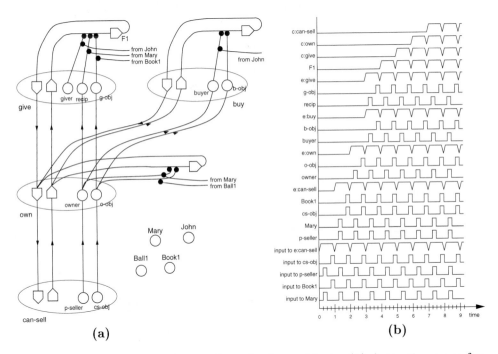

                    (a)   (b)

Figure 22.1 (a) An example encoding of rules and facts. (b) Activation trace for the query *can-sell(Mary,Book1)?*.

22.2.1 Terminology

We clarify some terminology before proceeding with a description of knowledge representation and reasoning in SHRUTI. A *predicate* is a relation. For example, *give(x,y,z)* is a predicate which represents the three-place relation: x gives y to z. Here x, y and z constitute the *arguments* or *roles* of the *give* predicate. A *fact* is a partially or completely instantiated predicate—like *give(John,Mary,Book1)*. Entities which are bound to predicate arguments are *fillers*. A *rule* specifies the systematic correspondence between predicate arguments. The rule $\forall x,y,z$ [*give(x,y,z)* $\Rightarrow$ *own(y,z)*] states that "if x gives y to z, then y owns z." A *query* is a fact whose truth we would like to ascertain. The term *entity* or *concept* is used to collectively refer to types (or categories) and instances (or individuals, sometimes referred to as *constants*). An *is-a relation* or *is-a fact* captures the superconcept-subconcept relation between types, and the *instance-of* relation between types and instances. Predicates, along with associated rules and facts, constitute the *rule-base* while concepts and their associated *is-a* relations constitute the *type hierarchy*. Predicates, concepts, facts, rules and *is-a* relations constitute *knowledge base elements*.

22.2.2 Knowledge Encoding and Inference in Backward Reasoning

Figure 22.1a illustrates how long-term knowledge is encoded in the rule-based reasoning system. The network encodes the following rules and facts:

$\forall x,y,z$ [*give(x,y,z)* $\Rightarrow$ *own(y,z)*],
$\forall x,y$ [*buy(x,y)* $\Rightarrow$ *own(x,y)*],
$\forall x,y$ [*own(x,y)* $\Rightarrow$ *can-sell(x,y)*],
give(John,Mary,Book1),
buy(John,x), and
own(Mary,Ball1).

The rule $\forall x,y,z$ [*give(x,y,z)* $\Rightarrow$ *own(y,z)*] states that "if x gives z to y, then y owns z." The other two rules are interpreted similarly. The facts *give(John,Mary, Book1)* and *own(Mary,Ball1)* represent "John gave Mary Book1" and "Mary owns Ball1" respectively, while *buy(John,x)* states that "John bought *something*."

Rule and fact encoding (Figure 22.1a) makes use of ρ-**btu** nodes (depicted as circles) and τ-**and** nodes (depicted as pentagons). On receiving a spike train, a ρ-btu node produces a spike train that is synchronous (i.e., in-phase) with the driving input, as long as the inter-spike distance, π, lies in the interval $[\pi_{min}, \pi_{max}]$. Here π_{min} and π_{max} are the minimum and maximum inter-spike gaps—i.e., minimum and maximum period of oscillation—for which the system can sustain synchronous activity [10]. A τ-and node behaves like a temporal AND node, and becomes active on receiving an uninterrupted pulse train. On becoming active, a τ-and node produces an output pulse train comparable to the input pulse train. The maximum number of distinct entities that may participate in an episode of reasoning is bounded by $\lfloor \pi_{max}/\omega \rfloor$ where we define ω to be the width of the window of synchronization—nodes firing with a lag or lead of less than $\omega/2$ are considered to be in synchrony. However, each distinct entity may participate in any number of bindings.

Each entity in the domain is encoded by a ρ-btu node. An n-ary predicate P is encoded by a pair of τ-and nodes and n ρ-btu nodes, one for each of the n arguments. One of the τ-and nodes is referred to as the *enabler*, *e:P*, and the other as the *collector*, *c:P*. In Figure 22.1a, enablers point upward while collectors point downward. The enabler *e:P* becomes active whenever the system is being queried about *P*. On the other hand, the system activates the collector *c:P* of a predicate *P* whenever the system wants to assert that the current dynamic bindings of the arguments of *P* match, or follow from, the knowledge encoded in the system. A rule is encoded by connecting (i) the collector of the antecedent predicate to the collector of the consequent predicate, (ii) the enabler of the consequent predicate to the enabler of the antecedent predicate, and (iii) the argument nodes of the consequent predicate to the argument nodes of the antecedent predicate in accordance with the correspondence between these arguments specified in the rule. A fact is encoded using a τ-and node that receives an input from the enabler of the associated predicate. This input is modified by *inhibitory modifiers*—links that impinge upon and inhibit other links[3]—from the argument nodes of the associated predicate. If an argument is bound to an entity in the fact, then the modifier from such an argument node is in turn modified by an inhibitory modifier from the appropriate entity node. The output of the τ-and node is connected to the collector of the associated predicate.

The Inference Process

Posing a query[4] to the system involves specifying the query predicate and its argument bindings. The query predicate is specified by activating its enabler with a pulse train of width and periodicity π . Argument bindings are specified by activating each entity, and the argument nodes bound to that entity, in a distinct *phase*, phases being non-overlapping time intervals within a period of oscillation.

We illustrate the reasoning process with the help of an example. Consider the query *can-sell(Mary, Book1)?* (i.e., Can Mary sell Book1?) The query is posed by (i) Activating the *enabler e:can-sell*; (ii) Activating *Mary* and *p-seller* in the same phase (say, ρ_1), and (iii) Activating *Book1* and *cs-obj* in some other phase (say, ρ_2). As a result of these inputs, *Mary* and *p-seller* fire synchronously in phase ρ_1 of every period of oscillation, while *Book1* and *cs-obj* fire synchronously in phase ρ_2. See Figure 22.1b. The activation from the *can-sell* predicate propagates to the *own*, *give* and *buy* predicates via the links encoding the rules. Eventually, as shown in Figure 22.1b, *Mary, p-seller, owner, buyer* and *recip* will all be active in phase ρ_1, while *Book1, cs-obj, o-obj, g-obj* and *b-obj* would be active in phase ρ_2. The activation of *e:can-sell* causes the enablers of all other predicates to go active. In effect, the system is asking itself three more queries—*own(Mary,Book1)?*, *give(x, Mary,Book1)?* (i.e., Did *someone* give Mary Book1?), and *buy(Mary,Book1)?*. The τ-and node F1, associated with the fact *give(John,Mary,Book1)* becomes active as a result of the uninterrupted activation it receives from *e:give*, thereby answering *give(x,Mary,Book1)?* affirmatively. The activation from F1 spreads downward to *c:give*, *c:own* and *c:can-sell*. Activation of *c:can-sell* signals an affirmative answer to the original query *can-sell(Mary,Book1)?*.

---

[3]A pulse propagating along an inhibitory modifier will block a pulse propagating along the link it impinges upon. In Figure 22.1a, inhibitory modifiers are shown as links ending in solid circles.

[4]We consider only yes-no queries. SHRUTI can also handle wh-queries [10].

The Type Hierarchy and Multiple Dynamic Instantiation of Predicates

Integrating a type hierarchy with the reasoning system allows the use of types (categories) as well as instances in rules, facts, and queries. Extending the reasoning system to incorporate multiple instantiation of predicates provides SHRUTI with the ability to simultaneously represent multiple dynamic facts pertaining to a predicate. Taken together, these extensions enable the reasoning system to represent and effectively reason with more complex rules and facts, and complex inferential dependencies including bounded symmetry, transitivity and recursion. The reader is referred to [6] for details.

22.2.3   Constraints on Rules and Inferences

SHRUTI is an *efficient* inference system. The size of a network encoding a given knowledge base is *at most linear* in the size of the knowledge base. The time taken to answer a query is proportional to the maximum of the time taken for activation to spread in the (i) rule-base and (ii) in the type hierarchy.

SHRUTI is also a *limited* inference system, and imposes several psychologically and biologically motivated constraints on the form of rules and facts that can be represented by the system and used in the reasoning process. These constraints make reasoning tractable and arise from the following fundamental restrictions, the motivations for which are discussed in [10] and [6]: (i) The number of distinct entities that can participate in any given episode of reasoning is bounded, and is typically a small number in the 7–10 range; (ii) The depth of reasoning is also bounded, and is generally a small value of about five; (iii) The number of predicate instantiations is limited to a small value around three.

22.3   Mapping SHRUTI onto Parallel Machines

SHRUTI is a structured connectionist network, which is one flavor of a massively parallel architecture. If we assign one simple processor to each node in the connectionist network and assume each link to be a communication channel between the processors, we have a specialized massively parallel system. Alternatively, we could simulate connectionist models on existing parallel machines. In [5], we argue that general purpose MIMD machines—i.e., distributed memory parallel machines—offer the best architecture for the simulation of structured connectionist networks.

There are several features of structured connectionist networks that facilitates their mapping onto parallel machines:

- Structured connectionist models are inherently parallel. However, in order to maximize the benefit of parallelism, the granularity of mapping must be tailored to the computational capabilities of the MPP processors.

- Given the simplicity of messages exchanged by nodes, it suffices to use interprocessor communication schemes optimized for short message packets—complex messages and communication protocols are unnecessary.

- Such networks are sparsely interconnected and hence, spreading activation touches only a small fraction of the nodes in the network.

In addition to the above, we make the following key assumptions:

- Since a knowledge representation system must be able to support any well-formed query as defined in Section 22.4.2, the source of initial activation and the depth to which it will propagate are unknown. This being the case, the system should be such that it will provide good performance *on average*.

- An episode of reasoning being very short, dynamic load balancing on the parallel machine is infeasible. We need to ensure that the static distribution of the knowledge base will guarantee good dynamic load balancing on average.

- The networks we deal with are large, since the system has to reason with very large knowledge bases.

Finally, as stated in Section 22.2, SHRUTI is a *limited* inference system, and imposes several psychologically and/or biologically motivated constraints on reasoning:

- The number of distinct entities that can participate in an episode of reasoning is bounded. This restricts the number of active entities, and hence, the amount of information contained in an instantiation. In turn, this limits the amount of information that must be communicated between predicates.

- Entities and predicates can represent only a limited number of dynamic instantiations. Entities and predicates therefore have a bounded number of banks, which constrains both space and time requirements.

- The depth of inference is bounded. This constrains the spread of activation in the network and therefore directly affects response time and resource usage.

In terms of mapping SHRUTI onto parallel machines, we exploit these constraints as much as possible in order to achieve efficient resource utilization and rapid response time. Of course, all these constraints are elastic and can be relaxed (incrementally) if one is willing to pay the associated performance penalty.

22.4 SHRUTI on the CM-5—Design and Implementation

This section describes the design and implementation of the SPMD asynchronous message passing parallel reflexive reasoning system—SHRUTI-CM5.

22.4.1 The Connection Machine CM-5

The Connection Machine model CM-5 [11] is an MIMD machine consisting of 32 to 1024 powerful processors. Each processing node is a general-purpose computer which can execute instructions autonomously and perform interprocessor communication. Each processor can have up to 32 megabytes of local memory and optional vector processing hardware. The processors constitute the leaves of a *fat tree* interconnection network, where the bandwidth increases as one approaches the root of the tree. Every CM-5 system has one or more control processors which perform managerial and diagnostic functions. A low-latency control network provides tightly coupled communications including synchronization, broadcasting, global reduction and scan operations. A high bandwidth data network provides loosely coupled interprocessor communication. A standard network interface connects nodes and I/O units to the control and data networks. The virtual machine emerging from a combination of the hardware and operating system consists of a control processor acting as a partition manager, a set of processing nodes, facilities for interprocessor communication and a UNIX-like programming interface. A typical user task consists of a process running on the partition manager and a process running on each of the processing nodes. SHRUTI-CM5 uses the CM-5 in message-passing SPMD mode where all communication, synchronization and data layout are under the program's explicit control.

As discussed in Section 22.1.1, though the CM-5 is technically a proprietary massively parallel supercomputer, it still conforms to the MIMD computing paradigm. It is therefore logically identical to a cluster computer constituted by independent workstations connected together by a high performance network.

22.4.2 The SHRUTI-CM5 Knowledge Base

We describe, at an abstract level, the knowledge representation and reasoning capabilities of SHRUTI-CM5. We limit ourselves to a brief description and refer the reader to [5], [10] and [6] for details regarding the form of the knowledge base, the propagation of activation under various conditions and an exhaustive listing of constraints that knowledge base elements must satisfy.

SHRUTI-CM5 is a mapping of SHRUTI onto the CM-5. Thus, SHRUTI-CM5 supports a rule-base, which can consist of rules and facts. In its most general form, rules are of the form:

$$\exists w_1{:}W_1, \ldots, w_p{:}W_p \ \forall x_1, \ldots, x_r, y_1{:}Y_1, \ldots, y_s{:}Y_s \ [\ P_1(\ldots) \wedge \cdots \wedge P_n(\ldots) \Rightarrow$$
$$\exists z_1, \ldots, z_t \ Q(\ldots)\ ].$$

$W_1, \ldots, W_p$ and $Y_1, \ldots, Y_s$ are types, and hence, represent concepts in the type hierarchy. The arguments of P_i $(1 \leq i \leq n)$ can be constants or any of the variables except $z_1, \ldots, z_t$. The arguments of Q are constants or any of the variables. In addition, rules must satisfy the constraints listed in Section 22.2.3.

Facts in SHRUTI-CM5 are of the form:

$$\exists x_1, \ldots, x_r, y_1{:}Y_1, \ldots, y_s{:}Y_s \ \forall z_1{:}Z_1, \ldots, z_t{:}Z_t \ [\ P(\ldots) \ ].$$

The arguments of P are either constants or any of the variables, with the constraint that a given x_i ($1 \le i \le r$) cannot occur in multiple argument positions.

The type hierarchy is specified by two kinds of *is-a* relations: *default is-a* relations and *labeled is-a* relations. Default *is-a* relations are of the form *is-a* (A, B), and explicates the fact that A is a subconcept (or instance) of B.[5] Labeled *is-a* relations have the form *is-a* R (A, B), where R is a relation. Such relations are interpreted[6] to mean A R B, i.e., $A \to^R B$.

Queries can be posed both to the rule-base and to the type-hierarchy. Rule-based queries have the form

$$\exists x_1, \ldots, x_r, y_1{:}Y_1, \ldots, y_s{:}Y_s \ \forall z_1{:}Z_1, \ldots, z_t{:}Z_t \ [\ P(\ldots) \ ] \ \textsf{rule-type?}$$

and result in activating the given query predicate and the entities which function as role-fillers for the predicate. Type hierarchy queries take the form: *is-a* relation (A, B)?. The system activates A in some phase ρ and waits for B to become active in the same phase. If B is a variable instead of a concept, we have an *enumeration* query.[7]

22.4.3   Design Considerations

In addition to the issues raised in Section 22.3, several other design details must be resolved when mapping SHRUTI onto any parallel machine. We discuss some of these in this section, and point out how they are handled when the target machine is the CM-5.

Granularity of Mapping

For effective mapping, the SHRUTI network encoding a knowledge base must be partitioned among the processors in the machine. The network partitioning can be specified at different levels of granularity. At the fine-grained *network-level*, the partitioning would be at the level of the basic nodes and links constituting the network. With *knowledge-level* mapping, knowledge base elements like predicates, concepts, facts, rules and *is-a* relations would form the primitives. The behavior of these primitives would be directly simulated without recourse to the underlying nodes and links constituting the primitive.

---

[5] Default *is-a* relations are encoded such that activation propagating upward reaches all super-concepts; activation propagating downward sets off a trail to reach subconcepts, superconcepts and superconcepts of subconcepts [6].

[6] Unlike default *is-a* relations, labeled *is-a* relations support only unidirectional activation propagation, from A to B.

[7] For enumeration queries, activation from A is propagated for a fixed number of steps. The active concepts in the system can then be enumerated.

The individual processing elements on the CM-5 are full-fledged SPARC processors. A subnetwork in the connectionist model can therefore be implemented on a processor using appropriate data structures and associated procedures without necessarily mimicking the detailed behavior of individual nodes and links in the subnetwork. We therefore argue that knowledge-level partitioning is the appropriate granularity for mapping SHRUTI onto the CM-5. Not only does this result in a faster and more efficient system, it also provides a conceptually clean mapping for the knowledge engineer or system designer to use.

Representing Synchrony

Temporal synchrony is a distinguishing feature of SHRUTI. Representing dynamic bindings using synchronous firing of connectionist nodes, and relating this to the spiking of neurons, is crucial in deriving several of the constraints and in defining reflexive reasoning.

SHRUTI-CM5 however, represents synchrony by using "tags" or "markers"—integers which take on a small number of values representing the phases in a cycle. Though temporal synchrony can be simulated on the CM-5 by using repeated processor synchronization, we have opted against this approach since such fine-grained and repeated processor synchronization would unnecessarily slow down the system. Although temporal synchrony is not explicitly used, we still exploit the characteristics and constraints derived from SHRUTI's temporal synchrony approach to reasoning.

Processor Allocation

Having chosen an appropriate granularity for encoding, the knowledge base can be viewed as a graph structure imposed on a collection of primitive knowledge base elements. With knowledge-level partitioning, predicates and concepts constitute the nodes of the graph, while rules and *is-a* relations represent links. In order to map the knowledge base onto an MPP machine, these primitive elements should be partitioned among the MPP processors. The *processor allocation scheme* directs the assignment of knowledge base elements to processors in the MPP. SHRUTI-CM5 supports two major processor allocation schemes: *random processor allocation* and *q-based processor allocation*.

Random Processor Allocation   Random processor allocation involves allocating knowledge elements to random processors. Every predicate and concept in the knowledge base is allocated to a random processor. When a predicate P is allocated to a processor p, all rules with P as the consequent, and all facts pertaining to P are assigned to processor p. In the type hierarchy, a relation of the form *is-a R* (A, B) is assigned to the processor housing A.

q-Based Processor Allocation   This processor allocation scheme is aimed at achieving a specified value of q (Section 22.5). q represents the probability of finding related elements on the same processor. In other words, for every predicate P, a fraction q of all the antecedent predicates of rules with consequent P will be located on the same processor as P. Random processor allocation is actually a special case of q-based allocation with $q = \frac{1}{N}$, where N is the number of processors in the parallel machine.

Attaining a specified value of q can be an arbitrarily hard task. In fact, depending on the structure of the knowledge base, it may be impossible to achieve certain q values. This being the case, the q-based processor allocation scheme tries to achieve a q value reasonably close to the target q value.

Load Balancing and Communication

Striking a compromise between load balancing and locality is an important aspect of mapping SHRUTI onto MPPs. In order to fully utilize the parallelism of the machine, computations must be uniformly distributed on all the processors. At the same time, interprocessor communication should also be minimized. Moreover, in a spreading activation system, activation originates at a small number of sources and spreads to some fraction of the network. Since the mix of queries posed to the system is not known in advance, the origin of activation is unknown. Hence, one can only aim at attaining optimal performance on an average (see Section 22.3). The processor allocation scheme is critical in achieving a balance between computation and communication.

SHRUTI-CM5 uses CMMD library functions [12] for broadcasting and synchronization, while almost all interprocessor communication is achieved using CMAML (CM Active Message Library) routines. *Active messages* provide efficient, low-latency interprocessor communication for short messages [12], [13]. Active messages are asynchronous (non-blocking) and have very low communication overhead. A processor can send off an active message and continue processing without having to wait for the message to be delivered to its destination—thereby overlapping computation and communication. When the message arrives at the destination, a handler procedure is automatically invoked to process the message. The use of active messages improves communication performance by about an order of magnitude compared with the usual send/receive protocol. The main restriction on such messages is their size—they can carry only 16 bytes of information. However, given the constraints on the number of entities involved in dynamic bindings (≈ 10), there is an excellent match between the size of an active message and the amount of variable binding information that needs to be communicated between predicate instances during reasoning as specified by SHRUTI. SHRUTI-CM5 exploits this match to the fullest extent.

22.4.4   Encoding the Knowledge Base

In the SHRUTI-CM5 system, the knowledge base is encoded by presenting rules and facts expressed in a human readable, first-order-logic-like syntax as shown in Figure 22.2.

```
/* Rules */
Forall x,y,z      [ give(x,y,z) => own(y,z) ];
Forall x,y        [ own(x,y) => can_sell(x,y) ];
Forall x,y        [ sibling(x,y) & born_together(x,y) => twins(x,y) ];
Forall x,y        [ sibling(x,y) => sibling(y,x) ];
Forall x:Animal, y:Animal [ preys_on(x,y) => scared_of(y,x) ];
Forall x,y,z Exists t     [ move(x,y,z) => present(x,z,t) ];

/* Facts */
give (John,Mary,Book1);
sibling(John, x);
Forall x:Cat, y:Bird [ preys_on(x,y) ];
Exists x:Robin [ own(Mary,x) ];

/* Type hierarchy */
is-a (Bird,Animal);
is-a (Cat,Animal);
is-a (Canary,Bird);
```

Figure 22.2 A knowledge base fragment in SHRUTI-CM5 syntax.

Knowledge encoding in SHRUTI-CM5 is a two-part process. First, a serial preprocessor running on a workstation processes the input knowledge base and partitions it into as many chunks as there are processors on the CM-5 partition. Second, each processor on the CM-5 independently and asynchronously reads and encodes the fragment of the knowledge base assigned to it by the preprocessor.

Each predicate and concept—nodes in the knowledge base graph—in the system is assigned to a processor, and is encoded on that processor using suitable data structures. The number of concept and predicate banks (and hence, instantiations) are bounded by system constants K1 and K2, corresponding to the multiple instantiation constants for concepts and predicates respectively.

Rules and *is-a* relations—links in the knowledge base—are also encoded using data structures, as are facts in the system. Rule structures are allocated on the processor containing the consequent predicate. In addition to linking the consequent and antecedent predicates, this structure also: keeps track of activation transformations (argument mappings) from the consequent to each antecedent predicate; identifies variables and conditions that need to be checked before firing the rule; maintains variables for determining query depth; and tracks collector activation. Fact structures are located on the processor containing the fact predicate and maintain pointers to concepts that are fillers for the predicate arguments. Structures for *is-a* relations are housed on the processor containing the first concept of the relation. Both rule and *is-a* links are labeled with the link type.

22.4.5   Spreading Activation and Inference

After the knowledge base has been encoded, queries can be posed in the rule-base or in the type-hierarchy (Section 22.4.2). Queries in the rule-base result in activating the relevant predicate and concepts as described in Section 22.2.2. Type hierarchy queries are posed by activating the first concept of the *is-a* relation. As noted in Section 22.4.3, integer markers are used to represent SHRUTI phases. The number of phases the system supports is dictated by the size of the active message (Table 22.1).

```
initialize statistics collection variables;

while (termination condition not met) {
  /* propagate activation in the type hierarchy */
  spread bottom-up activation;
  spread top-down activation;

  /* propagate activation in the rule-base */
  reverse-propagate collector activation;
  check fact matches;
  propagate enabler activation by rule-firing;

  update statistics collection variables;
}
```

Figure 22.3 The main propagation loop used in spreading activation during an episode of reasoning.

After a query has been posed to the system, the reasoning episode can be run to spread activation from the query predicate and/or concepts. The activation propagation loop is shown in Figure 22.3. Every processor in the CM-5 partition executes this loop independently and asynchronously. The steps in the loop are executed sequentially. Each step involves scanning the respective frontiers and taking appropriate action, as detailed in Section 22.4.5. After every iteration through the loop, each processor checks if the reasoning episode should be terminated. If termination conditions are satisfied, or if the global termination flag has been set by another processor, the processor breaks out of the loop and waits for other processors to do the same. When all processors exit the loop, they synchronize and output the results of the reasoning episode.

The termination condition in the activation propagation loop is met under two conditions: (i) An answer to the query is found or (ii) no answer is found after a specified number of iterations. The latter termination criterion is in keeping with the constraint that reflexive reasoning can occur only up to a bounded depth.

Interaction Between the Rule-Base and Type Hierarchy

Activation in the type hierarchy and rule-base spread independently of each other. But when matching facts or checking preconditions for firing rules, the firing phase of predicate arguments must be compared with the firing phase of respective concepts in the system. In order to make this efficient, whenever any concept becomes active by virtue of a default *is-a* relation (see Section 22.4.2), the firing phase of that concept is broadcast to all processors using a series of active messages. The processors cache this information and use it during fact matching and rule firing.

Since only default *is-a* relations play a role in answering rule-based queries, entity activation is not broadcast when the concept instantiation arrives via a labeled (i.e., non-default) *is-a* link. No interaction between the rule-base and type hierarchy is needed when dealing with type hierarchy queries.

Activation Frontiers

Each processing node maintains several activation "frontiers" for both the rule-base and the type hierarchy. Each frontier is essentially a list of predicates or concepts that are active and which need to be considered in the current activation propagation step. Several frontiers are maintained: (i) a rule-frontier consisting of consequent predicates of rules under consideration in the current step; (ii) a fact-frontier consisting of predicates for which fact matches need to be checked; (iii) a reverse-propagation-frontier for handling reverse-propagation of collector activation; and (iv) a type-hierarchy-frontier for activation propagation in the type hierarchy.

During each propagation step, all frontiers are consistently updated in preparation for the next step in the iteration. Frontier elements are deleted after performing the required operation. A frontier element will reappear in the frontier for the *next* propagation step only if the operation attempted in the current step was unsuccessful. This ensures that the same operation—like firing a specific rule, matching a fact or traversing an *is-a* link—is not unnecessarily repeated. All frontiers are created and deleted asynchronously on *each* processor. The frontier elements keep track of, among other things, the hop number (depth) of the instantiation, the link tag associated with the incoming instantiation, and the bank number under consideration.

Frontier Propagation

Frontier propagation algorithms are composed of a basic loop that traverses the frontier and processes frontier elements. Different frontiers require different processing, as dictated by the SHRUTI system architecture. Processing rule-, reverse-propagation- and type-hierarchy-frontiers result in activation propagation. Activation propagation is effected using active messages supported by CMAML routines. Sending an active message results in invoking a handler procedure either directly (for local destinations) or by sending an active message (for non-local destinations). Handler procedures for each type of frontier properly interpret the incoming message, direct the activation to the intended knowledge element, update book-keeping

Table 22.1 Active Message Structure for Rule-Base Activation Propagation

Bytes 0–3	4 bits	Enabler activation
	28 bits	Predicate arguments
Bytes 4–7	32 bits	Translation table index for destination predicate
Bytes 8–11	6 bits	Bank number
	6 bits	Hop number (depth)
	10 bits	Originating (source) processor index
	10 bits	Instantiation tag
Bytes 12–15	32 bits	Memory address of rule structure

information, and build a new frontier for the next iteration. A detailed description of the frontier propagation algorithms and their handler functions appears in [5].

Rule-frontier propagation results in spreading activation in the rule-base. All information needed to spread activation for a single predicate bank is contained in a single active message. The structure of this active message—i.e., the utilization of the 16 bytes of space available in a single active message—is shown in Table 22.1. Note how the restriction on the size of the active message constrains several of the system parameters. For example, the entire instantiation—including enabler and all argument activations—has to fit in 32 bits (bytes 0–3); SHRUTI-CM5 uses 4 bits for the enabler and a maximum of 7 arguments with 4 bits for each.

Fact-frontier propagation checks fact matches for predicates, and does not involve activation propagation. Concept instantiations are retrieved from the local entity cache on the processor. The cache is maintained as a hash table and access is therefore very fast. If the predicate collector does not become active, i.e., there were no successful fact matches, we need to recheck fact matches again since activation propagation in the type hierarchy could result in a fact match the next time around. Such predicates are added back into the fact-frontier for the next iteration.

Collector activation is reverse propagated when the reverse-propagation-frontier is processed. The activation value of the collector of the predicate originating the instantiation is computed as a function of the incoming antecedent predicate collector activations. By default, SHRUTI-CM5 uses a unit threshold function.

Type-hierarchy frontier propagation is used to spread activation in the type hierarchy. The type hierarchy frontier is scanned once, and for every entity on the frontier, bottom-up activation is propagated. If an entity appears in a default *is-a* relation, top-down activation is also propagated (Section 22.4.2). The 16 bytes (four 32-bit integers) of the active message are utilized as shown in Table 22.2.[8] As for

---

[8]In the active message structures for both the rule-base and the type-hierarchy (Tables 22.1 and 22.2), the *instantiation tag* field is used to implement selective activation traversal. Whenever the instantiation tag has a non-default value, activation can propagate on a link if and only if the link label matches the instantiation tag. This mechanism is used to ensure proper activation propagation in the presence of labeled *is-a* relations.

The location of predicates and concepts is encoded using *translation table indexes*. On a given

predicates, newly activated entities are added to the type-hierarchy frontier for the next iteration.

Multiple instantiation of predicates and concepts is handled procedurally. Whenever a predicate or concept receives activation, it is compared with existing activation in its banks. If the incoming activation is not already represented, it is deposited into the next available bank. The procedure ensures that (i) any predicate or concept represents at most a bounded number of instantiations (the number being decided by the multiple instantiation constants K1 and K2), and (ii) a given instantiation is represented at most once so that no two banks of a predicate or concept represent the same instantiation.

During a reasoning episode, SHRUTI-CM5 can be configured to collect statistics about various aspects of the system such as knowledge base parameters, processor communication and computation, and the reasoning process.

Table 22.2 Active Message Structure for Type Hierarchy Activation Propagation

Bytes 0–3	Translation table index for destination entity
Bytes 4–7	Entity activation
Bytes 8–11	Instantiation hop number (depth)
Bytes 12–15	Instantiation tag

22.5   SHRUTI-CM5—**A Mathematical Analysis**

A detailed mathematical analysis of SHRUTI-CM5 is presented in [5]. Here, we present a summary of the analysis, with emphasis on results and implications.

22.5.1   Motivation

The mathematical analysis of mapping of SHRUTI onto parallel machines is motivated by an attempt to derive general guidelines for effective implementation on massively parallel machines. We base our analysis on distributed memory massively parallel processors (MPPs) where processors operate autonomously and interprocessor communication is achieved by message passing. The results of the analysis provide pointers on efficient encoding of large knowledge bases on general purpose massively parallel machines. We also apply the results to validate the design of SHRUTI-CM5.

The analysis is based on the assumption that the crucial factor in effectively mapping SHRUTI onto MPPs is to appropriately control the distribution of knowledge base primitives among the processors of the MPP. Other than knowledge base distribution, most of the other factors that affect implementation efficiency—including

---

processor, this index to used to lookup the memory address of the structure encoding the predicate or concept under consideration.

the message passing overhead, knowledge base characteristics like number of predicates, branching factor, etc.—are beyond our control. Thus, given a particular machine and a knowledge base to be encoded on that machine, the assignment of knowledge base elements to the processors in the machine is the only major factor that is entirely under the control of the system designer. The analysis is aimed at deriving guidelines on optimum placement of knowledge base elements taking machine and knowledge base parameters into consideration. The analysis is based on the *average* case and yields optimum performance on average.

Processor assignment should take into account two factors—*load balancing* and *locality*. Load balancing attempts to maximally utilize available parallelism by providing a reasonably balanced load for all the processors in the machine. Locality, on the other hand, is aimed at minimizing communication overhead by clustering related elements on the same or nearby processors. The analysis introduces a single metric—the probability of finding related elements on the same processor—which is a measure of locality and implicitly determines load balance. We optimize response time with respect to this metric and study the results with a view toward designing large-scale knowledge base systems.

22.5.2   A Summary of the Analysis

Let $\mathbf{T}$ be the average response time for a given query Q. This time $\mathbf{T}$ is made up of two components:

$$\mathbf{T} = \mathbf{T}_{rb} + \mathbf{T}_{th} \tag{22.5.1}$$

where $\mathbf{T}_{rb}$ is the time needed to spread rule-base activation and $\mathbf{T}_{th}$ is the time needed to spread activation in the type hierarchy.

Defining q

In the process of spreading activation, predicates in the rule-base and entities in the type hierarchy need to communicate with other predicates and entities. These other predicates and entities could be located on the same processor or on another processor. Let prob(s) be the probability of finding related elements on the same processor. Thus, given a rule $P(\ldots) \Rightarrow Q(\ldots)$, prob($s$) is the probability that both P and Q are on the same processor. Similarly for A and B given *is-a(A,B)*. Let prob(c) $= 1 - $ prob(s) be the probability that related elements are on different processors.

We use q to denote prob(s), the probability of finding related elements on the same processor. Then, prob(c) $= 1 - q$. Let E_1 and E_2 be two related elements. Let E_1 be assigned to processor p. Then, E_2 is also assigned to p with probability q. With probability $1 - q$, E_2 is assigned to a processor other than p. When this happens, E_2 has a uniform probability of being assigned to any processor other than p. Thus, q is a measure of locality; the uniform assignment probability when two elements are on different processors ensures load balancing, subject to the locality requirements of q.

Since the rule-base and type hierarchy could have different connectivity characteristics, q_{th} and q_{rb} are used to represent q for the type hierarchy and rule-base, respectively.

Query Response Time

Using a series of derivations, in conjunction with simplifying assumptions and approximations, we obtain (see [5]):

$$\mathbf{T}_{rb} = \left\{ \frac{b_f^{D+1} q_{rb}^{D+1} - 1}{b_f q_{rb} - 1} + \frac{b_f^{D+1} - 1}{N(b_f - 1)} \right\} t_s \left\{ B_{rb} q_{rb} + (B_{rb} + 2) k_c (1 - q_{rb}) + K_{o_{rb}} \right\}$$

(22.5.2)

$$\mathbf{T}_{th} = \left\{ \frac{B_{th}^{D+1} q_{th}^{D+1} - 1}{B_{th} q_{th} - 1} + \frac{B_{th}^{D+1} - 1}{N(B_{th} - 1)} \right\} k_n \, t_s \left\{ B_{th} q_{th} + (B_{th} + 2) k_c (1 - q_{th}) + K_{o_{th}} \right\}$$

(22.5.3)

where

B_{rb} $B_{rb} = b_f + b_r$.

B_{th} $B_{th} = b_u + b_d$.

b_d Average downward branching factor, i.e., number of subconcepts (arising from default *is-a* relation) for an entity in the knowledge base.

b_f Average forward branching factor for predicates in the knowledge base, i.e., the average number of rules with the same predicate as consequent.

b_r Average reverse branching factor for predicates, i.e., average number of rules with the same predicate in the antecedent.

b_u Average upward branching factor, i.e., the number of *is-a* relations with the same entity as the first argument.

D Total number of iterations needed to answer a query Q. An iteration is defined below.

Hop Denotes activation traversing a rule or *is-a* link. Reverse propagation of collector activation is not considered to be a hop.

Iteration The computation needed to processes all knowledge base elements receiving activation which has traveled i hops constitutes *iteration i*. This includes the computation needed to process collector activation. One iteration could span several passes through the body of the activation propagation loop (Figure 22.3), and each pass could partially advance iterations for several i.

$K_{o_{rb}}$ The fixed, communication independent, cost for spreading activation and fact matching in the rule base. $K_{o_{rb}} = (B_{rb} + 2) k_{o_{rb}} + f k_{of}$, where $f k_{of}$ is the computational cost for fact matching.

$K_{o_{th}}$ The fixed, communication independent, cost for spreading activation in the type hierarchy. $K_{o_{th}} = (B_{th} + 2) k_{o_{th}}$.

k_c Communication cost. $k_c = \frac{t_c}{t_s}$.

k_n Number of entities appearing in the query Q.

$k_{O_{rb}}$ $(k_{O_{th}})$ Computational cost of spreading activation in the rule-base (type hierarchy). $k_{O_{rb}} = \frac{t_{O_{rb}}}{t_s}$ $(k_{O_{th}} = \frac{t_{O_{th}}}{t_s})$.

N Number of processors in the MPP machine, numbered from 0 to $N - 1$.

q Probability of finding related elements on the same processor.

q_{rb} (q_{th}) Value of q in the rule-base (type hierarchy).

$t_{O_{rb}}$ $(t_{O_{th}})$ Component of computation time, independent of the location of predicates (concepts), needed to process rule-base (type hierarchy) activation propagation.

t_s Time needed to call an empty *local* procedure on any processor.

t_c Time needed to call an empty procedure on a *remote* processor.

In order to minimize query response time $\mathbf{T}$ (Equation 22.5.1), we need to:

minimize $\mathbf{T}_{rb}$ with respect to q_{rb}, $0 \le q_{rb} \le 1$, **and**,
minimize $\mathbf{T}_{th}$ with respect to q_{th}, $0 \le q_{th} \le 1$.

To minimize $\mathbf{T}_{rb}$, we equate the derivative of Equation 22.5.2 to zero, and solve for q_{rb} to obtain those values of q_{rb} at which $\mathbf{T}_{rb}$ is stationary. $\mathbf{T}_{rb}$, and hence, $\frac{d\mathbf{T}_{rb}}{dq_{rb}}$, could be a high degree polynomial in q_{rb}, depending on the value of D, and may not have analytical solutions. We would therefore need to solve $\frac{d\mathbf{T}_{rb}}{dq_{rb}} = 0$ numerically to determine its roots. Since $0 \le q_{rb} \le 1$, we need to concern ourselves with only those values of q_{rb} in the interval $[0,1]$. $\mathbf{T}_{rb}$ has a minimum for $q_{rb} = q$, subject to the constraint $q \in [0, 1]$, if $\frac{d^2\mathbf{T}_{rb}}{dq_{rb}^2}\big|_{q_{rb}=q} > 0$. Similarly, $\mathbf{T}_{th}$ has a minimum for $q_{th} = q$, subject to the constraint $q \in [0, 1]$ if $\frac{d^2\mathbf{T}_{th}}{dq_{th}^2}\big|_{q_{th}=q} > 0$.

Example   Suppose the parameters in Equations 22.5.2 and 22.5.3 are set to: $B_{th} = 5$; $B_{rb} = 8$; $K_{O_{rb}} = 375$; $K_{O_{th}} = 175$; $k_c = 10$; $k_n = 1$; $N = 32$; $D = 10$ and $t_s = 10^{-6}$ sec. We have

$$\frac{d\mathbf{T}_{rb}}{dq_{rb}} = -35.0929 + 0.02283q_{rb} + 0.171225q_{rb}^2 + 1.1415q_{rb}^3 +$$
$$7.13437q_{rb}^4 + 42.8062q_{rb}^5 + 249.703q_{rb}^6 + 1426.88q_{rb}^7 +$$
$$8026.17q_{rb}^8 + 44589.8q_{rb}^9 - 9882.81q_{rb}^{10}$$

$$\frac{d\mathbf{T}_{th}}{dq_{th}} = -24.7944 + 0.0116q_{th} + 0.087q_{th}^2 + 0.58q_{th}^3 +$$
$$3.625q_{th}^4 + 21.75q_{th}^5 + 126.875q_{th}^6 + 725q_{th}^7 +$$
$$4078.13q_{th}^8 + 22656.3q_{th}^9 - 6982.42q_{th}^{10}$$

Numerically solving $\frac{d\mathbf{T}_{rb}}{dq_{rb}} = 0$ gives $q_{rb} \approx 0.43$. The equation has ten roots of which eight are imaginary. The two real roots are $q_{rb} = 0.428494$ and $q_{rb} = 4.69177$. Thus, $q_{rb} = 0.43$ is the only root in the interval $[0,1]$ and is a minimum since $\frac{d^2\mathbf{T}_{rb}}{dq_{rb}^2}\big|_{q_{rb}=0.43} = 689.473$ is positive. Similarly, we find the minimum of $\mathbf{T}_{th}$ to be at $q_{th} = 0.45$. Thus, for the parameter values listed above, the optimal values of q_{rb} and q_{th} are given by

$$q_{rb} = 0.43$$
$$q_{th} = 0.45$$

Figure 22.4 plots the variation of $\mathbf{T}_{rb}$ as q_{rb} varies in the interval $[0,1]$.

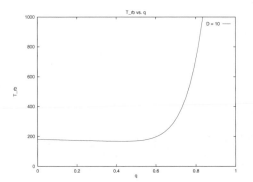 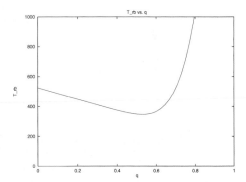

Figure 22.4 $\mathbf{T}_{rb}$ versus q_{rb}, when $k_c \approx k_{o_{rb}}$ (left, $k_c = 10$) and when $k_c \gg k_{o_{rb}}$ (right, $k_c = 100$).

22.5.3   Implications of the Analysis

Properties of $\mathbf{T}_{rb}$ and $\mathbf{T}_{th}$

Graphic exploration of the properties of $\mathbf{T}_{rb}$ and $\mathbf{T}_{th}$ indicate the following characteristics:

- Response time $\mathbf{T} = \mathbf{T}_{rb} + \mathbf{T}_{th}$ is quite close to optimal as long as q_{rb} and q_{th} have values below some "threshold." Response time increases rapidly when the q values increase beyond this threshold. This is more clearly illustrated by Figure 22.4, and is applicable as long as k_c is small, or comparable, to the computation cost ($k_{o_{rb}}$ and $k_{o_{th}}$) of processing a knowledge base element.

- When the cost of communication k_c becomes significantly large in comparison with the computation cost, system performance begins to deteriorate for small values of q, as can be seen in Figure 22.5. Under these conditions, deviating from the optimal values of q_{rb} imposes significant performance penalties. Figure 22.4 plots the variation of $\mathbf{T}_{rb}$ when k_c is significantly large. $\mathbf{T}_{th}$ behaves similarly.

- If the communication cost is much smaller than the computational cost of a knowledge base element, then $\mathbf{T}_{rb}$ and $\mathbf{T}_{th}$ are monotonically increasing, with a minimum value at $q_{rb} = q_{th} = 0$. In such a situation, the smaller the

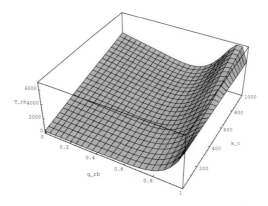

Figure 22.5 $\mathbf{T}_{rb}$ versus k_c and q_{rb}.

value of q, the better the response time. In other words, load balancing takes precedence over locality.

- Changing most of the other parameters results in shifting the "threshold," but does not significantly change the shape of the $\mathbf{T}_{rb}$ and $\mathbf{T}_{th}$ curves.

- As expected, reducing computational costs $k_{o_{rb}}$ and $k_{o_{th}}$ reduces the response time.

Estimating Parameters

The various parameters appearing in Equations 22.5.2 and 22.5.3 depend on the MPP machine, the knowledge base and the characteristics of the parallel reflexive reasoning system implementation. The machine parameters t_s and k_c can be determined by running relevant tests on the target machine. The number of processors on the machine fixes N. The computational costs $k_{o_{rb}}$, $k_{o_{th}}$, etc., depend on the characteristics of the parallel reflexive reasoning system, and can be estimated by running tests using the implementation in question. The branching factors B_{rb} and B_{th} are dependent on the knowledge base. These can be estimated by scanning the knowledge base and determining the average branching factors for the rule-base and type hierarchy. The query being posed determines k_n. For SHRUTI-CM5, estimates of these parameters are: $t_s \approx 5$ μsec and $k_c \approx 5$ since $t_c \approx 25$ μsec; based on experiments, k_o values range from 10–100, and knowledge base branching factors range from 2–10 (see Section 22.6).

Performance—Relation to Computation and Communication Costs

Response time is close to optimal for small values of q when the communication cost is small or comparable to the computation costs—i.e., load balancing is more important than locality. Thus, on machines like the CM-5, where communication is very efficient, especially when using low-overhead communication mechanisms like active messages, it is advantageous to aim for small q values. Fortunately, it is easy to obtain small q values using random processor allocation.

The analysis also provides guidance for distributing knowledge base elements when using more expensive communication schemes. For example, when mapping SHRUTI onto a network of workstations, we can use the results of the analysis to determine optimal distributions of a knowledge base using optimal q values.

Random Processor Allocation

When random processor allocation is used, predicates and entities are uniformly distributed over the processors of the MPP. We therefore have

$$q_{rb} = q_{th} = \frac{1}{N} \qquad (22.5.4)$$

When $N \gg 1$, i.e., the machine has a reasonably large number of processors, the above equation yields relatively small values for q_{rb} and q_{th}. For example, on a 32 node CM-5, we would have $q_{rb} = q_{th} = 0.03$. When the communication cost k_c is small compared to the computational cost of a primitive element, the analysis indicates that system performance, on average, is very close to optimal.

Furthermore, random processor allocation has the significant advantage of allowing incremental knowledge base encoding and processing, without the need for expensive static analysis of the entire knowledge base to ensure optimal processor allocation.

22.6   SHRUTI-CM5–**Experiments with Large Knowledge Bases**

In this section we present experimental results from running SHRUTI-CM5 on large knowledge bases. SHRUTI-CM5 has been tested using (i) artificial knowledge bases containing over half a million rules and facts, and (ii) WordNet, a real-world lexical database [7]. Results from these experiments bring out the effectiveness of SHRUTI-CM5 as a real-time reasoning system. We also experimentally validate some of the predictions made by the analysis in Section 22.5.

22.6.1   **Experiments with Random Knowledge Bases**

Part of the experimentation with SHRUTI-CM5 has been carried out using randomly generated *structured* knowledge bases. Though the individual knowledge base elements are generated at random, these elements are organized into *domains*, thereby imposing structure on the knowledge base. Each domain is a cluster of predicates along with their associated rules and facts. Domains can be of two types: *target* domains, which correspond to "expert" knowledge about various real-world domains, and *special* domains, which represent basic cognitive and perceptual knowledge about the world. A typical structured knowledge base consists of several target domains and a small number of special domains. The predicates within each domain are richly interconnected by rules. Predicates in each target domain are also richly connected by rules to predicates in the special domains. Predicates across different target domains, however, are sparsely connected. Predicates in two different special domains are left unconnected. The structure imposed on the knowledge base is a gross attempt to mimic a plausible structuring of real-world knowledge bases. This is motivated by the notion that knowledge about complex domains is learned and grounded in metaphorical mappings from certain basic, perceptually grounded domains [4].

In experimenting with SHRUTI-CM5, artificial knowledge bases used have over half a million elements. We present detailed results for a knowledge base identified as kb1, with about 250,000 rules, 250,000 facts and 50,000 predicates organized into 3 special domains and 150 target domains. Complete specification of kb1 and experimental results for the other knowledge bases are reported in [5].

Knowledge base kb1, containing about 500,000 elements, is split into five fragments of about 100,000 elements each. These fragments are loaded successively to investigate the effect of knowledge base size. Of the 500–600 queries generated, some 300 were answered and had depths ranging from 0 (fact retrieval) to 8. These queries were repeatedly run 5 times and the resulting data were used to investigate the performance of SHRUTI-CM5. In the experimental results plotted below, points represent average values, point ranges shown are 95% confidence intervals, while the curves shown are piece-wise best-fits. The curves are mostly quadratic best-fits, while some are exponential or linear best-fits.

Most of the experimentation has been carried out on a 32 node CM-5, while some have been run on 64 and 128 node machines. All experiments with random knowledge bases use random processor allocation. Furthermore, the reasoning episodes elicit little activity in the type hierarchy.

Knowledge Base Size and Query Depth

Figures 22.6–22.8 show the performance of SHRUTI-CM5 with random knowledge base kb1. Figure 22.6 plots response time for varying query depths and knowledge base sizes. When the knowledge base size is about 200,000 or smaller, the response time for different query depths is essentially linear since activation is, for the most part, confined to the query domain (the target domain in which the query was posed) and source domains. As the size of the knowledge base increases, with a proportional increase in average branching factor, the curve for each knowledge base size can be partitioned into two parts: For depths up to about 3, the response time increases steeply as all predicates in the query target domain and source domains become completely active; beyond that, the rate of response time increase is lower and depends on the number of active predicates in other target domains, and hence, on the number of rules that link predicates in different target domains. As the knowledge base size increases, one would expect the number of inter-domain rules to increase, and hence, the response time increases at higher rates, as brought out by the top three curves in the figure.

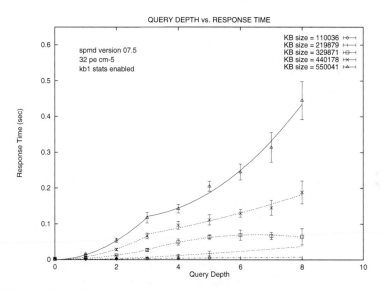

Figure 22.6 Query depth vs. response time. `Kb1` on a 32 PE CM-5.

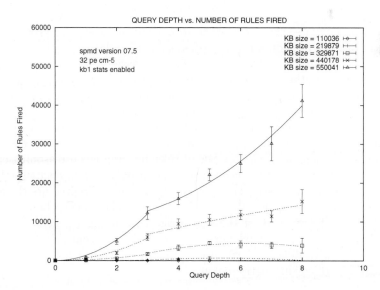

Figure 22.7 Query depth vs. number of rules fired in a reasoning episode. `Kb1` on a 32 PE CM-5.

Since firing a rule requires an active message and could potentially activate a new predicate, the number of rules fired (Figure 22.7), the number of active messages exchanged, and the number of active predicates in the knowledge base are closely related and influence response time, as is evident from the similarity between

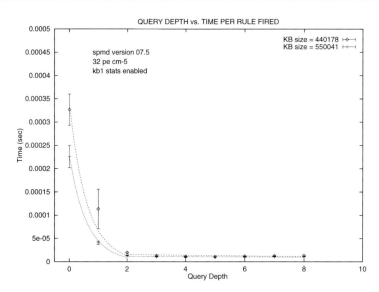

Figure 22.8 Query depth vs. time needed to fire a rule. Kb1 on a 32 PE CM-5.

Figure 22.7 and Figure 22.6. Note that response time would be proportional to the number of rules fired only if the processor load is relatively balanced; random processor allocation ensures that this is indeed the case.

Figure 22.8 shows the time needed to fire a rule as a function of knowledge base size and query depth. If r rules fire in a reasoning episode which takes t sec, we compute time per rule as $\frac{t}{r}$ sec. In plotting this graph, we are assuming that the computational cost of processing rules constitutes a major fraction, if not all, of the response time. In SHRUTI-CM5 with random knowledge bases, this assumption is valid when a reasonably large number of rules fire in a given reasoning episode. Under these conditions, the time needed per rule firing settles to a small, relatively constant value of about 8 μsec. The "time-per-rule" metric represents the average time needed to process a rule. We therefore expect this value to be constant for a given machine, irrespective of the knowledge base under consideration. That this is indeed the case is brought out in [5], where we present results from other knowledge bases with different structure and density. We discuss the effect of the CM-5 partition size on this metric below.

Effect of Parallelism

The speedup obtained for various query depths when running SHRUTI-CM5 on 64 and 128 node machines as compared to its performance on a 32 PE CM-5 is shown in Figure 22.9. The speedup is computed by taking the ratio of *average* response times for each knowledge base size and query depth. The maximum speedup possible for 64 and 128 node machines (over a 32 node machine) is 2 and 4, respectively. But the graphs in Figure 22.9 have values which are larger in some cases. This can be explained by the fact that the reasoning episodes run asynchronously; the number of rules fired and the number of active predicates could vary randomly. In fact, we observe that the number of rules fired is lesser in some cases and results in a faster termination of the reasoning episode.

The experimental results also show that the time-per-rule metric has a value of about 4 μsec on the 64 PE CM-5 and about 2 μsec on the 128 PE CM-5. We recall that the value was about 8 μsec for a 32 PE CM-5. These results can be related as follows: If r rules fire in a reasoning episode which takes t sec, we compute time per rule as $\frac{t}{r}$ sec. If the computational load is reasonably balanced—as is the case with random processor allocation—each of the N processors in the machine handles $\frac{r}{N}$ rules in t sec. Time per rule *per processor* would therefore be $\mathcal{T} = N\frac{t}{r}$. $\mathcal{T}$ is the time taken, on average, by any given processor to fire a single rule (subject to the assumptions stated earlier). Thus, $\mathcal{T}$ should remain constant irrespective of the number of processors on the machine and the structure of the knowledge base under consideration. We note that this is indeed the case:

$$32 \cdot 8 \; \mu\text{sec} = 64 \cdot 4 \; \mu\text{sec} = 128 \cdot 2 \; \mu\text{sec} = 256 \; \mu\text{sec}.$$

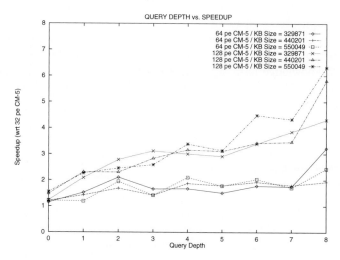

Figure 22.9 Speedup curves for 64 PE and 128 PE CM-5.

Real-Time Reasoning

As shown in the previous section, the time per rule per processor is approximately $\mathcal{T} = 256 \; \mu\text{sec}$. In other words, a processor takes 256 μsec to process a single rule. If $|KB|$ is the size of the knowledge base, and a fraction r of this knowledge base becomes active in an average reasoning episode,[9] the average number of rules fired

---

[9]We are still assuming that the computation cost is predominantly from the rule-base, and the computation is uniformly distributed on all the processors of the machine.

is $|KB| \cdot r$ and the average response time of SHRUTI-CM5 on a N processor CM-5 is $T = \frac{|KB|r\mathcal{T}}{N}$. In a real-time reasoning system, let T_{max} be the maximum response time that the application can tolerate. Then, we require:

$$T_{max} \leq \frac{k|KB|r\mathcal{T}}{N}$$

where k is a factor of safety whose value depends on the severity of the penalty for response time exceeding T_{max}. Based on this equation, we can estimate the largest knowledge base that will provide real-time responses on a given CM-5 partition. Conversely, given a knowledge base, we can determine the size of the CM-5 partition needed in order to obtain real-time performance.

22.6.2   Experiments with WordNet

WordNet is an on-line lexical database which attempts to organize information in terms of word meanings and their interrelationships [7]. One of the main reasons we have encoded WordNet on SHRUTI-CM5 is to evaluate its performance with large, non-random knowledge bases. In addition, we expect the parallel rapid reasoning ability of SHRUTI-CM5 and its rule-based reasoning capability to enhance the usability and applicability of WordNet.

WordNet (version 1.4) has about 95,000 words, grouped into 75,000 sets of synonymous words, or *synsets*. This database of about 75,000 synsets translates into a SHRUTI-CM5 knowledge base of about 880,000 *is-a* relations, using the mapping scheme detailed in [5]. The resulting knowledge base uses labeled *is-a* relations of the form *is-a R (A,B)* (which represents $A \rightarrow^R B$) to encode WordNet relations and synsets. For example, *is-a hypernym (Bird,Sparrow)* asserts that *Bird* is a hypernym (or superconcept) of *Sparrow*. Furthermore, the system supports both specific queries like *is-a hypernym (Bird,Sparrow)?* ("Is *Bird* a hypernym of *Sparrow*?") and enumeration queries like *is-a hypernym (Bird,x)?* ("Enumerate entities which have *Bird* as a hypernym").

Note that even though WordNet exercises only the type hierarchy of SHRUTI-CM5, the similarity of activation propagation in the type hierarchy and rule-base ensures that WordNet helps evaluate the effectiveness of SHRUTI-CM5 in terms of its ability to handle large knowledge bases in real-time.

Table 22.3 Average Response Time for a Sample of WordNet Queries

Query No.	SHRUTI-CM5 Query	Active Nodes	Response Time 32 PE CM-5	Response Time Serial	Speedup on CM-5
01	is-a hypernym (Bird,x)?	5150	0.02962	0.178118	6.013437
04	is-a hypernym (Entity,Sparrow)?	85312	0.274616	2.9662	10.801264
15	is-a similar (Heavy,Massive)?	181	0.0024312	0.0081617	3.357066
22	is-a haspart (Bird,x)?	120	0.0049411	0.0106783	2.161118

Table 22.3 lists 4 of the 34 queries used, along with response times, for the translated WordNet knowledge base on SHRUTI-CM5. Queries where the second

argument is a variable are enumeration queries. Queries were repeatedly run ten times and the times reported are average values. The number of nodes that are activated in the course of answering the query is shown in the column titled "active nodes." Column 5 of the table shows response time on a serial workstation for the WordNet queries. These times were obtained by compiling SHRUTI-CM5 to run on a serial SPARC server. The last column shows the speedup obtained on the CM-5 with respect to the serial workstation. The speedups are only approximate since the processor on the SPARC server and the CM-5 processing nodes are different, the CM-5 nodes being the slower of the two. We note that, with respect to serial SHRUTI-CM5, speedup on a 32 node CM-5 is better when the number of active elements is larger. This is to be expected, since effective use of parallelism will result when a large number of nodes are active—thereby providing better speedup.

22.6.3   Empirical Validation of the Analysis

As shown in [5], the actual response times for random knowledge bases and WordNet are very close to the values predicted by the analysis. The predicted and actual values agree closely as long as the assumptions made in the analysis are valid—which is the case when a large number of knowledge elements are active. The fact that the analysis accurately predicts performance with random knowledge bases and specialized real-world knowledge bases like WordNet, provides strong empirical validation of the theoretical analysis.

22.7   Conclusion

We described the design of an efficient knowledge representation and reasoning system capable of encoding very large knowledge bases and responding to a range of queries in real-time. In order to achieve speed and scalability we made use of massive parallelism in distributed memory parallel machines, and constrained the representational and inferential capabilities of the reasoning system according to the cognitively and biologically motivated limits suggested by SHRUTI.

Experiments show that the resulting system, SHRUTI-CM5 can effectively reason with respect to very large knowledge bases. We also mathematically analyzed the mapping of SHRUTI onto parallel machines from both a machine dependent and a machine independent point of view. This analysis relates average query response time to machine and knowledge base parameters. It also suggests an optimal mapping of a knowledge base onto the underlying parallel machine. The analysis also makes some interesting predictions about response time and its relation to computation and communication costs. One such prediction, validated by experimental data, indicates that average response time is close to optimal when knowledge base elements are mapped to random processors. In other words, load balancing is more critical than locality if communication cost is comparable to (or less than) the computational cost of processing a knowledge base element.

Applicability to Cluster Computing

In this work we made extensive use of the CM-5 for experimentation. However, almost all aspects of this work can be applied to any massively parallel (MPP) or symmetric multiprocessing (SMP) machine, including cluster computers, networks of workstations and clusters of SMP machines. The availability of message passing protocols like MPI makes it relatively easy to port SHRUTI-CM5 to other platforms. Similarly, the analysis presented here can be extended to other platforms.

The choice of an MPP machine like the CM-5 for experimentation was dictated more by availability than by anything else (Section 22.1.1.) We envision similar results with any machine that supports the equivalent of active messages. In Sections 22.3 and 22.4.3, we discuss general, machine independent aspects of mapping SHRUTI onto parallel machines—be they MPPs or cluster computers. The mathematical analysis in Section 22.5 is applicable to a range of parallel architectures when the various parmeter values are set appropriately. We would therefore like to highlight the fact that, even though most of the implementation and experimentation described here relate to MPPs, the basic design, analysis and mapping of SHRUTI onto parallel machines is applicable to a wide range of parallel architectures including cluster computers.

Furthermore, newer machines with faster processors have the potential for significant performance improvements. The CM-5 on which we ran our experiments (Section 22.6) had 32 MHz SPARC processors. Recent UltraSPARC workstations are an order of magnitude faster in raw speed. Our mathematical analysis suggests that a 10-fold increase in processor speed should lead to about a 10-fold increase in query response time, assuming that cluster computers based on the newer (and faster) processors would have networks which are comparable to the CM-5. In spite of advances in networking technology, it is a challenge to achieve communication performance comparable to the CM-5. Moreover, as processors get faster, communication overhead will start dominating query response time unless network performance improves proportionately. After all is said and done, we envision that efficient code running on modern cluster computers with fast, well-designed, state-of-the-art networks can achieve a 5—10-fold performance improvement over SHRUTI-CM5.

In summary, this work develops viable technology for supporting practical, large-scale real-time knowledge base systems on a wide variety of parallel architectures. It also provides new insights into mapping structured connectionist networks onto massively parallel machines. From a cognitive standpoint, the use of SHRUTI as the knowledge representation framework facilitates the exploration of common-sense reflexive reasoning.

22.8 Bibliography

[1] P. A. Carpenter and M. A. Just. Reading Comprehension as Eyes See It. In M. A. Just and P. A. Carpenter, (eds), *Cognitive Processes in Comprehension*. Erlbaum, 1977.

[2] J. Geller, H. Kitano and C. Suttner, (eds). *Parallel Processing for Artitificial Intelligence 3*. Elsevier Science, Amsterdam, 1997.

[3] R. V. Guha and D. B. Lenat. CYC: A Mid-Term Report. *AI Magazine*, vol 11(3), pages 32–59, 1990.

[4] G. Lakoff and M. Johnson. *Metaphors We Live By*. University of Chicago Press, Chicago, 1980.

[5] D. R. Mani. *The Design and Implementation of Massively Parallel Knowledge Representation and Reasoning Systems: A Connectionist Approach*. Ph.D. thesis, Department of Computer and Information Science, University of Pennsylvania, 1995.

[6] D. R. Mani and L. Shastri. Reflexive Reasoning with Multiple Instantiation in a Connectionist Reasoning System with a Type Hierarchy. *Connection Science*, vol 5(3 & 4), pages 205–242, 1993.

[7] G. A. Miller, R. Beckwith, C. Fellbaum, D. Gross, K. Miller and R. Tengi. Five Papers on WordNet. *Technical Report CSL-43*, Princeton University, 1990. Revised March 1993.

[8] L. Shastri. Why Semantic Networks? In J. F. Sowa, (ed), *Principles of Semantic Networks: Explorations in the Representation of Knowledge*. Morgan Kaufmann, San Mateo, CA, 1991.

[9] L. Shastri. Advances in SHRUTI—a Neurally Motivated Model of Relational Knowledge Representation and Rapid Inference Using Temporal Synchrony. *Applied Intelligence*, In Press, 1999.

[10] L. Shastri and V. Ajjanagadde. From Simple Associations to Systematic Reasoning: A Connectionist Representation of Rules, Variables and Dynamic Bindings Using Temporal Synchrony. *Behavioral and Brain Sciences*, vol 16(3), pages 417–494, 1993.

[11] TMC. Connection Machine CM-5 Technical Summary. *Technical Report CMD-TS5*, Thinking Machines Corporation, Cambridge, MA, 1991.

[12] TMC. *CMMD Reference Manual. Version 3.0.* Thinking Machines Corporation, Cambridge, MA, 1993.

[13] T. von Eicken, D. E. Culler, S. C. Goldstein, and K. E. Schauser. Active Messages: A Mechanism for Integrated Communication and Computation. In *Proceedings of the Nineteenth International Symposium on Computer Architecture*, ACM Press, 1992.

Chapter 23

MaRT: Lazy Evaluation for Parallel Ray Tracing

Sébastien Bermes,[1] Bernard Lécussan[1,2], and Christophe Coustet[3]

[1] ONERA-CERT, BP 4025 F-31055 Toulouse Cedex 4, France
[2] Supaero, BP 4032 F-31055 Toulouse Cedex, France
[3] META-CS, 99 av. Albert 1er, F-92500 Rueil-Malmaison, France

Email:*bermes@cert.fr, lecussan@cert.fr, coustet@cert.fr*

23.1 Introduction

23.1.1 Principles of Ray Tracing

Modeling the Imaged Scene

Ray tracing is a computational technique that can perform wave simulation at comparatively low cost. This technique can be applied in cases where the frequency of the simulated wave can be adapted to the minimal object size. This computational technique has been used for years in various application fields like image synthesis, seismic simulation, radar reflection and others.

In all of these application fields, ray tracing is done on a geometrical model made of surface primitives. Usually these primitives are triangular polygons, but when *polygon* is written in what follows, it can be read as *surface primitive*.

Depending on the case studied, the polygons can reflect either the sampling of a real object or the polygons can be the CAD representation of a virtual object. In the case where some spatial sampling of a real object is used, an infinity of equivalent sampling can be made. Additionally, changing the sampling accuracy can lead to a drastic change in the number of polygons, thus changing the magnitude of the ray tracing problem.

In addition to the geometrical description, the model describes the object regarding some relevant properties. To obtain a natural mapping of the properties on the geometry, it can be convenient to attribute a value for each property either to the polygons or to the polygon vertices. If either the resulting property sampling is not accurate enough or if a discontinue description is not desirable, the concerned properties can be interpolated to behave as continue ones.

In image synthesis, the basic mapped properties are color, reflectance and opacity. In addition, embedded in the texture description, many other properties can be mapped that are used to improve realism when rendering an image.

Simulating Waves with Rays

In the case where the problem is direct, as in seismic modeling or in spotlight simulation, the way in which the model is crossed by the wave coming from a given emitter is to be determined. Image synthesis, however, is a reverse problem where the characteristics of the wave coming to a given receiver have to be determined.

In the case that is of interest, that is to say, image synthesis, the way the scene is seen is to be determined. To do this, the received electro-magnetic wave (the received light) is discretized into a given number n of contributions coming from elementary directions. Each direction is explored reversely (that is, from the receiver to the model) to determine the observed color. This discretization leads to an image defined by n pixels, each of them having the color carried by the corresponding ray.

The ray tracing process consists in following the ray path through the model according to wave propagation principles. Thus, by following the initial propagation direction of the ray from the receiver to the model, the observed surface is found. This first calculation is a simple intersection problem between a segment (a part of the ray path) and a set of polygons (the description of the model). At the point where the first intersection occurs, if any, the observed color is to be determined. One sensible approach could mix the local color of the observed surface both with the color of the light illuminating it and with the color of the light coming indirectly from other surfaces. These indirect observations can occur through either a reflection process or a transmission process or both, according to the Snell-Descartes laws and the properties of the surface. The indirectly observed colors are determined in the same way through a new ray tracing process.

Computing Intersections—The Simplest Algorithm

The basic algorithm to discover an intersection point consists in testing for an intersection between the ray and every polygon in the model. If no intersection is found, the ray does not intersect the model and is processed in a specific way (the same given color could be attributed to all these rays). On the other hand, if there is at least one intersection, by sorting the intersection points according to their distance, it is easy to determine the first intersection along the ray path.

This algorithm clearly leads to a computation time proportional to the number of polygons of the model and cannot be applied to typically dimensioned models.

23.1.2   Accelerated Ray Tracing Techniques

As the previous algorithm suggests, the real limitation to the ray tracing technique is computation time spent in intersection calculations. Any attempt to improve the performances should be made here. More precisely, the first thing to do would be to lower the number of computed ray surface intersections.

Currently, the best acceleration techniques are those using space subdivision: Polygons are gathered in cubic space samples, called *voxels* (for volumic cell). For a given ray, first determine which voxels are along its path. Then search for an intersection with only the polygons in this succession of voxels, beginning with the first voxel crossed and stopping with the voxel where the first intersection occurs.

This algorithm introduces a preliminary calculation to find out the succession of crossed voxels, but as it saves most of the time spent in testing for ray-polygon intersections, the improvement is huge. The two main approaches to subdivide space are regular grids [1] and recursive subdivisions. A special case of recursive subdivision, where the subdivision factor is two, are the well known octrees [2]. As an octree is the simplest case of recursive subdivision, all the material in this chapter is based on octrees, but the same could apply to general recursive subdivisions.

While a regular grid is a regular subdivision of space, an octree is recursive and irregular: A voxel is subdivided in eight smaller voxels only if it contains too many surfaces to be efficiently handled at once (see Figure 23.1 for an example in 2D).

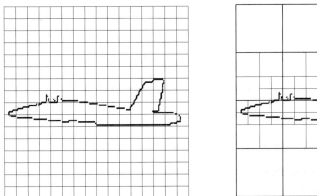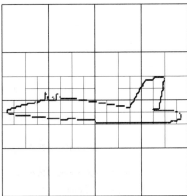

Figure 23.1 Regular Grid Subdivided Space vs. Octree Subdivided Space.

With a regular grid, all the voxels have the same size, and the most appropriate one has to be determined. Remembering that the main reason to subdivide space is to decrease the number of segment polygon intersection tests, it can be concluded that smaller is better insofar as a smaller voxel size further reduces the number of polygons in the fullest voxels.

Unfortunately, the amount of memory needed to voxelize a problem of the typical size at this level is more than one order of magnitude over the memory available on common computers. Despite the fact that regular grids determine the succession of voxels very efficiently, the memory cost involved makes them unusable.

On the other hand, by using slightly more complex data structures, octrees, lead to an increased cost in finding the succession of voxels, but with substantial savings in memory. Approaches based on recursive subdivisions can be considered as one of the most appropriate on common computers.

23.1.3   The Time-Memory Balance

In an octree, voxels have different sizes. Empty voxels have the maximum possible size (because an empty voxel is never subdivided); the others are subdivided at a given level. Once more, the size the most appropriate seems to be obtained by subdividing every voxel until a smaller voxel size has reduced the number of polygons in the fullest voxels. But by using this basic rule, the memory available on a common computer is just large enough to voxelize a typical small model. The point is that on a real world computer, an algorithm that does not comply with the available memory size cannot be used.

The available memory size has to be introduced in the subdivision criteria to obtain this new voxelization policy: The octree can be subdivided until a smaller voxel size has reduced the number of polygons in the fullest voxels and has complied with the actual memory size.

To increase the efficiency of ray tracing, a low level subdivision of space is desirable, leading to a huge amount of very small voxels. As, for conventional problems, the available memory is not large enough to subdivide all of the model at this desirable level, a compromise has to be found: Some parts of the model are not subdivided at the desirable level.

Memory, then, is a kind of potential: When used properly in the model subdivision, memory leads to performance improvement (be careful not to waste it!). Any memory saving is a potential computation time improvement.

23.2   On Ray Tracing Parallelization Techniques

As explained in the previous Section, in the basic ray tracing algorithm, one ray is cast for each pixel of the frame and all the rays are independent. This makes two basic parallelization strategies straightforward: Either distribute a certain number of rays to each processor, each processor working on one part of the frame, or partition the whole data base into many sub-volumes which are loaded into the local memory of each processor and cast all the rays on each sub-volume [3].

The first method is conventionally called the Image Parallel approach where each processor must have the complete scene description in its local memory.

The second method is named the Object Space approach where each processor computes the whole ray tracing related to the allocated object parts. The size and shape of each sub-volume can be statically or dynamically determined to optimize the workload among processors.

The parallelization of the ray tracing algorithm uses the classically hierarchical bounding volume tree [5] to reduce the number of intersection tests between rays and polygons. As the percentage of intersection tests in ray tracing computation represents more than 90% of the overall computation, the construction and the distribution of the tree is the crucial point of the algorithm.

23.2.1   The Image Parallel Approach

The main steps of the Image Parallel algorithm are as follows:

1. The master processor replicates the data base file on each computer file system; this task is part of a preprocessing step.

2. It builds the tree over the whole extent of the complete data base; this is done in parallel on each processor and takes the same amount of execution time as does the whole tree built on each processor's local memory.

3. It then computes ray tracing for the subset of rays assigned to each processor; this is done in parallel, but each ray will take a different amount of time to compute, depending on the complexity of the intersections that occur.

4. It collects results and display image; this is also a sequential task.

The main drawback of this approach is that the size of the scene data base is limited by the size of the local memory of the processor with the lowest memory. There have been many schemes proposed by authors [4], [6] to solve this. But these solutions induce extra communication costs to access remote data.

Furthermore, as only a subset of rays is cast on each processor, only part of the whole hierarchical tree is needed; the subtrees which are outside the scope of the local rays are built during step 2 but not used.

23.2.2   The Object Parallel Approach

The main steps of the Object Parallel strategy are as follows:

1. The master processor parses the data base file and does the data base partition; this task is part of a preprocessing step.

2. It then loads the data partition on the main memory of each processor; this is a sequential step.

3. Then it builds the tree over the part of the data base allocated to each processor; this is done in parallel on each processor but will take a different amount of time to compute, depending upon the complexity of the sub-volume.

4. Object Parallel Strategy computes ray tracing to the assigned regions on each processor; this is done in parallel, but the processing cost of each task could be different and communication messages could be needed to fetch remote data allocated on the neighboring processor.

5. It collects results and displays an image: this is also a sequential task.

During step 3, the ray information must be communicated to the processors assigned to the particular portion of the data base through which the rays propagate. As communication could be costly, data partionning algorithms are needed to balance the workload among processors in order to reduce some of the communication overhead. The main difficulty of this approach is to find an optimum between two opposite requirements - allocating small scattered regions to improve load balance versus allocating big contiguous regions by exploiting ray coherence to limit the number of communications.

23.2.3   Parallel Computation Analysis

Speedup

Much research has been done in the efficient implementation of parallel ray tracing algorithms to achieve a real speedup with several processors [4], [6].

A common misunderstanding of speedup evaluation is to measure speedup with respect to the version computed on one processor; sometimes, it could be read that super linear speedup could be reached, which is in fact wrong. Speedup obtained with N processors must always be measured with the respect to the best sequential version, as stated by Equation 23.2.1.

$$\text{Speedup} = \frac{\text{best sequential version computation time}}{\text{execution time with N processors}} \qquad (23.2.1)$$

Another classical pitfall is to consider the speedup of only the main processing task instead of all the steps of the algorithm; in fact, according to the Amdahl's law (see Equation 23.2.2), the sequential part of a parallel computation drastically reduces the speedup achieved with a parallel machine [9].

$$\text{Speedup} = \frac{1}{(1 - \text{fraction}_{enhanced}) + (\text{fraction}_{enhanced}/\text{speedup}_{enhanced})} \qquad (23.2.2)$$

Amdahl's law states that "the performance improvement to be gained from using parallel resources is limited by the fraction of the time those resources can be really used."

As an example, consider a process where 1% of the total time is sequential and 99% of the computation can be distributed over 100 processors; the theoretical maximum speedup which can be obtained is:

$$\text{Speedup} = \frac{1}{(1 - 0.99) + (0.99/100)} = 50.25$$

The overall process computation time could not be greater than 50 times the sequential version, but 100 processors have to be used. So, one of the major goals of parallel implementation must be to reduce the sequential part of the algorithm as much as possible before trying to optimize the workload among parallel processors.

Communication Overhead

As described previously, parallel implementation of the ray tracing algorithm needs communication between processors to fetch remote data allocated on neighboring processors or to send ray information to the particular portion of the data base through which the rays propagate. Because improvement is continually made on processor performance and network bandwidth, it is interesting to look at the different costs involved in communication between two processors to understand where the bottleneck is in the process of sending a message. For example, take a conventional system with a 500 MHz clock frequency processor, one instruction by cycle and 2 Gigabit/s network bandwidth. Emission can be split into the following phases where each cost is indicated in processor cycles. For simplicity of the demonstration, messages of 1K byte length are considered (see Figure 23.2).

l : time for the emitter to place the message in an output buffer.

b : determines the emitter to network bandwidth.

n : time to prepare each packet of the message and place it in an output queue for transmission.

m : time to activate the message handler.

h : time needed for the message handler.

w : hardware link latency.

Figure 23.2 Communication Parameter Costs (in Processor Instructions).

This shows that on today's real system, communication overhead is close to 4,000 instructions, which implies large granularity tasks to amortize this cost. Furthermore, it is illusive to believe that technological improvement can come in the future unless hardware support is not forthcoming to reduce protocol costs. This means that the parallel algorithm must reduce the number of messages as much as possible or bypass the problem by overlapping the communication cost with useful computation. In any case, the 500 instructions overhead at the beginning of the protocol cannot be avoided.

23.2.4   Synthesis

Many lessons can be drawn from previous analysis to conceive an efficient parallel solution of ray tracing algorithm. First, reduce the sequential part of the parallel version as much as possible. Second, find independent tasks to limit the number of messages while keeping all the processors busy. And third, make large task granularity to efficiently exploit the processor pipe-line.

Thus, ray tracing algorithm restructuring seems to be the only way to improve performance on parallel architecture while respecting those requirements. A new image parallel algorithm is proposed which bypasses the main drawbacks of the conventional approach. This is summarized in the following steps:

1. In a preprocessing step, replicate the data base file on each file system of distributed computers.

2. Assign a certain number of rays to each processor, but build only the necessary part of the tree needed for local rays in each local memory.

3. Compute ray tracing for the subset of all rays assigned to each processor. Find an optimum for task granularity to achieve an acceptable workload for each processor.

4. Collect the results and display the image.

In this way, there is no more remote data access for part of the tree and the sequential part of the algorithm is limited to step 4. The major points are to determine an algorithm that will dynamically assign part of the tree needed in each processor and to reduce the load imbalance in order to keep each processor busy as much as possible. This clearly demonstrates that the hybrid method which combines static and dynamic strategy produces high performance on a variety of images and large computer systems with hundred of processors [8]. In the next chapter, the detailed solution to implement step 2 and step 3 will be explained and experimental results will be given.

23.3   MaRT: a Lazy Ray Tracer

In this paragraph, the principles of the lazy ray tracer are discussed. The basis is a dynamically generated acceleration data structure: the lazy octree.

23.3.1   On Lazy Evaluation

Lazy evaluation comes from functional languages where, as opposed to imperative languages, no sequence of action is given but all of the calculus is evaluated with functions. In such a language, a program is nothing but a set of functions. Each function results in calling up other functions. Running a program means calling one function with various arguments.

One way for evaluating functional programs, called *graph reduction*, consists in representing the calculus as a graph tree, where nodes are functions, the branches are its arguments and leaves are values. Executing a program consists in reducing its associated tree to a minimal representation called *normal form*. When trying to reduce a given node (i.e., evaluating a function from its arguments), either first reduce all child branches, then evaluate the function on these leaf arguments, or start the function evaluation and reduce the child branches only when necessary. The first approach is called *strict evaluation*, the second one *lazy evaluation*.

Lazy evaluation defines potentially infinite data; in the following example a function is defined that builds the list of prime numbers, without any limit a priori:

```
build_prime_list (n)
 if (is_prime(n),
     return ( cons ( n, build_prime_list ( n + 1 ))),
     return ( build_prime_list (n+1)))
```

Where cons (a, l) adds a in head of the l list.

This is a recursive function without a limit test. This could not possibly run with strict evaluation, as the calculus tree is infinite and could never be reduced.

The following function call examples will give those results:

```
affect(PRIME_LIST, build_prime_list(1))
-> 1
nth(4, PRIME_LIST)
-> 5
nth(6, PRIME_LIST)
-> 11
nth(2, PRIME_LIST)
-> 2
```

Lazy evaluation delays the evaluation of `build_prime_list` as long as possible. In the above process, the affectation does not effectively call the function, but just associates the data definition `PRIME_LIST` to a given calculus tree. The following calls will make the evaluation of `build_prime_list` necessary, but only as long as the data is useful. For the first call to `nth`, only the first four prime numbers are actually computed. Two more are built in the next call, and the last one needs no new calculus, as the prime list has already been constructed up to the sixth element.

Unfortunately, lazy evaluation has a cost, as delaying evaluation also means storing the data necessary to resume the evaluation when needed. Though full lazy programming is to be avoided, it is possible to localize the parts of the program that will most benefit from laziness, and to limit lazy evaluation for those specific functionalities.

Lazy evaluation will be used to define the MaRT acceleration data structure, an octree built the same way the prime list was built.

23.3.2   The Lazy Octree

Description

The lazy octree is a potentially infinite tree. This means that no actual limitation needs to be defined for its construction, as limits will come from ray tracing. To explain this more clearly, how to simulate lazy evaluation on such a structure will be described. These techniques could be implemented in any imperative language.

Voxels in the tree can have three different status:

- Empty: The voxel contains no surfaces.

- Node: The voxel is not empty, and its eight child voxels are already built.

- Leaf: The voxel is not empty, but its child voxels are not yet built.

Lazy evaluation will allow a leaf voxel to be transformed into a node voxel. This process is called voxel evaluation. At the beginning of a simulation, i.e., before the first ray is cast, the octree is reduced to a single leaf voxel. The octree will be actually built during the ray tracing process.

During the voxel evaluation process, all the surface-child voxel intersections have to be computed. Though a full lazy process would delay those computations, allowing some child voxels to be fully computed and some others not, it appears to be cheaper to build all child voxels at once. First, it is faster to project a surface onto a set of adjacent child voxels than to separately compute each surface-child voxels projection, and does not cost much in the upper levels of the octree. Second, in the lower levels of the octree, statistics show that if one child voxel has to be built, most of the others will, too.

Ray-Voxel Intersection

Each time a ray hits a voxel, it is to be decided whether the polygon description of the voxel is sufficient or not for an analytic computation. Usually this boundary condition depends on the number of surfaces in the voxel, or on the relative size of the voxel compared to the ray solid angle. If this boundary condition is not reached, the intersection with all child voxels along the ray path has to be computed. If the voxel is a leaf voxel, it is evaluated in order to transform it into a node voxel.

In order to avoid expensive tests during ray-voxel intersection computation, some boundary conditions can flag a voxel. For a node voxel, it is always faster to explore the child voxels, since they are already built. These node voxels can be flagged "go deeper," i.e., each time a ray hits a node voxel it considers that no boundary condition has been reached. A leaf voxel that fits a ray-independent boundary condition (for example, due to the number of surfaces) can be flagged "stop here," as the boundary condition will be the same for all rays. For ray-dependent boundary conditions, a valid (and speed improving) approximation is to say that the condition test for the first ray that hits the voxel will give the same result as for all the other rays. Thus for each voxel, the test is necessary only the first time the voxel is hit, and the test result can flag "go deeper" or "stop here" to the voxel.

Contrary to methods using a static octree, most voxels actually built were hit at least once by a ray, and no useless voxel was built. This can result in large amounts of memory saves due to hidden parts of a scene: As no rays cross those areas, no voxels are built there. If the ray uses a solid angle method to avoid a deeper exploration, it can also save voxel construction in deep octree branches.

Figure 23.3 gives an example of the evaluation state of an octree after a phase of ray tracing. Rays were shot from the top left corner down to the whole area. No secondary rays were shot. White voxels are empty voxels, black are leaf voxels flagged "stop here," and the others are unflagged leaf voxels that were not hit by rays. Some of these voxels would be node voxels in a static octree, thus laziness can avoid the construction of useless data.

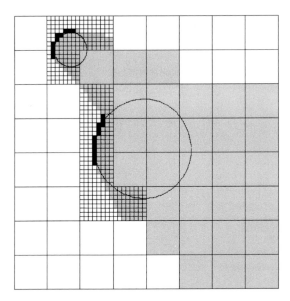

Figure 23.3 Example of Lazy Evaluation on an Octree.

23.3.3   Lazy Construction of Polygon Data

The lazy construction of the octree can save large amounts of memory size. But in very complex scenes — containing hundreds of thousands or millions of surfaces — the simple loading of the surface data can dramatically increase the total memory cost. One part of this data cannot be compressed without the risk of an expensive dynamic uncompression, such as the vertices for a polygon description, and the vertex list describing a polygon.

But what about that memory cost in the case of a scene described with triangular polygons? Each polygon has 3 vertex pointers plus 1 texture pointer, for a total amount of $4 \times 4 = 16$ bytes. Statistically there is one vertex for two polygons, each vertex costs $8 \times 4 = 32$ bytes in single precision or 64 in double. The total incompressible amount for n polygons is $n \times (16 + 32/2) = n \times 32$ bytes in single precision or $n \times (16 + 64/2) = n \times 48$ bytes in double precision.

Additionally, several coefficients are usually pre-computed for each polygon. This will highly improve the polygon-ray and polygon-voxel intersection computation speed. These coefficients can be quite burdensome in the total memory size: About 15 floating point coefficients are needed for each polygon, which results in 60 bytes in single precision or 120 in double. With these coefficients, the initial data size is nearly tripled.

However, those coefficients are not systematically useful for ray tracing: All polygons will not necessarily be hit by rays, and many voxel-polygon intersection can be solved without the use of these coefficients in the case where one vertex belongs to the voxel. Laziness can be used to allocate and compute those coefficients only when needed. Assume that the coefficient list for each polygon is empty and non allocated at the beginning of the ray tracing process. Each time the coefficient list becomes actually useful, it is allocated and computed. It costs only one pointer test for each access and it can save a large amount of memory.

23.4   Parallel MaRT

23.4.1   Implementation of Parallel MaRT

A Natural Data Balance

The simplest way to parallelize ray tracing for the best load balance is to segment a picture in small sub-pictures and dynamically distribute the computation of those sub-pictures to the processors. In the case of a distributed memory parallel system, the problem is to distribute data according to what each processor actually needs. Lazy evaluation of the octree and lazy construction of polygon data enables a natural data distribution over the processors: each processor will build only the data it needs, without having to build the entire data structure or to copy data from a remote processor.

But the efficiency of lazy evaluation in term of memory cost strongly depends on the coherence of rays. So the main points to pay attention to are the distribution of the sub-picture tasks over processors, and the coherence of various tasks in terms of ray space.

Task Granularity

The granularity (the sub-pictures size) has to follow two rules for the best results:

- Be large enough to reduce the communication overhead.

- Create many more sub-pictures than processors to minimize inactivity.

The experiments show that 10x10 pixel sub-pictures bring little overhead, which becomes negligible for 50x50 pixel sub-pictures. Such a granularity works with the second rule above, as most processed pictures will have hundreds of sub-pictures.

Task Coherence

The task coherence problem is closely linked to the laziness efficiency. The goal is to try to have each processor work on the smallest space area possible, and to avoid data redundancy with other processors.

In a sub-picture task scheme, data redundancy can be described in two categories. First, high level redundancy is around the upper levels of the octree. Processors all need to fully develop the first levels of the octree. As these voxels are very often read by the ray tracing process, avoiding this redundancy would bring an unacceptable overhead. The second redundancy is the one associated with low levels of the octree. Unlike the previous one, this redundancy can be partially avoided with task coherence. An important part of this redundancy is due to the adjacency of sub-pictures tasks treated by two different processors: Along the edge of the sub-picture, rays are nearly the same and need the same octree data to compute. The main goal of task coherence is to have processors work on adjacent sub-pictures and to share as few sub-picture edges as possible with other processors.

One accurate and simple way to achieve task coherence is to select the first sub-picture task of each processor uniformly on the edges of the main picture, and to choose the others as close as possible to the first one.

In comparison with a random task distribution, a test on picture f1 (Figure 23.4) shows that a coherent distribution saves 30% of memory space and 13% of cpu time. Thus this distribution is not the most coherent that can be hoped for, and results could be improved even more with a better distribution scheme.

Sequential and Parallel Parts of the Process

The only fully sequential parts of the implementation are input and output. All of the ray tracing process is fully distributed.

Voxelization is separately computed on each processor, according to the lazy evaluation process. A part of redundancy is to be expected, essentially for the upper levels of the octree, but as each processor develops only the data it needs, the voxelization process can not be considered as sequential.

23.4.2 Results

Test Scenes

Parallelization of ray tracing algorithms can avoid the main pitfalls by not taking into account the voxelization time or by considering the large images calculated on a small number of computers. Thanks to a large granularity and by ignoring the sequential part of the algorithm, it is possible to speed up the parallel computer by 90%. The research tests presented hereafter do not avoid these difficulties. What is interesting is the speedup of the parallel computer and the increased memory needed for the whole image computation in different cases.

Four test scenes with increasing number of surfaces were chosen to study the efficiency of laziness. All scenes have reflective surfaces which make the rays go in any direction of space, reducing the ray space coherence.

The description of the four scenes follows (see Table 23.1).

Table 23.1 Test Scenes

Name	f1	f2	g8	g9
Number of surfaces	59,840	210,040	786,432	3,145,728
Number of rays	642,222	765,176	2,766,478	2,839,037
Data size (MB)	2	7	25	101
Max data size (MB)	6	21	77	302
Total static size (MB)	55	127	132	335

Data size: the incompressible size (it includes the vertices and the triangle).

Max data size: the sum of data size and the maximal polygon size (i.e., with allocation of all polygon coefficients).

Total static size: the total size needed for a non-lazy simulation (Max data size + Max octree size).

Figure 23.4 shows the corresponding pictures. All pictures are 500x500 pixels.

Simulations

The simulations were run on a homogeneous Ethernet network of HP workstations 715/33 (each with 64 MB) and an IBM SP2 parallel architecture (each processor with 256 MB).

Figures 23.5 and 23.6 show the evolution of the speedup (see Equation 23.2.1) with the number of processors. I/O times are not taken into account in the recorded times.

Figures 23.7 and 23.8 show the evolution of the Memory factor. The memory factor is given by the formula:

$$\text{Memory factor} = \text{Total static size/Max total lazy size} \qquad (23.4.1)$$

where Max total lazy size is the maximal size used among the processors.

All speed results for g8 and g9 do not appear, for memory limitation reasons: g8 could not be simulated on the HP network except with 16 processors, and g9

*f*1   *f*2

*g*8   *g*9

Figure 23.4 Test pictures.

could not be loaded at all, due to the incompressible data size. On the parallel architecture, g9 could be run only with nine processors, so any sequential reference for the speedup calculus is unavailable.

Analysis of Speed Factors

A first important remark is that the results are similar on both architectures. This tends to prove that communication overhead is nearly negligible, as it would be much higher on the network than on the parallel architecture.

Now look at the speedup. In Table 23.2 the maximal theoretical speedup was evaluated in the case of a statically pre-built octree. In such a case, the max speedup for n processors would be:

$$\text{Max speedup} = \frac{\text{Total time}}{(\text{Voxelization time} + \text{Ray Tracing time} / \text{ n})} \qquad (23.4.2)$$

The lazy speedup shown in Figures 23.5 and 23.6 is much better than the the-

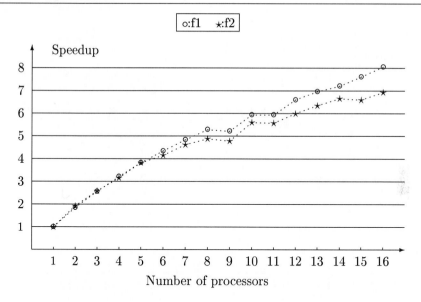

Figure 23.5 CPU results for a network of workstations.

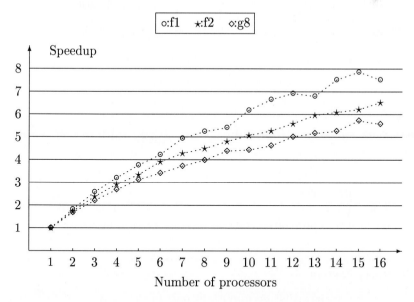

Figure 23.6 CPU results for a parallel architecture.

oretical non-lazy speedup given in Table 23.2, which proves that one part of the voxelization process was distributed over the processors: Lazy evaluation gives a natural data distribution over the processors. A reverse calculus from speedup

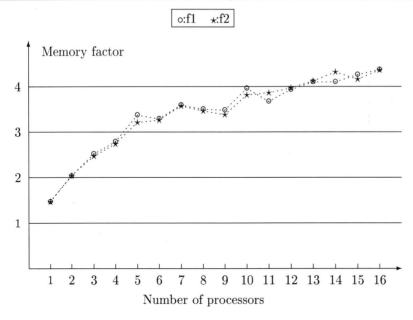

Figure 23.7 Memory cost results for a network of workstations.

Table 23.2 Theoretical Non-Lazy Speedup

Name	f1	f2	g8	g9
Seq. voxelization time / Total seq. time	26%	39%	27%	27%
Non-lazy max speedup (8 proc.)	2.8	2.2	2.7	2.7
Non-lazy max speedup (16 proc.)	3.2	2.3	3.1	3.1

shows that the percentage of non distributed cpu time ranges from 7% to 8% for f1 and f2, and from 12% to 14% for g8. In conclusion, lazy evaluation distributes voxelization time with an approximative ratio of 70% for f1, 80% for f2 and 50% for g8.

Analysis of Memory Factors

The memory factors also show that an important part of the data was distributed over the processors. The reverse calculus shows that for f1 and f2, 82% of the total sequential size was distributed over the processors, 50% for g8 and 45% for g9, which is coherent with the voxelization time distribution.

The relatively low results for pictures g8 and g9 can be explained by the fact that the task distribution algorithm shows a weakness in the middle of the picture, where the last sub-pictures to be computed are attributed to processors with little

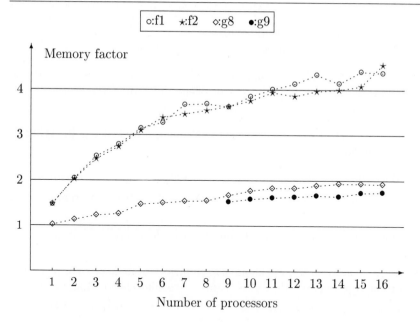

Figure 23.8 Memory Cost Results for a Parallel Architecture.

regard to coherence. For pictures g8 and g9, the center of the picture is one of the critical areas in term of surface density.

Conditions of Efficiency

Lazy evaluation for voxelization is a process for which improvement cannot be evaluated a priori. Experimentation shows that its cost compared to static voxelization is negligible, but what it brings can vary a lot with the simulation test.

Though the results previously stated are not favorable tests, as most of the octree is built in the sequential version, the high percentage of distributed voxelization proves that lazy evaluation can greatly improve performance in a wide range of simulation tests.

Another point is that conditions of efficiency are not dependent on architecture, as communications are limited to their simplest expression, i.e., task distribution. So it appears that the main conditional point is the task distribution scheme. As the first priority for task distribution is load balance, the choice of task affectation to processors is the main point that could achieve a good data balance.

23.5   Concluding Remarks

In this chapter, a methodology to implement real large applications on distributed computers is presented. The chosen application is parallel ray tracing, which is the basic algorithm for simulating wave propagation used, for example, for rendering a realistic image, in computational electro-magnetic or seismic simulation.

The proposed methodology can be summarized as follows:

1. Find the best sequential algorithm for the considered application; determine a reference execution time to solve the problem and deduce the limitations in time and memory size of the solution.

2. Find a parallel algorithm to overcome the sequential limitations in trying to respect five major rules:

   (a) Reduce the sequential part of the parallel algorithm as much as possible.

   (b) Build all needed data structures locally and try to limit remote data accesses.

   (c) Define coarse-grained task granularity to effectively exploit processor throughput.

   (d) Determine a fair static workload of each processor and try to improve the solution by a dynamic algorithm in order to achieve better load balancing.

   (e) Compare the solution to the sequential algorithm in terms of the ratio cost/performance and show the effective speedup.

The methodology applied to ray tracing problem has led to the notion of lazy evaluation of tree data structures and heuristics to improve the sequential process of ray-voxel intersection. This algorithm has given efficient results in term of space and time in sequential computation.

Lazy evaluation has been used to assign dynamically part of the overall tree to local processor without data migration. There may be some redundancies in memory allocation, depending on the scene, but with an acceptable cost. A static task granularity was defined with a set of rays computed by each processor.

Results show that the process of effective parallelization of efficient sequential algorithms is not a trivial task. The difficulty arises when the number of processors and the throughput of each processor are increased.

Clear distinction must be made between concurrent process distribution and problem solving parallelization. In the first case, the main issue is to achieve an acceptable workload of each processor managing a lot of heavy processes on a network of computers. Costs of workload analysis and communication overhead are marginal relative to process execution times. In parallel computation, the solution consists in finding efficient sets of separate tasks,in limiting the number of messages as much as possible and in finding an effective load balancing at runtime, thus avoiding time consuming processor workload analysis and costly tasks or data migrations.

Acknowledgments

We would like to thank A. Hachicha, D. Baudoin, E. Martin and G. Jacotot for their help in the performance measurement. Guy Durrieu and Edith Roques also have contributed to the final version of this chapter. The IBM SP2 performances were measured on a IBM SP2 provided by CNRS under program GDR/ANM.

23.6   Bibliography

[1] John Amanatides and Andrew Woo. A Fast Voxel Traversal Algorithm for Ray Tracing. *Proceedings of Eurographics 1987*, pages 3-9, August 1987.

[2] Andrew S. Glassner. Space Subdivision for Fast Ray-Tracing. *IEEE Computer Graphics and Applications*, vol 4(10), pages 15-22, October 84.

[3] S. A. Green. *Parallel Processing for Computer Graphics*. The MIT Press, London 1989.

[4] D. Badouel, K. Bouatouch and T. Priol. Ray Tracing on Distributed Memory Parallel Computers: Strategies for Distributing Computation and Data. *IEEE Computer Graphics and Applications*, vol 14(4), pages 69-77, July 1994.

[5] T. Kay and J. Kajiya. Ray Tracing Complex Scenes. *ACM Computer Graphics* 20(4), pages 269-278, 1986.

[6] Tonh-Yee Lee et al. Parallel Implementation of a Ray Tracing Algorithm for Distributed Memory Parallel Computers. *Concurrency: Practice and Experience*, vol 9(10), pages 947-965, 1997.

[7] E. Reinhard and F. W. Jansen. Rendering Large Scenes using Parallel Ray Tracing. *Parallel Computing Special Issues on Applications, Parallel Graphics and Visualisation*, vol 23(7), pages 873-885, 1997.

[8] A. Heirich and J. Arvo. A Competitive Analysis of Load Balancing Strategies for Parallel Ray Tracing. *Journal of Supercomputing*, vol 12(1 and 2), pages 57-68, 1998.

[9] J. L. Hennessy and D. A. Patterson. *Computer Architecture: A Quantitative Approach—Second Edition*. Morgan Kaufmann Publishers, Inc., 1996.

Chapter 24

Fast Content-Based Image Retrieval

JANE YOU AND HONG SHEN

School of Computing and Information Technology
Griffith University,
Nathan Campus, Brisbane, Australia

Email: {*you, hong*}*@cit.gu.edu.au*

24.1 Introduction

The last few years have seen an intense interest in multimedia systems which involve computer networks, databases, distributed computing, data compression, document processing, user interfaces, computer graphics, pattern recognition and artificial intelligence. The wide applications of multimedia systems include digital libraries, consumer video on demand, interactive TV, arts, medicine, publishing, meeting room support and training, education and entertainment. Images are being created at an ever-increasing rate as one type of multimedia data with advances in scanning, networking, compression and video technology. The generation of large on-line collections of images has resulted in a need for new methods which can

- find all images similar to an input image,
- identify images containing a specified object,
- recognize images featured by specified colour, texture or shape.

Determining how to query and retrieve an image by its content from large image databases is an active research area related to many computer science fields. Its applications cover a wide range including defence and civilian satellites, military reconnaissance and surveillance flights, fingerprinting and mug-shot-capturing, scientific experiments, biomedical imaging, and home entertainment systems. Yet, the search methodologies used to find pictorial information are still limited due to difficult research problems such as extraction of semantic and nonsemantic information, and efficient and effective information retrieval. Recent research has been focussed on the introduction of novel image representations and data models, efficient and robust query-processing algorithms, intelligent query interfaces, and domain-independent system architectures [1].

Traditionally, designing an image retrieval technique involves three primary issues:

- image feature extraction and representation,
- similarity measure,
- access or retrieval method, i.e., image indexing and searching.

Although existing techniques resolve these design issues in various ways, the significant connections and combinations among these three issues have not been investigated in a natural way.

Content-Based Image Retrieval (CBIR) is viewed as part of information retrieval. In general, previous approaches to CBIR fall into two categories: attribute-based retrieval and image-interpretation-based retrieval [2]. The first approach is database-oriented by modeling image contents as a set of attributes and managing them within the framework of conventional database-management systems. Such attribute-based representation of image contents requires high level image feature extraction and results in less scope for posing *ad hoc* queries to the image database. The second approach is based on the integration of feature-extraction and object-recognition during the management of image databases to overcome the limitation of attribute-based retrieval. Nevertheless, it is computationally expensive, difficult and somehow domain independent for object recognition. Recent research in CBIR recognizes the need for synergy between these two approaches. Currently a large proportion of research into CBIR has been centered on issues such as which image features are extracted, the level of abstraction manifested in the features, and the degree of desired domain independence [1]. Thus, appropriate techniques for image feature extraction and similarity matching will benefit image identification in developing CBIR systems.

At first glance, an image query and retrieval task appears deceptively simple because humans seem to be so good at finding information from a large image collection in terms of its colors, textures, shapes and object positions. Unfortunately, in an unconstrained environment, such a task is beyond the reach of current technology in image understanding. Research on ways to extend and improve query methods for image retrieval is widespread, and various results have been presented in workshops, conferences and surveys. Regardless of which approach is used, in general, an image retrieval system featuring generic query classes (i.e., color, texture, sketch, shape, volume, spatial constraints, browsing, objective attributes, subjective attributes, motion, text and domain concepts) will be powerful to deal with diverse applications. It is believed that a sophisticated graphical interface which integrates several generic queries based on natural and efficient schemes will provide a unified view of querying the image database.

The advances in image feature extraction/representation and similarity measure play a pivotal role in image identification and retrieval. Processing an image retrieval request involves three main steps: query feature selection, formulation of possibly similar images, and formulation of the final response set. Thus, dynamic image feature extraction, guided search and knowledge-based hierarchical matching will have significant potential to enable both image identification and image retrieval to be performed more effectively.

In general, image retrieval involves the execution of a large number of operations on large sets of structured data, requiring considerable execution time if performed in a sequential manner. The need to implement the related tasks in parallel arises from the speed requirements of real-time applications such as industrial on-line inspection, medical imaging, and autonomous navigation. In addition, the design of parallel algorithms has drawn more attention due to the commercial availability of parallel machines. However, the pioneering research mostly relies on specialized multiprocessor architectures for fast processing. A general methodology which is suitable to arbitrary imaging tasks on different parallel machines with various architectural features has not yet emerged. It is noted that the advanced technology of computer networks has made very high-speed networks available (Gig-bit/sec.). So there is significant benefit to be gained by utilizing a distributed computer system to replace the specialized machines for the parallel implementation of image processing tasks. We propose to use the divide-and-conquer method to implement the relevant image retrieval algorithms in parallel on a network of workstation clusters. In the following sections of this chapter, we will discuss the relevant issues, including: the traditional approaches to detect image features, our proposal of wavelet based image feature extraction scheme for image retrieval, image similarity measures, dynamic image searching, our parallel implementation strategies and the experimental results.

24.2   Image Feature Extraction

In the computer vision approach to retrieval, the user wants to find an image with certain attributes. These attributes are computed from pixel values and may correspond to local color, texture, or matched filter response, the shape or arrangement of regions defined by those attributes[3] To fulfill a request, the system gives each image a relevance score, and presents them to the user in order of relevance. Although there are searches on limited domains where one image feature or model may always be the best, in general, the one-feature solution will be too brittle, and a relatively small set of multiple image features or models (less than a dozen) will give the best performance. In this section we summarize a wide range of traditional approaches to image feature extraction. Instead of applying different techniques to extract and represent various image features, we further describe a wavelet based approach to extract three types of features – colours, textures and shapes for effective content-based image retrieval.

24.2.1   An Overview

The extraction of features such as edges, curves and texture properties is useful in a variety of applications including target recognition, character recognition, scene analysis, and biomedical and industrial applications. An image feature is a distinguishing primitive characteristic or attribute of an image field. Some features are natural in the sense that such features are defined by the visual appearance of an image, while other so-called artificial features result from specific manipulations or measurements of an image. The brightness of a region of pixels, edge outlines of objects, and gray scale textural regions are examples of natural features. Image amplitude histograms and spatial frequency spectra are regarded as artificial features.

Amplitude Features

The measure of image amplitude is the most basic of all image features. Such measurement can be made in terms of spectral value, luminance, tristimulus values, or other units at specific image points or over neighborhoods. In general, image amplitude measurements are of major importance in the isolation of objects within pictures (symbolic description) and in the labelling of such objects (interpretation).

Histogram Features

A discrete image array $I(i,j)$ sometimes can be represented as a sample of a two-dimensional stochastic process described by a joint probability distribution model. The histograms, developed for estimating image probability distribution in terms of measured image amplitude features, can be utilized to generate a class of image features. The shape of an image histogram provides many clues as to the character of the image.

Transform Coefficient Features

Transform coefficient feature extraction has proved practical in several applications, such as land usage classification and disease diagnosis from radiographs, in which the transform domain features are used as inputs to a pattern recognition classification system. Normally the coefficients of a two-dimensional transform specify the amplitude of the brightness patterns (two-dimensional basis functions) of a transformation such that the weighted sum of the brightness patterns is identical to the image. Thus the coefficients may be considered to indicate the correlation of a particular brightness pattern with an image field. However, in practice, image detection cannot be performed simply by monitoring the value of the appropriate transform coefficient because objects to be detected within an image are often of complex shape and brightness distribution, and do not correspond exactly to the more primitive brightness patterns of most image transforms.

Spot and Line Features

An image spot is a relatively small region whose amplitude differs significantly from its neighborhood. The problem of detecting and then segmenting isolated points in an image applies in both noise removal and particle analysis. Spatial-mask processing is viewed as a simple and fast method, in which the input image is filtered by the spot enhancement mask followed by thresholding. The mask used is a composite mask in the form of

$$M(i,j) = M_S(i,j) * M_L(i,j)$$

where $M_S(i,j)$ is one of the low-pass filter smoothing masks and $M_L(i,j)$ is the Laplacian mask.

A line segment is defined by its amplitude cross section, which must be U-shaped in a positive or negative sense over some extended region. The detection of lines in an image is a more complex procedure than the fairly straightforward procedure of point detection, which, however, is also based on spatial-mask processing.

Edge Features

Changes or discontinuities in an image attribute such as luminance, tristimulus value, or texture are fundamentally important primitive features of an image since they often provide an indication of the physical extent of objects within the image. Image edges are interpreted as arising from various types of discontinuities in the scene: occluding edges are discontinuities in range; convex or concave edges are discontinuities in surface slope; shadow edges are discontinuities in luminance; boundary segments are detected by global discontinuities; texture edges are discontinuities between textured regions.

The classical approaches to edge detection, reviewed by Davis[6], include high emphasis filtering, gradient operations, optimal techniques and a dynamic programming formulation of the edge detection problem. Several notable new techniques for edge detection have been developed, such as new classes of operators, Marr's edge detection theory, multidimensional edge detection, and the facet model-based approach.

Texture Features

Textural properties of image regions are often used to characterize natural scenes as exhibiting a repetitive structure. Though there is no rigid description of what texture is, the extraction of texture features in terms of texture primitives, structural models, statistical models and texture gradients attracts much attention to classification or segmentation of the image into differently textured regions. The notion of a primitive is central to both artificial and natural texture. A visual primitive is viewed as exhibiting certain invariant properties repeatedly occurring in different positions, deformations, and orientations inside a given area. Artificial textures consist of arrangements of primitives, such as line segments, dots, stars, or alphanumeric characters, placed against a neutral background. Natural textures are images of natural scenes containing semirepetitive arrangements of pixels.

For highly patterned textures, when the primitives are determined, it is important to describe the placement of primitives. A powerful way of describing the rules that govern textural structure is through a grammar, which describes how to generate patterns by applying rewriting rules to a small number of symbols. Though there is no unique grammar for a given texture due to many choices for rules and symbols, shape grammars, tree grammars, and array grammars are three of the basic formal ones.

Multidimensional Edge Features

Modern scanning techniques, such as computed tomography, have found wide applications in medicine and industry by producing true three-dimensional imagery of internal structures. The first stage in finding structures in these images, like that for standard two-dimensional images, is to evaluate a local edge operator over the image. If an edge segment in two dimensions is modeled as an oriented unit line segment that separates units (i.e., pixels) of different intensities, then in three dimensions, an edge can be defined as an oriented unit plane that separates unit volumes (i.e., voxels) of different intensities. Therefore, edge elements in two dimensions become surface elements in three dimensions; and the two-dimensional image gradient, when generalized to three dimensions, is the local surface normal. As in the two-dimensional case, many different basis operators can be used for 3-D edge detection and boundary tracking.

Color Edge Features

The previous description of image feature extraction is concerned with only black and white pictures; however, color images in particular provide more information in the real world. Color images may be described quantitatively at each pixel by a set of three tristimulus values g_1, g_2, g_3, which are proportional to the amount of red, green, and blue primary lights required to match the pixel color. The luminance of the color is a weighted sum of the tristimulus values in the form of

$$g = \alpha_1 g_1 + \alpha_2 g_2 + \alpha_3 g_3$$

where the weight coefficients α_i are constants.

An edge in a color image could be defined as existing only if the luminance field contains an edge. However, this definition ignores discontinuities in hue and saturation in regions of constant luminance. Another approach would be to examine each of the tristimulus arrays separately and to judge a color edge to be present only if an edge exists simultaneously in all arrays. A third definition would be to define an edge as existing if the vector difference between the tritimulus value vectors of two colors exceeds some threshold level.

24.2.2   Wavelet Based Multiple Image Feature Extraction

In the previous section we have summarized a wide range of algorithms for image feature extraction. In contrast to the traditional approaches to apply different techniques for different features [3], in the work reported here we propose a unique scheme to extract different features based on wavelet transform. The following highlights how to extract and represent three basic types of features – colour, texture and shape based on wavelet transform.

Wavelet Transform

Wavelet transforms offer the promise of compact representation and efficient detection of image components that match the waveshape of the chosen wavelet. Although wavelet transforms are relatively new on the image processing scene, there have been many applications in practice including image compression, image enhancement and image fusion. As described in [9], the wavelet transform includes the following key features:

- A basic wavelet is an oscillatory function that dies out as $|x| \to \infty$. Its spectrum resembles the transfer function of a bandpass filter.

- A set of basis functions for a wavelet transform can be generated from dilations and translations of a basic wavelet.

- The continuous wavelet transform represents a signal as a function of two variables: time and scale. It represents an image as a function of three variables: two for spatial position and one for scale.

- The wavelet series expansion represents a periodic or finite-length signal with a series of coefficients.

- The discrete wavelet transform represents an N-point signal with N coefficients. It represents an N-by-N image with N^2 coefficients.

- The Haar transform based on Haar functions is the simplest discrete wavelet transform.

- The Discrete Wavelet Transform (DWT) can be implemented directly or indirectly by the Fast Wavelet Transform (FWT, or herringbone) algorithm.

- The separable two-dimensional DWT can also be implemented by the FWT algorithm.

- Biorthogonal wavelet systems permit the DWT to use less restricted (e.g., symmetric) wavelets with compact support.

Given the set of orthonormal wavelets, the wavelet series expansion of the bandlimited continuous function $f(t)$ is

$$c_{j,k} = \int_{-\infty}^{\infty} f(t)\Psi_{j,k}(t)dt \quad \text{and} \quad f(t) = \sum_{j,k} c_{j,k}\Psi_{j,k}(t)$$

and the discrete wavelet transform of the sampled function is

$$c_{j,k} = \sum_i f(n)\Psi_{j,k}(n) \quad \text{and} \quad f(n0 = \sum_{j,k}\Psi_{j,k}(n)$$

where $n = 2^j + k$ for $j = 0, 1, ..., \log_2(N) - 1$, $k = 0, 1, ..., 2^j - 1$.

The concept of the above one-dimension wavelet representation can be extended to two dimensions easily[9]. Considering the case of unitary image transforms, we assume that the two-dimensional scaling function is separable, that is,

$$\phi(x, y) = \phi(x)\phi(y)$$

where $\phi(x)$ is a one-dimensional scaling function. If $\Psi(x)$ is its companion wavelet expressed by

$$\Psi(t) = \sum_k h_l(k)\phi(2t - k)$$

where $h_l(k) = (-1)^k h_0(-k + 1)$ and $h_0(k) = h_0(k) = <\phi_{1,0}(t), \phi_{0,k}(t)>$ and $\phi_{j,k}(t) = 2^{j/2}\phi(s^j t - k)$ for $j = 0, 1, ...,$ $k = 0, 1, ..., 2^j - 1$ then the three two-dimensional basic wavelets

$$\Psi^1(x, y) = \phi(x)\Psi(y) \quad \Psi^2(x, y) = \Psi(x)\phi(y) \quad \Psi^3(x, y) = \Psi(x)\Psi(y)$$

establish the foundation for a two-dimensional wavelet transform.

Color Histogram Features

Color is an important image feature. Color histograms provide for a global image color representation which has been used in many CBIR systems. As reported in [7], such chrominance information can be extracted from histograms of successive approximation quantization (SAQ) of wavelet coefficients. The SAQ scheme progressively decomposes the wavelet coefficients into quantization layers according to their importance, and generates a sequence of histograms in accordance with different resolutions. When a YUV color model is used, we will extract the histograms from each Y-, U-, and V-sub-image by applying biorthogonal wavelet transform, coefficient quantization and entropy coding.

Texture Features

Historically, structural and statistical approaches have been adopted for texture feature extraction[8]. The structural approach assumes the texture is characterized by some primitives following a placement rule. In the statistical approach, texture is regarded as a sample from a probability distribution on the image space and defined by a stochastic model or characterized by a set of statistical features. Here we adopted a wavelet based approach to represent texture features[4]. When an image is decomposed into de-correlated subimages through a wavelet filter bank, each sub-image represents the feature of some scale and orientation of the original image. Thus, the related wavelet coefficients can be used for texture feature representation. If an image is decomposed into three wavelet layers, there will be 10 sub-images.

For each sub-image, the standard deviation of the wavelet coefficients is calculated to represent its texture feature component. Consequently, 10 standard deviations corresponding to 10 sub-images are used as the texture representation for the image. The following represents its vector form:

$$F_t = [f_{t1}, f_{t2}, ..., f_{t10}]$$

Shape Feature

Visual shape of an object is another important datum in real world. In general, it is difficult to uniquely describe an object's shape in terms of alphanumeric descriptors[10]. We proposed to combine invariant moments computing and B-Spline curve representation to capture shape features in conjunction with wavelet coefficients. There are two key issues involved – B-spline representation of an object in its original image and moments description of the object at different scales and resolutions of sub-images via wavelet transform. The B-splines are regarded as one of the most efficient curve representations and possess very attractive properties such as spatial uniqueness, boundedness and continuity, local shape controllability, and invariance to affine transformations. For a given set of n ordered corner points $((x_1, y_1), (x_2, y_2), ...(x_n, y_n))$, we aim to fit a real-valued B-spline to such observed curve data. We aim to find an approximate B-spline such that the "error" measure between the observed data and their corresponding B-spline curve values is small. If we deal with a closed cubic B-spline with $m+1$ parameters $C_0, C_1, ..., C_m$, (control points), the curve can be modeled as a linear combination of four cubic polynomials in the parameter t, where t is normalized for each such segment between 0 and 1 $(0 \leq t \leq 1)$, i.e.,

$$r_i(t) = C_{i-1}Q_0(t) + C_iQ_1(t) + C_{i+1}Q_2(t) + C_{i+2}Q_3$$

where

$$Q_k(t) = a_{k0}t^3 + a_{k1}t^2 + a_{k2}t + a_{k3} \qquad k = 0, 1, 2, 3$$

In order to determine the error distance between the curve data and their corresponding B-spline points, the minimum mean square error estimation (MMSE) is used to determine the final B-spline representation of the given curve data by interative B-spline parameter estimation. This B-spline representation of object boundary will be used for final retrieval output by curve matching when the query image is presented by a sketch or contains clear object boundaries.

It is known that the area-normalized central moments computed relative to the principal axis are invariant under magnification, translation, and rotation of the object. Therefore, they are powerful measurements in the analysis of 2D shapes. Important information about a shape such as its size, center location and orientation are all moment-based attributes. A number of other useful shape features such as maximum and minimum moments of inertia, moment invariants, shape spreadness and shape elongation can also be derived from moments. For a given $M \times N$ size of image I, its $(p, q)th$ central moment is expressed as below:

$$\mu_{pq} = \sum_{i=0}^{M-1} \sum_{j=0}^{N-1} (i - \overline{x})^p (j - \overline{y})^q I(i, j)$$

where

$$\overline{x} = \frac{\sum_{i=0}^{M-1} \sum_{j=0}^{N-1} i \times I(i,j)}{\sum_{i=0}^{M-1} \sum_{j=0}^{N-1} I(i,j)}, \qquad \overline{y} = \frac{\sum_{i=0}^{M-1} \sum_{j=0}^{N-1} j \times I(i,j)}{\sum_{i=0}^{M-1} \sum_{j=0}^{N-1} I(i,j)}.$$

The normalised central moments, denoted by η_{pq}, are defined as

$$\eta_{pq} = \frac{\mu_{pq}}{\mu^{\gamma}_{00}}, \qquad \text{where } \gamma = (p+q)/2 + 1, \, p+q = 2,3,...$$

In the work reported here, we apply a wavelet transform to decompose the original image into a collection of subbands ranging from low to high resolution. The related first-, second- and third-normalised central moments for each subimage are computed and the average values of the same moment category for all subbands are used as individual shape feature components. Thus, the image shape feature vector is defined as

$$F_s = [\eta_{01}, \eta_{10}, \eta_{11}, \eta_{02}, \eta_{20}, \eta_{03}, \eta_{12}, \eta_{21}, \eta_{30}].$$

24.3   Dynamic Image Indexing

Fast searching and indexing is a key issue for efficient information retrieval. Indexing tabular data for exact matching or range searches in traditional databases is a well-understood problem, and structures like B-trees provide efficient access mechanisms. However, in the context of similarity matching for visual images, traditional indexing methods may not be appropriate. Consequently, data structures for fast access of high-dimensional features for spatial relationships have to be developed. As detailed in the above section, we introduce a general wavelet based scheme for image feature extraction and representation. Three features – colour, texture and shape – are considered and each is associated with an individual feature vector. How to organize the index structure with these features to facilitate image query? We propose a three-bits component code (CTS) to characterize the status of each individual image with the following specifications:

- The left bit C represents colour status:

  1 – a colour image,

  0 – a black and white image.

- The middle bit T represents texture status:

  1 – a texture image,

  0 – a non-texture image.

- The right bit S represents shape status:

  1 – an image with clear object(s),

  0 – an image without any objects.

The component code will facilitate the hierarchical structure of indexing and searching. Each individual image is classified into different image groups according to its component code. Within each group, images are further ranked with respect to their individual feature vectors or measurements. The searching process will start with the image group which has the same component code as the query image, which speeds up the processing by filtering out irrelevant images from the image collection. The following Table 24.1 shows data fields of each image:

Table 24.1 Data Fields of Each Image

Name of Data Field	Data Type
Image Name (ID)	string (integer)
Component Code	binary (integer)
Y-histogram	array of floats
U-histogram	array of floats
V-histogram	array of floats
Texture Vector	array of floats
B-spline curve	array of floats
Moment Vector	array of floats

24.4   Image Similarity Measurement

The second key issue in image retrieval is the measure of image similarity. We aim to combine image feature extraction and representation techniques in IP with the term weighting and relevance feedback techniques in IR for effective content-based retrieval. When an image is represented by a list of feature classes associated with the corresponding feature vectors, we will be able to solve two further problems:

- how to convert each feature vector to a weight vector for feature similarity measurement and

- how to combine multiple feature classes for image similarity measurement.

Firstly, we will normalize each component in a feature vector to the same importance by applying Gaussian normalization. We will then introduce the relevance feedback procedure to dynamically adjust the weights by putting more emphasis on relevant components and less emphasis on non-relevant components. We will use Cosine distance to measure the similarity between two weight vectors.

Secondly, we will combine similarity measurements of individual feature classes to measure image similarity. Rather than combining different features by fixed weights as reported in some research and industrial systems [1], based on our previous work, we will use the fuzziness membership to assign different relevance scores to different feature classes and combine ranks of different features with unequal weights to get a new similarity measurement for images.

24.5   Image Searching

The third key issue in image retrieval is image searching, which is concerned with locating images which best match a query image provided by a user. In contrast to the current approaches which often use fixed matching criteria to select candidate images, we propose selective matching criteria associated with user's query for flexible searching. Our system will support two types of queries:

a) to pose a query by image sample and
b) to use a simple sketch as a query.

In the case of query by image sample, the searching follows multiple feature extraction and image similarity measurement described above. Based on the nature of the query image, the user can add additional component weights during the combination of image features for image similarity measurement. In the case of query by a simple sketch provided a user, we will apply B-spline based curve matching scheme to identify the most suitable candidates from image database. In the case of query by sample image, we will use the proposed image component code to guide the searching for the most appropriate candidates in terms of colour, texture and shape from database.

In the case of B-spline based curving matching, the problem is to find a classifier that allocates the sampled data to one of the object curves. A residual error-based matching is described in [11]. We extended their algorithm by introducing parallel sorting algorithm to identify the candidate with the minimum error. Let $C_0(p), C_1(p), ..., C_m(p)$ be the set of $m+1$ control points associated with the B-spline $r_p(t')$ that approximates the pth object curve observed at the standard position, and let $(r_1, r_2, ..., r_N)$ be the set of observed N sampled ordered (in clockwise direction) data curve points. The sum of the residual errors of the data to the pth B-spline can be described as

$$d_p{}^2 = \sum_{j=1}^{N} \| r_j - r_p(t'_j) \|^2$$

The sample is allocated to the class for which $d_p{}^2$ is minimum.

24.6   Parallel Implementation

Content-based image retrieval involves many types of computing, ranging from two-dimensional correlation and convolution, to image transformation, geometric computing and graph analysis. In general, image-related computing can be summarized as the execution of a large number of operations on large sets of structured data.

One of the basic data structure in vision algorithm is the two-dimensional array. In many cases a vision task is performed by the application of a set of operations to all the elements of the image array. When such a task is implemented in sequential, it is computationally intensive. Thus the conventional sequential computers are too slow to perform complex image retrieval tasks in real time. However, the speed-up in computing can be achieved by performing different operations concurrently on each element of the array. Such a parallel method lies in the fact that several operators can be applied to the image simultaneously (MIMD style); or the same operator can be proceeded at different parts of the image at the same time (SIMD style).

In essence, there are two main types of parallelism – data parallelism and functional parallelism. In data parallelism, the processors execute the same instruction on separate pieces of the data, which we refer to as SIMD. The functional parallelism, where the processors perform different parts of the task on the same data, may be referred as MISD. The combination of these paradigms leads to MIMD architecture, which is more powerful but more difficult to program correctly.

With the advent of multiprocessor architectures, new problems arose: how to optimize the use of a greater number of computing resources (processors, memories, connections, etc.); how much concurrency and how much pipelining etc. Emphasis has now been given to the interconnections among the computational units so as to increase the flexibility of the architecture (including reconfiguration possibilities) to provide both static and, sometimes, dynamic hardware matching to tasks.

In contrast to the conventional parallel solutions which relied on specialized parallel machine, we explored the potential of distributed systems for parallelism. It is noted that the advanced technology of computer network has made very high-speed network available (Gigbit/sec.). Thus a distributed computer system can be utilized to replace the specialized machines for the implementation of vision tasks and dynamic load balancing for resource allocation. A divide-and-conquer policy can be adopted for such a scheme, where a complex task is divided into a number of sub-tasks, and those sub-tasks are later reorganized into clusters according to granularity before being mapped on computers for simultaneous implementation. Due to the nature of parallel processing used in this scheme, the operation speed can be increased and real-time issues are considered by coordinating the priorities of tasks.

24.6.1 Divide-and-Conquer Parallel Algorithms

A divide-and-conquer approach to vision computing can be easily implemented in a networking environment. An image is partitioned into subimages and distributed over nodes in the network. The local processing results such as two-dimensional matrix operation, feature detection and transformation for each subimage are merged over the entire image. Figure 24.1 shows the partitioning and processing for parallel component labeling, where the boundary connectivity of neighboring subimages is represented as a graph. Hence, the original image represented in one large two-dimensional matrix ($256 * 256$, or $512 * 512$, or $1024 * 1024$) is broken into a number of small matrices (subimages). The success of the parallel implementation using PVM on a cluster of workstations depends on the effective communication pattern between workstations. In the work reported in this chapter, the master/slave parallel programming paradigm is adopted. Each workstation represents a node in the network. One node is selected as the master and is responsible for spawning slave nodes that process subimages.

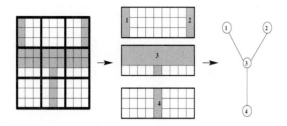

Figure 24.1 Divide images for parallel labeling.

24.7   Experimental Results

Parallel computation has been used successfully in many areas of computer science to speed up the computation required to solve a problem. In contrast to the conventional parallel implementation where either the dedicated hardware or the software is required, the parallel implementation of our proposed image retrieval algorithms is carried out on a network of workstation clusters. Both PVM and TreadMarks DSM packages are used in our test and their performance is reported in this section.

24.7.1   Parallel Wavelet Transform Using PVM

We adopted a divide-and-conquer approach and implement the wavelet transform in a networking environment using PVM (Parallel Virtual Machine). An image is partitioned into subimages and distributed over nodes in the network. The local processing results such as matrix operation and transformation for each subimage are merged over the entire image. It should be pointed out that the success of the parallel implementation using PVM on a cluster of workstations depends on the effective communication pattern between workstations. In the work reported in this chapter, the master/slave parallel programming paradigm is adopted. Each workstation represents a node in the network. One node is selected as the master, and is responsible for spawning slave nodes that process subimages. In our PVM based parallel implementation, the tasks for the master node include reading and segmenting image data, sending sub-image data to each slaves, coordinating the wavelet transform produced by slaves, and collecting the result from slaves for the final output. Table 24.2 shows different execution times with different numbers of slaves for the wavelet transform on 512×512 image based on pyramid algorithm. The sequential processing is performed on a single SPARC ELC station while the parallel implementation is on a 8-node structure using SPARC ELC stations.

Table 24.2 Wavelet Transform – the Execution Time Vs. the Number of Slaves

No. of Slaves	Execution Time (Sec.)
1	36.76
2	24.94
4	17.94
8	12.45

24.8   Parallel Image Feature Extraction – PVM Vs. DSM

The advantages and potentials of a general distributed shared memory system for parallel image processing is demonstrated by the performance comparison listed in Table 24.3, where different numbers of processes were invoked by means of both PVM and DSM on the 512×512 size image for image feature extraction. The parallel performance improvement is measured by the following ratio:

$$\gamma = T_p/T_s$$

where T_s refers to the sequential execution time and T_p refers to the parallel execution time. It is clear that DSM increases the speed better due to its fewer communication overheads. It is expected that the overall performance will be further improved by introducing dynamic task scheduling for parallelism.

Table 24.3 The Performance Comparison of DSM and PVM

number of processes	execution time (DSM)	execution time (PVM)
1	1.45 sec.	1.77 sec.
2	0.80 sec.	1.41 sec.
4	0.52 sec.	1.17 sec.
8	0.48 sec.	1.13 sec.
16	0.22 sec.	0.27 sec.
32	0.12 sec.	0.27 sec.

24.8.1   Hierarchical Image Matching in a PVM Environment

The hierarchical image matching scheme was first proposed by Borgefors[13] in order to reduce the computation required to match two images. This section details our extension of this scheme by introducing a guided search strategy to avoid the blind searching for the best fit between the given patterns. In order to avoid such a blind searching, a guided search strategy is essential to reduce computation burden. Our extension of the hierarchical image matching scheme (H.I.M.S) was based on a guided searching algorithm that searches first at the low level, coarse grained images, to the high level, fine grained images. To do this, we needed to obtain a Hausdorff distance approximation for each possible window combination of the template and target image at the lowest resolution. Those that returned a Hausdorff distance approximation equal to the lowest Hausdorff distance for those images were investigated at the higher resolution. The following summarizes the key steps involved in a H.I.M.S algorithm, and Figure 24.2 shows a binary image pyramid for guided search.

```
create image pyramid
for all combinations of windows
at lowest level
    get value of match for this combination
    if low value add to lowest list
end-for
for each remaining level
    remove area from lowest list
    get match value for this area
    if low value add to lowest list
end-for
```

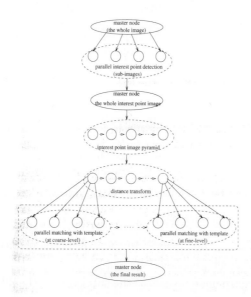

Figure 24.2 The structure of hierarchical image matching.

As emphasized before, the execution time of the matching can be reduced by utilizing a number of processors to perform multiple tasks in parallel. While most of the sequential execution time is spent on distance transform and matching measurement due to cache misses on a single processor, our investigation shows that the distributed computers can meet the high computational and memory access demands in image processing. Our initial parallel implementation of the matching scheme for object recognition was performed on a low-cost heterogeneous PVM (Parallel Virtual Machine) network. The following summarizes the main steps of implementation.

- Step 1: The detection of interesting points

    - 1.1 The master node reads in original image,
    - 1.2 The master node assigns one quarter of the partitioned image to each corresponding slave node,
    - 1.3 Each slave node performs Moravec operator to obtain the sub-region of interest point image,
    - 1.4 The master node collects the processed subregions from each slave node and combines them to obtain the complete interest point image,
    - 1.5 The master node calculates the histogram of the interest point image and determines the sequences of threshold value to build up the interest point image pyramid in the following stage.

- Step 2: The creation of interest point pyramid

    - 2.1 The master node assigns one quarter of the partitioned interest point image to each corresponding slave node together with a selected threshold value,
    - 2.2 Each slave node performs thresholding to obtain the subregion of the binary image,
    - 2.3 The master node collects the processed data from each slave node and combines them to get the completed binary image corresponding to the selected threshold value in order to create a pyramid.

- Step 3: The distance transform

    - 3.1 The master node assigns one quarter of the partitioned binary image to each corresponding slave node,
    - 3.2 Each slave node initializes the subregion of the distance image based on the binary image,
    - 3.3 Each slave node applies 3-4 DT mask to perform distance transform and the subregion of the final distance image is created,
    - 3.4 The master node collects the processed data from each slave node and combines them to create the distance image.

- Step 4: The matching procedure

    - 4.1 The master node assigns one quarter of the partitioned distance image and the interest image of the template to each corresponding slave node,
    - 4.2 Each slave node imposes the interest image of the template over the distance image and calculate the root mean square average for optimization,
    - 4.3 Each slave node passes a number of possible areas to the master node for further comparison.

- Step 5: The master node outputs the final result of matching.

To evaluate the performance gain, a system was implemented on a group of networked workstations (8 DECstations), where PVM (Parallel Virtual Machine) was used to provide a parallel execution environment. Based on the developed system, a number of experiments were carried out to measure the effectiveness of using the hierarchical approach in matching, and to measure the speedup of using parallel guided matching against using sequential matching. The results are shown in Table 24.4 and Table 24.5, respectively. The following diagrams are examples of object identification and localization using our hierarchical matching scheme, where Figure 24.3 is a 300×300 target image with a certain object to be identified and Figure 24.4 shows the matching result of our hierarchical scheme, which returns a match at position $(56, 142)$.

Table 24.4 Hierarchical Image Matching Scheme

Pyramid levels	image 1 (256×256)	image 2 (362×362)
1	239.66 sec.	544.27 sec.
2	21.36 sec.	38.12 sec.
3	1.9 sec.	4.32 sec.
4	1.32 sec.	2.18 sec.
5	1.28 sec.	2.14 sec.

Table 24.5 Matching a Rotated Template Image

Matching method	image 1 (256×256)	image 2 (362×362)
sequential	209.45 sec.	410.13 sec.
parallel	32.7 sec.	67 sec.

Figure 24.3 Target image.

Figure 24.4 Template image.

24.9 Conclusion

We conclude that the wavelet based image feature extraction with respect to colors, textures and shapes is powerful for image representation. The conversion of image feature vector to weight vector using the relevance feedback technique provides a general approach to measuring multiple feature similarities. The use of image component code facilitates dynamic image indexing and searching. The calculation burden can be further reduced by means of parallel implementation over a workstation cluster while no dedicated software and hardware architectures are required. The proposed algorithms for feature extraction, image indexing and searching are simple to implement in parallel. The performance evaluation of our distributed image matching system shows that the general message-passing models over existing networks are highly effective and scalable. Consequently, parallelism of a particular algorithm can be implemented on the networked computer systems to speed up the execution time. Such an extension will be suitable to many other applications. The potential gain in parallel can be further achieved by load balancing consideration to distribute resources properly, which can reduce the execution time and simplify communication requirement between those sub-tasks.

24.10   Bibliography

[1] A.D. Narasimhalu (ed). Special Issue on Content-Based Retrieval. *ACM Multimedia Systems*, vol.3(1), February 1995.

[2] R. Jain. NSF Workshop on Visual Information Management Systems. *SIGmod Record*, vol.22(3), pages 57-75, December 1993.

[3] T.M. Caelli and D. Reye. On the Classification of Image Regions by Color, Texture and Shape. *Pattern Recognition*, vol.26(4), pages 461-470, 1993.

[4] T.S. Huang, S. Mehrotra, and K. Ramchandran. Multimedia Analysis and Retrieval System (MARS) Project. *Proc. of 33rd Annual Clinic on Library Application of Data Processing – Digital Image Access and Retrieval*, 1996.

[5] M. Flickner, H. Sawhney, W. Niblack, and J. Ashley. Query by Image and Video Content: The QBIC System. *IEEE Computer*, vol.28(9), pages 23-32, September 1995.

[6] L.S. Davis. A Survey of Edge Detection Techniques. *Comput. Graphics Image Process.*, vol.4, pages 248-270, 1975.

[7] M.J. Swain and D.H. Ballard. Colour Indexing. *Int. Journal of Computer Vision*, vol.7(1), pages 11-32, 1991.

[8] R.M. Haralick. Statistical and Structural Approaches to Texture. *Proc. IEEE*, vol.67, pages 786-804, 1979.

[9] K.R. Castleman. *Digital Image Processing*. Prentice-Hall, 1996.

[10] R. Mehrotra and J.E. Gary. Similar-shape Retrieval in Shape Data Management. *IEEE Trans. Computer*, vol.28(9), pages 57-62, 1995.

[11] F.S. Cohen, Z. Huang and Z. Yang. Invariant Matching and Identification of Curves Using B-splines Curve Representation. *IEEE Trans. on Image Processing*, vol.4(1), pages 1-10, 1995.

[12] R. Picard. A Society of Models for Video and Image Libraries. *IBM Systems Journal*, April 1996.

[13] G. Borgefors. Hierarchical Chamfer Matching: A Parametric Edge Matching Algorithm. *IEEE Trans. Patt. Anal. Machine Intell.*, vol. PAMI-10, pages 849-865, 1988.

[14] D.P. Huttenlocher, G.A. Klanderman and W.J. Rucklidge. Comparing Images Using the Hausdorff Distance. *IEEE Trans. Patt. Anal. Machine Intell.*, vol. PAMI-15, pages 850-863, 1993.

Chapter 25

Climate Ocean Modeling

PING WANG, BENNY N. CHENG, AND YI CHAO

Jet Propulsion Laboratory
California Institute of Technology, USA

Email: {*wangp@rockymt, bnc@pacific, yc@comp*}.*jpl.nasa.gov*

25.1 Introduction

Ocean modeling plays an important role in both understanding the current climatic conditions and predicting the future climate change. However, modeling the ocean circulation at various spatial scales is a very challenging computational task. In contrast to the atmosphere, where the dominant weather system has a spatial scale of thousands of kilometers, much of the ocean energy is associated with mesoscale eddies (equivalent to the storms in the atmosphere) with a spatial scale of hundreds of kilometers near the equator to ten kilometers at high latitudes. A minimum ocean model is at least 100 times more computationally demanding than a typical atmospheric model.

Thus, it was not until recently that eddy-permitting (or eddy-resolving) calculations could be carried out on a basin to global scale. Using the vector supercomputers (e.g., Cray Y-MP) at the National Center for Atmospheric Research (NCAR), decade-long ocean model integrations have been carried out at 1/4 degree ocean model [1], which was the first model with performance exceeding 1 billion floating-point-operation-per-second (1 Gflops/s). With the advance of massively parallel computing technology, decade-long integrations at 1/6 degree resolution have been conducted at Los Alamos National Laboratory (LANL) [2] and the Jet Propulsion Laboratory (JPL) [3] on the CM-5 and Cray T3D, respectively. Recently, a 10-year integration at 1/10 degree resolution was made at LANL using CM-5, and a six-year integration at 1/12 degree resolution was made on the T3D at the Pittsburgh Supercomputer Center [4]. Despite the recent progress in eddy-resolving ocean modeling, it is apparent that we are far from convergence in resolution, because each of these higher resolution calculations shows additional features that were not resolved in a coarser resolution model. Furthermore, increasing the spatial resolution can sometimes degrade the solution at coarser resolutions, suggesting the need for more experimentation with eddy-resolving models.

Implementing a well-designed parallel ocean code and improving the computational efficiency of the ocean model will significantly reduce the total research time to complete these studies. There are many challenges in designing an efficient ocean modeling code on parallel systems, such as how to deal with an irregular computing geometry on a parallel system and how to port a code from one system to other systems. With an efficient ocean model on multiple platforms, one can maximize the limited computational resources available for climate ocean modeling.

In this chapter, we report on our experiences running one of the most widely used ocean models on a variety of parallel computer systems. One of our objectives is to improve the computational efficiency of the ocean model on parallel computers such that one can reduce the time in conducting scientific studies. We also want to emphasize the portability of the ocean model across a variety of parallel platforms, ranging from the most powerful supercomputers to affordable desktop parallel PC clusters (Beowulf-class system). Our experiences in porting and optimizing the ocean model on a variety of parallel systems are described. Scientific results from an Atlantic Ocean model with high resolutions have been obtained using 256 processors on the Cray T3D.

25.2   Model Description

The ocean model used in this study is the most widely used ocean general circulation models (OGCM) in the community. The OGCM is based on the Parallel Ocean Program (POP) developed at Los Alamos National Laboratory [2]. This ocean model evolved from the Bryan-Cox three-dimensional primitive equations ocean model [5] [6], developed at NOAA Geophysical Fluid Dynamics Laboratory (GFDL), and later known as the Semtner and Chervin model or the Modular Ocean Model (MOM) [7]. Currently, there are hundreds of users within the so-called Bryan-Cox ocean model family, making it the most dominant OGCM code in the climate research community.

The OGCM solves the three-dimensional primitive equations with the finite difference technique. The equations are separated into barotropic (the vertical mean) and baroclinic (departures from the vertical mean) components. The baroclinic component is three-dimensional, and uses explicit leapfrog time stepping. It parallelizes very well on massively parallel computers. The barotropic component is two-dimensional, and solved implicitly. It differs from the original Bryan-Cox formulation in that it removes the rigid-lid approximation and treats the sea surface height as a prognostic variable (i.e., free-surface). The free-surface model is superior to the rigid-lid model because it provides more accurate solution to the governing equations. More importantly, the free-surface model tremendously reduces the global communication required by the rigid-lid model.

Building upon the original ocean model developed at LANL, the JPL ocean model has been significantly optimized. In [8], several optimization strategies were described, including memory optimization, effective use of arithmetic pipelines, and usage of optimized libraries. Such a model improvement allows one to perform ocean modeling at increasingly higher spatial resolutions for climate studies. In this chapter, we focus on how to deal with an irregular computing geometry on a parallel system and how to port a code from one system to other systems.

25.3 Parallel Partition on Irregular Geometries

25.3.1 A Simple Partition

Domain decomposition techniques are widely used in parallel computing community. This method is simply to split a computation domain to n subdomains such that each processor can work on just one subdomain. Once n processors are applied, a significant speed-up should be achieved—a total processing time T is reduced to T/n. In order to design a parallel code by use of the domain decomposition techniques, partition of a computation domain is the first issue encountered. Computation domains of ocean models are usually irregular. A simple method to deal with irregular geometries is to use a rectangular geometry to approximate an irregular domain. In this case, a partitioning structure can be easily designed according to a regular node mesh, which can be a 1D, 2D, or 3D partition.

Here, a simple 2D partition is given. For an $(M \times N)$ two-dimensional partition, in which $(M \times N)$ is equal to $NPES$ (total processors), neighbors are to the north, south, east, and west. The following example first converts MY_PE (current processor) to coordinates in the abstract topology(2D torus):

$i = MOD(MY\_PE, M)$

$j = MY\_PE/M$

The coordinate of MY_PE in the abstract topology is (i, j). i and j were chosen in such a way that MY_PE is equal to $(i + M \times j)$.

This kind of partition gives a 2D mesh which divides a rectangular domain into $(M \times N)$ subdomains such that each processor needs to work on only one subdomain. But for ocean modeling, there are practically no rectangular geometries. If this simple 2D partition is applied, computing efficiency will deteriorate as some processors are idle on non-ocean areas which are inside the 2D partition domain. For instance, the original POP code used a 2D partition to divide the 3D ocean domain into subdomains in a rectangular computing geometry. Figure 25.1 shows the 2D partition on the North Atlantic Ocean. Here, about 36% of the processors are idle on land while other processors are working on the ocean domain. So designing a flexible partitioning structure, which works on only the ocean area, will dramatically save computing resources, leading to significant speed-up via an efficient partition.

25.3.2 An Efficient Partition

Recently we have developed a new irregular partition for ocean modeling. In order to achieve load balance, and to exploit parallelism as much as possible, a general and

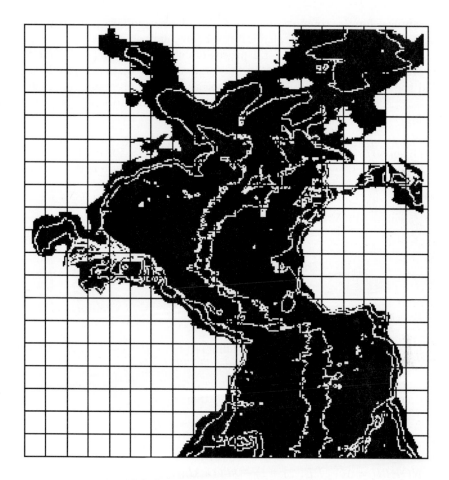

Figure 25.1 The original 2D partition over the North Atlantic Ocean. The contour lines represent the ocean depth of 1000 meters.

portable parallel structure based on domain decomposition techniques is designed for the three-dimensional ocean domain. It has 2D partitioning features and works on any irregular geometry, and the communication pattern on the subdomains has been designed as a virtual torus. MPI software is used for communication, which is required when subdomains on each processor need neighboring boundary data information. Because of the portability of this software, the code can be executed on any parallel system which supports the MPI library.

The main idea of this approach is to eliminate idle processors from the original 2D rectangular partition and to find the nearest neighboring processors which are active. Assume $NPES$ are used for computation and a rectangular 2D mesh ($M \times$

N) is applied for the computational domain. Since we know the irregular ocean topography G, it is easy to calculate total idle number of processors K caused by the 2D mesh. A target of total processors should be equal to $(NPES - K)$ if all processors work on only the ocean domain. Now the major problem is how to find the locations of the nearest neighboring non-idle processors for each active processor. A detailed procedure for locating neighboring processors is given in the following.

1. Given an original total number of processors $NPES$, 2D mesh $M \times N$, ocean topography G, calculate total idle processors K and get a new target number of total processors $NEWPES$.

2. Calculate idle processors mesh $IDLE$ as the following:

$$IDLE(i,j) = \begin{cases} 0 & \text{if processor is active} \\ 1 & \text{if processor is idle} \end{cases}$$

Here i,j are indices for the original 2D mesh.

3. For each PE, calculate the total number of idle processors whose indices are smaller than $MY\_PE(i,j)$, and save as $ITOTAL(i,j)$.

4. Calculate neighboring processors' locations for each PE by

$$EAST = MY\_PE(i+1,j) - ITOTAL(i+1,j)$$

$$WEST = MY\_PE(i-1,j) - ITOTAL(i-1,j)$$

$$NORTH = MY\_PE(i,j+1) - ITOTAL(i,j+1)$$

$$SOUTH = MY\_PE(i,j-1) - ITOTAL(i,j-1)$$

5. Modify boundary conditions and other input data files.

6. Perform ocean modeling on $(MPES-K)$ processors by use of new neighboring information computed in 4 and MPI software for communication.

The above procedure is very straightforward, efficient, and easy to use. We have successfully applied this procedure to the ocean modeling code for the North Atlantic Ocean (Figure 25.2), and it gives excellent results. All idle processors are eliminated, and the computing efficiency has been improved by 34%. This simple approach can be easily used for any problem which has an irregular computing domain and is parallelized by domain decomposition techniques, and it leads to significant speed-up.

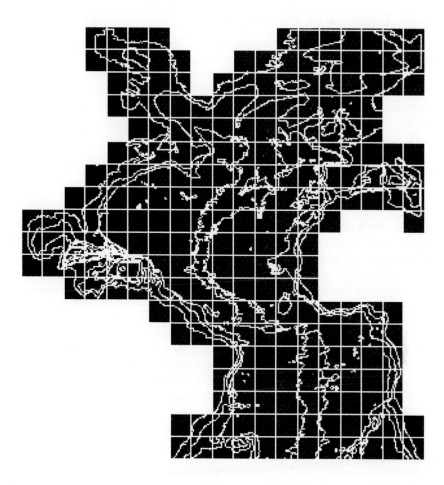

Figure 25.2 The new 2D partition over the North Atlantic Ocean. The contour lines represent the ocean depth of 1000 meters.

25.4   Ocean Modeling on Various Systems

Three-dimensional time-dependent ocean models require a large amount of memory and processing time to run realistic simulations. The significant computational resources of massively parallel supercomputers promise to make such studies feasible. But the dedicated processing time needed by the user to run the model is quite limiting, as most systems are shared by multiple users. Access to other systems should ease the computational traffic jam. Therefore, we need to make the code portable to various systems in order to take advantage of various available computing systems.

25.4.1   Overview of Parallel Systems

In order to port the ocean code to a variety of different systems, ranging from the most powerful supercomputers to affordable desktop parallel PC clusters (Beowulf-class system), understanding of these systems is necessary. Here, four typical parallel systems, the Cray T3D, the Cray T3E, the HP SPP2000, and the Beowulf cluster system, are considered. A brief description of those systems, which are the major computing resources used for the present study, is given here. Major features for each system are summarized in Table 25.1.

The Cray T3D at the Jet Propulsion Laboratory (JPL), a scalable parallel system, has 256 compute nodes with 150 Mflops peak performance and 64 Mbytes memory per node. Physically it has a distributed-memory.

The Cray T3E at the Goddard Space Flight Center, currently one of the most powerful MIMD computers available, has 1024 compute nodes with 600 Mflops peak performance and 128 Megabytes memory per node. It is a scalable parallel system with a distributed-memory structure. This machine improves application performance, by three to four times, over that of the previous generation Cray T3D.

The HP SPP2000 (Exemplar) at JPL and California Institute of Technology has 16 hypernodes, with each hypernode consisting of 16 PA-8000 processors and a single pool of 4 GB of shared physical memory. The overall architecture of the Exemplar is a hierarchical Scalable Parallel Processor(SPP). The topology of the 16 hypernodes connected by CTI(Coherent Toroidal Interconnect) is a 4×4 toroidal mesh. This supports a variety of programming models, including global shared-memory programming models and explicit message passing models.

The Beowulf system at JPL has 16 processors interconnected by 100 base T Fast Ethernet. Each processor includes a single Intel Pentium Pro 200 MHz microprocessor, which has a peak speed of 200 Mflops, 128 Megabytes of DRAM, 2.5 Gbytes of IDE disk, and PCI bus backplane, and an assortment of other devices. It is a loosely-coupled, distributed-memory system, running message-passing parallel programs that do not assume a shared-memory space across processors.

All those systems support a Fortran 90 compiler and MPI software for message passing. The Cray T3D and T3E also support the lower level Cray library, shmem, used for passing data between processors. The Beowulf system at JPL runs the Linux operating system, and the NAG Fortran 90 compiler is installed on this system. Other systems run their own operating systems and Fortran 90 compilers. Since all the above systems support explicit message passing models, theoretically, any Fortran 90 code using the domain decomposition techniques and MPI software should be able to execute on these systems.

Table 25.1 Parallel Computing Systems

Systems	# of Processors	Mflops/node	Memory
Beowulf	16	200	128 MB/node
Cray T3D	256	150	64 MB/node
Cray T3E-600	1024	600	128 MB/node
HP SPP2000	256	720	64 GB (shared-memory)

Recently we have ported the North Atlantic POP code to several distributed-memory and shared-memory systems, including the four systems described above. Porting a code to different systems requires some basic knowledge about the hardware and software. The ocean code runs well on some platforms, such as CM-2 Connection Machine, but it was not a simple issue to compile and run the ocean code on a new system. To run the ocean code on recently developed computing systems produces challenges. Each compiler on each system has its own features, so some modifications of makefile files and source codes are required for porting a code from one system to another. Many problems were encountered during the process of porting the code, and some major problems are reported in the following sections.

The compilation of ocean code on various parallel systems was the first problem encountered. Many error messages were generated at the initial compilation on a new system. Problems also vary on each systems. Details for porting the code from one system to another system and general optimization strategies for each system are described in the following.

25.4.2 Cray T3D

The ocean code (POP) used in our present study was originally written for the Connection Machine. The code was ported to the Cray T3D using SHMEM-based message passing. Since the code on the Cray T3D was time-consuming when large problems were encountered, improving the code performance was considered essential.

During the last few years, the JPL ocean modeling group has significantly optimized the POP code on the Cray T3D. Optimization methods included unrolling loops, both manually and through the compiler, rewriting code to equivalence multi-dimensional arrays as one-dimensional arrays, simplification of algebra, reductions in the number of divide operations, use of mask arrays to trade fast floating point work for slow comparisons and branches, explicitly rewriting statements in array notation as loops, and using optimized libraries. All of these contributed to the large decrease in time required to solve ocean modeling problems. The optimized code runs about 2.5 times faster than the original code, which gives significant performance improvements for modeling ocean at fine resolutions. A detailed description of this work was reported in [8].

25.4.3   Cray T3E

During the process of porting the optimized POP code from the Cray T3D to the Cray T3E, several problems were encountered at the initial compilation. First, the assembler code for the Cray T3D could not used for the Cray T3E; it had to be replaced by Fortran calls. This was easily accomplished by utilizing some of the Fortran calls originally written for the CM5 machine. Most of the assembly calls originated in the stencil routines, and the replacement Fortran codes were subsequently optimized for the Cray T3E. After other changes of the source code, the code was compiled successfully. However, the code ran slower than that on the Cray T3D. Theoretically, the Cray T3E should improve application performance by three to four times over that of the previous generation Cray T3D because of the hardware differences. The slowdown is due to the replacement of the assembler code with Fortran calls, and the entire code was not optimized on the Cray T3E.

Next, optimization of the code was considered for improvement of code performance. The STREAMS environment was turned on. This resulted in timing runs on par with the optimized T3D code. At the same time, the optimization options "$-scalar3 - unroll3$" were used. Changes were also made for BLAS (fast math) routines by use of SHMEM calls as the BLAS library is not optimized on the Cray T3E. At this stage, the updated code ran about two times faster than the code on the Cray T3D.

Another major speed-up was obtained by replacing all the default double precision reals with single precision reals. This was done by using a script to automate the conversion and resulted in another 50% speed-up. After all those modifications, the code ran about four times faster than the code on the Cray T3D. The final version was tested for an application on the North Atlantic region. It ran successfully; the results are given in the next section.

25.4.4   HP SPP2000

Porting the POP code from the standard distribution at LANL to the HP SPP2000 was also considered. The POP code with MPI version developed for the SGI machine was taken as the basic code. Since the code contains mixed single and double precision variables, it causes some problems when MPI calls are used. Implementation of all variables as double precision (real*8) variables was necessary. A script was written to convert all single precision variables to double precision ones. SIGNAL calls were replaced by function calls. Calls to SGI timer routines were replaced by corresponding calls to MPI timers. IO routines were modified to reflect the MPI topology specified in the ocean model setup. Finally, specific HP X-class exemplar compiler's optimization options " $+DA2.0N + DS2.0a - O3 + Oaggressive + Odataprefetch$" were applied to speed up the code. The modified code ran well on this system, and results are given in the next section.

25.4.5   Beowulf System-PC Clusters

The code for the HP SPP2000 was also ported to the Beowulf cluster system running on Linux. The NAG Fortran 90 compiler was used. Options "$-mismatch\_all -dusty$" had to be applied for compilation. Minor changes for the source code were made, such as the signal calls and timing calls. Double precision was applied for all REAL variables. After those modifications, the code was compiled successfully. Then the option "$-O$" was used for automatic optimization to improve the code's performance, and it ran well on the Beowulf system.

25.4.6   Code Performance and Intercomparisons

Currently the ocean code has been successfully ported to several parallel systems. After all these efforts, the POP code with the new partition, using the virtual torus topology described in the previous section, executes well on the HP SPP2000, the Cray T3E, T3D, and the Beowulf system. It should be easy to port the POP code to any parallel system which supports MPI.

Various code performance tests have been carried out among those systems. In order to maximize the performance of the ocean code, the use of parallel software tools and compiler options has been fully explored. For example, on the HP Exemplar the options "$-O3 + Oaggressive + Odataprefetch$" are used for running the ocean code. In order to compare the performance on each system, 16 processors are used for the parallel code due to the current maximum number of nodes on the JPL Beowulf system, and MPI software are used for message passing. Here, a model with grid sizes $180 \times 180 \times 20$, $360 \times 180 \times 20$, $360 \times 360 \times 20$, and $720 \times 360 \times 20$ is tested on those machines.

The results are shown in Figure 25.3, which lists the wallclock time for a 1-day integration for the four systems described earlier. The HP SPP2000 gives the best performance, and the Cray T3E shows better performance than the Cray T3D and the Beowulf. But it is interesting to note that the 16-node Beowulf system is slightly faster than the Cray T3D, and the difference is growing with the grid size used. This is because each PC of the Beowulf system being faster than a Cray T3D single node, but the communication on the Beowulf is slower than that on the Cray T3D. Overall, for a moderate grid size such as $180 \times 180 \times 20$, the communication plays a significant role. Hence, the discrepancy in time for the entire computation on the four systems depends on the difference in the network connections and the hardware. Once the grid size increases, the computation becomes dominant. Then the discrepancy in time is more consistent with the differences in the hardware.

As shown in Figure 25.3, the results on the Beowulf system are very promising: the code runs slightly faster than that on the Cray T3D and also reaches half the speed of the Cray T3E and HP Exemplar. These results are very interesting for the scientific computing community because of the low cost of the Beowulf system. Currently, the Pentium II 300 Mhz or 400 Mhz is available, and a faster network with a Gigabit rate of transfer instead of 100 Mbit is available at a reasonable price. More importantly, the price for these commodity products will drop dramatically with

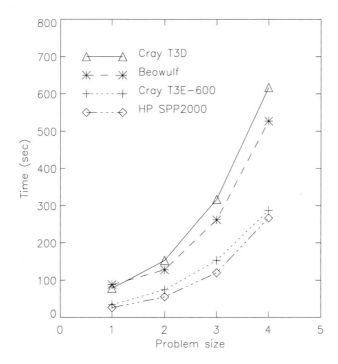

Figure 25.3 Ocean modeling on different parallel systems with grid size (1) 180x180x20, (2) 360x180x20, (3) 360x360x20, (4) 720x360x20.

time, so it is a very cost-effective way to perform large-scale scientific computing. It is quite feasible to build a dedicated Beowulf parallel system for a specific application such as ocean modeling at a fraction of the price for commercial parallel systems.

25.5   Scientific Results

Using 256-processor Cray T3D, we have conducted a 40-year integration of an Atlantic Ocean model with a spatial resolution of 1/6 degree and 37 vertical level. Figure 1.4 shows a snapshot of simulated surface current in the Gulf Stream region. The Gulf Stream is clearly simulated and plays a key role in the heat transport in the North Atlantic Ocean. Currently, we are coupling this 1/6 degree Atlantic Ocean model with a global atmospheric model on the Cray T3E. With the much bigger memory on the HP SPP-2000, it is anticipated that we can run a 1/12 degree Atlantic Ocean model.

In a regional application, we have studied the temporal and spatial evolution

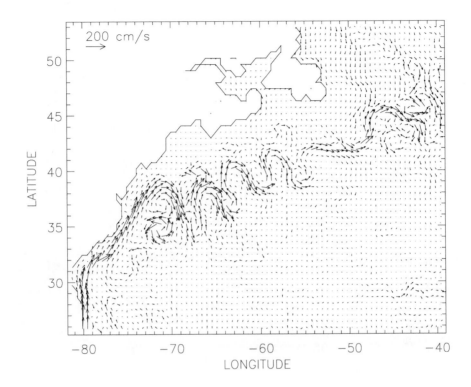

Figure 25.4 Snapshot of surface current in the Gulf Stream region simulated by the 1/6 degree Atlantic Ocean model.

of mesoscale eddies in the Gulf of Mexico (Figure 25.5). The eddies in the Gulf of Mexico are quite regular, appearing about every 10 months. In comparison with observations, the above described 1/6 degree North Atlantic Ocean model is able to reproduce major features of these eddies in the Gulf of Mexico, including their amplitudes, spatial and time scales, and propagation speed. Accurate descriptions and understanding of these eddies in the Gulf of Mexico are crucial for coastal monitoring and forecasting, which are of great benefit to regional fishery and oil industries.

25.6   Summary

In this chapter, we have developed an efficient, flexible, and portable parallel partitioning structure which can be used for any irregular ocean geometry. It has 2D partitioning features and works on any irregular geometry, and the communication pattern on the subdomains has been designed as a virtual torus. MPI software is

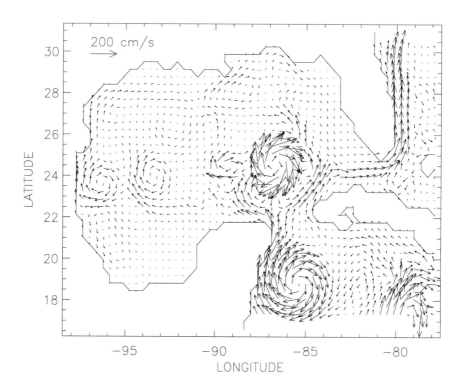

Figure 25.5 Snapshot of surface current in the Gulf of Mexico simulated by the 1/6 degree Atlantic Ocean model.

used for communication which is required when subdomains on each processor need neighboring boundary data information. This partitioning structure has dramatically saved computing resources, leading to a significant speed-up. Because of the portability of this software, the code can be executed on any parallel system which supports the MPI library. This feature allows us to study various ocean problems with different geometries on parallel systems.

We have also successfully ported the most widely used three-dimensional time-dependent ocean general circulation models to various distributed-memory and shared-memory systems, including the scalable parallel Cray T3E-600, the shared-memory HP SPP2000, and the 16-node PC cluster Beowulf system. Detailed descriptions of porting the ocean code from one system to another system have been reported. The comparison of wallclock time for a fixed number of time steps gives very useful information on the code performance of these advanced hardware systems. These discrepancies are due to the differences in the hardware of each system and the network connection used. The code scales very well on different systems as the problem's size increases with a fixed total number of processors. The code can be easily ported to any parallel system which supports a Fortran 90 compiler and MPI. In particular, the Beowulf system (pile of PCs) makes high resolution ocean computing a reality for the low-cost parallel supercomputing community.

Interesting scientific results have been obtained from the North Atlantic Ocean model, using a large number of processors. In spite of the difficulties associated with the high-resolution simulation of the ocean model, our present results illustrated here clearly demonstrate the great potential for applying our current approach to solving much more complicated ocean flow in realistic, time-dependent, three-dimensional geometries using parallel systems with large grid sizes.

Acknowledgments

The research described in this chapter was performed at the Jet Propulsion Laboratory (JPL), California Institute of Technology, under contract to the National Aeronautics and Space Administration. The Cray Supercomputers, the HP SPP2000, and the Beowulf system used to produce the results in this chapter were provided with funding from the NASA offices of Mission to Planet Earth, Aeronautics, and Space Science.

25.7   Bibliography

[1] A.J. Semtner and R.M. Chervin. Ocean-General Circulation from a Global Eddy-Resolving Model. *J. Geophys. Research Oceans*, vol. 97, 1992.

[2] R.D. Smith, J.K. Dukowicz, and R.C. Malone. Parallel Ocean General Circulation Modeling. *Physica D*, vol. 60, pages 38-61, 1992.

[3] Y. Chao, A. Gangopadhyay, F.O. Bryan, W.R. Holland. Modeling the Gulf Stream System: How Far From Reality? *Geophys. Research Letters*, vol. 23, pages 3155-3158, 1996.

[4] R.D. Smith and E. Chassignet. Personal Communication, 1998.

[5] K. Bryan. Numerical Method for the Study of the World Ocean Circulation. *J. Comp. Physics*, vol. 4, pages 1687-1712, 1969.

[6] M.D. Cox, Primitive Equation, 3-Dimensional Model of the Ocean. *Tech. Report 1*, GFDL/NOAA, Princeton, NJ, 1984.

[7] R. Pacanowski, R.K. Dixon, and A. Rosati. Modular Ocean Model User's Guide. *GFDL Ocean Group Tech. Report 2*, NOAA, Princeton, NJ, 1992.

[8] P. Wang, D. S. Katz, and Y. Chao. Optimization of a Parallel Ocean General Circulation Model, *Proceedings of Supercomputing 97*, San Jose, California, November, 1997.

Chapter 26

Computational Electromagnetics

DANIEL S. KATZ AND TOM CWIK

Jet Propulsion Laboratory
California Institute of Technology
Pasadena, California, 91109, USA

Email: {*Daniel.S.Katz, cwik*}*@jpl.nasa.gov*

26.1   Introduction

Current computational developments at the Jet Propulsion Laboratory (JPL) are motivated by the NASA/JPL goal of reducing payload in future space missions while increasing mission capability through miniaturization of active and passive sensors, analytical instruments and communication systems. Typical system requirements include the detection of particular spectral lines or bands, associated data processing, and communication of the acquired data to other systems, including the transmission of processed data to Earth via telecommunication systems. Each of these systems can include various electromagnetic components that require analysis and optimization over a complex design space. Specifications are being pushed by the demands of miniaturization as well as improved performance and/or greater fidelity in the imaging and telecommunication system. Because an experimental exploration of the design space is impractical, the use of reliable software design tools executing on high performance computers is being advanced. These tools use models based on the fundamental physics and mathematics of the component or system being studied, and they strive to have convenient turn-around times and interfaces that allow effective usage. These tools are then integrated into an optimization environment, and, using the available memory capacity and computational speed of high performance parallel platforms, simulation of the components to be optimized proceeds.

Electromagnetic components and systems at JPL can be selectively grouped into classes related to a) instruments and devices used for passive and active sensing, typically in the infrared to optical portions of the spectrum; b) components for filtering and guiding of energy for telecommunication or sensor applications; and c) antennas used for telescopes in the millimeter wave portion of the spectrum and for telecommunication in the microwave spectrum. Design efforts in the instrument and device class include finite element modeling of light coupling structures in quantum well infrared photodetectors and frequency selective surface integral equation models of near-infrared filters. Component design includes a wide range of waveguide couplers, horns and dichroic plates for radio frequency telecommunication and for millimeter wave sensors. These components are typically modeled using mode matching methods. Antenna design for telescopes and telecommunication systems involves physical optics analysis of beam-waveguide systems. Additionally, recent advances have led to integrated environments where electromagnetic models are coupled with structural and thermal models to allow design simulations of millimeter-wave telescopes that include surface distortions due to thermal loads on the telescope resulting from deep space trajectories. Finally, integrated environments call for optimization methods to be inserted into the design process to assist the designer through multi-parameter design spaces.

To fully carry out the goal of integrated design in an environment that includes optimization, high computational speeds and memory capacities are essential. These requirements can most easily be met by using parallel computing platforms. A wide range of electromagnetic codes has been ported to or developed for parallel machines at JPL. Initial work involved porting finite difference time domain and integral equation codes to a succession of distributed memory machines. This effort resulted in an understanding of machine performance and data decomposition for electromagnetic models that scaled with the number of processors and memory available. [1] Additional work involved the development of finite element methods, including unstructured mesh decomposition techniques on distributed memory machines. [2] Currently, parallel adaptive mesh refinement algorithms are being developed to solve these problems more efficiently. [3] The exploration of global optimization methods has also begun, using parallel genetic algorithms integrated with electromagnetic models for grating structures. [4] The parallel platforms that have been used in these projects have consisted of either one-of-a-kind machines or relatively expensive (though powerful) commercial computers, with the cost or availability of the parallel machines limiting their usefulness. Recently, a new class of parallel machines has become available. These machines, known as Beowulf-class computers, are built from commodity-off-the-shelf components connected together with commodity-off-the-shelf networking hardware and can achieve sustained performance equal to 10-100 personal computers.

Hyglac is an early Beowulf-class system, currently located at JPL. It consists of 16 nodes interconnected by 100Base-T Fast Ethernet. Each node include a single Intel Pentium Pro 200 MHz microprocessor, 128 MBytes of DRAM, 2.5 GBytes of IDE disk, and a PCI bus backplane. All nodes have a video card and a floppy drive, and a single monitor and keyboard are switched between the nodes. One node also has a CD-ROM drive. Because technology is evolving extremely quickly and price performance and price feature curves are also changing very quickly, no two Beowulfs ever look exactly alike. Of course, this is also because the components are almost always acquired from a mix of vendors and distributors. The power of de facto standards for interoperability of subsystems has generated an open market that provides a wealth of choices for customizing one's own version of Beowulf, or just maximizing cost advantage as prices fluctuate among sources. A Beowulf-class system runs the Linux [5] operating system, freely available over the Net or in low-cost and convenient CD-ROM distributions. In addition, publicly available parallel processing libraries such as MPI [6] and PVM [7] are used to harness the power of parallelism for large application programs. A small Beowulf system such as Hyglac costs less than \$20K (as of July 1998), including all incidental components such as low-cost packaging, taking advantage of appropriate discounts.

This chapter discusses results obtained on two Beowulf systems. Hyglac consists of 16 nodes interconnected by a 16 port Bay Networks 28115/ADV 100Base-T Fast Ethernet switch. The network switch is built around a 1.6 Gbps switch fabric, thus allowing up to 8 simultaneous 100 Mbps streams between 8 pairs of nodes. Naegling, a Beowulf system at Caltech, has a larger number (between 64 and 110, depending on the needs of various projects) of CPUs which are individually the same as those on Hyglac. It also has a small number of CPUs that contain 300 MHz Pentium II processors. It uses a network switch that consists of two 80-port Fast Ethernet switches, connected by a 4 Gbit/s link. Each switch has a backplane bandwidth that should be sufficient for the full 80 ports.

Previously, a suite of 6 application codes was studied on Hyglac. [8] These included the three electromagnetic applications that are discussed in this chapter, as well as other science and engineering applications. There was a wide range in the amount of data being communicated as well as the pattern of communication across processors, and it was determined that the amount of communication was the most important factor in predicting Beowulf performance for each application. Because the electromagnetic applications ran well on Hyglac, two of them were further studied on Naegling. [9] This chapter reprises some of that study, discusses an additional application, and attempts to provide more detailed analysis of the three applications.

All of the applications use MPI or PVM for communication between processors and run on other platforms. It is useful to examine some measured data from a few machines that are available at JPL to understand what part of the code performance is dependent on the code itself, and what part is dependant on the platform. Table 26.1 shows that the Beowulf systems (Hyglac and Naegling) have lower peak computation rates that the Cray systems (T3D and T3E-600), by factors of 1.5 to 3, similar memory sizes, and lower communication rates, by factors of 4 to 18. This implies that communications performance of the applications will be much worse than computational performance, as compared with the Cray systems, and explains why the amount of communication versus the amount of computation can be used to predict performance on the Beowulf systems.

Table 26.1 Comparison of Measured Data for Four Machines (Communications Data Is for Application-to-Application Communication Using MPI)

Parameter	Hyglac	Naegling	T3D	T3E-600
CPU Speed (MHz)	200	200	150	300
Peak Rate (MFLOP/s)	200	200	300	600
MEMORY (Mbyte)	128	128	64	128
Communication Latency (μs)	150	322	35	18
Communication Throughput (Mbit/s)	66	78	225	1200

26.2   Physical Optics Method

The software described in this section [10] is used to design and analyze reflector antennas and telescope systems. It is based simply on a discrete approximation of the radiation integral. [11] This calculation replaces the actual reflector surface with a triangularly faceted representation so that the reflector resembles a geodesic dome. The Physical Optics (PO) current is assumed to be constant in magnitude and phase over each facet, so the radiation integral is reduced to a simple summation. This program has proven to be surprisingly robust and useful for the analysis of arbitrary reflectors, particularly when the near-field is desired and the surface derivatives are not known.

The PO code has been developed and used at JPL over the last 30 years. Systems that were designed and analyzed using this code include the Deep Space Network (DSN) antennas (used for communication with spacecraft), and the Microwave Instrument for the Rosetta Orbiter (MIRO) antenna system (used to measure surface temperature gradient, outgassing, and temperature of gasses in the coma of the comet P/54 Wirtanen).

The PO code (generally) considers a dual-reflector calculation (as can be seen in Figure 26.1), which can be thought of as five sequential operations: (1) creating a mesh with N triangles on the first reflector; (2) computing the currents on the first reflector using the standard PO approximation; (3) creating a mesh with M triangles on the second reflector; (4) computing the currents on the second reflector by utilizing the currents on the first reflector as the field generator; and (5) computing the required field values by summing the fields from the currents on the second reflector. The most time-consuming part of the calculation is the computation of currents on the second reflector due to the currents on the first, since for N triangles on the first reflector, each of the M triangles on the second reflector requires an N-element sum over the first.

Because of its simplicity, the algorithm has proven to be extremely easy to adapt to the parallel computing architecture of a modest number of large-grain computing elements such as are used in Beowulf-class machines. At this time, the code has

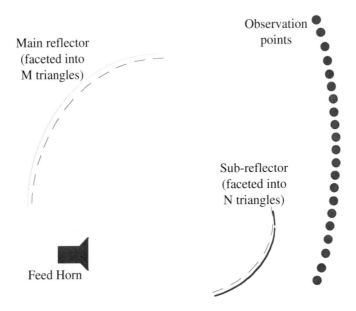

Figure 26.1 The dual reflector Physical Optics problem, showing the source, the two reflectors, and the observation points.

been parallelized by distributing the M triangles on the second reflector over all the processors, and having all processors store the complete set of currents on the N triangles of the first reflector (though the computation of these currents is done in parallel.) Also, the calculation of observed field data has been parallelized. The main steps listed above are thus all performed in parallel, using simply a small number of global sums, and a single all-to-all gather. There are also sequential operations involved, such as I/O and the triangulation of the reflector surfaces, some of which potentially could be performed in parallel, but this would require a serious effort, which has not been done at this time.

While examining the performance of the PO code, two different compilers were compared (Gnu g77 and Absoft f77) using the best optimization flags on the Beowulf system. One set of indicative results from these runs are shown in Tables 26.2 and 26.3. For this code, the Absoft compiler produced code that was approximately 30% faster, and this compiler was used hereafter.

It should be mentioned that the computation of the radiation integral in two places (in parts II and III, where the definition of the parts is given below) originally had code of the form:

```
CEJK = CDEXP(-AJ*AKR)
```

where `AJ = (0.D0,1.D0)`. This can be rewritten as:

```
CEJK = DCMPLX(DCOS(AKR),-DSIN(AKR))
```

On the T3D and T3E, these two changes led to improved results (the runtimes were reduced by 35 to 40%.) When these changes were applied to the Beowulf code using the second compiler, no significant performance change was observed, leading to the conclusion that one of the optimizations performed by this compiler was similar to this hand-optimization.

Table 26.2 Timing Results (in Minutes) for PO Code, for M=40,000, N=4,900, Using the Gnu g77 Compiler

Number of Processors	I	II	III	Total
1	0.0850	64.3	1.64	66.0
4	0.0515	16.2	0.431	16.7
16	0.0437	4.18	0.110	4.33

Table 26.3 Timing Results (in Minutes) for PO Code, for M=40,000, N=4,900, Using the Absoft f77 Compiler

Number of Processors	I	II	III	Total
1	0.0482	46.4	0.932	47.4
4	0.0303	11.6	0.237	11.9
16	0.0308	2.93	0.0652	3.03

The timings for each physical optics run are broken down into three parts. Part I is input I/O and triangulation of the main reflector surface, some of which is done in parallel. Part II is triangulation of the sub-reflector surface, evaluation of the currents on the sub-reflector, and evaluation of the currents on the main reflector. As stated previously, the triangulation of the sub-reflector and evaluation of the currents on those triangles is done redundantly, while evaluation of the currents on the main reflector is done in parallel. Part III is evaluation of far fields (parallel) and I/O (on only one processor).

It may be observed from Tables 26.4, 26.5, and 26.6 that the Beowulf code performs slightly better than the T3D code, both in terms of absolute performance as well as scaling from 1 to 64 processors. (Tables 26.4 and 26.5 contain results obtained on Hyglac, and Table 26.6 contains results obtained on Naegling.) This performance difference can be explained by the faster CPU on the Beowulf versus the T3D, and the very simple and limited communication not enabling the T3D's faster network to influence the results. The scaling difference is more a function of I/O, which is both more direct and simpler on the Beowulf, and thus faster. By reducing this part of the sequential time, scaling performance is improved. Another way to look at this is to compare the results in the three tables. Clearly, scaling is better in the larger test case, in which I/O is a smaller percentage of overall time.

It is also clear that the communications network used on Naegling is behaving as designed for the PO code running on 4, 16, or 64 processors. Since the majority of communication is single word global sums, this basically demonstrates that the network has reasonable latency for this code.

Table 26.4 Timing Results (in Seconds) for PO Code, for M=40,000, N=400

Number of Processors	Beowulf			T3D		
	I	II	III	I	II	III
1	3.19	230	56.0	14.5	249	56.4
4	1.85	57.7	14.2	8.94	62.5	14.7
16	1.52	14.6	3.86	8.97	16.6	4.13

Table 26.5 Timing Results (in Minutes) for PO Code, for M=40,000, N=4,900

Number of Processors	Beowulf			T3D		
	I	II	III	I	II	III
1	0.0482	46.4	0.932	0.254	48.7	0.941
4	0.0303	11.6	0.237	0.149	12.2	0.240
16	0.0308	2.93	0.0652	0.138	3.09	0.0749

Table 26.6 Timing Results (in Minutes) for PO Code, for M=160,000, N=10,000

Number of Processors	Beowulf			T3D		
	I	II	III	I	II	III
4	0.0950	94.6	0.845	0.546	101	0.965
16	0.0992	23.9	0.794	0.463	25.6	0.355
64	0.0950	6.38	0.541	0.520	6.93	0.116

Tables 26.7, 26.8, and 26.9 show comparisons of complete runtime for the three test problems sizes, for the Beowulf, T3D, and T3E-600 systems. These demonstrate good performance on the two Beowulf-class machines when compared with the T3D in terms of overall performance, as well as when compared with the T3E-600 in terms of price-performance. For all three test cases, the Beowulf scaling is better than the T3D scaling, but the results are fairly close for the largest test case, where the Beowulf being used is Naegling. This can be explained in large part by I/O requirements and timings on the various machines. The I/O is close to constant for all test cases over all machine sizes, so in some way it acts as serial code that hurts scaling performance. The I/O is the fastest on Hyglac, and slowest on the T3D. This is due to the number of nodes being used on the Beowulf machines, since disks are NFS-mounted, and the more nodes there are, the slower the performance

is using NFS. The T3D forces all I/O to travel through its Y-MP front end, which causes it to be very slow. Scaling on the T3D is generally as good as the small Beowulf, and faster than the large Beowulf, again due mostly to I/O. It may be observed that the speedup of the second test case on the T3E is superlinear in going from 1 to 4 processors. This is probably caused by a change in the ratio of some of the size of some of the local arrays to the cache size dropping below 1.

Table 26.7 Timing Results (in Seconds) for Complete PO Code, for M=40,000, N=400

Number of Processors	Beowulf(Hyglac)	Cray T3D	Cray T3E-600
1	289	320	107
4	73.8	86.1	29.6
16	20.0	29.2	8.36

Table 26.8 Timing Results (in Minutes) for Complete PO Code, for M=40,000, N=4,900

Number of Processors	Beowulf(Hyglac)	Cray T3D	Cray T3E-600
1	47.4	49.4	18.4
4	11.9	12.6	4.43
16	3.03	3.30	1.14

Table 26.9 Timing Results (in Minutes) for Complete PO Code, for M=160,000, N=10,000

Number of Processors	Beowulf(Naegling)	Cray T3D	Cray T3E-600
4	95.5	102	35.1
16	24.8	26.4	8.84
64	7.02	7.57	2.30

A hardware monitoring tool was used on the T3E to measure the number of floating point operations in the M=40,000, N=4,900 test case as 1.32×10^{11} floating point operations. This gives a rate of 46, 44, and 120 MFLOP/s on one processor of the Beowulf, T3D, and T3E-600, respectively. These are fairly good (23, 29, and 20% of peak, respectively) for RISC processors running Fortran code.

A few tests have been run for small test cases using 300 MHz Pentium II nodes on Naegling. They have shown a speedup of 40% for the computation part of the code over the 200 MHz Pentium Pro nodes.

26.3 Finite-Difference Time-Domain Method

The software described in this section can be used for finding antenna patterns, electromagnetic scattering from targets, fields within small electronic circuits and boards, as well as in bioelectromagnetic and photonic simulations. The method directly produces results in the time domain (transient fields), and, by some fairly simple post-processing (Fourier transforms), can produce results in the frequency domain at a number of frequencies. Models can include a variety of materials, including inhomogeneous, anisotropic and non-linear materials.

Finite-differencing was introduced by Yee in the mid 1960s as an efficient way of solving Maxwell's time-dependent curl equations. [12] His method involved sampling a continuous electromagnetic field in a finite region at equidistant points in a spatial lattice, and at equidistant time intervals. Spatial and time intervals have been chosen to avoid aliasing and to provide stability for the time-marching system. [13] The propagation of waves from a source, assumed to be turned on at time $t = 0$, is computed at each of the spatial lattice points by using the finite-difference equations to march forward in time. This process continues until a desired final state has been reached (often the steady state). This method has been demonstrated to be accurate for solving equations with millions of field unknowns in a relatively efficient manner on sequential and parallel computers.

This version of the FDTD algorithm uses a uniform Cartesian grid, and describes the object being studied as a combination of cubic cells and square faces. More complex versions exist for more accurately modeling curved surfaces and thin features, such as wires or composite materials, but these versions are often based on a Cartesian code, with small modification in regions where objects do not align themselves with the coarse grid. The vast majority of both the operations required and the physical region that is modeled is a Cartesian grid, and thus, this is the key work to be run in parallel efficiently.

This code is second order in both space and time. Using the sampling method chosen by Yee, updating a given field component requires knowledge of that same component one time step previously, as well as knowledge of additional field components within a planar region with size one square spatial cell. A typical update has a cross-shaped stencil, and looks like:

$$A_z(x,y,z,t) = C_a(x,y,z) \times A_z(x,y,z,t-\Delta t) +$$
$$C_b(x,y,z) \times \left(\begin{array}{l} B_x(x,y+\Delta x,z,t-\Delta t/2)- \\ B_x(x,y-\Delta x,z,t-\Delta t/2)+ \\ B_y(x+\Delta x,y,z,t-\Delta t/2)- \\ B_y(x-\Delta x,y,z,t-\Delta t/2) \end{array} \right) \quad (26.3.1)$$

where A_z and (B_x, B_y) are field components (either electric or magnetic), and C_a and C_b are simply coefficients that are not functions of time.

The parallelization is done in a very straightforward manner: by decomposing the three-dimensional physical domain being studied over the processors using a two-dimensional decomposition (over x and y). All values of z for a given (x,y) are located on the same processor. As the update stencil requires data one cell away from the component being updated in each direction, at the edges of the decomposed regions, an additional plane of cells from a neighboring region is needed. As neighboring regions are located on neighboring processors, this introduces communications. The data that is required to be communicated is referred to a ghost cell data (or ghost cells). This is illustrated in Figure 26.2 for a distribution on a 4 by 4 grid of processors.

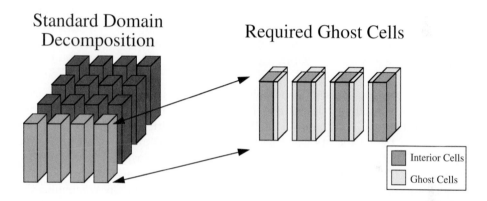

Figure 26.2 The relation between the 2-D decomposition of the 3-D grid and the required ghost cell communication.

All FDTD results that are shown in this section use a fixed size local (per processor) grid of 69 × 69 × 76 cells. The overall grid sizes therefore range from 69 × 69 × 76 to 552 × 552 × 76 (on 1 to 64 processors). (All Beowulf results are from Naegling.) This is the largest local problem size that may be solved on the T3D, and while the other machines have more local memory and could solve larger problems, it seems more fair to use the same amount of local work for these comparisons. In general, the FDTD method requires 10 to 20 points per wavelength for accurate solutions, and a boundary region of 10 to 20 cells in each direction is also needed. These grid sizes therefore correspond to scattering targets ranging in size from 5 × 5 × 5 to 53 × 53 × 5 wavelengths.

Both available compilers were used on the Beowulf version of the FDTD code. While the results are not tabulated in this chapter, the gnu g77 compiler produced code which ran faster than the code produced by the Absoft f77 compiler. (Again, both compilers were used with their best optimization flags.) However, the results were just a few percent different, rather than on the scale of the differences shown by the PO code. All results shown here are from the gnu g77 compiler.

Table 26.10 shows results on various machines and various numbers of processors in units of CPU seconds per simulated time step. Complete simulations might require hundreds to hundreds of thousands of time steps, and the results can be scaled accordingly, if complete simulation times are desired. Results are shown broken into computation and communication times, where communication includes send, receive, and buffer copy times.

Table 26.10 Timing Results (in Computation - Communication CPU Seconds per Time Step) for FDTD Code, for Fixed Problem Size per Processor of 69 × 69 × 76 Cells

Number of Processors	Beowulf	Cray T3D	Cray T3E-600
1	2.44 - 0.0	2.71 - 0.0	0.851 - 0.0
4	2.46 - 0.097	2.79 - 0.026	0.859 - 0.019
16	2.46 - 0.21	2.79 - 0.024	0.859 - 0.051
64	2.46 - 0.32	2.74 - 0.076	0.859 - 0.052

It is clear that the Beowulf and T3D computation times are comparable, while the T3E times are about three times faster. This is reasonable, given the relative clock rates (200, 150, and 300 MHz) and peak performances (200, 150, 600 MFLOP/s) of the CPUs. As with the PO code, the T3D attains the highest fraction of peak performance; the higher clock rate of the Beowulf gives it a slightly better performance than the T3D, and the T3E obtains about the same fraction of peak performance as the Beowulf. As this code has much more communication that the PO code, there is a clear difference of an order of magnitude between the communication times on the Beowulf and the T3D and T3E. However, since this is still a relatively small amount of communication compared with the amount of computation, it doesn't really effect the overall results.

It should also be noted that the use of 300 MHz Pentium II nodes produces a speedup of 20% for the computation part of the code. This improves the Beowulf as compared with the Cray platforms. If the delivered performance of PC-class CPUs continues to increase faster than that of workstation CPUs, future Beowulf-class machines will become more and more competitive with vendor-produced parallel computers.

26.4   Finite-Element Integral-Equation Coupled Method

The finite element modeling software (discussed in greater detail in [14], [15]) begins with mesh data constructed on a workstation using a commercially available CAD meshing package. Because the electromagnetic scattering simulation is an open region problem (scattered fields exist in all space to infinity), the mesh must be truncated at a surface that maintains accuracy in the modeled fields, and limits the volume of free space that is meshed. Local, absorbing boundary conditions can be used to truncate the mesh, but these may be problematic because they become more accurate as the truncating surface is removed from the scatterer, requiring greater computational expense, and they may be problem dependent. The approach used in this section solves the three-dimensional vector Helmholtz wave equation, using a coupled finite element—integral equation method. A specific integral equation (boundary element) formulation that efficiently and accurately truncates the computational domain is used. A partitioned system of equations results from the combination of discretizing the volume in and around the scatterer using the finite element method, and discretizing the surface using the integral equation method. This system of equations is solved using a two-step solution, combining a sparse iterative solver and a dense factorization method. The matrix equation assembly, solution, and the calculation of observable quantities are all computed in parallel, utilizing a varying number of processors for each stage of the calculation.

In this section, one of the three codes that make up the complete finite-element integral-equation electromagnetic analysis package is discussed. This software package was originally implemented in parallel on the Cray T3D massively parallel processor, using both Cray Adaptive Fortran (CRAFT) compiler constructs to simplify portions of the code that operate on the irregular data to build the matrix problem, and optimized message passing constructs on portions of the code that operate on regular data and require optimum machine performance to solve the matrix problem. The complete discussion of the parallel algorithm is given in [2].

This software is used similarly to the finite-difference software, except that it computes results in the frequency domain, rather than in the time domain. It is also much simpler to input complex geometric structures into this code than into the FDTD code, by using commonly available commercial CAD packages.

The complete finite-element code (PHOEBUS) builds a large sparse matrix and solves it for many right hand sides. The matrix equation is:

$$\begin{vmatrix} \mathbf{K} & \mathbf{C} & \mathbf{0} \\ \mathbf{C}^\dagger & \mathbf{0} & \mathbf{Z_0} \\ \mathbf{0} & \mathbf{Z_M} & \mathbf{Z_J} \end{vmatrix} \begin{vmatrix} \mathbf{H} \\ \mathbf{M} \\ \mathbf{J} \end{vmatrix} = \begin{vmatrix} \mathbf{0} \\ \mathbf{0} \\ \mathbf{V_i} \end{vmatrix} \qquad (26.4.1)$$

where the symbol † indicates the adjoint of a matrix. Both $\mathbf{K}$ and $\mathbf{C}$ are sparse, $\mathbf{Z_0}$ is tri-diagonal, and $\mathbf{Z_M}$ and $\mathbf{Z_J}$ are banded. In particular, the system is complex, non-symmetric, and non-Hermitian. The sparsity of the system is shown in Figure 26.3 for a case with only several hundred finite element unknowns. For larger, representative cases, the number of finite element unknowns will grow into hundreds of thousands while the number of columns in $\mathbf{C}$ will be several hundred to several thousand.

The solution to this matrix equation system is completed in two steps. Initially, $\mathbf{H}$ in the first equation in (26.4.1) is written as $\mathbf{H} = -\mathbf{K}^{-1}\mathbf{C}\mathbf{M}$ and substituted into the second equation, resulting in

$$\begin{vmatrix} \mathbf{Z_K} & \mathbf{Z_0} \\ \mathbf{Z_M} & \mathbf{Z_J} \end{vmatrix} \begin{vmatrix} \mathbf{M} \\ \mathbf{J} \end{vmatrix} = \begin{vmatrix} \mathbf{0} \\ \mathbf{V_i} \end{vmatrix} \qquad (26.4.2)$$

where $\mathbf{Z_K} = -\mathbf{C}^\dagger\mathbf{K}^{-1}\mathbf{C}$. This relatively small system is then solved directly for $\mathbf{M}$

and **J**. By solving the system in two steps, the interior solution is decoupled from the incident field $\mathbf{V_i}$, allowing for efficient solutions when many excitation fields are present, as in monostatic radar cross section simulations. This section discusses only the code used in the first step, as the code used in the second step is quite straightforward.

The relative numbers of unknowns in **H** and **M** (or **J**) make the calculation of $\mathbf{K^{-1}C}$ the major computational expense. This operation is the solution of a system of equations, $\mathbf{KX} = \mathbf{C}$, where **C** is a rectangular matrix with a potentially large number of columns in the case of electrically large scatterers. The solution is accomplished by using a symmetric variant of the quasi-minimum residual (QMR) iterative algorithm. The resulting overall matrix (26.4.2) is treated as being dense, and the solution of this second system is accomplished via a direct dense LU decomposition, since its size is relatively small.

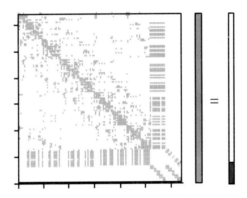

Figure 26.3 Scatter plot graphically showing structure of system of equations. Darkened spaces indicate non-zero matrix entries.

After the steps of building and distributing the matrix have been completed on a workstation or one processor of a parallel computer, or on multiple processors of a parallel computer using a data parallel language, the solution of the matrix for each of the right hand sides is done on the parallel computer, using a code written with a message passing model. This portion of the overall problem usually requires over 98% of the complete problem time, and again, it is the work done by the code considered in this section.

After the matrix is been built, reordered to minimize and equalize row bandwidth, and distributed into files, these files are read into the message passing matrix solution code. A block-like iterative scheme (quasi-minimal residual) is used for the matrix solve, in which a matrix-vector multiply is the dominant component. Figure 26.4 illustrates the process performed on a single processor in the matrix-vector multiply.

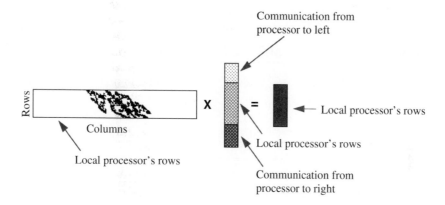

Figure 26.4 A representation of the work required in each processor to perform a matrix-vector multiply.

Because the matrix has been distributed in a one-dimensional processor grid, it makes sense to distribute the vectors similarly. The processor doing each portion of the multiply must acquire portions of the vector from its neighboring processors, as determined by the column extent of non-zeros in its portion of the matrix, and then perform the floating point operations of the multiply. The resultant vector is local to this processor, and no further communication is required.

Tables 26.11 (and 26.12) show performance data for this QMR code, running on 16 (and 64) processors, and solving a matrix problem formed from a model of a dielectric cylinder, with radius $= 1$ cm, height $= 10$ cm, permittivity $= 4.0$, and frequency $= 5.0$ GHz. The matrix is complex, with 43,791 (and 101,694) rows having an average of 16 non-zero elements per row. The physical problem requires solving this matrix for 116 right hand sides. The items in this table are measurements of the time spent in each part of the matrix solution for all right hand sides, in CPU seconds. Again, the two Beowulf compilers produced code that ran with nearly identical speed.

The computation in the matrix-vector multiply is 55% faster on the Beowulf CPU than on the T3D CPU. This is due to a combination of increased clock speed and increased cache size. The communication is about 10 times slower on the Beowulf compared with the T3D (both using MPI), which is reasonable, given that this problem requires a large number of messages of both small and large length, as well as a fairly large number of small-size global sums. With messages of this size, this code is obtaining as much throughput as is possible with MPI. All of the global sums are included in the data of the Other Work row, which also contains a large number of vector-vector operations (including dot products, norms, scales, copies.) The increase in time of this work from the T3D to the Beowulf can be viewed as a

Table 26.11 CPU Seconds Required for Each Portion of the Matrix Solution for 116 Right Hand Sides, 43,791 Edges, Using 16 Processors

Type of Work	T3D(shmem)	T3D(MPI)	Beowulf(MPI)
Matrix-Vector Multiply Computation	1290	1290	1502
Matrix-Vector Multiply Communication	114	272	1720
Other	407	415	1211
Total	1800	1980	4433

Table 26.12 CPU Seconds Required for Each Portion of the Matrix Solution for 116 Right Hand Sides, 101,694 Edges, Using 64 Processors

Type of Work	T3D(shmem)	T3D(MPI)	Beowulf(MPI)
Matrix-Vector Multiply Computation	868	919	1034
Matrix-Vector Multiply Communication	157	254	2059
Other	323	323	923
Total	1348	1496	4016

function of decreased memory-bandwidth, as there is almost no cache reuse in this work.

Overall, this problem is almost three times slower on the Beowulf than the T3D, due to a combination of communication speed, memory-bandwidth, and amount of communication. As with the previous codes, limited studies have been performed using 300 MHz Pentium II nodes. They have shown a speedup of 40% for the computation part of the code. Even with this factor, this code has decent but not outstanding price-performance, compared with the current value of a T3D. Faster communication is needed for the Beowulf version of the code to be truly comparable.

26.5 Conclusions

The intent of this chapter was to discuss the Beowulf class of computers, focusing on communication performance, since the computation performance of the personal computer CPU which forms the building block of the Beowulf is well-understood, and to reach some conclusions about what this performance implies regarding the feasibility of using this type machine to run electromagnetic codes in an institutional science and engineering environment, such as at JPL.

This chapter has shown that for both parallel calculation of the radiation integral and parallel finite-difference time-domain calculations, a Beowulf-class computer provides slightly better performance that a Cray T3D, at a much lower cost. The limited amount of communication in the physical optics code defines it as being in the heart of the regime in which Beowulf-class computing is appropriate, and thus it makes a good test code for an examination of code performance and scaling, as well as an examination of compiler options and other optimizations. The FDTD code contains more communication, but the amount is still fairly small when compared with the amount of computation, and this code is a good example of domain decomposition PDE solvers. (The timing results from this code show trends that are very similar to the results of other domain decomposition PDE solvers that have been examined at JPL.)

The physical optics software had the best performance, primarily due to its almost embarrassingly parallel nature. The limited communications required by the software led to very good overall performance, due mostly to the CPU speed of the Beowulf being 33% faster than that of the T3D. This code is superior in both absolute performance and price-performance on the Beowulf than on the T3D.

The electromagnetic finite-element software performed similarly to the finite-difference software, in that computation was faster, and communication was slower. The unique aspect of this code is the large amount of BLAS 1-type operations that are performed with data moved from main memory, rather than from cache. This work is substantially slower than similar work on the T3D. The reason for this is a combination of poorer memory-CPU throughput, and lack of optimized BLAS routines for the JPL Beowulf. BLAS routines which have been optimized for the Pentium Pro CPU under Linux have recently been released, and they will be examined in the near future. These new routines are expected to improve the performance on the PHOEBUS code. Overall, even without this change, this code has acceptable performance on the Beowulf.

An interesting observation is that for Beowulf-class computing, using commodity hardware, the user also must be concerned with commodity software, including compilers. Compared with the T3D, where Cray supplies and updates the best compiler it has available, the Beowulf system has many compilers available from various vendors, and it is not clear that any one always produces better code than the others. In addition to the compilers used in this chapter, at least one other exists (to which the authors did not have good access.) The various compilers also accept various extensions to Fortran, which may make compilation of any given code difficult or impossible without re-writing on some of it, unless, of course, the code was written strictly in standard Fortran 77 (or Fortran 90), which seems to be extremely uncommon.

It is also interesting to notice that the use of hand-optimizations produces indeterminate results in the final runtimes, again depending on which compiler and which machine are used. Specific compiler optimization flags have not been discussed in this chapter, but the set of flags that was used in each case was the set that produced the fastest running code, and in most but not all cases, various compiler flag options produced greater variation in runtimes than any hand optimizations. The implications of this are that the user be certain there are no gross inefficiencies in the code to be compiled, and that it is more important to choose the correct compiler and compiler flags.

Overall, this chapter has examined and validated the choice of a Beowulf-class computer for the physical optics application (and other similar low-communication applications), the finite-difference time-domain application (and other domain decomposition PDE solvers), and the finite-element application (and other similar sparse iterative algorithms). It has examined performance of these codes in terms of comparison with the Cray T3D and T3E, scaling, and compiler issues, and pointed out some features of which users of Beowulf-systems should be aware.

Acknowledgments

The work described was performed at the Jet Propulsion Laboratory, California Institute of Technology, under contract with the National Aeronautics and Space Administration. The Cray T3D supercomputer used in this investigation was provided by funding from the NASA Offices of Earth Science, Aeronautics, and Space Science. Part of the research reported here was performed using the Beowulf system operated by the Center for Advanced Computing Research at Caltech; access to this facility was provided by Caltech. Access to the Cray T3E-600 was provided by the Earth and Space Science (ESS) component of the NASA High Performance Computing and Communication (HPCC) program. The authors also wish to gratefully acknowledge Charles Norton's help with LaTeX.

26.6 Bibliography

[1] J. Patterson, T. Cwik, R. Ferraro, N. Jacobi, P. Liewer, T. Lockhart, G. Lyzenga, J. Parker, and D. Simoni. Parallel Computation Applied to Electromagnetic Scattering and Radiation Analysis. *Electromagnetics*, vol. 10(1-2), pages 21-39, 1990.

[2] T. Cwik, D. S. Katz, C. Zuffada and V. Jamnejad. The Application of Scalable Distributed Memory Computers to the Finite Element Modeling of Electromagnetic Scattering and Radiation. *International Journal on Numerical Methods in Engineering*, vol. 41(4), pages 759-776, 1998.

[3] J. Z. Lou, C. D. Norton, and T. Cwik. A Robust and Scalable Software Library for Parallel Adaptive Refinement on Unstructured Meshes. 1998 HPCCP/CAS Workshop, NASA Ames Research Center, Moffett Field, California, 1998.

[4] C. Zuffada, and T. Cwik. Synthesis of Novel All-Dielectric grating Filters Using Genetic Algorithms. *IEEE Transactions on Antennas and Propagation*, vol. 46(5), pages 657-663, 1998.

[5] K. Husain, T. Parker et al. *Red Hat Linux Unleashed*. Sams Publishing, Indianapolis, Indiana, 1996.

[6] M. Snir, S. W. Otto, S. Huss-Lederman, D. W. Walker, and J. Dongarra. *MPI: The Complete Reference*. The MIT Press, Cambridge, Massachusetts, 1996.

[7] A. Giest, A. Beguelin, J. Dongarra, W. Jiang, R. Manchek, and V. Sunderam. *PVM: A Users' Guide and Tutorial for Networked and Parallel Computing*. The MIT Press, Cambridge, Massachusetts, 1994.

[8] D. S. Katz, T. Cwik, B. H. Kwan, J. Z. Lou, P. L. Springer, T. Sterling, and P. Wang. An Assessment of a Beowulf System for a Wide Class of Analysis and Design Software. *Advances in Engineering Software*, vol. 26(3-6), pages 451-461, July 1998.

[9] D. S. Katz, T. Cwik, and T. Sterling. An Examination of the Performance of Two Electromagnetic Simulations on a Beowulf-Class Computer. *High Performance Computing Systems and Applications*, J. Schaeffer, ed, Kluwer Academic Press, Norwell, Massachusetts, 1998.

[10] W. A. Imbriale and T. Cwik. A Simple Physical Optics Algorithm Perfect for Parallel Computing Architecture. *10th Annual Review of Progress in Appl. Comp. Electromag.*, pages 434-441, Monterey, California, 1994.

[11] W. A. Imbriale and R. Hodges. Linear Phase Approximation in the Triangular Facet Near-Field Physical Optics Computer Program. *Applied Computational Electromagnetics Society Journal*, vol. 6, 1991.

[12] K. S. Yee. Numerical Solution of Initial Boundary Value Problems involving Maxwell's Equations in Isotropic Media. *IEEE Transactions on Antennas and Propagation*, vol. 14(5), pages 302-307, 1966.

[13] A. Taflove. *Computational Electrodynamics: The Finite-Difference Time-Domain Method*. Artech House, Norwood, Massachusetts, 1995.

[14] T. Cwik, C. Zuffada, and V. Jamnejad. Efficient Coupling of Finite Element and Integral Equation Representations for Three-Dimensional Modeling. *Finite Element Software for Microwave Engineering*, T. Itoh, G. Pelosi, and P. Silvester, eds, John Wiley and Sons, Inc., New York, 1996.

[15] T. Cwik, C. Zuffada, and V. Jamnejad. Modeling Three-Dimensional Scatterers Using a Coupled Finite Element—Integral Equation Representation. *IEEE Transactions on Antennas and Propagation*, vol. 44(4), pages 453-459, 1996.

Chapter 27

CFD Simulation: A Case Study in Software Engineering

PETER LUKSCH

LRR-TUM
Institut für Informatik
Technische Universität München, Germany

Email: *Peter.Luksch@in.tum.de*

27.1 Introduction

Computational Fluid Dynamics (CFD) is one of the Grand Challenge Applications that have been and still are the driving forces behind the development of parallel computer architectures. Today, mature simulation algorithms are available in a number of commercial software packages. Although modeling technology still is an area of active research, the main obstacle to widespread use of simulation technology today is its demand for compute resources. Only a combination of efficient and robust state-of-the-art numeric algorithms and parallel computation can overcome these limitations.

In recent years, quite a few projects have been around that have parallelized applications in scientific computing such as CFD. For instance, within the scope of the EUROPORT initiative, a number of industrial codes from different domains of scientific computing have been parallelized. Almost all these projects focused on the specific application under consideration; they did not attempt to generalize or even document their lessons learned. As a consequence, there is no generally accepted method to parallelize large software packages.

Unlike many earlier projects, the interdisciplinary project SEMPA[1] (see Table 27.1) has aimed at documenting the lessons learned during parallelization of TfC, a state of the art CFD simulation package developed by AEA Technology. An

---

[1] Software Engineering Methods for Parallel Applications in Scientific Computing. The project has been funded by the German Ministry for Education, Science, Research and Technology, bmb+f.

Table 27.1 The SEMPA Project Team

Institution	Domain/Contribution	Project Members
TU München, Inst.f.Informatik LRR-TUM, Prof. A.Bode wwwbode.in.tum.de	computer science parallel processing	P.Luksch, U.Maier M.Weidmann, S.Rathmayer
AEA Technology GmbH www.aeat.co.uk/cfx/CFXDe.html	mechanical engineering CFD software TASCflow, TfC[a], CFX	G.Scheuerer F.Unger
ICAIII, Universität Stuttgart Prof. G.Wittum www.ica3.uni-stuttgart.de	applied numerical analysis adaptive multigrid methods	P.Bastian, V.Reichenberger
GENIAS Software GmbH www.genias.de	high performance computing batch queuing system CODINE	W.Gentzsch F.Ferstl, A.Haas
project information: wwwbode.in.tum.de/Par/appls/proj/sempa_e.html		

[a]TASCflow for CAD

efficient and scalable parallelization of TfC, ParTfC, has been implemented that will be integrated into future releases of AEA's CFX software. In addition, a software engineering process has been defined, documented and consequently applied in the design and implementation of ParTfC that the partners involved will use in future parallelization projects. SEMPA has not been restricted to parallelization alone. The project successfully demonstrated the application of object oriented software technology in the domain of scientific computing. Starting with TfC's key module as a case study, a complete object oriented re-design of TfC has been carried out and implemented in C++ and Java. The problem of making efficient use of parallel scientific software is addressed, too. A resource manager has been developed that enables production runs of parallel software like ParTfC to execute in batch mode, making use of resources currently not claimed by interactive users.

27.2   TfC – a State-of-the-Art Industrial CFD Package

Before going into details about its parallelization and its object oriented re-design, we have to provide the necessary background on TfC, which is presented in more detail in [3].

TfC is an industrial CFD package developed and marketed by AEA Technology, GmbH. The software can be applied to a wide range of flow problems, including laminar and turbulent viscous flows, steady or transient, isothermal or convective, incompressible or compressible (subsonic, transonic and supersonic). Application fields include pump design, turbomachines, fans, hydraulic turbines, building ventilation, pollutant transport, combustors, nuclear reactors, heat exchangers, automotive, aerodynamics, pneumatics, ballistics, projectiles, rocket motors and many more.

TfC solves the mass momentum and scalar transport equations in three-dimensional space on hybrid unstructured grids. It implements a second order finite volume discretization. The system of linear equations that is assembled in the

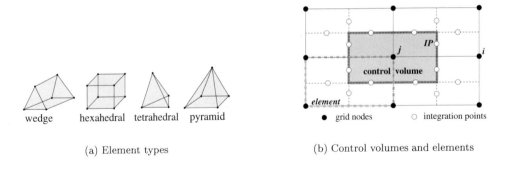

| wedge | hexahedral | tetrahedral | pyramid | | ● grid nodes | ○ integration points |

(a) Element types   (b) Control volumes and elements

Figure 27.1 TfC finite volume discretization.

discretization phase is solved by an algebraic multigrid method (AMG).

Hybrid Unstructured Grids   TfC has four types of elements that are defined by their topology: hexahedral, wedge, tetrahedral and pyramid elements (see Figure 27.1) each of which has its specific advantages. Any combination of elements from these types that fills space is a legal grid, but not necessarily a good one. Grid generation is the task of experienced engineers using advanced software tools.

An unstructured grid cannot be represented efficiently by regular data structures such as matrices. TfC uses linked lists to store node connectivity.

The Simulation Algorithm   Flow simulation in TfC essentially is an iterative loop of discretization and solution of a system of linear equations (see Figure 27.2). The discretization transforms the non-linear equations into linear ones, which are then solved by an algebraic multigrid solver. The iteration terminates if either the solution has converged or a maximum iteration count has been reached. In instationary computations, this process is repeated for each time step.

> **TfC MainControlLoop** (stationary simulation)
>   TimeSteps = 0
>   converged = false
>   **while** TimeSteps < MaxTimeSteps **or** not converged **do**
>   TimeSteps = TimeSteps + 1
>   **discretization and equation assembly**
>   **Algebraic Multigrid solver**
>   **od**

Figure 27.2 TfC main control loop.

Finite Volume Discretization   For each control volume, the integrated transport equation has to be solved:

$$\frac{\partial}{\partial t} \underbrace{\int_{V} \rho\phi dV}_{\text{transient}} + \underbrace{\oint_{A} \vec{n}\vec{U}\rho\phi dA}_{\text{advection}} = \underbrace{\oint_{A} \vec{n} J dA}_{\text{diffusion}} + \underbrace{\int_{V} S_{\phi} dV}_{\text{source}} \qquad (27.2.1)$$

Each term is discretized individually (see [3] for more detail), resulting in one linear equation per control volume. The transported quantity ϕ (e.g., velocity, pressure, enthalpy) at some grid node is expressed as a linear combination of nodal values ϕ and nodal gradients $\nabla\phi$ at its neighbor nodes.

Equation assembly is executed in an element based way, as illustrated in Figure 27.1.[2] The surface of a control volume consists of a number of faces. Flux through a face is approximated by the flux at the integration point times the face's area. For each element, fluxes through its faces are computed and added to the corresponding coefficients in the equations' of the adjacent control volumes. In Figure 27.1, the flux through integration point IP contributes to coefficients a_{ij} and a_{ji} in the equations for control volumes i and j. In the system of linear equations that results from discretization, there are non-zero coefficients only for neighboring nodes. Thus, the matrix is very sparse and structurally symmetric, i.e., a_{ij} non-zero implies a_{ji} non-zero. Since TfC uses unstructured grids, the matrix does not have any particular structure such as a band matrix.

The Algebraic Multigrid Solver (AMG)   The system of linear equations assembled by finite volume discretization defines the coefficients at the finest grid (level 1) of the AMG solver. For simplicity of drawing, we use a structured two-dimensional grid to illustrate the principle of algebraic multigrid. Note that TfC actually uses three-dimensional unstructured hybrid grids.

The basic idea behind multigrid is to define a hierarchy of grids, as illustrated in Figure 27.3. Computation proceeds from coarse to fine grids and vice versa. At each grid level, an iterative solver is executed, the so-called smoother. At the coarsest grid, an exact solver is used. The process of "passing" a result to the next coarser grid is referred to as *restriction*; *prolongation* "passes" the result to the next finer level in the grid hierarchy. Typical patterns for traversing the grid hierarchy are V- and W-cycles.

The objective in this iterative process, of course, is to reduce the error in the solution. If we think of the error function as being a superposition of harmonic sine waves, we see, by means of Fourier analysis, that iterative solvers quickly reduce those error components whose wavelength is short compared to the width of the grid, while leaving long wavelength components almost unchanged. In a hierarchy of grids, any wavelength is short compared to the width of some grid. Thus, all components of the error are "smoothed" during a V- or W-cycle.

---

[2]For simplicity of drawing, we display structured grids in Figures 27.1, 27.3, and 27.4.

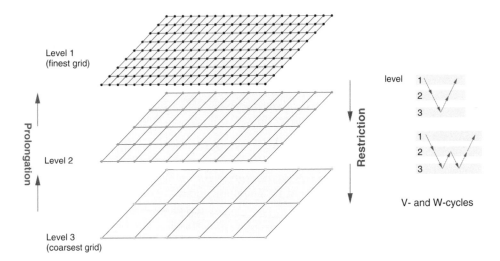

Figure 27.3 Multigrid hierarchy.

A coarse grid (level $i+1$) is generated by partitioning the nodes at the finer grid (level i) into blocks. Each of these blocks defines one node at grid level $i + 1$. In a structured two-dimensional grid, coarsening could be implemented by "omitting" every second grid line which results in a coarsening factor of four. The coarsening factor is the ratio between the number of nodes in the fine grid to the number of nodes in the coarse grid. Coarsening is much more complex with unstructured grids. The objective is to maximize the coarsening factor without compromising the smoothing effect. To achieve this, coarsening should proceed in the direction of small grid width, since error components in that direction are smoothed well at the current grid level. In addition, blocks should be "well shaped" in order to minimize connectivity in the coarse grid.

As explained in [5], the effect of smoothing depends not only on the grid's geometry but also on the current coefficient values. In *algebraic* multigrid, coarsening proceeds in the direction of *strong* coefficients. For some node i, all coefficients whose absolute value is more than some threshold percentage of the maximum coefficient value at that node, are defined to be *strong*. The coarsening procedure will add the nodes connected to i by strong coefficients to the block i belongs to. This is illustrated in Figure 27.4: Assume that coefficients with absolute values of 5 or more are defined "strong." Then the four marked nodes would be mapped into a block that corresponds to a node at the next coarser grid level.

In TfC's AMG implementation, the strategy of *coarsening in the strong coefficient direction* is complemented by a number of sophisticated heuristics that control the size and shape of the resulting blocks. TfC's AMG uses a modified ILU0 solver as its smoother. In general, ILUe solvers perform a lower-upper decomposition of

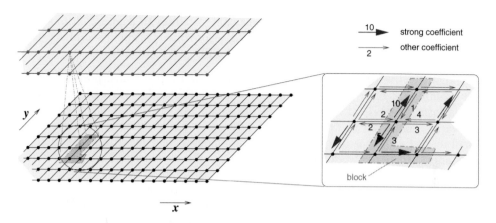

Figure 27.4 Algebraic multigrid: coarsening in the strong coefficient direction.

the matrix but update only elements that lie within a "bandwidth" of e from the main diagonal, which limits undesired fill-ins to the sparse matrix. TfC's ILU0 smoother actually updates only the main diagonal, i.e., $e = 0$. For more detailed information on AMG, we refer to the literature [5], [6].

27.3   Requirements for Parallel CFD Simulation

The main motivation for parallelizing software, of course, is to speed up program execution. In scientific computing, another – very important – driving force behind parallelization is the desire to be able to solve larger problems. The size of the problems CFD users want to deal with is at least an order of magnitude beyond the capabilities of today's workstations – with respect to memory requirements and CPU time. For turbulent flow, statistical models are used that simplify physical behavior since the resource requirements of exact simulation would exceed the capacity of today's computers. To CFD users, scaleup (the ability to deal with larger models) is at least as important as speedup. Parallel processing on distributed memory systems increases both CPU power and memory capacity. In particular, it allows the use of all resources available in a network of workstations (NOW) for simulations that exceed the resources of a single host.

User Interface   In order to be useful in practice, a parallel CFD software package must be fully compatible to the pre- and post-processing tools used with its sequential counterpart. Users of commercial CFD software often use a variety of third party pre- and post-processing tools; any change in the interface to pre- and post-processing therefore should be avoided. Ideally, the user should be completely unaware of parallel execution – except, of course, for execution time and the size of the problems he or she can deal with.

Users also expect the parallel version of the program to support all modeling options available in the sequential code and to provide checkpointing and restart facilities as are usually available in sequential CFD programs.

Portability Given the rapid development of hardware platforms, portability is a key requirement of any complex software system. Portability across a wide range of platforms is of equal importance to the vendor and the users of parallel CFD software. Compared to other types of software, CFD vendors serve a relatively small market. The customers' hardware equipment is very heterogeneous, ranging from a few networked workstations or PCs at small companies to high performance MPPs or supercomputers at large research facilities. Only software that is available for a large portion of this spectrum can be commercially successful.

While standardization in parallel programming models has made significant progress over the last years, there is little standardization in CFD software. As a consequence, a model design for CFD package A cannot be used directly by CFD package B. Lack of interoperability forces CFD users to commit themselves to a specific vendor once they start to develop a complex model. They are dependent on that vendor's ability to make his software available on the latest hardware platforms.

Efficiency and Scalability With parallel CFD simulation, two aspects of efficiency are relevant. Obviously, runtime efficiency is a critical issue. The second critical issue is memory efficiency. The total amount of main memory required by the parallel code should not be significantly larger than the memory requirement of the sequential program.

Many earlier parallelization projects have reported performance figures only for hardware configurations with up to four or eight processing nodes. Usually, no reasons are given in the publications why larger configurations have not been considered. Bottlenecks may have prevented simulations on more processors, or larger hardware configurations haven't been available, in which case potential bottlenecks could not be detected.

With CFD, there are two scenarios for parallel computing: to be able to solve larger problems in the same time (scaled work-load), or to speed up simulation of current (fixed) work-loads so that simulation tools can be used interactively rather than running in batch mode over night. The second scenario is a rather long-term objective since it would require computation speed to increase by at least five orders of magnitude. Since it is of primary concern that CFD users are able to deal with larger models, we are currently concerned with the first scenario. Our scalability requirements can be stated as follows: The parallel CFD program should deliver good efficiency on most of today's common parallel hardware platforms. On networks of LAN connected workstations where the parallel CFD program has to share resources with other users, efficiency requirements will be less strict than for MPPs or SMPs. We assume that the work-load scales with the number of processor nodes, i.e., partitions are sufficiently large to keep the CPU busy.

In the scaled work-load model, figures for speedup s_n and efficiency e_n in their classical definitions

$$s_n = \frac{T_s}{T_n} \quad , \quad e_n = \frac{s_n}{n} = \frac{T_s}{nT_n} \tag{27.3.1}$$

(where T_s is the runtime of the sequential program, T_n the runtime of the parallel program on n nodes) often cannot be given in practice. The reason is that a model large enough to justify the use of, say, 128 nodes on a distributed memory multiprocessor, cannot be computed on a single processor due to resource restrictions. We therefore "scale" the definitions of speedup and efficiency by comparing the runtime on n processors to the runtime of the same work-load on some smaller number k of processors, and refer to these definitions as *incremental speedup* $S_{inc}(k,n)$ and *incremental efficiency* $E_{inc}(k,n)$:

$$S_{inc}(k,n) = \frac{T_k}{T_n} \quad , \quad E_{inc}(k,n) = \frac{k}{n}S_{inc}(k,n) = \frac{kT_k}{nT_n} \tag{27.3.2}$$

So, if the parallel program takes 12 hours to complete on 32 processors and 8 hours on 64 processors, $S_{inc}(k,n) = 1.5$ and $E_{inc}(k,n) = 0.75$. The design requirement for ParTfC has been to achieve an (incremental) efficiency of 0.7 or more on all MPP and SMP configurations that are available for benchmark runs.[3] On (heterogeneous) NOWs that run in multi-user operation, it is very difficult to obtain meaningful performance figures for parallel applications. In addition, the main motivation for using these platforms is to be able to deal with larger models using existing hardware. Therefore, we didn't explicitly state an efficiency requirement for NOWs.

Maintainability FORTRAN is still the dominant language in scientific computing due to the large base of existing software and libraries and widespread availability of compilers that produce very efficient code. Many software systems have a long history of development that dates back to the time when FORTRAN was the latest programming language. These legacy systems often are poorly structured (code is subdivided into subroutines by author rather than by function) and there is little documentation. This type of software is becoming increasingly difficult to maintain as more software developers get involved, new features are added, and the software grows in size.

For a vendor of scientific software, consequent application of software engineering principles becomes increasingly important in order to keep his software manageable. Bad habits that have been common in scientific programming for a long time have to be overcome. The size of modern scientific software systems is best illustrated with some figures from practice: The CFD part alone (i.e., not including the interfaces to pre- and post-processing) of TfC has more than 100,000 lines of FORTRAN code and more than 500 subroutines. TfC currently implements only a part of the modeling

---

[3]Note that this requirement does not specify a range for n and k in equation 27.3.2. In practice, $n \le 64$; k is determined by the smallest configuration the work-load used in the benchmark can be simulated on.

options available in its predecessor TASCflow, which uses block-structured grids. TASCflow has about 450,000 lines of codes and more than 700 subroutines.

TfC by no means is a legacy system. The software is structured very well and comprehensive documentation for CFD developers is available. Modular design, documentation and the excellent support by AEA's experts have been key contributions to the success of parallelization and object oriented re-design of TfC. Unlike many other scientific codes, TfC exploits nearly all of FORTRAN's support for structured modular software design.

In the long term, however, the growing size of scientific software will require application of object oriented software technology, which is steadily spreading in many application domains other than scientific computing. In the SEMPA project, we took the following approach: ParTfC has been developed based on the FORTRAN code of TfC based on PVM. At the same time, object oriented technologies have been investigated in the case study of re-designing the Algebraic Multigrid solver.

Optimized Resource Utilization for Production Runs   NOWs are available at almost any company or research facility that is likely to use CFD software. Studies such as [1] have shown that workstation resources are unused most of the time. From this background it seems an attractive option to use those 90% idle resources in NOWs to execute batch jobs. Batch queueing systems assign unused resources to jobs previously submitted by users for batch execution. Actually, there are a number of public domain and commercial batch queueing systems for sequential jobs, e.g., CODINE,[4] LSF,[5] CONDOR;[6] the chapter "Job and Resource Management Systems" in Volume 1 gives an overview of the state-of-the-art in resource management. Most vendors claim their software supports parallel batch jobs. In fact, those batch queueing systems allow a parallel batch job to be started. But they have control only over the initial process of that parallel application. They cannot control any processes dynamically created by that initial process, i.e., a parallel application could "congest" the cluster without taking care of interactive users by dynamically spawning new tasks. In particular, there is no way of moving away a task from a host that is claimed for an interactive session by some user.

In order to use NOWs efficiently for production runs of parallel programs, a resource management system is required that is able to handle both sequential and parallel jobs. It has to manage a "peaceful" coexistence of interactive users and batch jobs. Having fixed time slots for batch-only and interactive-only use does not seem a viable solution in times of flexible working hours. Also, this approach would not make use of resources that are idle during interactive operation. The resource manager has to control resource utilization. When submitting a parallel batch job, users specify their resource requirements. For instance, a parallel CFD job could specify: architecture: Sun/Solaris or SGI/Irix, 8–32 processors, minimum memory per processor: 128 MB, maximum CPU time: 7 hours. The resource manager has

---

[4]http://www.genias.de/products/codine/index.html
[5]http://www.platform.com
[6]http://www.cs.wisc.edu/condor

to collect accounting information on resource consumption. It also has to enforce resource limitation, e.g., by terminating a batch job that exceeds its maximum CPU time or that attempts to allocate more than its maximum number of processors.

Usually, interactive users have priority over batch jobs. In certain exceptional, situations, however, the system administrator must be able to assign top priority to urgent batch jobs. In general, if a workstation is claimed by an interactive user, all batch activity has to be removed from that host as soon as possible. The user should not be aware of the fact that "his" workstation is used for batch processing. For a parallel application, this usually means that one or more of its tasks have to be migrated. Migration should be transparent to the application; i.e., the other tasks should not be aware of the fact that some task has migrated to another host. In addition, the delay in computation should be minimized. If the resource manager cannot find a host where to migrate the task(s) and the minimum resource requirements specified for the batch jobs can no longer be met, the whole job has to be suspended and is resumed as soon as the resource manager detects that sufficient resources are available.

27.4   Design and Implementation of ParTfC

The software engineering process defined in SEMPA for the parallelization of scientific programs is best explained in the context of the case study in which it has been developed and evaluated: the parallelization of TfC.

Accuracy and robustness of simulation software are at least as important to users as performance. Therefore, state-of-the-art numerical methods and sophisticated parallelization techniques have to be applied. Interdisciplinary collaboration of application domain experts (e.g., mechanical engineers) and computer scientists is necessary for a parallelization project to be successful. In particular, project members must gain a sound understanding of the problems and the methods in each other's discipline. This has been the main motivation for setting up the interdisciplinary SEMPA project team.

The Software Engineering Process   There is a vast body of literature on software engineering processes and methods; see, e.g., [8]. In the scientific computing domain, however, developers have not been accustomed to following a formally defined software engineering process. So, the primary issue is to have some software engineering process at all and to actually apply it consequently. Especially in interdisciplinary projects, where people with different backgrounds and methods cooperate, it turns out to be mandatory to have a well-defined design process.

The software engineering process used in the design of ParTfC has been developed based on the software engineering guidelines used by AEA (which at that time still was ASC) when developing TfC. These guidelines have been adapted to the task of parallelizing existing (sequential) software. The process model is hierarchical and combines software models known from literature. Its top level resembles the waterfall model and is illustrated in Figure 27.5. When existing code is to be

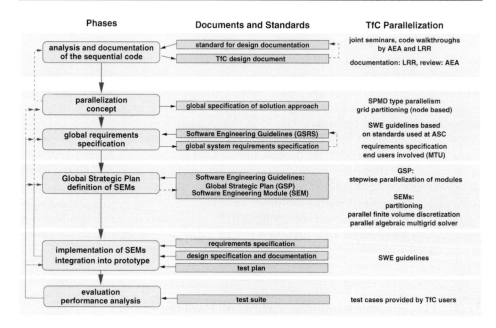

Phases	Documents and Standards	TfC Parallelization
analysis and documentation of the sequential code	standard for design documentation / TfC design document	joint seminars, code walkthroughs by AEA and LRR / documentation: LRR, review: AEA
parallelization concept	global specification of solution approach	SPMD type parallelism / grid partitioning (node based)
global requirements specification	Software Engineering Guidelines (GSRS) / global system requirements specification	SWE guidelines based on standards used at ASC / requirements specification end users involved (MTU)
Global Strategic Plan definition of SEMs	Software Engineering Guidelines: Global Strategic Plan (GSP) Software Engineering Module (SEM)	GSP: stepwise parallelization of modules / SEMs: partitioning parallel finite volume discretization parallel algebraic multigrid solver
implementation of SEMs integration into prototype	requirements specification / design specification and documentation / test plan	SWE guidelines
evaluation performance analysis	test suite	test cases provided by TfC users

Figure 27.5 The software design process of ParTfC.

parallelized, the first stage in the project is to analyze that code and to document those aspects that may be relevant to parallelization. Then possible parallelization strategies are identified and compared. In most cases, one approach can be clearly favored over the alternatives.

The next step in the process is the global requirements specification. One might argue that requirements should be set at the project start. However, some knowledge about the program and potential parallelization strategies is necessary to estimate what requirements the parallel program can reasonably be expected to meet. Requirements are useless if they are not quantified. We distinguish functional requirements from attributes. A functional requirement is one that either is met or is not met. An example is: "The parallel program must have a restart mechanism." Functional requirements are assigned priorities: *Essential* ones must definitely be met, otherwise the product is considered useless; *conditional* ones enhance the software product but their absence wouldn't make it useless; *optional* ones that have "nice to have" features. Attributes are requirements that can be quantified, e.g., "efficiency is at least 0.65." For each attribute, values are specified for the *worst*, *defined* and *best case*. A solution that does not achieve the worst case is considered to be a failure. If the defined case value is achieved, the project is considered to be successful. The best case value describes an upper limit to an attribute. There are, however, a number of attributes to which no really meaningful best values can be given.

The global strategic plan (GSP) sets the road-map for the project, i.e., it defines software engineering modules (SEMs) and their dependence. A SEM is a work-package that has a well-defined interface and that can be completed by a relatively small team in a few months. Progress is checked periodically in project meetings. Progress is checked against the time schedule and the GSP. If required, the GSP is revised according to the experience made so far. Finally, a detailed work and time schedule is set up for the next period.

Since SEMs are of limited complexity, a less formal approach to software engineering can be applied. Usually it is sufficient to require a formal specification of requirements to the SEM and a design document for future maintenance of the software module. Completed SEMs are subsequently integrated into the parallel prototype according to the GSP. The parallel program is validated using a representative suite of test cases. Another suite of test cases is used for performance analysis. The following sections describe how this process has been applied in the design of TfC.

Program Analysis and Identification of Parallelism   With TfC, quite comprehensive documentation has been available that is intended for use by CFD developers who integrate new modeling features. However, many issues relevant to parallelization were not covered in that documentation. We have analyzed TfC in a series of joint meetings of engineers from AEA and computer scientists from LRR-TUM. Results have been documented at LRR-TUM and reviewed at AEA. Finally, we have defined a standard that fitted the collection of documents into a comprehensive design documentation for the developers of ParTfC. This procedure has been quite time-consuming, but paid off immediately: The general strategy of parallelization was agreed on in a single meeting.

The Parallelization Strategy   Since TfC is a grid based application, SPMD parallelization is a natural approach. Each process actually simulates a certain region in space. In ParTfC the nodes of the grid are partitioned.[7] In order to avoid communication in the discretization phase, each partition is augmented by an overlap region as illustrated in Figure 27.6. Each task of the parallel program is assigned a partition of the grid nodes, the core nodes. The task processes all elements that have at least one of its core nodes. The discretization phase thus completely assembles all equations $\sum_j a_{i,j} x_j = r_i$ for all its core nodes i.

Going Parallel Step by Step   The GSP subdivides the design of ParTfC into three SEMs: grid partitioning, parallelization of global control and finite volume discretization, and parallel algebraic multigrid. These modules are subsequently integrated into the sequential program, replacing their sequential counterparts. Thus TfC gradually evolves into a parallel program; intermediate versions being partially parallel. ParTfC has been developed based on the PVM message passing library and has then been ported to MPI.

---

[7]Alternatively, one could have partitioned the elements.

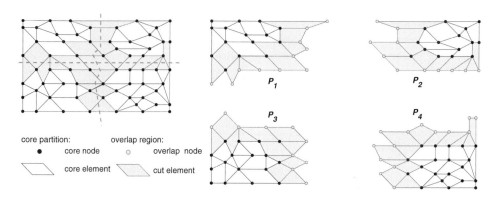

Figure 27.6 Data partitioning in ParTfC.

Partitioning the Grid   An unstructured hybrid grid as used in TfC can be viewed as a general graph. A number of graph partitioning algorithms have been published and implemented in a series of software packages. In ParTfC, we have used the MeTiS package,[8] which implements multilevel graph partitioning, a state-of-the-art algorithm. In addition, recursive coordinate bisection and simple coordinate bisection in a user defined direction have been implemented. MeTiS generated high quality partitioning for our test cases but required a substantial amount of main memory. The alternate methods require less runtime and memory; their results, however, are inferior in quality to those generated by MeTiS.

After the core partitions have been determined, the overlap region is determined as illustrated in Figure 27.6. Next, communication data structures have to be set up. For each partition i, a list of nodes k is set up from which nodal values ϕ_k and gradients $(\nabla\phi)_k$ have to be received from partition j. We refer to that list as $R_{i \leftarrow j}$. The process that owns partition i (P_i for short) also needs – for each neighbor partition j – a list of nodes whose values and gradients it has to send to the process that has that partition. Since the set of nodes in $S_{j \rightarrow i}$ is identical to that in $R_{i \leftarrow j}$, it is sufficient to compute only one of the lists and then communicate it.

To be compatible with the existing pre-/post-processing environment, ParTfC had to use the same file structure and formats as the sequential program, which, of course, are not optimized for retrieving geometry information for individual partitions. In ParTfC, all I/O is done by one dedicated process ("master"), which distributes geometry information read from the files to the other processes. From that stream of information, the other processes build the data structures for their partitions. Results are collected and merged by the "master" process and written to file. File I/O and centralized control such as residual computation are the only functions that distinguish the "master" from its "slaves." Much care has been taken to

---

[8]http://www-users.cs.umn.edu/~karypis/metis/metis.html

make sure that no process, not even the master, has to build data structures whose size is proportional to the total model size. Thus, scalability is not limited by any bottleneck inherent to the parallel computation.

Parallelizing Global Control and Finite Volume Discretization   Nodal values and gradients are exchanged once per iteration of the *while* loop of Figure 27.2. In ParTfC, a node in some partition has a local and a global number. Global node numbers are identical to TfC's node numbers and therefore identify a node uniquely. Local node numbers are assigned autonomously by processes during initialization of ParTfC and therefore do not uniquely identify a node. The $R_{i \leftarrow j}$ and $S_{j \rightarrow i}$ lists are sorted by global node numbers after initialization is complete. Throughout the computation, ϕ and $\nabla \phi$ values are packed into and unpacked from messages in that order. The message itself does not contain any node numbers.

The discretization phase processes element by element. This procedure is essentially left unchanged in ParTfC. Since overlap elements have been added to the partition, each process P completely assembles all equations (in residual form):

$$\sum_{1 \leq j \leq N} a_{ij} \Delta x_i = r_i \qquad (27.4.1)$$

for the nodes i in its core partition. These equations, however, have coefficients a_{ik} where node k is not in P's core partition but in its overlap region. For each of these nodes we add the equation

$$a_{kk} \Delta x_k = 0 \qquad (27.4.2)$$

Δx_k values are updated in each iteration of the main control loop (cf. Figure 27.2).

Parallel Algebraic Multigrid   The parallel AMG solver exchanges data after each solver sweep (i.e. smoother call). The ILU0 smoother is left unchanged, i.e. the smoother is applied to the local set of equations only (equations 27.4.1 and 27.4.2). $R_{i \leftarrow j}$ and $S_{j \rightarrow i}$ have to be built for each grid level. Except for the finest grid, all grids are constructed dynamically each time AMG is called.

Coarse grids are computed in the parallel solver using the same algorithm as in the sequential program. There is, however, one restriction: All nodes in a block must belong to the same partition, i.e., blocks are not allowed to stretch across partition boundaries. Thus, each process can determine the coarse grid structure of its partition autonomously. In order to determine the connectivity in the generated coarse grid, processes have to communicate. Consider a coarse grid block named A in P_i that has fine grid nodes i, j, k. A connects to those blocks at P_j that have neighbors of i, j, k. Since P_i doesn't know about the result of P_j's coarse grid generation, communication is required.

At the coarsest grid, an exact solver is executed. Since the coarsest grid typically has very few nodes, the solution is computed sequentially. The solver dynamically makes a tradeoff between speedup gained and overhead caused by parallel execution. If partitions become too small to justify the overhead of parallel execution, the

Table 27.2 Results for Test Case "Flow Around a Cylinder" on a Cray T3E

	Number of Partitions								
	2	4	8	16	24	32	64	96	128
Time steps	10	10	10	10	10	10	10	10	10
G1 (81,375 nodes) runtime [sec]	500	273	152	89		74	53		
G2 (625,250 nodes) runtime [sec]				606	443	345			
G3 (1,360,775 nodes) runtime [sec]							448	332	296

system of equations is collected on a single process and multigrid computation is continued sequentially. When moving back up in the grid hierarchy (toward finer grids), the equations are again distributed to all processes. The algorithms for restriction and prolongation are unaffected by parallel execution and therefore have been left unchanged.

Performance Evaluation   A number of test cases with up to 1,360,775 grid nodes have been simulated on a variety of hardware platforms: clusters of UNIX and NT workstations, shared memory multiprocessors such as DEC alpha servers, HP S-Class, NEC SX4, SGI PowerChallenge, SGI Origin 2000, distributed memory multiprocessors such as Cray T3E and IBM SP2.

For all test cases, the numerical behavior of ParTfC has been identical to that of TfC. In particular, the number of time steps needed to converge has either been identical or has differed by only one. That means that parallelization had no negative effect on convergence. Efficiencies[9] of more than 75% have been measured on almost all platforms, provided that partitions have been reasonable large. On SMPs, efficiencies of more then 85% have been observed for most cases. Memory overhead has been negligible. Only if partitions were quite small did efficiency drop below 70%, and the overlap contained more than 10% of the nodes.

Table 27.2 shows the results for the largest configuration tested so far.[10] As already mentioned, running the same model on any number of processors in a range between 1 and 256 is impossible or at least not reasonable. We see for grid G1 that efficiency drops for more than 16 nodes, since partitions are getting too small. On 32 processors, each partition has only 2,500 nodes on the average. The maximum partition size a processor of that Cray T3E can deal with is about 40,000. Therefore, grid G3 cannot be simulated on 32 or fewer processors. We give performance figures only for a range of processor numbers where partitions are of reasonable size. The figures for G3 indicate an incremental speedup of 1.5 from 64 to 128 processors, which corresponds to an incremental efficiency of 0.75.

Our benchmark results indicate that ParTfC is well scalable, at least up to 128

---

[9]absolute efficiencies e_n for test cases that execute on a single processor, incremental efficiencies $E(k,n)$ otherwise.

[10]The short runtimes are due to the fact that only a small number of iterations has been executed for the benchmarks. An actual production run would require much more iterations to complete. Few iterations are sufficient for benchmark purposes since all potential overhead occurs within the scope of one iteration of the main control loop.

processors. We have been unable to simulate a grid larger than G3 of test case "flow around a cylinder" because no workstation has been available that could pre-processes such a large model. This pre-/post-processing bottleneck will be discussed in Section 27.6.2. On some of the platforms, we have compared the PVM and MPI versions of ParTfC. No significant differences in total program performance have been observed. So far, we have not presented performance figures for NOWs. Since there is no meaningful measure for parallel performance in a heterogeneous multi-user environment, ParTfC's performance on this type of platform is very hard to evaluate. However, most users of this type of low-cost platform will be more concerned about the size of problems they can deal with. ParTfC exhibits excellent scalability with respect to memory requirements and therefore meets their requirements.

Lessons learned   Consequent application of the software engineering process described in Section 27.4 has been a key prerequisite for the success of ParTfC. It has provided the basis for efficient communication and productive cooperation in an interdisciplinary team of mechanical engineers, computer scientists, and numerical analysts. In particular, the effort spent in achieving a sound understanding of the sequential program before starting parallelization has paid off. Although quite time consuming in the initial phase, this approach resulted in a sound concept for parallelization that has proved to be successful. The global requirements specification has helped to avoid solutions that might have been easier and faster to implement than those actually adopted but would have compromised scalability or other key requirements.

The two level software engineering process has turned out to be very effective. The global strategic plan that has been periodically revised in meetings approximately every three months has made progress and problems visible to all project members. At the level of SEMs, the process has been revised throughout the project. The initial version of our guidelines had a waterfall-like process model. From the experience gained in the first SEM, we adopted a less formal model where a design document is the only deliverable document for a SEM. Since with ParTfC, requirements for SEMs have been quite clear from the GSP, we have omitted the requirements specification at the level of SEMs. In general, however, we believe that SEM requirements should be defined explicitly.

In a larger project, our software engineering process possibly would have to be extended to more than two levels. Then, the GSP defines SEMs that themselves are decomposed into work packages. In this hierarchy of SEMs, the software engineering process will be more formalized at the higher level and less formalized at the lower level.

27.5   Object Oriented Design of Scientific Software

As scientific computing software grows in complexity over time, object oriented technology becomes an indispensable means of keeping systems maintainable. However, the scientific computing community is still reluctant to make use of this technology, which already is in widespread use in a number of other application domains. Our objective has been to demonstrate within the scope of the SEMPA project that object orientation is worth to be considered for real world scientific computing applications. To that end, we chose TfC's key numeric module, the AMG solver, as a case study for demonstrating the potential of OO. The numerical core of TfC has been redesigned according to object oriented principles and implemented in C++.

AMG has been chosen as the initial case study for object orientation (OO) because it has a well-defined interface to the rest of the program. Despite its limited size (in terms of lines of code), AMG is the numerical heart of TfC and it exhibits considerable complexity with respect to control flow and data structures. Therefore, it has been a particular challenge to demonstrate that an object oriented implementation in C++ or Java can achieve numerical accuracy and reasonable runtime efficiency in such a case study of practical relevance. AMG solves equations of the form

$$Ax = R, \qquad A \in \left(\mathbb{R}^{d \times d} \right)^{n \times n}, x, R \in \left(\mathbb{R}^d \right)^n \qquad (27.5.1)$$

A is the *stiffness matrix* that results from the discretization phase. x is the solution vector, and R the residual vector. d denotes the *number of degrees of freedom* in the equation, i.e., the number of physical properties to be computed for each grid node. For the coupled mass/momentum equation, $d = 4$; for each node the three components of velocity, u_x, u_y, u_z, and pressure, p, are determined. For scalar equations, where only one property (e.g., enthalpy) is computed per node, $d = 1$. Matrix elements are themselves matrices of dimension d; vector elements are themselves vectors of dimension d.

Although even larger in size (lines of code) than the FORTRAN code, the C++ code of AMG is much easier to understand to someone who is not familiar with the program. Since all code related to accessing and administrating data structures is encapsulated in classes, the source code of the AMG algorithm itself is very compact. Actually, it looks very similar to the pseudo code notation we have used in the design document of TfC to describe the AMG solver. So a great deal of the design documentation that took us quite some time to write for the FORTRAN program is already present in the C++ sources.

Performance is a critical issue in scientific computing that is often used as an argument against OO. Actually, the initial version of the C++ AMG solver was quite slow. A number of optimizations, however, reduced runtime considerably. One of them demonstrates the benefits of encapsulation with respect to modularity. The initial version of the C++ solver used a sparse matrix data structure where the time required for element insertion increased with the number of elements already

in the matrix. Since matrices are created in each iteration of the main control loop
for all levels except the finest grid, this operation is performance critical. Therefore,
the original data structure was replaced in the *Matrix* class by a new sparse matrix
data structure which was based on the C++ standard template library and achieves
element insertion in constant time. While changing the matrix data structure would
have implied changes in many places all over the FORTRAN sources, only one class
had to be modified in the C++ solver.

After some initial optimizations, preliminary benchmarks have indicate runtimes
between 1.5 and 7 times the runtime of the FORTRAN solver, which, of course, still
is too slow for the OO solver to be used in a production environment. However,
optimization of the OO code still is in progress. In addition, performance improved
further by using advanced compilers such as the KAI[11] or EPC[12] C++ compilers.
We expect further optimizations to the code and the use of latest compiler technology to make the runtime difference between C++ and FORTRAN almost disappear
in the foreseeable future.

Due to the success of the OO AMG project, we decided to develop an object oriented re-design of the rest of TfC's CFD part, which essentially consists of the finite
volume discretization module. More detailed information on the class structure of
OOTfC can be found in [3].

In recent years, Java has established itself as the standard for platform independent object oriented programming. Java comes with comprehensive support for
distributed computing in the Internet. Since we plan to use the object oriented
TfC prototype as the basis for future research projects in meta-computing, we have
chosen Java as the implementation language for future software development. The
C++ version of AMG has been ported to Java.

27.6   Productive Use of Parallel Scientific Computing Software

Speedup and scaleup by parallel execution are two factors among others that contribute to productivity in using scientific computing software. Other important
factors are optimized utilization of hardware resources and turnaround time, i.e.,
the time an engineer has to wait until he or she can see the effect of a design change
in simulation results.

27.6.1   Resource Management in Workstation Clusters

We have developed a resource management system for PVM applications that meets
the requirements stated in Section 27.3. The SEMPA resource manager makes use of
the CoCheck consistent checkpointing and process migration mechanism, the PVM
tasker and resource manager interfaces, and the batch queuing system CODINE,
which is marketed by GENIAS.

---

[11]http://www.kai.com

[12]www.epc.co.uk

CoCheck [9] provides a mechanism to generate consistent checkpoints of parallel applications. CoCheck guarantees that a consistent set of checkpoints is written, i.e., it takes care of in transit messages, etc. To checkpoint an individual task, it relies on a single process checkpointing mechanism provided by a batch queuing system or by the operating system.

Resource Management is decentralized. When starting a parallel job, the batch queuing system selects a set of hosts according to the job's resource requirements specification. This virtual machine then is administrated by the virtual machine resource manager, VM-RM, which is part of the SEMPA resource manager. PVM itself provides only the interface that redirects PVM calls like *pvm_addhost* and a default resource manager. PVM's default resource manager has been replaced by the VM-RM, which interacts with the batch queuing system.

Task migration may be required by the batch queuing system if it detects that an interactive user claims access to a host of the virtual machine. The batch queuing system will attempt to replace that host by another idle host. If no such host is found, the task(s) from the removed hosts are distributed onto the remaining hosts, provided that the smaller virtual machine still meets the job's resource requirements. If not, the whole job is suspended, i.e., a checkpoint is written to disk, all tasks are terminated and the virtual machine is cleaned up.

The VM-RM may request task migration if it finds that a host in its virtual machine is overloaded and another host has low load. If that host is outside the virtual machine, VM-RM will request the batch queueing system to add it.

Task migration requires a checkpointing and restart mechanism. The SEMPA resource manager supports both application level and system checkpoints. Many scientific computing applications have a checkpointing mechanism that saves the current state to disk. Computation then can restart from that state. Application level checkpoints usually are much smaller than system level checkpoints since they contain only the relevant state variables. In addition, with application level checkpoints processes can migrate across platforms, e.g., from a Sparc to a PowerPC based workstation.

CoCheck's system level checkpoints can be written either to disk or be directly transferred to a remote process. In the latter case, a new process is created on the destination processor first. Then the checkpoint is written directly into the address space of that process so that the new process has the same state as the suspended one. Now the new process can replace the checkpointed one which is discarded. Migration is transparent to the application, since the application uses virtual task identifiers which are mapped to physical task identifiers by the checkpointing library.

The SEMPA resource manager has been tested using ParTfC as work-load. It is, however, hard to evaluate a resource management system outside a real-world production environment. Even in such an environment there are a number of factors that are hard to quantify, e.g., the impact of batch processing on interactive users.

Since we didn't have a production environment available, we can't give figures on system throughput. We have done some measurements of overhead and load balancing. The overhead introduced by resource management is minimal and can be neglected for long running applications like a CFD simulation. In order to evaluate the effect of load balancing on a job's runtime, we have compared runtimes of ParTfC simulations in a load balanced and in a load imbalanced cluster. Load imbalance has been achieved by running an additional (load producing) process on one host. In our test cases, load balancing actually decreased the job's run time. For large simulation models, however, the gain in speed has been much less significant than for small ones. This trend has been observed for both application and system level checkpointing. It is due to the fact that migration overhead increases with the size of state information to be transferred. Therefore, the threshold value for load imbalance should be determined depending on model size.

We have compared ParTfC's checkpointing mechanism to CoCheck's transparent checkpointing. ParTfC uses the same mechanism as its sequential counterpart; i.e., it writes the result (nodal values for all physical properties) to file. This checkpointing/restart mechanism is almost free, since mechanisms to read in initial values and to write out results have to be implemented anyway. However, ParTfC's mechanism requires the whole application to be checkpointed, stopped, and restarted while CoCheck's migration mechanism can checkpoint and migrate one task only while the others are stopped only until the migration has completed. Therefore, CoCheck's migration mechanism performs better. If checkpoints could be written for individual tasks (i.e., partitions), application level checkpointing possibly could outperform system level checkpointing.

Only a basic set of resource management strategies have been implemented so far. The node status reporter [7] provides detailed information on a host's resource utilization, so that different strategies can be implemented and be compared. Based on the on-line monitoring interface specification OMIS[13] [2], future research will aim to make the resource manager inter-operate with other tools.

27.6.2   The Pre- and Post-Processing Bottlenecks

The current mode of using scientific software is batch oriented. Having set up a model, the engineer submits the compute job, which usually takes hours or days to complete. The result data are written to disk and read by some post-processing tool. This traditional approach has been adopted for ParTfC for the sake of backwards compatibility to existing pre- and post-processing tools. It has, however, a number of drawbacks. With post-mortem result visualization, the user has to wait until the computation has completed before he can see whether something has gone wrong. Erroneous behavior (e.g., caused by bad parameter settings) often could be detected very early in the simulation if its state could be monitored on-line.

While parallel computation allows one to deal with really large models, these models often cannot be generated by the pre-processing software that executes on a single workstation due to lack of memory. The same applies for post-processing. Therefore, new concepts for model generation and result visualization are required to fully exploit the potential scalable parallel simulation offers.

---

[13]http://wwwbode.in.tum.de/~omis

The post-processing problem is addressed by a current project at LRR-TUM. OViD (On line Visualization and Debugging) [4] defines a concept for on-line visualization of scientific computations. A server interfaces to the parallel computation on the one side and to a visualization tool on the other side. The parallel application has to be instrumented to interact with the server. Visualization is based on objects that have to be defined for the individual application. In addition, interaction points have to be defined; i.e., points in the source code where the objects have a consistent state that can be used for visualization. Developers of scientific applications can easily apply this method to their code. The second interface also is very general. It allows software developers to easily adapt their current post-processing tool to access the OViD server rather than files. Of course, the OViD interface offers a much richer functionality than a file interface. To make use of them, the visualization tool will have to be extended. The main advantage for the user, however, is that he can stay with the post-processing tool he is used to and will subsequently get additional functionality as the tool developers make use of the interactive services the interface provides.

With this interactive approach to visualization, the amount of data that has to be transferred between the compute server and the user's workstation can be reduced in a variety of ways. Object data is delivered on demand only to avoid unnecessary network traffic. On-line data selection and compression can be applied at the server side. Careful selection of the type of representation that is transferred can further reduce network traffic. For instance, if a face model is sufficient for the visualization function requested by the user, the amount of data to be transferred is reduced by an order of magnitude if the server provides a face representation rather than the full geometry.

Coupling the visualization tool with a parallel source level debugger increases productivity during program development and maintenance. Erroneous numerical behavior is extremely difficult to observe with current source level debuggers, especially if the problem occurs with a very large model. Bad behavior is best detected with the application specific visualization tool, since it provides the appropriate view of the current state. To track down the problem further, a (parallel) source code debugger provides provides the appropriate view.

27.6.3 Network Based Collaborative Design Environments

Usually, a number of individuals in different organizations at different places are involved in a CFD project. A typical scenario involves the CFD software vendor, the user who designs and simulates a model, and possibly a university group in a mechanical engineering department that is developing a new modeling feature. Currently, these groups exchange data by mailing tapes, and they have to meet frequently to analyze problems. They would be much more productive if they could interact in a network based environment (Internet or intranet) where they could share a common view of the current state of the computation under consideration.

Therefore, future research in scientific computing will have to address collaborative design environments that allow distributed teams to share a common view of the current state of the computation under consideration and to interact with it on-line. Some issues related to such an environment already have been addressed in projects at LRR-TUM. OViD allows an arbitrary number of tools to attach to the parallel computation at runtime. With OOTfC, a demonstration prototype of an Internet browser based visualization tool has been implemented.

27.7   Bibliography

[1] Philip Krueger and Rohit Chawla. The Stealth Distributed Scheduler. In *Proceedings of the IEEE 11th International Conference on Distributed Computing Systems*, pages 336–343, Los Alamitos, CA, 1991.

[2] Thomas Ludwig, Roland Wismüller, Vaidy Sunderam, and Arndt Bode. *OMIS — On-line Monitoring Interface Specification (Version 2.0)*, vol. 9 of *Research Report Series LRR-TUM, Arndt Bode, ed.* Shaker-Verlag, Aachen, July 1997.

[3] Peter Luksch, Ursula Maier, Sabine Rathmayer, Matthias Weidmann, Friedemann Unger, Peter Bastian, Volker Reichenberger, and Andreas Haas. SEMPA: Software Engineering Methods for Parallel Applications in Scientific Computing, Project Report, vol. 12 of *Research Report Series LRR-TUM*, Arndt Bode, ed. Shaker-Verlag, Aachen, September 1998. http://wwwbode.in.tum.de/archiv/Projektberichte/SEMPA-Schlussberichte/Schlussberichte.

[4] Sabine Rathmayer and Michael Lenke. A Tool for On-Line Visualization and Interactive Steering of Parallel HPC Applications. *11th International Parallel Processing Symposium*, IEEE Computer Society, 1997.

[5] Michael J. Raw. A Coupled Algebraic Multigrid Method for the 3D Navier-Stokes Equations. In *Fast Solvers for Flow Problems, Proceedings of the 10th GAMM-Seminar, Notes on Numerical Fluid Mechanics*, vol. 49, pages 204–215. Vieweg-Verlag, Braunschweig, Wiesbaden, 1995.

[6] Michael J. Raw. Robustness of Coupled Algebraic Multigrid for the Navier-Stokes equations. In *34th Aerospace Sciences Meeting & Exhibit*. American Institute of Aeoronautics and Astronautics, January 1996.

[7] Christian Röder. Load Management Techniques in Distributed Heterogeneous Systems, vol. 11 of *Research Report Series LRR-TUM*, Arndt Bode, ed. Shaker-Verlag, Aachen, 1998.

[8] Ian Sommerville. *Software Engineering*. Addison Wesley, 1996.

[9] Georg Stellner and Jim Pruyne. Resource Management and Checkpointing for PVM. In *Proceedings of the Second European PVM User Group Meeting*, pages 131–136, Lyon, September 1995.

Chapter 28

Quantum Reactive Scattering Calculations

RANIERI BARAGLIA[†], RENATO FERRINI[†], DOMENICO LAFORENZA[†],
ANTONIO LAGANÀ[‡]

[†] CNUCE, CNR
via S. Maria, 36
Pisa, Italy

[‡] Dipartimento di Chimica
via Elce di Sotto
Perugia, Italy

Email: (R.Baraglia, R.Ferrini, D.Laforenza)@cnuce.cnr.it
lag@reaction.chm.unipg.it

28.1 Introduction

The modeling of complex gas phase systems (such as those for simulating cold plasmas, spacecraft propellers, air pollution, etc.) is based on the solution of fluid dynamics and chemical kinetics equations [1]. The most difficult task in such modeling is to assemble the chemical kinetics since a complete data base of the efficiency parameters of intervening reactions is not available. This information is difficult to supply experimentally due to the range of conditions necessary for the modeling, though it can occasionally be derived by an interpolation of available experimental data. However, this is generally not possible and there is no alternative to make a direct a priori calculation of efficiency parameters such as rate coefficients and cross-sections of the intervening elementary processes.

From a theoretical point of view, an elementary reaction is a many body problem concerning the collision of two or more molecular aggregates. Due to the low probability of collisions of three or more molecules, the theory has been developed mainly for two molecule (bi-molecular) collisions.

The most popular recent theoretical advances are based on classical mechanics. Classical mechanics describes elementary processes in terms of the time evolution of the positions and momenta of N pointwise masses. Related computational procedures can be efficiently implemented on parallel machines or large metacomputers (once a few basic precautions have been taken) because of the easy-to-decouple nature of related algorithms [2]. Once the state-to-state reactive probabilities have been calculated by integrating classical equations of motions for a suitable sample of initial conditions, rate coefficients or cross-sections of the intervening processes can be evaluated by averaging over the unobserved variables.

Unfortunately, pure quantum effects (such as thresholds, resonances, interferences, etc.) cannot be properly dealt with by classical mechanics. To this end, rigorous quantum treatments need to be used. However, because of the associated heavy demand of computational resources, these treatments lead only to tractable computational procedures for low energy and fairly light three or four atom reactions. Moreover, due to the strongly coupled nature of related numerical algorithms, an efficient implementation on parallel architectures is extremely difficult to achieve.

This chapter is organized as follows: First, we illustrate how the problem of calculating quantum reaction probabilities has been decomposed and how related algorithms can be organized. Then we analyze the parallel models adopted to implement one of these algorithms on massively parallel architectures. Finally, we discuss the performances measured when implementing the code on some parallel architectures.

28.2 The Many Body Problem: Description, Decomposition, and Solutions

The problem examined here is how to calculate efficiency parameters (rate coefficients and cross-sections) of elementary reactive processes using quantum means. For bimolecular reactions of atom diatom system, the evaluation of state-(vj)-to-state $(v'j')$ rate coefficients $(k_{vj,v'j'}(T))$ at a given temperature T is based on the calculation of the state-to-state cross-section using the following equation:

$$k_{vj,v'j'}(T) = \left(\frac{8}{\pi \mu k_B^3 T^3} \right)^{1/2} \int_0^\infty E_{tr} \sigma_{vj,v'j'} e^{-E_{tr}/k_B T} dE_{tr} \qquad (28.2.1)$$

In equation 28.2.1, E_{tr} is the translational energy of the system, μ is the reduced mass of the two collision partners, and k_B is the Botzmann constant. The state-to-state cross-section $(\sigma_{vj,v'j'})$ can be calculated by averaging over the unobserved variables the square modulus of the corresponding element of the scattering **S** matrix.

28.2.1   The Decomposition of the Problem and the Mathematical Formalism

The mathematical problem of calculating the $\mathbf{S}$ matrix of a reactive scattering process is usually tackled by constructing the wavefunction that describes both asymptotic and intermediate complex arrangements. This wavefunction can be calculated by integrating the time dependent Schrödinger equation

$$i\hbar\frac{\partial}{\partial t}Z\left(\{\mathbf{w}\},\{\mathbf{W}\},t\right) = \mathbf{H}Z\left(\{\mathbf{w}\},\{\mathbf{W}\},t\right) \qquad (28.2.2)$$

where Z is the global wavefunction of the molecular system, $\mathbf{H}$ is the total many body Hamiltonian, t is time, and $\{\mathbf{w}\}$ and $\{\mathbf{W}\}$ are the electronic and nuclear coordinate sets, respectively.

The Separation of Nuclear Motion

The size of the problem can be initially reduced by partitioning the total Hamiltonian into an electronic operator $\mathbf{H}_e$ (including contributions for fixed nuclei interactions) and a nuclear kinetic energy operator $\mathbf{T}_N$ and by expanding the global wavefunction Z in terms of the adiabatic electronic wavefunctions $\Phi_k^e(\{\mathbf{w}\};\{\mathbf{W}\})$. These wavefunctions are eigenfunctions of the fixed nuclei equation

$$\mathbf{H}_e\left(\{\mathbf{w}\};\{\mathbf{W}\}\right)\Phi_k^e(\{\mathbf{w}\};\{\mathbf{W}\}) = V_k(\{\mathbf{W}\})\Phi_k^e(\{\mathbf{w}\};\{\mathbf{W}\}) \qquad (28.2.3)$$

which only parametrically depends on the nuclear positions. The ensemble of $V_k(\{\mathbf{W}\})$ values at various nuclear geometries is the Potential Energy Surface (PES) on which the motion of the N nuclei of the system takes place. By substituting the expansion of Z into equation 28.2.3, we obtain a set of coupled differential equations which describe the nuclear motion. Coupling matrices also contain terms related to electronic motion. These are often assumed to be negligible, as is usually the case in thermal reactions. Consequently, we can write the time dependent Schrödinger equation

$$i\hbar\frac{\partial}{\partial t}Z\left(\{\mathbf{w}\},\{\mathbf{W}\},t\right) = \mathbf{H}_N(\{\mathbf{W}\})\Xi(\{\mathbf{W}\}) = [\mathbf{T}_N(\{\mathbf{W}\}) + V(\{\mathbf{W}\})]\,\Xi(\{\mathbf{W}\})$$
$$(28.2.4)$$

where the index k of the potential energy surface V_k has been dropped for the sake of simplicity. In the same equation, the $\Xi(\{\mathbf{W}\})$ wavefunctions are the functions which describe nuclear positions. Nuclear wavefunctions are given as coefficients of the global wavefunction expansion of Z in terms of Φ^es.

Center of Mass and Time Separation

The problem can be further reduced (without introducing additional approximations) by separating the motion of the center of mass and by factorizing the time dependence in the system wavefunction (this means that the system can be described by a stationary wave) [3]. As a result, the size of the calculation is reduced to $3N$-3 since for N nuclei N-1 position vectors with respect to the center of mass are needed to describe the system. Consequently, for a three atom (A, B, C) system there are six variables and the related stationary Schrödinger equation can be formulated as

$$[\mathbf{H}_N - E]\,\Xi(\mathbf{R}_\tau,\mathbf{r}_\tau) = \left[-\frac{\hbar^2}{2\mu}(\nabla^2_{\mathbf{R}_\tau} + \nabla^2_{\mathbf{r}_\tau}) + V(R_\tau,r_\tau,\Theta_\tau) - E\right]\Xi(\mathbf{R}_\tau,\mathbf{r}_\tau) = 0$$

$$(28.2.5)$$

where E is the total energy of the system, $\mathbf{R}_\tau$ and $\mathbf{r}_\tau$ the mass scaled atom-diatom Jacobi coordinates, and $\Xi(\mathbf{R}_\tau,\mathbf{r}_\tau)$ the time independent nuclear wavefunction. As usual, Jacobi coordinates are labeled after the arrangement τ (τ = 1, 2 and 3 means A + BC, B + CA and C + BA, respectively) to which they refer.

As we shall discuss later, we could decide not to discorporate the time dependence at this stage and keep the time dependence for use as a continuity variable for the numerical integration of the scattering equations.

Partial Wave Decomposition

To further reduce the dimensionality of the problem to three dimensions (3D), we can reformulate the atom diatom Hamiltonian as follows:

$$\mathbf{H}_N = -\frac{\hbar^2}{2\mu}\left(\frac{1}{R_\tau}\frac{\partial^2}{\partial R_\tau^2}R_\tau + \frac{1}{r_\tau}\frac{\partial^2}{\partial r_\tau^2}r_\tau\right) + \frac{(\mathbf{J}-\mathbf{j}_\tau)^2}{2\mu R_\tau{}^2} + \frac{\mathbf{j}_\tau^2}{2\mu r_\tau{}^2} + V(R_\tau,r_\tau,\Theta_\tau)$$

$$(28.2.6)$$

where $\mathbf{J}$ is equal to the sum of $\mathbf{j}_\tau$ and $\mathbf{l}_\tau$ ($\mathbf{J}$, $\mathbf{j}_\tau$ and $\mathbf{l}_\tau$ are the total, the rotational and the orbital angular momentum operators of the system, respectively), and Θ_τ is the angle formed by $\mathbf{R}_\tau$ and $\mathbf{r}_\tau$. This makes it convenient to expand the $\Xi(\mathbf{R}_\tau,\mathbf{r}_\tau)$ wavefunction in terms of the $\Psi^{JMp}(\mathbf{R}_\tau,\mathbf{r}_\tau)$ partial waves, which are eigenfunctions of the modulus J of the total angular momentum $\mathbf{J}$, of its projection M on a space fixed reference axis, and of the parity p. It is also useful to adopt a body fixed Cartesian reference frame. To do this, the frame can be rotated to allow the z axis to lie along the $\mathbf{R}_\tau$ vector and the xz plane to coincide with the molecular plane (in this system, the projection of the total angular momentum $\mathbf{J}$ is Ω). The body fixed frame allows the three orientation angles (the α, β and γ Euler angles) of the reference frame to be separated from the three internal coordinates R_τ, r_τ and Θ_τ.

Dimensionality Reduction and Dynamical Approximations

To reduce the size of the problem from three to two (2D) or one (1D) dimensions, we need to introduce dynamical approximations. Typically, these approximations consist of substituting an operator with a constant (sudden), or decoupling a degree of freedom (adiabatic). Typical examples of reduced dimensionality methods are the Centrifugal Sudden (CS) approximation and the Energy Sudden (ES) approximation. Like the exact close coupled treatment, they are based on the solution of a 2D bound state problem. However, the partial decoupling introduced by the approximation allows the calculations to be separated into smaller independent blocks and the related computing to be reduced.

In our investigation we focused on the Reactive Infinite Order Sudden (RIOS) approximation [4], which is the simultaneous introduction of the CS and ES approximations. In the RIOS treatment, the scattering equations are reduced to a set of fixed collision angle two mathematical dimension differential equations

$$\left[-\frac{\hbar^2}{2\mu} \left(\frac{1}{R_\tau} \frac{\partial^2}{\partial R_\tau{}^2} R_\tau + \frac{1}{r_\tau} \frac{\partial^2}{\partial r_\tau{}^2} r_\tau - \frac{A_\tau}{R_\tau{}^2} - \frac{B_\tau}{r_\tau{}^2} \right) + V(R_\tau, r_\tau; \Theta_\tau) - E \right]$$

$$\Xi^{RIOS}(R_\tau, r_\tau; \Theta_\tau) = 0 \qquad (28.2.7)$$

where $A_\tau = \hbar^{-2} l_\tau (l_\tau + 1)$ and $B_\tau = \hbar^{-2} j_\tau (j_\tau + 1)$ since the approximation consists in substituting the diatomic rotation $\mathbf{j}_\tau^2$ and atom diatom orbiting $\mathbf{l}_\tau^2$ operators with fixed values.

28.2.2   The Integration of Scattering Equations

There are various techniques for integrating scattering equations which depend on the theoretical formulation chosen for the many body problem. The most direct one is the method which integrates in time equation 28.2.4 (see reference [3]). On the other hand, when time is factored out, we can still consider all the spatial variables in the same manner, expand the solution as a linear combination of functions of all variables, and solve variationally the resulting set of linear equations. The most popular method, however, singles out from the spatial variables a privileged coordinate to be taken as a reaction coordinate. The expansion is then made in terms of the functions of the remaining local (bound) variables in the reaction coordinate. By averaging the bound coordinates, we obtain a set of coupled differential equations in the reaction coordinate which are then integrated by propagating the solution from the origin to the asymptotes.

The Propagation Method

In the RIOS code, equation 28.2.7 is integrated by partitioning the R_λ and r_λ planes (defined by a fixed value of Θ_λ in both reactant $\lambda = \alpha$ and product $\lambda = \beta$ channels) into a polar and a Cartesian subdomain. The α and β planes intersect at the straight line connecting the origin $R_\lambda = r_\lambda = 0$ to the ridge which separates the related entrance and exit regions. For each arrangement channel λ, the integration is carried out from the separation line to a value of R_λ large enough to ensure that the atom-diatom interaction is negligible. In the short range, Cartesian coordinates are replaced by circular coordinates centered on a classically forbidden inaccessible point (turning center) located on the intersection line.

To carry out the numerical integration, each arrangement channel is segmented into several small polar ($N_{\lambda p}$) and Cartesian ($N_{\lambda c}$) sectors. Within each sector i, the fixed Θ_λ RIOS wavefunction $\Xi^{RIOS}(R_\lambda, r_\lambda; \Theta_\lambda)$ is expanded in terms of the $\phi^i(r_\lambda; R_\lambda, \Theta_\lambda)$ eigenfunctions calculated by solving the one-dimensional bound state equation in r_λ

$$\left[\frac{\partial^2}{\partial r_\lambda^2} + \frac{2\mu}{\hbar^2} \left(V(r_\lambda; R_\lambda^i, \Theta_\lambda) - \varepsilon_\lambda^i \right) \right] \phi^i(r_\lambda; R_\lambda^i, \Theta_\lambda) = 0 \qquad (28.2.8)$$

at R_λ^i the midpoint value of R_λ for sector i (a similar expression is obtained in the polar coordinate σ_λ). To this end, the potential is calculated on N_g evenly spaced grid points along r_λ (or σ_λ in the polar region) and the eigenfunctions are calculated using a propagation method.

By truncating the expansion to the first N_v terms, substituting the expansion into equation 28.2.7 and averaging on r_λ, we obtain a set of N_v coupled equations of the type (here again, a similar expression is obtained when using η_λ in the polar region)

$$\left[\frac{d^2}{dR_\lambda^2} - \mathbf{D}_\lambda^l(E, \Theta_\lambda) \right] \psi_v^l(R_\lambda; \Theta_\lambda) = 0 \qquad (28.2.9)$$

where $\mathbf{D}_\lambda^l(E, \Theta_\lambda)$ is the coupling matrix and $\psi_v^l(R_\lambda; \Theta_\lambda)$ are the coefficients of the expansion of $\Xi^{RIOS}(R_\lambda, r_\lambda; \Theta_\lambda)$ for a given energy E and a fixed value of l (the j label is dropped from the notation since in the RIOS approach, the $j \neq 0$ results can be obtained from the $j = 0$ ones by a simple energy scaling).

For all the desired values of E and every value of l contributing to reaction, equation 28.2.9 is integrated by propagating the solution through the various sectors. This is performed by using a recursive algorithm which matches intrasector analytical solutions to those of the next sector at the common border. After matching the solutions of the α and β channel (hereafter, in fact, we shall drop the label λ from the equations) and imposing the appropriate boundary conditions at the asymptotes, we can estimate the detailed state v to state v' fixed Θ **S** matrix elements ($S_{lv,v'}(\Theta, E)$).

The Computer Algorithms

Various computer algorithms have been designed to implement the numerical procedures. In particular, a first order initial value technique has been adopted for the time dependent method; a solver of a set of linear (integral) equations constrained to a minimization of a reference quantity has been used for the variational method, and a propagation technique for the RIOS method. For illustrative purposes, the scheme of the RIOS method for which parallelization has been investigated in depth is given in Figure 28.1.

The main differences between full and reduced dimensionality treatments are in the reduced size of the bound state problem (and thus the smaller size of the coupling matrix), the partitioning of the calculations into several N_Θ decoupled

---

SECTION I
Input general data
Calculate quantities of common use
SECTION II
subsection *a*
IF (first run) THEN
      LOOP on N_Θ angles
            LOOP on N_S sectors
                  Generate fixed angle one dimensional cuts of the potential
                  Calculate related eigenvalues and eigenfunctions
                  Calculate overlap integrals and fixed coupling matrix
                  Store eigenvalues, overlaps and coupling matrix
            END the sector loop
      END the Θ loop
ENDIF
subsection *b*
LOOP on N_Θ angles
      Read the fixed angle energy independent coupling matrix
      LOOP on N_E energies
            Embed the energy dependence into the coupling matrix
            LOOP on l quantum numbers
                  LOOP on N_S sectors
                      Propagate the **R** matrix through the sectors
                  END the sector loop
                  Calculate and store detailed **S** matrix elements
                  IF (converged with l) exit l loop
            END the l loop
            Calculate the fixed angle, fixed energy contribution to the cross-section
      END the energy loop
END the angle loop

Figure 28.1 Scheme of the RIOS Algorithm.

fixed angle calculations (leading to an additional loop over the values of the angle Θ), and the reduction of the angular momentum quantum numbers to l. Quite often, as is the case for the two approaches considered here, reduced dimensionality methods are designed so that the bound state problem is one-dimensional and only some of the internal degrees of freedom are explicitly considered. This means that *subsection a*, in which the basis set and related overlap and coupling matrices are calculated, has little time consumption and moderate memory occupation. As a result, *subsection b* is also less demanding in terms of computer resources.

28.3 Parallelization Strategies

The parallelization of RIOS has been pushed to different levels and the related computational code has been implemented on several computer architectures.

In order to adopt an efficient parallelization strategy, some aspects of the problem decomposition of the RIOS method have been analyzed [5]. As shown in Figure

28.1, the main body of the computation is performed in $SECTION\ II$, which has two steps: *subsection a* and *subsection b*.

In *subsection a*, the coupling matrix is computed. The various routines perform, for a given value of Θ, the following tasks:

1. divide the integration domain into many small sectors;

2. generate sector one-dimensional eigenfunctions and eigenvalues;

3. compute the sector coupling matrix and overlaps between eigenfunctions of adjacent sectors.

In *subsection b*, the solution is calculated by propagating the **R** matrix (*i.e.*, the matrix of the ratio between the function χ and its derivative) for a given value of E and l (a $E_k l_m$ pair), using the coupling matrix produced in *subsection a*.

To design a suitable parallel model, we examine the cpu and memory requirements of the code as well as its possible order dependencies. As a result:

1. the partitioning of the integration domain into sectors has a limited memory and cpu time demand, and is free of order-dependent constructs at an intersector level;

2. the generation of the one-dimensional eigenfunctions and eigenvalues for each sector creates a large demand for processor time and is free of order-dependent constructs at an intersector level;

3. the computation of the sector coupling matrix has a large memory demand (calculated quantities must be stored in large matrices) and an order dependence at an intersector level. This dependence is not recursive because it needs only eigenfunctions and eigenvalues of one sector (which is an order independent calculation) to be passed to the next one;

4. the propagation of the solution is, on the other hand, strictly order dependent at an intersector level because the propagation of the solution through the various sectors is a recursive algorithm which builds the value of the R matrix at one sector from the one at the previous sector.

The above described features allow the exploitation of parallelism at various levels of complexity. The parameter considered to express the level of computational complexity is usually the granularity (*i.e.*, the amount of computational work assigned to a single process).

The commonly used procedure is to refer to parallel computational models (*i.e.*, task farm and pipeline [6]). Since the structure of RIOS is quite complex, a combination of models rather than a single one might be the optimum solution. Unfortunately, there is no unique correspondence between the parameters of the physical problem and the parameters of the algorithm. Therefore, the validity of a model may be confined to a limited range of values of physical parameters.

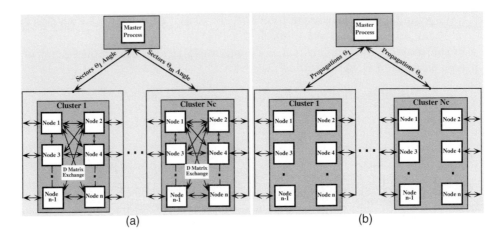

Figure 28.2 Sketch of task farm model for *subsection a* (a) and *subsection b* (b).

28.3.1   Task Farm Model

As shown in Figure 28.1, the number of operations performed by RIOS is proportional to the number of angles, sectors and gridpoints $(N_\Theta N_s N_g)$ when performing the cut of the potential energy channel; to the number of angles, sectors, gridpoints and bound functions $(N_\Theta N_s N_g N_v)$ when calculating sector eigenvalues and eigenfunctions; to the number of angles, sectors and the squared number of gridpoints and bound functions $(N_\Theta N_s N_g^2 N_v^2)$ when calculating overlap integrals between adjacent sectors; and to the number of angles, sectors and the squared number of bound functions $(N_\Theta N_s N_v^2)$ when propagating the solution for a given pair of E and l values.

Because of the very high turnaround time of fixed angle calculations, on single processor mainframes, it was more convenient to run individual jobs for single Θ values, and consider a small number N_E of energies and all the l quantum number values needed to obtain converged contributions to the cross-sections.

Parallelization Phase

A static data decomposition can be used to parallelize *subsection a*. To this end, sectors can be grouped into blocks of approximately the same size and each block is assigned to a different processor for execution. The number of sector blocks generated obviously depends on the number of processors available on the machine used. In order to overlap communication and processing, the part of the sector coupling matrix calculated for a particular sector on a given node is broadcast to all other nodes as soon as it has been calculated. To reduce the occupation of the message buffer, each receiving node reads buffer messages before executing the computation. At the end of *subsection a*, the coupling matrix is stored in the memory of all the nodes. This means that the computation of *subsection b* can start immediately after the last coupling matrix contribution has been calculated and broadcast.

If a coarse granularity scheme is adopted for parallelizing *subsection b* (*i.e.*, the distribution of one angle or one energy to each node at a time), the recursive structure of the propagation is kept within the node computation. In this way node operations are independent and thus a task farm model can be adopted. The parallelism can be exploited both at a high level by distributing the calculations at different fixed Θ values, and at a lower level by distributing fixed E_k, l_m pair propagations.

The task farm model requires one node to act as a master. The work unit is the fixed angle calculation that the master program assigns to each node. The master node assigns to the slave nodes a packet of work units of a predetermined granularity for a set of E_k, l_m pairs. The slaves carry out sequentially the calculations for the assigned work packet.

A sketch of the model structure for the first phase *subsection a* and the second phase *subsection b* is given in Figures 28.2 (a) and 28.2 (b), respectively.

Inefficiency Factors

A close analysis of the structure of the task farm model highlights several potential sources of inefficiency. The following factors are possible sources for computational inefficiency in parallel calculations:

1. The synchronization time between *subsection a* and *b*, denoted as $S_{a,b}(\Theta)$, which may make the slave nodes of the cluster remain idle until the last node has finished calculations of the coupling matrix section and broadcast this section to the other nodes.

2. The unproductive time, denoted as $U(\Theta)$, associated with still running propagations after convergence has been reached.

3. The synchronization time between *subsection b* and *subsection a* at the end of each angle computation, denoted as $S_{b,a}(\Theta)$.

4. The time associated with the final load imbalance, , denoted as R_{lu}. This makes all the remaining processors wait for the one that carries out the last propagation.

Another factor that may be a source of inefficiency for a task farm organization of the code is the fact that when the number of processors used is small, the master node may not be fully utilized.

Optimization Phase

To improve the efficiency of the parallel model, we have clustered the nodes of a parallel machine into N_C groups (clusters) of approximately the same N_{CN} size. The master process is in charge of coordinating the calculations of both sections *subsection a* and *subsection b*. In *subsection a*, it assigns statically to each slave of a given cluster the construction of a section of the fixed angle energy independent coupling matrix **D** for a given block of sectors. In *subsection b*, it assigns dynamically to each slave of a given cluster the propagation for a given value of Θ. In this way parallelism is exploited both at a Θ (high) level (by simultaneously treating different values of the angle Θ on different clusters), and at a lower level (by simultaneously treating either statically the calculation of **D** portions for blocks of sectors in *subsection a* or dynamically the propagation of the solution for fixed E and l values in *subsection b*). Because of this organization of the code, an increase in either the number of angle values considered for the angular averaging, or in the amount of execution time required for the propagation, can be managed easily. However, memory problems may arise at a node level when the number of sectors is increased, and at a master level when the number of energies and/or the number of the l values is increased.

To reduce $S_{a,b}(\Theta)$, $S_{b,a}(\Theta)$ and R_{lu}, we relieved the master from the task of coordinating the whole calculation by allowing the nodes to communicate directly with each other and with the master.

The minimization of the $S_{a,b}(\Theta)$, $S_{b,a}(\Theta)$ and R_{lu} factors can be enhanced by dynamically resizing the clusters at runtime, though this introduces an overhead associated with the time needed to supply the new **D** matrix to the nodes that have been moved to a different cluster. Since $S_{a,b}(\Theta)$ is quite small and $S_{b,a}(\Theta)$ can be reduced by using small clusters [7], the dynamic resizing of the clusters affects above all the minimization of R_{lu}.

When resizing the clusters, the transfer of the new **D** matrix from the master to the moved nodes is quite inefficient because of its size. We found it more convenient to perform the transfer via a interprocessor communication. This goal is assigned to the first node of the cluster that becomes free after executing an $E_k l_m$ propagation. Using a single node to carry out the transfer of the **D** matrix is more efficient than using many nodes because of the time associated with the coordination of the various nodes at the beginning and at the end of the transfer process.

28.3.2   Pipeline Model

In order to assess the scale-up properties of the parallel implementation of the RIOS approach, some parameters can be stressed up to their limit values. For example, at the higher level of the parallel model N_Θ could be increased or, at the lower level, N_S, N_v, N_E and N_l could be increased. An increase in N_Θ and N_S leads to a linear increase in computing time, while an increase in N_v and N_E to a quadratic one. However, for example, an increase of N_l beyond a certain limit has no effect at all, since convergence with l will be reached in any case at a smaller value of this quantum number. The most dramatic effect on memory demand is associated with an increase in N_S and N_v because, as already mentioned, the dimension of the coupling matrix is proportional to their maximum value.

Unfortunately, the dependence of memory and time consumption on the calcu-

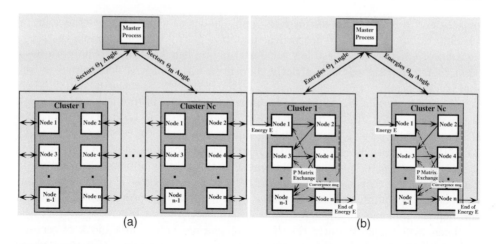

Figure 28.3 Sketch of pipeline model for *subsection a* (a) and *subsection b* (b).

lation parameters is not so simple since some of them are not independent variables. They are, in fact, indirect functions of the (usually more than one) physical parameters of the problem. An even more drastic demand for memory and cpu time is associated with the restoration of the full dimensionality of the code when RIOS constraints on the motion of the system are released.

In massively parallel architectures an increase in cpu demand is, in principle, less of a problem since a scale up of the number of nodes may always be assumed. A more severe limitation to a scale up is associated with the size of the node memory. To cope with a large increase in memory demand, the only practical solution is to push the parallelization to a finer grain, though there is an obvious price to pay in terms of synchronization and communication times. The solution we adopted for RIOS is to push parallelization at a sector level for *subsection b*. This means that a limited number of sectors per node had to be assigned. For these sectors, however, node calculation involves not only eigenvalues, eigenfunctions, overlaps and the coupling matrix, but also the related fraction of propagation.

Parallelization Phase

As shown in Figure 28.3 (a), *subsection a* has the same structure as in the task farm model [9], [8]. Each node deals with the calculation of a portion of the coupling matrix **D**. The only structural difference for this subsection is that at the end of the calculation there is no need for the nodes to distribute the portion of **D** that they have computed. Moreover, the various routines act as in the task farm model and need the same duplication of calculations at the edges between different sector blocks.

On the other hand, the structure of the model, for *subsection b*, is radically altered. In fact, in this approach each node is no longer responsible for carrying out the entire propagation for an $E_k l_m$ pair. Nodes simply propagate the solution through the block of sectors for which they have calculated the coupling matrix in *subsection a*. However, these few local sector propagations have to be performed (and therefore assigned) in a strictly sequential way, which is determined by the sector numbering.

A suitable parallel model for this approach is the pipeline model. In this model, the propagation for all $E_k l_m$ pairs (say $k = 1$ and $l = 0$ *i.e.* $E_1 l_0$) starts at node 0 for the first block of sectors whose coupling matrix resides in the memory of the node. Then the propagation continues on the next node for the next block of sectors. This means that, when the propagation of the **P** matrix for the first block of sectors is completed, node 0 sends the calculated **P** matrix to node 1 (**P** is a matrix that collects the **R** matrix and all the other data necessary to propagate the solution through the pipeline steps).

Then, while node 0 starts the $E_1 l_1$ propagation for the first block of sectors, node 1 takes care of the $E_1 l_0$ propagation for the second block of sectors whose coupling matrix resides in its memory. At the end of this operation, nodes 0 and 1 transfer their results to nodes 1 and 2, respectively. In this way, as is typical of pipeline models, the solution is propagated from the first block of sectors to the last one. The price paid to adopt this model is that all the nodes are idle for a time interval proportional to their distance from node 0 (pipeline start-up time). However, several pipes can be activated at the same time for different $E_k l_m$ pairs, thus allowing a larger number of nodes to be active from the very beginning.

Figure 28.3 (b) shows the pipeline model related to *subsection b*.

Convergence with l is checked by the last processor in the pipe. When convergence has been reached, this processor sends a message (dashed line in Figure 28.3 (b)) to the remaining nodes to allow them to terminate the propagation for other l values of the same energy. When this message is read by a node, all actions related to terminating calculations for a given energy value are undertaken, such as resetting messages residing in the buffers concerned with convergence, and getting ready to generate the coupling matrix for a different angle (when necessary).

Inefficiency Factors

The parameters of the pipeline model of the RIOS method affect the performance of the parallel program. During the execution, after the completion of the operations of *subsection a*, the nodes wait for a time that is roughly proportional to the node number and to the time spent by the first node to propagate and transfer the **P** matrix. All the nodes are actively working on different $E_k l_m$ pairs only when the propagation for $E_1 l_0$ has reached the last node of the pipe. The time that is wasted includes the startup time (the time needed to fill up the pipe), the synchronization time (the time needed to transfer and/or receive the results from one sector block to the next one) and, finally, the unused time (the time spent carrying out the propagation for those $E_k l_m$ pairs which will not contribute to the final result because convergence has already been reached).

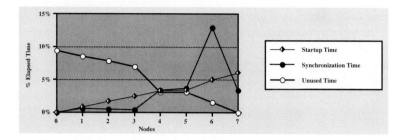

Figure 28.4 Wasted times of the pipeline model plotted as a function of the number of nodes.

These quantities were found not to depend on the size of the machine used, although they were found to be sensitive to the size of the clusters. To shows the origin of this, Figure 28.4 plots the fraction of elapsed time associated with these three sources of inefficiency as a function of the number of nodes (pipelines of 8 nodes were used).

The increase in the startup time and the decrease in unused time as the number of nodes increases is not surprising, though there is a lack of smoothness due to the need to discretize the assignment of the number of sectors to the various nodes. The synchronization time, on the other hand, shows an anomaly for nodes 5, 6 and 7. Intuitively, the synchronization time should be approximately the same for all the nodes. The fact that this is not true is due to the different nature of the sectors assigned to nodes 6 and 7, and partly also to node 5. In fact, Cartesian sectors are assigned to nodes 6 and 7 (fully), and node 5 (partially). The propagation for these sectors is less time consuming than for polar sectors due to the weaker coupling of related equations. Another factor of heterogeneity is the fact that node 7, unlike all the other ones, does not need to forward the propagation result to the next node since it contains the last sector.

Optimization Phase

One way to reduce the inefficiency times, is to organize the sectors into blocks made up of a different number of sectors. Increasing and decreasing the number of sectors for higher numbered nodes leads, in any case, to an increase in synchronization time in *subsection a*. However, in *subsection b*, an increase of the block size with the number of nodes leads to a reduced startup time and a reduced synchronization time (node $n + 1$ has to wait less to obtain the **P** matrix from node n), especially if **P** is forwarded while node $n + 1$ is still busy carrying out the propagation of the previous $E_k l_m$ pair. However, this occurs at the expense of unused time. In fact, by the time the last node has reached convergence, the number of $E_k l_m$ pairs propagated by the lower numbered nodes is larger. However, when a scheme based on blocks of decreasing sizes is adopted, both the startup time and the synchronization time become longer, while the unused time is reduced.

With regard to a constant block size, an increasing size reduces both the startup time and the synchronization time. In fact, since node $n + 1$ is slower than node n in executing its own portion of propagation, it has to wait for a starter time to obtain the $\mathbf{P}$ matrix. At the same time, the unused time increases because the lower numbered nodes are faster in executing their part of the job. As a result, lower numbered nodes have already propagated a large number of $E_k l_m$ pairs when the last node detects that convergence has been reached. On the other hand, a block size that decreases with the number of nodes makes both the startup time and the synchronization time longer while it makes the unused time shorter.

To optimize the sector distribution with respect to the workload balance, a linear increase with the node number was adopted. The function was constrained to be normalized and to have a positive angular coefficient. This gave us the freedom to adjust only one parameter. We chose to vary the number of sectors assigned to the first node of the pipeline.

By using this linear function, several tests of the program were run by using parameters of a typical moderately light three different atom system (like $Li + FH$ [10], [11]). The minimum elapsed time was measured when choosing a small angular coefficient. This confirms that the optimum choice is a sector distribution which slowly increases with the number of nodes.

Also, some propagation calculations for the pipeline model may be carried out after convergence has been reached. The time associated with these unused calculations is large when an increasing distribution of sectors is adopted. To minimize this time, we took advantage of the fact that contributions to the cross-section are constantly monitored and a *preconvergence state* can be defined. This is a state in which a reactive probability is lower than a threshold value. Consequently, when the last node, which carries out the final propagation and the convergence check, finds that fixed l contributions to the cross-section (at a given E value) have become smaller than the threshold value, a message is issued to the first node making it start the propagation for the first l value of the next energy. If this preconvergence state does not lead to an actual convergence when completing the active fixed l calculations for that energy, the last node of the pipe issues another message allowing the first node to start further calculations with larger l values. Only the convergence message closes the work for a given energy and resets memory buffers.

Another improvement consists in partitioning the nodes into clusters and assigning the calculations for different angle values to different clusters (computations for different angle values are decoupled). The main advantage of partitioning the machine into clusters is that the startup time associated with shorter pipelines is reduced. For the same reason synchronization and unused times are also reduced. Partitioning into clusters also reduces the final load imbalance because it leads to a better distribution of the workload.

However, a decrease in the number of nodes in the pipeline increases the size of the sector block assigned to each node. This increases the memory request, which may end up exceeding the capacity of the node memory.

The clustering requires that the distribution among the clusters of the fixed angle calculations is managed by a master, as it is in a task farm model. Therefore, the optimized parallel model turns out to be a hybrid task farm of pipelines.

The following sections describe the execution of the task farm and pipeline implementations of the RIOS code on the distributed memory (Cray T3E), the distributed shared virtual memory (SGI Origin 2000) and the heterogeneous distributed computers. The runs were made using the typical values for production calculations of the reactive cross-section of $Li + FH$.

28.4   Parallel Implementations on CRAY T3E

For the implementation on a Cray T3E distributed memory system a coarse grain task farm model seems to be the right solution because of the very high performance of the node processor of the Cray machine. On the other hand, the large number of processor elements available for this architecture implies that a fine grain task farm implementation should give the best performance. Moreover, a fine grain implementation improves the load distribution among the nodes. The best choice is thus a task farm model with a *medium* grain.

28.4.1   Task Farm Model

To parallelize the RIOS code on the Cray T3E the N nodes of the machine are gathered in N_C clusters and fixed angle calculations are distributed to different clusters of nodes. Since the Cray T3E uses the SPMD paradigm, one node has to be used to run the master process. In this way one processing element is not available for the execution process. This model often leads to clusters having different dimensions. At runtime this cluster configuration could lead to larger final load imbalance time.

Due to the higher processor performance, the work packet assigned to each slave node is the whole fixed E propagation. Since all fixed l calculations for the same energy E are carried out sequentially by the same node, the convergence check is internal to the node and there is no unused time $U(\Theta)$.

Moreover, by dynamically resizing the clusters dimension at runtime, the R_{lu} time is also reduced.

28.4.2   Pipeline Model

Since each processor of the Cray T3E has a sufficiently large local memory, the execution of a large RIOS problem is still possible even without resorting to the use of the pipeline model. Nevertheless, it is important to implement this model as well in order to exploit the speed of the communication network, and this is particularly true in view of the implementation of higher dimensionality codes.

The implementation of the optimized pipeline model implies that one node of the Cray T3E is used as a master node. The remaining nodes are slave nodes and can be partitioned into clusters. Each cluster carries out a fixed angle calculation by using a pipeline mechanism. At each step of the pipeline process, a node performs the calculation of a portion of a $E_k l_m$ propagation.

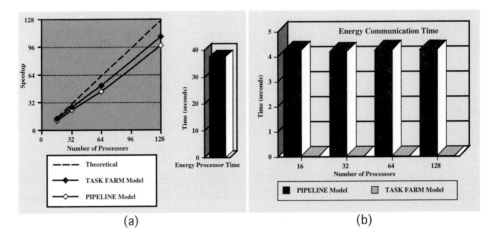

(a)   (b)

Figure 28.5 Speed-ups (a) and interprocessor communication times (b) of the task farm and pipeline model on a Cray T3E architecture.

28.4.3   Performance Evaluation

The Task Farm and Pipeline versions of RIOS were run on a Cray T3E-1200 having 128 nodes with a local memory of 256 Mbytes, and using the following parameters: 64 angles, 80 (fairly high) energies, 400 sectors, 80 quantum numbers and 15 vibrational states. The nodes of the machine are grouped into 15 clusters of 8 nodes, and 1 cluster of 7 nodes. In all the runs the main inefficiency factors (*i.e.*, startup time, synchronization time and final load imbalance time) of the task farm and pipeline models were monitored. Figure 28.5 (a) gives the speed-up values of the two versions of the RIOS program when varying the number of processors. The speed-up values shown in the figure indicate that the performance of the two models was satisfactory. Moreover, the figure shows that the task farm version leads to better performances than the pipeline version. In Figure 28.5 (a) the average cpu time required to carry out the propagation at fixed E is also shown.

The average communication, synchronization and load imbalance times were analysed to investigate the decrease in speed-up with respect to the theoretical speed-up when the number of the processors increases. In order to compare the values measured on the Cray T3E-1200 with those measured on other parallel architectures, communication, synchronization and load imbalance times were normalized with respect to the number of computed energies.

Interprocessor communication times include the time spent while transferring data and waiting to read the buffer message. In the task farm model, the largest fraction of time spent in communicating in *subsection a* is associated with the broadcasting of the various blocks of the **D** matrix from the computing node to all other nodes, and in *subsection b* with the transfer of the **D** matrix to nodes moved from an inactive (stopped) to an active cluster. In the pipeline model, the interproces-

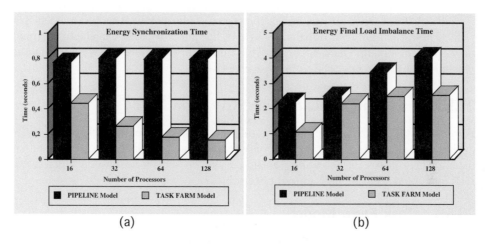

Figure 28.6 Synchronization (a) and load imbalance times (b) of the task farm and pipeline model on a Cray T3E architecture.

sor communication time includes the startup times that are associated with the different fixed energy calculations.

As shown in Figure 28.5 (b) the communication time of the pipeline model is larger than that of the task farm model. The main reason for this is that in the pipeline model for each energy the nodes have to wait for the pipe to be filled (startup time). This time remains roughly constant for single energy computations in all runs.

Figure 28.6 (a) reports the single energy synchronization time, measured for the pipeline and the task farm models when varying the number of processors. In the task farm model, the synchronization time is made up of both $S_{a,b}$ waiting times between *subsection a* and *subsection b*, in which the slave nodes of one cluster are idle until all the nodes end their work, and $S_{b,a}$ waiting time between *subsection b* and *subsection a*, at the end of an angle computation.

In the pipeline model, the synchronization time is the time needed to transfer and/or receive the **P** matrix from one node to the next one at each step of the propagation process. As shown in Figure 28.6 (a), the synchronization times of the pipeline model are longer than those of the task farm model. In all the tests, the synchronization times of the pipeline model remain constant since the computation carried out by nodes in *subsection b* is about the same. On the other hand, synchronization times in the task farm model depend on the different computations associated with a given energy and a given angle.

The final load imbalance of the two parallel versions is shown in Figure 28.6 (b). In the task farm model, the possibility of resizing the cluster at runtime (when one cluster has accomplished the assigned work, the freed nodes are distributed among the active clusters) allows us to reduce the idle time of slave nodes waiting for the one that carries out the last propagation. This optimization phase leads to a reduction in the final load imbalance. The technique of resizing the clusters cannot be used in the pipeline model, because it is impossible to insert a new node into the pipeline chain when the related process is active.

28.5   Parallel Implemention on SGI Origin 2000

For distributed shared virtual memory architectures, the most suitable choice is the exploitation of the coarse grain RIOS approach. Since the large size of the shared memory guarantees the scalability of the parallel code even for large problems, the task farm model is the most appropriate solution.

28.5.1   Task Farm Model

In this implementation, the node on which the master process runs also spawns a slave process, and each slave node receives a packet of work consisting of a fixed whole E propagation. This gives a better level of parallelism and removes the unused time $U(\Theta)$ since the convergence check is made directly by the slave node. If the problem is very large the parallelism could be exploited at an angle level.

The final load imbalance time R_{lu} is reduced by dynamically resizing the clusters. Otherwise, the synchronization time $S_{a,b}(\Theta)$ and the synchronization time $S_{b,a}(\Theta)$ are not removed.

28.5.2   Performance Evaluation

The task farm model of the RIOS method was run on the SGI Origin 2000 with 16 processing elements and a global shared memory of 8 Gbytes. In all the runs the following parameters were used: 16 angles, 8 (fairly high) energies, 400 sectors, 80 quantum numbers and 15 vibrational states. The nodes of the system were grouped into clusters of 5 nodes, and the following three tests were conducted by using 1, 2 and 3 clusters, respectively, and a master node.

Figure 28.7 (a) shows the speed-up values obtained by running the RIOS task farm version in the three tests. The figure also reports the average processor time required for the propagation of an energy.

Figure 28.7 (b) shows the average communication and synchronization times and the final load imbalance time for single energy propagation. Interprocessor communication times are negligible while synchronization times $S_{b,a}(\Theta)$ are larger than the load imbalance time R_{lu}. The reason for this can be found in the following angle calculations: execution stream of the clusters, the computational time of single energy, and the technique used for dynamically resizing the clusters.

28.6   Parallel Implementation on a Metacomputer

Metacomputing allows the combined computational power of several platforms to be used in order to enhance the performance and to exploit the heterogeneity of

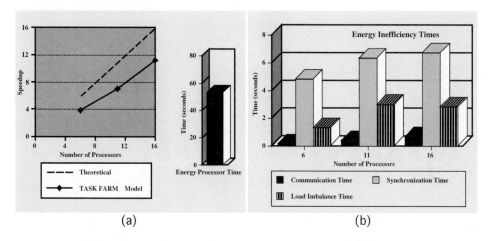

(a)   (b)

Figure 28.7 Speed-ups (a) and inefficiency times (b) of the task farm model on the ORIGIN 2000 architecture.

the different architectures. Therefore, RIOS can be executed on a metacomputer by performing the code that best exploits the architectural characteristics of the metacomputers [12]. On MPP systems and clusters of workstations, the RIOS task farm code can be used. When the node memory becomes a limitation to perform the task farm code, a pipeline code can be adopted. The metacomputer used for conducting our experiments consisted of an 8-node IBM SP2, an 128-node nCUBE2, and a cluster of 4 workstations HP 9000/735 with 128, 4 and 32 Mbytes per node, respectively. All the machines were connected by a 10 Mbit/s Ethernet.

28.6.1 Implementation Issues

The parallel model adopted on the above mentioned metacomputer is a task farm. In order to coordinate the execution of several slave processes running on different machines, the master process includes the functionalities of both the task farm and pipeline models described above. The master process dispatches work packets with different granularities because a medium-grain task farm, a coarse-grain task farm and a pipeline code were adopted on an IBM SP2, a cluster of workstations, and on the nCUBE2, respectively. The IBM SP2 nodes are grouped into clusters and a work distribution at energy level was performed; instead, in the cluster of workstations, there was a work distribution at angle level.

The Parallel Virtual Machine (PVM) [13] was chosen as the communication library for the metacomputer. In order to integrate the nCUBE2 machine into the metacomputer, a *converter* process running on the master node was implemented. The converter translates the message passing primitives from PVM to equivalent nCUBE2 native ones.

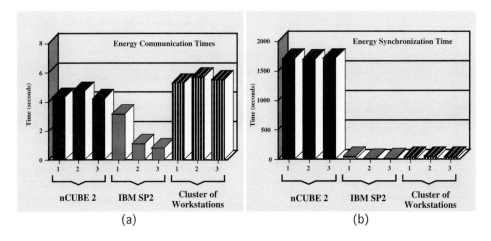

Figure 28.8 Communication (a), synchronization (b) times running the RIOS code on a metacomputer.

28.6.2 Performance Evaluation

The experiments were conducted on three metacomputer configurations:

1. First Configuration:

   (a) 64-node nCUBE2, partitioned into 4 clusters of 16 nodes each;

   (b) 8-node of IBM SP2, grouped into 1 cluster;

   (c) 4-workstation HP 9000/735 cluster.

2. Second Configuration:

   (a) 64-node nCUBE2, partitioned into 4 clusters of 16 nodes each;

   (b) 8-node IBM SP2, grouped into 2 clusters of 4 nodes each;

   (c) 4-workstation HP 9000/735 cluster.

3. Third Configuration:

   (a) 64-node nCUBE2, partitioned into 4 clusters of 16 nodes each;

   (b) 8-node IBM SP2, grouped into 3 clusters of 3, 3 and 2 nodes respectively,

   (c) 4-workstation HP 9000/735 cluster.

In all the runs, the parameters of the RIOS code were: 48 angles, 8 (fairly high) energies, 400 sectors, 80 quantum numbers and 15 vibrational states. In Figures 28.8 and 28.9, the average times of the communication, synchronization and final load imbalance measured for a single energy propagation are shown. In the figures, the

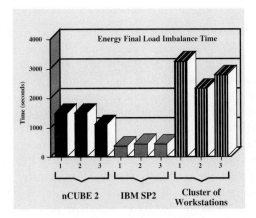

Figure 28.9 Final load imbalance times running the RIOS code on a metacomputer.

numbers 1, 2 and 3 denote the metacomputer configurations adopted for the tests. Figure 28.8 (a) shows that the interprocessor communication time of nCUBE2 and of the cluster of workstations remains almost constant. There are minor variations due to the different angle values computed in each run. On the other hand, the IBM SP2 communication times are different since a different partitioning was used in each run. The large communication time in the first test is mainly due to the communication time needed in *subsection a* to broadcast the sections of the **D** matrix computed by the nodes. This time decreases when the number of clusters of the IBM SP2 increases.

The synchronization times shown in Figure 28.8 (b) were obtained for the IBM SP2 and the workstation cluster by adding the time $S_{a,b}(\Theta)$ and the time $S_{b,a}(\Theta)$, while for nCUBE2 they were obtained by adding the pipeline startup times and the pipeline flush times when the convergence is reached. The large nCUBE2 synchronization times are due to the management of the pipeline.

Figure 28.9 shows the times associated with the final load imbalance required for a single energy propagation. These times are large for the cluster of workstations due to the coarse grain adopted. Moreover, the final load imbalance times are quite large on the nCUBE2 due to the different durations of the fixed angle calculation assigned to each node cluster of the nCUBE2. On the other hand, on the IBM SP2 the final load imbalance time remains constant in the three tests.

28.7   Concluding Remarks

Quantum theoretical chemistry has always been on the leading edge of innovative computing during the mainframe and vector computing era. On these machines, high performing reactive scattering codes have been successfully implemented using both time-independent and time-dependent approaches as well as propagation and variational methods.

Progress in innovative computing has recently almost exclusively concentrated on parallel architectures. The computing power offered by these machines seems to be the ideal ground for a fast development of computational procedures that can deal with the massive production of chemical information needed to accurately model chemical processes intervening in atmospheric phenomena, material technology, pollution, and combustion. Unfortunately, for chemical computational applications, this development is not as fast as it could be. This can be ascribed to the reluctance of chemists to implement their complex codes (which are mainly designed for sequential machines) on parallel architectures before definite standards have been set and smart compilers developed. However, the design of smart compilers is strongly related to the identification of a reduced set of efficient parallel models. This needs to be supported by an extensive and detailed analysis of computationally demanding applications.

In this chapter, several elementary and composite models suitable for parallelizing time independent quantum reactive scattering codes have been examined, and an attempt to establish relationships between the parameters of the physical models and the parameters of the algorithmic models has been made. The efficiencies of various simple and composite parallel models when applied to the calculation of reactive properties have been compared in terms of the speed-ups measured for the RIOS program implemented on different platforms. Extensions to higher dimensionality treatments have also been considered, especially intervening on the section dealing with the construction of the coupling matrix.

28.8   Bibliography

[1] M.Capitelli, and J.N. Barsdley. *Non Equilibrium Processes in Partially Ionized Gases*. Plenum, New York, 1990.

[2] A. Laganà, E. Garcia, O. Gervasi, R. Baraglia, D. Laforenza, and R. Perego. $D+D_2$ Quasiclassical Rate Constant Calculations on Parallel Computers. *Theoretica Chimica Acta*, vol. 79(323), pages 323–333, Springer-Verlag, 1991.

[3] G.C. Schatz, and M.A. Ratner, *Quantum Mechanics in Chemistry*. Prentice Hall International, 1993.

[4] M. Baer, E. Garcia, A. Laganà, and O. Gervasi. *Chem. Phys. Letters*, vol. 158(362), pages 362–368, 1989.

[5] G. Fox, R. D. Williams, and P. C. Messina. *Parallel Computing Works!* Morgan Kaufmann Publishers, Inc, 1994.

[6] A.J.G. Hey. Experiment in MIMD Parallelism. *Proc. of International Conference PARLE'89*, pages 28–42, 1989.

[7] R. Baraglia, D. Laforenza, and A. Laganà. Parallelization Strategies for a Reduced Dimensionality Calculation of Quantum Reactive Scattering Cross-Section on a Hypercube Machine. *Lecture Notes in Computer Science*, vol. 919, pages 554–561, 1995.

[8] R. Baraglia, R. Ferrini, D. Laforenza, and A. Laganà. On the Optimization of a Task Farm Model for the Parallel Integration of a Two-Dimensional Schrödinger Equations on Distributed Memory Architectures. *ICA3PP, IEEE Third International Conference on Algorithms and Architectures for Parallel Processing*, pages 543–556, December 1997.

[9] R. Baraglia, R. Ferrini, D. Laforenza, and A. Laganà. An Optimized Task Farm Model to Integrate Reduced Dimensionality Schrödinger Equations on Distributed Memory Architectures. *International Journal Future Generation Computer System*, 1998 (in the press).

[10] A. Laganà, E. Garcia, and O. Gervasi. *J. Chem. Phys.*, vol. 89, pages 7238–7241, 1988.

[11] E. Garcia, O. Gervasi, and A. Laganà. Approximate Quantum Techniques for Atom Diatom Reactions. A. Laganà, (ed.) *Supercomputer Algorithms for Reactivity, Dynamics and Kinetics of Small Molecules*. Dordrecht, Kluwer, pages 271–294, 1989.

[12] R. Baraglia, R. Ferrini, D. Laforenza, and A. Laganà. Metacomputing to Overcome the Power Limits of a Single Machine. *Lecture Notes in Computer Science*, vol. 1225, pages 980–986, 1997.

[13] A. L. Beguelin, J. J. Dongarra, G. A. Geist, W. Jiang, R. Mancheck, and V. S. Sunderam. *PVM: Parallel Virtual Machine: A Users' Guide and Tutorial for Networked Parallel Computing*. The MIT Press, 1994.

[14] R. Baraglia, R. Ferrini, D. Laforenza, and A. Laganà. An Optimized Pipeline Model to Integrate 2D Schrödinger Equations. *MPCS 98 Third International Conference on Massively Parallel Computing Systems*. Colorado Springs, Colorado, April 1998.

[15] R. Baraglia, R. Ferrini, D. Laforenza, and A. Laganà. On the Optimization of a Pipeline Model to Integrate Reduced Dimensionality Schrödinger Equations for Distributed Memory Architectures. *The International Journal of Supercomputer Applications and High Performance Computing*, 1998.

Chapter 29

Biomedical Applications Modeling

SUCHENDRA BHANDARKAR, SRIDHAR CHIRRAVURI, AND SALEM MACHAKA

Department of Computer Science
The University of Georgia
Athens, Georgia 30602–7404, USA

Email: *suchi@cs.uga.edu, chirravu@cs.uga.edu, machaka@cs.uga.edu*

29.1   Introduction

In this chapter we present two biomedical applications of cluster computing using PVM [15]. The first deals with the problem of chromosome reconstruction via ordering of clones from a genomic library. This problem of chromosome reconstruction or physical mapping is central to the field of molecular genetics and can be shown to be isomorphic to the classical NP-complete *Optimal Linear Arrangement* (OLA) problem. We propose parallel algorithms for simulated annealing (SA) and microcanonical annealing (MCA) and apply them to this problem. The second problem deals with the analysis of heart rate variability (HRV) from an electrocardiograph (EKG) signal. An EKG measures the electrical activity of the heart and when plotted as a function of time, it exhibits certain characteristic peaks called R peaks which reflect the dominant electrocardiac phases. The instantaneous heart rate is computed as the inverse of the time period between two successive R peaks and is observed to be a highly complex non-linear function of time. The Kolmogorov (K_2) entropy, a commonly used measure of the HRV, characterizes the non-linear complexity of electrocardiac activity. We design a parallel algorithm for the computation of K_2 entropy and show its utility in real-time analysis of HRV. We describe the implementation of the above algorithms on a cluster of UNIX workstations running PVM. We also analyze and discuss the convergence, speed-up and scalability characteristics of the various parallel algorithms.

604

29.2   The Chromosome Reconstruction Problem

A central problem in genetics, right from its very inception, is that of creating maps of entire chromosomes which could then be used to reconstruct the chromosome's DNA sequence. These maps are central to the understanding of the structure of genes, their function and their evolution. The large number of DNA markers and the ease with which molecular markers are assayed have shifted the problem focus from the experimental collection of data to the computational issues of assembling entire maps.

Chromosomal maps fall into two broad categories – *genetic maps* and *physical maps*. Genetic maps, which are of low resolution (i.e., 1–10 million base pairs (Mb)), represent an ordering of genetic markers along a chromosome where the distance between two genetic markers is inversely proportional to their recombination frequency. While genetic maps narrow the search for genes to a particular chromosomal region, it is a physical map that ultimately allows the recovery and molecular manipulation of genes of interest. A physical map is defined as a partial ordering of distinguishable DNA fragments or *clones* by their position along the entire chromosome where the clones may or may not contain genetic markers. A physical map has a much higher resolution than a genetic map of the same chromosome (i.e., 10–100 thousand base pairs (Kb)).

29.2.1   Physical Mapping via Clone Ordering

The specific technique, discussed in this chapter, for generating a physical map is one based on determining an ordering of clones from a library that optimizes a prespecified objective function [7]. The optimal ordering of clones, with respect to their position along a chromosome, is then deemed to constitute a physical map. Previous work in the Department of Genetics at the University of Georgia resulted in a physical mapping algorithm ODS (**O**rdering **D**NA **S**equences) based on simulated annealing [7]. The physical mapping approach in ODS can be summarized as follows:

(i) Each DNA fragment or clone in the library is scored for the presence or absence of specific oligonucleotide sites or *probes* by a series of biochemical experiments. This results in the assignment of a digital *signature* to each clone.

(ii) The *Hamming* distance $d(C_i, C_j)$ between two clonal signatures C_i and C_j is defined to be the measure of dissimilarity between their signatures.

(iii) The total linking distance D for an ordering is defined as the sum of the Hamming distances between all pairs of successive clones in the ordering:

$$D = \sum_{i=1}^{n-1} d(C_i, C_{i+1}) \tag{29.2.1}$$

(iv) The desired (i.e., optimal) ordering or physical map is deemed to be that which results in minimization of the total linking distance D. This ordering criterion is based on the intuitive rationale that clones with similar digital signatures tend to overlap along the chromosome and hence should be placed next to each other on the physical map.

Let D_m denote the minimum linking distance associated with the space of all possible clonal orderings and D_0 the linking distance associated with the *true* ordering. It can be shown that

$$\lim_{n \to \infty} prob(|D_m - D_0| > \epsilon) = 0 \qquad (29.2.2)$$

That is to say, D_m converges in probability to D_0 as the size n of the clonal library grows [16]. This result provides the formal basis for the physical mapping algorithm ODS. Figure 29.1 shows the physical map of Chromosome IV of the fungus *Aspergillus nidulans* constructed using ODS.

The problem of computing such an optimal clone ordering or physical map can be shown to be isomorphic to the classical NP-complete *Optimal Linear Arrangement* (OLA) problem [8]. No polynomial-time algorithm for finding the optimal solution to the OLA problem is known except for some simple cases that deal with error-free data [4]. Stochastic optimization algorithms such as SA [9] or MCA [6] are capable of avoiding local optima in the solution space and producing solutions that are close to a global optimum in polynomial time on average. One of the drawbacks of a serial implementation of SA and MCA is that the annealing schedules necessary to obtain a solution close to a global optimum, are computationally intensive. Parallel processing on a cluster of workstations is one of the ways in which this drawback can be alleviated [2].

29.3   PVM Algorithms for Chromosome Reconstruction

29.3.1   Simulated Annealing and Microcanonical Annealing

Stochastic optimization algorithms such as simulated annealing (SA) [9] and microcanonical annealing (MCA) [6] are a subcategory of stochastic hill-climbing search techniques and are characterized by their capacity to escape from local optima in the objective function. A single iteration of a stochastic optimization algorithm consists of three phases: (i) perturb, (ii) evaluate, and (iii) decide.

In the perturb phase, the current solution $\mathbf{x}_i$ to a multivariate objective function $E(\mathbf{x})$ which is to be minimized (i.e., the linking distance D in our case), is systematically perturbed to yield another candidate solution $\mathbf{x}_j$. In our case, the clone ordering is permuted by reversing the ordering within a randomly chosen block of clones. In the evaluate phase, $E(\mathbf{x}_j)$ (i.e., the linking distance D for the new clone ordering) is computed. In the decide phase, $\mathbf{x}_j$ is accepted and replaces $\mathbf{x}_i$ *probabilistically* using a stochastic decision function. The stochastic decision function is *annealed* in a manner such that the search process resembles a random search in

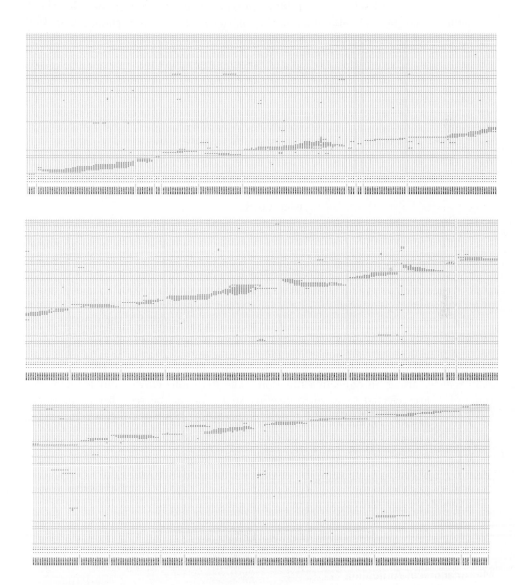

Figure 29.1 An ordered physical map of *Aspergillus nidulans* Chromosome IV.

the earlier stages and a greedy local search or a deterministic hill-climbing search in the latter stages. The major difference between SA and MCA arises from the difference in the stochastic decision function used in the decision phase. But their common feature is that, starting from an initial solution, they generate, in the limit, an ergodic Markov chain of solution states which asymptotically converges to a stationary Boltzmann distribution. The Boltzmann distribution asymptotically converges to a globally optimal solution when subject to the annealing process [9].

Simulated Annealing

In the decide phase of SA, the new candidate solution $\mathbf{x}_j$ is accepted with probability p, which is computed using the Metropolis function given by:

$$
p = \begin{cases} 1 & \text{if } E(\mathbf{x}_j) < E(\mathbf{x}_i) \\ \exp\left(-\frac{E(\mathbf{x}_j) - E(\mathbf{x}_i)}{T}\right) & \text{if } E(\mathbf{x}_j) \geq E(\mathbf{x}_i) \end{cases} \tag{29.3.1}
$$

or the Boltzmann function $B(T)$ given by:

$$
p = B(T) = \frac{1}{1 + \exp\left(\frac{E(\mathbf{x}_j) - E(\mathbf{x}_i)}{T}\right)} \tag{29.3.2}
$$

at a given value of temperature T, whereas $\mathbf{x}_i$ is retained with probability $(1 - p)$.

The Metropolis function and the Boltzmann function give SA the capability of *probabilistically* accepting new candidate solutions that are locally suboptimal compared to the current solution, thus enabling it to climb out of local minima. Several iterations of SA are carried out for a given value of T, which is then systematically reduced using an annealing function. The iterations carried out for a single value of T are referred to as an *annealing step*. As can be seen from equations (29.3.1) and (29.3.2), at sufficiently high temperatures, SA resembles a completely random search, whereas at lower temperatures it acquires the characteristics of a deterministic hill-climbing search or local greedy search.

Both the Metropolis function and the Boltzmann function ensure that SA generates an asymptotically ergodic (and hence stationary) Markov chain of solution states at a given temperature value. It has been shown that logarithmic annealing schedules of the form $T_k = R / \log k$ for some value of $R > 0$ are asymptotically good, i.e., they ensure asymptotic convergence to a global minimum with unit probability in the limit $k \to \infty$ [9].

Microcanonical Annealing

MCA models a physical system whose total energy, i.e., sum of kinetic energy and potential energy, is always conserved. The potential energy of the system is the multivariate objective function $E(\mathbf{x})$ to be minimized, whereas the kinetic energy $E_k > 0$ is represented by a demon or a collection of demons. In the latter case, the total kinetic energy is the sum of all the demon energies. The demon energy (or energies) serve(s) to provide the system with an extra degree (or degrees) of freedom, enabling MCA to escape from local minima.

In the decide phase of MCA, if $E(\mathbf{x}_j) < E(\mathbf{x}_i)$ then $\mathbf{x}_j$ is accepted as the new solution. If $E(\mathbf{x}_j) \geq E(\mathbf{x}_i)$ then $\mathbf{x}_j$ is accepted as the new solution only if $E_k \geq E(\mathbf{x}_j) - E(\mathbf{x}_i)$. If $E(\mathbf{x}_j) \geq E(\mathbf{x}_i)$ and $E_k < E(\mathbf{x}_j) - E(\mathbf{x}_i)$ then the current solution $\mathbf{x}_i$ is retained. In the event that $\mathbf{x}_j$ is accepted as the new solution, the kinetic energy demon is updated $E_k^{n+1} = E_k^n + [E(\mathbf{x}_i) - E(\mathbf{x}_j)]$ in order to ensure the conservation of the total energy. The kinetic energy parameter E_k is annealed in a manner similar to the temperature parameter T in SA. MCA can also be shown to converge to a global minimum with unit probability given a logarithmic annealing schedule [6].

29.3.2   Parallel SA and MCA Using PVM

As described earlier, a candidate solution in the serial SA or MCA algorithm can be considered to be an element of an asymptotically ergodic first-order Markov chain of solution states. Consequently, we have formulated and implemented two models of parallel SA (PSA) and parallel MCA (PMCA) algorithms based on the distribution of the Markov chain of solution states using PVM.

- The Non-Interacting Local Markov chain (NILM) PSA and PMCA algorithms.

- The Periodically Interacting Local Markov chain (PILM) PSA and PMCA algorithms.

In the NILM PSA and NILM PMCA algorithms, each processor within the PVM system runs an independent version of the serial SA or MCA algorithm, respectively. In essence, there are as many Markov chains of solution states as there are physical processors within the PVM system. Each Markov chain is local to a given processor, and at any instant of time, each processor maintains a candidate solution which is an element of its local Markov chain of solution states. The serial SA or MCA algorithm run asynchronously on each processor, i.e., at each temperature value or kinetic energy value, each processor iterates through the perturb-evaluate-accept cycle COUNT_LIMIT number of times concurrently (but asynchronously) with all the other processors.

A parallel random number generator is used to generate the Markov chains of solution states in the perturb phase. By assigning a distinct seed to each processor at the start of execution, we ensure the independence of the Markov chains on the various processors. The evaluation function and the decision function (for PSA and PMCA) are executed concurrently on the solution state within each processor. On termination of the annealing processes on all the processors, the best solution is selected from among all the solutions on the individual processors. The NILM model is essentially that of multiple independent searches.

The PILM PSA or PILM PMCA algorithm is similar to its NILM counterpart except for one major difference. Just before the parameter T or E_k is updated using the annealing function, the best candidate solution from among those in all the processors is selected and duplicated on all the other processors. The goal of this synchronization procedure is to focus the search in the more promising regions of the solution space, which suggests that the PILM PSA or PILM PMCA algorithm should be potentially superior to its NILM counterpart. The PILM model is essentially that of multiple periodically interacting searches.

In the case of all the four algorithms, NILM PSA, NILM PMCA, PILM PSA and PILM PMCA, a *master process* is used as the overall controlling process. The master process runs on one of the processors within the PVM system. The master process spawns child processes on each of the other processors, broadcasts the data subsets needed by each child process, collects the final results from each of the child processes and terminates the child processes. In addition to the above-mentioned functions for task initiation, task coordination and task termination, the master process also runs its own version of the SA or MCA algorithm just as any of its child processes.

In the case of the PILM PSA and the PILM PMCA algorithms, at the end of the COUNT_LIMIT number of perturb-evaluate-decide iterations at each temperature or kinetic energy value, the master process collects the results from each child process along with its own result, broadcasts the best result to all the child processes, and also replaces its own result with the best result. The master process updates its temperature or kinetic energy value using the annealing function and proceeds with its local version of the SA or MCA algorithm. On reaching the final temperature or kinetic energy value, the master process collects the final results from each of the child processes along with its own, selects the best result as the final solution and terminates the child processes. The master process for the NILM PSA or NILM PMCA algorithms is similar to that of its PILM counterpart except for the absence of periodic interaction between the master process and any of the child processes during the annealing procedure. The master process for all the four algorithms is depicted in Figure 29.2.

The child process, in the case of the PILM PSA and PILM PMCA algorithms, collects the clonal data and certain initialization parameters from the master process. Each of the child processes runs an independent version of the SA or MCA algorithm on its data set. The child processes interact periodically with the master process. At the end of COUNT_LIMIT iterations at each temperature or kinetic energy value, each child process sends its result to the master process and waits for the master process to transmit the best result thus far. On receipt of the best result, each child process updates its temperature or kinetic energy value using the annealing function and proceeds with its local version of the SA or MCA algorithm on the received result. When the final value of the temperature or kinetic energy is reached, each child process transmits its result to the master process. The child process, in the case of the NILM PSA or NILM PMCA, algorithm, is similar to that of its PILM counterpart except for the absence of periodic interaction between the master process and any of the child processes. The child process for all the four algorithms is depicted in Figure 29.3.

```
master()
 beginmaster
  Phase 1: Initial Setup
  (a) Spawn Child Processes;
  (b) Read Input: clonal data, clonal distance matrix and
      initial seeds for the parallel random number generator;
  (c) Broadcast the input to all spawned child processes;

  Phase 2: The Annealing Algorithm and Process Coordination
   In the case of PSA:
     T = T_max; Finished = (T <= T_min);
   In the case of PMCA:
     E_k = E_max; Finished = (E_k <= E_min);

   while (not Finished)
    beginwhile
     for (Count = 1; Count <= COUNT_LIMIT; Count = Count + 1)
      beginfor
       (a) Perturb Phase: same as serial SA or MCA;
       (b) Evaluate Phase: same as serial SA or MCA;
       (c) Decide Phase:
       if PSA: SA decision criterion;
       if PMCA: MCA decision criterion;
      endfor

     In the case of PILM PSA or PILM PMCA:
       (a) Receive clone ordering from each child process;
       (b) Select best clone ordering;
       (c) Send best clone ordering to each child process;

     if PSA: Update temperature T = A(T);
     if PMCA: Update kinetic energy E_k = A(E_k);
    endwhile

  Phase 3: Output Result;
   (a) Receive clone ordering from each child process;
   (b) Select best clone ordering;

 endmaster;
```

Figure 29.2 The master process for PILM/NILM PSA/PMCA algorithms.

```
child()
 beginchild
  Phase 1: Initial Setup
   Receive Input from Master Process: clonal data, clonal distance
   matrix and initial seeds for parallel random number generator;

  Phase 2: Annealing Algorithm and Coordination with Master Process;
   In the case of PSA:
     T = T_max; Finished = (T <= T_min);
   In the case of PMCA:
     E_k = E_max; Finished = (E_k <= E_min);
   while (not Finished)
    beginwhile
     for (Count = 1; Count <= COUNT_LIMIT; Count = Count +1)
      beginfor
       (a) Perturb Phase: same as serial SA or MCA;
       (b) Evaluate Phase: same as serial SA or MCA;
       (c) Decide Phase:
             if PSA: SA decision criterion;
             if PMCA: MCA decision criterion;
      endfor
     In the case of PILM PSA or PILM PMCA:
      (a) Send clone ordering to Master process;
      (b) Receive best clone ordering from Master process;
      if PSA: Update temperature T = A(T);
      if PMCA: Update kinetic energy E_k = A(E_k);
    endwhile

  Phase 3:
   Send clone ordering to Master Process and Exit;
 endchild;
```

Figure 29.3 The child process for the PILM/NILM PSA/PMCA algorithms.

29.4   Heart Rate Variability and Kolmogorov Entropy

An EKG signal measures the electrocardiac activity of the heart. A typical EKG signal, when plotted as a function of time, exhibits certain characteristic peaks, called R peaks, which reflect the dominant electrical phases of the underlying heart beat phenomenon. The instantaneous heart rate is computed as the inverse of the time interval between two consecutive R peaks in the EKG signal and is typically a very complex function of time. In most biological systems, the heart rate is monitored and continuously adjusted by a complex and highly sensitive regulatory mechanism that responds to several extracardiac stimuli [13]. For example, variations in the instantaneous heart rate may be caused by several factors such as body position, physical activity, body temperature, respiration rate, blood volume, blood pressure and emotional state [12]. We use the term *heart rate variability* (HRV) to denote the fact that the instantaneous heart rate is a complex nonlinear function of time. It is imperative in many situations to be able to characterize and measure HRV from the EKG signal in order to *quantitatively* analyze the underlying cardiac activity.

It is difficult to reconstruct a complex dynamic system such as the heart, which is believed to have several degrees of freedom, using a relatively few time series data points from the EKG. Consequently, several mathematical techniques have been developed to characterize the HRV. These techniques include classical techniques based on the computation of statistical parameters of time series data such as the mean, standard deviation, power spectrum and autoregression (AR) [12]. The more recent techniques are based on the computation of parameters that characterize the underlying nonlinear chaotic dynamics of the HRV such as the correlation-dimension, Lyapunov exponents [1], Kolmogorov (i.e., K_2) entropy [11] and Approximate Entropy (ApEn) [12].

The HRV is not only a measure of the nonlinear complexity of the underlying heart rate data, but also has significant clinical ramifications. *Qualitative* analysis of the HRV has often been used as an indicator of cardiovascular health by cardiologists [14]. The heart rate of healthy persons is known to have less regularity (i.e., higher degree of chaos) than the heart rate of cardiac patients [10]. More specifically, low HRV in patients with an acute myocardial infraction often implies greater risk for short-term cardiac morbidity and mortality [3]. HRV analysis has been used successfully in humans to noninvasively evaluate autonomic responses to specific maneuvers and drugs, as well as responses to more chronic pre-existing pathologic conditions [12]. For example, low HRV in a fetus is an early indication of fetal distress [3]. Due to its close association with cardiovascular health, it is important to be able to *quantitatively* measure and analyze HRV.

29.4.1 K_2 Entropy

Kolmogorov formulated a method to compute the *entropy* and *correlation dimension* of chaotic dynamic systems [11]. Grassberger and Procaccia [11] developed a measure, namely, the K_2 entropy, as an estimate of the asymptotic lower bound for the metric Kolmogorov entropy computed from time series data. The algorithm used to compute K$_2$ entropy can also be used to estimate a good lower bound for the correlation dimension of complex dynamic systems. The serial computation of K$_2$ entropy from time series data is described as follows:

Consider a time series with N points. Let x_i denote the *ith* point in the time series. The time series data can be vectorized by constructing d-dimensional vectors where each vector consists of d consecutive points in the time series $\mathbf{X}_i^d = (x_i, x_{i+1}, x_{i+2}, \ldots, x_{i+d-1})$. In such a d-dimensional vectorization (or embedding) of the time series data, the correlation integral $C_d(\epsilon)$ is defined as the limiting ratio of the number of vector pairs with distance (in d-dimensional Euclidean space $\mathcal{R}^d$) between them not exceeding ϵ to the square of the number of points in the time series, i.e., N^2:

$$C_d(\epsilon) = \lim_{N \to \infty} \left[\frac{1}{N^2} \left| \left\{ (n,m) \text{ such that } \left[\sum_{i=1}^{d} |x_{n+i} - x_{m+i}|^2 \right]^{1/2} < \epsilon \right\} \right| \right] \quad (29.4.1)$$

The K$_2$ entropy, is given by:

$$K_2 = \lim_{\epsilon \to 0} \lim_{d \to \infty} \left[\frac{1}{\tau} \ln \frac{C_d(\epsilon)}{C_{d+1}(\epsilon)} \right] \quad (29.4.2)$$

In our case, the Takens constant τ was assumed to be unity. The K$_2$ entropy is a *quantitative* measure of the complexity or degree of chaotic behavior of the dynamic system underlying the time series data. In general, lower values of K$_2$ entropy indicate a certain degree of order (or periodicity) in the behavior of the dynamic system, whereas a higher values of K$_2$ entropy indicate more complex or chaotic behavior. The K$_2$ entropy values are interpreted and classified as follows:

1. K$_2$ entropy $= 0$ implies that the dynamic system is either *constant* or *periodic*,

2. K$_2$ entropy $>> 1$ (approaching ∞) implies that the dynamic system is *random*, and

3. $0 <$ K$_2$ entropy $<< \infty$ implies that the dynamic system is *chaotic*.

For the purpose of verification of the algorithms for computation of the correlation integral and the K$_2$ entropy, a model system, i.e., the Henon system, was considered. The Henon system is a model chaotic system whose time series data points are generated using the recurrence equations [1]:

$$\begin{aligned} X_{n+1} &= \alpha - X_n^2 + \beta Y_n \\ Y_{n+1} &= X_n \text{ where } \alpha = 1.4, \ \beta = 0.3 \end{aligned} \quad (29.4.3)$$

The Henon system is known to have a characteristic K$_2$ entropy of 0.325 and a correlation dimension of 1.22 [11].

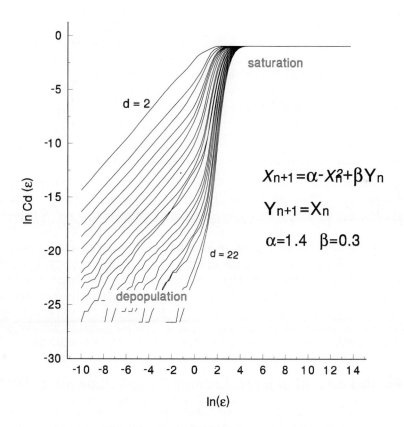

Figure 29.4 Correlation integral curves for the Henon system.

Figure 29.4 shows the plot of $C_d(\epsilon)$ as a function of ϵ on a dual logarithmic (i.e., log-log) scale for various values of the embedding dimension d for the Henon model system. This plot is referred to as the correlation integral (i.e., C_d) plot and the curves in the plot are referred to as the d-curves. With reference to the C_d plot in Figure 29.4, the region where all the d-curves merge into a single horizontal line is called the *saturation* region. In the saturation region, the d-dimensional distances between all possible vector pairs are contained within a hypersphere of radius ϵ, resulting in an asymptotic value of unity for $C_d(\epsilon)$ (equation (29.4.1)).

The *depopulation* region in the C_d plot is characterized by small values of ϵ where there are very few or no vector pairs whose inter-vector distances in $\mathcal{R}^d$ are less than the value of ϵ. The depopulation region (Figure 29.4) is characterized by the abrupt termination of the d-curves for small values of ϵ. This is particularly noticeable in the case of d-curves at higher dimensional embeddings (i.e., higher d values) where the possibility of finding vector pairs with inter-vector distances less than ϵ reduces dramatically.

The *scaling* region in the C_d plot is defined as the one between the saturation and depopulation regions where all the d-curves have a constant slope and are parallel to each other (Figure 29.4). The K_2 entropy is computed as the asymptotic distance between successive d-curves in the scaling region in the limit $d \to \infty$. The correlation-dimension is computed as the asymptotic slope of the d-curves in the scaling region in the limit $d \to \infty$.

29.4.2   Serial Computation of the Correlation Integral

The computational complexity of the serial algorithm for the computation of K_2 entropy stems primarily from the computation of C_d (equation (29.4.1)). When computing the K_2 entropy with a maximum embedding dimension $D << N$ (where N = number of time series data points), there are approximately $N \cdot (N-1)/2$ d-dimensional vector pairs (where $d \leq D$) to be considered. From equation (29.4.1) and the outline of the serial algorithm given in Figure 29.5, it can be shown that the computational complexity of the serial algorithm is $O(N^2 D^2)$. For large values of N, the computation on conventional single/serial processor systems becomes quite unwieldy, and the high response time severely limits the usefulness of the algorithm for many time-critical and real-life applications [5]. This is the primary motivation for considering a parallel algorithm on a PVM system of UNIX workstations.

29.5   A Parallel Algorithm for K_2 Entropy Computation using PVM

The PVM algorithm is designed by partitioning the outermost loop (with loop index d) of the serial algorithm (Figure 29.5) and having different processors iterate through the outermost loop for different ranges for parameter d. The master process spawns the child processes, broadcasts the time series data to all the child processes and awaits the results of the child processes. On receipt of the results of each of the child processes, the master process computes the correlation integral C_d by assembling the `CompareVec` matrices received from each of the child processes. Each child process receives the time series data from the master process and computes its share of the outermost loop partition. On completion, it sends its `CompareVec` matrix to the master process. The master and slave processes are depicted in Figures 29.6 and 29.7, respectively.

```
for (d=1; d < D; d++)
beginfor

 /* Find the correlation-integral Cd(epsilon) by embedding
    the time-series data points in the d-th dimension */

 for (n = 1; n < (N-2*d+1); n++)
 beginfor
  for (m = n; m < (N-1); m++)
  beginfor
   distance = 0;
   for (i = 0, i < (d-1); i++)
   beginfor
    distance = distance + (X[n+i]-X[m+i]) * (X[n+i]-X[m+i]);
   endfor

   distance = sqrt(distance); /* Euclidean distance */

   i = 0;
   for (eps = 0; eps <= eps_final; eps = eps + eps_increment)
   beginfor
    if ( distance <= eps ) CompareVec[i] = CompareVec[i] + 2.0;
    i = i+1;
   endfor
  endfor
 endfor

/* Print the values of correlation-integral Cd(epsilon) */

 for (i = 0; i <= eps_final/eps_increment; i++)
  if (CompareVec[i] > 0) print(log(CompareVec[i]));
endfor
```

Figure 29.5 Serial algorithm for the computation of C_d.

```
master()
beginmaster
 Phase 1: Initial Setup
 (a) Spawn Child Processes;
 (b) Read Input: time series data;
 (c) Computer the range [d_min, d_max] for each child process;
 /* The [d_min, d_max] ranges for the child processes are
    non-overlapping */
 (d) Broadcast time series data to all child processes;
 (e) Transmit the [d_min, d_max] range to each child process;

 Phase 2: Collect Results
 (a) Receive CompareVec[][] matrix from each child process;
 (b) Assemble the CompareVec[][] matrices in CompareVecSum[][];
 (c) Print results:
     for (d = 1; d < D; d++)
      for (i = 0; i <= eps_final/eps_increment; i++)
       if (CompareVecSum[d][i] > 0) print(log(CompareVecSum[d][i]));
endmaster
```

Figure 29.6 Master process for parallel computation of C_d.

29.6   Optimal Scaling Region Determination Algorithm

The scaling region in a C_d plot is the one where all the d-curves are optimally parallel to each other [11]. Grassberger and Procaccia [11] present a manual procedure for determining the scaling region by visual inspection of the C_d plot. We present a serial exhaustive search algorithm for determination of the optimal scaling region in the C_d plot.

The objective function for the exhaustive search algorithm is formulated so as to have a minimum in the scaling region, where all the d-curves are optimally parallel to each other. The search algorithm proceeds by exhaustively constructing straight lines (with varying slopes and y-intercepts) that intersect the d-curves in the C_d plot. For each candidate line of intersection, the objective function value is computed as the summation of squared errors. Each error term in the summation is defined to be the deviation of the candidate line of intersection from the normal to that particular d-curve at the point of intersection. Note that the value of the objective function would generally be high in the depopulation region where all the d-curves have different slopes. However, in the saturation region, the objective function would have a very low value (generally zero), which is not desirable. In order to prevent the objective function from straying into the saturation region, the value of the objective function is normalized by dividing it by the *local* entropy. We define *local*

```
child()
beginchild
 Phase 1: Initial Setup
 (a) Receive time series data from master process;
 (b) Receive  [d_min, d_max] value from child process;

 Phase 2: Compute Correlation Integral in the range
 for (d = d_min; d <= d_max; d++)
 beginfor
  for (n = 1; n < (N-2*d+1); n++)
  beginfor
   for (m = n; m < (N-1); m++)
   beginfor
    distance = 0;
    for (i = 0, i < (d-1); i++)
    beginfor
     distance = distance + (X[n+i]-X[m+i]) * (X[n+i]-X[m+i]);
    endfor

    distance = sqrt(distance); /* Euclidean distance */
    i = 0;
    for (eps = 0; eps <= eps_final; eps = eps + increment)
    beginfor
     if ( distance <= eps ) CompareVec[d][i] = CompareVec[d][i] + 2.0;
     i = i+1;
    endfor
   endfor
  endfor
 endfor

 Phase 3: Transmit CompareVec[][] matrix to master process;

endchild
```

Figure 29.7 Child process for parallel computation of C_d.

entropy of the C_d plot with respect to a straight line as the vertical distance between two successive d-curves with the highest possible d values intersecting that straight line. It must be noted that there may exist some areas in the depopulation region where local entropy cannot be defined. This normalization procedure effectively penalizes the objective function (i.e., forces it to have a high value) in and around the saturation region. In the actual implementation, values of local entropy close to zero were replaced by a small positive constant to avoid overflow error. The normalized objective function is computed exhaustively for several candidate intersection lines characterized by the angle of the slope (measured in degrees) and the y-intercept. The global minimum on the objective function surface yields the angle of the slope and y-intercept of a line that is optimally orthogonal to all the d-curves and whose intersection points with the d-curves lie entirely within the scaling region. We define these intersection points to constitute the *optimal scaling region*.

29.7 Experimental Results

29.7.1 Chromosome Reconstruction

The PSA and PMCA algorithms were implemented on a PVM system comprised of a cluster of eight SUN SPARC5 UNIX workstations using C as the programming language. The various algorithms were run on a clone data set derived from Chromosome IV of the fungus *Aspergillus nidulans*, which was made available to us by Professor Jonathan Arnold, Department of Genetics, University of Georgia. The data set consisted of 592 clones with each clone having a 115 bit signature.

In order to obtain a fair comparison between the various PSA and PMCA algorithms, the product (denoted by λ) of the number of processors n and the maximum number of iterations performed by a single processor at a given temperature or kinetic energy value (i.e., COUNT_LIMIT) was kept constant. For example, if one of the algorithms is run with 4 processors with COUNT_LIMIT = 50,000 then with 2 processors, COUNT_LIMIT would be 100,000 and with 1 processor, COUNT_LIMIT would be 200,000.

It was observed that the NILM PSA algorithm had a faster rate of convergence than the PILM PSA algorithm in terms of execution time. However, the PILM PSA algorithm was found to have a faster rate of convergence in terms of the number of iterations. This can be attributed to the fact that, although the PILM PSA algorithm needs fewer iterations than the NILM PSA algorithm, the average time per iteration in the case of the PILM PSA algorithm is greater. This is due to the overhead of interprocessor communication and synchronization entailed during the periodic interaction between the master process and the child processes in the case of the PILM PSA algorithm.

Table 29.1 shows the speed-up results for all the four algorithms: NILM PSA, PILM PSA, NILM PMCA and PILM PMCA for a varying number of processors n and varying values of λ. For a given value of n, varying the value of λ directly affects the the interprocessor communication overhead ratio $\tau = T_{comm}/T_{cpu}$ where

T_{comm} is the total time spent in interprocessor communication and T_{cpu} is the total time spent in computation. A higher value of λ for a given value of n implies a lower value for τ and vice versa. For a linking distance equal to the optimal value of 550, the NILM PSA algorithm is seen to have a speed-up of 3.1 for $n = 8$ and $\lambda = 200,000$ and a speed-up of 6.1 for $n = 8$ and $\lambda = 1,200,000$. This result is expected since the interprocessor communication overhead ratio τ is lower at higher values of λ, resulting in a higher speed-up. The PILM PSA algorithm is seen to have a speed-up of 3.0 for $n = 8$ and $\lambda = 200,000$ and a speed-up of 4.7 for $n = 8$ and $\lambda = 1,200,000$. As expected, the PILM PSA algorithm has a lower speed-up than the NILM PSA algorithm for given values of n and λ due to its higher interprocessor communication overhead. As also expected, for a given value of n the speed-up of the PILM PSA algorithm shows an increasing trend with increasing λ.

We observe that the parallelization of the MCA algorithm does not result in any speed-up (Table 29.1). On the contrary, there is a degradation in performance as the number of processors is increased. This phenomena can be explained by the fact that the serial MCA algorithm is considerably faster than the SA algorithm for the same number of iterations. For given values of n and λ, the interprocessor communication overhead ratio τ is far greater in the case of the PMCA algorithm as compared to the PSA algorithm. The interprocessor communication overhead dominates the performance of the PMCA algorithm for smaller values of λ, resulting in a degradation in performance as the number of processors is increased. As expected, the NILM PMCA and PILM PMCA algorithms show an increasing trend in speed-up (just as their PSA counterparts) with increasing λ for a given value of n. The NILM PMCA algorithm shows a speed-up of 0.4 for $n = 8$ and $\lambda = 200,000$ and a speed-up of 1.3 for $n = 8$ and $\lambda = 1,200,000$ (Table 29.1). The PILM PMCA algorithm, on the other hand, shows a speed-up of 0.6 for $n = 8$ and $\lambda = 200,000$ and a speed-up of 2.1 for $n = 8$ and $\lambda = 1,200,000$ (Table 29.1).

29.7.2   K$_2$ Entropy Computation

The correlation integral C_d was computed for the model Henon system (Figure 29.4) on the 8-node SUN SPARC5 workstation cluster using PVM. The runtime statistics of the parallel algorithm are tabulated in Table 29.2 for a varying number of processors and varying number of time series data points. As can be seen in Table 29.2, the speed-up is acceptable for all data sizes. For a given data size, the speed-up is slightly sublinear in the number of processors. For a given number of processors, the speed-up improves with increasing data size. Both these observations are consistent with our expectations since the communication overhead ratio τ increases with increasing number of processors for a given data size and decreases with increasing data size for a given number of processors.

The values for the K$_2$ entropy and correlation-dimension of the model Henon system, computed using the parallel algorithm for the computation of C_d in conjunction with the serial algorithm for determination of the optimal scaling region, agrees well with the values reported by Grassberger and Procaccia [11], as shown in

Table 29.1 Speed-up Results for the PSA and PMCA Algorithms

λ	n	Linking Distance = 550			
		NILM PSA	PILM PSA	NILM PMCA	PILM PMCA
	1	1.0	1.0	1.0	1.0
	2	1.8	1.4	0.8	0.8
200,000	4	3.0	1.8	0.8	1.0
	6	3.4	2.7	0.6	0.9
	8	3.1	3.0	0.4	0.6
	1	1.0	1.0	1.0	1.0
	2	2.1	1.4	0.8	1.2
400,000	4	3.9	1.8	0.9	1.4
	6	5.8	2.9	0.9	1.2
	8	5.5	3.5	0.6	1.1
	1	1.0	1.0	1.0	1.0
	2	2.2	1.2	1.4	1.3
800,000	4	3.7	1.9	2.0	1.7
	6	6.3	3.2	1.6	1.9
	8	5.4	3.5	1.2	1.5
	1	1.0	1.0	1.0	1.0
	2	1.8	1.5	1.6	1.7
1,000,000	4	4.5	2.0	1.9	1.7
	6	5.5	3.3	1.5	1.9
	8	5.5	4.7	1.6	2.4
	1	1.0	1.0	1.0	1.0
	2	2.3	1.5	1.4	1.3
1,200,000	4	4.7	1.9	1.8	1.1
	6	6.7	4.7	2.1	1.6
	8	6.1	4.7	1.3	2.1

Table 29.3. Since Grassberger and Procaccia obtained the values of the K_2 entropy and correlation-dimension for the Henon system manually (i.e., by visual inspection of the C_d plot), a precise comparison based on numerical accuracy, between their results and ours, is not possible.

In most medical applications requiring off-line analysis of EKG data, a data set containing a bare minimum of 1800 heart rate points (i.e., 10 minutes of heart rate data at a sampling rate of 3 Hz) is needed. A data set of larger size would obviously improve the precision of the subsequent analysis. A turnaround time of one minute for the off-line analysis of 1800 heart rate data points would be considered acceptable - a capability that is currently provided by the 8-node PVM system. On-line analysis of EKG data (during cardiac surgery, for example) would require a turn around time in the millisecond range, which is 3–4 orders of magnitude

Table 29.2 Runtime Statistics of the Parallel Algorithm for Computation of the Correlation Integral C_d of the Henon System, T: Execution Time (min), σ: Speed-up

No. of Processors	No. of Data Points							
	2K		4K		8K		16K	
	T	σ	T	σ	T	σ	T	σ
1	5.21	1.00	9.13	1.00	27.32	1.00	248.74	1.00
2	2.86	1.82	4.94	1.85	14.30	1.91	128.22	1.94
4	1.52	3.41	2.64	3.46	7.83	3.49	70.07	3.55
6	1.01	5.16	1.75	5.22	5.16	5.29	46.67	5.33
8	0.75	6.95	1.30	7.02	3.82	7.15	34.26	7.26

Table 29.3 Comparison of Results for the Model Henon System. K_2: K_2 Entropy, CD: Correlation Dimension

	K_2	CD
Grassberger and Procaccia	0.325	1.22
PVM Implementation	0.334	1.24

smaller than that of our current PVM implementation. We intend to address this issue in our future research.

29.8 Conclusions

In this chapter, we presented PVM-based parallel algorithms for two very important biomedical problems: chromosome reconstruction and heart-rate variability analysis. We designed and analyzed two models for a parallel simulated annealing (PSA) algorithm and two models for a parallel microcanonical annealing (PMCA) algorithm in the context of chromosome reconstruction via clone ordering. These models were based on the decomposition of the Markov chain of solution states across multiple processors and were termed as the Periodically Interacting Local Markov chain (PILM) model and the Non-Interacting Local Markov chain (NILM) model. The algorithms were implemented on a PVM system comprised of eight SUN SPARC5 workstations running UNIX.

Between the NILM PSA and PILM PSA models, the former showed faster convergence to the globally optimal solution and higher speed-up as well. This could be attributed to the higher interprocessor communication overhead associated with the PILM PSA model. Both, the PILM and the NILM PMCA models showed very little improvement in terms of speed of convergence and speed-up over the serial

MCA algorithm. This can be attributed to the fact that the PMCA algorithm has a higher interprocessor communication overhead ratio τ, compared to the PSA algorithm. In other words, since the serial MCA algorithm is inherently fast and computationally efficient, the performance of the PMCA algorithm was dominated by the interprocessor communication overhead, leading to an overall performance degradation as the number of processors was increased. This was further corroborated by our observation that decreasing the value of τ (by increasing the number of iterations of the PMCA algorithm performed by each processor for a given kinetic energy value) improved the speed-up characteristics of the NILM and PILM PMCA algorithms.

In this chapter, we also presented a PVM-based parallel algorithm for heart rate variability analysis. We designed a parallel algorithm for the computation of the correlation integral and a serial exhaustive search-based algorithm for the determination of the optimal scaling region in the correlation integral plot. These algorithms were used to compute the K_2 entropy and the correlation dimension of experimental heart rate data. These algorithms were also verified on the model Henon system. The parallel algorithm for the computation of the correlation integral showed very good speed-up on the 8-node PVM system and could be readily applied to real life situations which call for timely analysis of chaotic time series data arising from an underlying complex dynamic system. The application of the PVM algorithm as an on-line prognostic/diagnostic tool for determining cardiovascular health needs to be further explored.

Acknowledgments

This research was partly funded by an NRICGP grant by the US Department of Agriculture to Dr. Suchendra Bhandarkar.

29.9   Bibliography

[1] G.L. Baker and J.P. Gollub. *Chaotic Dynamics, An Introduction.* Cambridge University Press, New York, 1990.

[2] S.M. Bhandarkar and S. Machaka. Chromosome Reconstruction from Physical Maps Using a Cluster of Workstations. *Jour. Supercomputing*, vol 11(1), pages 61–86, 1997.

[3] J.T. Bigger, J. Fleiss, J.L. Fleiss, R.C. Steinman, L.M. Rolnitzky, R.E. Kleiger and J.N. Rottman. Frequency–Domain Measures of Heart Period Variability and Mortality after Myocardial Infraction. *Circulation*, vol 85(1), pages 164–171, 1992.

[4] K.S. Booth and G.S. Lueker. Testing for the Consecutive One's Property, Interval Graphs and Graph Planarity using pq-Tree Algorithms. *Jour. Comput. Systems Sci.* vol 13, pages 335–379, 1976.

[5] S. Chirravuri, S.M. Bhandarkar and D. Whitmire. A Massively Parallel Algorithm for K_2 Entropy Computation: Case Studies of Model Systems and *In Vivo* Data. *Intl. Jour. Supercomputer Appl. and High Perf. Computing*, vol 9(4), pages 296–311, 1995.

[6] M. Creutz. Microcanonical Monte Carlo Simulation. *Physics Review Letters*, vol 50(19), pages 1411–1414, May 1983.

[7] A.J. Cuticchia, J. Arnold, and W. E. Timberlake. ODS: Ordering DNA Sequences—A Physical Mapping Algorithm based on Simulated Annealing. *CABIOS*, vol 9, pages 215–219, 1993.

[8] M.S. Garey and D.S. Johnson. *Computers and Intractability: A Guide to the Theory of NP–Completeness*. W.H. Freeman, New York, 1979.

[9] S. Geman and D. Geman. Stochastic Relaxation, Gibbs Distribution and the Bayesian Restoration of Images. *IEEE Trans. Pattern Analysis and Machine Intelligence*, vol 6(6), pages 721–741, 1984.

[10] A.L. Goldberger and B.J. West. Fractals in Physiology and Medicine. *Yale Jour. Biology and Medicine*, vol 60, pages 421–435, 1987.

[11] P. Grassberger and I. Procaccia. Estimation of Kolmogorov Entropy from a Chaotic Signal. *Physical Review A*, vol 28(4), pages 2591–2593, 1983.

[12] R. Introna, E. Yodlowski, J. Pruett, N. Montano, A. Porta and R. Crumrine. Sympathovagal Effects of Spinal Anesthesia Assessed by Heart Rate Variability Analysis. *Anesthesia and Analgesia*, vol 80(2), pages 315–321, 1995.

[13] R.E. Phillips and M.K. Feeney. *The Cardiac Rhythms*. W.B. Saunders Publishing Company, Philadelphia, PA, 1973.

[14] S.M. Ryan, A.L. Goldberger, S.M. Pincus, J. Mietus and L.A. Lipsitz. Gender–Related and Age–Related Differences in Heart Rate Dynamics - Are Women More Complex Than Men? *Jour. of The American College of Cardiology*, vol 24(7), pages 1700–1707, 1994.

[15] V. Sunderam. PVM: A Framework for Parallel Distributed Computing. *Concurrency: Practice and Experience*, vol 2(2), pages 315–339, 1990.

[16] M. Xiong, H.J. Chen, R.A. Prade, Y. Wang, J. Griffith, W.E. Timberlake, and J. Arnold. On the Consistency of a Physical Mapping Method to Reconstruct a Chromosome *In Vitro*. *Genetics*, vol 142(1), pages 267–284, 1996.

Appendix A

Glossary[1]

adaptive Taking available information into account. For example, an adaptive mesh-generating algorithm generates a finer resolution mesh near to discontinuities such as boundaries and corners. An adaptive routing algorithm may send identical messages in different directions at different times, depending on the local density information it has on message traffic.

address mask In Internet communications, a 32-bit long mask used to select an IP address for subnet addressing. The mask selects the network portion of the IP address and one or more bits of the local LAN address.

address space A region of a computer's total memory within which addresses are contiguous and may refer to one another directly. A shared memory computer has only one user-visible address space; a disjoint memory computer can have several.

address translation In networking, the process of converting external addresses into standardized network addresses and vice versa. This facilitates the interconnection of multiple networks each of which has its own address plan.

Amdahl's Law A rule first formalized by Gene Amdahl in 1967, which states that if F is the fraction of a calculation that is serial and 1-F the fraction that can be parallelized, then the speed-up that can be achieved using P processors is: $\frac{1}{F+\frac{1-F}{P}}$ which has a limiting value of $\frac{1}{F}$ for an infinite number of processors. It does not matter how many processors are employed, if a calculation has a 10% serial component, the maximum speedup obtainable is 10.

ANSI American National Standards Institute, a United States-based organization which develops standards and defines interfaces for telecommunications, among other things.

AppleTalk Apple Computer's proprietary network suite of protocols.

---

[1]A modified version by Mark Baker and Rajkumar Buyya. The original version (Courtesy of Geoffrey Fox) can be found at "The National HPCC Software Exchange (NHSE) HPCC Roadmap" Website: `http://nhse.npac.syr.edu/roadmap/`

Applets An application interface where referencing (perhaps by a mouse click) a remote application as a hyperlink to a server causes it to be downloaded and run on the client.

architecture The basic plan along which a computer has been constructed. Popular parallel architectures include processor arrays, bus-based multiprocessors (with caches of various sizes and structures) and disjoint memory multicomputers.

ARP Address Resolution Protocol under TCP/IP used to dynamically bind a high-level IP address to a low-level physical hardware address. ARP is limited to a single physical network that supports hardware broadcasting.

ARPAnet The U.S. Advanced Research Project Agency network, which was the first large multi-site computer network.

associative address A method whereby access is made to an item whose key matches an access key, as distinct from an access to an item at a specific address in memory. See "associative memory."

associative memory Memory that can be accessed by content rather than by address; content addressable is often used synonymously. An associative memory permits its user to specify part of a pattern or key and retrieve the values associated with that pattern. The tuple space used to implement the generative communication model is an associative memory.

asynchronous A method of transmission which does not require a common clock, but separates fields of data by stop and start bits.

Asynchronous Transfer Mode A broadband cell relay protocol that cuts subscriber data into fixed size packets for transfer across the wide area network.

atomic Not interruptible. An atomic operation is one that always appears to have been executed as a unit.

automatic vectorization A compiler that takes code written in a serial language (often Fortran or C) and translates it into vector instructions. The vector instructions may be machine specific or in a source form such as array extensions or as subroutine calls to a vector library.

auxiliary memory Memory that is usually large in capacity, but slow and inexpensive, often a rotating magnetic or optical memory, whose main function is to store large volumes of data and programs not being actively used by the processors.

bandwidth The communications capacity (measured in bits per second) of a transmission line or of a specific path through the network. Contiguous bandwidth is a synonym for consecutive grouped channels in multiplexers, switches, or DACs; i.e., 256kbps (4 64kbps channels).

bank conflict A bank "busy-wait" situation. Memory chip speeds are relatively slow when required to deliver a single word, so supercomputer memories are placed in a large number of independent banks (usually a power of two). A vector of data, laid out contiguously in memory with one component per successive bank, can be accessed at one word per cycle (despite the intrinsic slowness of the chips) through the use of pipelined delivery of vector-component words at high bandwidth. When the number of banks is a power of two, then vectors requiring strides of a power of two can run into a bank conflict.

bank cycle time The time, measured in clock cycles, taken by a memory bank between the honoring of one request to fetch or store a data item and accepting another such request. On most supercomputers, this value is either four or eight clock cycles.

barrier A point in a program at which barrier synchronization occurs.

barrier synchronization An event in which two or more processes belonging to some implicit or explicit group block until all members of the group have blocked. They may then all proceed. No member of the group may pass a barrier until all processes in the group have reached it.

benchmark A quantitative measure of performance for a computing system. The measure may be in terms of computational performance, which is often rated in FLOPS, or in terms of memory speed, or communications bandwidth or some more application-oriented measure such as LIPS or OLTPS. A collection of benchmark results for many computer systems is available online from the National Software Exchange.

BISDN Broadband Integrated Services Digital Network is a packet switching technique which uses packets of fixed length, resulting in lower processing and higher speeds.

bisection bandwidth The rate at which communication can take place between one half of a computer and the other. A low bisection bandwidth, or a large disparity between the maximum and minimum bisection bandwidths achieved by cutting the computer's elements in different ways, is a warning that communications bottlenecks may arise in some calculations.

bit-addressable Allowing direct access to individual bits, rather than requiring bits to be selected by applying arithmetic or other operations to whole words. The local memory of each processing element in many processor arrays is bit-addressable.

BLAS Basic Linear Algebra Software is a suite of very basic linear algebra routines, out of which almost any other matrix calculation can be built. See the National Software Exchange for the BLAS source and documentation.

block To suspend one's own operation, or the operation of another process. A process may block itself, or be blocked by the system, until some event occurs. If all processes are simultaneously blocked, and no external event can cause any of them to become unblocked, then deadlock has occurred. The term, "block," is also often used to refer to a chunk of data or program.

blocking An operation that causes the process executing it to block. Usually applied to communications operations, where it implies that the communicating process cannot perform any other operations until the communication has completed.

BPS Bytes Per Second is a unit of memory access speed or communications transfer speed.

bridge A LAN internetworking device that filters and passes data between LANs based on Layer 2 (MAC layer) information. Bridges do not use any routing algorithms.

broadcast To send a message to all possible recipients. Broadcast can be implemented as a repeated send, but is more efficiently implemented by using spanning trees and having each node in the tree propagate the message to its descendants.

buffer A temporary storage area in memory. Many methods for routing messages between processors use buffers at the source and destination, or at intermediate processors. See also packet switching, virtual cut-through and wormhole routing.

bus A single physical communications medium shared by two or more devices. The network shared by processors in many distributed computers is a bus, as is the shared data path in many multiprocessors.

busy-waiting A situation whereby processor cycles are used to test a variable until it assumes a desired value.

cache A high-speed memory, local to a single processor, whose data transfers are carried out automatically in hardware. Items are brought into a cache when they are referenced, while any changes to values in a cache are automatically written when they are no longer needed, when the cache becomes full, or when some other process attempts to access them.

cache consistency The problem of ensuring that the values associated with a particular variable in the caches of several processors are never visibly different.

cache hit A cache access that successfully finds the requested data.

cache line The unit in which data is fetched from memory to cache.

cache miss A cache access that fails to find the requested data. The cache must then be filled from main memory at the expense of time.

CAD Computer-Aided Design; a term which can encompass all facets of the use of computers in manufacturing, although the term CAM is also in use.

CAE Computer-Aided Engineering, like CAD, but usually applied to the use of computers in fields such as civil and nautical engineering.

CAM Computer-Aided Manufacturing.

CCITT Consultative Committee International Telephone and Telegraph is an international organization which develops standards and defines interfaces for telecommunications.

cell relay Packet switching technique which uses packets of fixed length, resulting in lower processing speeds. Also known as BISDN and ATM.

cellular automata A system made up of many discrete cells, each of which may be in one of a finite number of states. A cell or automaton may change state only at fixed, regular intervals, and only in accordance with fixed rules that depend on the cell's own values and the values of neighbors within a certain proximity.

CFD Computational Fluid Dynamics; the simulation or prediction of fluid flow using computers, a field which has generally required twice the computing power available at any given time.

channel A point-to-point connection between two processes through which messages can be sent. Programming systems that rely on channels are sometimes called connection-oriented, to distinguish them from the more widespread connectionless systems in which messages are sent to named destinations rather than through named channels.

circuit switching A switching method where a dedicated path is set up between the transmitter and receiver. The connection is transparent, meaning that the switches do not try to interpret the data.

CISC Complicated Instruction Set Computer; a computer that provides many powerful but complicated instructions. This term is also applied to software designs that give users a large number of complex basic operations.

CLNP Connectionless Network Protocol, also known as ISO-IP. This protocol provides a datagram service and is OSI's equivalent to IP.

clock cycle The fundamental period of time in a computer. Current technology will typically have this measured in nanoseconds.

clock time Physical or elapsed time, as seen by an external observer. Nonrelativistic time. In small computer systems where all components can be synchronized, clock time and logical time may be the same everywhere, but in large systems it may be difficult for a processor to correlate the events it sees with the clock time an external observer would see. The clock times of events define a complete order on those events.

CLTP Connectionless Transport Protocol, which provides end-to-end transport data addressing and is OSI's equivalent to UDP.

clustered computing A commonly found computing environment consists of many workstations connected by a local area network. The workstations, which have become increasingly powerful over the years, can together be viewed as a significant computing resource. This resource is commonly known as cluster of workstations, and can be generalized to a heterogeneous collection of machines with arbitrary architecture.

cluster middleware A layer that resides between the operating system and user-level environment and offers single system image and system availability services.

CMIS Is the service performed by the Common Management Internet Protocol.

co-processor An additional processor attached to a main processor, to accelerate arithmetic, I/O or graphics operations.

combining Joining messages together as they traverse a network. Combining may be done to reduce the total traffic in the network, to reduce the number of times the start-up penalty of messaging is incurred, or to reduce the number of messages reaching a particular destination.

combining switch An element of an interconnection network that can combine certain types of requests into one request and produce a response that mimics serial execution of the requests.

communication overhead A measure of the additional workload incurred in a parallel algorithm due to communication between the nodes of the parallel system.

compiler directives Special keywords often specified as comments in the source code, but recognized by the compiler as providing additional information from the user for use in optimization.

compiler optimization Rearranging or eliminating sections of a program during compilation to achieve higher performance. Compiler optimization is usually applied only within basic blocks and must account for the possible dependence of one section of a program on another.

compcomms ratio The ratio of the number of calculations a process does to the total size of the messages it sends. A process that performs a few calculations and then sends a single short message may have the same computation-to-communication ratio as a process that performs millions of calculations and then sends many large messages. The ratio may also be measured by the ratio of the time spent calculating to the time spent communicating, in which case the ratio's value depends on the relative speeds of the processor and communications medium, and on the startup cost and latency of communication.

concurrent computer A generic category, often used synonymously with parallel computer to include both multicomputer and multiprocessor.

concurrent processing Simultaneous execution of instructions by two or more processors within a computer.

condition synchronization Process of delaying the continued execution of a process until some data object it shares with another process is in an appropriate state.

configuration A particular selection of the types of processes that could make up a parallel program. Configuration is trivial in the SPMD model, in which every processor runs a single identical process, but can be complicated in the general MIMD case, particularly if user-level processes rely on libraries that may themselves require extra processes.

contention Conflict that arises when two or more requests are made concurrently for a resource that cannot be shared. Processes running on a single processor may contend for CPU time, or a network may suffer from contention if several messages attempt to traverse the same link at the same time.

context switching Saving the state of one process and replacing it with that of another that is time sharing the same processor. If little time is required to switch contexts, processor overloading can be an effective way to hide latency in a message passing system.

control process A process which controls the execution of a program on a concurrent computer. The major tasks performed by the control process are to initiate execution of the necessary code on each node and to provide I/O and other service facilities for the nodes.

COW or NOW Clusters of Workstations (COW) are a particular HPDC environment where often one will use optimized network links and interfaces to achieve high performance. A COW (if homogeneous) is particularly close to a classic homogeneous MPP built with the same CPU chipsets as workstations. Proponents of COW's will claim that use of commodity workstation nodes allows them to track technology better than MPP's. MPP proponents note that their optimized designs deliver higher performance, which outweighs the increased cost of low-volume designs, and effective performance loss due to later (maybe only months) adoption of a given technology by the MPP compared to commodity markets.

CPU Central Processing Unit of a sequential computer system. Sometimes used to mean one processor element of a concurrent computer system.

critical section A section of program that can be executed by, at most, one process at a time.

CSP Communicating Sequential Processes; an approach to parallelism in which anonymous processes communicate by sending messages through named point-to-point channels. CSP was coined by Hoare in 1985. All communication is synchronous in that the process that reaches the communication operation first is blocked until a complementary process reaches the same operation.

cycle Cycle of the computer clock is an electronic signal that counts a single unit of time within a computer.

cycle time The length of a single cycle of a computer function such as a memory cycle or processor cycle.

DACS Digital Access Cross-connect System is a switch that enables test access and switching of digital signals in a T system.

data cache A cache that holds data but does not hold instructions.

data dependency A situation existing between two statements if one statement can store into a location that is later accessed by the other statement.

data-driven A data flow architecture in which execution of instructions depends on availability of operands.

data locality and caching A key to sequential parallel and distributed computing is data locality. This concept involves minimizing "distance" between processor and data. In sequential computing, this implies "caching" data in fast memory and arranging computation to minimize access to data not in cache. In parallel and distributed computing, one uses migration and replication to minimize the time a given node spends accessing data stored on another node.

data parallelism A model of parallel computing in which a single operation can be applied to all elements of a data structure simultaneously. Typically, these data structures are arrays, and the operations are arithmetic and act independently on every array element, or reduction operations.

dataflow A model of parallel computing in which programs are represented as dependence graphs and each operation is automatically blocked until the values on which it depends are available. The parallel functional and parallel logic programming models are very similar to the dataflow model.

deadlock A situation in which each possible activity is blocked, waiting on some other activity that is also blocked. If a directed graph represents how activities depend on others, then deadlock arises if and only if there is a cycle in this graph.

declustered A file system that distributes blocks of individual files among several disks. This contrasts with a traditional file system, in which all blocks of a single file are placed on the same disk.

decomposition A division of a data structure into substructures that can be distributed separately, or a technique for dividing a computation into subcomputations that can be executed separately. The most common decomposition strategies in parallel computing are: functional decomposition, geometric decomposition, and iterative decomposition.

demand-driven Data flow architecture in which execution of an instruction depends upon both availability of its operands and a request for the result.

dependence The relationship of a calculation B to a calculation A if changes to A, or to the ordering of A and B, could affect B. If A and B are calculations in a program, for example, then B is dependent on A if B uses values calculated by A. There are four types of dependence: true dependence, where B uses values calculated by A; antidependence, where A uses values overwritten by B; output dependence, where A and B both write to the same variables; control dependence, where B's execution is controlled by values set in A. Dependence is also used in message routing to mean that some activity X cannot proceed until another activity Y has completed. For example, if X and Y are messages attempting to pass through a region with limited buffer space, and Y currently holds some or all of the buffer, X may depend on Y's releasing some buffer space before proceeding.

dependence analysis An analysis by compiler or precompiler that reveals which portions of a program depend on the prior completion of other portions of the program. Dependency analysis usually relates statements in an iterative code construct.

direct mapping A cache that has a set associativity of one so that each item has a unique place in the cache at which it can be stored.

direct naming A message passing scheme in which source and destination designators are the names of processes.

directed graph A graph in which the edges have an orientation, denoted by arrowheads.

disjoint memory Memory that appears to the user to be divided among many separate address spaces. In a multicomputer, each processor typically has its own private memory and manages requests to it from processes running on other processors. Disjoint memory is more commonly called distributed memory, but the memory of many shared memory computers is physically distributed.

disk striping Technique of interleaving a disk file across two or more disk drives to enhance input/output performance. The performance gain is a function of the number of drives and channels used.

distributed computer A computer made up of many smaller and potentially independent computers, such as a network of workstations. This architecture is increasingly studied because of its cost-effectiveness and flexibility. Distributed computers are often heterogeneous.

distributed computing The use of networked heterogeneous computers to solve a single problem. The nodes (individual computers) are typically loosely coupled.

distributed memory Memory that is physically distributed among several modules. A distributed memory architecture may appear to users to have a single address space and a single shared memory or may appear as disjoint memory made up of many separate address spaces.

DMA Direct Memory Access; allows devices on a bus to access memory without requiring intervention by the CPU.

domain That part of a larger computing resource allocated for the sole use of a specific user or group of users. See also space sharing.

DRAM Dynamic RAM; memory which periodically needs refreshing, and is therefore usually slower than SRAM but is cheaper to produce.

dusty deck A term applied to old programs (usually Fortran or Cobol). The term is derived from the image of a deck of punched cards grown dusty over the years.

dynamic decomposition A task allocation policy that assumes tasks are generated at execution time.

eager evaluation A scheduling policy under which each computation begins as soon as its inputs are ready or its necessary preconditions have been satisfied. This is the scheduling policy used in most programs, but contrasts with the lazy evaluation policy often used in functional and logic programming.

efficiency A measure of hardware utilization, equal to the ratio of speed-up achieved on P processors to P itself.

embarrassingly parallel A class of problems that can be broken up into parts, which can be executed essentially independently on a parallel or distributed computer.

EPROM Electronically programmable ROM; a memory whose contents can be changed using special hardware. This usually involves removing the chips from their environment in order to "burn" a new pattern into them.

ethernet A LAN protocol that supports high-speed communications in the local area. Usually rates are at 10Mbps.

explicitly parallel Language semantics that describe which computations are independent and can be performed in parallel. See also "implicitly parallel."

fairness A property of a concurrent system. If a system is fair, then in the long run all processes are served equally. No process has preferential access to semaphores and, in particular, no process can livelock.

FDDI Fast Digital Data Interface; a standard for fiber optic communications systems.

fetch-and-add A computer synchronization instruction that updates a word in memory, returns the value before the update, and produces a set of results as if the processors executed in some arbitrary order.

FIFO First In, First Out, a queue.

file server A process running on a computer that provides access to files for remote user systems.

file system The hardware used for nonvolatile data storage; the system software that controls this hardware; the architecture of this hardware and software. A parallel file system is one that can be read or written to by many processors simultaneously.

FLOPS Floating Point Operations Per Second; a measure of memory access performance, equal to the rat eat which a machine can perform single-precision floating-point calculations.

Flynn's Taxonomy A classification system for architectures that has two axes: the number of instructions streams executing concurrently, and the number of data sets to which those instructions are being applied. The scheme was proposed by Flynn in 1966.

fork To create a new process that is a copy of its immediate parent.

FPU Floating Point Unit; either a separate chip or an area of silicon on the CPU specialized to accelerate floating point arithmetic.

functional unit Functionally independent part of the ALU, each of which performs a specific function, for example: address calculation, floating-point add, or floating-point multiply.

GaAs Gallium Arsenide; an relatively new semiconductor material, still not yet fully mastered by chip manufacturers. GaAs components can run much faster than silicon-based components.

Gantt chart A diagram used to illustrate a deterministic schedule.

generative communication A model of parallel computing in which processes that have been spawned dynamically turn into data upon completion, and data may be stored in tuples in one or more shared tuple spaces. A process may add tuples to a tuple space, or remove then by matching against their contents.

granularity The size of operations done by a process between communications events. A fine grained process may perform only a few arithmetic operations between processing one message and the next, whereas a coarse grained process may perform millions.

guard A logical condition that controls whether a communication operation can take place. Guards are usually defined as part of the syntax and semantics of CSP-based languages.

heterogeneous Containing components of more than one kind. A heterogeneous architecture may be one in which some components are processors, and others memories, or it may be one that uses different types of processor together.

high-order interleaving Memory interleaving strategy based on high-order bits of an address.

HiPPI High Performance Parallel Interface; a point-to-point 100 MByte/sec interface standard used for networking components of high performance multicomputers together.

hit ratio The ratio of the number of times data requested from a cache is found (or hit) to the number of times it is not found (or missed).

homogeneous Made up of identical components. A homogeneous architecture is one in which each element is of the same type; processor arrays and multicomputers are usually homogeneous. See also heterogeneous.

hop A network connection between two distant nodes.

hot-spot contention An interference phenomenon observed in multiprocessors caused by memory access statistics being slightly skewed from a uniform distribution to favor a specific memory module.

HPCC An acronym for High Performance Computing and Communications, which is the field of information addressed by this glossary.

hypercube A topology of which each node is the vertex of a d-Dimensional cube. In a binary hypercube, each node is connected to n others, and its co-ordinates are one of the 2^n different n-bit sequences of binary digits. Most early American multicomputers used hypercubic topologies, and so the term "hypercube" is sometimes used as a synonym for multicomputers.

I/O Refers to the hardware and software mechanisms connecting a computer with its environment. This includes connections between the computer and its disk and bulk storage system and also connections to user terminals, graphics systems, and networks to other computer systems or devices. Standard I/O is a particular software package developed under UNIX for the C programming language.

ICMP Internet Control Message Protocol, which is used to handle errors and control messages at the Internet protocol layer. ICMP is considered to be part of IP and is used to test whether a destination is reachable and responding.

IEEE 802.3 The standard for Carrier Sense Multiple Access with Collision Detection is one of the most used LAN protocols.

implicitly parallel Language semantics that do not allow the user to explicitly describe which computations are independent and can be performed in parallel. For an implicitly parallel language, the compiler must deduce or prove independence in order to make use of parallel hardware. The comparative difficulty of the deduction separates implicitly parallel languages from explicitly parallel ones.

information A collection of related data objects.

instruction buffering Process of prefetching instructions with the goal of never making the processor wait for an instruction to be fetched. This is sometimes also known as instruction look-ahead.

instruction cache A cache memory that holds only instructions.

instruction pipelining Strategy of allowing more than one instruction to be in some stage of execution at the same time. See also MISD.

instruction scheduling A strategy of a compiler to analyze the outcome of the operations specified in a program and to issue instructions in an optimal manner. That is, the instructions are not necessarily issued in the order specified by the programmer, but in an order that optimally uses the registers, functional units and memory paths of the computer, while at the same time guaranteeing correct results for the computation.

instruction set The set of low level instructions that a computer is capable of executing. Programs expressed in a high level language must ultimately be reduced to these.

instruction stream Sequence of instructions performed by a computer.

interactive vectorizer An interactive program to help a user vectorize source code.

interconnection network The system of logic and conductors that connects the processors in a parallel computer system. Some examples are bus, mesh, hypercube and Omega networks.

interleaved memory Memory divide into a number of modules or banks that can be accessed simultaneously.

interprocessor communication The passing of data and information among the processors of a parallel computer during the execution of a parallel program.

interprocessor contention Conflicts caused when multiple CPU's compete for shared system resources. For example, memory bank conflicts for a user's code in global memory architectures are caused by other processors running independent applications.

interrupt-driven system A system whose processes communicate by message passing in such a way that when a message is delivered to its destination process, it interrupts execution of that process and initiates execution of an interrupt handler process, which stores the message for subsequent retrieval. On completion of the interrupt-handler process (which sets some flag or sends some signal to denote an available message), the original process resumes execution.

interval routing A routing algorithm that assigns an integer identifier to each possible destination and then labels the outgoing links of each node with a single contiguous interval or window so that a message can be routed simply by sending it out the link in whose interval its destination identifier falls.

IP The Internet Protocol that defines the unit of information passed between systems that provides a basic packet delivery service. It handles best effort connectionless delivery service and includes ICMP.

IP address The Internet Protocol address which is a 32-bit address assigned to a host. The IP address has a host component and a network component.

IPX Integrated Packet Exchange, for example, Stratacom's Packet switch for public and private T1 and E1 networks.

ISO International Standards Organization, which, among other things, sets standards for programming languages.

Java A distributed computing language (Web Technology) developed by Sun, which is based on C++, but supports Applets.

join To wait for the termination of one or more descendent processes that were forked at some earlier time.

Kermit A public domain file transfer and terminal emulation program. Similar in functionality to uucp.

kernel A process providing basic services. A service kernel can run on every processor to support minimal operating system services, while a routing kernel can handle or forward incoming messages.

key Unique object of a search.

knowledge Information plus semantic meaning.

LAN Local Area Network, a network of multiple interconnected data terminals or devices within a local area to facilitate data transfer. Most notable of LAN topologies is ethernet, token ring, FDDI, etc.

LAP Link Access Procedure is a modified form of HDLC that CCITT specified for X.25 networks. LAP-B is link access procedures- balanced and is the X.25 implementation of SDLC and similarly, LAP-D is the ISDN and frame relay implementation of SDLC.

LAPACK A Linear Algebra Software Package, which has been mounted on a wide range of platforms. It evolved from the older LINPACK package from Netlib.

latency The time taken to service a request or deliver a message which is independent of the size or nature of the operation. The latency of a message passing system is the minimum time to deliver a message, even one of zero length that does not have to leave the source processor; the latency of a file system is the time required to decode and execute a null operation.

light-weight process A process which executes concurrently with other processes, in the same address space and in an unprotected fashion. Light-weight processes are used by systems such as MACH to reduce the overhead of process startup.

linear speed-up Speed-up that is directly proportional to the number of processors used. According to Amdahl's Law, linear speed-up is not possible for a problem that contains any sequential portion, no matter how small. Gustafson's Law however, states that linear speed-up can be achieved if the problem size is increased as well as the number of processor employed.

link A one-to-one connection between two processors or nodes in a multicomputer.

link loading The amount of communication traffic carried by a link, or by the most heavily loaded link in the system. As link loading increases, both latency and contention are likely to increase.

LINPACK A linear algebra software package, which has been mounted on a wide range of platforms. It has now been superceded by LAPACK. also a set of widely quoted performance benchmarks based on linear algebra and available from the National Software Exchange.

livelock A situation in which a process is forever blocked because another process has preferential access to a resource needed by both processes.

LIW Long Instruction Words: the use of long (64 or more bits) instruction words in a processor to improve its ability to pipeline calculations.

load balance The degree to which work is evenly distributed among available processors. A program executes most quickly when it is perfectly load balanced, that is, when every processor has a share of the total amount of work to perform so that all processors complete their assigned tasks at the same time. One measure of load imbalance is the ratio of the difference between the finishing times of the first and last processors to complete their portion of the calculation to the time taken by the last processor.

locality The degree to which the computations done by a processor depend only on data values held in memory that is close to that processor, or the degree to which computations done on a point in some data structure depend only on values near that point. Locality can be measured by the ratio of local to nonlocal data accesses, or by the distribution of distances of, or times taken by, nonlocal accesses.

lock Any device or algorithm whose use guarantees that only one process can perform some action or use some resource at a time.

logic The branch of mathematics that investigates the relationships between premises and conclusions of arguments.

logical time Elapsed time as seen from within processes. This may differ from clock time, because processes can block or be suspended during multitasking and because they can run at different speeds. The logical times of events define only a partial order on those events.

loose synchronization A program running on a concurrent computer is said to be running in loose synchronization if the nodes are constrained to intermittently synchronize with each other via some communication. Frequently, some global computational parameter such as a time or iteration count provides a natural synchronization reference. This parameter divides the running program into compute and communication cycles.

loose and tight coupling Here, coupling refers to linking of computers in a network. Tight refers to low latency, high bandwidth; loose to high latency and/or low bandwidths. There is no clear dividing line between "loose" or ""tight."

MACH A microkernel-based operating system developed by Carnegie Mellon University.

macrotasking Technique of dividing a computation into two or more large tasks to be executed in parallel. Typically, the tasks are subroutine calls executed in parallel.

mailbox An address used as a source or destination designator in a message.

mapping Often used to indicate an allocation of processes to processors; allocating work to processes is usually called scheduling.

marshall To compact the values of several variables, arrays, or structures into a single contiguous block of memory; copying values out of a block of memory is called unmarshalling. In most message passing systems, data must be marshalled to be sent in a single message.

mask A Boolean array or array-valued expression used to control where a data parallel operation has effect; the operation is executed only where array elements are true.

MPP The strict definition of Massively Parallel Processing is a machine with many interconnected processors, where "many" is dependent on the state of the art. Currently, the majority of high-end machines have fewer than 256 processors. A more practical definition of an MPP is a machine whose architecture is capable of having many processors - that is, it is scalable. In particular, machines with a distributed memory design (in comparison with shared memory designs) are usually synonymous with MPPs since they are not limited to a certain number of processors. In this sense, "many" is a number larger than the current largest number of processors in a shared-memory machine.

MFlops 10^6 Flops.

memory bank conflict A condition that occurs when a memory unit receives a request to fetch or store a data item prior to completion of its bank cycle time since its last such request.

memory protection Any system that prevents one process from accessing a region of memory being used by another. Memory protection is supported both in hardware and by the operating system of most serial computers, and by the hardware kernel and service kernel of the processors in most parallel computers.

mesh A topology in which nodes form a regular acyclic d-dimensional grid, and each edge is parallel to a grid axis and joins two nodes that are adjacent along that axis. The architecture of many multicomputers is a two- or three-dimensional mesh; meshes are also the basis of many scientific calculations, in which each node represents a point in space, and the edges define the neighbors of a node.

message passing A style of interprocess communication in which processes send discrete messages to one another. Some computer architectures are called message passing architectures because they support this model in hardware, although message passing has often been used to construct operating systems and network software for uniprocessors and distributed computers.

message typing The association of information with a message that identifies the nature of its contents. Most message passing systems automatically transfer information about a message's sender to its receiver. Many also require the sender to specify a type for the message, and let the receiver select which types of messages it is willing to receive.

MPI The Message Passing Interface standardizes the communication subroutine libraries used for programming on massively parallel computers such as Intel's Paragon and Cray's T3D, as well as networks of workstations. MPI not only unifies within a common framework programs written in a variety of exiting (and currently incompatible) parallel languages, but allows for future portability of programs between machines.

metacomputer This term describes a collection of heterogeneous computers networked by a high-speed wide area network. Such an environment would recognize the strengths of each machine in the metacomputer and use it accordingly to efficiently solve so-called metaproblems. The World Wide Web has the potential to be a physical realization of a Metacomputer.

metaproblem This term describes a class of problem which is outside the scope of a single computer architectures, but is instead best run on a Metacomputer with many disparate designs. These problems consist of many constituent sub-problems. An example is the design and manufacture of a modern aircraft, which presents problems in geometry grid generation, fluid flow, acoustics, structural analysis, operational research, visualization, and database management. The Metacomputer for such a Metaproblem would be networked workstations, array processors, vector supercomputers, massively parallel processors, and visualization engines.

message-oriented language A programming language in which process interaction is strictly through message passing.

microtasking The technique of employing parallelism at the DO-loop level. Different iterations of a loop are executed in parallel on different processors.

MIMD Multiple Instruction, Multiple Data; a category of Flynn's taxonomy in which many instruction streams are concurrently applied to multiple data sets. A MIMD architecture is one in which heterogeneous processes may execute at different rates.

MIPS one Million Instructions Per Second. A performance rating usually referring to integer or non-floating point instructions.

module A memory bank, often used in the context of interleaved memory.

MOPS one Million Operations Per Second. Usually used for a general operation, either integer, floating point or otherwise.

motherboard A printed circuit board or card on which other boards or cards can be mounted. Motherboards will generally have a number of slots for other boards, by which means the computer system may be expanded. When all the slots are used up, however, it is usually difficult to expand further, and this is the manufacturer's way of telling you to buy a bigger system.

multicast To send a message to many, but not necessarily all, possible recipient processes.

multicomputer A computer in which processors can execute separate instruction streams, have their own private memories and cannot directly access one another's memories. Most multicomputers are disjoint memory machines, constructed by joining nodes (each containing a microprocessor and some memory) via links.

multigrid method A method for solving partial differential equations in which an approximate solution on a coarse resolution grid is used to obtain an improved solution on a finer resolution grid. The method reduces long wavelength components of the error or residual by iterating between a hierarchy of coarse and fine resolution grids.

multiprogramming The ability of a computer system to time share its (at least one) CPU with more than one program at once.

multitasking Executing many processes on a single processor. This is usually done by time-slicing the execution of individual processes and performing a context switch each time a process is swapped in or out, but is supported by special-purpose hardware in some computers. Most operating systems support multitasking, but it can be costly if the need to switch large caches or execution pipelines makes context switching expensive in time.

mutual exclusion A situation in which at most one process can be engaged in a specified activity at any time. Semaphores are often used to implement this.

$n^{1/2}$ The minimum vector length on which a pipelined architecture delivers one-half of its theoretical peak performance. The larger $n^{1/2}$ is, the longer calculations must be to amortize the startup cost of the pipeline. This measure was coined by Hockney and Jesshope in 1988.

NeTBIOS Network Basic Input/Output System that provides a Session layer interface between network applications running on a PC and the underlying protocol software of the Transport and Network layers on the OSI model. Normally a LAN protocol.

network A physical communication medium. A network may consist of one or more buses, a switch, or the links joining processors in a multicomputer.

NFS Network File System is a protocol developed to use IP and allow a set of computers to access each other's file systems as if they were on the local host.

node Generic term used to refer to an entity that accesses a network.

non-blocking An operation that does not block the execution of the process using it. Usually applied to communications operations, where it implies that the communicating process may perform other operations before the communication has completed.

non-deterministic model A task model in which the execution time of each task is represented by a random variable.

NUMA Non-Uniform Memory Access; not supporting constant time read and write operations. In most NUMA architectures, memory is organized hierarchically, so that some portions can be read and written more quickly by some processors than by others.

operating system That software responsible for providing standard services and supporting standard operations such as multitasking and file access.

operation oriented language A programming language using remote procedure calls as the principle means for interprocess communication and synchronization.

optimal Cannot be bettered. An optimal mapping is one that yields the best possible load balance; an optimal parallel algorithm is one that has the lowest possible time-processor product.

optimization problem A problem whose solution involves satisfying a set of constraints and minimizing (or maximizing) and objective function.

OSF Open Software Foundation; an organization established by a number of the major computer manufacturers to set software standards.

packet switching A routing technique in which intermediate nodes wait until they have received the whole of a message before forwarding any of it. Packet switching often requires a large amount of buffer space, and contention for access to this space can lead to deadlock.

page The smallest unit of a virtual memory system. The system maintains separate virtual-to-physical translation information for each page.

parallel computer A computer system made up of many identifiable processing units working together in parallel. The term is often used synonymously with concurrent computer to include both multiprocessor and multicomputer.

parallel slackness Hiding the latency of communication by giving each processor many different tasks, and having them work on the tasks that are ready while other tasks are blocked (waiting on communication or other operations).

PVM Parallel Virtual Machine was developed at Emory and Tennessee Universities, and Oak Ridge National Laboratory. It supports the message passing programming model on a network of heterogeneous computers (http://www.epm.ornl.gov/pvm/).

parallelization Turning a serial computation into a parallel one. Also sometimes turning a vector computation into a parallel one. This may be done automatically by a parallelizing compiler or (more usually) by rewriting (parts of) the program so that it uses some parallel paradigm.

parsing Process whereby a compiler analyzes the syntax of a program to establish the relationship among operators, operands, and other tokens of a program. Parsing does not involve any semantic analysis.

partitioning Process of restructuring a program or algorithm into independent computational segments. The goal is to have multiple processors simultaneously work on these independent computational segments.

percentage parallelization The percentage of processor expenditure processed in parallel on a single job. It is not usually possible to achieve 100 percent of an application's processing time to be shared equally on all processors. See Amdahl's Law.

percentage vectorization The percentage of an application executing in vector mode. This percentage may be calculated as a percentage of CPU time or as the percentage of lines of code (usually Fortran) in vector instructions. The two approaches are not consistent and may give very different ratings. The first calculation method leads to performance improvement as measured by

CPU time, while the second method measures the success rate of the compiler in converting scalar code to vector code. The former is the more meaningful hardware performance measure.

performance model A formula that predicts the speed, efficiency, memory requirements, or other execution characteristics of a program on a particular architecture.

ping The Packet Internet Groper is a program useful in testing and debugging LAN/WAN troubles. It sends out an echo and expects a specified host to respond back in a specified time frame.

pipe A communication primitive which involves the transmission of information through a linearly connected subset of the nodes of a parallel computer.

pipelining Overlapping the execution of two or more operations. Pipelining is used within processors by prefetching instructions on the assumption that no branches are going to preempt their execution; in vector processors, in which application of a single operation to the elements of a vector or vectors may be pipelined to decrease the time needed to complete the aggregate operation; and in multiprocessors and multicomputers, in which a process may send a request for values before it reaches the computation that requires them.

polling Involves a node inspecting the communication hardware (typically a flag bit) to see if information has arrived or departed. Polling is an alternative to an interrupt driven system. The natural synchronization of the nodes imposed by polling is used in the implementation of blocking communications primitives.

ports A variant of mailboxes allowing multiple client processes but only a single server process.

POSIX A standard of definition of the interface to the UNIX operating system.

PRAM Parallel Random Access Machine; a theoretical model of parallel computation in which an arbitrary but finite number of processors can access any value in an arbitrarily large shared memory in a single time step. Processors may execute different instruction streams, but work synchronously. The three most important variations of the PRAM are: EREW (Exclusive read, exclusive write); any memory location may be accessed only once in any one step. CREW (Concurrent read, exclusive write); any memory location may be read any number of times during a single step, but only written to once, with the write taking place after the reads. CRCW (Concurrent read, concurrent write); any memory location may be written to or read from any number of times during a single step. A CRCW PRAM model must define some rule for resolving multiple writes, such as giving priority to the lowest-numbered processor or choosing among processors randomly. The PRAM is popular because it is theoretically tractable and because it gives algorithm designers a common target. However, PRAMs cannot be emulated optimally on all architectures.

prefetch To fetch or load a data entity or program instruction from memory in advance of actually starting to process it. Processors that have prefetch instructions can avoid some of the bottlenecks that arise from a memory system that is slower than processing speed.

private memory Memory that appears to the user to be divided between many address spaces, each of which can be accessed by only one process. Most operating systems rely on some memory protection mechanism to prevent one process from accessing the private memory of another; in disjoint memory machines, the problem is usually finding a way to emulate shared memory using a set of private memories.

procedure oriented language A programming language in which process communication and synchronization are accomplished through the use of of shared variables.

process The fundamental entity of the software implementation on a computer system. A process is a sequentially executing piece of code that runs on one processing unit of the system.

process creation The act of forking or spawning a new process. If a system permits only static process creation, then all processes are created at the same logical time, and no process may interact with any other until all have been created. If a system permits dynamic process creation, then one process can create another at any time. Most first and second generation multicomputers supported only static process creation, while most multiprocessors, and most operating systems on uniprocessors, support dynamic process creation.

process group A set of processes that can be treated as a single entity for some purposes, such as synchronization and broadcast or multicast operations. In some parallel programming systems there is only one process group, which implicitly contains all processes; in others, programmers can assign processes to groups statically when configuring their program, or dynamically by having processes create, join and leave groups during execution.

process migration Changing the processor responsible for executing a process during the lifetime of that process. Process migration is sometimes used to dynamically load balance a program or system.

processor array A computer that consists of a regular mesh of simple processing elements, under the direction of a single control processor. Processor arrays are usually SIMD machines, and are primarily used to support data parallel computations.

processor overloading Mapping many processes to a single processor, so that parallel slackness can be exploited.

PVC Permanent Virtual Circuit is a permanent logical connection between two end points which is carrying user frame relay encapsulated data.

race condition A situation in which the final result of operations being executed by two or more processes depends on the order in which those processes execute. For example, if two processes A and B are to write different values VA and VB to the same variable, then the final value of the variable is determined by the order in which A and B are scheduled.

RAID Redundant Array of Inexpensive Disks; a file system containing many disks, some of which are used to hold redundant copies of data or error correction codes to increase reliability. RAIDs are often used as parallel access file systems, where the sheer size of storage capacity required precludes using more conventional (but more expensive) disk technology.

RAM Random Access Memory; computer memory which can be written to and read from in any order.

randomized routing A routing technique in which each message is sent to a randomly chosen node, which then forwards it to its final destination. Theory and practice show that this can greatly reduce the amount of contention for access to links in a multicomputer.

RDBMS Relational DataBase Management System; software to manage a database in which data are stored by attribute.

redundant computation Calculations that are carried out more than once or by more than one processor. Computations may be done redundantly because it is cheaper to have every processor calculate a value for itself than to have one processor calculate the value and then broadcast it, or because processes may not have enough memory to store all the values they calculate and may need to overwrite some during execution.

rendezvous When the server side of a remote procedure call is specified by using an accept statement or similar construct.

reply message Passing of results back to the client in a remote procedure call.

RGB Red-Green-Blue; the most common form of color display hardware.

ring A topology in which each node is connected to two others to form a closed loop.

RIP Routing Information Packet is an IGP supplied with BSD networking Unix.

RISC Reduced Instruction Set Computer; a computer that provides only a few simple instructions but executes them extremely quickly. RISC machines typically rely on instruction prefetching and caching to achieve higher performance than CISC machines. The term is also applied to software designs that give users a small number of simple but efficient operations.

ROM Read Only Memory; a computer memory which cannot be written to during normal operation.

routing The act of moving a message from its source to its destination. A routing technique is a way of handling the message as it passes through individual nodes.

routing algorithm A rule for deciding, at any intermediate node, where to send a message next.

RPC Remote Procedure Call is a popular model for implementing distributed client-server computing environments. It is an alternative to inter-process communication (IPC) which allows remote systems to execute a set of procedures to share information.

scalable Capable of being increased in size, or more accurately, capable of delivering an increase in performance proportional to an increase in size. A scalable architecture is one that can be used as a design for arbitrarily large machines, or one whose increase in performance is linear in the amount of hardware invested. The term is also applied to programming systems, although its meaning is less clear in these cases. It is generally used to imply that the methods and algorithms employed in such systems are, in principle, capable of performing correctly equally well on large and small hardware systems.

ScaLAPACK A Linear Algebra Software Package, which has been mounted on a wide range of platforms. This is a version of LAPACK suitable for distributed memory computer systems. The software is available from the National Software Exchange.

scalar processor A computer in the traditional Von Neumann sense of operating only on scalar data.

scheduling Deciding the order in which the calculations in a program are to be executed, and by which processes. Allocating processes to processors is usually called mapping.

scoreboard A hardware device that maintains the state of machine resources to enable instructions to execute without conflict at the earliest opportunity.

SCSI Small Computer Systems Interface; a hardware standard for interfacing to devices such as disks.

secondary memory A larger but slower memory than primary memory. Access to secondary memory often requires special instructions, such as I/O instructions.

self-scheduling Automatically allocating work to processes. If T tasks are to be done by P processors, and P < T, then they may be self-scheduled by keeping them in a central pool from which each processor claims a new job when it finishes executing its old one.

semaphore A data type for controlling concurrency. A semaphore can be initialized to any non negative integer value. After that, only two operations may be applied to it: "signal," which increments the semaphore's value by one, and "wait," which blocks its caller until the semaphore's value is greater than zero, then decrements the semaphore. The value of a semaphore typically represents the amount of some resource that is currently available, while waiting on a semaphore forces processes to block until some of that resource can be claimed. A binary semaphore is one that can take on only the values 0 and 1.

sequential bottleneck A part of a computation for which there is little or no parallelism.

sequential computer Synonymous with a Von Neumann architecture computer and is a "conventional" computer in which only one processing element works on a problem at a given time.

serialize To put potentially concurrent operations in a strictly sequential order. If concurrent processes must claim a lock before doing some operation, for example, then their operations will be serialized.

set associative A cache structure in which all tags in a particular set are compared with an access key in order to access an item in cache. The set may have as few as one element or as many elements as there are lines in the full cache.

shared memory Memory that appears to the user to be contained in a single address space and that can be accessed by any process. In a uniprocessor or multiprocessor there is typically a single memory unit, or several memory units interleaved to give the appearance of a single memory unit.

shared variables Variables to which two or more processes have access, or the model of parallel computing in which interprocess communication and synchronization are managed through such variables.

single system image A property of cluster that makes network of computers appear as a single system.

SIMD Single Instruction, Multiple Data; a category of Flynn's taxonomy in which a single instruction stream is concurrently applied to multiple data sets. A

SIMD architecture is one in which homogeneous processes synchronously execute the same instructions on their own data, or one in which an operation can be executed on vectors of fixed or varying size.

SISD Single Instruction, Single Data; a category of Flynn's taxonomy in which a single instruction stream is serially applied to a single data set. Most uniprocessors are SISD machines.

SLIP Serial Line Internet Protocol is used to run IP over serial lines, telephone circuits or RS-232 cables connecting two hosts.

SMTP Simple Mail Transfer Protocol is the Internet's electronic mail protocol.

SNMP Simple Network Management Protocol, a network management tool used in TCP/IP based networks that is used to manage the network equipment and processes. Usually graphic on an X-window display.

space sharing Dividing the resources of a parallel computer among many programs so they can run simultaneously without affecting one another's performance.

spanning tree A tree containing a subset of the links in a graph which reaches every node in that graph. A spanning tree can always be constructed so that its depth (the greatest distance between its root and any leaf) is no greater than the diameter of the graph. Spanning trees are frequently used to implement broadcast operations.

SPARC Scalable Processor ARChitecture; a family of chips which can be manufactured using a variety of technologies, but still be compatible in some ways.

spawn To create a new process with arbitrary initial memory contents and instructions.

speed-up The ratio of two program execution times, particularly when times are from execution on 1 and P nodes of the same computer. Speed-up is usually discussed as a function of the number of processors, but is also a function (implicitly) of the problem size.

spin lock An implementation of the lock primitive that causes a processor to retest a semaphore until it changes value. Busy-waits will spin until the lock is free.

spinning A process waiting for the value of a spin lock to change is said to be spinning.

SPMD Single Program, Multiple Data; a category sometimes added to Flynn's taxonomy to describe programs made up of many instances of a single type of process, each executing the same code independently. SPMD can be viewed either as an extension of SIMD, or as a restriction of MIMD.

SQL Standard Query Language; a standard for adding data to, or recovering data from, databases.

SRAM Static RAM; memory which stores data in such a way that it requires no memory refresh cycle and hence has low power consumption. Generally, this type of RAM is faster but more expensive than DRAM.

startup cost The time taken to initiate any transaction with some entity. The startup cost of a message passing system, for example, is the time needed to send a message of zero length to nowhere.

subnet address An extension of the IP address that allows a network to be autonomous by itself and still be a subsection of a larger user network.

supercomputer A time-dependent term which refers to the class of most powerful computer systems worldwide at the time of reference.

superlinear speed-up Speed-up that is greater than an amount proportional to the number of processors used. While superlinear speed-up is theoretically impossible, in practice it may occur because distributing a problem among many processors may increase the effective total size of the cache being used, or because distribution may change the order in which nondeterministic operations are carried out, which can lead to earlier termination of the program.

swap To exchange two items. The term refers to swapping a section of real memory (contents) for a section of virtual memory.

switch A physical communication medium containing nodes that perform only communications functions. Examples include crossbar switches, in which N+M buses cross orthogonally at NM switching points to connect N objects of one type to M objects of another, and multistage switches in which several layers of switching nodes connect N objects of one type to N objects of another type.

SMP A Symmetric Multiprocessor supports a shared memory programming model; typically, with a UMA memory system, and a collection of up to 32 nodes connected with a bus.

synchronization The act of bringing two or more processes to known points in their execution at the same clock time. Explicit synchronization is not needed in SIMD programs (in which every processor either executes the same operation as every other or does nothing), but is often necessary in SPMD and MIMD programs. The time wasted by processes waiting for other processes to synchronize with them can be a major source of inefficiency in parallel programs.

synchronous Occurring at the same clock time. For example, if a communication event is synchronous, then there is some moment at which both the sender and the receiver are engaged in the operation.

T1 Transmission facility at digital service (DS1) level 1 with 1.544Mbps in North America and 2.048Mbps in Europe.

T3 Transmission facility at digital service (DS3) level 3 with 44.736Mbps. STS1 or OC1 at 51.84Mbps is the Sonet equivalent for broadband services. Sometimes called a 45meg circuit.

task farming A technique for implementing self-scheduling calculations. In a task farm, a source process generates a pool of jobs, while a sink process consumes results. In between, one or more worker processes repeatedly claim jobs from the source, turn them into results, dispatch those results to the sink, and claim their next jobs. If the number of jobs is much greater than the number of workers, task farming can be an effective way to load balance a computation.

TCP Transmission Control Protocol is the main transport protocol in the Internet protocol suite. It provides reliable, stateful and connection/stream oriented end-to-end connectivity.

TCP/IP Is a compound acronym used synonymously with transmission control protocol TCP, which is an Internet protocol.

telnet An application that provides virtual terminal services for a wide variety of remote systems. It allows a user at one site to interact with applications at other sites as if the user's terminal is local.

TFlops 10^{12} Flops.

thrashing A phenomenon of virtual memory systems that occurs when the program, by the manner in which it is referencing its data and instructions, regularly causes the next memory locations referenced to be overwritten by recent or current instructions. The result is that referenced items are rarely in the machine's physical memory and almost always must be fetched from secondary storage, usually a disk. Cache thrashing involves a similar situation between cache and physical memory.

thread A lightweight or small granularity process.

throughput Number of results produced per unit time.

TLB Translation Look-aside Buffer; the memory cache of the most recently used page table entries within the memory management unit.

token ring Token ring is an IBM based LAN protocol that uses a ring shaped network topology. Token ring has speeds at 4Mbps and 16Mbps. A distinguishing packet is transferred from machine to machine and only the machine that is in control of the token is able to transmit.

topology A family of graphs created using the same general rule or that share certain properties. The processors in a multicomputer, and the circuits in a switch, are usually laid out using one of several topologies, including the mesh, the hypercube, the butterfly, the torus and the shuffle exchange network.

torus A topology in which nodes form a regular cyclic d-dimensional grid, and each edge is parallel to a grid axis and joins two nodes that are adjacent along that axis. The architecture of some multicomputers is a two- or three-dimensional torus.

tuple An ordered sequence of fixed length of values of arbitrary types. Tuples are used for both data storage and interprocess communication in the generative communication paradigm.

tuple space A repository (like an associative memory) for tuples in a generative communication system.

UART Universal Asynchronous Receive-Transmit; a standard protocol for device drivers.

UDP User Datagram Protocol is a transport layer protocol in the Internet protocol suite. UDP uses IP for packet delivery, and is unreliable, connectionless, and stateless. However, UDP does not use handshaking before exchanging data and therefore acknowledgments and guaranteed delivery are not available. UDP relies on higher protocol layers to provide end-to-end data delivery and integrity.

UMA Uniform Memory Access; permitting any memory element to be read or written in the same, constant time.

uniprocessor A computer containing a single processor. The term is generally synonymous with scalar processor.

UNIX An OS originally developed by AT&T which, in various incarnations, is now available on most types of supercomputer.

utilization Percentage of time a processor spends executing useful tasks during execution of a program.

vector processor A computer designed to apply arithmetic operations to long vectors or arrays. Most vector processors rely heavily on pipelining to achieve high performance.

vector register A storage device that acts as an intermediate memory between a computer's functional units and main memory.

virtual channel A logical point-to-point connection between two processes. Many virtual channels may time share a single link to hide latency and to avoid deadlock.

virtual concurrent computer A computer system that is programmed as a concurrent computer of some number of nodes P, but which is implemented on either a real concurrent computer of some number of nodes less than P or on a uniprocessor running software to emulate the environment of a concurrent machine. Such an emulation system is said to provide virtual nodes to the user.

virtual cut-through A technique for routing messages in which the head and tail of the message both proceed as rapidly as they can. If the head is blocked because a link it wants to cross is being used by some other message, the tail continues to advance, and the message's contents are put into buffers on intermediate nodes.

virtual memory A system that stores portions of an address space that are not being actively used in in some medium other than main high-speed memory, such as a disk or slower auxiliary memory medium. When a reference is made to a value not presently in main memory, the virtual memory manager must swap some values in main memory for the values required. Virtual memory is used by almost all uniprocessors and multiprocessors, but is not available on some array processors and multicomputers, which still employ real memory storage only on each node.

virtual shared memory Memory that appears to users to constitute a single address space, but which is actually physically disjoint. Virtual shared memory is often implemented using some combination of hashing and local caching.

VLSI Very Large Scale Integration; applied to technologies capable of putting hundreds of thousands or more components on a single chip, or sometimes applied to those chips so manufactured.

VMS Virtual Machine System; an operating system developed by DEC and widely used on VAX machines. Popularity of this OS is probably waning in favor of UNIX like systems.

Von Neumann architecture Used to describe any computer which does not employ concurrency or parallelism. Named after John Von Neumann (1903-1957) who is credited with the invention of the basic architecture of current sequential computers.

WAN Wide Area Network, a network of circuits spanning a large region or global in proportions, that is used to transmit data between widespread subscribers.

Web clients and servers A distributed set of clients (requesters and receivers of services) and servers (receiving and satisfying requests from clients) using Web technologies.

working set Those values from shared memory that a process has copied into its private memory, or those pages of virtual memory being used by a process. Changes a process makes to the values in its working set are not automatically seen by other processes.

wormhole routing A technique for routing messages in which the head of the message establishes a path, which is reserved for the message until the tail has passed through it. Unlike virtual cut-through, the tail proceeds at a rate dictated by the progress of the head, which reduces the demand for intermediate buffering.

write-in cache A cache in which writes to memory are stored in the cache and written to memory only when a rewritten item is removed from cache. This is also referred to as write-back cache.

write-through cache A cache in which writes to memory are performed concurrently both in cache and in main memory.

X.25 Is the CCITT standard protocol for transport-level network services and was originally created for connecting terminals to computers. It provides reliable stream-oriented transmission services and is widely used in Europe. TCP/IP can be implemented as a layer above X.25.

X.400 Is a CCITT protocol for electronic mail.

X.500 Is a CCITT protocol for electronic mail.

XDR eXternal Data Representation is a standard for machine independent data structures.

Index